Extraordinary Lives

**www.readersdigest.co.uk**

Published in the United Kingdom by Vivat Direct Limited
(t/a Reader's Digest), 157 Edgware Road,
London W2 2HR



Printed in Portugal
ISBN 978 0 276 44650 4

# Extraordinary Lives

# Contents

**That's Another Story**
Julie Walters

9

Having delighted audiences with her screen and West End stage successes for more than twenty-five years, Julie Walters has been described as the nation's most popular actress and comedienne. In her candid and entertaining autobiography, she reveals the highs and lows of a remarkable career, recalling her childhood in Birmingham, her days at a convent school, and her decision to take up nursing to appease her mother. Unable to suppress her real ambition to be an actress, though, she was soon auditioning for drama school . . .

**Knave of Spades**
Alan Titchmarsh
163

Mention the name of Alan Titchmarsh and many people will think of television's favourite gardener—the star of *Gardeners' World* and *Ground Force*. It's true that gardening remains Titchmarsh's abiding love, but he also fronts a variety of documentaries, hosts a daytime chat show and presents music programmes, as well as writing best-selling novels, gardening books, and now his memoirs. Told in the same easy-going, humorous manner that captivates his audiences, *Knave of Spades* is a warm, self-deprecating, joyous read.

## Dear Fatty
Dawn French

297

It's become a cliché in Britain to call somebody in the entertainment field a national institution, but that's exactly what Dawn French is. Her career has spanned three decades, from her days as one half of the much-loved duo of French and Saunders, to her more recent role as the Vicar of Dibley, and she is utterly successful in everything she does. Here, in the hilarious, honest and heartfelt *Dear Fatty*, she describes the ups and downs of her journey, chronicling the extraordinary rise of a complex,unstoppable woman.

## The Time of My Life
Patrick Swayze & Lisa Niemi

479

Patrick Swayze met Lisa Niemi when they were little children who shared a burning desire: to be a dancer. Over the next thirty years, Swayze made a name for himself on stage, screen and television, and will be best remembered for his stunning performances in *Dirty Dancing* and *Ghost*. His soul mate and wife, Lisa, who became a successful writer and director, was always by his side. This heartwarming memoir of Swayze's life, richly enhanced by an uplifting and enduring love, is testament to his strength and passion.

Julie Walters
That's Another Story

In January 1970, I had my audition for a place at Manchester Polytechnic School of Theatre . . . I had been asked to prepare three pieces, one of which had to be Shakespeare. I chose Lady Macbeth.

I was interviewed on the day by Edward Argent, the principal of the school.

'So you want to be an actress?' He was a round, teddy-bearish man.

'No. I am an actress,' I said. 'Whether I am employed as such is another matter, but that's what I am; I am an actress.'

Julie Walters in 'That's Another Story'

# One

'Five years ago today . . .'

It's my mother's voice. She is at the foot of the stairs, calling out the story of my birth, as she did on so many birthdays.

'Ten years ago today . . .'

It is Irish, a Mayo voice worn at the edges, giving it a husky quality, which, she told me once, some men had found alluring.

'Fifteen years ago today . . .'

Now it is soft with memory. I was the fifth and final child to be born, each delivery producing its own particular trauma.

The first, my brother Tommy, arrived in 1942. He continually scratched at his face, until eventually he was taken into hospital where his tiny hands were bandaged to prevent further harm. When Kevin, the second, was born three years later, my mother's screams of 'Put him back!' apparently reached the outskirts of Birmingham. This, according to my mother, was due to the inordinate size of his head. The third, Mary, was stillborn, and in order to get me to eat eggs my mother had told me that it was Mary's refusal to do so that had caused her demise. One day I challenged the assertion, pointing out that a dead baby wouldn't have been able to speak let alone have much of an appetite. And anyway, I went on, where is her grave? My mother went quiet. I was beginning to think she had made the whole thing up, that there never was a Mary, until my father chimed in with awful innocence, 'Well, she was incinerated, wasn't she?' That was the first time I ever saw her cry and I didn't understand her grief, at least not for about another thirty years.

The penultimate birth was a miscarriage. Then, after she was told it would be too dangerous to have any more children, I came along in 1950, on February 22, at three o'clock in the afternoon.

'My waters broke . . .' A slight vibrato begins. 'Your father and I got on the bus.' She knows I need to know and that she needs to recount it. 'They should never have given me that fish dinner . . .' I am now in St Chad's Hospital, watching my mother, the said fish dinner having been thrown up over the counterpane. She is about to give birth. 'The cord was round your neck.'

'God, Mum, I feel as if I was actually there.' She ignores this.

'They got in the priest. They could save only one of us . . . Your father had to choose.' My mother's incomparable sense of drama now removes all vibrato from her voice and this last statement is made with a terrible flat resignation. Like the best of actors, she knows that less is more.

'I chose you.' My father chipped in on this only once that I remember. His voice is gentle, with a big, full, Birmingham inner-city accent. He is sitting, his hair full of plaster dust, weathered far beyond his years, in the kitchen at 69 Bishopton Road, smelling of turps and house paint and years of cigarettes. The cigarettes weren't just in his clothes; they were in his skin. He had smoked since he was ten. Even though he died in 1971, I can summon up that smell in an instant.

'He chose you.' Her voice is that of a sad, bewildered child. 'The priest had to give me the last rites.'

'Yes, but you were all right in the end.'

'Extreme unction.'

'Yeah but—oh blimey . . .' He knows when to give up.

'They took you away. I didn't see you for a whole week.'

No one speaks.

'Happy birthday, Julie.'

NUMBER 69 Bishopton Road was a big, draughty, end-of-terrace house. There was a song in the fifties, 'This Old House', with lyrics like, 'Ain't got time to fix the windows, ain't got time to fix the floors.' As a small child, whose universe began and ended at our back gate, I presumed it was being sung specifically about our house.

Similarly once, while I was watching *Watch with Mother* on my own, aged about three, a kindly lady sat holding a teddy bear, saying, 'Look, Teddy, there is a little girl watching us and she's got a teddy just like you!' I was into the kitchen, screaming at my mother that the lady on television could not only see me but she had spoken to me. Only when I asked my father why, when there were Tom cats, were there not any Kev cats, and he explained that Tom cats were not named after my older brother, did it dawn on me that the sun didn't shine out of my arse.

At the far end of Bishopton Road was Lightwoods Park, right on the border of Bearwood, which is part of the Black Country and Birmingham. As a child I was forbidden to go to the park unaccompanied because of 'strange men'. Lightwoods Park, which covered about ten acres, had a bandstand. There were a set of swings, a seesaw and a conical roundabout in the shape of a witch's hat, the top of which was balanced on top of a tall pole. Next to this play area was the pond, upon which people sailed their model boats and suchlike, while in hot weather it became a muddy soup of children and dogs, paddling and swimming.

Never were my mother's warnings to keep out of the park fiercer than during the summer holidays when the annual funfair came for a week. I found the smell of hot dogs, diesel and candy floss, the loud pop music, half drowned out by the noise of generators, totally alluring, and I loved rides like the bumper cars where muscle-bound young men in dirty jeans would take your money and jump on the back of your car, or better still on the waltzers, where the more you screamed the faster they would whip you round. According to my mother, 'No decent girl would be interested in boys like those, low types from God knows where.' Needless to say I went every year. The fairground boys—poignantly described in Victoria Wood's song 'I Want to be Fourteen Again', '. . . the coloured lights reflected in the Brylcreem in his hair . . .'—played leading roles in a fantasy of mine about living in a caravan, working on a stall involving goldfish and smelling of petrol.

Our end of the street formed the junction with Long Hyde Road. Only about 100 yards long, there were rarely more than two or three cars parked in it, one of them being my father's. Dad always owned a car and the first I remember was a small, bright yellow van, which my father referred to as Sally.

Sally had no side windows at the back, just two little square ones in the back doors, and so her rear consisted of a dark space that was always full of tools, paint and the general detritus of my father's work life. Yet if we went out in Sally as a family, she would be transformed: Dad would shift everything out of the back and sling in an old bus seat for my brothers and me to sit on. It had a silky, soft pile if you ran your hand across it, a jazzy brown and green pattern against a beige background, and the whole thing was edged in brown leather. This worked really well unless we had to stop suddenly. The seat would abruptly tip over backwards, sending us sprawling. So any journey would mainly be spent scrambling about in the semidarkness, getting the seat upright again in time for the three of us with a united scream of 'Daaaaaaaad!' to be sent flying once more. Every journey ended like this as we pulled up outside the house, accompanied by my grandmother's declaration, if she was with us, of 'We've landed!'

Sally was eventually replaced by a far superior Ford Esquire estate. It was a sedate grey colour and its main advantage was that the estate bit at the back served as extra passenger space for small persons. The small person was inevitably me, and it meant that not only could I travel staring out of the back window, making faces or breathing on the glass and writing back-to-front messages, like 'ylimaf neila na yb detcudba gnieb ma I !!pleH' for the driver behind to ignore, but I could avoid being poked by my brothers.

The other advantage of this new acquisition was that Dermot Boyle, the boy who lived opposite, with whom I played on a regular basis, was envious. Mr Boyle was a builder's labourer from Kerry who, as my dad would say, liked a drink. He had permanently wet lips that appeared to work independently of the rest of his face. They flopped around clumsily, an impediment to words buoyed up on clouds of alcoholic breath and accompanied by blizzards of spit. Mr Boyle was severely shortsighted, which meant he was forced to wear glasses with lenses so thick that his eyes were tiny blue dots. We often stood giggling at the upstairs window, behind the nets, watching Pat Boyle wobble up the street on his push-bike and stand swaying, trying to get his key in the front-door lock, his face jammed right up against it. Eventually, the door would be opened by the long-suffering Mrs Boyle and Pat would go lurching forwards like a pantomime drunk, Mrs B berating him. The irony was that Mrs Boyle, who never took a drink in her life, died of liver cancer and Mr Boyle, who was rarely sober, died of natural causes.

I am ashamed to say that I exploited Dermot's envy of our car to the maximum. If he happened to be out playing, I would sit provocatively on the front bumper, caressing its shiny chrome with one hand, the other stretched backwards across the bonnet, chatting inanely on while secretly clocking Dermot's reaction. He would sit on the kerb, usually eating a piece of his mother's home-made cake, squirming and covering his eyes. At last he would run off, mid-conversation, shouting 'Stop it!', spraying cake crumbs as he went.

A couple of years later we went up several rungs on the status-symbol ladder of car ownership, acquiring a two-tone Vauxhall Victor estate, in green and cream. I couldn't wait to torment Dermot with it. In fact my father had hardly got out after bringing it home than I was draped across its bonnet in true motor-show fashion, while the hapless Dermot tried not to look, his face turning cherry red in an attempt to control his rage. My father never ever told me off, but that day, on his way into the house, he wheeled round and shouted, 'Gerroff, ya daft cat, you'll scratch the paintwork!' Whereupon, out of the blue, a bird shat on the bonnet right next to me, splattering the fingers of my left hand.

I jumped down and ran into the house, feeling vaguely ashamed, while Dad whipped out an old handkerchief from his pocket and began lovingly to wipe the bonnet clean. I guess Dermot and I were even-stevens after that, and years later, on a visit home, I remember asking my mother to whom the flash car belonged that was parked opposite. 'Oh, Dermot is home to stay.' I felt my own little dart of envy; I wasn't to pass my driving test until I was thirty-seven.

It was here on Long Hyde Road, which ran along the side of our house, that I would spend my time playing with neighbourhood children. My first crush developed when I was about five. More accurately, I experienced my first feelings of loss. I'd been playing regularly with a boy called Robert, who had pale blond hair, and suddenly he was going away; the family were moving house. He stood there, eating a piece of bread and butter as he broke the news. I remember him not looking at me as he spoke and then running off, leaving four little crusts on the top of the wall. Somehow it was the sight of those crusts that sparked off the grief of this separation. I picked one up and ate it. I kept the other pieces in one of my father's old cigarette packets until they went a bluish-green colour. I don't remember much else about this boy's family, except the reporting some years later of the death of Robert's older brother in a climbing accident on Snowdon. Again the image of the small blond head slid into my mind like a frame of film, as it has continued to do on the odd occasion ever since.

Long Hyde Road was almost permanently marked out with white chalk for rounders or hopscotch, and a couple of times the whole length of the pavement was marked out into four wobbly lanes for an athletics tournament organised by my brothers. Tommy and Kevin, at least in my eyes, were the cocks of the neighbourhood, heroes who made other boys look pitiably inadequate. To say I was proud of them could not be more of an understatement. They were the very best at everything, and I as their little sister basked not only in their glory but also in their protection.

They were knights in shining armour. This is best illustrated in an incident that occurred when I was about seven.

There was a boy in the next street who, whenever I walked past his house, would leap out and attack me with his big plastic space gun. He would hold me there for about twenty minutes or so, his gun pinning my chest to the wall while my head and shoulders were stuck in the privet hedge above. On some occasions he was accompanied by the family boxer dog, which he would whip up into a frenzy so that it would leap about, eyes flashing and long globules of saliva swinging from its jaws. The thing would jump up at me, its pink willy ready for action, and it would attempt to mount me. It was rape by proxy. Needless to say I would walk miles out of my way to avoid this awful boy and his oversexed dog, but one day, mistakenly thinking he was on holiday, I got caught again. Arriving home upset, I blurted out to my older brother Tommy what had happened. Within minutes, he went round to the child's house and not only thrashed him but did so in front of his astonished parents. The boy never came near me again.

Our house was north-facing and we didn't get central heating until 1963. Ice on the inside of the bedroom windows was usual throughout the winter. On the coldest nights my parents would simply pile the beds with coats, and the weight would make turning over in bed a feat of strength that wasn't worth the effort. The cold meant that the seat nearest the fire in the kitchen was fiercely fought over; once won, it would be given up only for the direst of emergencies. I remember Tommy managing to stay put for a record-breaking length of time, eventually jumping up with a howl to find that his Wellington boot had melted with the heat and had welded itself onto his leg. He still bears the scars.

The house was on three storeys. The front door opened onto an oddly shaped hallway, one wall of which was almost all window. This was because the previous owner had an electrical shop and had built the hall on to display his radios. There were two doors off it, one leading into the front room, my father's office. It smelt of tobacco and ink and him, and in the corner was his big roll-top desk, from which he ran his building and decorating business. It also contained the piano, upon which I wrote hundreds of songs, all sounding very similar and which I sang at the top of my voice, hoping that someone would say, 'My God, that's brilliant!' instead of 'For Christ's sake, shut up!'

The other door led to the sitting room, which held the television. We were one of the first in our road to have one, and on important occasions like the Grand National, the Cup Final or the Queen's Speech, neighbours would be invited in to watch. It was a similar story with the telephone. Most people hadn't got one and so if there was an urgent need for a neighbour to contact someone, they would use ours, always offering to pay. This would invariably result in the same scenario: my mother and one of her friends sitting at the kitchen table, pushing a couple of coppers back and forth, with 'No! No! I couldn't take it from you!' and 'Now don't be silly, Mary, just take it!' This could go on for up to half an hour, until eventually my mother gave in.

The most important feature of the sitting room was the three-piece suite with its sofa, the back of which was the perfect height for saddling and mounting. Most nights after school I would jump on its back and go for a hack, my school satchel the saddle, its strap the bridle. I can remember a teacher once asking me why some of my exercise books seemed to be bent in such a peculiar way. 'Have you been sitting on them?' After this incident I made sure my satchel was empty before saddling up.

It was on this sofa that my addiction to *Coronation Street* started back in December 1960, watching the first episode with my mother. I am slightly ashamed to say that when my own daughter was born and I brought her home, that very evening I was sitting in front of the television, holding her, and when the theme for *Corrie* came on she turned her little week-old head towards the television in recognition. She remembered it from the womb. It was on that sofa that I would lie on a Saturday afternoon, the curtains drawn, watching the afternoon film. They were generally films from the thirties and forties, with Bette Davis being my favourite.

She was unique: there was an exciting, un-Hollywoodish reality and lack of vanity in her performances, and she always played strong women who had to be reckoned with.

I can still feel the rough, bobbly texture of that sofa with its maroon and grey upholstery, and smell its musty aroma as it warmed up on a winter's night in front of the four-bar Magicoal electric fire. We were allowed to have this on, just two bars, if the weather was really cold; anything warmer than Arctic and my mother's voice would shoot up an octave to register panic at the thought of a potentially colossal bill. Her fear of being in debt, and her resultant husbandry—to the extent that she would walk several miles to save a halfpenny on a pound of carrots—meant that no bill ever went unpaid.

The door out of the sitting room opened onto a little hall, on the left of which, down a couple of stone steps, was the pantry. It was a small, dark room, cool even in summer, with shelves laden with tinned food, a constant supply of my mother's rock cakes and, on the floor, a huge basket full of clean, unironed laundry. I loved my mother's rock cakes but their texture was the endless butt of jokes. I can remember my father mending a hole in the roof and shouting down to me in the garden, 'Oh blimey! Hand us up one of your mother's rock cakes.' Once, my brother Kevin and I played a game of cricket with one. It lasted for several overs and it wasn't until my brother hit a whacking great six that it finally disintegrated into a cloud of crumbs.

The pantry was brilliant for pretending to be Mrs Waller, who ran a small grocery shop over the road. Mrs Waller didn't so much run the corner shop as reign over it. A handsome woman in a pristine pink nylon overall that shushed every time she moved, she had beautifully waved honey-blonde hair and perfect make-up. If there was ever more than one customer she would throw her head back, as if she was about to sing an aria, and call, 'Trevaaaaar!' Trevor was her awkward teenage son with whom she appeared to be endlessly disgruntled. If Trevaaar was not available her husband would be summoned. A bespectacled, careworn man would appear through the plastic strips of curtain that hung across the doorway and stand there mutely. Without deigning even to look at him, she would bark instructions: 'Mrs Jordan's ham, please.' The men in Mrs Waller's life were a source of regret to her and she had a particular tone of voice reserved only for them. It was strident and imperious and every syllable screamed, 'I am too good for you!' But when I walked into the shop, her face would lift into a pretty pink smile and I would have penny bars of chocolate and twopenny chews thrust into my hand. Poor Trevor! If only he'd been a Tina.

Next to the pantry were the stairs, which like the little hall itself were covered with the same brown carpet, enlivened by a small motif in black repeated at regular intervals. Not long after my father had laid this carpet, my mother and I went into Freeman, Hardy & Willis on the Bearwood Road and there it was, our new carpet, all over the shop!

'Mum, I—'

That's as far as I got. I was dragged outside, my arm only just remaining in its socket and my mother's hot breath steaming up my ear: 'Don't mention the carpet!' My father was the shopfitter for Freeman, Hardy & Willis.

At eighteen months I had trodden on my nightdress while going up these stairs to bed and put a tooth through my lip, which still sports a tiny hairline scar today. These stairs were where, on dark nights, I had shouted endless 'Good nights' to my parents, stopping each time to wait for the comfort of their reply, and where I sang made-up songs as loud as I could so that any menace hiding behind the dark crack of a door would know how unafraid I was. They were also where I prepared for a possible career in bus conducting, charging up and down them wearing my father's old Box Brownie as a ticket machine.

Opposite the pantry and the stairs was the middle door; this opened at the side of the house onto the garden. The middle door was where everyone called; only strangers knocked at the front door. Here the milk was delivered, the milk cart being pulled by a big brown and white horse. My mother would shout, 'Get out there with a bucket and shovel, the milkman's coming,' then she would keep watch from an upstairs window and shout, 'Too late, SHE'S got it!' thus referring to a neighbour who was already scooping the steaming heap of horse dung with a satisfied smirk.

Our coal was also delivered by a horse-drawn cart. Mr Charlton of Charlton Brothers, Coal Merchants, would lumber up the garden path, followed by a couple of his minions, to the coal house, each with a hundredweight sack of coal on his back. He was an almost Dickensian figure, sporting a nautical-looking black cap, and a thick black leather jerkin. On his feet were a pair of huge hobnailed boots. He was completely black from head to toe, while his face was like an amateur actor's, blacked up to play Othello. The only bits that escaped were two pink crescents, one behind each ear, his pale grey eyes and his pure white hair. This last was only visible when, in a gentlemanly gesture, he would remove his hat to receive payment of his bill.

Next to the middle door was the kitchen. This was the room in which we mainly lived, as a family. My earliest memories are of this room: of clambering out of my pram, down onto a sofa, and finding Nelly, our black-and-white cat, buried beneath copies of the *Daily Mirror* and the *Reveille*. One of the few times I saw my mother cry was when Nelly died. She was at least twenty years old, but no one could be quite sure as she was already adult when she turned up out of nowhere and muscled her way in at number 69, ejecting the resident tomcat in the process. During her reign she had over a hundred kittens, mostly delivered in the bottom drawer of my mother's dressing table. Mum, cooing like a proud grandmother, fed any weaklings with an eardropper full of warm milk. There were times, when the births were at their most prolific, that the kittens would disappear soon after delivery and it was announced that Nelly had suffocated them by accidentally sitting on them, but I remember my father coming in from outside with an empty bucket. It was never discussed.

Nelly wasn't an affectionate cat. Too much stroking and the

claws would be out like a flash. When I was a child my hands and arms were permanently striped from Nelly's bad-tempered lashings, but Mum adored her and reserved a special voice with which to address her, high-pitched and squeaky with delight.

Strangely, the kitchen was not a kitchen at all. The real kitchen, which was called the scullery, was a tiny room next to it. The 'kitchen' was a smallish room with three easy chairs, their thin foam cushions usually balanced on top of a heap of newspapers. There was a large Singer sewing machine on elaborate wrought-iron legs, upon which our mother made a lot of our and her own clothes. In one corner stood a large kitchen cabinet on which we made golden syrup or jam sandwiches when we came in from school, and in the other corner was a big old-fashioned radio.

This was of great fascination. I loved turning the tuning dial and being plunged into some fuzzy foreign world called Hamburg or Bordeaux. It was a comfort to hear its familiar drone from other parts of the house. It meant that you were not alone, that life was being lived, and the voices of the BBC Light Programme promised that we were in safe hands. The first sound of the day, as I lay in bed, was the low drone of the shipping forecast vibrating up through the floorboards as my mother got ready for work. On Sundays our lunch, or dinner as it was called, was eaten to *Round the Horne*, *Beyond Our Ken* and *Hancock's Half Hour*. We took our meals round the Formica-topped table in the bay window, but as we grew older we collected our plates and took them off to eat watching television or doing homework, leaving my poor mother to eat by herself, as my father always came in much later. My sister-in-law tells of how she came round to be introduced to the family for the first time. She says that once the meal had been served suddenly there was no one in the room but herself and my mother and, with my mother nipping in and out, she virtually ate alone.

The scullery was where as small children we stood in the big old sink and washed. Water would have to be boiled up on the gas stove as there wasn't a hot tap. It was where my father shaved. I would stand on a little table next to him so that I could watch the pleasing process of shaving foam and bristles being removed in sharp, smooth tracts. I cannot deny that to this day a whiff of Old Spice does cause a distant thrill.

The bathroom upstairs was used only once a week when the immersion heater was put on, closely monitored by my mother; otherwise it was a room in which from November through to May you could see your breath. Lying in a hot bath meant lying shrouded in steam so thick that you could barely make out the taps at the other end. When I was growing up the bedroom was purely for sleeping. It never occurred to anyone then that people might 'need their space'. Apart from the lavatory, the only other room with a lock was the bathroom. Once ensconced in the warmth of the water, the clouds of white steam concealing the room, one could be transported for at least half an hour. With its echoey acoustic, a girl could hone to near perfection her impersonations of Sandie Shaw ('Always Something There to Remind Me'), the Ronettes ('Be My Baby') and the Supremes ('Baby Love'). And then, of course, the water would become tepid and the steam would turn to condensation. I can recall the pall of disappointment that would descend as the bleak old bathroom would gradually reveal itself out of the mist. It was lying in this bath, aged eighteen, knowing I was to embark on a nursing course in a matter of weeks, that I felt safe enough, under cover of the hot tap running at full tilt, to say in a small voice, 'I want to be an actress.' Words I had never spoken before. To anyone.

The scullery led in turn onto a sort of outhouse extension, which was called 'the back place'. In the corner there was a drain, and there was always a smell of soapsuds in the air from the seemingly endless rounds of washing and washing-up. In winter it also smelt of geraniums and coal dust, while in the summer the soapy freshness of the drain often turned a tad fetid. It was built on before our time to incorporate the coal house and the outside toilet, the latter referred to by my brother Kevin, for some unfathomable reason, as the Lah Pom. I preferred the upstairs toilet and rarely used the Lah Pom as it was often home to at least a couple of large house spiders. I was terrified of the creatures.

This is illustrated by an incident in 1979, when I was working on a play at the Hampstead Theatre Club and renting a flat. One evening I went to run a bath only to find a spider the size of a Bentley attempting to climb up the side of it. After letting out an unstoppable scream and trying to flush it down the plughole, I ended up phoning the director of the play and asking whether he would get rid of it. After coming some way across town, and with much hilarity, Mike Leigh humanely disposed of the thing and then went back to finish his tea.

The back place acted as an overflow to my father's garage, and it was here that, on coming in late at night as a teenager, I would reach up and blindly scrabble about on a dusty old shelf to find the key to the middle door. It was also home to a succession of pet rodents that I kept when aged about eleven and where I attempted to breed a couple of my best mice for business purposes. I pinned an advert onto the garage door: FOR SALE, ATTRACTIVE DOMESTICATED BABY MICE, TWO SHILLINGS EACH, OR TWO FOR THREE AND ELEVEN. The breeding programme went rather better than I had anticipated, and within a couple of weeks there were eight or nine tiny brown mice, no bigger than a thumbnail. Before I could separate them they had bred and bred again. I remember only one small girl and her friend enquiring about the mice. However, when they clapped eyes on them they wanted a reduction in price, claiming, 'They'm brown! They ent proper pet mice. Pet mice am white.'

'Yes they are. Pet mice can be any colour.'

'No they cor. I'll tek two for a bob.'

Needless to say there was no sale. I then became increasingly desperate as their numbers grew. Finally I came down one morning to find that the babies had eaten an escape route out of the wooden box in which they were being kept and had disappeared into a tangled heap of assorted piping that my father had dumped on the shelf. For years whenever we went out into the back place there was the sound of tiny scurrying feet across the stone floor.

Upstairs, there were three bedrooms. My parents' room was at the front of the house and in the corner stood a large mahogany wardrobe where our Christmas presents were hidden every year. A quick recce in about the third week of December would usually give the game away. It was where I came across my beloved red and yellow scooter, upon which for years I went everywhere.

My parents slept in a creaky old bed with a dark walnut headboard, and it was into this that I would creep every Saturday morning, once my mother had gone out, to cuddle up to my dad. On several occasions, seeing him get out of bed, I thought I had caught a glimpse through the flies of his pyjamas of something odd hanging round his nether regions. I subsequently asked my mother whether he was 'the same as me down below'. She instantly looked away and, with what I now see as total embarrassment, said, 'Yes, yes, yes, yes, yes, yes, yes . . .'. I thought the yeses were never going to stop and, in my innocence, regarded them as simply an expression of absolute confirmation. You can therefore imagine my surprise when, around the same time, I came across my brothers in fits of laughter, having put elastic bands on their willies. I could only deduce from this that the willy detached itself and fell off at some point before boys grew into men and that perhaps the elastic band had something to do with it. I remember fiercely debating this theory with several of my contemporaries, thinking how uninformed they were.

I could spend a whole afternoon in my parents' bedroom, going through the bottom drawer of my mother's dressing table, leafing through the personal things of her past. It was where I felt I could discover clues to her, like a detective: clues to the girl she once was before we came along. It was full of photographs of her as a young woman, dark and handsome. It is said that a lot of people living along the west coast of Ireland have dark complexions, and this is attributed to the fact that the Spanish Armada crashed on the rocks there. My mother, with her dark hair and eyes and olive skin, could easily have passed for Spanish, but when questioned about this she was outraged, claiming that 'The Irish met them with pitchforks!' To which my father replied, 'I think the Irish met them with something else, Mary!'

In these photographs her dark, strong features were set in an unsmiling, no-nonsense face, against an alien, sepia background. The images were peopled by worn, dusty-looking folk, staring pale-eyed at the camera with a self-consciousness that enthralled me and drew me in. There was a shabby leather handbag full of letters and postcards, from close friends and distant relatives long ago, from California and Australia and, of course, Ireland: chatty, intimate letters to a girl we never knew, who didn't yet know us. I would read the same letters over and over again, and stare at the same photographs, often employing a magnifying glass, hoping against hope that I would discover a vital secret.

Up until about six or seven I slept in the room next door to my parents. It was here during the Christmas of 1955 that I shared my brothers' double bed with my Auntie Agnes who was visiting from London. Auntie Agnes was my mother's younger unmarried sister. In her youth she had been quite beautiful and, we were told, she was never short of admirers. As a young girl, however, she developed an abscess on her hip that resulted in crippling arthritis, and she ended up with one leg being several inches shorter than the other. This plus regular migraines served to completely incapacitate her in late middle age. She would have no truck with men and she lived alone in a bedsit in Shepherd's Bush.

When she came to visit, it was usually cut short by some sort of argument between the sisters, resulting in Auntie Agnes flouncing out and taking a black cab to New Street station to board the train to London. My mother would no more take a cab than boil her own head. In fact the only time a black cab was ever seen in our street to my knowledge was when Auntie Agnes came to stay.

Their relationship was beset by a petty competitiveness. My mother once sent her a silk scarf for Christmas. Needless to say, she had not bought it; it was a gift that had been given to her by a work colleague. On receiving it my aunt sent it back immediately with a curt little note saying that she never wore silk next to her skin. During a visit one Christmas to her sister's flat, my mother, noting the paucity of cards that Agnes, 'the poor lonely thing', had received, asked in her best innocent-little-girl voice, 'How many did you get?'

'Oh . . .' my aunt began, but that was it, my mother came straight back with 'I had eighty-two!'

It was here, in this big, sagging double bed that I have my earliest memory of wetting the bed. Bed-wetting for me was a nightmarish saga that lasted through to the beginnings of puberty. Every night I begged God to spare me the usual morning humiliation of having to confess to my mother that I'd 'done it again' only to wake up at the familiar stench of ammonia and the cold, soggy tangle of pyjamas and sheets. How my mother managed, going out to work full-time as she did, with three children, Grandma and no washing machine, is simply unimaginable to me. Today the sheets would be whipped into a machine, then into the tumble drier and be back on the bed before a person could say 'incontinence pad'. Instead they had to be boiled in a bucket on the gas stove, rinsed, put through the mangle in the back yard and then transferred to the washing line, in all weathers, maybe taking days to dry.

The whole thing made staying at friends' houses out of the question unless my mother had words, and this brought its own shame: the whispered conversations in the hallway as we were about to leave; the friend's face as she greedily cottoned onto my secret and then no one mentioning it, culminating in my not daring to allow myself to sleep at all and so returning home exhausted. The only time my bed-wetting didn't provoke my mother's wrath was that Christmas when Auntie Agnes came to stay.

At the opposite end of the landing from my parents' bedroom was the back bedroom into which I moved after my grandmother passed away. With the airing cupboard in the corner and the toilet next door, there was a continual sound of dripping, whooshing and ticking of pipes. It was here that I lay in the dark, wood-framed bed that my grandmother had died in, listening under the covers to Radio Luxembourg on my father's big blue Bush transistor radio, until late at night when a hand smelling of Boots soap and fags came and retrieved it.

It was here one awful autumn in 1967 that I lay for a whole

month in disbelief at my being dumped by my first love, Bob. I endlessly pored over his letters, which I kept in an old sewing box under the bed, called my Bob Box. It was a relationship that was never consummated, its physical side consisting of a lot of snogging to the Beach Boys' 'God Only Knows' and well-mannered groping.

The only time we could have done the deed was when a group of us from school, who my parents thought were all girls, spent a weekend in a caravan somewhere in mid-Wales, the boys turning up later after our dads had dropped us off. Bob and I spent hours in frenzied snogging on a very narrow bunk once the lights went out but in an act of gallantry he placed the sheet between us, so that should his passion reach uncontrollable heights there would be this crisp white contraceptive to save the day. However, it wasn't the sheet that eventually cooled our ardour. It was the sound of whispering coming from the bunk opposite ours, where one of my friends was sleeping with a boy who was new to the group. The whispering then became more urgent.

'No! No! No!' And then, 'No, please, you're hurting me.' And with every 'No' I remember that Bob squeezed me to him as if I were the one calling out. For several minutes this poor girl's pleas hissed out into the silence, punctuated by pitiful sobs, which eventually died into whimpers. No one spoke or moved. Were my adult self to be transported back there, I would have spoken out and put a stop to what was going on. But back then we weren't sure, and one of the boys the next day, when his girlfriend expressed her concern, was reported to have said, 'Oh, she was all right. She must have wanted him to or she wouldn't have got into bed with him.'

Bob and I lasted only the length of the summer holidays, but in my memory the time was idyllically stretched. I have no photographs but in my blurry memory he is tall, dark and handsome, easily outclassing the normal run of suitor. So I thought myself lucky. There had been two or three before him, but they felt more like practice until the real thing came along. My dates with them involved mainly writhing about, while trying to keep straying hands out of my bra in case they should happen upon the handkerchiefs stuffed therein, as we sat in the back row of the Princess Hall Cinema on Smethwick High Street.

It always seemed as if few of the audience had gone to see the film. People would be talking, running up and down the aisles, or throwing things. Once, bizarrely, I saw half a grapefruit fly through the air and land on a chap's head like a chic little hat. On one occasion someone set fire to his seat. When the anarchy reached a certain pitch the manager would storm down to the front and scream, 'That's it! All the one and nines out!' And those in the cheap seats would be shown the door.

My dates with Bob were on another plane. He had just left school, grammar school to boot; having done A levels, he was going to teacher-training college; my brothers didn't sneer and, most importantly, my mother approved. So when he came home for the weekend after being away at college for about a month and told me in his front room—the room that I had left on so many occasions with my lips and chin raw from kissing—that he thought it was best that we finished, it was as if he was suddenly speaking Urdu and, indeed, everything in that familiar room instantly became unfamiliar. He walked me to the bus-stop. I don't know what was said and I probably couldn't have told you then either, overwhelmed by the terrible need to get away and cry.

As I sat on top of the bus, the tears began and they never really let up for about a month. Under any other circumstances my mother would have harangued me for taking to my bed, and at the time, though I didn't understand it, I was grateful for her silence. I questioned her about it much later, wondering what on earth she had made of the whole thing.

She said, 'We guessed that you had a broken heart, but we didn't like to say anything. We thought it best.'

I'm not sure why I was immensely touched by the fact that they had known all along. I know that their silence was born out of an inability to deal with 'feelings', but it was also born out of recognition, sympathy and, of course, wisdom.

The main advantage of the back bedroom was that just below

the sash window there was the roof of the back place. The roof joined onto the garden wall, which was about six feet high and separated us from number 68. This meant that it was possible to get down over the roof, onto the wall, down onto the dustbin placed conveniently beneath, and out into the world. It was also possible to do the thing in reverse if, as sometimes happened, the key to the middle door hadn't been left on the shelf in the back place.

At around sixteen or seventeen, I started going to clubs with Chris, my best friend from school. She was strikingly beautiful, with a mane of dark brown hair and blue eyes fringed by almost doll-like lashes, causing male heads to whip round to look wherever we went. My mother thought that I was just spending the evening round at Chris's house. We would head to Birmingham made up to pull, or at least impress, the thought of pulling a stranger in a nightclub being a little scary. Once on the number 9 bus, we would go straight upstairs onto the back seat. Then Christine would open her handbag and take out a bottle of Estée Lauder's Youth Dew. She would first spray both of our necks just below each ear and then, employing a huge circular movement, she would totally enshroud us in a cloud of the stuff. Next out of the bag came a little pack of Beechnut spearmint chewing gum. To finish off, out would come the Consulate menthol cigarettes. We were good at communicating solely by gesture or look. This was mainly down to the fact that Chris had a not insubstantial stutter.

We both purported to be Mods, which meant that we wore leather jackets over twin-sets and pearls, below-the-knee pencil skirts and clumpy shoes. On our nights out in town, however, we donned more slinky evening attire and Chris would often do our hair. One of the fashions of the day was a soft set of bubbly, bouncing curls, and Chris made a valiant effort at achieving this look for the two of us with the help of a set of rollers and a couple of litres of cheap hair lacquer. This liquid set the curls into rigid little pompoms all over the head and the whole thing was rendered highly inflammable. There were terrible tales of girls bending their heads to light a cigarette and their whole hair catching alight, burning it down to the scalp.

There was an occasion once, after I'd started work, when I went out on a Sunday night. There wasn't time on the Monday morning to comb out the stiff curls with their solid lacquered finish. After I had slept on it for several hours, my hair had taken on a very odd shape, completely flat on one side, while wildly frizzing out on the other. I slipped into the office and sat at my desk. Within minutes the boss was at my elbow, hissing in my ear: 'You're late! And take that silly wig off your head!'

On these nights out we would most often end up at the Locarno, a large club in the centre of Birmingham. In my memory, it was enormous and divided into several bars and a couple of dance floors, each appealing to a different age group, one for what we thought of as middle-aged people but who were most likely folk in their early twenties. Here the music was live and the band tended to play rock-and-roll, Elvis Presley, Frank Ifield, Tom Jones, the Beatles. No matter what, it always seemed to finish off with couples draped over each other, moving slowly round the room to 'I Remember You' by Frank Ifield and, later, 'Hey Jude'. At some point midway through the evening we would look in on our way to the toilets with the intention of mocking the 'aged' dancers.

On one of these occasions I was asked to dance by a tall, gaunt-looking Irishman with an engaging smile. After a few minutes jigging around he started to have a coughing fit and during the course of it something flew down the front of my dress. I remembered the cigarette in his hand and, seeing that it was no longer there, began to jump up and down. By this time the man was on the floor, flailing about among the feet of the nearby dancers. I shouted down to him not to bother about his fag, that my friend had some, but he was having none of it, getting up and lurching out of the room without a word. Later that night on the bus home, I reached down to adjust the handkerchief padding of my ill-fitting bra, and entangled in it was a pair of false teeth on a little pink plate.

With my knickers hanging down in the garden at 69 Bishopton Road, Smethwick—a sign of things to come.

A day out with Mum and Dad, Kevin and Tommy in Blackpool—a rare portrait of all the family together at the same time.

On midsummer's eve 1969, I met and fell in love with my first proper boyfriend, whom I shall name 'DT'. I confided to DT that I wanted to be an actress.

A scene from 'Educating Rita' with Michael Caine. He was funny, friendly and direct, with a working-class down-to-earthiness that put me at my ease straight away.

The Golden Globes, 1984, for 'Educating Rita'. My outfit was pronounced the worst there by one publication, but as this was Hollywood, I took it as a compliment.

Victoria Wood and me in the early days. We met at the Bush Theatre in West London in 1978, slipping easily into friendship during rehearsals of 'In at the Death'.

Mrs Overall, the cleaner, in 'Acorn Antiques', a sketch written by Victoria Wood and based on a badly made soap opera. She is my favourite character of all time.

With my husband Grant Roffey, the very handsome man that I met in a bar in Fulham.

The other room at the Locarno was presided over by a DJ playing mainly Tamla Motown, which was our kind of music. 'This Old Heart of Mine' by the Isley Brothers along with 'The Harlem Shuffle' by Bob & Earl never fail to summon up the Locarno for me. We would throw our bags down and, fag in hand, coolly shift from foot to foot, our shoulders lifting and dropping to the beat in a kind of lazy shrug.

Christine was a good few inches taller than my five foot three and a half and could easily peruse the dance floor over the top of my head, where groups of young men lurked and perused us back. I would watch her face and await the signal that meant we were being approached by two eligible contenders. This would be an excited widening of the eyes and the hint of a smile. If, on the other hand, we were being approached by two chaps that she considered inferior, she would throw me a look of horror that befitted the heroine in a silent movie.

She was very conscious of her height. However, it was guaranteed that if two blokes came over, one tall and the other short, it would be the short one that made a beeline for Chris, as if her height was a challenge. She would generally ignore them by staring imperiously into the middle distance above their heads.

On one occasion, a particularly small man suddenly appeared from nowhere, right in front of her, and started to cavort about in a sort of awful homage to Mick Jagger, with much leaping up onto the toes of one foot and clapping his hands above his head, all done side on to Christine, like a matador with a bull. It was as if he were trying to show how virile he was, yet at the same time proving the exact opposite. This, of course, we found irritatingly uncool and Christine stopped dead and stood there, staring down at him; but the man didn't notice, too wrapped up in his dance. Finally he threw his hands up into the air above his head and Christine caught hold of them with one hand and shouted directly into his face, 'Can't you see I'm taller than you!' In unison we left the floor, cackling cruelly as we went.

On these nights we would most likely get home somewhere

between midnight and one o'clock. My parents, having gone to bed at about ten thirty, assumed that we had got in not long after that. On many occasions when they had forgotten to leave the key out I scaled that wall onto the roof and in through the bedroom window in evening clothes and high heels, having downed several rum and blacks.

Across the yard from the back place was a double garage, built by my father. It housed my dad's car and that of Reg Wood, his sometime partner. There was a poignant little echo twenty years later, when I teamed up with Victoria for the Granada television series *Wood and Walters*. As well as the cars, the garage was home to the guinea pig, imaginatively named Guinea.

Guinea pottered round the garden during the day, going back into the garage at night, usually when my dad came home from work. Guinea always ran out and watched as my father drove his car in, returning to his cage when the parking was complete. My father said that had Guinea lived much longer, he would have started shouting, 'That's it! Left hand down a bit! You've gorrit!' For six years he led an uneventful life until we introduced him to a female guinea pig called Janet. He went berserk, trying to mount this poor creature in a very agitated fashion. After a few hours, during which I left them, thinking that things would calm down, I went in to check on them, only to find Guinea stone dead and Janet lying exhausted in the corner.

Many years later my daughter had a couple of guinea pigs of her own, a large grey male called Robin and a tiny chestnut one called Rosette. Remembering Guinea's right-to-roam lifestyle, I suggested that Robin and Rosette should graze to their hearts' content on the little lawn at the back of our house. They got on fine for at least half an hour, whereupon Maisie came screaming into the house, 'They're dead! They're dead!' I ran out into the garden, expecting them both to be prostrate from shagging, only to find that Plato, our black and white tomcat, had attacked them, having Rosette for first course and Robin for second. I suffered many years of 'You saids' from Maisie, but I honestly thought all would be well. It remains a mystery to this day how Guinea survived unmolested when he was surrounded by a neighbourhood full of cats, not to mention our own formidable Nelly.

The garage was also the venue for my first theatrical triumphs. These were shows put on by my brother Tommy, with me very much in a supporting role. We bullied local children into getting threepence from their mothers, then proceeded to lock them in while we terrorised them with our made-up dramas, mainly inspired by some television play or other and involving a lot of my mother's old lipstick and cast-off dresses.

It all came to a stop during one of my brother's magic acts. He would stand there, in a magician's cape and hat, and tell the audience that he was going to make me disappear by putting me in the special cabinet. This he had made himself out of bits of old wood. We had rehearsed and rehearsed, and all that I was required to do was to step into this cabinet. While waving his wand about, Tommy would declaim in a high, moany sort of voice some mysterious incantation; then, touching the cupboard with the tip of his magic wand, he would close the door. After this there would be more magic-speak, rising in speed and volume to increase the dramatic tension. Meanwhile, inside the cabinet I was simply meant to slip behind a bit of old red blanket that was hanging down at the back, so that when my brother at last opened the door I would have 'disappeared'. The blanket's real function was to conceal a gap between it and the back wall of the cupboard.

However, one summer holiday the magic show did not go to plan. We had gone through the usual procedure of my brother introducing me as his assistant, whereupon I would parade about with much waving of arms, dramatically indicating the various facets of the 'amazing magic box'. Of course I wasn't allowed to speak and was given a good whack once when I had offered to tell them where I had actually gone during the period of my magical disappearance. On this particular day, I dutifully got into the cabinet as usual. Whether I was feeling mutinous, as the whacking incident had rankled, I don't know, but the thought of pricking the bubble of my brother's pomposity as he preened and strutted about was terrifying, exciting and, above all, funny.

The door was duly whisked open with a grand flourish, Tommy announcing with great assurance that, as everyone could see, I had vanished. He didn't notice for what seemed like an age that I was still standing there. It was only when the children began to titter that he cottoned on. He wheeled round, and I can still see the shock in his eyes, made more vivid by the bright-red hieroglyphics painted on his cheeks and forehead with my mother's lipstick. The look of shock changed briefly to one of hurt, followed, in a second, by a flash of anger as he came towards me. I jumped out of the box and ran out across the yard and into the back place, where I locked myself in the dreaded spider-ridden Lah Pom.

After the children had been dismissed, my brother came to find me, and having been given several assurances that he would not hit me I opened the door. He said, 'It's all right.' And I could see that he wasn't in fact angry at all. 'Why did you do it?' His expression was one of bafflement. I had betrayed him, and I guess it could be said that this was an early lesson in stage trust, but there was something else, and I think it was a little touch of respect. He had caught a glimpse of the future actor in me, creating the drama and grabbing the limelight.

A year or so later a man knocked on the door with a script in his hand. He was from our parish church and, having told my mother they were doing a play at the church hall, asked whether I would like a part in it. He gave me the script and I scurried off upstairs to read it. I have little memory of it, except that my character had quite a few lines in the form of a single speech and the play was a Bible story of some sort. My mother made this man a cup of tea, and by the time he had drunk it, I was downstairs again, performing my part, the script held behind my back, the speech having gone effortlessly in. When I did come to perform it, it was my brother Tommy who rushed to tell me, with wonder in his voice, that not only was I really good but that I was the best! It is something he has done ever since.

# *Two*

I got my first suntan during a heatwave in 1966 when I was preparing for my GCEs. I sat out in the back yard on a kitchen chair, head back, eyes closed. When I went back into the house, I found that my face had turned a bright, not unattractive, brownish pink. And there began an addiction, which I still have. It made everything look better. My hair, which was still vaguely blonde, looked blonder; my eyes looked browner, and my skin looked brighter and healthier, but above all I looked as if I had been somewhere exciting and exotic. It was in the sixties that people started to take holidays to Spain, and so gradually suntans, which were very rare after a holiday in an English seaside resort, began to be something of a status symbol. In our own street, the first people to go abroad on a regular basis were a family at the bottom end of Long Hyde Road. They were an attractive lot, in a flashy, television-advert sort of way, a pretty blonde mother and daughter and a darkly handsome father and son. But what set them aside from the rest of us was that once a year they would go off somewhere, looking similar to everyone else, and return a couple of weeks later as another species: bronzed, relaxed, transformed into world travellers.

The Walters took their yearly week away within the confines of the United Kingdom and came home looking much the same as when they left. We holidayed in Wales, camping with a couple of other families. We had caravan holidays in Weymouth, Margate and Weston-super-Mare, and even now the smell of Calor Gas takes me right back there, snuggling down under the covers on a narrow bunk bed. But the holiday location I most remember was Blackpool.

All five of us would pack into our Ford Esquire car, the roof rack piled high with a motley collection of suitcases, and head off on a journey that took about six hours as there were no motorways. I always had to sit in the middle, my two brothers on either side, and Kevin was invariably carsick.

There were a couple of mysterious remedies employed to stave this off. One was a small chain suspended from underneath the rear bumper and the other one was Kevin having to wear a brown-paper vest. As neither worked, the smell of vomit, petrol fumes and cigarette smoke was the perennial accompaniment to these journeys, my brother insisting on the last, claiming that it would prevent the first. My father, having been given the excuse to smoke continually, did so and we spent the whole journey in an eye-watering fug, my brother with his head in a carrier bag, and the rest of us playing I Spy and eating the cheese-and-tomato sandwiches that my mother had made before we set out. The game of I Spy would stop on the approach to Blackpool and be replaced by 'The first one to see the tower!' and then, 'The first one to see the sea!'

We always stayed at number 26 Empress Drive, a bed and breakfast that was run by a Mrs McGinn. Empress Drive was a quiet residential street, lined with neat terraced Edwardian houses, with bright-white fronts, well-kept privet hedges and gleaming windows. Inside, number 26 smelt of fresh paint, clean carpets and lavender furniture polish. Every nook and cranny was dust-free and polished to a military shine. Once inside, we were encouraged by my mother to speak in little more than a whisper. Breakfast was a self-conscious ritual, where the crunch of toast was deafening.

After breakfast we would gather our things for the day, because we were not allowed back in until the evening. If the weather was fine—that is, not actually raining—we would walk down to the North Shore and my parents would ensconce themselves in a couple of deck chairs, both of them, whatever the weather, fully dressed, my father on occasion wearing a suit, albeit with sandals and socks. I would strip down to my stretchy ruched bathing costume, having underdressed back at the b. & b. in order not to have to go through the embarrassing palaver of trying to change on the beach. It was bad enough at the end of the day, wobbling about on one foot as you tried to remove a sodden swimming costume.

I would run off to the sea with my mother's cries of 'Don't go out too far!' hanging in the air after me. Before I was born, Kevin, who would have been two at the time, had nearly drowned in a pothole at Sandersfoot but was saved by a family friend, himself only a boy. He had held on to Kevin after seeing him in trouble, until my father reached them after running flat out across jagged rocks and stones. Then, with terrible irony, when he was a young man my brother's saviour was himself drowned, after being swept away by a freak wave while on holiday. So my parents were ever vigilant when any of us were in the sea.

In the event of inclement weather we would walk down the Golden Mile, an exciting string of shops selling 'Kiss Me Quick' hats, plastic miniatures of the tower and all sorts of incongruous items made out of sugar, such as giant baby's dummies, false teeth or women's breasts. I remember on one occasion seeing an elderly woman sucking with great enthusiasm on a pink phallus, wrapped in a bit of cellophane. I instantly knew from my giggling parents' reaction that it was somehow lewd. There were shops selling every piece of crockery imaginable with *Blackpool* plastered all over it. It was thrilling, and I believe that at one time or another I bought all of the above, excluding, that is, the body parts.

The very best, though, was the funfair. We visited this only once during the whole holiday because it was deemed too expensive. My abiding memory is of the Mad Mouse, a small bullet-shaped carriage built to hold two people. The track was high up over the water. It started teasingly slowly up a steep incline until it reached the first corner, round which it would abruptly swerve at break-neck speed, making the passenger feel that the little car was going to career off the edge and plummet into the water below. It was heaven! After going on it the first time, I was so gloriously terrified that my right arm was paralysed. I had to go on it again, several times, to get the feeling back.

I went back to Blackpool in the 1990s to film *Wide-Eyed and Legless* for the BBC and was thrilled to find that I would be staying at the Imperial Hotel on the front. As a child, whenever we drove past it, my mother would say with a wistful little laugh, 'Oh, the Imperial.' And my father would chime in with respectful resonance, 'Oo ah, I'd love to see inside that.'

As I stood at reception, checking in, I felt a lump gather in my throat, and at the earliest opportunity I went in search of Empress Drive. As always happens when you revisit a place you frequented as a child, everything was smaller. The street was narrower and shorter, and the houses a little grimier, poorer, less cared for. I walked back to the hotel feeling as if the sight of that road was an assault on my perfect bubble of memory; but the memory is robust and the Empress Drive of the 1950s is still preserved within it, in all its bright, optimistic glory.

I NOTICE as I write down the memories of my life that I tend constantly to refer to my mother and far less to my father. This is because my mum was the centre of the family, whereas my dad tended to hover on the edge of our life.

Thomas Walters was born in 1909. The family lived in Icknield Port Road in Ladywood, a poor inner-city suburb of Birmingham widely regarded as a slum. He was the second youngest of six children, comprising four older sisters and a younger brother. His father was killed during the Battle of the Somme in 1916. He often told us how he was sent to the headmaster's office and, aged seven, holding the hand of his five-year-old brother, was told bluntly, 'You'd better get off home to your mother, your dad's been killed.'

I think it is significant that he himself didn't have a father for much of his growing up, for he seemed ill at ease with some of the requisites of fatherhood. Dealing with my brothers he seemed to shrink back, and it was my mother who was always at the forefront when it came to family discussion. If an argument were to take place, he would disappear. There was one incident between Kevin and myself, when he was eighteen and I was thirteen, where I hurled an ashtray at him. I missed and hit my father on the knuckle. Instead of intervening, Dad simply said, 'I'm getting out of here,' and left the room. He seemed to have little connection with his sons and, although proud, I believe he felt reduced by their academic achievements. However, it was his sense of humour that was the basis of his survival. When my brother Tommy announced he had won a scholarship to Cambridge to study for a PhD, my father was reading the *Smethwick Telephone*, our local rag, and without looking up he said, 'I can't see any adverts for philosophers in the Situations Vacant.'

He was a slightly built, wiry man with dark curly hair, swept back and tamed by a daily dose of brilliantine. Both of my parents being small, dark-eyed and dark-haired, they were often mistaken for brother and sister. Dad always looked older than his years, his face hollow-cheeked, weathered and deeply riven with lines. Even when he was smiling, there was a permanent expression of worry etched deep into his face.

I was his favourite and was in no doubt whatsoever of his love for me. My love for him, however, felt more like pain: it hurt and was suffused with pity. As a child, I fretted about him and for him. This, I think, was in part because of his physical appearance. His smoking habit, having started in childhood, kept him very thin. When questioned by us as to why he never went into the sea while on holiday, he said, 'Last time I went swimming, everyone thought it was a pair of braces floating in the water.'

But it was also due to the way my mother related to him. She constantly referred to him as 'your poor father' while commenting favourably about other, bigger men: 'Oh, he's a fine figure of a man.' She spoke in reverential terms about men in professional positions, 'He's a bank manager!' or 'He's a doctor!' Her voice lowered in register, indicating the deep respect she felt for a man in such a position. I don't think these things were said with any malice towards my father. I think they were born more out of insensitivity, together with frustration about her own position in life; but they fuelled the fear and pity that I felt for him, and my brothers took much pleasure in whipping up these feelings with merciless teasing.

One incident has stayed with me. I was about five and there had been a snowstorm with high winds which had brought our garden fence down. I watched, helpless, at the kitchen window as my dad struggled alone with the six-foot-high fence as the wind tossed it this way and that, its force sending him staggering. He looked small, David against the Goliath of the elements, and there was no one to help, all three of us having been told to stay indoors. I felt wretched watching this pitiful little scene, while my brothers cranked it up several notches: 'Oh poor Dad, look, he can't lift the fence. Ahhh, poor Dad.' I was conscious that he was a lot older than other people's dads, forty-one when I was born, and this was a source of embarrassment; I felt guilty that I changed the subject when the age of people's parents was being discussed.

He met my mum while drinking in the Leebridge Tavern on Dudley Road in Ladywood, where she was working as a barmaid, the job she landed when she first came to England. He set her on a pedestal instantly, I suspect feeling that he had been lucky to catch this attractive, intelligent woman who was a cut above those around him. No one could make my mother laugh as my father could. Many a time I would walk into the kitchen and find her doubled up, unable to get her breath, because of some joke Dad had relayed to her. He would be laughing too but his laughter was more to do with the pleasure of watching hers. They courted for six months and then married in 1941. My father was never called up. Instead he worked at Lucas Electrics, making munitions.

His great pleasure in life was a pint with his cronies at the Dog Inn or the King's Head on the Hagley Road. The Dog Inn was a place for a quiet drink with other regulars, whereas the King's Head was where Dad went to 'see a man about a dog', which presumably meant he was meeting a business associate. My mother continually complained, 'Oh, your father's down the pub again,' and related to us how she had seen people ruin their lives by drinking their money away. His other love was horse racing. He studied form and was often to be found in front of the television, fag in mouth, watching the racing on a weekday afternoon when my mother thought he was at work. He had several large wins, which paid for cars and holidays, but when he died his account was pretty much in the red.

When the war was over he started his decorating business. Although he was wholly uneducated, leaving school at fourteen, he had an eye for colour and form, and a strong visual sense. This could be seen in the way he dressed and in the few oil paintings he did, two of which were hung in a local art gallery. He started in his fifties, and generally liked to paint portraits. He did a telling self-portrait; a portrait of me at about twenty-one, which I found embarrassing at the time, because it touched on my adolescent awkwardness; and a beautiful painting of three children, eyes fixed on the painter as if they were staring down the lens of a camera.

My father's work life seemed to take a huge toll on him. His hands, always cut and misshapen with bruises, were yet another catalyst for my pity. As a child I would hold them, moved and pained by their appearance, and Dad would just laugh, amused by my concern. He became increasingly tired as the years went by, unable to get up in the mornings. During the school holidays, my mother used to ring up every morning from her office in her tea break to see whether he had gone to work. At night he would fall asleep in the chair, head back, mouth open, snoring.

He broke his ankle while painting a ceiling, aged around fifty. It took a long time to heal and afterwards he always walked with a limp. This, plus a heart attack when he was fifty-two, blamed largely on the forty Park Drive ciggies a day that he was smoking, aged him terribly. One day he walked into the GP's surgery, thinking he was suffering from indigestion. The doctor listened to his heart and sent him straight to hospital. The heart specialist said it was imperative that he give up smoking. My father refused point-blank, stating that smoking was 'the only pleasure I've got left'. The heart attack simply confirmed what I feared as a child, that my 'poor father' hadn't the strength to withstand the blows that life seemed to be dealing him.

A couple of months before his death I was sitting with him in the kitchen, having come home from college for the weekend, when he said, 'I don't think I've got a lot longer left, Bab, but I want you to know that it's all right because I've had a good life and I'm tired now.' He died, aged sixty-two, in 1971, of another heart attack, this time a massive one that killed him more or less instantly. He was lying in bed with my mother, chatting. She asked him a question and he didn't answer, just hiccupped and died. It had been a beautiful July day; he had been up on the roof, mending it; but, more importantly, he had won on the horses.

BRIDGET O'BRIEN, my maternal grandmother, had come to live with us towards the end of the war after the death of my grandfather, having found the farm they ran together just outside Castlebar, County Mayo, too much for her alone. None of her four children, of which my mother was the eldest, was prepared to take it on. Because my mother was the cleverest of the four, her parents had earmarked her to run it and look after them in their old age. Having plans of her own, she ran away, aged twenty-six, telling them that she was just going to visit England, and she never came back. Then when she announced six months later that she was going to marry a builder, a letter came from her mother, demanding that she should 'come home at once!' and commenting, disparagingly, 'marrying a man in overalls indeed!'

I don't think Grandma acknowledged my father once during the whole fifteen years she was with us, except for the odd sneering lift of her nose. Tommy also got short shrift, due to the fact that he was born before she arrived, and also because of his resemblance to my father. Kevin, born not long after she arrived, was her out-and-out favourite. This, I think, was because he looked like her favourite son, Martin, and, more importantly, her late husband, Patrick. I fell somewhere in between, and feel now that I was probably lucky to be neither loved nor hated by her.

She had suffered a couple of strokes even before I was born, and my brothers used to say, 'At the third stroke she will be seventy-eight.' It turned out that she had in fact suffered a whole series of tiny cerebral bleeds, which had an effect similar to Alzheimer's disease. She would frequently get up in the small hours, dressed only in a pair of truss-pink knee-length bloomers and a pair of brown fluffy zip-up boots, and she would disappear into the night.

The first we would hear of it would be a phone call from the local post office where she would always end up at a godforsaken hour, banging on the door. My father was duly summoned by a fairly pissed-off postmaster to go and pick her up. Then there would be a bit of a scuffle where he, the postmaster and the postmaster's wife would attempt to get my grandmother into her dressing gown. This was no mean feat, as Grandma's strength was legendary. The whole post office debacle would invariably end, after my grandmother's repeated claims that she had no idea who my father was, with her getting into his van with her usual imperious lift of the nose.

Things seemed to take a turn for the worse when a pigeon shat on her head in Trafalgar Square. We had gone on a day-trip to London in my father's Ford Esquire estate. The M1 had just been built and I must have been about nine. Things were fine on the way down but after the pigeon incident she became rather quiet. Then when we were about halfway back up the motorway she announced that she was going to 'get up now and make the tea', whereupon she attempted to get out of the car. My mother instructed us to sit on her, which we did, but every few minutes, she would start again: 'I'll get up now and make the tea.' Eventually we managed to distract her with a pile of magazines, and she began to shred them into thin strips. By the time we reached home, the car was like a giant hamster's nest.

I remember us getting out and my mother's face, livid, some of the strips trapped among the curls of her newly permed hair: '*Now* you can get up and make the bloody tea!' My grandmother closed her eyes in a world-weary way, then up went the nose and out she got. As she walked up the garden path like a world leader on a state visit, my brother shouted from the car, 'Grandma's wet on the seat . . . Eeeeeew . . .'

From then on she had her own special seat next to the fire in the kitchen. She ate all her meals sitting in it. One evening, we turned round and there was my grandmother performing the delicate task of eating a soft-boiled egg with a huge pair of coal tongs, her face blackened with coal and sticky with yolk. It was the seat in which she did everything, literally. I can remember the priest once getting up out of it with a damp patch on the back of his cassock and us all staring silently as he waved a jolly goodbye at the gate. So we were on full alert when visitors arrived, ready to head them off at the first sign that they might wish to take the weight off their feet.

My poor mother did what she could about my grandmother's incontinence, but with three children and a full-time job, she couldn't always give it her whole attention. I can remember feeling very angry seeing her, exhausted after a full day's work, clearing up yet another of my grandmother's deposits.

One day, I saw Grandma walk up the middle of our small strip of garden, which Mum had lovingly tended. I watched as lupins, gladioli and pansies were mashed underfoot and at the same time small, hard turds were dropping out from under her old black skirt as she walked along, just like a horse. My dad then erected some chicken wire round the garden to stop her wandering onto it, but this had to be taken down when one day we found her spread-eagled, flat on her face with both feet stuck in the chicken wire.

For several years after the war my mother kept chickens for eggs and occasionally, at Christmas, one would be dispatched for lunch, my grandmother doing the honours. These birds would invariably be a little tough, so one year a turkey was bought to be raised for the following Christmas. However, when it came to it my mother refused to allow it to be put down. So it became a pet.

It grew to an enormous size, strutting round and seeing off

anyone who had the audacity to come in through the back gate. Tradesmen were terrified of it. When the milkman came in with his daily delivery, the turkey would run the full length of the garden and, like an overfilled jumbo, take off just as he reached the end. As the milkman was bending down to put the milk on the step, the turkey would fly at him with a fearsome squawk, its awful talons to the fore. My mother refused to get rid of him, stating that he was as good as a watchdog. This state of affairs continued until one day Kevin, three at the time, came running into the house, screaming. The thing was on his head, its talons embedded in his scalp. So Grandma was dispatched to do the dispatching.

Grandma was a whiz at dispatching. Legend would have it that she could dispatch, pluck and draw a bird in about ten minutes. The other thing she was good at was making sugar sandwiches, something my mother would never allow: squares of white bread slathered in butter and thickly covered in white sugar. When I came in from school these treats were produced with pleasure.

She was also an endless source of entertainment, introducing into our vocabulary words that no one has ever been able to explain. 'Ahhh, she's like a maharather in bad weather!' is one example, and we children were often referred to as 'wee goms' as in 'get up out of bed, you wee gom!' When she sat down to watch television, she never really understood that whoever was on television at the time couldn't hear her. If there was a drama on, she would join in with the dialogue: 'How dare you speak to her like that!' She was hard of hearing and would often shout, 'What did you say? Speak up, man!' Her eyesight wasn't too good either, and once, while watching a ballet, she suddenly stood up and said, 'How dare you display yourself in front of me like that!' and marched out of the room. She had thought that the male dancer, instead of wearing tights, was naked from the waist down.

Grandma was a good playmate too, and you could engage her in most games of make-believe. I have one vivid memory of telling her that she had just started school, as I had done in reality only days earlier. She became completely immersed in this. I can see her face now and can remember being quite frightened by its sudden transformation. It became strangely lopsided, the small, brown eyes moist and shining, her mouth stretched wide into a grin, clearly showing that she had but one yellow tooth in the middle of her upper jaw. She began to babble excitedly about learning to read and write, and then she wrote her maiden name in a childish scrawl several times on the paper I had given her. Two or three years after she died this had a rather strange repercussion.

I must have been about twelve at the time, and I had decided to move up into the unused attic room at the top of the house. It was a large, cold room with a big sash window, looking down over the street. One wall was papered with front covers of *Punch* magazine from when Tommy had slept there briefly. It felt wonderfully removed from the rest of the house, as no one ever went up there.

On the first night that I was to spend in this room, I got into bed, excited by the fact that I had a light suspended above my pillow that I could switch on by pulling a cord. I was reading my comic when the light suddenly went out, so I yanked it back on. This happened again several times. In the end I gave up and snuggled down to go to sleep. Just as I was drifting off, the light came back on again. I pulled the cord to turn it off but on it came again. This time, my heart hammering, I quickly put an arm out from under the blankets and snapped it off. '*Stop it!*' I shouted, and it did. I lay there for some time, unable to sleep, wondering whether the light did this every night, when suddenly the door to the room was flung open, pushing the tattered old floor rug back with a mighty squeak. I stayed under the covers, sick with fear. I told myself it must be a draught, and eventually I fell into a fitful sleep.

When I awoke next day the door was still wide open but the morning light had removed all threat. It was when I got up that I noticed a small piece of paper a couple of feet from the bed. I recognised it immediately. It was the paper I had given my grandmother some seven years earlier, on her 'first day at school'.

I couldn't work out where it had come from, but then I remembered that outside the door, on the landing, was the trunk my grandmother had brought with her from Ireland filled with various items of her belongings. But why would this scrap of paper have been kept in her trunk? Maybe she had treasured it, but even so, if it had been put in her trunk, with its heavy wooden lid, how did it get out of there and into this room, which I had cleaned thoroughly the day before, and how did this stiff old door open with such force? Well, suffice it to say I never slept up there again.

Grandma died in 1960. As she lay dying I would sit by her bed and moisten her lips with a tiny brush dipped in water, fascinated once again by the transformation of her face, this time with an unrecognisable peace that softened her features. I saw for the first time that there was beauty in her face.

I'm asked time and time again about why I choose to play people older than myself: Mrs Overall, or Robert Lindsay's mother in *GBH*, or, more recently, Evie in the film *Driving Lessons*. I believe the main reason is that I want to re-create the fun and the calamity that was caused by my grandmother in our house for almost the whole of my childhood years.

This conundrum was partly solved when I was involved in an *Omnibus* for BBC Television about my life. I went back to the west of Ireland to the place where my mother was born. The thatched cottage that she had been brought up in had long since been demolished, but I spoke to the people who had lived next door. When I asked them about my grandmother, the woman they described came as a revelation. She was lively, energetic and funny, loved by the local children and always welcoming with an apple to give them from the orchard. I was shocked, feeling both deprived of that woman that they had all known and saddened when I thought of the confused, cantankerous old woman I had grown up with. It made no sense to me, and then I remembered the beauty of that face as she lay dying, with its secret smile, and somehow it did.

# Three

'Now you're a proper schoolgirl!' I felt my stomach tighten. I was standing in the kitchen, wearing a white blouse, with a navy, silver and yellow tie under a navy-blue gym-slip that almost reached my ankles. It would have been the beginning of January 1955, and in a week or so I was about to start school at the kindergarten of a convent preparatory school in Birmingham.

My mother had talked about my new school in reverential tones. 'Oh, you'll learn how to speak properly,' whereupon she would launch into an awful attempt at a middle-class English accent: 'You'll be mixing with doctors' daughters and the like.' I was uncomfortable with her talking in this way and even then saw it as some sort of betrayal. Clearly the way we spoke and the fact that I was a builder's daughter meant that I was quite simply not good enough, so I started that school ashamed of who I was.

I was to be taken to school by Mary, the older sister of one of Kevin's friends. Her mum ran a clothing catalogue, and every Monday night I was dispatched to pay our instalment, or the 'club money' as it was called. Her dad was usually there, ensconced in his armchair. He was from Southern Ireland, older than his wife and gently spoken. When I was very small he would take me on his knee and tell me stories of fairies and elves in a dramatic voice that could make the hair on the back of my neck stand up, but he would always end in a burst of laughter and a rough, bristly cuddle.

I loved these Monday nights. I would be sat down in front of the television and given tea in a china cup and saucer, plus a piece of fruit-cake, while I watched *Bonanza*. Their own children were older than me and off out or in another room doing their homework. In fact I can remember feeling disappointed if any of the children were there because their mum and dad might have been distracted from their pampering of me.

Mary was their middle child, seven or eight years older than me, a pupil at the senior school, next door to the prep. She was a pretty girl with long dark hair and a massive amount of good sense. The journey to school consisted in part of a fifteen-minute bus ride towards the city centre. On that first morning I was just about to step down at the stop when, with a sweep of her arm, Mary pushed me aside and leapt from the bus. Then she stood in the path of a speeding bicycle, thus preventing what might have been a rather nasty collision. She struck a pose like Superwoman, while the cyclist, with a squeaking of brakes, ended up with his handlebars pressed hard up against her tightly belted regulation gabardine mac. Mary held the cyclist there, their faces just inches apart, while she waved me and several other passengers safely off the bus. Words were exchanged but I cannot remember what they were, except that his were said with an angry scowl. What I do know is that, without a doubt, she came off best.

After this act of bravery I was in complete awe and rarely dared to speak a word to her on our subsequent journeys. I even put up with her spitting on her handkerchief and cleaning my face with it. So I was not a little relieved when at six years old I was allowed to travel to and from school by myself.

The school was situated in a middle-class residential road, full of large detached houses. It consisted of two wings at the centre of which was the chapel. One wing was the school itself and the other was the nuns' living quarters.

There was no playground as such: we would be sent out to play on the drive or sometimes, as a special treat, 'down the field'. The field was a green area at the back of the school, the other side of which was the Edgbaston reservoir. No sports were ever taught or played there, although I do seem to remember the odd beanbag being flung about. Weather permitting, at lunchtime and mid-morning break we were sent out onto the drive to play. Alongside it was a strip of lawn, upon which we were forbidden to tread. Many a child, myself included, had been summarily thrashed about the legs for simply letting the back of a heel touch it. So when I visited the school almost thirty years later I was filled with devilment to find that piece of lawn still there.

It was in the mid-eighties and I was up in Birmingham filming for the *Victoria Wood Christmas Special.* Finding myself with a couple of hours to spare, I decided to go and take a look. The school was just as manicured and pristine as I remembered it. And there was the piece of lawn, the cause and location of my humiliating public slapping. It was with joy in my heart, therefore, and a pair of high-heeled boots on my feet, that I tramped up and down several times, digging my heels deep into the turf. I was hoping that one of the Sisters would appear and tell me to get off the grass. In fantasyland I know exactly how I would have acted. I would have stood there, feet apart, hands on hips, and said: 'Please . . . make my day . . . Go on! Try and slap my legs.'

The nuns were of the classic penguin variety, wearing black habits and veils that billowed out behind them like giant bat wings. Under the veil was a starched white wimple and covering their bosoms a stiff white scapular, upon which hung a black wooden crucifix. Dangling from the waist was a set of rosary beads that clacked and jingled when they moved, the sound of which served as a warning that a nun was in the vicinity.

'My name is Sister Cecilia.'

She had a big, pale, bespectacled face and was the teacher in charge of the kindergarten. There was a tension that hung in the air at this place. For not only did the Sisters dispense helpful gems like, 'Don't cross your legs, you never saw the Virgin Mary cross hers,' and offer strictures that patent-leather shoes were not to be worn because they reflected your nether regions, they also administered random slaps to the head, meted out for such misdemeanours as whispering in class. During my first couple of weeks an incident occurred that was to set the tone.

After many homilies as to how careful we were going to have to be, the kindergarten was delivered of a set of new desks; their metal legs were still wrapped in brown paper, wound round them in strips. Sister Cecilia warned us sternly that under no circumstances were we to undo this wrapping. Within a day or two one of the legs on my desk was beginning to unravel! Then as if in a bid for freedom, another leg revealed itself and then another. I looked on appalled and helpless. Each time Sister Cecilia came near me I expected the thwack to the side of my head, but somehow I managed to escape it. Soon other people's desk legs began to undo. One brave soul decided to inform Sister of what was happening to her desk and to tell her that she had nothing to do with it. She was dragged from her place and thrashed on the legs. I can see the two of them now, the girl wih her cardigan half pulled off, careering into the front row of desks and knocking a chair flying, tears racing down her cheeks, and Sister Cecilia's large white hand in a blur of slapping.

Eventually, one Sunday night, in a state of terror at the thought of going to school on the Monday, I confessed to my parents in an explosion of gulping tears the awful tale of the mutinous desk legs. They stood dumbfounded and then, unable to calm me, my father went off to telephone the Mother Superior. I waited, in my pyjamas by the kitchen fire, sick to my stomach.

When he returned my father was smiling. 'There's no problem.'

'But what did she say?'

'She laughed . . . She said it doesn't matter, Bab . . .'

It doesn't matter! It was incredible to me that the fear and trepidation of the previous weeks could be solved by two adults in a matter of minutes; but it seems that it was, for when I went into school the next day, we were told to remove the wrapping from our desk legs. Thus was the desk-leg saga brought to a close.

However, I never went into that school without fear of what was in store, and there was plenty in store over the coming years — the elocution lessons my mother had spoken of with such reverence being one of the unhappiest experiences. These were to be taken by a lay teacher. In some ways I could cope with the inappropriate nature of the punishments handed out by the nuns because they were like a different species. But I felt let down by the lay teachers when they displayed the same lack of compassion and understanding. None of the teaching staff seemed to have any joy in them, and they appeared angry and unhappy. The elocution teacher was no exception.

The classes were held in a prefabricated hut at the back of the school. My abiding memory is of standing at the front of the class reading from a book. Throughout I had consistently pronounced words that had a long A, such as 'daft', in the same way as words with a short A, such as 'cat'. This was the way I spoke then and how I speak today; it was the way we all pronounced such words at home; I simply couldn't bring myself to say this long A.

After the reading the teacher wrote out on the blackboard a list of words that were supposed to be pronounced in this way and asked me to read them out. I didn't get past the first one, which was 'bath'. Something in me refused to say it the way she wanted, and every time I said 'bath' with a short A she walloped my hand with a ruler. I can't recall how long I stood there but I know that I never gave in. It felt like some kind of final frontier to my self-worth. I was defending who I was. If I gave her what she wanted, I would be confirming my mother's fears—that we were not good enough—and I simply couldn't do that.

This difficulty with Standard English, or Received Pronunciation as it was then called, followed me to drama school many years later and beyond. It was not that I refused to speak it for a role, but that it caused me a certain discomfort. It gradually ceased to be a problem as I came, in later years, to be more accepting of who I was. My mother was forever disappointed that I didn't come home speaking like the doctors' daughters of her imagination, and I was unable at the time to express why I couldn't.

I'm not going to list every punishment that took place at this school, but there is one more that remains distinct in my memory. I was eight or nine years old. Our teacher was Sister Ignatius, a towering figure with a florid face and thick, black, beetle brows. She had a booming voice and a nasty temper. One day she had had reason to leave the classroom for a few minutes, leaving the form captain in charge. There was total silence. Suddenly one of the girls said, 'Isn't it quiet without Sister?' The minute Sister

Ignatius returned, the form captain, a humourless swot of a girl, saw fit to report this innocent remark. The nun then launched herself at the child who had had the audacity to speak, the first blow knocking her clean off her chair. She then set about beating her while the girl lay cowering on the floor, trying to protect herself. After a minute or so of thrashing, Sister Ignatius dragged the child into a small room off the back of the classroom. She slammed the door behind them and continued to beat her.

We sat frozen. Not a look was exchanged as we listened to the raining down of blow after blow. When the nun emerged, purple faced and enraged, we were forbidden to speak to the girl. She was shut in the room for the rest of the day. We were told to send her to Coventry until instructed to do otherwise, and I still experience a sense of shame when I think of her standing alone at break times and dinnertimes in the days that followed, all of us fearful of what would happen should we dare to talk to her.

How on earth we learned anything under this tyranny is beyond me. Long division? Forget it! If you didn't get it the first time, it was better, at least in my book, to copy someone else's rather than suffer the humiliation that might result if you got it wrong. In year six, I would spend library hour reading a book from cover to cover without taking in a single word. All of Arthur Ransome's apparently wonderful novels simply passed in and out of my head in a blur of meaningless verbiage. It felt as if the whole set-up was a club that I would never belong to, even down to reading a book for pleasure.

But something surprisingly healing did emerge from my time at this school. Even more surprisingly, it was during Sister Ignatius's terrible reign. On the odd afternoon we would play the miming game whereby she would get us up individually to do a mime and the other children would have to guess what it was. I can still recall the euphoria I felt on hearing that nun's laughter the first time I stood out front, and I can see the classroom on that day, flooded with afternoon sun: how colourful and beautiful it suddenly looked. I also experienced a sense of power. I had, however briefly, quelled this woman's anger and unhappiness and somehow made her safe.

'You should go on the stage!' she said in her big, cracked voice, still giggling. I knew then that in her laughter and in the laughing faces of my classmates lay my salvation and the building blocks for my self-esteem.

My mother's ambition was for me to pass from the prep school up to the senior school, but I knew there wasn't a chance in hell and so did she. She had already been hauled in when I was in year three and told that there was every likelihood that she was wasting her nine guineas a term. I wasn't keeping up. Mum said virtually nothing afterwards but her disappointment was palpable. 'Oh, Julie . . . Oh dear . . .' I felt the same humiliation and helplessness as I had when I had wet the bed.

As predicted I didn't get into the senior school, but this could hardly be called a disappointment. It meant that if I passed the eleven-plus examination—and the alternative was unthinkable—I would go to Holly Lodge Grammar School for Girls in Smethwick, where there wasn't a nun in sight; my brothers were already going to Holly Lodge Grammar School for Boys. As it was, I nearly didn't get in there either. A letter came, stating that I had failed the exam. My chest tightens now as I recall my mother breaking the news as if I had been found guilty of some heinous crime. I felt as if I had failed my whole life and all I had to look forward to was years of shame at a secondary-modern school. I went around in a state of total dejection for days, wanting to hide away as I heard my mother broadcast the news of my failure to friends and family.

Then, a week or so later, a letter came from Holly Lodge. It seemed I hadn't failed; I was what the letter referred to as 'borderline', and the school were willing to take me if I promised to work hard. I felt as a prisoner must do on death row after being given a reprieve.

Arriving at Holly Lodge was like getting into your own bed after sleeping on someone else's floor. People spoke as I did; they lived in houses like mine; their brothers knew mine; older girls from the years above came up to me in the corridor and said, 'Are you Kevin Walters's sister?' I grew inches taller with pride. In short, I knew that this was where I belonged.

They also taught PE, which hitherto I had been deprived of. Like my brothers before me, I loved sport and at Holly Lodge spent most dinner hours and time after school in the winter playing hockey, with Saturday mornings playing for one of the school teams. Once or twice the PE mistress invited the local Sikh boys' team to practise with us. They were gentle and friendly boys, but their long-limbed grace made us girls feel like a herd of carthorses. The Sikhs would practise shooting by placing a chair in the centre of the goal and hitting balls from the halfway line straight between the legs with deadly accuracy. They put us to shame.

At the end of the hockey season the first-eleven girls would play a match with the first-eleven boys' football team from the school across the way. Every year I would watch from the sidelines and every year I would be more and more turned on by the spectacle of big, hunky sixth-form boys tackling our girls in sometimes quite ferocious tussles that looked as if, at any moment, in a parallel universe at least, they would fling their sticks aside and rip their clothes off. When it came to my turn to play them, I could barely run for the lust of it.

But for some, the highlight of the hockey season was the game we played against the staff. The thought of wrapping my stick across the shins of a certain teacher who had accused me of cheating, when I hadn't, was almost sublime, but when it came to it, I couldn't do it, because she was a different person on the pitch, sweet, smiling and vulnerable. In fact, this was true of all of them, with the exception of a male teacher who had the unsavoury reputation of slithering up to girls during lessons and placing his great hoof on the corner of their desk, thus thrusting his baggy old crotch at them. His too-close-for-comfort tutoring had to be punished. So of course a huge cheer came from the crowd when he was helped limping from the pitch, having been given a mighty thwack across the ankle by our towering centre half.

During the summer terms I spent my free time preparing for

the Smethwick interschools athletics championships. I was a sprinter and usually competed in the 200 metres and the relay, the winning of either being almost a matter of life and death. To contemplate coming second or third filled me with a sickening anxiety; indeed, I frequently threw up after a race, whatever the outcome of it. When I came third in the 200 metres, the first time I had ever run it, I hid in the toilets, vomiting and crying at the same time, which is actually quite difficult, and then waited until everyone else had gone home. Facing them seemed an impossibility. I went home in dread of telling my mother. She wasn't an 'Oh well, it's the taking part that counts' sort of person.

When, still at primary school, Kevin told her with pride that he had come third in a maths test, she shot back instantly with, 'Who came first?' and when he told her, she said, 'Oh, he's clever!' reserving all her praise for some other child. Worse still, when my other brother Tommy got a first-class degree from Birmingham University, she just said, 'Ah well, they're turning them away from the Harwell nuclear plant with firsts.' So when I told her of the disaster that had occurred, I was shocked at her gentle response. 'It doesn't matter. Forget about it,' she said without looking at me. I presumed that she must have sensed my distress and, had I been pleased with the result, it would have been another story.

I never lost that race again and became Worcestershire 200-metres champion in 1966. As a result of this, an athletics scout from Smethwick Harriers took me under his wing. However, I had torn a muscle in my hip, so instead of continuing with the sprinting, which would have damaged the muscle further, we embarked on a course of training that involved walking. This was not your normal walking; no, this was a mode of walking that no mentally fit human being would employ to go anywhere for fear of attracting the wrong kind of attention. It involved a pumping arm action, which was fair enough, but also involved arching the back and making the arse stick out in a baboon-like fashion. With legs straight, always having to keep one foot on the ground at any one time, it resulted in a somewhat vulgar mincing, at speed, with the hips and bottom swaying exaggeratedly from side to side.

This was competitive walking, and most athletics meetings had several walking races as part of the day's events. I endured the humiliation of this by going training either early in the morning or at dusk, and even then I couldn't escape the smirks, occasionally accompanied by heckles alluding to the possibility that I might have shat myself.

It all came to an abrupt end when, at an athletics meeting, I entered a walking event for the first time. I set off at a cracking pace, leaving the others way behind. At the point of lapping them for the first time, after only a lap and a half, and thinking, these people are hopeless, I started to tire. Throughout the subsequent laps they began to overtake me, one by one. When the last one passed me, panic began to balloon in my chest. I simply couldn't be the last person over that finishing line.

So I concocted a plan and, minutes later, I started to stagger and wobbled off the track onto the grass. After reeling round for a few seconds, I collapsed and lay there, clutching my stomach. I waited. First there were shouts and then the thud of feet on turf as a couple of St John Ambulance men came running towards me. A stretcher was thrown to the ground, right in my eyeline. The day was going to end well after all! This was more than I could have hoped for, being carried off on a stretcher by two burly ambulance men, the centre of a drama; the young girl who all but had the race in the bag, only to have it snatched from her grasp by a mystery illness. The girl who had soldiered on, in agonising pain, until she could take no more: she is nothing less than a heroine!

Then the coach arrived. 'It's all right, fellas, you won't be needing that.'

Surely he wasn't talking about the stretcher!

'She's just run out of breath. I told you, didn't I, to pace yourself? What were you playing at?'

'My stomach . . . I can't get up!'

'Don't be so silly, of course you can. It's just a bit of stitch.'

And with that he sent my knights in shining armour away.

'Come on! On your feet. You'll get cold down there.'

I wanted to rise up and lamp him one on the chin. Then others started to arrive and gawp.

'Is she all right?'

'Course she is! She just went off like shit off a shovel and then found she'd got no puff!'

Oh, the humiliation! Now I was no longer the tragic heroine, but the idiot who had whizzed off at a ridiculous speed, got a stitch and had to stop; it was almost worth telling the truth! I never did, but the coach knew, and I knew that he knew, and he knew that I knew that he knew. I never went back.

I started my time at Holly Lodge in Form 3C. This was the bottom class of four streams and here I made my friends, some of whom I am still in touch with today. On the first day, our teacher, a grim-faced young woman who taught history and seemed to be in a permanent state of resentment, took the register. After each name was called the appropriate girl shouted out, 'Here!' When my turn came, just as I was about to answer, I felt a slight prick in my left buttock and my 'Here' popped out in a falsetto yelp, causing the teacher to pause with a baleful look over the top of her Edna Everage glasses. I turned to be met with a huge smile from the girl behind. She had stuck her compass point into my bum cheek. We bonded in that moment. Not that I want you to think, dear reader, that the piercing of one of my body parts is mandatory for the forming of friendships on my part, but this girl had huge charisma and attracted round her a little clique of which I was proud to be a member.

It was at her twelfth birthday party, during a game of Postman's Knock, that I had my first kiss from a boy who lived across the road from her. He was a couple of years older, with cornflower-blue eyes, and was made more attractive by the fact that his father was in prison for robbing gas meters. It was exciting knowing what my mother's reaction would be if she were to discover this liaison, which, needless to say, in due course she did. Kevin spotted me with him one day and not only did he tell the boy to clear off, but he then told my mother I was mixing with a rough lad from a certain part of Smethwick. I was duly forbidden to 'go hanging about the bottom end of Smethwick'. I tried to explain that there was no 'bottom end', it was all 'bottom', but she wouldn't have it and so I continued to go in secret.

I felt instantly at ease with the girls in my class and was able to let go of most of the self-consciousness that I had suffered at the prep with regard to where I lived (I never invited anyone home), what my parents did for a living, where we went on holiday (the summer before my last year at the prep, we went to Margate, and, while there, made a day-trip to Calais). When I went back to the prep school after the summer holidays, girls were discussing their two or three weeks in Italy, Scotland and Cornwall. So when I was asked where we had been, I said, heart racing, that we had toured the south coast and been to France. Inevitably one of these girls asked where in France had we gone. I was at a loss and had to admit it was Calais.

'What? You got off the ferry and didn't go any further?'

I tried to laugh it off. 'Yes.'

'But Calais is horrible. People race to get out of it.'

I was paralysed by my dissembling and stood there, my face boiling. The little group dispersed, suddenly distracted by the clanging of the bell for lessons to begin. As I went to my desk, the girl next to me said, 'I went on a day-trip to Calais once. I loved it.' I wanted to cry.

At Holly Lodge, I slowly began to discover a pride, both in my family and in my home. I recognised my peers and found my place among them pretty quickly. I was the cheeky clown, calling out in class with comments to make the other girls, and sometimes the teachers, laugh. I would impersonate the headmistress, my grandmother, various pop stars: anything to get those laughs. I recognised a power in it: it enabled me to be seen. It stopped the world from being overwhelming and it was a lethal weapon.

The school had a drama society, but because of my daily performances in class I had little use for it. Also I wasn't keen on the girls who belonged to it, thinking them uppity and cliquey. Only once did I appear in one of the school's drama productions, put on with the boys' school, and that was as Moth in *A Midsummer Night's Dream* in my first year. I found it thrilling: not only the opportunity to perform, but also a chance to rehearse in the out-of-bounds boys' school. I conducted myself in rehearsals much the same as I did in lessons: making everyone laugh and constantly interrupting the male teacher, on whom I had a bit of a crush.

Finally, one day, this teacher dragged me in gorgeous masterly fashion to one side and said, 'Do you know why I cast you as Moth?'

'No,' I said, looking up flirtatiously.

'It's because, like a moth, you are a bloody nuisance!'

The thrill I felt, standing backstage on that first night, listening to the chatter of an expectant audience, my face plastered in greasepaint, dressed in my costume of pink and lilac muslin, is basically the same stomach-churning, mouth-drying, heart-banging thrill that I feel nowadays waiting in the wings to go on. And wherever it may be, that warm, dark space behind the scenery, half lit by the spill from the stage, filled with apprehension and expectancy, will always remind me of that night long ago, on the creaking, cramped side-stage of the school hall at Holly Lodge. However, I never went for any more parts, preferring the instant fix I got from clowning in class.

Despite its genteel name, Holly Lodge Grammar was by no means a school for young ladies. Although we had a uniform, I found that many of the older girls distorted it out of all recognition. Berets were folded in half and pinned onto the back of the head with a couple of hairgrips. Hair would then be backcombed and lacquered up and over the top, so that the thing was barely visible. Ties were left loose; blouse collars were worn up with the tips turned down; skirts were rolled over at the waist and hoicked, St Trinian-like, up to mid-thigh—often, until tights came in, revealing stocking tops and suspenders. In the first two or three years I was there, shoes tended to be flat but with pointed toes and steel caps on the heels, so that the noise as girls walked along the stone corridors in large numbers was like something out of heavy industry, and any slipping or skidding would cause sparks to fly.

Out of school, en masse, some of these girls could be an alarming sight, trailing along Smethwick High Street, striking sparks, arms linked, four abreast, making passers-by jump into the road. Discipline varied hugely from class to class. Certain teachers hadn't got the personality required to get our attention and their classes were nothing short of mayhem, with everyone talking, wandering around willy-nilly, and completely ignoring the teacher's pleas to sit down and be quiet. On one occasion we barricaded the door with desks so that the teacher couldn't get in. I can remember a teacher giving up and leaving in tears more than once.

My insecurity, although greatly reduced, still manifested itself. For instance, I would never customise my uniform; my uniform made me feel safe and I never looked forward to non-uniform days, feeling awkward in whatever I wore. Doing something different with your blazer or your skirt meant putting your head above the parapet. I never felt good enough about myself to do that. Choosing to personalise your uniform was a sign of wanting to be grown up and part of me didn't want that; I wanted to be little and cute and funny, and to be loved for it. Even graduating from socks to tights was a cause for anxiety. So I put it off lest anyone should say: who do you think you are? Because I didn't know.

This anxiety about clothes and my appearance reached a crescendo at around the age of fourteen or fifteen, when one of the coolest girls in the class was taking a group to see *Thank Your Lucky Stars* for her birthday, and I was invited. This was a weekly Saturday-night pop show, filmed in front of a live audience in Birmingham's Alpha Studios. It boasted the first network television appearance of the Beatles.

A couple of weeks before we were due to go, I began to get into a state about what I should wear. Nothing was good enough. I scoured the shops and nothing was right. I had no idea. So, just as in the walking race, I concocted a plan. I would be ill and unable to go. Two days before the event, I took to my bed, claiming that I felt sick. At lunchtime I had some soup and proceeded to make myself vomit it up. I continued to do this until the day after the girl's birthday, but by this time I really did feel poorly. The doctor prescribed some kind of antibiotic. For two whole weeks I lay prostrate on the sitting-room sofa, every turn of my head making me retch, unable to keep anything down. I was secretly thrilled that I had the power to make this happen, and I was lapping up my mother's concern until the doctor returned for the third time and started to talk of possible hospitalisation.

Now I really was scared. The next day, with monumental effort, I arose from my sickbed and looked in the mirror. It was the face of someone else. My hair was flat with grease; my skin had gone sheet-white; my lips were virtually the same colour as my skin, and my eyes were enormous. This last effect I would quite like to have kept. I stared into eyes that were strange yet familiar, and watched as big, shiny tears welled up. I touched the glass and whispered, 'I'm so sorry.'

And so began my recovery. When I finally returned to school, people gawped as I passed them in the corridor and didn't want to tackle me at hockey practice lest, as one friend put it, I should 'snap'. Although I had taken some pleasure in my power to make myself ill, I was frightened by the fact that I could make myself believe I was sick and by the way my body then took over. What if I couldn't have come back?

Throughout my time at Holly Lodge I felt younger than my peers. With the onset of puberty a lot of the girls in my class suddenly appeared a good few years older than me. Some looked as if they could be about thirty with a couple of kids, while others looked as if they were about nine. I was of the nine-year-old variety. A lot of them were sexually active. I had no experience apart from a bit of kissing and fumbling. My sex education started when playing in Lightwoods Park aged about eight. One of my friends drew my attention to two dogs, one mounting the other, and said, 'That's what your mum and dad do.' I did my best to rid my head of the image of my mother on all fours and my dad slavering behind her.

Once, I laboured under the delusion, born of a rumour, that if a girl had splayed feet, it meant that she had lost her virginity. This didn't make sense when I looked at a girl a couple of years above, who was from a very religious family, wore very long skirts and was nicknamed 'Miss Smethwick 1918', but I still believed it. It didn't occur to me that my mother's feet, for instance, pointed straight out in front. I was also told that you could get pregnant by sitting in a married man's bathwater, so I always gave the bath a good rinse if my father had been in before me.

My mother never broached the subject of sex education until I was sixteen, when she asked, 'Do you know about periods, Julie?'

'I should hope so, Mum, I've been having them for two years.'

She knew this of course, but obviously had not known how to tackle the issue. My periods starting late didn't help in the maturity stakes. The actual moment took place when I was staying with relatives of a friend and didn't feel I could ask for assistance, so I ended up shoving a pillowcase between my legs. I went home on the bus in some discomfort and got off it walking like John Wayne. When I look back, it seems that there was something engineered about my immaturity. If I played a childish role I felt safe, but despite setting myself apart in this way I managed to maintain a prominent position in the group, by being good at sport and playing the jester.

There was also insecurity around food. For the midmorning break, which we referred to as 'lunch', people brought in sandwiches, crisps and fruit. I never did this. I spent the whole of the break begging titbits off the other girls. They quite rightly got miffed: 'For Christ's sake, why don't you bring your own?'

I had always blamed this odd behaviour on the fact that my mother would never fund a daily packet of crisps, and that I felt I would be shown up by whatever food I brought in. Seeing as some girls brought in plain bread and butter, I don't think that this can really be the case. Rather, I think it had more to do with the fact that if I had nothing, nothing could be taken from me. As I was the younger sister of two brothers, anything was open season. Even now I feel enraged when anyone takes food off my plate.

As the years went by at Holly Lodge, my confidence grew and my schoolwork gradually improved. I became good at French, English and Geography, and I got four GCEs, English Literature, English Language, French and Geography, while failing everything else. Once I was in the sixth form things quickly began to slide. Many of my friends had left as, particularly in working-class families, the imperative was to get a job. At the start of the new academic year various girls from different forms were working alongside each other for the first time and so the whole dynamic changed. It was to be the setting for a very shameful episode.

I had become friends with an entirely new group. This little clique was led by a girl who possessed a wicked sense of humour. Like the others in our group I was both captivated and in awe of her. After a few weeks she started to take against a certain girl, making snide comments about her, often followed by crude cartoons of her victim, which sometimes ended up on the sixth-form notice board. Although underneath I felt guilty about being part of this bullying, I did nothing to discourage it. In fact I, along with the others, joined in with vicious gossip about the poor girl that made our leader hoot with delight and made us, in turn, glow with pride.

But then it began to escalate. A plan was hatched to rub butter on the pedals of her bicycle and put pepper in her beret. I wanted nothing to do with it, yet lacked the courage to walk away. This girl had been a good friend of mine and I felt heartsore at the undeserved grief that I knew we were causing her, watching as her bubbly personality seemed to melt away. When it came to carrying out the plan, I said that I would keep watch from the library window upstairs. I just sat at a table staring blindly at some reference book, wishing I was somewhere else. I feel huge shame today at my cowardice and regret when I think of her sitting in the classroom later that afternoon, her face burning from the pepper, her eyes smarting and bloodshot.

A couple of evenings after this, someone knocked at the front door. I found our victim's mother standing there. I was very scared, knowing of course why she had come and worried that my mother, who was only in the kitchen, might walk in at any moment. She made a little speech in a voice I thought was both angry and close to tears. She said that her daughter was desperately upset and didn't deserve this treatment; it wasn't fair and why were we doing it? I stood there dumbly, unable to answer any of her questions. Just as she was about to walk off, she turned round and said, 'She's got a heart of gold.' I knew it was true. I went straight to my bedroom, flung myself on the bed and cried myself to sleep. I told the others the next day that the girl's mother had turned up at my door. They were shocked and said little, fearing there could be repercussions of some sort, and the whole sorry episode drew to a close.

The incident was duly filed away, in 'the never to be looked at again' file at the back of my head, but several years ago I decided to write to the girl we had bullied. I apologised for the pain she must have suffered and for my cowardice at not sticking up for her. She, of course, was generous in her forgiveness and made light of it all. It is a tribute to her strength of character that she withstood our childish bitchery, and I'm reminded of this every time I read of yet another child being kept off school or even committing suicide as a result of bullying.

The work in the lower sixth was a lot more challenging and so, it seemed, was getting up in the morning. Having overslept, I would amble in, in the late morning or at dinnertime, until I got so far behind that I couldn't make head nor tail of geography A level, and Molière's *L'Avare* might as well have been written in Mandarin. Eventually at the end of the lower-sixth year, Mr Taylor, our deputy head, took me to one side and gave me a letter addressed to my parents. 'Julia . . .' Teachers always called me Julia. 'We don't want you to come back next year. You will never get your A levels now; you are too far behind. You haven't put in the work. And we don't like your subversive influence.'

I looked up into the intense blue eyes while scrabbling for the meaning of 'subversive'. Did it refer to my truancy? Or could it have referred to the time when I had thrown a metal chair at a thin wooden partition, on the other side of which was our straight-faced form teacher who was in the process of teaching the upper-sixth French group? It was reported that the resulting clatter had almost caused her to collapse with fright.

I went home that afternoon, posted the letter to my parents in a dustbin and told my mother that I had reached a momentous decision: I would take up nursing. There was no need for me to stay on at school; I would prefer to get a job for a year and save some money (the word 'save' was always a good one with my mother). Surprisingly, without any discussion, she agreed. I went straight upstairs and looked up 'subversive'.

# Four

My first full-time job was in an insurance office in Birmingham. Prior to this, aged about fifteen, I had been employed on a Saturday at C&A Modes where, along with my friend Chris, I unpacked assorted items of clothing. We then found more interesting employment at a sweetshop. Every Wednesday night and all day Sunday we were left to our own devices and gorged ourselves freely on crisps, ice lollies, Bassett's sherbet fountains (a personal favourite) and Caramac chocolate. We gave away packets of cigarettes to boys we fancied and spent hours on the telephone, playing daft tricks on members of the public, asking them lewd questions about their sex lives. Needless to say, it was not a job that lasted long, once the absentee proprietor cottoned on.

The insurance office, on the other hand, was a proper job. I was in charge of finding the files that corresponded to the post that came in each morning. I soon tired of the tedious nature of the work and would spend time staring wistfully out of the window, longing to be away from what I began to see as a kind of prison. Post began to pile up, and eventually I resorted to putting it down the toilets. This practice was brought to a close when I came in one morning to find that the ladies' toilets were closed due to flooding. Luckily the blockage was cleared, the offending substance being too wet and mushy to be identified, but I wasn't the only junior with a red face that morning.

I sat next to a girl called Linda and would spend most of the day trying to make her laugh. The names of various clients sent us both into purple-faced hysteria, often causing Linda to get under her desk so as not to be seen by Miss Kelly, our spinsterly section leader. Sometimes I would scour the filing cabinets for names to make my new friend laugh. Cornelius Crack was a favourite; John Smellie and Katarina Balls were others that can still get me going today. Every so often this behaviour would be punctuated by a serious bollocking from Miss Kelly.

Linda was fifteen and had already been at the place for about six months.

'How old am ya?' she asked on my first day there.

'Seventeen,' I replied.

'Am yer engaged?'

'No.'

'Blimey! If I ent engaged by the time I'm seventeen, I'll kill me bloomin' self.'

About ten years later, I saw a woman I'm sure was her, pushing a baby in a stroller along Smethwick High Street with two other children in tow. She had a badly bruised eye and a swollen and cut lip.

At the age of eighteen, in May 1968, I enrolled in the Queen Elizabeth Hospital School of Nursing in Edgbaston. My mother was never prouder, before or since. It is what she would have wanted for herself, had she had the opportunity. Frustratingly, her parents sent her younger sister, Agnes, to England to train as a nurse, but she became a secretary instead.

After six weeks in the preliminary nursing school, my first ward was an ophthalmic ward, dealing mainly with cataract operations. The ward Sister, a Sister Hartwell, had lived in the nursing home across the road from the hospital since she was seventeen. This detail I found both depressing and claustrophobic, as at this point she was apparently sixty-seven. She never called me by my name: it was always 'Come here, Little Nurse' or 'Where's the little nurse?' booming embarrassingly from one end of the corridor to the other. Her huge blue eyes peered piercingly at you through thick dark lashes, over half-moon glasses perched midway down a largish Roman nose. You might be engaged in some nursing activity and suddenly she would be at your side, a little closer than was comfortable, staring directly at your face. She was equally eccentric when dealing with the patients.

In order to administer drugs, in the form of drops, to the eye, it was first necessary to dilate the tear duct, which was done with a small, pointed, sharp-looking implement. Sister would get up onto the bed, shouting at the patient to relax and keep still. Then on her knees, wobbling about millimetres from their face with the said implement, she would, while peering myopically through her half-glasses, attempt to dilate the tear duct. If she didn't succeed the first time, she would loudly berate the patient, blaming their inability to keep still.

I dreaded this procedure because it often resulted in her shouting in exasperation, 'Little Nurse! Get up here now, you, and finish this off!' On one occasion, just as I started to move towards a patient with this dilating tool, she slapped me on the arse with such force I nearly blinded the poor woman I was trying to treat. 'What are you playing at? Get up there on the bed. You can't do this standing by the bed, you're too small, Little Nurse.'

When I lost my fear of her, I became very fond of this Sister. Apart from being scarily hilarious, she was immensely kind and I know she was fond of me. Although I worked on several different wards, my experience on this one was unlike any other.

I never really settled into nursing, feeling that I couldn't possibly be up to the task as well as ultimately knowing that I was there to please my mother and to fulfil her ambition rather than my own. I was terrified of being given any responsibility, constantly doubting my own ability. Mind you, this wasn't without cause.

Within the first few weeks on the wards, I whipped out what I thought were my forceps, which were used to clamp off tubing. In this instance the tubing concerned linked a bag of blood that was being used in a blood transfusion to the patient. Snapping them onto the tube, I found that it was not the forceps at all but my surgical scissors. I was sent back to the nurses' home to change, looking as if I had just performed major abdominal surgery with a blunt kitchen knife.

Another unfortunate incident occurred, involving a faulty bedpan washer. Bedpans were placed in these contraptions, the door would be closed and then for several minutes the thing would spray the pans with hot water with the force of a fire hose. On this occasion, no sooner had I closed the door than it fell open again almost immediately, but sadly not before the water had started to spray. Luckily, because the machine was faulty, the water was breathtakingly cold and it hit me full in the face and chest, sending me reeling backwards against the sluice-room wall, where I remained in shock until the cycle had finished. While I stood there, being battered by the spray, the staff nurse came in and stood looking at me with an amused smirk on her face. When the water finally stopped, she said, 'What is this? *Carry on Nursing*?' And then wearily, 'Go and get changed.' And so ensued another embarrassing walk back to the nurses' home in disarray.

I never got into any serious trouble, but I came close to it once when I was working on a men's surgical ward. I was on the night shift, and on this particular ward the consultant in charge insisted on every patient giving a midstream specimen of urine. This process involved first cleaning the area with cotton-wool balls dipped into a mild disinfectant, which was poured into a small foil gallipot. Then the patient would begin to urinate, catching some pee midstream in another little pot.

One night after most of the men had gone to sleep an old man appeared like an apparition. He should have been admitted earlier and, for some reason, he had turned up at eleven o'clock. I showed him to his bed and went to make a cup of tea for him, leaving him to get into his pyjamas. When I returned he was in bed and it was only then that I remembered the required specimen.

'Mr Jackson, I'm going to need a specimen of urine from you before you go to sleep,' I whispered.

I waited, he smiled.

'I need you to do a specimen,' I said a little louder.

'WHAT?' This was extremely loud and rasping, and several people nearby started to stir. I tried to keep my own voice down.

'We are going to have to be very quiet, Mr Jackson, because everyone is asleep.'

'Fat bloody chance!' came a weary voice from the next bed.

'YES . . . GOOD NIGHT.' And he slid down under the covers.

'No, Mr Jackson. You can't go to sleep yet.'

'No, neither can we!' came a voice from the bed opposite.

I pulled the covers back, at which Mr Jackson shot up and looked at me as if I was an intruder. 'WHAT'S GOIN' ON?'

By now everyone was awake, and requests for cups of tea or exasperated moans were coming from all directions. After much negotiation, I managed to get him out of bed and part manhandled him down the ward and into the toilets. Once inside I showed him the pack containing the foil container of disinfectant and explained. 'Mr Jackson, I want you to clean yourself with this.' I dipped the cotton-wool balls into the disinfectant and pointed at his flies. At this he sprang back, protecting his nethers like a footballer defending himself from a free kick.

'WHAT'S YOUR GAME? I'M OLD ENOUGH TO BE YOUR GRANDFATHER!'

'No, no, Mr Jackson, I just want a specimen.'

And I went through the instructions, with him nodding and loudly affirming his understanding at every stage. Then with fingers crossed I left him to it. Half an hour or so later I went to check in the toilets, to find that the pot containing the disinfectant was empty but so was the specimen jar, and the old man had gone. When I went back to his bed, he was again snuggled down under the covers and this time clearly asleep, so I waited until morning.

‘’Morning, Mr Jackson, what did you do with your specimen?’

‘YES, YES,’ he said dismissively. ‘I DRANK THE MEDICINE.’

‘Oh my God,’ I murmured ever so quietly when I realised that he had in fact drunk the disinfectant and simply had a pee straight into the toilet.

‘AND WHAT’S MORE IT GAVE ME A BELLYACHE!’

‘Oh my God!’ I said again and went to confess to the senior nurse. I was hauled up in front of the assistant matron, who explained how irresponsible it was to leave an old deaf man etc., etc., etc.

I messed up quite a bit during my eighteen months of training, but none of my cockups came anywhere near that of a poor girl in my set. She was on a ward filled with elderly women and she got the brilliant idea that, instead of going round each old dear and cleaning her false teeth, she would collect all the dentures in a big bowl and wash them all together. She only realised her gaffe when it was too late and had to guess whose belonged to whom. Patients were complaining of sore gums for weeks after, and night after night when they were all asleep, she went round whipping dentures off the bedside lockers and swapping them round, still trying to match the right teeth to the right mouth.

I encountered death many times while nursing, but never got used to the shock of finding a bed empty when arriving on duty and discovering that someone you had got to know, whose family you had chatted with, was now dead. The first time this happened, I had come on duty for the afternoon shift and the ward was frantically busy. Usually at the beginning of a shift the senior nurse going off duty would give notes on all the patients, so that those coming on duty would be up to speed. But on this particular day they were still carrying out their various duties and it was clear that help was needed. At the top of the ward was Mr Claydon’s bed. He was a long-stay patient and had been unconscious for a couple of weeks. Seeing that the curtains were closed round his bed, I decided that this was where I would start. I went in and immediately began chatting. We were told that unconscious patients could more than likely hear what you said, as hearing was the last sense to go in a coma. Hospital gossip had it that a nurse who had talked about how fat a female patient was while she was unconscious was slapped across the face by the woman when she came round, the woman having heard everything.

Mr Claydon was lying on his back and next to him on the table was a bowl of tepid water. Someone was obviously intending giving him a bed-bath. Thinking the water a little too cool, I set off to get some more hot. The ward Sister asked what I was doing. When I said I was getting some nice hot water for Mr Claydon, she said, 'It doesn't need to be hot, he's not exactly going to complain, is he?' I was speechless: to treat a vulnerable patient like this, even when run off your feet, was unconscionable.

I ignored her, and when I returned to Mr Claydon's bed he was in much the same position. I began the preparations for his bath, getting his toilet bag and towel from his bedside locker, while plucking at a large bunch of black grapes in his fruit bowl and talking away as I did so.

'I expect your wife will be in soon, so we'll get you nice and fresh for her.' And so forth.

I pulled the sheet down and proceeded to wash him, while telling him how busy the ward was. At one point the staff nurse popped her head through the curtains and said, 'Oh! Are you doing this? Good.' Shortly afterwards she popped her head through again and said, 'You do know he's dead, don't you?'

Immediately, almost as a reflex action, I spat out the grape I had been eating, which landed splat in the middle of her apron bib. It stayed there, all chewed and purple, for a second or two and then dropped to the floor. We both stared at it.

'Oh no! I've been eating his grapes!'

'Well, they're  no different now to what they were half an hour ago when he was still alive. You've been stuffing them down you all week. His wife must be wondering how come he gets through so many, considering he's been in a coma. Now, do you know how to lay him out?'

'Erm . . . no.'

'Well, just carry on and wash him and then I'll be back to show you what to do.'

No sooner had she left than I began to turn him onto his side so that I could wash his back, and as I did so he let out a long, low, sinister moan. I was so shocked that I jumped back and, in doing so, banged into his locker, sending his false teeth, which were in a jar on top of it, flying to the floor and skidding out under the curtain into the ward beyond.

'He's not dead!' I shouted. 'There's been a mistake!'

With that the same staff nurse came back through the curtains, brandishing the teeth and, putting the top set together with the bottom ones to make them work like a mouth, said in a ventriloquist's voice, 'Oh yes I am! I was just having a moan about you eating all my bloody grapes!'

She then went on to explain that the moan that I had heard was simply air passing through his vocal cords as he was being moved.

Death on a ward was a disturbing experience for the other patients, and some ward Sisters were more sensitive in this regard than others. Later in my training I worked on a women's medical ward, which was mainly populated by the elderly, so that death was more frequent than on other wards, and they had the unobtrusive laying-out procedure down to a fine art. When a corpse was being taken down to the mortuary, it was transported on a special trolley. This looked like a normal gurney, but underneath the mattress was a secret compartment, into which the body would be put. We were instructed that if anyone were to die on our watch, we were to play it down, so that the other patients were unaware of what was going on. And so it was one lunchtime when I was sent on ahead of the main course with the soup trolley. The first patient was an ancient woman, Mrs Kent. She was sitting up in bed, her head resting on the pillows, staring down at her hands.

'Mrs Kent? Your dinner's here. Are you going to eat some soup for me?'

I touched her arm and instantly knew from the bluish discoloration round her lips, and the inordinate stillness around her, that there was a good chance she might have popped her clogs. After surreptitiously feeling for her pulse and finding that there wasn't one, I decided that the best course of action was to carry on with the soups. I ladled hers into a bowl and put it in front of her.

'Mrs Kent, here's your soup; eat it up now, while it's hot.'

I took her hand, wrapped her already icy fingers round the spoon and placed it in the soup. Now she looked as though she was poised on the brink of sampling her soup and was examining it first, which was fair enough as only the week before someone had found a cotton-wool ball in theirs. I then continued on up the ward, handing out soup to the other patients. When I reached the far end, a couple of the old ladies drew my attention to the fact that Mrs Kent had toppled face first into her soup.

'That soup's hot, Nurse! She must have fallen asleep!'

I rushed back to her. Then, remembering my instructions to keep the whole thing low-key, I slowed down and spoke calmly to the corpse that was Mrs Kent.

'Now what's going on here, Florrie? It's very bad manners to suck your soup up like that. You're going to get it everywhere.'

With a little laugh I lifted her face out of the bowl. Her nose and mouth were covered in a thick coating of pea soup. This I quickly remedied with a paper napkin, while the hand into which I had forced the spoon was raised up, holding the spoon as if she were going to attack someone with it. I tried to make the hand, which was level with her ear, come back down, but I couldn't budge it. By this time other patients were beginning to take notice.

'What's up with Florrie? Is she playing up?'

'Yes, I think she needs the bedpan.'

And with that I drew the curtain round the bed and told Sister, who instructed me to lay Mrs Kent out with as little fuss as possible. When I returned Mrs Kent was still in the same position, arm raised. I proceeded to remove the spoon from her hand, but the fingers were clasped round the handle, rigid and tight. With a lot of cracking of finger joints, I managed to free it. I then began to carry out the procedure of laying out, which involved washing, labelling the body and tying the two big toes together, then placing the corpse in a shroud, which I couldn't quite close owing to the fact that her arm still refused to lie down. Eventually Mrs Kent was wheeled off in the secret gurney and no one said a word.

Sister suddenly collared me and said, 'Did you get her teeth?'

'. . . Her teeth?'

'Yes, you'll need to take her teeth out and put them with her belongings. Go on and catch the porter, he won't have got far.'

I chased after him, catching him just as he was in the lift and about to take Mrs Kent down to the basement. I jumped in.

The porter was somewhat strange-looking, like Herman Munster's better-looking cousin or a member of the Addams family on work experience. He had a rather large head and a livid-looking scar across the side of his forehead. He never spoke as far as I knew. I didn't relish being alone in the lift with him alongside a corpse going down to the mortuary.

'I've been sent to get her teeth.'

He opened the top of the gurney and pulled back the shroud without saying a word. Mrs Kent greeted me with her raised arm, but when I tried to open her mouth in order to retrieve the teeth, it proved impossible. It was set solid in a kind of snarl and the teeth, which were tantalisingly visible, were a lurid green colour, owing to a coating of pea soup. Not wanting to be in the mortuary any longer than was necessary, I hopped up onto the gurney. Just as I was wrestling with Mrs Kent's jaw, the lift juddered to a halt at the second floor, the door opened and a cocky medical student stood there, staring.

'What on earth are you doing?' he said with a snigger.

'I'm just having a last snog before they put her in the fridge.'

'God, if anyone sees you . . .'

'I'm trying to take her teeth out, for Christ's sake!'

'Why? Does she owe you money?'

And with a click of the jaw, out they came.

Later that day, carrying a small polythene bag containing all Mrs Kent's belongings, I entered the visitors' room. There are few things more poignant than the bag of belongings handed over to relatives when a patient dies. In this case, a wedding ring, a little bottle of eau de cologne, a toilet bag and those teeth. Her daughter, a woman of about fifty, was standing there looking lost and red-eyed. When I handed her the bag she looked inside.

'Oh, her teeth,' she said, sounding as if she was about to cry. 'She never let anyone see her without those.'

Not long before I made my decision to leave nursing, I worked on the Coronary Care Unit, an entirely stressful experience. Virtually every patient was wired up to a machine that measured his or her heart rate by means of electrodes. When I was alone on night duty, the senior nurse having gone for dinner, I would constantly check the patients and their machines for any sign of heart failure.

I knew what to do should someone's heart stop as I had played a part in saving a patient's life, when on another ward a man had keeled over. I gave him mouth-to-mouth and cardiac massage, together with another nurse, until the crash team arrived and his heart did, in fact, start again as a direct result of our efforts. It was a tremendous feeling, giving me huge confidence and an illusion of omnipotence for at least a couple of days, but I still found the responsibility of this unit overwhelming. My nerves weren't helped by the fact that the electrodes were constantly coming unstuck and each time it happened it would set off the alarm—a high-pitched beep—and the electronic graph would flatline.

During my first week, one of the alarms, attached to a huge Irish labourer, was activated. Quick as a flash, a diminutive medical student vaulted the cot-side and proceeded to carry out cardiac massage by bashing his breastbone with some force; I was once told that if you broke the sternum you had done a good job. The Irishman rose up and, thinking he was the victim of an assault, punched the student in the face, knocking him clean out.

I wasn't much enamoured with the operating theatre either. I was too short to watch my first operation, the repair of a hernia, and was given a stool to stand on. I was dreading the scalpel making the first cut into the flesh, but once this was over I found it fascinating, not least the conversations between the surgeon and the anaesthetist, gossiping and telling jokes. On one occasion the theatre Sister was hit in the centre of her forehead by a splash of blood and the surgeon said, 'Oh, changed your religion?' All this while sorting through the innards of an unconscious human being.

The most interesting operation I saw was on the brain of a woman with Parkinson's disease, which involved drilling holes in her skull. The drill, of the hand variety, bore a close resemblance to one my dad had in the shed and made a similar sound as it cracked slowly through the bone. Once the brain had been reached, it was the surgeon's task to locate the overactive cell that was causing the patient's tremor, then try to zap its nucleus, which he did by watching a monitor in another room entirely. It was like *The Golden Shot*: 'Up a bit . . . Now left and down a wee bit.'

Once I was summoned to help clean up after a major operation. I plunged my hand into a sink filled with bloody water, in order to pull out the plug, and found something soft lying on the bottom. On taking it out, I found it to be a man's severed leg, from a below-the-knee amputation. I flung it away from me across the room, at which the nurse helping me said, 'Oh, not you as well! That thing has been tossed about like a caber all afternoon.'

My experience on the Coronary Care Unit and in the theatres, I believe, went a long way to convincing me that perhaps I wasn't in the right profession. There was a side of nursing, however, that I loved. It was the feeding and the washing of patients, making their beds, eating their grapes, chatting and making friends. I ended up writing to several ex-patients for some time after I had given up the profession. Other people fell in love with doctors, but not me: I fell in love with the patients. There was something about having a man captive in a bed and seeing to his every need.

My favourite ward was a men's medical. Thirty men, all on bed rest! I used to long for the odd shift when I would be left in charge. As soon as the staff nurse had gone, I would shout, 'OK, you horrible lot, who's got chocolates and who's got a nice grape? Come on, the wife must have brought you in something nice.' I would then do my version of tap-dancing round the ward, picking up the odd chocolate here and grape there, while cracking jokes and telling stories. At the end of the shift, I would go round and kiss them all good night. On the cheek, of course.

Another ward I had adored was a men's surgical, dealing mainly with peripheral vascular disease, caused almost entirely by smoking. The men on the ward were all of a particular type: small, thin, wiry and funny. It took a few days for me to realise that the reason I got on so well with them was that they reminded me of my own father.

One of the symptoms of this condition was called intermittent claudication, which meant that after walking a certain distance the patient would experience pain in the calf muscle, presumably because enough blood couldn't get through to it via the ravaged mveins. One weekend I went home and heard my parents talking.

'Well, you've probably pulled a muscle, that's all.'

'No, if it was a pulled muscle, it'd hurt all the time I was walking, but, like, I was walking down to the post office and after about thirty yards I suddenly got the pain. I rubbed my leg and it went off and just as I got to the post office it was coming on again.'

'Well, that's strange, I don't know what that would be.'

But I did, I knew exactly what it was.

'Dad, get it checked out.'

'No, it's all right, it's just old age.'

'Dad, you're sixty, not eighty. Go and see the doctor.'

'Nah, don't you worry about me.'

But as ever I did.

NOTHING WAS GOING to keep me in nursing. When Sister Ignatius had said to me, 'You should go on the stage,' she wasn't telling me anything I didn't already know. I had always known that what I really wanted to do was act. I had to do something. But what?

I rang the British Drama League and told a very posh-sounding woman that I wanted to become an actress. What should I do?

She said, 'Well, really you should go to university.'

'But I've only got four O levels.'

'Then you can't.' And that was the end of that.

On midsummer's eve 1969, I met and fell in love with my first proper boyfriend, whom I shall call DT. It was a sublime period in which I staggered about the wards, completely knackered after nights of unbridled shagging. I had discovered sex in a big way, but it hadn't all been smooth going. It took me three days to lose my virginity because I was so tense: clamped shut, I suppose. However, after those three days, there was no stopping me.

Meeting DT was a revelation on every level. He came from a middle-class family in a well-to-do part of Birmingham. Entering his house for the first time was like entering a foreign country. There was a spacious sitting room with a grand piano in one corner and French windows that opened out onto a large garden which was a far cry from the little rectangles of earth round our way. This garden had a pond and a willow tree, and from the branch of a large oak hung a tyre for people to swing on—for fun! It was a garden built for the pleasure of being outside.

The kitchen had the wonderful, hitherto alien, aroma of freshly ground coffee and garlic. It boasted a dishwasher, which in those days was referred to as a washing-up machine. Next to the kitchen was the breakfast room: a room whose sole purpose was to sit and eat breakfast in! The dining room being another room entirely!

Upstairs, Mr and Mrs T had an en suite bathroom, a luxury I didn't come across for another ten years, and then only in a hotel. They read the *Daily Telegraph*, cooked spaghetti Bolognese, and spoke without a trace of a Birmingham accent. At dinner they drank wine. They called dinner, lunch; tea, supper; while dinner itself you ate at eight o'clock in the evening.

The September of the year that we met, DT went up to Manchester Polytechnic, now Manchester Metropolitan University, to study sociology. I was heartsore, and any will I had left to continue nursing disappeared almost immediately. Every day that I had off was spent getting to Manchester at the earliest opportunity, staying until the last possible moment and coming home miserable. On one such visit I confided to DT that I wanted to become an actress, whereupon he told me that there was a drama course right there at the poly and why didn't I apply? An audition was set up for the following January. Now all that was left to do was give in my notice to the school of nursing and *tell my mother*.

I went home to talk to my brother Tommy, because, apart from Sister Ignatius, he was the only person who had ever said that I should become an actress. Once again, he was encouraging and said that I should go for it, especially while I had DT's emotional support. I went to see my other brother, Kevin, and his wife Jill, both of whom reiterated Tommy's sentiments, Kevin offering to be there when I told my mother, a task I dreaded.

On the appointed evening, I took my father aside to brief him of my impending change of career and, as I thought, he said if that's what I wanted, I must do it. Finally, with my brothers and my dad standing in between my mother and me, I broke the news.

'Mum? I'm going to leave nursing. I want to be an actress.'

'Don't be ridiculous! Has she gone mad?'

'Well, if it's what she wants . . .' My dad was trying to mediate.

'Don't talk so bloody daft! She'll ruin her life.'

'She doesn't have to stay in nursing if it's not what she wants.'

This was from Kevin, with a touch of the old teenage insolence. He and Mum had rarely seen eye to eye.

'You'll be in the gutter before you're twenty!'

Tommy joined the fray: 'There's no point in her staying in a job that makes her miserable. She should go for it while she's young.'

'I might have expected that from you!'

Tommy had had a couple of stabs career-wise before embarking on his degree in theology at Birmingham University, one at teacher-training college and the other when he entered the Jesuits, staying only a matter of weeks. My mother had wept bitterly on the day that he left home to join, thinking that she would never see him again, and then she had gone totally mad, calling him every name under the sun, when she'd heard he'd packed it in.

'Acting!' This was said with utter contempt. 'You've been

watching too much television! May the great God look to me!'

And that was it, it was all over. I then announced I would be moving up to Manchester, where I would get a job for a year before hopefully getting into college. The course I had applied for was also a teaching course, which went a long way to assuaging my mother's anxiety, but it also left her disappointed, in that she could no longer live out her own ambition to be a nurse through me.

I MOVED TO MANCHESTER in November 1969 to live with DT. After a week or two, we found a bedsit in Maple Avenue, Chorlton-cum-Hardy, in the attic of a Victorian house, with a tiny kitchen tucked into the eaves. Downstairs, on the first floor, we had the use of a bathroom that we shared with the rest of the house.

One evening, just days after we had moved in, I arrived home, thrilled at having found a job, to see a small envelope had been posted under our door. On opening it, I saw a square of folded paper containing a little clump of dark pubic hair, and on the paper was written, 'Found in the bathroom. Yours, I believe.' It was unsigned. I was mortified. It was obviously meant for me as DT had gorgeous bright-red hair. Someone must have used the bathroom immediately after me and . . . Oh, it was too awful to contemplate. After this incident I chose to wash standing at the sink in the freezing kitchen.

My parents, even my father, thought that I was living with a friend from school and that DT was living elsewhere. It would have been too much, on top of abandoning nursing, to tell them the truth. When recently I played the role of Mary Whitehouse, the self-styled moral campaigner, it brought my rebellious, anti-establishment, nineteen-year-old self into sharp focus. Although my mother thought Mary Whitehouse a 'bit of an old fuddy-duddy', when it came to sex before marriage she virtually shared the same views.

After I'd been in Manchester for a year my parents finally came to visit. There was a frantic hiding of all things DT, but I failed to put away my birth-control pills, which my mother's hawk eyes spotted straight away. She never said anything, or even remotely hinted at it; it was Tommy who told me years later how she'd seen them on the bathroom shelf and was somewhat miffed.

Once I settled into living with DT, I began to realise that there was something wrong with my sleep. I would frequently shoot up in bed in the middle of the night, often screaming, my heart banging, covered in sweat. As the years went on it became increasingly worse. Every single night I would have a disturbance of one sort or another. On a good night, it would be brief. However, on a bad night, this waking could happen every hour.

These night terrors were not like a normal nightmare. There was no story to them; it was more like a terrifying image presenting itself to my psyche. The image would often involve dark water and drowning. I would see the water rising up the bedroom windows and wake knowing that I was the only one who could do anything about it. I would then get up, trying to work out what was going on, pacing round, staring hard out of the window, and then beginning to not know why I was doing so. The remnants of this conundrum would sometimes filter into the next day, leaving me with the troubling sensation that something vital had been left undone.

When I was away from home I started to dread going to sleep, much the same as I had as a child and had feared wetting the bed. This wasn't helped by my propensity to sleepwalk. Once, while staying in a hotel on location, I walked out of the hotel room stark naked and was only woken by the sharp click of the door as it closed behind me. Luckily a female guest was returning to her room and got me a towel to wrap round myself, allowing me to sit in her room while she called the receptionist to come and let me into my own.

Frequently, I would wake up thinking that there was someone in the bed next to me who I couldn't identify, and I would end up nudging my long-suffering husband awake, asking, 'Who are you?' How my marriage has survived these nightly disturbances is nothing short of a miracle. I was eventually to find salvation in the form of acupuncture at the ripe old age of forty-eight, after thirty years of badly disrupted sleep. Then, just as I started to get a good night's sleep, the menopause started, but that's another story.

In the year prior to college, I did a series of temporary jobs: counting cigarettes for Carreras; as a sales assistant in a shoe shop; plus a myriad of others, the worst of which was in a factory where I spent my days screwing tops onto large cans of oil.

I found my new life of cohabitation challenging and exciting. In the tiny kitchen at Maple Avenue, DT gave me my first cookery lessons. How to boil potatoes and how to make spaghetti Bolognese, two 'skills' that have formed the basis of the cook I am today!

It was here that the exploding haggis incident occurred. I had just left the kitchen when a bang brought me running back in to find the innards of a haggis, which had been boiling on the stove, dripping from the ceiling. The downstairs neighbour stood on the landing looking a touch scared. This was after the pubic-hair business and, unsure whether this neighbour was the author of the note, I was struck dumb. The two of us just stood there, him wondering what had happened and me picturing him picking my pubes out of the bath.

One Saturday, I invited a couple of friends round. Lunch was to consist of a quiche plus some salad, followed by apple crumble and custard. I was totally thrilled with the result as I got the two dishes out of the oven. They looked cookery-book perfect, golden and delicious, but when we came to eat the quiche, no one could get their knife through the pastry. One friend placed his knifetip down vertically and banged on the end of the handle, hammer-and-chisel style. I have never made pastry since.

In January 1970, I had my audition for Manchester Polytechnic School of Theatre. I had been asked to prepare three pieces, one of which had to be Shakespeare. I chose Lady Macbeth, *Macbeth* being the only Shakespeare I knew, having studied it at O level. The other two I barely remember, except that one was a character contemplating suicide, and the other was from a play by Clemence Dane, whom I had never heard of. I was interviewed by Edward Argent, the principal, who was wearing a black velvet jacket. I recall thinking that this was a good sign as I was wearing my new black velvet trouser-suit with bell-bottoms.

‘So you want to be an actress?’ He was a round, teddy-bearish man, with dark, twinkling eyes, thick dark hair and a full beard.

‘No. I am an actress,’ I said. ‘Whether I am employed as such is another matter, but that’s what I am.’ I believed that absolutely and felt that if he were to turn me down, it would be his loss.

‘So, do you think you’ll be able to learn anything here, then?’

‘Oh yes, I’ll be learning about the actress that I am and how to use what I have.’

He then asked me to perform my pieces. Never since have I performed anything, first time, with such confidence. First of all I did my Lady M, the ‘screw your courage to the sticking place’ speech, feeling totally in tune with every single line. Buoyed up by this, I went on to the suicide speech. Again I soared through it, convinced that I was completely at one with the character.

Edward Argent didn’t say anything straight away, just creaked slightly in his chair. ‘Mmm, that was interesting and very, very good.’ I felt as if I might just float up into the air, but then, ‘Tell me, why did you choose to play a man’s part?’

‘Oh . . .’ I laughed; what the hell was he talking about? And then I realised that because I’d bought a book of audition speeches, I didn’t know the plays that the speeches were taken from and therefore, of course, I didn’t know the characters either.

‘Oh, I just thought it would be . . . you know . . . Oh, what the hell, I had no idea it was a man, I just liked it and I wanted to play that speech and express those feelings.’

Now he laughed. ‘I like your honesty, good for you. Now what else have you got for me?’

‘I bet you can’t wait!’ I laughed nervously. ‘It’s by Clemence Dane and before you ask, no, I don’t know anything about him, but I think he must be pretty good, judging from this speech anyway.’

‘Oh yes . . . Incidentally, Clemence Dane is a woman.’

About three weeks later, I received a letter accepting me on the course, but this depended on my gaining one more GCE, as five were required in order to teach. I embarked on a course at a college in Stockport to study anatomy and physiology. It was now

February, and with the exams in June I thought it best to choose a subject I already had some knowledge of. Because of my nursing course, this seemed to be the best choice and, indeed, I managed to pass it with a grade two, my best grade to date.

In the summer of 1970, DT and I decided to hitchhike down to Arcachon on the southwest coast of France, camping as we went. He had borrowed an old tent belonging to his father. It was stowed in an ancient, stained, green canvas tote bag. Our first stop was at a campsite in the Bois de Boulogne on the outskirts of Paris. We arrived just as people were preparing their evening meals. I looked round at the colourful, state-of-the-art tents. Some had separate bedrooms and covered extensions to sit out under. People were cooking elaborate meals on full gas ranges, while others were drinking wine at elegantly laid-out tables. There was that smell of coffee and garlic wafting in the air, which made me excited about setting up camp and cooking our first meal out in the open. Then DT got the tent out.

It just wouldn't come out and required me to hold the bottom of the bag while DT tugged it free. When he finally did so, it came out so suddenly that he went careering backwards and fell on top of a child's beach ball, causing it to burst with a bang and the child to burst into tears. I went to the rescue with my school French.

'*Oh, pardonnez-nous! Nous achèterons un bal nouveau.*'

I noticed the man opposite begin to titter and mutter something into the tent. This brought his wife out, who stood and joined in, both openly enjoying the scene. Then the child's father came over.

'*Oh, je me remercie! Mon ami est un imbécile! Pardonnez-nous, s'il vous plaît!*'

'It's all right, love, he's got another one.' And he laughed a big fat-bellied Barnsley laugh. Scooping up the bawling child, he made to leave, but as he passed the spilt contents of the tote bag, he said, 'Good God! Where did you get this from? The Imperial War Museum?' Another big-bellied laugh. 'When was this last used? The Crimea?'

Secretly I was a bit miffed, but putting a brave face on it DT and I started to erect the cause of the hilarity. It was made from extremely thick and heavy canvas, and every crease and fold was full of long-dead flies, spiders and cobwebs.

'Oh! Brought your insect collection with you, have you?'

More laughter, and by now we had attracted a small audience. Putting the tent up then became an activity for the entire camp. The man opposite brought over his mallet and was knocking in the wooden tent pegs, while the Barnsley couple were trying to lay flat the thin ground sheet, while laughing at the age of the thing. Finally it was up. We got out our primus stove and I heated up some frankfurters and beans, but every so often a little group would gather and watch us as if we were an exhibit.

It was an idyllic holiday. Camping among the cypress trees at Arcachon and sitting at the pavement cafés, sipping huge cups of milky coffee while we observed the passing folk, is set like crystal in my mind. Even taking into account the antiquated tent and the Spanish lorry driver who offered us a lift from Arcachon to Calais on the way home and proceeded to molest me as I sat between him and DT—something I tolerated in silence because the lift was so valuable but which I avenged with a knee to the balls in the car park at the ferry terminal while DT was in the lavatory—it set a joyous bench mark for every holiday that has followed since.

## *Five*

From the moment I started at the School of Theatre, I felt as if I belonged. It was as if I had been struggling uphill in the wrong gear all my life. Now, everything made sense. However, I did have a little trouble staying awake in the history of theatre classes, and I tended to try to get out of the make-up classes, which I found a trial because I might have to remove the thick eye make-up I daubed on every morning. I hadn't allowed a single person to see me devoid of eye make-up for about three years—in fact, from the moment I realised the effect it had on my eyes, making them darker and larger. Without it I thought myself ugly in the extreme. I had, and of course have, tiny eyes; nowadays this rarely crosses my mind but back then eyes simply had to be huge. Girls wanted to look like Twiggy, waiflike, stick-limbed, eyes wide with innocence. So my eye make-up started at my browbone and very nearly finished at my cheek.

This belief that I became attractive to others only when I had emphasised my eyes with a black pencil line went on until my thirties. It was largely cured by having to be made up for filming. When I first started out, I would go into the make-up bus with a tiny line round my eyes and a light scraping of mascara, only to have it wiped off instantly. So, of course, I would try a little less and then a little less still, until it just wasn't worth it any more, and what a relief it was to finally accept the way I looked.

In the second year of make-up classes we turned to the making of Greek masks, which were composed of plaster of Paris. We were sent home with some of the necessary materials to practise making and applying it. Usually people made casts of their arms and legs, but I decided that DT's penis might be more interesting and he, probably thinking it might perk up our sex life, agreed to it.

The first step in the procedure, in order to facilitate the easy removal of the plaster when dry, was to apply Vaseline and, as you might imagine, this also produced an effect that made the member more conducive to the application of the plaster. Once this was on, all we had to do was wait for it to dry. It looked marvellous and we were both thrilled, but probably for entirely different reasons. Half an hour later, when it was nail-tapping dry, I gingerly began to try to slide it off, but this brought a huge scream from DT. I couldn't understand it; I had slathered him with Vaseline. But on closer inspection some of the hairs on his testicles were deeply embedded in the plaster.

I tried to get the kitchen scissors that I had been using in between the plaster and the bollocks, but they were too big. I then tried to employ a pair of nail clippers, but the thought of them clipping his scrotum sent DT into a total panic.

'We'll have to go to hospital. They'll have to cut it off!'

'Isn't that a bit drastic?'

'I mean cut the plaster off! This isn't funny!'

He was now trying to pace round the room with his trousers round his ankles, holding the plaster cast in place. The thought of taking him to the hospital on the bus, trying to conceal this huge white erection protruding rudely from his trousers, was too much. I had a terrible urge to laugh. The plaster of Paris had made his member look almost twice its natural size and, as it was already sizable, with his long curly hair and beard he resembled one of those Greek statues that you can buy in tacky tourist shops, of tiny men with disproportionately large phalluses, which are supposed to be fertility symbols.

'I'll go downstairs and see if they've got some nail scissors.'

DT didn't say anything, he just looked at me as if to say, 'Why did I ever listen to you?'

I went off to knock on the downstairs neighbour's door. She was a trainee solicitor who lived by herself and I was never sure, with her neat and anal look, that she wasn't the phantom pube collector.

'I was just wondering if I could borrow a pair of nail scissors?'

'Well, I've got scissors but . . . what's it for?'

'Oh, trimming my boyfriend's beard.' She disappeared and came back seconds later with a pair of long, pointed scissors in a plastic sheath. 'These are my best hair scissors and they can be used only for hair; anything else will blunt them.'

'Don't worry, I'll take great care of them.'

I managed to slip the scissors down between cast and scrotum, and snip the first pubes free, after which it was plain sailing. It was a perfect cast, coming away completely intact. I think DT was pretty chuffed with it, as it took pride of place on the mantelpiece for some months, prompting admiring glances from female visitors—as well as several male ones, come to think of it. When I went to place the scissors back in their sheath, I noticed one or two of his pubes were still attached to the blades. I couldn't resist leaving one. I then waited to see whether it would reappear under the door in a little envelope, but it never did.

In the summer holidays after my first year at college, I was working as a ward orderly at the General Hospital in Birmingham. I loved the job and had far greater success in it than I ever had in my original nursing role, largely because less was expected of me and my nursing experience bumped me up above the others in terms of competence. My mother thought I was staying in the nurses' home, whereas I was renting a room with DT in Varna Road in the Birmingham red-light district.

One Friday morning—Friday, July 23, 1971—to be exact, I had come on duty and was immediately summoned to the matron's office. A weary-looking woman sat at the other side of the desk. I could think of no reason why I should have been summoned. Had someone made a complaint?

'Your father passed away last night. Your mother has been trying to contact you; she was under the impression you were living here.'

I sat staring at her, aware that I still had the same half-smile on my face that I was wearing when I entered the room. My parents ... My parents think ... No, my mother ...? I couldn't make the syntax of what she had said fit into any sensible order.

'I presume you were expecting this?'

Dad was dead; I'd got it now. A gunshot through the centre of my chest and I was still smiling the stupid smile. 'Oh yes, yes, we were ... expecting it.'

No we weren't, no we weren't! I stood up, and the smile started to shift with a series of muscular twitches in my cheeks.

'You'd better get home to your mother, she'll be needing you.'

Outside, in the long, echoing Victorian corridor, where the endless cacophony of the hospital could swallow up every human sound imaginable, I let out a trapped yelp of sorrow; the smile was gone and the tears came. My Auntie Clare, my mum's sister-in-law, picked me up from the hospital and, driving the wrong way round the one-way system in Birmingham city centre, dropped me at the flat of my brother Kevin. As soon as we looked at each other, his face became a mask of silent pain. We raced home to Bishopton Road in Kevin's Mini van, the two of us in a fog of feeling that neither could express, and then suddenly my brother went flying headlong into the back of the car in front. The driver got out and began to shout and swear at my brother.

I jumped from the car and screamed at the man: 'You leave my brother alone, our dad's just died, we've got to get home!'

He didn't say another word, even apologising for an accident for which he was in no way responsible.

I was anxious about seeing my mother. How was I to make sense of her without my father? I was almost expecting to see a piece of her physically missing. She was sitting in one of the easy chairs in the kitchen and looked up as I came in, her face bright red and tear-stained, helpless with grief.

'We were five and now we're only four.'

I didn't cry again until the funeral a week or so later. I had felt oddly numb, possibly because my mother was so upset and I felt I needed to be strong. In the days that followed we started to sort out my father's belongings. I found a lock of my hair from years ago when it was blonde and a diary from when I was fourteen, full of mundane facts like: 'Went to school' and 'Hockey practice' in a childish scrawl, and then I found ten Park Drive tipped. I took them out into the yard and stamped on them.

In some ways, my mum flowered after my father's death. She started going out more, attending a night school to learn French, and asking me on one occasion whether I'd like to have a *coup d'état*, thinking she was offering me a cup of tea. She began to take the foreign holidays she had yearned for all her life, my father having had no interest. One of these was a trip to Lourdes organised by the church. She came back with conjunctivitis and was most put out when we suggested that she might have contracted it from the holy waters. She seemed to worry less, and when after some time I asked her whether she would ever consider marrying again—after all, she was only fifty-six when Dad died—she said, 'Good Gad, no. Why should I spend my old age clearing up after some old man?'

She died in 1989. I stood in a field and screamed at a pale sky until my voice went ragged, 'Where are you? *Where . . .?*'

I had driven back from Birmingham to our house in Sussex a couple of days after the funeral, berating my new Mini for having so little power, only to discover that I had driven the entire journey with the handbrake on. I stood in that field until the sky went black, hoping for a sign that this incredible energy that was my mother was still in the world, unable to comprehend how her huge presence and extraordinary drive were no longer here.

The love between us was combative and competitive, but I never doubted its power. The mourning of her was hard and painful, and some of it was carried out in public. In the West End stage production of *Frankie and Johnny in the Clair de Lune* later that year, the character of Frankie has a very moving speech about her mother, and every night I cried for the loss of my own mother as I spoke the lines. The following year, I was allowed to mourn her further, in Peter Hall's production of Tennessee Williams's *The Rose Tattoo*, through the character of Serafina, who continually cries for a sign from her dead husband.

The mourning continues to this day, but now it is softened by a bit of understanding of what it is to be a mum and, of course, it has mellowed with age. I no longer look for signs as once I did; there is no need. They are everywhere.

LATER IN THE SUMMER of 1971, DT and I took off overland in a Mini to Istanbul with another couple from London, whom we had met when I was working at the hospital. Both were students at Birmingham University and the chap, whom we code-named Rupert, was the owner of the said Mini. He was one of those car anoraks who spent all his free time sniffing round the vehicle, twiddling and tweaking, and although DT was meant to share the driving with him, Rupert could never quite bring himself to let him take the precious wheel. People often refer to their cars as 'she', but somehow when Rupert did it had a greater resonance. Interestingly, he called his girlfriend, who did all the navigating, by her surname, firing orders at her as we went along.

'Henman? Passports!' or 'Henman? Chewing gum!' or 'Henman? Consult map, please!'

Almost as an omen, one of the wheels began to wobble free as we drove off down the Balham High Road, just minutes into the first leg of our big adventure. We went through France, Germany, Austria, Italy, Hungary, Bulgaria, Romania, Greece and finally Turkey, with Rupert driving as if a homicidal maniac were in hot pursuit. DT and I were squashed into the back seat with assorted belongings crammed round us. Convinced it would prevent the engine from overheating, Rupert insisted that we had the heater on inside the car, which became unbelievably stifling as soon as we crossed the Channel. I'm not sure when we discovered we might have made a mistake embarking on that trip, but it was probably on the Balham High Road.

In Romania we travelled through the High Carpathians, where huge mountains on either side of the road almost touched in places, leaving just a tiny blue crack of sky above us. In the little towns, the local people crowded round the car, stroking it. They were saying its name, incredulously, over and over again, almost chanting with wonder, 'Owstin Meenee!'

The people simply couldn't believe that we had travelled all that distance, from London, England, and by this time neither could we. When we passed through the border between Hungary and Romania, Rupert surpassed himself with his tactful cockney charm. As the Hungarian border guards were walking round the car, one of them signalled for him to open the boot. Rupert swaggered round to the back to flip it open and, as they rooted through, he pointed at the contents and said with a smirk, 'Yeah, bombs! Yeah, there's bombs in there, mate! Yeah, that's it, bombs!'

If DT and I could have slid down our seats and disappeared, we would have, but we were forced to cringe, sitting up in full view of anyone who cared to look. Clearly thinking that these men couldn't speak English, Rupert made an exploding sound, blowing his cheeks out and throwing his hands into the air, just so that they got the full picture. Whereupon the guard, in perfect English, of course, said, 'Take everything out, please.'

We were there for hours as they emptied the contents of every single container onto the ground: soap powder, shampoo, orange squash etc., all of which we would have to replace. By now DT and I were furtively discussing where we could jump ship. However, we stayed the course and arrived in Istanbul.

On our return journey, the plan was to take a ferry from Igoumenitsa in Greece to Otranto in Italy. Smaller than we had imagined, our boat was called the *Rumba*. Once the car was sardined in on the little deck below, we scrambled up to the top deck to sunbathe. It was a perfect Mediterranean day, with a cloudless blue sky and a sea that barely moved. After the cramped, sweaty conditions of the car, I have to say it felt like the *QE2*.

Everything was perfect until we pulled out of Corfu harbour, our only port of call, and a wind came from nowhere to tickle the surface of the sea. To begin with this was a welcome relief from the relentless sun but, as we left the harbour behind, the water became choppy and turbulent. Within minutes it became very difficult to stand as the *Rumba* lurched from port to starboard and then from bow to stern, shoving its windswept passengers into drunken little scurries to grab hold of whatever solid thing they could. This, I thought, was the Mediterranean—surely the storm wouldn't last long?

Four hours later, we had barely moved, the *Rumba* now being lifted up almost vertically by huge dark waves and eighty-mile-an-hour winds. The deck was virtually deserted, everyone having taken refuge in the cramped little bar below, where apparently the floor was covered with vomit that slid from side to side with every lurch of the boat. The only people on deck were a couple of blokes retching over the side and me, lying on the deck, wrapped in my sleeping-bag, weak from continuous nausea. DT had gone off to find somewhere for us to shelter, so when I felt a hand upon my shoulder, I thought it was him.

'Oh, missy!' It was one of the Greek sailors. 'I take you to lie down.'

He had a kind, weather-beaten face and I was too weak to argue.

'Come.' And with that he scooped me up and carried me down some stairs into a small cabin that smelt of oil and TCP.

'Come, you sleep here, the captain's cabin.'

He lowered me gently onto a bunk, made me drink half a tumbler of water, pulled a coarse blanket up over me and stuck a piece of cotton wool in each of my ears. The blanket stank of diesel and aftershave, but I managed to fall into a deep sleep.

I had no idea how long I'd been asleep when an icy hand pushing back the hair from my forehead woke me up. I opened my eyes and it was pitch-black; there was a smell of garlic, French cigarettes and that aftershave. A face that I could barely make out, but which I knew didn't belong to my sailor friend or DT, was almost level with mine. As my eyes adjusted to the dark, I could see the outline of a big, round face with a full beard.

'I come sleep with you. This . . . my bed. I sleep now.'

And with that he began to get into the narrow bunk. My head was pounding as he squashed himself in and began to kiss my face.

'No, please . . . I am sick . . . please.'

'It is OK. You are like daughter.'

I quickly turned my back on him, praying that this wouldn't make matters worse.

When freezing fingers fumbled under my sweater and round my waist, I felt panic begin to rise, bringing with it a fresh wave of nausea. I shifted onto my back, trying to shove his hands away.

'Is OK. I sleep with you . . . like daughter.'

Poor bloody daughter! I bet she doesn't look forward to you coming home from the sea! The hands slid downwards.

Then it came to me, a trick I'd learned at school. I took in a very deep breath and then let out a long, loud, resounding burp. It stopped him in his tracks. Then I sat up. 'Oh, I'm . . . going to be sick . . . sick . . . Please, sick . . . sick . . .'

He jumped from the bed and switched on the light. My assailant was a huge man wearing nothing but a pullover and a grubby-looking pair of Y-fronts stuck into the crack of his not insubstantial bottom. With his back to me, he was rummaging through a heap of clutter on top of a small cabinet.

'Wait, wait! I have . . .'

He turned, offering a conical-shaped paper party hat. Then the water that the sailor had made me drink when he put me to bed came shooting up like a fire hydrant. As I grabbed the hat, the water spurted out of my mouth to land, hot and splashing, on the bare feet of the man. He instantly jumped back, grabbing his shoes and trousers, saying simply, 'I go now.'

Yeah, you do that. And too weak to get up, I flopped back down in the bed and slept until morning.

Thirteen hours later the same bloke who had tried to molest me came and woke me up to disembark. 'We here now. We in Otranto.'

He was wearing a big smile as if we had both been on a long and jolly journey. I got weakly to my feet, whereupon he gave me a huge hug and kissed me on the forehead.

'You like my daughter.'

It took me days to recover, but needless to say I did and I have never really suffered from motion sickness since.

DURING MY LAST two years at the poly, I moved into a bedsit at the top of a tall Victorian house in Demesne Road, Whalley Range. DT had gone off to Bristol to do an MA and the two of us had decided that we would get married the following summer. Despite the fact that or street was pronounced De Main Road, all the bus drdivers shouted 'Dmeznee!' as the bus approached the stop.

All of us in the house in 'Dmeznee Road' were from the polytechnic, and the place was presided over by Dolores, a kind of caretaker who lived in the basement. She was a thin, reedy Irish woman with long dyed blue-black hair, which after a week or two would sport snow-white roots, giving her a badger-like appearance. She wore her hair pinned up, and you could plot her movements through the house by following the trail of hairpins or the smell of stale cigarettes, as she was never without a Rothmans Kingsize hanging from her bottom lip.

Dolores was lonely and would often hover about, purporting to dust but actually waiting to catch people as they came in from college, whereupon she would pounce with tales of woe. We all tried to avoid having to go down to her room. She had an amazing skill for keeping people metaphorically pinned to the wall, unleashing torrents of verbiage at them before they had time to think of an escape route.

One Saturday night I was cooking a meal when the electricity ran out, so I was forced to go down and cadge some shillings off her to feed the meter. When she opened the door, she had the look a hunter might have on spotting a prize prey.

'Hello! Are you not out this Saturday night?' She'd already clasped hold of my arm to prevent any escape.

'No. How are you?'

As soon as I said this, I knew it was a mistake.

'I have cancer.'

Oh my God and it's a big one. 'Oh . . . oh . . . I . . . I'm so . . . I'm so sorry.'

'Yes, I had this pain and I finally went to the doctor and . . .'

I didn't speak for another sixty-five minutes. Halfway through her monologue, around the part where she was describing what they had found on her first set of X-rays, I remembered that I'd left the sweet and sour pork bubbling away on top of the gas stove. I had to listen while she told me what the doctor had said of her prognosis, what the operation would entail, plus the details of her Uncle Pat's tumour and his eventual demise, before I managed to get a word in edgeways about the imminent fire that was about to break out at the top of the house.

As I rushed up the stairs, a dreadful smell of burning met me full on. The pork was no longer recognisable, and what you might call extreme caramelisation had taken place. From then on I kept my own stash of shillings.

Dolores was a close relative of the theatrical landlady, a legendary figure in the acting world. I imagine there are few of them left today. When I was looking for accommodation in Sheffield in 1980, an actor friend told me about an experience he had had while staying in digs there. He had a room in a house run by a slightly brassy woman with a twinkle in her eye. One night he returned late to find the landlady going at it hammer and tongs, completely naked on the kitchen table, with the young stage manager who had just moved in. Mortified, the actor squeezed past them, muttering something about being 'terribly sorry', when the woman looked over the top of the stage manager's shoulder and, still going at it, said, 'Good night, Mr Simmons. Sleep well.'

The next day he tried to creep out of the house without bumping into her, to save them both from embarrassment, but just as he was leaving she rushed down the stairs and said, 'Oh, Mr Simmons, I'm sorry about last night. You must think I'm a terrible flirt.'

I stayed briefly in some digs in Leicester in 1985 with three other actors. On my first morning there, before going in for rehearsals, we were all round the breakfast table eating our boiled eggs. One of the actors was ensconced with his newspaper in the downstairs lavatory, which was situated just off the kitchen. There was a rapping on the lavatory door and loudly and clearly the landlady shouted, 'Oh, oh, Mr Harcourt? Do remember, no solids in the downstairs toilet. Thank you.'

In the first term of our second year at college, we were scheduled to do teaching practice. I was placed in a primary school in north Manchester and given several different age groups to teach. At this point both my brothers and my sister-in-law were teachers, and it gave me a peek into their lives. I loved teaching and saw how close in many ways it was to acting. It was necessary to give a kind of performance to keep children interested in what you had to say. The six weeks' practice culminated in a nativity play, which

I had helped to get together, along with one of the class teachers, Mrs Forbes, a nice woman I immediately took to.

On the afternoon of the first performance I sat to the side of the little stage with a small cassette player at the ready, in full view of the audience. With a sign from Mrs Forbes, who was standing on the other side of the stage, I pressed the play button. Mrs Forbes's sign was achieved by waving her arm slowly from side to side as if she were on a crowded beach and needed to be seen.

My first cue was a beautiful rendition of 'In the Bleak Midwinter', which in turn was the cue for Mary and Joseph to trudge wearily across the stage. Then after another huge wave from Mrs Forbes, I faded the music out and the narration began, read by one of the eleven-year-olds, describing how Mary and Joseph had walked for miles, battling through the wind and the snow. This was my next cue, but instead of a howling gale, out from the cassette came the sound of pouring rain, accompanied by great claps of thunder. Mary and Joseph looked helplessly towards Mrs Forbes, who was now doing big winding actions with her hand, interspersed with dragging her forefinger across her throat.

In panic mode, I tried to fast-forward the tape and it whizzed on to a police siren, at which Mrs Forbes's winding action now went up a notch. I then decided that perhaps rewind was the best course of action, randomly stopping and inwardly begging the gods to make something sensible come out, but this time we were treated to gunshots and the galloping of horses.

On hearing the shots Joseph threw Mary to the ground, causing her to scream. Covering her with his cowl, he proceeded to hold the unseen gunmen at bay and pick them off one at a time with his staff, miraculously turned into a rifle. Now Mrs Forbes was fairly whipping her hand across her throat. I pressed stop, plunging us into a sudden silence. Everyone froze. Joseph directed a last shot at the enemy. Silence. Then from underneath the cowl Mary yelped, '*Ow!* You're on my hair!' and the narrator said, 'Joseph killed every one of those muggers, and they went on their way towards Bethlehem.'

My second and final teaching practice, in the third year, was a very different experience. It was to take place at a girls' secondary school, close to my bedsit. I was teaching all years except the sixth form and, almost without exception, the bottom streams. On my first day, I was sitting down for lunch in the canteen with the girls when an altercation started at the next table. A male teacher in his mid-forties was asking a girl to leave as she was in the wrong sitting, and she was refusing to go. Suddenly, a towering girl, about six feet tall, squared up to this poor bloke. 'You lay one finger on her and you got me to deal with!'

He tried to ignore her and carried on, in a calm, quiet voice, trying to reason with the girl who wouldn't go. Eventually he made the mistake of touching her lightly on the arm, whereupon the Amazon launched a shocking attack, hurling punches and kicks, and lashing out at his face. Girls and staff alike were open-mouthed as the two of them became locked in a fierce struggle in which his shirt was ripped from button to armpit and her blouse was torn open, sending buttons flying.

They fell to the floor, the girl viciously grabbing at the man's face and hair. They were right next to a set of stone steps and, suddenly rolling over and over, they began to tumble down them. Every time she was on top, the girl would grab his hair and bang his head with a sickening thud on the step. When they hit the bottom they lay there without moving. Then the girl stood up and swaggered off, complaining about a broken nail. The teacher got slowly to his feet, stunned and ashen-faced, his hair standing up in messy, spiky clumps. There was a trickle of blood from his nose, his lip was cut and he had bitten his tongue. I turned to the teacher next to me and said, 'Please, tell me I won't be teaching her.'

Fortunately, I wasn't. I was given what they referred to as 'the Easter leavers'. These were girls who were not going to do GCEs, but would leave at Easter, some aged just fifteen. This meant that they had absolutely no interest in any form of schoolwork. I knew that if I was going to survive, I had to get them on my side.

I told them how I was on teaching practice and my every move was being watched, so I needed their help. I asked them to get out their Shakespeare textbook and have it open on the desk as if we might be discussing it, should the teacher that was monitoring me walk past and look through the window. It was a gamble but one that paid off, because they thought the whole subterfuge was a gas. I assured them that we wouldn't in fact be studying Shakespeare because I knew very little about it and what I really liked in terms of drama was modern stuff about real people's lives. That was it; from then on we were friends.

We talked casually, with girls sitting on top of their desks and lounging about with their feet up on chairs. This informality was a battle I was prepared to forgo in exchange for their participation and interest. One girl kept watch; every time a teacher came down the corridor the girls would jump down behind their desks, burying their heads in their Shakespeares. We discussed everything, from their feelings about being 'left to rot', as one girl so aptly put it, because they weren't academic, to abortion and racism, and we started off with the fight in the canteen.

'Did anyone see that fight in the canteen? Blimey! What was all that about?'

And they were off. Should men be allowed to teach in a single-sex school? Was there a racist element, with the girl involved being black and the teacher being white? How do black girls view white men in authority? How are teachers meant to keep control? Every time they got loud, I'd ask them to pipe down, reiterating the fact that I would be in trouble with the teacher if she heard the noise, and they were totally with me.

After a week or so I got them to act out some of the topics that we were discussing. Mother–daughter relationships is the topic that has stayed with me. A small black girl, looking much younger than her years, improvised a situation bringing in elements from her own life, living in a one-bedroom flat with her mother who was a prostitute and drug addict. It was some of the most honest, raw and moving acting I have seen to date.

These girls weren't going to get their GCEs but they were

highly intelligent, articulate and passionate once they engaged. I became hugely fond of them and felt that I had shared real intimacy with them, brought about by the power of drama. They could express their fears and hopes through it, and it promoted discussion and understanding of some of the bewildering elements of their lives. And I personally learned that drama was more than just acting lines off a page. It was therapeutic; it helped to develop emotional intelligence and the use of language and communication skills; it was educational for both performer and audience alike. I think, if taught moderately well, it is a vital part of a healthy education.

DT AND I had decided that we would marry in Bristol, where he was studying for his MA, in the summer of 1973. Everyone was thrilled; my mother approved, and he had bought me a gorgeous antique engagement ring, set with three vibrant turquoise stones. Three weeks before the wedding day, on one of his weekend visits to Manchester, I shot up in bed in the middle of the night, filled with only one, very certain thought.

'Oh, DT . . . I'm so sorry!' I couldn't get out any more than that. I was paralysed by gulps and sobs.

'What? What is it, love?' He sat up and put his arm round me.

Eventually I managed, 'I can't get married. I'm just not ready. There's too much of life to do first. I just can't!'

And I knew it to be right because the relief was enormous, as if something had been surgically removed, something that I hadn't even registered as being a problem; now that it was gone I was light as air.

But I loved DT and hurting him was painful.

'Look, DT, let's carry on as we are. I just don't want to get married.' And finally he stopped asking why.

We lay there in silence and then, 'DT? Can we still go on the honeymoon?'

We were going to Lisbon and I couldn't give *that* up, and neither could he.

I wasn't looking forward to telling my mother, but to my surprise she said, 'Thank God you found out it wasn't right now and not after you'd got married.' And then, 'So you weren't pregnant, then?'

A couple of months later we did go off on our 'honeymoon', staying in a pension in Lisbon for a couple of nights, then hitchhiking north and stopping in a little fishing village just south of Oporto. With no accommodation booked, we were given the address of the local doctor who, it seemed, had a room that he occasionally let out to tourists. It was an attic room in the eaves of the family house with a ceiling that sloped down to the floor. There was very little space but it was perfectly adequate.

We spent the days reading, lying on the beach sunbathing, and eating freshly caught sardines barbecued at the water's edge by the fishermen's wives. Our evenings were passed in the cafés and bars, and we only returned to our room late at night.

One night I was awoken by a creaking sound, and on opening my eyes was met by the creepy sight of a shadowy figure moving slowly about the room. I was paralysed with fright and buried my head under the covers. DT was dead to the world. I gradually slid into a fitful sleep. The next day I was convinced I had seen a ghost and endured much teasing from DT. The following two nights I slept very lightly, but there was no repetition of the event.

On our last night we got back to our room with the intention of making an early start in the morning, so we decided to pack our things. I had lost a flip-flop and was on all fours looking for it under our bed when from somewhere close behind me came what sounded like a low snarl. I screeched and backed away towards the door. At that moment, DT returned from downstairs, where he had been paying the doctor.

'Bloody hell, DT, there's something living in here.'

'What? What is it?'

'I just heard it growling. I think it came from behind there!'

Opposite our bed, running along the bottom half of the sloping roof, was an old green curtain on a length of saggy wire. I had looked behind it when we first moved in, and there were just some cardboard boxes, a pile of towels and a heap of old clothing. DT moved towards it on tiptoe, pulling a cartoon expression of angst by baring his teeth and making big scared eyes. Just as he bent down to peep inside, there was, somewhat comic in its timing, a long-drawn-out fart. He jumped up and fell back onto the bed.

We stared for a moment as a sulphurous odour filled the room.

'Oh my God, DT, I'm scared! What is it?'

'I don't know. Do you think it's human?'

We were now talking in stage whispers.

DT gingerly got up off the bed and, with one hand covering his nose and mouth against the stench, he began to pull the curtain back. We both peered into the gloom until our eyes became accustomed to it. There seemed to be a hunched shape on the ground, and we could hear it breathing, deep and slumberous. Not only was it human but I recognised its profile.

On one or two occasions when we had popped back to the room during the day, we had passed an ancient woman on the steps to our attic dressed in the classic widow's garb of long black skirt and shawl. She was apparently the doctor's mother and never spoke a word to us, and yet there she was sharing our room! She must have got up at dawn before we woke and gone to bed while we were out in the evening. I guess it was her room, but the doctor saw a chance to make a little extra cash and shoved her behind the curtain. We went into hysterics, thinking about our lovemaking on the previous nights and wondering whether she had lain there, perhaps getting a bit of a kick from what she heard.

I slept soundly that night. At least I did after DT opened a window in the roof.

DT and I split up for good the following year, going through a wistful little ceremony where we divided up our few domestic acquisitions. I can see them laid out on the floor of my bedsit, with DT and me looking down at them. There was a motley set of cutlery, a plastic pedal bin and a washing-up bowl. We focused our pain on the bowl, which was the subject of some discussion, although not enough to prevent us from being good friends thereafter.

# *Six*

We did major productions at the Manchester Polytechnic. In the first year we put on a play titled *The Dark of the Moon*, a strange piece set in the Appalachian Mountains. I suppose it was chosen because it had a huge cast, and although it wasn't a musical, members of the cast were required to sing. I played the dark witch and can remember little about the experience, except that we put it on in the studio theatre, which in fact was a derelict church with holes in the roof through which rain fell and pigeons shat on a regular basis.

The studio was situated next to the art college at All Saints and was where we were based. We also had the use of a derelict shop on the corner opposite for voice classes and rehearsals, while movement classes were held in the art-college gymnasium. The 'make-do' nature of the old church and the filthy old shop premises gave the course a feeling of having been shoved in as an unwanted afterthought, which did little to promote a sense of belonging and even less for student self-esteem. In fact, in our second year a demonstration was organised to protest, but I don't recall many turning up. Although I attended the protest, in reality I loved the School of Theatre as it was, with its makeshift, leaky, falling-down premises, and I felt that something of importance was lost when, in 1973, it moved to the Capitol building in Didsbury, an old television studio with all the character of a civic toilet.

The second-year production, *Summer Folk* by Maxim Gorky, was staged in the University Theatre. I played Varya, the female lead, and the moment I stepped out onto that stage for the technical rehearsal, I knew that I was home. I felt for the first time in my life that I had a voice, and that this is how it would be heard, and this was how I would be seen and measured.

Our third-year production was *The Playboy of the Western*

*World* by J. M. Synge, in which I played Pegeen Mike. It was staged at the Library Theatre, the main repertory theatre situated underneath the huge circular library in St Peter's Square. This venue made it feel real and professional. To be able to inhabit an Irish accent, for the play was set in the west of Ireland, and to be able to use it to express a complex character instead of my usual comic caricature of my mother or grandmother, was a deep thrill.

It was here at the Library Theatre that I did one of my very first auditions for a job: the Sylvia Plath poem 'Daddy', my beloved Lady M. and a piece from *Juno and the Paycock*. The woman who took the audition, whose name I have completely obliterated from my memory, was in a grim mood. It was cold and draughty and she was wrapped up in a vast winter coat and swathed round the neck and mouth with a big woolly scarf, so that I could barely hear a word that she said. The speed with which she got me in and out was bloody rude. I didn't get the job, unsurprisingly, and subsequently discovered that she had had all her teeth out on the morning of my audition. Nice of her to turn up, really.

I applied to Granada Television and was awarded a bursary for a one-year postgraduate course in acting and stage production at the Stables Theatre, next door to the studios. About fourteen students enrolled in the autumn of 1973. We functioned like a complete company, with student actors, student directors, student stage designers and student administrators.

After getting off to a wobbly start by staging a mutiny over the choice of our first play, *The Hollow* by Agatha Christie (the lecturer's argument being that this was the kind of unexciting thing we could expect to be doing in rep), we went on to do *'Tis Pity She's a Whore*. Guess who I played? Then a little-known piece, titled *He Who Gets Slapped*, set in a tatty French circus, in which I played a lion tamer. Our final production was *The Marriage of Figaro*, in which I took the part of the maid. It was during the preparation for this that I started to audition for work. I heard that the Everyman Theatre in Liverpool needed a couple of actors for the summer, so I applied.

The Everyman was one of the most unique, innovative and exciting repertory theatres of the day. Alan Dossor was the director, but at this point he was taking time off and Jonathan Pryce, the actor, was directing while he was away. Therefore it was Jonathan who took my audition. One of my pieces was again *Juno and the Paycock*, which I had left till last, considering it my *coup de grâce*. I couldn't wait to do it, but when I told Jonathan what my final piece was to be, he announced that he had played it only recently. This would not normally present a problem but I had decided to beef the piece up a little, generally rewriting it to suit myself, even adding a little song at one point in it. It never struck me that (a) perhaps I should play the script as written or (b) that anyone would even notice or care. Nevertheless, I still launched into it, thinking my version a great improvement on Sean O'Casey's. Luckily Jonathan found it funny, but looking back he was more likely to have been amused by my youthful conceit than my comic invention. He gave me the job and I started work on June 14, 1974.

From the minute I stepped down from the train at Lime Street station, I knew that I would love Liverpool. As I was struggling with a huge bag, a short, rotund woman who happened to be walking by said, 'Let me carry that for ya. You've got enough to carry!' And she carried my heaviest bag to the taxi rank for me.

Then when I told the taxi driver that I wanted to go to the Everyman Theatre, he said, 'It's only up the road, you know, love?'

'I know but it's really steep and I've got too much to carry.'

He drove me there and refused any payment.

'No! Go on, girl. You gerron that stage and knock 'em dead.'

The theatre was situated at the top of Hope Street. The Catholic cathedral, which the locals referred to as Paddy's Wigwam, stood at one end and the magnificent Protestant cathedral at the other. It had been arranged for me to stay in a bedsit on the top floor of a Georgian house in Canning Street, a five minute walk from the theatre. Below me in another bedsit, also working at the theatre, was Geoffrey Durham, who later became the magician, the Great Soprendo, and the husband of Victoria Wood.

He was a fantastic actor. One of my fondest memories is of Geoff making a splendid entrance in a production of Brecht's *Coriolanus* at the Everyman. As we did not have enough actors, he was playing the whole of the Roman army. He walked on with a majestic presence but, unbeknown to him, a wire coat hanger had become attached to his bent elbow and was swinging from his sleeve like a handbag. I entered soon after, playing Coriolanus's wife, I'm ashamed to say crying with laughter, my face twitching with the effort of keeping it straight.

I had been taken on at the Everyman to replace a member of the cast of a show staged in a pub titled *Flash Harry*. The main company were leaving to go down to London because the show they were in was transferring to the West End, a musical about the Beatles, titled *John, Paul, George, Ringo and Bert*, whose book and music were both written by Willy Russell. It turned out to be a huge hit in the West End, going on to similar success on Broadway.

*Flash Harry*, on the other hand, was a raucously funny show about a Liverpool flasher in which, among other things, I was to play his mother. My first spot in the show involved a monologue on the trials and tribulations of being the parent of a misunderstood flasher, and I stood at the microphone, knitting a long woollen willy warmer as I spoke. I had to learn the Scouse accent, for which Winnie, the cleaner at the theatre, was drafted in to teach me.

The show was a bit of a free-for-all, hanging loosely round the central tale of the flasher and his escapades, and our contribution was pretty much left up to us. Geoff Durham did his own brilliant version of the song, 'The Laughing Policeman'. So when I told Roger Phillips, our director, that I did a passing impersonation of Shirley Bassey, a sparkly dress with huge holes cut into it was fished out of wardrobe, a wig was bought from Woolworth's and Birley Shassey was born. I absolutely loved doing it! The number I chose was 'Hey, Big Spender', with my innuendo-filled version of 'Goldfinger' as an encore. Accompanied by Roger on the tinny old Everyman piano, I would wander down off the stage, sashaying round the tables and draping myself over dockers and the like, singing, 'I don't cock my pork for every man I see!' in some of the roughest pubs in the universe.

The audiences were at least as funny as we were, and every time we took a breath in, there was the possibility of a sharp one-liner being pinged at us from somewhere in the crowd. We rarely had any real trouble, which was quite something, as the punters didn't pay to see the show; we were generally booked by the landlord and just turned up in the pub and got started. 'It's the long 'airs from the Everyman's' is how I once heard us described.

Later on in the season, during the run-up to Christmas, we did *Dick Whittington and his Pussy*. Matthew Kelly played Dick and I played his Pussy, in a manner of speaking. As you might imagine, it was packed with gags about genitalia. 'Would you like to see my Pussy?' or 'Have you seen my Dick?' You get the picture.

After we'd been performing it for about two weeks, we got word from the landlord of our next venue that someone had reported us to the vice squad, so could we possibly tone the show down somewhat as the boys in blue would be paying us a visit that very night. We held an emergency meeting, in which we removed the more salacious jokes and all the swearing. When we started the show there wasn't a policeman in sight, but just as we were beginning to go back to the old script, we spotted them coming in, supposedly incognito but unmistakable: huge, with very short hair (remember it was 1974), navy-blue overcoats and great big feet. So back we went to the expurgated version. This did not please the audience, some turning their backs and talking among themselves. A show that was normally a riotous one and a quarter hours long, ran for a measly twenty minutes without the risqué jokes. But the coppers left wondering what all the fuss was about.

My days in the pub shows were lessons in pure survival on stage. We had to entertain or go under. Alcohol played a large part in these shows. A great deal of beer, in my case bottled Guinness, was swilled, and I don't think I ever did one of those shows sober. I can remember standing outside pubs as we were about to go in, knowing that it would be the last time that I would see it with any clarity. My eight-stone frame probably absorbed a good three pints on most nights. I had to keep up with the lads, and the audience insisted on buying us drinks, so who was I to argue? I couldn't contemplate even one drink before a show nowadays.

My first production on the main stage of the Everyman was Shakespeare's *The Taming of the Shrew*, directed by Jonathan Pryce, with Petruchio making a spectacular first entrance on a motorbike to Eric Clapton's 'Layla'. Anarchy was never very far below the surface of an Everyman production. One night, while making his entrance, Nicholas Le Prevost tripped over a stage weight and, careering onto the stage, let rip with, 'Shit! . . . I' faith!'

I played the part of Bianca, Kate's sister, and hated every second of it. I thought the character a wimp and longed to play the Shrew. I had no time for Bianca's girlie nature, and this was reflected in a series of night terrors that went on throughout the run. I awoke to find myself ransacking the drawers of my dressing table, in search of the pink dress that I wore in the play. I would turn my mattress onto the floor, thinking it might be underneath. Every night the same thing happened: the sliver of light between the top of the curtain and the window frame would catch my eye and draw me back to reality. I never understood Bianca and was constantly looking for a way to make her mine. I guess the search for the dress was an echo of that search for the character.

In November 1974 we started rehearsals for the Everyman Christmas extravaganza, *The Cantrill Tales* by Chris Bond, and a new actor was to join our ranks. He walked into rehearsal on the first morning, wearing a pair of flared denim jeans, its skirt-like flares in pale pink cotton. I was in love! Or possibly lust: it remained to be decided. Even with the slightly theatrical spotted neckerchief round his neck, he would have looked more in keeping if he'd come to mend the boiler, but his charisma was all too evident. He had mad, impish eyes either side of a battered nose, and high, wide cheekbones.

It was Pete Postlethwaite. He moved into my bedsit almost

immediately and we slipped into a roller coaster of a relationship that lasted five years. He was the most stunning and intelligent of actors, brought up a Catholic, with a rough, working-class edge that I felt at home with. He took everything to the limit. His performance in Brecht's *Coriolanus* is one of the most riveting performances I have ever seen. His mother came one night, and during this particular performance a couple of girls in the circle started to giggle. On hearing this going on throughout an important speech, Pete leapt from the stage onto the edge of the circle, causing a collective gasp. He then jumped down among them, while remaining in character, and aimed a good portion of his monologue directly—and weirdly appropriately—at these poor girls, as if they were part of the crowd in the play. They sat there in petrified silence, as did the rest of the audience, probably fearing that they might be next in line. Afterwards, his mother said, 'Oh, Peter! You'll go round the bend if you carry on like that!'

One Friday night after the show, I was up at the bar, chatting to a guy and his friends who had befriended a lot of the actors. The guy grabbed hold of my hand.

'How would you like to go on a magical mystery tour?'

He then handed me what looked like a tiny bit of lead from a propelling pencil, stuck between two pieces of Sellotape.

'What is it?'

'A piece of heaven . . . It's a tab of acid. Just stick it in your mouth. It's totally harmless. What are you scared of?'

'I don't know. What will it do?'

'Jesus! You are a scaredy-cat, aren't you? It'll just make everything bright and fun for a couple of hours.'

I unstuck the two pieces of Sellotape and propelled the thing to the back of my throat; one swallow and it was gone. Some twenty minutes later, unaware of what I had done and unprepared for the consequences, I joined the group as they bundled into the street. We had walked no more than a few yards when I had to stop to do up my shoe. As I bent my head, everywhere around me was flooded a bright crimson, like blood through water. And so the trip began. We went into a darkly lit drinking den that I had never visited before, and I was plunged into something that looked like a Hogarth painting, its characters toothless and scruffy, in what went from eighteenth-century to modern garb and back again.

We then went on what was probably, for the others, a normal night out but for me was a succession of bizarre freak shows; the whole world was an out-of-control circus. At some point during the night I headed back to my bedsit where I began to wonder when the nightmare would end. I had become increasingly uncomfortable in the company of the people I was with, seeing in every glance and half-heard sentence a sneer or a slight or something much more threatening, the nature of which I could not pin down. Once back in my room I tried to make tea but became utterly distracted by a sweater I had washed earlier: like a scene from a horror film it appeared to be seething with worms, but I then realised that I was experiencing a hallucination, and that the worms were simply fibres sticking out of the wool.

I lay on my mattress on the floor, my muscles jumping and restless, and my attention was suddenly grabbed by a poster of Marilyn Monroe. Her face filled the frame, her big scarlet lips kissing out at the camera. Abruptly, with an unpleasant, wet snap, her tongue whipped out of her mouth. It was long, black and forked, like a snake's, slithering maniacally round her face. I ripped the poster from the wall, screwing it up and throwing it into the corner of the room. I stood over it and watched as it began slowly to unfurl, and I screamed as the tongue exploded through the crushed folds of paper to lash again round Marilyn's by now distorted face. I stamped on it repeatedly to no avail as the tongue still managed to emerge. Gingerly I picked it up by a corner and, keeping it at arm's length, I dropped it in the wastepaper bin and placed a dinner plate on top.

I lay back down on the bed. Then crashing into my mind came the thought that my small bedsit was in fact the universe in its entirety and that there was nothing else beyond it. Outside the door there were no other bedsits, there was no staircase, no Mikie, the downstairs drunk. Outside was a void and what we saw from the window an illusion.

I jumped up from the bed; please, God, this could not be true! I tentatively opened the door. Everything looked as it always did. I tiptoed down the stairs, every creak threatening to burst my eardrums, and at the bottom, half lit by the morning sun flooding through the window above the door, lay Mikie in his usual heap, but now he was a big snoring walrus and not frightening at all.

I began to laugh, the sort of laughter I long for, liberating and cathartic, and off I went into a beautiful, bright Liverpool morning, a sharp wind off the Mersey blowing away the thought that the world stopped at my door. About eight hours after it began, the trip finally started to come to an end by my being drawn, heavy and drained, into the Catholic cathedral. It was still early morning; I sat shivering in one of the back pews, the sun streaming down in bright, laserlike rays upon the altar. Then an altar boy entered like an actor on a stage, the sun making a halo of his hair. He was laying out, with great delicacy, the props that were necessary for the celebration of the Mass. Just a few hours later I was laying out my own props backstage at the Everyman for the Saturday matinée. I felt fuzzy and detached, and noticed that every time I bent forward the world went ever so slightly pink.

I STAYED AT the Everyman Theatre for eighteen months, with a summer season in Aberystwyth in the middle, to which almost the entire company decamped. One day during that summer Pete came home and produced a tiny black-and-white Jack Russell puppy from his pocket, claiming that, if he hadn't taken her there and then, the farmer would have shot her. My heart sank; what could I do? So she was christened Babs.

I felt blessed that I had got into the Everyman. Previously I had believed that theatre was the preserve of the middle classes, but here the audiences were a complete mixture; it felt as if we were reaching out to the entire community, on the front line of some kind of revolution. Two productions stick out: *Funny Peculiar* by

Mike Stott and *Breezeblock Park* by Willy Russell, new plays directed by Alan Dossor. He was fearlessly inventive and clever, handsome and moody, and I was terrified of him.

In *Funny Peculiar* I played an ordinary housewife and mother of a young baby who is pressurised by her husband to be more sexually liberated and eventually driven almost to breaking point. There is a cracking scene in which my character tries to express her pain and bewilderment. I had no idea how to tackle it; it was outside my life experience. Alan, immediately recognising my problem after the read-through, took me aside.

'Don't worry about that scene. We'll deal with it without the others present. Don't learn it.'

I was dreading it, this rehearsal with just the two of us; it felt as if I was going to have to recite a not-yet-invented times table for Sister Ignatius, with a wasp stuck under her wimple. In fact it was the best acting lesson I've ever had. The lines of the speech concerned were disjointed half-sentences and isolated words held together with a series of dots. We talked about Irene, who she was and what exactly the feeling was that propelled these words from her mouth. Again he said, 'I don't want you to learn it or to try to act it. I just want you to feel it.'

And once I got that feeling, it was deep and powerful, something that I have hankered after in numerous performances ever since. The lesson I learned—that emotional honesty is what draws an audience to you, that it is something that first comes from your core, and that this is true of every single part—has stayed with me and it is something I have tried to adhere to throughout my career.

*FUNNY PECULIAR* took me down to London and into the West End after a short season at the Mermaid Theatre. It transferred, in the spring of 1976, to the Garrick Theatre in Charing Cross Road, where Richard Beckinsale played Trevor, my husband, and Pete Postlethwaite replaced Kevin Lloyd as Desmond the baker in one of the funniest scenes ever to be staged. Suffice it to say that a lot of real cream buns were involved and the two characters embark literally on a bunfight. I have rarely heard laughter like it in a theatre since.

*Funny Peculiar* marked the first time that my mother came to see me in a play. She had rung up not long after we opened and both the show and I had been declared a hit. She said she wanted to come and see it, adding, 'I don't mind how you live,' meaning that she had guessed that I was living with Pete.

We had found ourselves a flat in Greek Street, Soho, with Babs, of course. It cost £25 per week and was on the second floor, with an office underneath us, an Italian restaurant on the ground floor and, in the tiny flat above us, a pair of overfriendly girls, visited by a succession of men into the small hours. The first thing my mother saw when she walked in and went over to the window was the sex shop opposite. She said nothing but laughed a little nervously. This just heightened my anxiety about her seeing the play, as it involved references to fellatio. The final scene of the play involved Trevor lying in a hospital bed with a cage over his legs and my character, Irene, putting her head down under the cage, to his obvious enjoyment. I was dreading seeing my mother afterwards. To my amazement she said, 'Oh, Julie, that *was* funny! You would keep looking under the sheets, wouldn't you?'

I stayed in the play at the Garrick for a year, during which Pete, Babs and I settled into our version of domesticity in Greek Street. Life in Soho was peculiarly suited to life in the theatre, in that, like us, the place came alive at night. The street had two nightclubs, Le Kilt and the Beat Route, so the flat had a constant thump, vibrating its floor and walls until about three in the morning. Spookily, on the door of the Beat Route at that time was a tall, dark, handsome doorman whom I was to marry years later. Grant must have seen me walk past on numerous occasions.

Once the clubs closed in the small hours, it was the turn of the dustcart. Crate upon crate of assorted bottles from these clubs, as well as the restaurants, would be hauled, smashing and clanging, into the back of the cart, a lengthy process lasting at least an hour. Throughout the night there would be various fracas, as groups of drunks would descend on the strip joints and brothels. So it was not until around three or four o'clock that any sort of peace would descend and we could go to bed. By day, which started for us in the early afternoon, the flat became a drop-in centre for any actor who happened to be in town. I longed for a bit of space of my own and frequently went to the theatre early to spend the afternoon in my dressing room, reading, with a cup of tea. The dressing room was my home away from home. It was here that I discovered a need for time and space alone, which I crave if I don't get enough.

Greek Street was not an ideal place to keep a dog, and taking her out for a wee last thing at night was not a walk in the park, if you get my drift. Pete always did that while I took her out during the day and was frequently pointed at by tourists and smirked at by office workers who obviously thought I was a prostitute. I suppose that walking the streets of Soho, with no bag and a small dog, given my penchant for lots of eye make-up, could have given the wrong impression.

One hot Sunday morning in 1976, I took Babs to Hyde Park and decided on a bit of a sunbathe in a deck chair. At first she settled down under the chair, but after a short time, and as more people began to arrive, she staked out an area round it. Anyone who had the audacity to cross over her boundary was seen off with a barrage of yapping. Eventually she palled up with a Border-collie type belonging to a man who was sunbathing just outside her designated protection zone. I enjoyed the sight of the two of them bounding around with great joyous leaps into the air.

The game then heightened in intensity, culminating in the two of them chasing one another round and round this man's deck chair, getting faster and faster, and then they both stopped dead and peed with shivering excitement, one after the other, on the man's clothing, which lay in a pile next to his chair. I leapt up in a panic and tried to catch Babs without waking the man. This resulted in my chasing her and the collie round his deck chair until, with a flattening rugby tackle, I pinned her to the ground. Just as I thought I'd escaped, the man woke up.

'Oh hi! . . . I'm just catching my dog. Time to go home now.'

'Oh yes,' he said, smiling sleepily at Babs. 'What's her name?'

'Babs . . . What's yours called?'

'Oh, I haven't got a dog.' The stench of dog pee was already rising off his clothes. The collie was nowhere to be seen.

'Oh . . . ah . . . OK. See ya.'

We always took Babs with us when performing in the theatre, once foolishly taking her on stage for the curtain call, where the sight of hundreds of people clapping caused her to evacuate her bowls there and then. Once in the theatre she would make the dressing room her home and then woe betide anyone with the temerity to enter. She had bitten more stage-doorkeepers than I care to think about, even cornering one poor dresser in my dressing room for the whole of the first act of *Funny Peculiar*.

I had Babs for seven years and was heartbroken when, having nowhere to live at the time and having exhausted the goodwill of all to whom I had farmed her out in the past, I was forced to give her away, albeit to a nice old pensioner who adored Jack Russells.

Directly across the street from the flat was number 59, a hostel for homeless women. On our first night in the flat, after being woken by the sound of breaking glass and unearthly wails, we flung up one of our windows to find that some poor soul was lying there lifeless on the pavement. The paramedics were in the process of manoeuvring her onto a stretcher. The police were also there, trying to calm the situation, while hanging out of the windows above were a motley group of women in varying states of déshabillé and mental disorder.

It was like a scene from *Marat Sade*. One of the women was waving a carrier bag down at a young policeman while shouting something unintelligible. Getting no response, she tipped the bag upside down and emptied its contents down into the street, where it landed on what turned out to be one of the inmates who had been dodging about, getting in the way. The woman was dressed only in a thin grey ankle-length nightdress. She instantly wheeled round, letting out an operatic scream. This scattered the little group of inmates who had gathered round the injured woman, and there were various cries of, 'Mind you don't step in it!' and from the woman herself, 'The dirty cow! Come down 'ere!' Then from above came a booming voice, surprisingly cultured.

'I won't be troubling myself, thank you very much. I think you'll find that that mess belongs to you, as I found it in your bed.'

Much cackling followed from various quarters. Then a bucket appeared at the window and, before another word was spoken, it was emptied of a liquid, the identity of which can only be guessed at, onto the heads of the group below. After a screaming match between the two protagonists people started to disperse.

'I don't know what she thinks she's looking at.' It was a loud, rasping, cockney voice, roughened by years of drink, cigarettes and God knows what else. 'It's rude to stare.'

At first we couldn't tell where it was coming from or to whom it was addressed.

'Yeah, you, ya little tom!'

It then became clear that it was coming from one of the top-floor windows. In the corner, backlit, was the silhouette of a big, round woman, her face, somewhat sinisterly, in complete darkness.

'What is she? Queen of all she surveys?' And then rather mysteriously, but megaphone-loud, '*You are what you eat!*'

Oh my God; I almost looked behind me to check that it really was me that she was shouting at, but as I was the only person that I knew of to be eating a banana in Greek Street at half past four on that particular morning, I pulled my head in so fast and pulled the window down with such a bang, that my banana got severed.

We lived in Greek Street for two years, and I don't think a single day went by without some comment from the woman opposite. It could be anything: 'How many fags have you had today?' or 'You're not wearin' that, are ya?'

I never made any reply, for fear of encouraging her, and all in all her observations, some too close to home for comfort, forced us to keep the curtains closed an awful lot of the time.

There are three characters whom I recall with something almost resembling fondness from number 59: the first was the above commentator; the second was the posh woman who screeched out into the night such gems as: 'If you do not remove your enormous crack from my vicinity, I shall be forced to fill it with my boot!' The third was 'Yella-Bellied Brenda'.

Brenda got her name because every so often she would take to the streets, chanting the phrase, 'Ya yella-bellied bastards!' over and over again at the top of her not inconsiderable voice. If the weather was inclement, she would actually shelter in the doorway of number 59 and shout her accusations from there, causing an absolute furore within. The bucket would frequently make an appearance on the windowsill above, the posh lady booming down: 'If you do not cease from these incantations, I shall be forced to take a drink and you know what will happen then!'

This was followed by the bucket being emptied of the suspicious-looking liquid onto the head of the hapless Brenda.

I am ashamed to say that this behaviour created huge entertainment for us opposite and, indeed, probably for our entire side of the street. It was like watching *Candid Camera.*

One night the window of the sex shop opposite was smashed by a drunken man, setting off the alarm and also Brenda. She came out and began to patrol the scene with her usual rant. The police arrived to find that the entire contents of the window—which consisted of several giant dildos and a couple of sets of extremely uncomfortable-looking underwear—had been looted. The window-smashing culprit clearly hadn't taken them as he was lying flat out in an alcoholic stupor, although several ladies from number 59 had been bobbing about. The police proceeded to manhandle the drunk up onto his feet, but on waking he became violent.

Meanwhile, Yella-Bellied Brenda was reaching a kind of hysteria with her own rantings. Once the police had wrestled the drunk into the back of the Black Maria, they shoved poor old Brenda inside too. For a short while there was a welcome silence, then Brenda started again with her 'Yella-bellied bastards'. The man joined in with some drunken response, while the old Black Maria shook as if a rugby scrum were taking place inside.

In the meantime the police had gone across the street to tackle some other altercation. By the time they returned a couple of hours later, the Black Maria was completely motionless; the man had long since gone silent, but dear old Yella-Belly was still going at it full pelt. It was a marvel that this woman never came near to losing her voice. At this point they opened the doors and let her out, but just before they slammed them shut again, a plaintive cry of 'Merciful heaven!' was heard quite clearly from within.

My husband, Grant, who had been a young policeman at West End Central, told me much later that number 59 Greek Street was well known to the police. They dreaded the inevitable call, and it was always palmed off onto the 'rookies', because no one else wanted the job. It seemed that the women used to get rather excited by the sight of these young men (Grant was then only eighteen) in their uniforms. Once inside the building, with its dimly lit corridors where haggard faces peered through the cracks of half-opened doors, the young men were subjected to harmless but nevertheless creepy catcalls, and a lot of exposing and propositioning went on. They were told back at the station that it was a home for old actresses. Grant said he'd always wondered what it was about acting that had made so many women go round the bend. And as I said to him at the time, that is an entirely different matter.

Greek Street eventually got to be too much. I used to think sometimes that people—and when I say people, I suppose I mean men, and when I say men, I suppose I mean drunks—came to Soho specifically to urinate. The door into our building was round at the side in Manette Street, and being sheltered and out of the way of the main thoroughfare, it was forever being mopped and disinfected by the restaurant on the ground floor. One morning not long before I moved out, I returned home after doing a bit of shopping to find a man brazenly pissing up against the door. Boiling with rage, I took a run at him and kicked him with some force up his bottom, causing him to pitch forward and nut the door with his forehead. He spun round—tall, bearded and unkempt-looking—and I immediately felt sorry for him; in fact I was on the verge of apologising when he began a tirade of screaming, frothing abuse. I backed away as he advanced on me, his flies still open, while propelling out a string of invective and becoming more agitated by the second. He proceeded to harangue me with a curious mixture of hell and damnation, added to the threat that he, himself, could rip my guts out and very much enjoy the experience. I turned tail and ran.

When I finished in *Funny Peculiar* in the spring of 1977, I discovered to my surprise that I had lost three-quarters of a stone in weight, which took me down to just under eight stone. This is a syndrome that has repeated itself throughout my career whenever I am engaged in a long run. No matter what I eat I can't seem to keep the weight on. I believe it has to do with the effort required for me to re-create the part every night and with the adrenalin rush that this produces.

Shortly after *Funny Peculiar* finished we tried to go down the same route with Willy Russell's hilarious *Breezeblock Park*, starting off at the Mermaid, with Wendy Craig in the central role. After a mauling by the critics we took it valiantly into the Whitehall Theatre, with Prunella Scales instead. Playing the very dim Vera, I had a ball. The show was adored by the audiences, and although the cast, myself included, were well received, the play was trounced once again by the critics, despite the fact that several of them were convulsed with laughter on press night. It came off after a few weeks with audiences roaring their approval to the last.

THE FOLLOWING YEAR, in the summer of 1978, I took a job at the Bush Theatre, a tiny space above a pub of the same name on Shepherd's Bush Green in West London. It was, and still is, a major force in the championing of new talent, especially writers. Our production was to be an evening of playlets by such luminaries as Snoo Wilson, Nigel Baldwin, Ken Campbell, Ron Hutchinson, Dusty Hughes, who also directed, and a young woman I'd never heard of, Victoria Wood.

The evening was to be titled *In at the Death*, and Victoria, fresh out of BBC1's *That's Life*, was to provide musical interludes between each sketch, one of which was the glorious 'Guy the Gorilla' ('died of chocolate, not usually a killer'), as well as writing a sketch of her own.

The sketches were based on small snippets from newspapers connected in some way with death. Ron Hutchinson's was set in Northern Ireland, based around a Ruby Murray lookalike contest; there was a brilliant sketch by Dusty Hughes about the people who turn up to gawp at road accidents, but the hit of the evening was Victoria's piece, entitled *Sex*, which involved a young woman, played by me, worried that she was pregnant and finding out from this other character, played by Victoria, that she hadn't even had sex. It brought the house down every night.

One line that I particularly remember as a rafter shaker was: 'Well, where are you in the menstrual cycle?'

'. . . Erm . . . Taurus.'

It was here at the Bush that our relationship was cemented, easily slipping into a friendship on the first day of rehearsals, when we discovered that we had Geoffrey Durham in common, who had lived underneath me when I was at the Everyman. It turned out that he was Vic's bloke, and so here was our first bond. The second, which Victoria informed me of over liver, boil (*sic*) and onions at the Bush café, was that we had met before. It turned out that she had auditioned at Manchester Polytechnic School of Theatre when I was a first-year there. I had been drafted in to usher the auditionees into the theatre to do their pieces and had spent the entire time trying to entertain them with stories of my nursing days and generally showing off. The image of this shy little girl, wearing glasses and throwing up in a bucket, flashed before me.

There was a third thing that bonded us. One evening after rehearsal, Vic and I were going somewhere or other in her newly acquired Mini van. We got lost in the backstreets of Shepherd's Bush and ended up in a cul-de-sac, so a three-point turn was necessary in order to get out. Victoria swung the car round with great aplomb and, being a non-driver at this stage of my life, I was hugely impressed by her skill and confidence. Then she backed up and we heard a bit of a crunch. She pulled tentatively forward to reveal that she had knocked down an entire garden wall. Our escape from that street, apart from the paroxysms of laughter, was worthy of a 1970s action thriller.

I fear that we gave the poor old director, Dusty Hughes, rather a hard time, or at least I did. I just felt that I knew best. I had come from the great Everyman, and some London-based, middle-class, university-educated bloke was not going to direct me. In those days I still laboured under the misapprehension that certain types of direction were tantamount to slurs on my acting ability. One day, Victoria and I hatched a devilish plan.

'Dusty! What sort of car have you got?'

He told us.

'Where is it parked?'

'Why?'

'We think it's being broken into!'

And off he shot. Then we decided on what we thought was the best way to play the particular sketch we had been rehearsing.

Dusty was a talented playwright, going on to win the London Theatre Critics Award for Most Promising Playwright in 1980, and he took our prank-playing at his expense in very good heart.

As ever, I was in my element fooling around, which took me right back into class-jester mode. One lunchtime, while for some reason we were hanging out of the office window upstairs, we spied Harold Pinter standing at the bus-stop in the street below.

'Harold! Hello, there! You write plays, don't you?' I called.

'Pardon?'

'You're a writer! We could do with one of those up here!'

A week after we opened we wrote 'H. Pinter (two tickets)' on the bookings list and scared the cast half to death, laughing our heads off backstage as we watched the other actors nervously upping their performances to impress the very absent Mr Pinter.

Backstage at the Bush consisted of an area approximately six feet by six feet and a set of stone steps leading down to the street. These were also used as the fire escape and the dressing room. It was extremely cramped with six actors all trying to get changed in this space, and Vic and I had many a private joke about the slack nature of a certain actor's underpants.

The show was well received on the whole and, on the final Saturday, David Leland, who was running a young writers' festival at the Crucible Theatre, Sheffield, asked Victoria to write a play for it. She said she would write something for me. I thought this was very kind, but couldn't ever imagine it happening, and went off to have a not particularly happy time at the Bristol Old Vic.

It was at Bristol that I was told the tale of an actor playing Macbeth during a matinée. He had started the famous speech, 'Tomorrow and tomorrow and tomorrow . . .', when an aged voice from the stalls was heard to say, 'Oh, that'll be Wednesday.'

And it was here that I read Victoria's wonderful new play *Talent*, which she had, indeed, written for me. My character was called Julie and my character's boyfriend was called Dave Walters. The play centred on a talent contest in a seedy Northern nightclub. Julie was entering the contest and Maureen, her best friend, played by Victoria, had come along for support. It fitted me like a glove. I knew this girl exactly, how she would speak, cry, laugh, and when she would breathe. And I wasn't free! It had to go ahead without me and I was mortified. The show was seen by Peter Eckersley, a Granada Television producer, who picked it up for television. This meant I had a chance to audition for the part.

It was a play with songs, two of which I was required to sing, one of my own choosing (Stevie Wonder's 'Isn't She Lovely?') plus one of the numbers from the show. The latter was a gorgeous, sardonically nostalgic song titled 'I Want to Be Fourteen Again'. When it came to my turn, Victoria played it in my key, a privilege I'm not entirely sure the rest of the auditionees enjoyed. Just as I was leaving, she said, under her breath, 'Don't worry, I'm going to play it in a really high key for everyone else!' I took it as a joke, but I'm not certain to this day whether it was.

Anyway, I got the part and there began a working friendship where Victoria gave me brilliant gift after brilliant gift. We followed

*Talent* with a sequel the following year titled *Nearly a Happy Ending*. This featured the same two characters, Julie and Maureen, and involved Maureen's attempts at losing her virginity at some awful sales conference in a dreary hotel. It was both hilarious and touching, and an amazingly generous vehicle for me. It was followed by another one-off comedy drama, *Happy Since I Met You*, in which I played opposite Duncan Preston, my character being a drama teacher and his a struggling actor. It was a gorgeously bittersweet comedy.

Peter Eckersley then decided that Victoria and I should have our own series, and so *Wood and Walters* was launched. Sadly Peter died in between the recording of the pilot and the making of the series, and we missed him hugely. It was never the same, and we felt that the series, which was his baby, suffered enormously without him.

We recorded it up at the Granada Studios in Manchester every Friday. As this took place in the middle of the day, the studio audience was mainly elderly people and we would go on set to be met by a bank of white heads, with comments pinging out into the often deafening silence. 'Who are these girls?', 'What's a boutique?' and once, 'We're missin' *Brideshead* for this!' This last became a private catch phrase for Victoria and me. At my BAFTA tribute in 2003 Victoria was sitting next to me, and just before she got up to make her speech, she handed me a scrap of paper on which she had written: 'We're missin' *Brideshead* for this!'

In 1984 Victoria asked me to join her in her new series *Victoria Wood as Seen on TV*. This could not have been a more different experience to the one at Granada. It was recorded on a Saturday night as if it were a live show. There was a sketch set in a shoe shop where I played a rather batty sales assistant and Vic played a customer. I wasn't sure how I should play it, but because the whole evening had a live-theatre feel to it, it put a creative edge on everything. Just as the lights went up for the sketch to begin, I decided to stumble about in the shop window, creating havoc and knocking shoes everywhere, and we were off; it was like the old Everyman days. The sketch was brilliantly written and would have worked anyway, but what was so gratifying for me was finding the character there and then, during the show itself. The studio audience had a ball. In one sketch, involving a very old waitress taking ages to serve soup to a couple, I thought we might have to stop, as the laughter went on and on and on.

As far as sketch writing is concerned, Victoria is in a league of her own. The soup sketch came out of the two of us ordering soup from an ancient waitress in a restaurant on Morecambe seafront. It probably took her a matter of minutes. Often when we were rehearsing, Geoff Posner, the director, would ask her to write some extra material. She would go off and ten minutes later would be back with something utterly hilarious.

It was in this series that my favourite character of all time was born: Mrs Overall. 'Acorn Antiques' was a sketch based on a badly made soap, inspired by the early *Crossroads*. It was set in an antiques shop situated in a fictional town called Manchesterford, run by the snobbish and imperious Miss Babs, played brilliantly by Celia Imrie. Mrs O was the cleaner, and what a gem of a part she was. We always filmed that particular sketch the day before the show, without an audience and thus without the consequent nerves and pressure. It was heaven. The very first time we were to record, all the elements of Mrs Overall came together at once. I was being made up, which consisted of a bit of lipstick making a tiny, pinched, dark red cupid's bow; I was also meant to be wearing a wig. Sitting in front of the make-up mirror with my hair restrained by a hairnet that made my head look rather small and pealike, I looked at Victoria. We both laughed, having the same thought at the same time: 'I don't need a wig, do I?' And so she was born. The public loved 'Acorn Antiques', a fan club was formed, and twenty years later people are still coming up to me in the street and firing Mrs Overall quotes at me.

In 1994 we did our second television film, *Pat and Margaret*. Pat was Margaret's famous older sister, from whom she had been separated at a young age. In the intervening years Pat had become a famous actress in a *Dynasty*-style television series, whereas

Margaret worked in a motorway service station café. In the story, the two sisters are brought together in a 'surprise, surprise'-type show, and from there the drama unfolds. As Pat, I believe I had some of the funniest speeches ever written. If only I could be that funny when I was that angry. However, my favourite line belonged to Pat and Margaret's mother, played by Shirley Stelfox. She said, on being confronted by her two daughters about her shortcomings as a mother, 'I didn't know what love was until I bred my first Afghan.'

I have played so many parts written by Victoria, and every one has been of the once-in-a-lifetime variety. Every one has made me laugh out loud and left me gagging to slip into their shoes. Petula, in the comedy series *Dinnerladies*, has got to be up there with the very best. *Dinnerladies* was set in a works canteen. Victoria played Bren, one of the ladies, and I played her somewhat eccentric mother. We had scene after scene together, where she gave me all the best lines and simply stood there more or less as a feed. Had I her talent for writing, I wouldn't be giving those punch lines to anyone else. But that's Victoria.

RETURNING TO LONDON from Bristol in 1979, my relationship with Pete having come to an end, I embarked on a play at Hampstead Theatre Club to be written and devised by Mike Leigh.

It was for me the ultimate acting experience. To begin with, the actors all worked on their own with Mike. First we made lists of the characters who had peopled our lives and discussed them with him. Then Mike picked a person from this list as a basis for the character that would eventually appear in the play. Gradually he started to put the actors together in group improvisations. In the course of these, I found that my best friend was to be Sheila Kelly and then that I was going out with Stephen Rea, whom I subsequently married and with whom I eventually had three children. For sixteen weeks we improvised continually so that these people became unutterably real, the fabric of their lives and the world in which they lived true and vivid. Now, thirty years later, I still can't go past the Catholic church on Quex Road, Kilburn, without thinking,

That's where Mick (Stephen Rea) and I got married.

The play was set in Kilburn, and most of the improvisations outside the rehearsal room took place in seedy pubs up and down Kilburn High Road, with Mike tucked away in a corner listening and watching the goings-on. He had instructed us not to come out of character unless blood was drawn. I played a rough, feisty, loud-mouthed woman called Dawn, whom I had based on someone who went to my school. On one occasion I rounded, in a Dawn-like way, on a navvy who was leering at me as I crossed the bar to the lavatory.

'Wharra you looking at?'

'Sometin' that needs a good seein' to.'

'You should be so bleedin' lucky!'

'Exactly my thoughts.' And then into his pint, 'Scrubber!'

'What did you call me?'

'I called you what you are—a scrubber!'

He was now looking pretty menacing and my heart—that is, Julie's heart—was pounding, whereas Dawn was up for a fight. There had to be a compromise. I turned on my heel, throwing a loud '*C—!*' over my shoulder, and disappeared into the ladies', where I collapsed onto the lavatory, hardly daring to breathe. Eventually Jean (Sheila Kelly) came to see where I was, and as Dawn I had to concoct a story involving constipation to explain my absence.

On the first night of the show, *Ecstasy*, about twenty minutes into the first half a woman stood up and declared in a loud voice, 'Who are these people? They're not actors!' and walked out. Mike was thrilled, indeed we all were. It was a compliment as far as we were concerned, a tribute to the realism of the piece.

On another occasion, halfway through the second half, Jim Broadbent suddenly declared, 'Oh God! I don't feel very well!' The audience giggled knowingly at this, obviously thinking they were into an *Abigail's Party* scenario, where one of the characters has a heart attack. However, on stage we were in panic mode.

'Am yer all right, Len?' I said, staying in character, to which Jim mumbled something unintelligible.

We tried to carry on, each trying to ascertain how ill he was by asking questions in character, until suddenly he stood up and blurted out, 'I think I'm having a stroke!' and blundered off the stage.

For a few seconds the place went deadly silent, all of us, actors and audience alike, reeling from being yanked out of Leigh world and plunged into the real one. Sheila Kelly then stood up and said, 'Is there a doctor in the house?' About twenty-nine people put their hands up. It was Hampstead, after all.

Finally one of them came backstage and tended to poor Jim, who was lying flat out on the floor of one of the dressing rooms, in extreme discomfort. It turned out to be a nasty virus from which he recovered in a few days, but more importantly, it was something for us all to dine out on for years to come.

During the play the characters spent a lot of their time drinking, and on the last night, the prop drinks were replaced by the real thing. I'm pretty sure it was Stephen Rea who was responsible, as I seem to remember him confiding in me before the show. What I remember clearly was the private glee we shared as Sheila and Jim discovered that their normal beverage was rather more warming than usual. Stephen, with the devil in him, insisted on filling up everyone's glass, with Sheila, ever the professional, realising she was fast getting drunk and trying to stop him, all of it conducted while remaining steadfastly in character. All I can say for my own part is that Dawn liked a drink and by the end of the show Julie was well and truly plastered.

# Seven

In the spring of 1980, while appearing in Victoria Wood's play *Good Fun* at the Sheffield Crucible Theatre, I was sent a script of a new play titled *Educating Rita* by Willy Russell. It had been commissioned by the Royal Shakespeare Company, with Mike Ockrent set to direct, and was to be put on in their studio theatre, which at that time was the Donmar Warehouse in Covent Garden.

I was immediately attracted to the character of Rita, a working-class hairdresser who embarks on an Open University degree. During the course of the play she finds herself marooned between her own working-class roots and the middle-class life she craves, sensing that in essence she is an outsider. All comes good in the end when she grasps that, through education, the most important thing she has gained is choice. There was not a scene in the play that I didn't identify with and, just like *Talent*, it felt like destiny.

At the time, *Good Fun* was rumoured to be going into the West End, and I couldn't face a long run, even though every night was a riot. My character, Betty, a cosmetics saleswoman, brought the house down. Her opening line after knocking on the door and being told to come in was: 'I'm sorry . . . I never lay my hand on a strange knob.' One night the hysteria grew to such a pitch that we simply couldn't continue. Nevertheless a three-month run in repertory, sharing half the week with another production, was a far more attractive deal than a run in the West End with eight shows a week for nine months, even though the difference in money would be huge. So I plumped for *Educating Rita*, thinking it would be all over by the autumn . . . How wrong could I be?

In the summer of 1980 I was renting a room in the flat of my friend, the actress Rosalind March, in Balham. We had both come out of long relationships, and we spent a lot of evenings with a bottle of wine, vindicating ourselves of any blame, while heaping it instead on the hapless men involved. We had met originally through the acting agency, Actorum, a couple of years earlier.

Actorum was an agency run by and for actors, and when members were unemployed they were expected to come into the office to man the phones, ring round for work and negotiate contracts. In practice some members were rarely, if ever, in the office and others were never out of it, which at times gave rise to a degree of, shall we say, bitterness. While there were people who were wonderfully efficient in the office, there were others who put only themselves up for parts. One such individual, who at this time was most certainly middle-aged and not what a girl would describe as good-looking, put himself forward to play Romeo at the Royal Shakespeare Company, no less, when actually, were it being cast at the time, *The Hobbit* would have been more appropriate.

When the Royal Shakespeare Company commissioned Willy Russell, apparently they were expecting a big musical like *John, Paul, George, Ringo and Bert*, which had enjoyed a massive success. What they got was a two-handed play with one set and no idea how to cast it. It was decided to cast it from outside the company, leaving Willy and Mike Ockrent to their own devices. We started rehearsals in June 1980.

Mark Kingston was to play Frank, the Open University lecturer, and the two of us hit it off immediately. Although I had identified with the character of Rita, when it came to act her I had real difficulty in finding her core and agonised through rehearsals about who she was, trying different approaches and using different characters from my own life as inspiration. I never truly found Rita until the first preview at the Donmar where somehow, through sheer terror and the life-or-death need to survive, she clicked gawkily into place. On that first night Mark and I stood holding hands backstage, waiting to go on, shaking with fear, both feeling that a blanket of humiliation was waiting to smother us.

How wrong could we be? I remember during the first-night interval Mike whooshing through the dressing rooms, making an O with his thumb and forefinger, and calling, 'Prima! Prima! Prima! Prima!' while Mark and I just stared at one another, thinking: Is he deluded? No, he was right; the next day the papers were full of praise and you couldn't get a seat.

One day I received a phone call from a Lewis Gilbert. He told me that he was a film director and he had come to see the play and had absolutely loved both it and me. He was going to film it and wanted me for the part but could not offer it to me just then as he had yet to raise the money. He would be in touch.

Approximately three months later he rang again. He had been in America, where potential investors had talked of Paul Newman and Dolly Parton in the roles of Frank and Rita. Well, I could think of two very good reasons why I couldn't compete with her. It seems that because I was an unknown I would be required to do a screen test, the very thought of which sent me into paroxysms of panic. It seemed a tiny pivot on which my life might move into another league, where I was to star in a major motion picture or, alternatively, where I would fail to make the grade and then have to live with rejection—not an easy one for me (remember the fiasco of the walking race?). What if I was too nervous to perform at all? What if the Americans wouldn't think I was good-looking enough? What if, what if, what if . . . However, salvation was at hand; a month later Lewis rang again.

'It's all right, darling, we've got Michael. You won't have to do a screen test now.'

At first I couldn't make any sense of this; I thought he could only be saying that I had not got the part.

'OK, dear . . .? Happy? You've got the part.'

'*Oh my garrrrrrrd!*'

'Now we've got Michael, we don't need a star to play your part.'

'Sorry? Michael who?'

'Caine, darling, Michael Caine is going to play Frank.'

I rang everyone I knew, including Duncan Preston. So when the phone rang and a deep Texan drawl said, 'Hi, am I speaking to Julie Walters?' I answered suspiciously, 'Yeeees?'

'My name is Herbie Oakes. I am the producer of your movie *Educating Rita* and—'

'Stop before you start! Very good, Duncan, but I know it's you and do you know how I know it's you? Because your Texan accent is soooooo bad!' And cackling manically I put the phone down.

I decided to ring Duncan back. He completely denied having just called me and, what is more, I believed him. *Oh my gaaaard!* I'm already off on the wrong foot. But the producing person rang back and I tried to explain and apologise.

'I'm so sorry, erm . . . Mr . . . Mr Hoax, er, no . . . Mr Oakes.'

He was charming and friendly, going on to explain that he had simply called to invite me round to his place for drinks so that I could meet Michael as well as some other people whose names went immediately out of my head. All I heard was Michael (*The Ipcress File*, *Get Carter*, *The Man Who Would Be King*, *Zulu*, *Alfie* and millions of other films too numerous to mention) Caine.

He was, as you might imagine, funny, friendly and direct, with a working-class down-to-earthiness that put me at my ease straight away. When I was leaving, Shakira, his wife, said, 'You are so lucky it's Michael.'

I mentioned this to Lewis.

'Oh yes, darling, when you think who else it could have been, she's absolutely right.'

I have spent the last twenty-five or so years trying to work out who on earth he might have been referring to.

We started shooting in August 1982 in Dublin. The play was set in northern England and in reality the university would more than likely have been some redbrick monstrosity, but Willy and Lewis wanted it to be intimidatingly otherworldly for Rita. So the beautiful, photogenic Trinity College, Dublin, was cast.

The filming lasted nine weeks, and with Lewis Gilbert at the helm it was an unstressed, light-hearted pleasure. He was delightfully absent-minded, and legend has it that once, after filming at Pinewood Studios, he drove the twenty miles to Shepperton Studios by mistake and berated the security man on the gate for not recognising the name of the film he was directing. He had an appealing clumsiness and would frequently walk onto the set knocking lamps this way and that, leaving cries of 'Relight!' in his wake, and once, when not quite concentrating, he crossed his legs and fell off the dolly. (This is a platform on wheels for the camera and not something that you blow up, dear reader.)

Michael was completely unstarry, preferring to be out on the set chatting to the crew rather than confined to his trailer. He loved good food and treated us to lavish meals in some of Dublin's and the surrounding area's finest eateries. He also gave me one of the best pieces of acting advice ever, which was: 'Save it for the take.'

There is a great temptation to do a scene at full pelt in rehearsal, if only to make sure that you actually can, but often there are lots of rehearsals and you can kill the freshness and spontaneity of the thing by constant repetition.

This happened the day we were shooting the scene when Rita comes back to tell Frank why she hadn't turned up to his house for dinner. It was meant to be tearful and from the moment I woke up I was preparing for it, even gulping my breakfast down on the verge of tears. The first shot was of Rita standing there crying through the rain-lashed window. In the very first rehearsal, I let it all out and then struggled to achieve any tears through the next five or six rehearsals, until Michael pointed out that it was not that close a shot and that they couldn't really see whether I was crying or not anyway. Another filming lesson: check the size of the shot. By the time it came to my close-up I had absolutely nothing left and it was then that Michael said: 'Save the special stuff for the take.' It has rung in my ears many, many times since.

The whole experience, being my first film, was a steep learning curve. I had performed the role innumerable times on stage, but that performance needed to be got rid of rather than utilised. It was a performance designed to reach people sitting in the back rows of a theatre, while I was now required to give a performance for an audience that for a lot of the time was just inches from my face. However, Lewis was always at hand: 'Too big, darling, it's not the Albert Hall!'

No one could have been more surprised than me by the success of the film. When I first saw it in a little screening room in Soho, I was appalled by my performance, thinking it over the top and amateurish, and I thought I would be dumped on from a great height by critics and public alike. I wanted to run and hide, so when Lewis mentioned that Columbia Pictures had bought it for release and there was talk of Oscar nominations, I thought he had gone completely off his rocker.

The film opened in London first, in the spring of 1983, with a royal premiere at the Odeon, Leicester Square, attended by the

Duke of Edinburgh. He sat in the row in front of me, and when the film finished he turned round to give me a thumbs up and a wink.

The following autumn the film was to open in the States, and I asked my friend Ros Toland, who had been the publicist for the film in Britain, to accompany me. She had a refreshingly irreverent attitude towards the Hollywood establishment as well as a wicked sense of humour. We flew to New York and were booked into a huge corner suite at the Plaza Hotel, looking directly out over Central Park. I fell for New York instantly. Everywhere I turned seemed to be a movie location; in fact the whole place felt like a film set. It was buzzy, neurotic, with an ambient sense of excitement and danger. I was enthralled by the city and still am.

The press junket began with twenty television interviews, one after the other, followed by a seemingly endless round of newspaper interviews. Michael, Lewis and I were each ensconced in separate rooms at the Plaza, visited in turn by individual journalists. That evening Michael took us to Elaine's, a famous restaurant frequented by celebrities. The walls were covered in their photographs, personally signed. So when I asked Michael where the ladies' was and he instructed me to turn left at Woody Allen, I went along the wall scanning the photos for Woody's portrait and ended up tripping over the real man's feet. We sat in the corner, with Michael pointing out anyone famous as they came in. 'That's Henry Mancini . . . you know, "Moon River".' The charming thing was that Michael was more famous than any of them.

Next stop was Los Angeles. We were checked into the Beverly Hills Hotel, a pink palace set in the heart of the highly manicured Beverly Hills, known for its celebrity clientele and its famous Polo Lounge, dubbed by Bette Midler the Polio Lounge.

It was Labor Day weekend, which gave us time to ourselves, so we headed to the pool. Ros and I sat there agog, chortling at the assembled clientele. I had never seen so much gold in one place. When one woman dived in it was a wonder she ever came up again. She was covered in what is nowadays referred to as bling and so, it seemed, was everyone else there: great lumps of the stuff hanging from ear lobes, necks and wrists, not pretty or subtle. A bank statement made into a sunhat would have been more aesthetically appealing, while creating a similar impression.

Just before we left I appeared on the *Tonight Show* with Johnny Carson and regaled him with stories of the Beverly Hills Hotel, such as how we were not allowed into the Polo Lounge because one of us was wearing denim, and that the most smartly dressed people there were the hookers. I also told him that, after staying there, fifty per cent of my luggage was now towelling. Johnny loved all this and invited me on the show twice in one week to talk about it further. Unfortunately the hotel didn't see the funny side of it, and I was never booked in there again.

I had always had a fascination for Los Angeles. Every Christmas we received a card from my mother's second cousins who lived there, the Takahashis. My great-aunt Margaret had gone to California from Ireland in the 1920s and worked as a waitress. One day she was taken ill and a Japanese doctor tended her. Even though neither could speak the other's language, they fell in love and subsequently got married. Their children in turn married Japanese-Americans. During the Second World War they were interned in a camp, even though they saw themselves as American. When my mother was a child at home in Ireland her cousin Margaret got in contact, and my mother had been writing to them, never having met them, ever since. So it was with great excitement that I contacted the Takahashis and told them I was in Los Angeles.

I was invited to dinner at their home downtown and felt instantly at ease with them. There was something strangely familiar that I couldn't quite name: a turn of phrase, the tone of someone's laugh, my mother's eyes surrounded by an Oriental face. They joked that they thought their small eyes were down to being Japanese, but having met me, they could see that they were in fact Irish eyes. I booked tickets for them for the Los Angeles premiere and enjoyed watching the Columbia Pictures representative who, after ushering them in, turned to a colleague and mouthed silently, 'Her *cousins*?'

Just as I was about to leave Los Angeles, a call came for me to appear on *Good Morning America* with the famous television journalist Barbara Walters. It was to happen the very next day in New York, so I was to fly there immediately. I arrived at the airport to find that the flight was delayed because LaGuardia airport in New York was fogbound. The plane eventually took off well past midnight. When we arrived in the vicinity of LaGuardia, an announcement was made to the effect that the airport was still fogbound and would we please be patient. They did not send Ros with me on this particular journey as it wasn't deemed necessary, so I was travelling alone, seated next to a man who was becoming increasingly nervous. Eventually the captain's voice came over the speaker system with the comforting announcement: 'It seems this fog just isn't going to lift so we are proposing that we land at Newark instead of LaGuardia as we are running out of fuel fast.'

With that the man sitting next to me jumped up out of his seat and shouted, '*You asshole!*'

We landed at Newark airport some twenty minutes later at about four o'clock in the morning. I hadn't a clue where Newark was. I couldn't remember where I was staying and, needless to say, the Columbia Pictures rep, for whom I had no contact number and who was meant to meet me off the flight about six hours earlier at another airport entirely, was not there. I had no dollars, as they were in my hotel room back in LA and I had been assured I would not need any money, as I would be met and taken everywhere.

Stiff with panic, I wandered out of the deserted airport in the vain hope that there would be a car waiting for me. No such luck. I went towards the taxi rank and heard a woman ask whether anyone wanted to share a cab into Manhattan. At exactly the same time the name of the hotel I was booked into popped into my head and I took her up on the offer, along with another woman and a man. I sat in the back of the cab, desperately trying to think how I was going to explain my lack of funds. When the cab pulled up outside my expensive-looking hotel it just exploded out of my mouth: 'Erm . . . I'm really sorry but I haven't got any money . . . Columbia Pictures were meant to be meeting me . . .'

'Oh, that's OK. Forget it.' This was the nice lady to my right.

'Columbia Pictures, huh?' This was the man sitting in the front, addressing me as if I were a half-wit claiming to be a brain surgeon.

'Yes, I've got a film opening here. I'm an actress. I'm on *Good Morning America* in the morning.' Me, squirming.

'It's fine, really.' The woman.

'You are a movie star appearing on *Good Morning America* and you can't pay for your cab ride?' The man.

'Yes, I know it sounds odd, but . . . I'm so sorry.'

'Yeah, you betcha it sounds odd.' The man, very cross and sneery. 'Yeah, whatever, lady. We'll pay.'

I skulked off into my posh hotel. It never crossed my mind that I could have got the hotel to pay the cab for me and saved myself the humiliation of trying to explain the unbelievable. Now I always make sure that I have cab money, a contact number and an address, no matter who says that they have organised everything.

After about an hour and a half's sleep I was sitting in front of a mirror at the studio, supposedly getting ready for the show. Even though there were magenta-coloured circles under my bloodshot eyes, I had for the first time in my life elected to wear no make-up, as the thought of touching my eyes was too much to bear. Never had the term 'red eye', the name given to the Los Angeles to New York flight, been more appropriate. Just before we went on air, I happened to mention to Barbara, who was sitting there in fully coiffured, beautifully dressed, perfumed splendour, that I hadn't bothered with make-up. Even beneath the perfection of her own freshly applied maquillage, I could see that she had paled at the thought of me appearing barefaced on national television, and when we went on air, she thought it so significant that she announced, 'She has no make-up on, everybody!' I saw a playback of the two of us afterwards and could see only too clearly why it is necessary to wear at least a modicum of slap, not only because of the draining effect of the powerful studio lighting, but also because up against Barbara's extraordinary hue I looked positively green.

From LA we went on a nine-week tour of America. Then on to all the major cities of Australia, followed by New Zealand, and finally the Netherlands and Scandinavia. I saw mainly the insides of hotel rooms, but there were days off where we were treated royally. In Los Angeles, through a connection of Ros's, we went to visit Tippi Hedren's ranch. Tippi, famous for appearing in Hitchcock's *The Birds* and *Marnie* and for being Melanie Griffith's mother, lived on an amazing spread in California, where she kept animals rescued from the circus. Among the elephants was one in particular, whose back I rode on, which spent its time rearing up onto its hind legs in a sad parody of its former days as a performer. There were lions lounging around on the tops of old buses, one of which I was able to sit down with and cuddle—admittedly he was ancient and had no teeth or claws, as these had been removed during his days as a circus performer. The most abiding image, however, was sitting in the kitchen when a fully grown tiger jumped in through the window just like a domestic cat.

Nothing on the tour quite compared to this, although there were highlights: in Denver, we were taken on a special plane ride over the Rockies; in Sydney, I was put up in a penthouse that the Queen had occupied only weeks before; everywhere we went, we flew first class and stayed in the most exclusive of hotels.

In every city there was a Rita waiting to meet me: that is, an actress playing the part in a theatre somewhere. Today I still get people writing to say how *Educating Rita* has given them the impetus to make changes in their lives. I have often been asked whether I get fed up with being so associated with this part, and I always answer that I would be thrilled to be remembered for anything, but to be remembered for this is a privilege.

Since *Rita* I have continued to make a steady stream of films, good, bad and indifferent, many of which have been arguably more accomplished in the acting stakes, but none has been met with the same warmth and recognition.

Mrs Weasley, in the Harry Potter films, probably comes close and does, of course, add a whole new audience of children. I must confess I love to see the look of wonder on their faces when they discover that the woman at the supermarket is none other than Mrs Weasley. It's usually their parents who point me out, and there is very often a fierce discussion as to how this person could possibly be Mrs Weasley, who as everyone knows is a rotund redhead. In the film, of course, I wear a red wig and padding; in fact my substantial bosoms were, for the first couple of films, stuffed with birdseed, which became a little worrying while filming at King's Cross station with the number of pigeons that there were pecking around on the platforms. However, without *Rita* I probably would never have been considered for the Harry Potter films, because it was *Rita* that got me recognition in the film world and, more importantly, in Hollywood.

I won my first film BAFTA for *Educating Rita* at a ceremony during which I got increasingly drunk. I had no idea how much I had drunk, as waiters never allowed your glass to be empty and I was too nervous to eat the dinner provided. I had no real expectations of winning, so when my name was called out by Michael Aspel, who was hosting the evening, I was unprepared. I tottered up onto the stage and stood there for several seconds, staring my BAFTA in the face, and then I said, 'Has anyone got a carrier bag? I can't go home on the tube with this.'

Muted laughter.

'Thank you . . . thank you . . . thank you . . . thank you . . . No, really . . . thank you . . . No, honestly . . . Thanks.'

As I left the stage, thinking my speech to be cleverly ironic, Michael said to a quietly embarrassed audience, 'She might at least have said, "Thank you",' and brought the house down.

After the ceremony I, along with fellow winners, was meant to be presented to the Princess Royal, but this proved impossible as I was under the table, literally, discussing the state of the film industry with an actor who was quite clearly as drunk as me but whose identity has now been completely obliterated from my memory.

Having played Rita on stage as well as film, I am often asked which of the two media I prefer, and I have to say that the theatre wins hands down. Nothing can compare with the adrenalin-fuelled excitement where each performance is unique, as is the relationship with each audience. Film is much more technical, where the story is told more by the director and his editor. It is shot out of sequence in tiny segments lasting only a matter of minutes, and once shot is set in aspic. It is not possible in film for the actor to experience the thrill of a story unfolding, in the way that the cinema audience does while watching, but in theatre the actor shares this with them. This is not to say that I don't enjoy film; it is far less stressful than theatre. You get a chance to do lines over and over again and you don't have to artificially project the character out over the stalls.

I have had the good fortune to be involved in two great productions at the Cottesloe Theatre at the National: the first one being Sam Shepard's *Fool for Love* in 1985 and the second Arthur Miller's *All My Sons* in 2000. Because of the intimacy of the space in which they were performed, these two experiences, along with *Rita* at the Donmar Warehouse, managed to combine the intimacy of film with the heart-pumping excitement and shared experience of live performance.

IN THE SPRING of 1982 I was offered a part in a BBC film written by Alan Bennett, titled *Intensive Care*. Unfortunately the actor playing the lead role was taken ill at the last minute and so Alan himself was drafted in to play the partly autobiographical role.

I was to play the part of a nurse who becomes sexually involved with Alan's character, and when the day of the read through arrived we were issued with new scripts that contained certain changes. The chief one was during the bed scene. The two characters are about to get undressed, and in the original they did so with some gusto. However, in the new script the lines had been changed. I now had to say how much I liked Alan's character's shirt: 'That's a nice shirt . . . keep it on.' When we actually came to shoot it, Alan was so nervous that the director brought down a bottle of whisky to calm his nerves. After much ribbing on my part, with Alan standing there giggling, and me screaming at him not to come into the bedroom yet while I mimed catching a just-lubricated Dutch cap that kept slipping from my grip like a wet bar of soap, all of which he endured with an embarrassed glee, we finally shot the scene. Afterwards, there was such a sense of post-coital relief that the two of us sat up in bed together and had a cigarette.

I have had the good fortune to work with Alan Bennett on five different occasions, including both *Talking Heads* series and a BBC play titled *Say Something Happened* with Thora Hird and Hugh Lloyd, and each production has had that familiar feeling of somehow coming home. The two *Talking Heads* were a sort of acting heaven, and the whole idea of talking directly to the camera appealed enormously to the storyteller in me. For my performance in *Say Something Happened*—where I played the part of a rookie social worker investigating an aged couple who had been put on the 'At Risk' register but finding that she, the social worker, was the one most at risk—I was nominated for my first BAFTA. The nomination was split between that and my performance in 1982 of Angie in Alan Bleasdale's *The Boys from the Blackstuff.*

This was the first time that I had played such a dramatic role, and the first time I recognised that I was voicing my own angst through the character. I found Angie's outpouring of anger and pain powerfully cathartic, and we all experienced the old Everyman feeling that we were involved in something ground-breaking and important. It is still a performance that is close to my heart. No one writes about the chaos and madness that runs through ordinary life like Alan Bleasdale. As a writer he is a total maverick; who else would cast me in the role of Robert Lindsay's mother in a television drama series? But that's just what he did for *GBH* in 1991. It was a role I relished: an Irish grandmother! To begin with, we tried all sorts of prosthetics to age my face, including having a full cast of it made. In the end we decided that the prosthetics looked artificial, creating a barrier between me and the audience, and becoming more of a distraction than anything else so that the viewer would be thinking: How did they do that?

I can recall saying at the time, let's just allow the wig, costumes and body language to do their stuff. And the excellent make-up artist—who could have had a field-day with latex wrinkling and the like, the BAFTA Craft Awards flashing neon in her mind's eye—was the first to say it had got to be done through acting. And so that is what we did.

Inside my own head I was definitely the character, but I still can't judge whether I got away with it or not. Who cares: I got to work with Robert Lindsay, with whom I felt an instant bond. We worked together again in 1994 on Alan's next project, the epic *Jake's Progress*, this time playing husband and wife. We had a glorious seven months in Ireland, ending every week with a breakneck dash to Dublin airport in order to get home.

WHEN THE POSSIBILITY of an Oscar nomination for *Educating Rita* was mooted, I thought it a ludicrous notion, but nevertheless it happened. I guess the inordinate amount of publicity I had done round the States had paid off. I was first nominated for, and subsequently won, a Golden Globe. I was also asked to co-host the ceremony for this with John Forsythe, who played the handsome patriarch in the American television series *Dynasty*. I thought that because of this I had probably not won, and therefore had not thought of anything to say. When my name was called out as the winner of Best Actress in a Musical or Comedy, all I could think of was a daft joke alluding to the fact that, as I was also running the show, it was a bit of a fix. At the time there had just been a scandal involving a bad actress whose billionaire husband had tried to buy her a Golden Globe. My joke went down like a cup of the cold proverbial and was lambasted in the press as tasteless.

The Oscars were like the Second Coming. During the week running up to them, it seemed that every daytime programme and news show was running a feature on them. There would be in-depth discussions of nominees' performances and whole programmes given over to what they might wear on the night. I remember seeing a long, lacy, wafty thing being proposed as my possible number for the big night and thinking: God, are they going to get a surprise! I was in fact wearing a knee-length, black-leather number, given to me by Elizabeth and David Emanuel, who had designed the wedding dress for the Princess of Wales. It was pronounced by one publication the worst outfit there, but, as this was Hollywood, I took it as a compliment.

My fellow nominees were Meryl Streep, Shirley MacLaine and Debra Winger, and according to the newspapers and the bookies I was the rank outsider. We all knew that it would be Shirley MacLaine who would end up holding the golden phallus. Her amazing career had spanned thirty-odd years in which she had never won an Oscar, and her performance in *Terms of Endearment*, for which she was nominated, deserved to be honoured. I suppose I was fairly relaxed about the whole thing. It would have been much more tense-making if I had thought that there was a possibility of winning.

I was thrilled to be in the same line-up as Meryl Streep. Although we were more or less the same age, I felt that she belonged to some other rarefied stratosphere that bore no relation to the let's-have-a-cup-of-tea world that I inhabited. The last thing I expected, dear reader, was twenty-three years later to be sitting on my arse in southern Greece, with my sprained ankle resting in the esteemed actress's lap while she shouted orders.

'Ice! Quick! Get it elevated!'—and a group of people were running this way and that, icing and elevating as if their lives depended on it. Then on Meryl's instruction I was carried through the streets of the village to my digs by the member of the crew most people fancied, which was a bit of a bonus. The film was *Mamma Mia!*, and when my agent rang to say I had been offered the part of Meryl Streep's friend in . . . I didn't wait for the rest, I screamed 'YES!!' It turned out to be a bit of a hit.

The day of the Academy Awards itself was a bit like a cross between Christmas and your wedding day; gifts arrived at my hotel room, of handmade chocolates, champagne and flowers from film companies, agents and people wanting to advertise their products and services. A blur of hairdressers, stylists and make-up artists came and went, until all there was left to do was go. I was being accompanied by my agent, Sara, and her friend Dan.

Just as we were about to leave, I heard a scream from Sara's bathroom. The zip in her dress had given up, spitting out a couple of teeth as it went. We stood there for several seconds, Sara pink with panic and Dan pulling the two sides of the zip together as if they might mend themselves. Eventually he remembered the sewing kit in the bathroom and did a sterling job of lashing the two bits together. With back-up from a couple of safety pins, we were off.

When we arrived at the theatre, there were huge crowds of overexcited people, gawping and screaming, and of course there was the red carpet. It must have taken us a good hour and a half to get up it, as we were waylaid by endless television crews and journalists. After the ceremony, there was a do with dinner and dancing. I was paraded round by a Columbia Pictures executive to meet various famous folk, three of whom stick in my memory. The first was Michael Jackson, who had a very little voice; the second was Mel Gibson, who was just very little. The third was Liza Minnelli, whom I had met before.

Just before we were to start filming *Educating Rita*, Michael Caine threw a party at Langan's Brasserie in London. A lot of us went on to a club called Tramp where, after a couple of hours, I found that I could not stand a minute longer the agony of my new cowboy boots, so I decided to go to the ladies' to take them off. Because I was wearing no hosiery whatsoever and my feet, after frenzied dancing, had swollen, their removal proved nigh-on impossible. As I sat on a chair, face crimson with effort, the door opened and in came Liza.

'Hi. Need a hand?'

'Oh . . . yes, please.' Whereupon she bent and pulled my boot off.

'Oh, my . . . you're bleeding. Do you want the other one off?'

'Yes, of course, Liza, and then fix me an ice-cold martini, call me a cab and you may take the rest of the night off.'

No, I didn't say that; just, 'Oh . . .'

She whipped it off and said, 'Wait here, I'll be right back.'

Within minutes she was back brandishing plasters, antiseptic and cotton wool; lifting my feet onto her lap, she gently bathed and dressed them.

'Oh, you should throw these boots away. Nothing should give you that much pain.'

I was wondering whether we were about to embark on a discussion about something more than blisters when she jumped up and lifted her skirt. I laughed nervously. I had read *The News of the World*, I knew what these Hollywood stars were capable of. She began to remove her tights. Oh my God! Liza, I'm not that way inclined—

'Here, put these on. It'll make getting the boots on and off easier. And trust me, throw 'em away.'

So when I met her at the Oscar bash some eighteen months later, I felt as if we were old friends.

'Julie, hi! Congratulations!' I noticed that Americans congratulate you after an awards ceremony, even if you haven't won, simply for being nominated. In Britain, you've simply lost and people look sorry for you, avoiding all eye contact.

She hugged me and whispered conspiratorially in my ear, 'Don't tell Shirley, but I voted for you.'

'Oh, thanks, that's nice. No, I won't tell her.'

I don't suppose she'll ever read this; I mean, after all, I haven't read *her* autobiography.

Then as I was being dragged off to be introduced to yet another weary megastar, I managed to get in, 'I've still got your tights!'

In 1984 the party to be at was Swifty Lazar's, and directly after the rather sedate dinner and dance, Willy Russell—who had also been nominated for, but not won, Best Adapted Screenplay—and I set off to find it. We jumped into a cab and instructed the driver to take us to Swifty Lazar's. The befuddled-looking cabby said he had never heard of such a restaurant, so we got into another taxi. Again, the driver had never heard of the place, so in frustration we decided to call it a night and never made the big post-Oscar party. We found out the next day that Swifty Lazar was not a restaurant but a famous Hollywood agent. The whole Oscars thing was a not-to-be-missed experience, but it has to be viewed for what it really is, a wonderful piece of marketing for the film industry; many a brilliant film and performance has gone unnoticed because there hasn't been the budget to sell it properly.

At my second Oscar experience in 2001, when I got the Best Supporting Actress nomination for Mrs Wilkinson in *Billy Elliot*, it was the *Vanity Fair* party that everyone wanted to get into. However, I chose Elton John's instead because he'd asked me personally at the premiere, plus there's always the chance that he might play the piano and do a turn.

No one could have predicted the phenomenal success of *Billy Elliot*. We all knew that it was funny and charming, but how were they going to sell a film about a miner's son who became a ballet dancer? Apparently things were looking grim until two people from Universal came to a screening and said, 'We like it.' From the moment a big studio showed an interest, everyone else did too.

In 2001, my second film BAFTA was for *Billy Elliot*; this was a very different experience from *Educating Rita*, as I was allowed to really create a character. Although it was already brilliantly written by Lee Hall, director Stephen Daldry and I would generate whole new scenes—something I have never been party to, before or since. All films, in my experience, are so schedule-dominated that there is never the room for such a 'luxury', but somehow Stephen managed it. I had real fun with the character, taking away any maternal instinct she might originally have had to steer her away from sentimentality. Then the choreographer, Peter Darling, told me how his dance teacher had smoked and called out instructions to her pupils while perusing the *Daily Mirror*. I couldn't resist that. I pored over documentaries about the little dance schools that seemed to be particular to the Northeast, where the film was set, and loved the fact that the majority of the teachers couldn't really dance themselves. This suited me perfectly, as dancing—choreographed dancing—was something that scared me and I already had the ghost of my experience on *Stepping Out* haunting me.

In that film, shot in 1990, Lewis Gilbert, for it was he, told me that although it was a film about a tap-dancing class, it didn't matter that I had never tap-danced.

'No, darling, don't worry. We can shoot round all that.'

Thank God I got Phil Collins's sister Carole to teach me a few steps, and even then I found it virtually impossible. Once we got to Toronto to start a three-week rehearsal period prior to filming, I found that, apart from Andrea Martin, I was the only person who had never tapped before. The ancient Hollywood-style choreographer, a scrotum in glasses, made us rehearse in a line-up that placed the most proficient dancer, Liza Minnelli, on the far right, with the dancers decreasing in skill as you moved left until you ended up with me at the other end. It was hell.

This was what was in my head as I went to my first rehearsal of *Billy Elliot*. Peter assured me I wouldn't have to do anything that was out of my ability range. Again I found it headachingly difficult to learn the steps. There was something terrifying in the fact that the music waited for no man, and it wasn't exactly music that had a nice sedate tempo. Unlike a play, where a momentary lapse could be covered by a pause, with dancing the music and the beat were relentless. When the day came to film the dance sequence with Jamie Bell, with whom I had yet to dance, I saw him in the corner doing some amazing-looking steps and asked him what scene they were from. He stared at me and said, 'It's our dance sequence.'

I was dumbfounded; I didn't even recognise the steps.

It was a long morning, all we had in which to film a sequence that should have taken several days. I was in the early stages of the menopause and I felt heavy and bloated. I started the morning unable to get the steps right and then, embarrassingly, was unable to prevent myself from crying. I went to a far corner of the room to hide my emotions, and then wished that I hadn't as it drew unwanted attention. It also meant that I would have to turn and face the assembled crew, who were all keen to get on with an impossible schedule.

Of course, when I did turn round, I was met with nothing but sympathy, which could have given rise to another blubbing session. With a massive intake of breath and a feeling of it's now or never, the camera rolled and I went through the dance for the first time ever without a hitch. We had it. I noticed that very recently when I shot *Mamma Mia!* I was less afraid of dance, and I think that the conquering of that little sequence in *Billy Elliot* had a lot to do with it.

# Eight

After the hoo-ha of the 1984 Oscars was over, I stayed around in Hollywood for a short time. I was introduced to a hotshot agent, did the rounds of casting folk and was even given a few scripts to peruse. But they didn't really know what to do with me; the scripts were all a bit Rita-esque, with some American screen-writer's ill-informed idea of what a working-class English girl was like. How could I summon up the enthusiasm to work on things like these when I had had the privilege of the likes of Alan Bennett's, Willy Russell's, Alan Bleasdale's and Victoria Wood's characters to perform?

So, much as I loved the idea of Hollywood, I knew where I wanted to be. I felt that the roles I wanted to play, and the projects I wanted to be a part of and that would fulfil me, were tied to my roots, and that there was a cultural divide that I could not comfort-ably cross; my real interest lay deep down in my own history and people. I also felt that the talent of British writers, technicians and directors was unrivalled.

So back home I came, travelling straight up to the Lake District on arrival, to shoot a film titled *She'll Be Wearing Pink Pyjamas*, about a group of women on an outward-bound course. The film looms large in my memory because of an incident that occurred after we'd been marooned up there for two or three weeks.

One evening we were all in the bar, bemoaning the fact that in a day or so's time we would have to remove our clothes for a particular scene set in a shower. Being naked in public is not something that I seek out in life, or in work for that matter. I had done it once before in Alan Bennett's *Intensive Care* and I was to do it once again on stage in *Frankie and Johnny in the Clair de Lune* in 1989, but that was in a very dim light. And then finally—I'm positive that I mean finally—I was to strip off in 2003 for *Calendar Girls*, but this was a very brief shot, after a pep talk from Helen Mirren, plus a glass of champagne, plus a seniority that gave us women total dominance of the set on that day.

However, back in 1984, I felt no such seniority, and the thought of a fairly long scene with dialogue while you soaped your lalas was not on my list of things I must do before I die. Then someone came up with the idea that we should refuse to do it unless the crew took their clothes off as well. In the excitement the idea developed into us telling the producers that there had been a recent ruling by Equity, the actors' union. Then Pauline Yates suggested that we get her husband, the actor Donald Churchill, to ring up pretending to be Peter Plouvier, the then general secretary of Equity. The next day a message was left asking the producer to ring Peter Plouvier at Equity urgently, along with Donald Churchill's telephone number.

The conversation went something like this:

'Yes, hello, Peter, you left a message for me to call you. I'm working on the film *Pink Pyjamas*.'

'I believe you have a scene involving several actresses having to appear naked. I'm afraid the Women's Committee have just passed a motion stating that should any female members of a cast be required to appear naked, then the same number of crew will have to appear naked too. I am sorry about this. I expect you could do without it but I'm afraid we are forced to comply.'

Nobody expected for a minute that the producer would believe a word of this. But, dear reader, he did.

On the day that the scene was to be shot, we arrived to find members of the crew in heavy discussion with the producers, some saying that they refused to undress. 'I'm not taking my clothes off! I have to bend down a lot . . .' Others were trying to negotiate a fee for revealing all.

'I'm not going to let a bunch of loony feminists ruin my film!' was heard being screamed from the producer's caravan.

By this time we were terrified, not of the scene but of the consequences of our prank once the truth was out. However, we felt we had to carry on. Inside the shower set the moment came for us to remove our dressing gowns. As soon as we did so, the sound boys whipped everything off as well. Many a sound technician would have felt diminished by the size of his boom, but not our man, may I say. Next to follow was Clive Tickner, our marvellous lighting cameraman, sitting there on the dolly, looking ravishing in nothing but a set of headphones. Eventually, the entire crew were naked except the director, who refused. Thereafter a lot of people went round inexplicably lifting their little fingers behind his back, especially when he said anything a mite pompous.

It is amazing how respectful men become when they, too, are naked. Once the scene was over we made our confession with a case of champagne placed strategically between us and them, to ease any embarrassment, and it was all taken in good heart. It is a story that still follows me round the world today. The film turned out to be a publicist's dream but a box-office disappointment, as was the film I did the following year in 1985.

This was *Car Trouble*, in which I starred with my dear friend Ian Charleson. *Car Trouble* was a comedy that revolved round an awful couple called Gerald and Jacqueline. He is the proud owner of an E-Type Jaguar, and Jacqueline takes a fancy to the dishy mechanic who services the said E-Type and ends up servicing her. The climax, for want of a better word, occurs when they are at it in the car and inadvertently slip the handbrake off in a mid-coitus frenzy, sending the car careering through woodland and down a bank. The two of them end up being stuck together, Jacqueline having gone into a trauma-induced spasm. *City Limits*, then *Time Out*'s rival what's-on magazine, called it 'a sizzling turd of a movie'.

However, *City Limits* was forgiven the following year when it gave me the award for Best Film Actress for my portrayal of Cynthia Payne, the Streatham-based madam, in the film *Personal Services*. David Leland had written a really affectionate, moving and funny script, and Terry Jones, of *Monty Python* fame, was to direct. But even though I was his and Terry's first choice for the role, the producers weren't so keen and I was forced to read on camera on three separate occasions before being finally offered the part. There was to be a press conference, at which Madame Cyn and I were to be centre stage, to announce the forthcoming production, so David and Terry organised a dinner so that the two of us could meet. I remember the restaurant as being exclusive and not entirely empty.

'Do you like sex, Julie?' Cynthia has just sat down.

'Erm . . . Well, it depends . . . on who it's with.' I giggle.

'A lot of my girls can take it or leave it, but you get a girl who actually likes it and you've struck gold.'

Cynthia has quite a loud, strident voice. In fact she is talking to me as if I were sitting inside a cupboard with the door shut. The man at the next table has a coughing fit.

'I couldn't be doing with it when I was on the game, I got too sore.'

A man and a woman have just entered the room, turned round and gone out again.

David coughs. 'Erm, shall I order for you, Cynthia? I know what you're like when you get talking.'

David knows Cynthia well, having apparently spent the last two years in her company researching this film. I notice that he has gone grey round the temples since I last saw him.

'Yes, David, you order. I like a man who can take the lead. All my lot want to be humiliated . . . here.'

She rummages in her bag and brings out several small black-and-white snaps. It takes me time to focus. 'He's a bank manager.'

There is a naked man lying, well, cowering, on the floor of a perfectly ordinary sitting room, covered in some dark substance.

'He likes to be covered in Hoover dust.'

Diners at the surrounding tables are now enveloped in total silence; there isn't even the scrape of a knife to be heard.

She produces another snap for my perusal. In it a group of elderly men are sitting round with cups of tea, being served biscuits by a couple of topless women in stockings and suspenders.

'That's one of my parties.'

'Oh . . . The gentlemen are quite—'

'Yes, I know, I prefer them old. They're easier to handle. A lot of mine are slaves.'

She then goes on to explain that she has clients who simply wish to be humiliated by a woman in high heels and the bonus is that they make no demands for sex. It is all about role-play, she says.

'I have my house scrupulously cleaned once a week by a man on his hands and knees wearing nothing but a suspender belt and stockings. As long as I kick him up the bum every so often he's fine. So if ever you need a cleaner I could easily find you someone, and the beauty of it is *they* pay *you*!'

There are now two waiters in the doorway, enjoying the show. Cynthia has moved on to regaling us about a man who wants to be frightened and she tells us how she and a friend took him out to a lonely spot in the countryside, where they ordered him to undress, tied him to a tree and then left him for a couple of hours.

'We gave him a slap and went shopping in Brighton. He used to love it, except one time we forgot about him and had to go back for him in the dark and we couldn't remember where we'd put him.'

More photos then appear, one of a huge man wrapped up in a blanket with a dummy in his mouth.

'He's a High Court judge. You should come to one of my parties, Julie, you'd love it.'

I managed to avoid this.

# Nine

The following year I was offered the role of another real person, the wife of Buster Edwards, one of the key players in the Great Train Robbery. Although in some ways it makes the job easier, playing a living person also brings with it a huge responsibility to do them justice. Unlike Cynthia, June was a very private person, and so I felt my responsibility to be even greater. I was excited to hear from Norma Heyman, the producer, that Phil Collins was set to play the lead, and in September 1987 we started rehearsals for *Buster*. We had been at it only a couple of days when I discovered that I was pregnant.

About eighteen months previously, I had met a very handsome man in a bar on the Fulham Road. I had just returned after playing Lady Macbeth opposite Bernard Hill in the Scottish play at Leicester Phoenix. It had been a huge success for me on many levels, not least because it was the first time I had not employed an accent of some sort. At the time I felt that the current prime minister, Margaret Thatcher, was a good model upon which to base my interpretation of the character. Lady M's vaulting ambition, whatever the human cost, seemed to be a perfect parallel, but during rehearsals I discovered the frail creature beneath the driven exterior. It is the only part I have ever wanted to play again, apart from Mrs Overall of course.

Once home in London, I went to the aforementioned bar to catch up with my best buddy, Ros March. We had met at the Fulham Boulevard for tea at four o'clock in the afternoon and were still there by nine o'clock in the evening, by which time the place was awash with so-called 'hooray Henrys', and Ros and I were three sheets to the wind. At some point I staggered up to the bar for yet more refreshments and, hearing all the 'Yah-yahing' going on, I announced at the top of my voice to Ros, but also for the benefit of those around me: 'I bet nobody here is a member of the Labour Party!'

With that a big, deep voice next to me said, 'I am, actually.'

I looked up and that was it: love, dear reader, or, most likely at that particular juncture, lust. We struck up a conversation, and then after saying good night he apparently spotted us staggering about outside, with me dropping ten-pound notes all over the place. Fearing for our safety he decided to walk us home. On reaching my door—I lived a matter of minutes away—I insisted on his coming in for a cup of tea, asking at the same time whether, as he was a man, he would mind taking a look at a) my shower, as I could read a novel in between each drop of water that came out of it, and (b) my washing machine, which for some reason I had been unable to empty.

As I stood watching, as my mother would have called him, this 'fine figure of a man' get down onto his haunches to inspect the machine, I was overcome with an overwhelming sense of exhilaration. When he dropped onto all fours for an even closer look and said, 'I think you probably need a pump,' I mistook his meaning and leapt, laughing with drunken glee, onto his back.

He shot to his feet, obviously thinking that this was an attack.

'No! No! I want you to have my children!' I cried reassuringly. 'Honestly, I'll give you reasonable access!'

Anyway, we have at this point been together for twenty-three years. He was right about the pump, in all senses; and a short and passionate eighteen months later we decided that we would, all things being equal, have a baby.

In the run-up to *Buster*, we realised that we had achieved our goal. When I broke the news to her, Norma decided that for insurance purposes it was probably better that it went no further than her. This was all very well, but I was suffering from sickness morning, noon and night, and every so often during rehearsals, which were mainly with Phil, I would have to rush to the lavatory. One of my quick exits occurred just when Phil, as Buster, was telling me he loved me and we were about to get into a clinch. That morning, my driver, Jeff, had asked me whether I was happy with his driving as he was concerned with the way I dashed, green-faced, from the car at the end of each journey. Then Norma grabbed me after rehearsals and said that Phil was wondering whether I had a problem with him, as my behaviour was so odd, so she was forced to spill the beans. There was much relief all round.

I WAS THRILLED to be pregnant. I had begun to feel empty during the couple of years prior to meeting Grant, wondering what my life was for. What was the purpose, apart from earning money, of rushing from project to project, never standing still to take life in?

A few months before I met him, I was shooting *The Secret Life of Adrian Mole*, in which I played Adrian's mother. While waiting around to start filming, I picked up a copy of *Punch*. On page one was a cartoon of a man sitting in front of a television, with a newspaper in his hand, shouting: 'Oh, look! There's something on television tonight that hasn't got Julie Walters in it!'

Although I joked about it, I felt upset. The point was punched home as I raced off that night to appear in Sam Shepard's *Fool for Love*. I began to question my life of constant work, the gaps filled with wild socialising fuelled by too much drink. It felt shallow, and meaningless. I knew there was more, and that night in the Fulham Boulevard, even through the fog of too much champagne, I knew somehow that I had found it.

Once the morning sickness was over, spot on three months, I felt wonderful. For the first time in my life I was suffused with calm. I loved the way I felt and looked: my skin rosy, my hair lustrous, even my eyes seemed to have taken on a new intensity of colour and depth.

'I've had a premonition!' This is Nora, one of the dressers on *Buster*. She is hovering in the doorway of my trailer and has caught me getting into my costume. 'You are going to have a boy!'

'Excuse me, are you Tracy Ullman?' This from a ginger-haired woman standing on the pavement outside.

'No, no, I'm not. Sorry.'

'Are you sure?'

'Yes, yes, I'm pretty sure I'm not Tracy Ullman.'

Nora now moves into the caravan so that the woman can enjoy an unimpeded view of me in my 1960s underwear.

'Of course she's not Tracy Ullman! This is Julie Walters!'

'Who?'

I'm thinking: can this get any more humiliating, when Nora closes the door swiftly then says, 'Yes, it's a boy! Let me hug you!'

I had thought that, if I ever were to have a child, I would have a girl. This wasn't a preference, but I suspect that at the back of my mind the thought lurked that because I had had a prickly relationship with my mother, a daughter would heal this to some extent, so Nora's news threw me completely. I began to imagine tiny boys with Grant's face running round the sitting room.

However, two weeks later an amniocentesis test proved that Nora was talking out of her considerable backside. I was definitely having a girl. The little bump had lost its anonymity: it was now a 'she' instead of an 'it', and we were thrilled. We set about discussing names. Clea came up, but put together with Grant's surname, Roffey, we could see that it didn't perhaps work. I suggested Anya; he said over his dead body. He suggested Kelly and I said over mine and then some! I then went out on a limb and suggested Coco; Grant went quiet on this one, but a friend talked me out of it, saying that to name a child after a night-time drink was almost tantamount to abuse. Then, some months down the line I came across a reproduction of a Victorian music-hall poster, and in the corner was the name Maisie.

During the latter part of my pregnancy, partly as an antidote to all the serious and alarming books on the subject which mainly left me feeling that I'd already got parenthood wrong and she wasn't even born yet, I decided to keep a diary. This turned into a small and slightly daft tome titled *Baby Talk*. It helped hugely to keep everything in perspective, and through it I discovered the joy and power of writing.

My daughter's birth was the most important event of my life

and, as it can't be topped, the telling of it will round off this tale. I was to have a Caesarean section a couple of weeks prior to the due date. This was decided by the consultant obstetrician because I had suffered high blood pressure, and it was also discovered that I was diabetic, so I was forced to have insulin injections every day; both conditions miraculously disappeared at the moment of birth. The consultant was concerned that I would either have a big baby, due to the diabetes, or a small one, due to the high blood pressure. Added to his concerns was the fact that Maisie was in a frank breech position, meaning that not only was she upside down and refused to turn, but also that her legs were up over the back of her head. When she was born the paediatrician unwrapped her from her blanket and gently flattened out her legs, but when he let go they sprang straight back up round her ears. He said that this would go in a day or two, adding that it was not the sort of habit you would wish her to have as a young woman.

On the Sunday night before she was to be delivered, I sat on the bed of my hospital room, overcome with inexplicable sadness. I ran a bath and soaked in it for a good hour. I tried to picture what my life would be like from eight fifteen onwards the next day, but, as anyone will tell you, nothing on this earth prepares you for life after birth. The sadness continued as I lay there and I began, as I had so often done, to talk to the little person inside. After a couple of minutes of explaining to my unborn daughter that in a few short hours her world would be opened up, she would be brought out into this one, and that we couldn't wait to meet her, my sadness was suddenly thrown into focus. We were now on the eve of a kind of parting, a forced and unnatural parting at that. I guess I felt I had failed her by not giving birth to her naturally, which seemed to be the root of my melancholy.

That night I woke in the small hours to go to the loo. As I walked into the bathroom, I thought that I was wetting myself and then realised that my waters had broken. I had a huge desire then to be holding her and I said, 'You're coming! You heard me! You clever girl!' And I cried and then the sobs turned into little giggles of pure joy, and the sadness floated up and out on the laughter, and I knew that what was happening was meant and was perfect.

I had a brief, heart-soaring moment when I got the notion into my head that, now that she was on her way, I might just be able to give birth naturally, but it was not to be; the Caesarean was to take place as scheduled and I would be taken down to theatre at eight o'clock. But at least now I was excited about the prospect.

'FIVE YEARS AGO today . . .'

I can hear my mother's voice, so close in note and tone to my own that they are one.

'Ten years ago today . . .' I am calling up the stairs, 'Dad and I went down to the theatre.' I think I hear her yawn. 'I had my epidural and I noticed your dad had disappeared.'

Grant laughs, he knows what's coming.

'Then I looked round and everyone else had disappeared as well—nurses, doctors!'

I've got her now, I can hear her listening.

'Don't exaggerate.' Grant is still laughing. He is sitting in his overalls in the kitchen, reading his *Farmers Weekly*, drinking a cup of tea and eating toast.

'A nurse came back in and I said, where is everyone? And she said, "Oh, your husband went a bit green, we had to take him out."'

I hear her go 'Ahhh . . .' Her sympathy is genuine.

'One minute, he's sitting there looking concerned; the next he's out cold, surrounded by nurses.'

Grant stops laughing. 'I never could stand hospitals.'

'It was a typical act of upstaging on your part.' Now I'm making myself laugh. 'You were so beautiful,' I tell her, 'so perfect.'

And she laughs, and she is.

# Alan Titchmarsh

## *Knave of Spades*

*Dad, probably worn down by both my unhappiness at school and my constant nagging about gardening . . . had finally made an appointment to see the headmaster.*

*'We think,' he said, when he returned home, 'that it might be better if you left school early. The headmaster said that if you had your mind set on it then we should let you be a gardener.'*

*If the high five had been invented I would have given him one. Instead, I wandered off into the garden. Birds sang, bees buzzed, but I don't think I heard them. Dad's words just echoed in my ears.*

*Alan Titchmarsh in 'Knave of Spades'*

## GREEN SHOOTS

It could have gone either way. I could have been a carpenter, rather than a gardener. The thing was, I was so desperate to leave school I almost didn't mind what I did. Almost.

I had failed my eleven-plus. Not spectacularly, just positively. I'd gone from the sooty Victorian stonework of Ilkley All Saints Junior School in Leeds Road to the brand-new glass-and-painted-panelwork secondary school on Valley Drive. They pulled it down in 2008, so at least I have the satisfaction of knowing that I outlived the place that caused me so much grief.

It came as a shock that, having been called 'Alan' by my teachers for the first seven years of my scholastic life, I was now 'Titchmarsh'.

Soft beggar. But it is so much more difficult to hide with a name like that than it is with Robertson, Smith or Brown. I still shudder slightly at the sound of my own name. I could have changed it to something less obtrusive when I started doing television, but the moment passed and so now I'm stuck with it.

Not that all the blame for my slow start can be laid entirely at the door of the school, or the teachers, come to that. I was a classic late developer. A bit of a dreamer. I meant well but, as one of my school reports remarked, 'Alan has very good intentions; what a pity they are not always fulfilled.'

The memories of those early years are as vivid as a stained-glass window. I cannot watch the film *Kes* without pangs of anxiety at young Billy Casper's feelings of isolation on the football pitch—always the last to be picked along with the 'fat boy'. I was the smallest in the class until I left school at fifteen and went to work in the greenhouses where I grew ten inches in the first year.

As inferiority complexes go it was fairly well developed. But I cannot claim that I was ever mistreated. Both parents were loving—my father in an understated Yorkshire way—and concerned to instil in my sister Kath and me a sense of duty, good manners, kindness and honesty. I was taught to walk on the outside of the pavement when accompanying a female—I still do—and to take off my school cap whenever I passed a lady, whenever a funeral cortege passed me and whenever I went indoors.

I could not leave the table without asking to do so, was not permitted to talk with my mouth full, went to church on Sunday and knelt by my bed each evening to say my prayers. Neighbours were 'Mr So-and-so' and 'Mrs So-and-so', aunts and uncles never referred to by their Christian names alone, and until I was well into double figures I never dared to answer my parents back. On the first occasion I disagreed with my mother's pronouncement on something, I don't know who was the more shocked, her or me.

By the time I was fifteen I was perhaps a little more assertive than it would appear from this confessional, but not much. The one thing I did know was that I was determined to leave school, even if the words of one of my teachers would ring in my ears for the rest of my life—'He'll never amount to much.' At least I have that much in common with Einstein.

Dad wasn't at all sure that leaving school at fifteen—before taking my O levels—was a good idea. Once it became clear that my mind was set on doing so, he took up a rearguard position: 'You'll need a trade.'

He had noticed that over the previous five years I had become more and more interested in gardening. I had built a polythene greenhouse in our back garden where a selection of plants had been cultivated, along with a cage of pet mice. Nature had always been an interest of mine. For a while it was touch and go whether I would be a gardener or a vet, but then the appearance of a cat in my greenhouse scared the mice literally to death and so plants started to seem like a more viable career path than animals.

My interest in nature had developed early on. It was so ingrained that I cannot say for certain when it began. I have always been fascinated by 'natural history', to use the more academic term that I never thought of using during my childhood and adolescence. I could lie on the lawn under a sheet of blackout material for hours on end, watching birds coming down to feed on the crumbs I had scattered on the lawn. I would scoop handfuls of frogspawn from the tarn on Ilkley Moor each spring and watch the full stops turn to commas and the commas into wriggling crotchets every year, even growing on the froglets in a small vivarium that Dad made for me from an old orange box and a sheet of glass left over from repairing the kitchen window. My required television viewing was *Zoo Quest* with David Attenborough, *Look* with Peter Scott and *On Safari* with Armand and Michaela Denis.

I joined the Wharfedale Naturalists' Society at the age of eight—their youngest member—and went to 'lantern lectures' about butterflies and birds, fungi and mammals in winter, and up the Dales on field trips in spring and summer.

Gardening seemed a natural extension of this passion for

everything that flew, crawled, swam or grew. I still think of gardeners as the only truly interactive naturalists. Birdwatchers watch birds, botanists look at flowers, but gardeners grow them, working hand in hand with nature rather than simply spectating.

Not that my wish to be a gardener impressed my father. He could never see gardening as 'a trade'. I found it hard to see why until, several years after I had taken up the spade, he confessed that both his father and his grandfather had been 'jobbing gardeners' and had made him weed for a penny a bucket. His own boredom with that task, and observation of the fact that neither of his male forebears had ever had more than a couple of ha'pennies to rub together, had put him off gardening for life. My grandfather's spade—which I use to this day—was employed by my father to mix concrete. It still carries the telltale traces.

Worried that he might not countenance my being a gardener, I offered joinery as an alternative trade, reasoning in my own mind that if I could not grow things for a living then at least I could spend all my spare time doing so. I had always been good with my hands—whether that meant knocking together my own greenhouse from timber offcuts my dad brought home, or building model stage and television studio sets from balsa wood and cardboard, so joinery was not such an odd choice.

Dad, probably worn down by both my unhappiness at school and my constant nagging about gardening and joinery, finally made an appointment for him and Mum to see the headmaster. Not that he told me about it. Not until he returned home anyway.

'We think,' he said, 'that it might be better if you left school early.'

My joy at the prospect of being released from Purgatory was tempered by the fact that they clearly thought the further education of this academic failure would be futile.

'To be a joiner?' I asked.

'No.'

'What then?'

'The headmaster said that there were plenty of joiners about but not enough gardeners, and that if you had your mind set on it then we should let you be a gardener.'

'Oh.'

If the high five had been invented I would have given him one. Instead, I wandered off into the garden. Birds sang, bees buzzed and the leaves of the old sycamore up at the top end rustled in the summer breeze, but I don't think I heard them. Dad's words just echoed in my ears over and over again. Some massive weight had been lifted from my shoulders. I blundered in a kind of delirium into my little polythene greenhouse among the geraniums and the spider plants, the false castor oils and the busy Lizzies. For a while I could not see much. I think I must have got something in my eye. I reached for the hanky in my left-hand pocket. I still have one there. An ancient tradition, but one that comes in handy—in cold weather, when eating spaghetti Bolognese, and in moments when life throws up things that catch you unawares.

DO I BELIEVE in 'green fingers'? Completely. Not that I think there is anything remotely mysterious or fanciful about the condition. If you look at the way plants behave, notice their likes and dislikes and act accordingly the chances are that they will grow for you. They are innately willing to do so and capable of doing so. Most of them grow in spite of us, rather than because of us, so it is up to us not to get in the way. Oh, and you'll also need a bit of patience. In a world of instant gratification, the pleasure involved in anticipation is sometimes difficult to get across.

While my dad had no patience at all with the garden in Nelson Road, where I spent the first sixteen years of my life, my mum pottered about in it in between washing and ironing, cooking and bringing up two children. She inherited her growing skills from her father, Herbert Hardisty, a council 'ganger' from the highways department, whose allotment on the banks of the River Wharfe initiated me, aged one, into the delights of home-grown food. Mum would push me there in my pram and park me among the bean rows while she helped her horny-handed father pull carrots and beetroots for summer salads. For a few years a small veg patch graced her own garden at Nelson Road, but soon her tastes became more ornamental. Not that she was into anything that remotely approached garden design. The area that passed for the lawn was rectangular, the washing line ran down its centre like a semi-permanent spine and the yard-wide borders that surrounded it were stuffed with a mixture of goldenrod, montbretia and Shasta daisies—perennial plants that were happy to hold their own come drought, deluge or badly aimed football.

My mum's way with plants was instinctive. When I started attending day-release classes and night school to learn my craft, I would come home and tell her what she was doing wrong, with the benefit of my newly acquired knowledge and all the confidence of youth.

'Oh,' she would say. 'I see.' And go on doing things in just the same way as she always had. Age and experience have since taught me that there is more than one way to root a cutting, and my mother could root the spokes of an old umbrella.

MY FIRST JOB came about as a result of a happy accident. Dad, though a plumber by trade, was also a part-time fireman and would be called out by the siren that wailed over the town, causing him to drop whatever he was doing, swap his slippers for his shoes and run to the fire station four streets away. He would spend Tuesday evenings on maintenance work there with the other part-timers—carpenters and electricians, decorators and council workmen—among them Wally Gell, who worked in the local parks department. One Tuesday night Dad mentioned that his lad wanted to be a gardener.

'Oh,' said Wally. 'We've a vacancy if he wants to apply.'

So one day in the summer of 1964 I put on a pair of jeans, a clean shirt and tie and a check sports jacket, polished my shoes and went on my bike to the council nursery half a mile away on Little Lane to meet the Parks Superintendent.

Hector Mutlow, FIPRA (Fellow of the Institute of Park and Recreation Administration), was a small, birdlike man with a shortie raincoat and a flat tweed cap. His voice had a tremulous, reedy quality that made him sound like a bassoon in need of tuning, with an occasional hint of the bagpipes.

I stood in front of him on the rough gravel drive of the nursery, hoping that my appearance would not let me down. I needed all the help I could get to secure the position for which I was desperate: Apprentice Gardener for Ilkley Urban District Council.

Hector Mutlow looked me up and down. It did not take long. There wasn't much to look at.

'So you want to be a gardener?'

'Yes.'

'Are you sure?'

'I think so, yes.'

'Well, I don't want you to do anything hasty, so why don't you come and work for me for a fortnight for nothing, and if you like it I'll take you on.'

I thanked him profusely. I think I heard bells ringing. Maybe a heavenly choir.

'Are you all right?'

The voice seemed to be coming from elsewhere. I pulled myself together. 'Yes. Fine. When do I start?'

'Right now if you want.' He looked over his shoulder and called to the man in the doorway of the old brick potting shed. 'Kenneth, do you want to show this lad what he'll be doing?'

Ken Wilson nodded. He was the parks department foreman, Hector Mutlow's number two, a wise and gentle man, balding, with kind eyes and a face that lit up when he smiled. In all the years I knew him he was always scrupulously fair, though if a job was not done well he would let you know, in that quiet-spoken but firm way he had. 'There are some plants over here saying "Alan, why don't you water me?"' was one of his favourites.

Ken came over, on that first day, and shook my hand, looking into my eyes and no doubt trying to work out how long I would last. He, too, wore a tie, but the jacket was off and the sleeves rolled up, his grey flannel trousers protected by a denim apron.

'You'd better follow me,' he said softly.

He led the way to an old Victorian greenhouse that was divided into three—two long, low, white-painted houses, joined by a higher central section. Following him, I climbed the two stone steps up to the first greenhouse and heard the clinking of the loose brass ferrule as he turned the knob and pushed open the door. Inside, carefully arranged on the shingle-topped staging were row after row of geraniums—scarlet, orange, pink and magenta, many of them with coloured leaves as well as bright flowers. Alongside them stood a swathe of neat, upright plants with feathery plumes of red and yellow—Prince of Wales' feathers, or celosia. They seemed to me to be unbelievably exotic.

The cathedral-like atmosphere—the stillness of the air and the silence, except for the rhythmic drip-drip-drip of water from the staging into the sunken concrete tanks beneath them—was awe-inspiring. Having walked me through these floral cathedrals, Ken Wilson said the three words which, at that point in my life, were the most thrilling I had ever heard: 'These are yours.'

At first I thought I must have misheard. 'Are you sure?'

He raised his eyebrows, and I realised the stupidity of my reply.

'Right,' was the best response I could manage.

'I'll leave you to get on with your watering then.' And with that he was gone.

I stood there, in that first greenhouse, quite still for a few moments, gazing at the colour on all sides, looking up at the white-painted rafters and down at the deep and seemingly bottomless tanks of rainwater beneath the staging. Gloop, drip, gloop, drip were the only sounds I heard in this otherwise silent haven.

I walked on towards the higher central greenhouse and opened the door to discover tall grevilleas, the Australian silk-bark oak, in pots on the floor, shooting upwards and diffusing the rays of the summer sun with their ferny fronds. The wall at the back of this tall lean-to that backed onto the potting shed was lime-washed bright white. In front of it were serried ranks of *Primula obconica* in pots on the staging. The next door led to the final greenhouse and more geraniums, not yet in flower. I turned and retraced my steps to the bottom door, suddenly aware of a thumping sound that was coming from my chest. It was definitely my heart, there was no doubt about that. But it was beating with fear as well as excitement. What if I got it wrong? What if they all died? But I took a grip of myself. Come on. I could grow plants. Here there were just more of them.

I was in my element. In *my* greenhouses, and if I managed to get through the next two weeks they'd let me keep them. I was fifteen. And all this was mine for the asking.

## GARDENER'S BOY

I got the job. I think they all knew from day one that I thought it was the best thing that had ever happened to me.

For four days of the week (the fifth was for studying) I worked in the parks department. The nursery staff—three of us plus a driver, with occasional input from the foreman—grew all the plants necessary for spring and summer bedding out in the flowerbeds and roundabouts in Ilkley and pot plants for floral decorations in the town hall and library, the King's Hall and Winter Gardens, Ilkley's two statuesque Edwardian assembly rooms.

There were a dozen or so men, mainly middle-aged, who made up the motley crew responsible for beautifying the 'Heather Spa', as Ilkley was referred to in its Victorian heyday. It had grown in size a century and a half previously thanks to the smelly yet health-giving properties of the chalybeate waters that erupted from natural springs on the moor. Castellated hotels called 'hydropathic establishments' were erected to cater for the gentry who wanted to 'take the waters'. With the passing of the hydropathic fad in the early twentieth century Ilkley had become the preferred residential area, along with Harrogate, for the wool merchants of Leeds and Bradford, and the 'hydros' had become hotels and colleges or else been pulled down to make room for more houses.

The rough north/south dividing line between the posh end and the working-class area of Ilkley is Brook Street, the town's main shopping thoroughfare. We lived in the working-class bit to the east—parallel streets of stone-built, slate-roofed terrace houses with back lanes between house and garden. Pleasant, but utilitarian. To the west of Brook Street is The Grove, the Bond Street of Ilkley, where Betty's Café—other branches in York, Harrogate and Northallerton—is the jewel in the crown.

Up King's Road and Grove Road to the west are larger detached houses, with spacious grounds backing onto the moors. The River Wharfe bisects the valley running east to west, at right angles to Brook Street, and on the higher slopes of both sides of the valley are the smartest houses of all, hidden from view by copses and woodland, and reached via curving gravel or tarmac drives.

In these houses, many of the men who worked by day for the parks department would earn a few extra shillings by working on summer evenings or Saturday mornings mowing and weeding, clipping hedges and digging vegetable plots.

My wage, as far as I can remember, amounted to £3 7s 6d. I gave it all to my mum, and she gave me back ten bob pocket money. While I was the lowest of the low in my newly appointed position, with indentures for a five-year apprenticeship and therefore a smaller sum of money since my employment was guaranteed, Mickey Ware was classed as a labourer and earned rather more. He was a year or so older than me, with a stubbly beard and a liking for Helen Shapiro.

In charge of us both was Ron Jeavons, married with two kids, tall and gangly, with thick glasses. It was Ron who gave me the budding knife I still use today. An apron and a budding knife were the regulation equipment of an apprentice in the nursery. The dark blue denim apron (it took a while to stop my mother calling it my 'pinny') came wrapped up in brown paper. The budding knife came in a small cardboard box labelled 'The Burbank'. But I never did lay my hands on it. Instead, Ron took his old one out of his apron pocket and gave me that. 'I could do with a new one,' he said. I would be lying if I said that I did not feel disappointed, but if I had known that the old knife he gave me would last—to date—forty-five years, then I might not have felt so bad. Under Ron's tutelage, and that of one or two of the rest of the team, I spent the next few years learning my trade.

DAD WOULD WAKE ME at around seven since we both needed to leave early for work. I didn't need to shave every day at fifteen, neither did we shower every morning in the 1960s—anyway, we hadn't got one, only a bath and that was for Friday nights or special occasions—so I was out of the door and on my bike for the ten-minute ride to the nursery on Little Lane once Dad had got a bowl of thick porridge down me.

The nursery itself was situated just outside the town centre and surrounded by council houses and small cul-de-sacs of pebble-dashed semis with names like Wheatlands that nodded an acknowledgment to their rural past. It comprised about eight acres, I should think, with areas of ground for growing wallflowers and shrubs, neatly arranged white-painted timber greenhouses and a series of sheds and lean-tos housing tools, vehicles and stacks of loam, peat and sand.

Work began at 7.45 a.m. The thirteen greenhouses, in which grew geraniums and ferns, hydrangeas and chrysanthemums, were heated by a coke-fired boiler the size of a small van, situated in a sunken boiler house in the centre of the nursery. Mickey and I took it in turns—week on, week off—to maintain and fuel this temperamental beast. In these days of automatic gas- or oil-fired central heating it is hard to believe just how labour-intensive were these earlier heating methods.

Picture me, on a cold winter's morning, clad in a donkey jacket (the sports jacket wore out) and will-power, bouncing all of my seven stone on the end of a six-foot-long steel poker trying to break up the clinker, a four-inch layer of metallic crust that seemed welded to the bottom of the boiler. Once broken up, it would be removed, while still red hot, with a large pair of tongs, and deposited in a metal dustbin that sat alongside the boiler. When it filled up—every couple of days—the bin had to be carried up the steps of the boiler house and the contents dumped outside, sometimes being used to create an ash path down the side of one of the greenhouses.

Once clinkered, it was then a matter of closing the front door for half an hour and opening up the damper to get the firebed roaring orange. Then I'd shovel in more coke and ram it to the back of the boiler with another long metal tool that looked like a gigantic draw-hoe. Once full, the damper would be left open for a while to get the coke going, and then shut down so that it did not burn too fast. Throughout the day this beast with a life of its own would be checked every couple of hours to make sure that it was burning evenly, and more fuel added until the final stoking up at night, when it was filled once more and left to burn, with threats and crossed fingers.

It was a relief when summer arrived and the boiler could be allowed to go out, although then that all-consuming task was just replaced with another one—watering.

Ron and Mickey had five greenhouses apiece, each around thirty feet long, and I had three. They would be checked for watering morning and evening, and for the first couple of years I worked there we were not allowed to use hosepipes.

'If you use a hosepipe you don't look at what you're doing,' was Ken's reasoning. Neither, in those first few years, did we use plastic pots. Each and every pot, in which we planted the thousands of plants we grew, was made of terracotta.

'Clay pots keep the roots cool,' Ken told me. They did, but being porous they also took a deal of watering. The technique of finding out which plants needed watering was simple and effective, but hugely time-consuming. We would dip a metal, two-gallon, long-spouted Haws watering can into the rainwater tank beneath the staging and, with this in one hand and a small long-handled mallet in the other, work our way down the staging on one side of the house and back up the other, checking to see which plants were thirsty. A smart tap on the rim of each pot with the mallet would produce either a dull thud (the rootball was moist) or a ringing sound (the plant was dry). If it rang, you watered it; if it went 'clunk', you didn't.

I left the nursery before the oil-fired boiler arrived, but I did live to see the advent of hosepipes and plastic pots. It speeded up our watering no end—you can't tell from tapping a plastic pot whether it is dry or not—but I don't think Ken ever quite trusted them.

All those pots. It doesn't take a mathematician to work out that the plants that fill thirteen thirty-foot greenhouses are going to need a lot of compost. Especially when they have to be given a new and larger pot and more compost every few months.

We got through so much on the nursery that we mixed our own. And so, aged fifteen, when others were learning by heart the words of 'Twist and Shout', 'Needles and Pins' and 'I Can't Get No Satisfaction', I was learning that the formula for John Innes Potting Compost No. 1 consisted of 7 parts by bulk partially sterilised loam, 3 parts by bulk granulated peat and 2 parts by bulk sharp sand, plus 4oz John Innes base fertiliser (2 parts by weight hoof and horn, one-eighth of an inch grist; 2 parts by weight superphosphate of lime and 1 part by weight sulphate of potash) plus three quarters of an ounce of ground limestone or chalk per bushel. This was doubled for John Innes No. 2 and trebled for John Innes No. 3. The impressive (or sad) thing, though I have no way of proving it to you, is that I was able to write this down from memory without looking it up.

It would take Mickey and me half a day to mix a six-foot-high and eight-foot-wide heap of John Innes, and to this day I have never seen a better mix of compost in any bag that I have bought.

All this manual labour needed fuelling. Dad's fortifying porridge would wear off after an hour or so, which meant that at around half past nine, when the driver had returned from distributing the men around town, I was grateful for the pork pies he handed round. These were fresh, oven-warm raised pies with golden-brown crunchy pastry and pink, peppery pork made by Michael at Thirkell's the pork butchers on Railway Road. I could manage two of them as a midmorning snack, drinking the liquefied jelly through the hole in the top, then crunching into the meat and pastry. At noon I'd be ready for lunch, sometimes nipping home on my bike for a poached egg or beans on toast, or else tucking into a sandwich and a KitKat washed down with a mug of sweet tea in the potting shed. At a quarter to five I'd head home for my tea—a hot main course followed by pudding—and Mum would usually knock up a sandwich or two for supper around ten. My waistline remained at twenty-eight inches until I was twenty-six years old.

You might think that life on the nursery was an arduous sort of existence. But the funny thing is, although we worked our socks off, it was one of the most enjoyable times of my life, simply because the reason for our hard graft was the plants we were growing. Every one of the men I worked with over the years, tough and unsentimental souls though they might be, would, at some point, say, 'Now just look at them! Don't they look wonderful?' And that was why we did it.

MICKEY WAS ALWAYS very cagey about girls. He didn't give a lot away. When we were mixing potting compost or taking cuttings he'd let slip enough to let me know that he was playing the field—going to a dance at the King's Hall in Ilkley, or the Queen's Hall in Burley-in-Wharfedale, and having a snog afterwards round the back. Maybe even a bit of a fumble. But he never said much. After a year or two he went completely silent on the subject and it wasn't long before he announced he was getting married. It seemed to me, from this experience, that when you met the right one you knew it straight away. I'd have been grateful to have met anyone.

There was the odd flirty dalliance at school—a kiss behind the curtains at a dance—but nothing serious. Not until Rosemary Pickering, the slender little redhead from Guiseley for whom I fell hook, line and everything else. I met her at a dance at the King's Hall and we held hands and kissed before she caught the bus home. She made my stomach feel funny—the first time it had been caused by something that hadn't been served up by Grandma. Our tune was 'Groovy Kind of Love'. It still makes me wistful.

I suppose we 'went out'—if you can call the odd youth-club encounter and Scout-hut dance 'going out'—for about three months, maybe once a week, but in the end she dumped me—just after my sixteenth birthday party. Looking back I think *I'd* have dumped me after that party. It consisted of eight of us sitting round our front room in chairs having a chat, eating crisps, nuts and Twiglets and drinking Coca-Cola. It was meant to be grown up. In reality it was deadly. I could see from the way she was sitting, opposite me, that Rosemary was wearing suspenders. It was of academic interest. She apologised for forgetting to bring me a present and said goodbye at the front door after doing her best to make polite conversation along with the other equally bewildered members of the youth club. I never saw her again. Well, not until seven years ago.

I'd written about this encounter in *Trowel and Error*. On an author tour, I was somewhere in Staffordshire, sitting at a table in a bookshop with, thankfully, a long queue in front of me. I handed up a signed copy and then looked for the next person in the queue. In front of me stood a sturdy middle-aged lady in a brown tweed coat. She smiled. I smiled back, and then the penny dropped.

'Rosemary,' I murmured.

'Hello,' she said.

'How are you?'

'I'm fine. I'm married now, with two sons.'

'Good heavens!' Not an original remark, or a very complimentary one, but the best I could manage under the circumstances.

We chatted for a few moments. 'Is it for you?' I asked. She nodded. I wrote something that I hope was meaningful, wondering if she would mind the fact that I had made reference to her in the book and revealed our short, innocent relationship to the wide world. I didn't have to wonder for long. As I handed her the book she smiled at me.

'I've read it already,' she said. 'Thank you for page ninety-three.'

JOE ROE, who was in charge of the cemetery down on the banks of the River Wharfe, was always popping into the nursery on his old bike, to ask us to send down more wallflowers for the graves, or to moan about something or other. He wasn't especially well disposed to me, for some reason. 'How's the council weedster?' he'd ask of me. I'd shrug. 'You know that's what they call you—all them others you left behind at school? Got a girl yet?'

I'd always try to change the subject, but Joe would bait me until he once again mounted his bike and rode back to the cemetery to dig a hole for some newly departed soul. 'The council weedster can't get a girl.' It wouldn't have hurt so much if it hadn't been true. Miserable old sod.

Mickey, to his credit, did his best to snap me out of it. 'Decoration this afternoon. Concert Club. You're coming.'

That perked me up. The floral decorations in the Town Hall, King's Hall and Winter Gardens were our only chance to get out. The Ilkley Concert Club was a rather up-market organisation that organised monthly recitals using world-class artists.

We loaded up the back of the Land Rover with peat-filled troughs, pots of primulas and celosias, ferns and pelargoniums, a few taller grevilleas for height and one or two spares of this and that, with the aim of making the front of the local stage look a little more like the Albert Hall but without obscuring the artist.

It was the middle of the afternoon. The concert was due to take place in the evening and the star of this particular performance was the clarinetist Janet Hilton. As Mickey and I entered the hall, one of us at each end of a heavy peat-filled trough, I could hear the soaring notes of the clarinet. The artist was rehearsing for the evening's performance. I glanced at Mickey. He pulled a face. Silently we walked up the steps at the side of the stage with the long black trough, and gently slid it into place.

We went out and brought in the other trough, sliding it onto the opposite side of the stage. The rehearsal was still under way. I don't think I had ever been in such close proximity to a world-class musician, and since my preference was for Handel and Schubert rather than Helen Shapiro I found myself quite carried away. Mickey, on the other hand, seemed rather taken with the soloist's legs. Her skirt, while not quite a mini, did show them off well.

We went back and forth the while, bringing in more plants, and when we had assembled our selection we began, on all fours, scooping holes in the peat and inserting them in what we considered to be a pleasing arrangement.

So it was that we both found ourselves at the feet of, and within a few feet of, the clarinetist as she finished one piece and prepared to begin another. I prayed that Mickey wouldn't say anything. That we would just carry on with our job silently while Janet Hilton ran through her pieces.

He glanced across at me with a glint in his eye and I knew that my wish was not to be granted.

Cocking his head in her direction, as if to make clear to me to whom the remark was directed, he said, 'There's someone here who's cleverer than you and me, Alan.'

Janet Hilton smiled indulgently. I could see she was embarrassed. But not nearly as embarrassed as me. Why did he have to use my name? Why couldn't he make his remark on his own account without having to rope me in? What did he mean, 'cleverer than us'? I wasn't stupid. I wasn't a concert performer but . . .

There was absolutely nothing I could say to redeem the situation. I could feel myself turning puce, and simply busied myself with making another hole in the peat for another pelargonium.

Janet Hilton began to play something by Weber, but she might as well have been playing Helen Shapiro's greatest hits for all I cared. After a few more minutes—the piece being mercifully too long to afford Mickey a second crack at a chat-up line—we slunk out of the hall with our spare plants and headed back to the nursery in the Land Rover.

THE FLORAL DECORATIONS were not only the high spot of the parks department nursery's life, they were the cause of its very existence. In my time there, between 1964 and 1968, the nursery on Little Lane grew all the plants needed for the town's beds and borders as well as the civic floral decorations. Between July and September, five of us would be responsible for preparing (slicing below a node and removing the lower leaves), inserting in four-inch clay flowerpots of cuttings compost topped with half an inch of sharp sand, and rooting—on the benches in the greenhouses—fifteen thousand individual pelargonium cuttings for the following year's display. Once rooted, the young plants were potted up individually in black polythene bag pots.

The floral highlight of the year was the annual Civic Ball, when the King's Hall and the Winter Gardens were transformed with hundreds upon hundreds of pot-grown plants that had been raised especially for this one date in the calendar in early November.

November is chrysanthemum time, and we had two long greenhouses devoted to them. Now chrysanths are an acquired taste and are rather out of fashion at the moment, but for me they have a nostalgic appeal, quite simply because for four years my life was bound up with them. The aroma given off by their crushed leaves is redolent of autumn—a sour yet fruity tang that signifies the fading of the year.

One greenhouse was filled exclusively with ferns, a humid corridor of *Nephrolepis exaltata* banked on either side. The plants themselves would be sprayed over daily, and so would the heating pipes beneath the staging, until clouds of steam obscured them from view. How they loved it! Verdant fountains of fronds cascaded over the front of the stone benchwork like some fantasy scene from *Lord of the Rings*.

Another house would boast hydrangeas—great domes of pink and white and electric blue—and yet another fibrous-rooted begonias, 'Mrs Clibran' and 'Optima', foot-high beauties with luscious pink and pale salmon flowers. Those were temperamental plants whose stems had to be tied individually to split green canes with thin strands of raffia so that they could be held upright. It was one of Ken's 'unwinding' jobs.

Keeping all these plants free of pests was a full-time job. All manner of noxious fluids and smokes would be brought into play. The chrysanthemum cuttings were dipped in a nicotine solution, hydrangeas were sprayed with a white oily preparation called Volck that made them shine and made it more difficult for insects to gain a foothold. Smoke bombs were let off in the greenhouses when an outbreak of red spider mite or whitefly was noticed, but for common-or-garden aphids—greenfly and blackfly—we would use a smouldering bonfire of nicotine shreds.

Looking back I am astounded at how cavalier we were with those chemical preparations, in the days before health and safety took hold. Look up 'nicotine' in the dictionary and you will discover that it is 'a toxic colourless or yellowish oily liquid which ... acts as a stimulant in small doses, but in larger amounts blocks the action of autonomic nerve and skeletal muscle cells'. Nasty stuff.

Picture us then, Mickey and me, deciding of an evening that the insect infestation in our greenhouses had got to the stage where it needed to be brought under control. We always fumigated, according to the instructions, in dull weather, not bright sunshine. As a result, it would be the last thing we did before we went home, so that the smoke could do its work overnight and we could open up the ventilators in the morning and allow in fresh air.

The technique with nicotine shreds, was to prise off the lid of the tin with a screwdriver, and then use the same implement to loosen the tightly packed shreds of nicotine-impregnated grey paper. A couple of piles of these shreds, about a foot across and six inches high, would be arranged on the path of the greenhouse—evenly spaced—and then set alight with a match. It was important that the shreds smouldered rather than blazed, so that the maximum amount of smoke was produced.

Having lit the two piles, we would beat a hasty retreat and then watch from outside the closed door of the greenhouse to make sure that they did not flare up. If they did, we would run back inside, with a handkerchief over nose and mouth, and stamp out the offending blaze until the heap smoked gently once more.

Our reward for all this came in the form of appreciative comments from those who attended the Civic Ball, which took two full days to dress with flowers. The entire balcony of the King's Hall would be filled with a bank of several hundred chrysanthemums, our two long greenhouses emptied for the occasion. The stage boxes down either side of the hall would billow with primulas, poor man's orchids and ferns, and the stage would sport a waterfall of foliage and flowers.

At the end of our preparations, late on the Friday afternoon, we would leave behind this botanical cornucopia, having transformed an elegant but urban Edwardian assembly hall into a magical wonderland. On Monday morning we took it all apart, when the sound of the music was no more than an echo, and the petals of the chrysanthemums littered the dance floor like confetti.

## RULES AND REGULATIONS

At least we were spared health and safety back in the sixties. We were expected to fall back on that old stalwart 'common sense', a facility much neglected in the twenty-first century. Nowadays all workmen must wear fluorescent jackets and all reversing lorries make that dreadful beeping sound. The net result is that when everyone wears a fluorescent yellow jacket absolutely no one stands out, and when the beeping is continuous the lorry might just as well be playing 'Land of Hope and Glory'.

I wouldn't mind if it were really done in the interests of *our* safety, but we know it's not. It's simply so that we don't have a leg to stand on when it comes to suing those who are responsible. Not that I'm a natural litigant. Those adverts for firms of solicitors who claim they can get you a fortune if you fall off a pavement leave me frothing with despair.

Being a man of the soil and a child of nature, I have a much more straightforward solution to two of the world's problems—overpopulation and litigation. I suggest that no warnings are printed on anything, all fluorescent jackets are consigned to a furnace and lorries stop beeping tomorrow. That way, all those who are stupid enough to take a sleeping tablet before they drive, tuck into the cashews when they know they have a nut allergy and walk under a lorry without looking both ways will be bumped off quite quickly, thus usefully reducing the population and leaving behind only those who possess the commodity that I am bemoaning—common sense. Darwin called it natural selection.

Ken Wilson called it 'using your noddle'. I did just that. Most of the time. Except when I said that of course I knew how to disbud carnations (for fear of looking stupid). I methodically took off *all* the flower buds, not just the small outer ones to let the large, central one develop, which is the more usual course of action. The look on Ken's face when I proudly stated that I had done the job is etched in my memory. My actions set back one of our floral displays by a good three months. I didn't do it again.

There were other rules that I learned more quickly—like 'Do not use your thumbs when potting up plants'. Ken would tell me that when he was in 'private service' the foreman would rap his knuckles with a bamboo cane if he caught him doing so—the reasoning behind this being that you can feel the pressure you are applying with your fingers much more sensitively than you can with your thumbs. His instructions stayed with me—I still can't bring myself to use my thumbs when potting up.

Neither can I leave doors open. It comes of working in greenhouses where heat cost money; a door left open in winter would send heating bills soaring and chill tender plants to the marrow. And so I shut doors, and drawers, and cupboards every time I pass them. It drives my family mad.

Ken's other rule was 'Every plant has a front and a back'; especially useful to know when 'staging up'—arranging plants on the greenhouse benches. Plants grow towards the light, as a result of which they tend to lean in one direction. I cannot plant anything in my garden without 'facing it up'.

One thing I did notice, within a few weeks of starting work, was the difference between people who were comfortable with plants and those who were wary of them. There is a sort of instinctive ease about handling plants. Sometimes it may seem rough or heavy-handed, but those who know plants know how robust they can be, and when their constitution is such that the gardener needs to be more careful.

Seedlings need treating with tenderness—the slightest squeeze of their fragile stems can kill them, which is why they are always held by the fat seed leaves or cotyledons when they are pricked out. That was another rule learned. But larger plants are surprisingly tough. Ken used to test the health of a mature cyclamen plant before it came into flower by turning the plant and the pot upside-down and balancing the dome of foliage on the palm of his hand. It told him if the plant had enough but not too much water, and showed that it was in the peak of health.

It's funny how some folk don't really understand watering, imagining that if you keep tipping the stuff on a plant then it will be happy. Some are—azaleas and ferns prefer to be damp at all times—but most other plants need watering only when the compost in the pot begins to feel dry to the touch. That is the key—*feel* the compost with your fingers. If it feels dusty it is dry, and you should apply water thoroughly until it runs out of the bottom of the pot. If, on the other hand, it feels like a freshly wrung-out flannel, then it is moist and the plant will be happy.

There were other rules about watering. 'Never water when the sun is shining' was one that I had heard often at home. I offered this advice to Ken. 'So you'd leave your plants asking for water all day, would you?' he asked. 'They'd be dead by evening.' Plants, I learned, need water when they are dry. It is best not to wet the foliage of hairy-leaved plants in sunny weather since they might scorch, but more harm is done by letting plants go thirsty than by watering them in bright sunshine. Watering morning and evening is better, which is what we always aimed to do on the nursery since evaporation is slower at those times and plants can consequently absorb more of it, but if a plant wilts due to dryness at the roots, cut your losses and give it a soak right there and then. It will be deeply grateful.

Rainwater or tap? Rainwater—or cooled boiled water—if you can, but most plants can cope with tap water, unless you live in an area of hard water and they are lime-haters. Potted azaleas and rhododendrons prefer rainwater, but many other plants are too tough to care.

New gardeners can start with easy-to-grow plants and progress to the trickier kinds. Today the moth orchid—phalaenopsis—is sold in garden centres and DIY stores all over the country. It is happy in any reasonably lit room, needs watering only once every two weeks and will keep its flowers for three or four months. Virtually indestructible, provided that you don't try to kill it with kindness. Gardenias, on the other hand, are absolute stinkers—insisting on a degree of humidity and a diet of rainwater, they will drop their flower buds and turn their leaves yellow if you do anything that is not to their liking. Geraniums are, I think, much more forgiving. Or pelargoniums, as I learned to call them.

LATIN NAMES ARE, for many aspiring gardeners, a nightmare. An impediment to the enjoyment of horticulture. To most of us a plant name is only of use when we want to tell someone else about it and make sure they know what we are on about. But that can give rise to confusion. Look up our native wild flowers in that wonderful book *The Englishman's Flora* by Geoffrey Grigson and you will discover that one man's lords and ladies (the common name for *Arum maculatum*) is another man's parson-in-the-pulpit. In Warwickshire they call it moll of the woods and in Wiltshire great dragon. Cross to the Isle of Wight and they'll talk about cocky baby, while in Devon they refer to it as cows and calves. It is pokers in Somerset and toad's meat in Cornwall. Confusing.

That's why we have these botanical names derived from Latin and Greek—a system devised by a Swede, Karl von Linné (Linnaeus) in the eighteenth century—so that gardeners and naturalists the world over could call a plant, or an animal for that matter, by the same name. It is a universal language, allowing, of course, for the vagaries of pronunciation. I went to the Bavarian Alps once and discovered that the plant I thought was *Saxifraga aizoides* was, to botanical-speaking Germans, *Sassifragga ite-so-eedez*. It took me ages to work out what they were on about. I hesitate to tell you how they pronounce the Latin name of the pine tree, *Pinus*.

In the days of my apprenticeship, armed with an increasing plant vocabulary from my City and Guilds course, I used to sit up late into the night, writing down these Latin names. The process was akin to writing lines as punishment. But it did help to din them into me and, having always loved words, it gave me an even richer form of language in which to indulge myself.

Some plant names have a delightful euphony: *Metasequoia glyptostroboides* and *Clematis viticella* 'Purpurea Plena Elegans' are two favourites. I love the swift and parasitic plangency of *Viscum album* (mistletoe) and the Greek scholar echoes of *Aesculus hippocastanum*, the horse chestnut.

I began to learn the descriptive qualities of these names. That the dahlia was named after Dr Dahl and so we should really say 'darlia', and that helianthus—sunflower—means quite literally 'sun-flower'. *Alba* means white and *nigra* black, *viridis* green and *rubra* red. Anything ending in '*ii*' is named after a man, and in '*ae*' a woman. The suffix '*ensis*' denotes a place. There are totally baffling epithets as well, with which to catch out friends who regard themselves as keen and well-informed gardeners. *Rhododendron ponticum* is a common plant, even a pest in many places. But ask for the meaning of its second name and you will invariably find the cognoscenti stumped. *Ponticum*? Simple—it means 'growing on the shores of the Black Sea'.

But there is a downside to plant names. It comes with age. There is a moment in life when they become more easily recalled than the names of people. It is a worrying time . . .

I CAN REMEMBER with crystal clarity the moment I discovered the particular brand of deep, saturating peacefulness that is to be found in a greenhouse. It is distinct from any other kind of enclosed tranquillity. It has not the cluttered dustiness of a garden shed, nor the lofty intimidation of a church or cathedral, though its peacefulness can rival both. It possesses a special kind of silence.

It is a distinct form of sanctuary where plants grow, concentrating their efforts on thriving, and so it has a kind of latent energy, possessed by no structure other than glass.

Not that my very first greenhouse was made of glass. That would have been way beyond my means. No, my first lean-to construction was erected during a weekend in the early 1960s against the stone wall of the midden at the bottom of the garden. This soot-blackened structure was really no more than a stone-built shed, built to store rubbish, but which had no use now other than to house old, rotting bikes. Its back wall abutted the garden and, facing east, was bathed in the morning sun. I reasoned that if I used that as the small wall at the far end of the greenhouse I could build away from it in a westerly direction, alongside the privet hedge, and have a greenhouse that faced south.

Over that weekend, I hammered and banged (a screwdriver not being a part of my armoury—much too slow) until a relatively sturdy framework had appeared. Holes were dug in the ground to support four upright posts, and a surplus bedhead and footboard were fastened to the two rear posts to make the back wall.

I was all set now—I had the framework in place and all I needed was something to cover it. For a rare moment in my life, maths came in useful. I calculated the amount of polythene I would need to cover the structure and took a trip to Hothersoll's in Leeds Road, where Mr Hothersoll cut off the required length with a large pair of scissors, rolled it up and handed it over in exchange for a few shillings. I cannot, even today, inhale the aroma of new polythene without being whisked back fifty years to that special weekend when I made my first greenhouse.

Back home I set to with drawing pins and covered the framework with the polythene. The door posed a bit of a problem. How to make it? I settled for a strip of polythene with a batten pinned along the bottom that could be rolled up to allow access and ventilation, and which could be held halfway up on a loop of string to allow a greater or lesser amount of air circulation. (It was this flimsy door that allowed in the neighbour's cat and so, a few weeks later, adjustments were made and I managed to acquire a timber frame which would make a proper hinged door.)

Cookie next door furnished me with rooted cuttings of busy Lizzies (she nipped them off her plants and popped them in jam jars on her windowsill, where they rooted in a few weeks), plantlets from her spider plant (chlorophytum—one of my first Latin names), a false castor oil and several geraniums from plant stalls at the church bazaar. Orange boxes and a couple of floorboards formed the staging, and I fastened a couple of shelves against the end wall to hold more plants as my collection grew. Woolworths supplied a small plastic watering can and a packet of Sangral which was, apparently, the last word in plant food.

But as any gardener will tell you, however large your greenhouse, you will always fill it. Mine was very small; it filled up very quickly. And it also filled my heart. You may remember, in *Citizen Kane*, the story of Rosebud. The great media baron, on his deathbed, having built a vast publishing empire and an enormous and luxurious mansion sitting in a grand estate called Xanadu, is heard to murmur 'Rosebud' as his life ebbs away. As the contents of his house are dispersed we see a small, painted sledge being thrown into the furnace. Upon it is painted the name 'Rosebud'. Citizen Kane was never happier than when he was a child, playing with that sledge—a time when life was true, and simple, and innocent—and that first little greenhouse will remain my personal 'Rosebud', so much pleasure did it give me.

But polythene is not durable, and the time came when I needed more space for my plants and a more permanent structure in which to grow them. I had started work now, and the enjoyment of looking after larger, proper greenhouses made of glass had turned my head. Mum and Dad gave the nod to a fully fledged greenhouse, if I could find one that I could afford.

I asked around at work. Albert's eyes lit up. 'I've got one on the allotment,' he said. 'I'm looking to sell it.'

'What's it like?' I asked, doing my best not to sound too excited, lest the price should escalate.

The man who started it all—Granddad Hardisty with his one-year-old grandson on his allotment by the River Wharfe.

In the greenhouse I built in the garden at Sunningdale. This photo, taken by Alison, appeared on the back cover of my first hardback book.

A young gardener's hero: Percy Thrower, television's original 'celebrity' gardener, first appeared in 'Gardening Club' in 1956.

Chelsea Flower Show 1985—Her Majesty T[he] Queen, a Gold Medal-winning garden, an[d] blazer and bow tie that won no prizes.

olving garden problems for BBC 'Breakfast ne' viewers in 1985, with presenter Nick oss trying to get a word in edgeways.

On the front cover of 'Amateur Gardening' magazine—what every celebrity gardener should have been wearing in 1983.

to the studio—fake sky, fake shed, but a nuine rugby shirt on the current affairs ogramme 'Nationwide', in 1980.

The Last Night of the Proms at the Royal Albert Hall—microphone and camera switched off so the presenter can give voice to 'Land of Hope and Glory'.

'It's sectional,' offered Albert.

I misheard him. Albert had sinus trouble and his speech was not always the clearest. I thought he'd said 'It's a Sexton,'—a proprietary brand of greenhouse I assumed. If it was a Sexton, I reasoned, it must be a proper greenhouse. A good one.

I went home and told Dad. 'We'd better go and have a look at it,' he said.

Albert had told me the precise location of his allotment on the banks of the river. Dad and I took the ten-minute walk and located it. The greenhouse was situated at one end, and it was clearly not of any brand known to man. It was constructed, both the sides and the flat roof, from old window frames. They were of different sizes and different colours, and some opened on hinges and some on sashes, which did give the structure a kind of rustic charm. But no one could have called it pretty. It suited Albert and his allotment, but I could not see Mum agreeing to let Albert's edifice—sectional or not—be erected in her garden.

Dad didn't say much. He didn't need to. I knew it was a non-starter and we walked home again, disconsolate.

I didn't mention it again at work for a while, except to tell Albert that his greenhouse was not quite what I was looking for. He seemed disappointed. Crestfallen in fact. And I had that terrible feeling that I still get when I am aware I have let somebody down. Disappointed them. For two pins I would have bought the greenhouse from him just to see him happy, but the five pounds he was asking was my entire budget. I felt a bit of a heel.

A few weeks later, Old Harry was working with me in the potting shed on the nursery taking geranium cuttings. 'You still looking for a greenhouse?' he asked.

'Yes.'

'You went to look at Albert's?'

'Yes.'

'Mmm. Not up to much?'

'Not really,' I muttered, guiltily.

'I might be getting rid of mine if you're still interested.'

'Oh. But I thought . . .' Harry was a keen gardener even in his spare time. He had won prizes at the local flower shows and liked nothing more than pottering in his greenhouse in Wyvil Crescent of an evening and at the weekend.

'With the missus in Arden Lea I'm going to have to move and I won't be able to take it with me.'

Arden Lea, once a large private house up Parish Ghyll Drive, was the local hospice, whose light and airy rooms looked out over Ilkley Moor. I was unsure what to say. 'I'm sorry,' was all I could manage.

My inept, brief condolences were brushed aside. In spite of the fact that Harry knew his wife was not long for this world, and that he would have to find a flat or a bungalow where he could live alone, he was not into self-pity, and that his beloved greenhouse could go to someone who would get as much pleasure out of it as he did seemed to be his main concern.

'I'll have to ask the wife. I'm going up tonight. I'll see what she says.' There the conversation ended, and Harry walked through from the potting shed into the greenhouse with another tray full of potted cuttings. I carried on, my head stuffed with a mixture of emotions—sympathy for Harry and his impending loss, and an anticipation of, at last, having my own proper place to grow things.

Harry's wife gave the go-ahead the following day and Dad and I went to look at the greenhouse. We found that it looked just like a greenhouse *should* look—painted dark green with a pointed roof and ventilators, and a proper door at one end. 'Better than Albert's?' asked Harry. My dad nodded and I handed over the five-pound note.

'You'll have to collect it, mind,' warned Harry.

'That's all right,' said Dad. 'I've got transport.'

I did wonder how it would fit in the Austin van, even when it came apart into sections. But I discovered that weekend that it was not the van that Dad had been referring to when he said that he had transport. It was a handcart.

Wyvil Crescent was about a mile from Nelson Road. At the age of sixteen I had reached a sensitive stage in my adolescence. It was hard enough to keep my head held high when watering the hanging baskets that hung from the lampposts in front of the smart shops along The Grove as my erstwhile fellow pupils, on their way to school, remarked 'Like the pinny!' But to have them accost me, on their way to football matches that Saturday morning, or going into town to hang out in the coffee bar, was more than flesh and blood could stand. We had to make that one-mile journey along one of Ilkley's busiest thoroughfares, with the handcart and its iron-rimmed wheels rattling along the tarmac. We pushed it, Dad and me, three times there and three times back. By the end of the morning, I awaited the onset of death by shame.

But that afternoon I forgot about the journey from hell and set about admiring the best five pounds I have ever spent. Not only had I acquired a greenhouse, but also all the paraphernalia that went with it. There were watering cans and syringes for spraying foliage or noxious chemicals. There were specially crafted aluminium dibbers and sieves of all sizes. There were one or two complicated-looking implements whose uses I had yet to divine, thermometers to show soil and air temperatures, and a propagating case with soil-warming cables and a real glass lid. An Aladdin paraffin heater would provide winter warmth (and a certain degree of heartache, I would later discover, in trying to regulate its performance), and a brand-new automatic ventilating arm would open the top window if I was away at work and the temperature rose too high.

Having caused me the greatest amount of embarrassment in living memory, Dad redeemed himself over the next couple of weeks by replacing the rotten timber beam at the foot of one end of the greenhouse, and by building the brick foundations on which it would sit. Within the month it was freshly painted in sparkling green livery, and up and running. I was sixteen, learning about gardening faster than a cat learns to climb, and master of my own destiny. Well, I had my own greenhouse, anyway. A proper one, with real glass in the windows and real ventilators that opened on hinges. And I bet Citizen Kane never had one of those.

# THE EDUCATION OF A GARDENER

They told me what I should do. Well, Ken did. 'You'll go to day release now—for your City and Guilds—and then to college for a year full-time. Askham Bryan probably; near York. Then to Kew, Wisley or the Royal Botanic Garden Edinburgh—they do a three-year diploma course. And then on to The Grotto . . .'

'The what?' I asked. It sounded like something Father Christmas sat in.

'The Grotto. It's the headquarters of the Institute of Park and Recreation Administration. Near Reading. Down south. Then you can become a Parks Superintendent, like Mr Mutlow.' There was a twinkle in his eye.

The whole thing came as a surprise to my dad when I went home and related this ten-year plan, for that's what it would mean—a five-year apprenticeship, a year at college, three at Kew, Wisley or Edinburgh and a final year at the odd-sounding 'Grotto'. You could become a brain surgeon in less time.

'Oh, I see,' was all Dad could manage by way of an opinion, having thought that 'a trade' was the best recommendation he could offer his son, his father and grandfather having gardened with only muscle power and determination to their name.

Mum murmured, 'We'll see', and it was left at that.

But before any of those aspirations could be made reality, the most immediate was my enrolment at the Shipley Art and Technical Institute near Bradford to study for my City and Guilds Stage 1 in Horticulture on one day and one evening a week. It was all a bit scary. But at least I would be learning about plants, which I was keen to do, rather than French verbs, which I wasn't.

Up until that point my performance, academically, had been distinctly average. I had managed the A stream in secondary school, but my class position was usually in the lower half of the thirty-odd pupils that made up class 4A.

I shot into the top two or three at Shipley Art and Technical Institute, a grim-looking Victorian building in Saltaire erected, according to a guidebook, 'in 1853 by Sir Titus Salt (d. 1876), the first man to manufacture Alpaca woollen fabrics in England. The station is close to the mills, and equally near is the church, built in the Byzantine style.'

The Institute was run in suitably Byzantine style by a little man called Taylor whom we rudely referred to as 'Hitler' though, to be honest, his deputy Mr Hilton had the moustache. Fortunately we students had little to do with him, meeting him only on our day of enrolment, and subsequently only ever seeing him through the plate-glass window of the reception area just inside the great oak doors of the Victorian building where he addressed his secretaries surrounded by great wall charts. He looked like a pocket-sized general planning a campaign.

Our lectures—on everything from 'Decorative Horticulture' to 'Soils and Manures', 'Calculations' and 'Fruit and Vegetable Growing'—took place either in lofty gloss-painted classrooms, like those I had left behind at junior school, or in the windowless basement of the building. Only in the third year of my course was the patch of waste ground at the rear, which overlooked Salt's Mill, turned into a garden of sorts.

The students—all male—were a mixed bag, drawn mostly from local authorities in the Bradford area. While intellectual pursuits might not have been high on their agenda they were, for the most part, a pleasant bunch, their broad Yorkshire accents echoing around the cavernous classrooms like booming bass drums.

We'd turn up at nine in the morning for lectures, break for coffee around 10.30 a.m. and then be allowed an hour for lunch at 12.30, which gave us just enough time—the three or four of us who thought we were more sophisticated than the rest—to nip down the road to the centre of Shipley so that we could patronise the Lai-Seng Chinese restaurant, situated on the first floor of the small and newly built shopping centre. A Chinese restaurant! At fifteen! They did a three-course meal for half a crown (twelve and a half pence) and the first course, without fail, was the best chicken soup I had ever tasted. We hadn't heard of monosodium glutamate back then.

In coffee and tea breaks the conversations turned to all manner of things unrelated to horticulture, if not to propagation. Keith, from a park somewhere in the depths of Bradford, sidled up to a couple of us one day and asked if we'd ever seen people 'at it'.

'What do you mean?' I asked.

'You know. Screwing . . .'

'No! 'Course I haven't.'

I think he knew from the nervous smile that I was telling the truth. Looking around furtively, he pulled a small, grubby envelope from his inside pocket. 'Look at these,' he said, laying down a series of small black-and-white photographs on the desk in front of me. There were just eight of them—these were the days of the Brownie 127, long before the world had gone digital. The photos showed a man and a woman in various positions on a three-piece suite. And on the hearth rug in front of the settee.

'Good, aren't they?' asked Keith.

I wasn't sure whether he meant the standard of photography or the technique of the couple involved. The best I could manage was 'Goodness!', which seemed a rather tame response to my first glimpse of what I suppose was pornography. I did think that some of the positions must have been uncomfortable and a bit risky.

This was not the only kind of daring that day release introduced me to. While not quite of the winkle-picker and drainpipe-trouser generation of ten years previously, I like to think that my dress sense developed in those first years at work, if not always for the better or with parental approval. The secondhand army combat jacket that I bought in Otley with my first week's wages was hastily returned and swapped for a couple of serviceable shirts.

I did, though, manage to get away with buying hipster trousers, a revelation in green tweed. Finished off with a wide brown leather belt, a pair of Hush Puppy Chelsea boots and a purple polo-necked jumper, I looked the bee's knees, I thought. The floppy fringe completed the picture. The only thing I lacked was transport. I had my bike, but longer journeys meant travelling by bus or train.

My bus journey to Shipley was a dull affair and it took the best part of an hour to cover the twelve miles up hill and down dale. Other lads had mopeds, and I envied quite desperately Dave Hollingsworth's Honda 50 with its scarlet and cream coachwork. But Chris Rigden had a proper motorbike, all chrome and throbbing saddle. I know it throbbed because he used to give me a lift as far as the bus station in Shipley, with the aim of making my journey home a little shorter. Each time I got on the back (without a crash helmet since they were not then compulsory) and wrapped my arms round his waist before he roared off down the road, I was convinced that I was about to die.

I never did get any motorised transport, in spite of the fact that I passed my driving test first time at the age of seventeen. I was quite desperate for something better than a bike, but as my father never tired of saying, 'It's not buying a car that costs money, it's keeping it on the road.'

I persuaded Dad to let me borrow his car now and then—a lumpy old Borgward with a column gear change whose row of unmarked buttons on the dashboard I had furnished with Letraset to remind me what they all did. At least I learned to double declutch on it, even if its back seat was the venue for little more than a chaste peck with a very occasional girlfriend. Nothing at all worth snapping with a Brownie 127.

Of all the vocations—and it is a vocation, not a job—that of gardener makes a man more aware of the seasons than any other. We have, as a race, lost the joys of what a monastic friend of mine calls 'the postponement of gratification'.

We can eat strawberries in December now, if we want, but having been picked before they were ripe and travelled from the Far East, their flavour cannot compete with a fresh and sun-ripened berry picked from the garden in June. I want parsnips and swedes in winter, not asparagus, which belongs to April. I look forward to the first raspberries, in spite of the fact that as a fruit they freeze well and I can, if I wish, enjoy them all the year round.

Gardeners know the seasons of the year not just for the crops they produce, but also for the effect they have on our daily work. Bitter days of winter mean more layers of clothing and frozen fingers—so cold that when run under a hot tap to thaw out they cause us such agony that we cry out in pain. It is better to let them warm up slowly than risk the gardener's version of 'the bends'.

On the nursery, when outside work had to be carried out in winter—the cleaning of greenhouse glass, for instance, or the repairing of broken panes—we would wrap ourselves up in as many layers as we could. The top one was always a tatty old gabardine overcoat, once fawn, now spattered with assorted colours of paint. It was one of several that hung behind the door of the potting shed and whose once-trim tails had so often been caught on nails and torn into shreds that Mickey and I, astride the greenhouse ridge on a windy day, looked like two distressed moths, our wings flapping in the breeze as we tried to keep our balance.

When digging in winter with the smooth-bladed spades from the toolshed (there was rivalry for the best one, worn to a shining heart shape by years of use), we would gradually shed the layers until, on even a chill February day, we were warm as toast in just shirtsleeves, digging the lumpen aromatic manure from the local stables into every spit with the eagerness and competitive spirit of youth, and wiping the sweat from our brows with our forearms as we stretched upright every few minutes to look at the rolling main of freshly cultivated earth that we left in our wake.

What Mickey had in muscle power, I could only match in wiriness, but in the space of that first year on the nursery I grew to five feet nine inches under glass, and developed a series of upper-back and shoulder muscles that are still as hard as iron.

Spring would bring a rash of weed growth to nursery paths and the beds of soil where wallflowers were sown and shrubs grown on. The once-bare earth would come to life in a haze of lime-green chickweed and yellow-dotted groundsel, and the race for survival would begin between cultivated plants and interlopers. The spade was back on its rusty nail now, and the argument would be over the favourite Dutch hoe.

Working backwards through the rows, we would slice off the annual weeds where their stems met their roots, with the words of Lennie Best, our 'Fruit and Vegetable' lecturer at the Institute, ringing in our ears—'Don't push it in too deep, lad—skim it across the surface. You're cuttin' 'em off not diggin' 'em up!'

The weeds, severed in their prime, would be left on the surface to shrivel up in the sun, if we had timed it properly. If we hadn't and a shower of rain followed, we'd be back out there a few days later skimming off the ones that had rerooted.

On the nursery, spring meant seed-sowing in tray after tray of seed compost. I won't bore you with the formula, but Mickey and I had to mix that, too. Begonias would be the first seeds to benefit from our mixture—dust-fine seeds, fox-brown and glossy, worth more, ounce for ounce, than gold, said Ron.

After these *Begonia semperflorens* came the antirrhinums, the French and African marigolds, the lobelia and alyssum, the tobacco plants and the petunias, giving us week after week of pricking out seedlings into wooden trays—six in one direction, seven in the other—forty-two plants to a tray. The trays came by the dozen from the local greengrocer. Once they held tomatoes—

they had 'Holland' on the sides in bright-red letters—but now they held serried ranks of embryo plants, which, when they grew up, would decorate the town with their jolly summer flowers.

The empty staging in some of our thirteen greenhouses was filled with hundreds of trays now, each sporting a rash of eager young seedlings. But some were not so eager to grow, and keeled over at compost level. Fungus disease. Damping off. We'd prise the lid off a tin of Cheshunt Compound, a lavender-grey powder that smells strongly of ammonia—one whiff was as effective at bringing you round after a night on the tiles as a bottle of smelling salts. It was mixed with water—a teaspoonful to a one-gallon can—and the pale purple brew used to dowse the affected trays. I was never convinced that it worked; it was rather like locking the stable door after the horse had bolted.

In between the pricking out of seedlings we were potting up literally thousands of rooted pelargonium cuttings. They, too, would be bedded out around the town come summer, and our greenhouses were now bursting with plants, not only on the staging, but also slung from shelves arranged on brackets above our heads on either side of the path, and in trays along the floor.

With the lengthening days came an even greater pressure on our time and a greater likelihood of plants drying out. The sun's rays were hot now, even in Yorkshire, and Mickey and I were stripped to the waist on the sunniest days, competing to see who would have the best tan by the end of summer. Mickey always won—thicker skin, I told him.

Our greenhouses had to be shaded to prevent the plants from being scorched, especially sun-sensitive species like ferns and hydrangeas, where one day of brilliant sunshine could dry their foliage to a crisp and ruin a whole year's work. We had no blinds and no sophisticated forms of ventilation. The roof vents were on simple metal stays and we had to judge how wide to open them, depending on the degree of cloud cover and the strength of the wind. On really warm days the door at the end of each greenhouse would be wedged open, too, except for the fernery, which was kept, always, as humid as a Turkish bath, its doors closed and just the merest crack of air allowed to creep through its ventilators.

'Go and put some air on,' was a frequent instruction in summer. That and damping down the floors of our greenhouses with water at two-hourly intervals was our only way of lowering the temperature, apart from shading them with a pale green version of whitewash by the name of Summer Cloud. It came in a green tin with an antiquated design, showing a man painting out the sun in a summer sky. Mickey and I would mix a bucketful apiece, whisking the green powder into water, and, armed with that and a long-handled brush, set about painting the glass of our greenhouses with a thin layer of 'green-wash' each April. From then on we could not see out of our greenhouses, and neither could others see in, until, in September, we had the deadly job of cleaning the stuff off with a scrubbing brush and a sharp jet of water.

Whenever the weather was warm and sunny and we had a lot of potting up to do, Mickey and I would carry a portable wooden potting bench outdoors, position it so we had our backs to the sun, and then load it up with compost and pots. The pressure was relieved a little when the men had taken away our trays of bedding plants—trailers full of them distributed round the town's flowerbeds and bedded out in a manic four-week period at the end of May and on into June. Now we would have to clean out our greenhouses and ready them for the pelargonium cuttings. This was the least popular job of the year—scrubbing the white-painted glazing bars with a disinfectant mixture that ran down your arms, then your body, finally and inevitably making its way into your underwear and down your legs.

The shingle on the benches would be scooped up into sieves and rinsed with a hosepipe and the central path of each greenhouse scrubbed free of green algae with a stiff, long-handled broom—a job that was undertaken every Friday throughout the year, along with liquid feeding in spring and summer.

From July to September the geranium cuttings would be brought in by Old Harry and Young Harry, having been cut from the plants now growing happily in the town's flowerbeds and bundled into great sheets of hessian. The two Harrys would carry them over their shoulders like a pair of Father Christmases. By the end of the summer, we'd need to have taken fifteen thousand of them to ensure that next year's display was every bit as good as this year's. Some we rooted in trays, others at the rate of five to a four-and-a-half inch clay flowerpot, but always the compost was topped with half an inch of sharp river sand to help guard against rotting off.

Autumn meant chrysanthemums. They would come indoors from their summer sojourn on the ash bed and need staking, tying and disbudding as well as regular watering and weekly feeding with the stinking manure-water. The newly divided pots of ferns would ask for tender nurturing and high humidity to 'get them away', and the thousands of geranium cuttings would have to be monitored for an outbreak of 'blackleg', a fungus disease that would rot off their stem bases with dire consequences. The sharp sand might help, but it did not guarantee success.

Bulbs would be potted up—narcissi and hyacinths for a spring display in the town hall, and the flower-filled troughs from inside the town hall and the library would be replenished with fresh new flowering plants and ferns every week, regardless of the season.

And then it would be winter. A quieter time, but always with some kind of job to do—cleaning, repairing, picking off dead leaves and flowers and restaging plants on their benches. There was always the boiler to keep topped up and clinkered, and if all else failed, there were flowerpots to wash in cold muddy water and seed trays to scrub clean while we waited for the turn of the year and the days to become longer.

From November through to February it would, for the most part, be dark when we started work and dark when we finished, and on some days the sky would remain the colour of an old army blanket and we would be grateful for the warmth our greenhouses provided. This was the time of year when we, the trio of nursery workers, knew we had the best time of it.

# SATURDAY JOBS

Expecting a gardener to like every aspect of gardening is like expecting a musician to like all music. Only a liar could claim to do so. I can't think of many gardening jobs I really hate—except the predictable ones like battling bindweed and mare's-tail. And growing gladioli. And pampas grass. And standard roses. But cultivating someone else's soil requires a particular kind of dedication.

It was Dad who got me into it, thinking, not unreasonably, that I could do with a few extra shillings to eke out my wages. He had been plumbing for the owner of a house up Rupert Road—one of the smarter residential thoroughfares on the Middleton side of Ilkley—for some time, and the man had indicated that he was a little short-staffed in the gardening department.

It was not a large garden. The area to the rear of the smart, large semi was laid to lawn and flanked by flower borders. In front of the house was a short tarmac drive and a shrubbery where holly and Portugal laurel, euonymus and olearia did their best to grow in dry, root-ridden soil.

I turned up at 9 a.m. on the first Saturday morning—I would not need any tools, I'd been told—and the owner of the house, a tall, kindly-looking gentleman, greeted me and showed me round. I admired the borders and the lawn and asked what he would like me to do. He took me to the front of the house, where the deep gloom of the shrubbery lowered over all, and asked me if I would mind 'tidying it up'. He did not need anything cut down, he said, just the soil worked over.

Every Saturday morning, for the next few months, I beavered away in the stygian darkness with a bent garden fork, trying to rid the grey dust of its dreary carpet of weeds. I fought to find some kind of satisfaction in the job, but there is not a lot to be had in a death-defying shrubbery. Did he want me to have a go in the back garden? I asked. The answer was negative. 'No. Just keep going in the shrubbery if you would.'

Each week a few more weeds would have reared their heads and battle would commence once more. I never did get to see the back garden, with its lawn and herbaceous borders—the 'regular' gardener who turned up midweek had the satisfaction of caring for them.

The only bright moment in the morning would be the appearance of a large cup of coffee and two biscuits. It would be left for me in the utility room, which could be entered from the outside of the house; there was no need for me to remove my wellies since newspaper had been laid on the floor. After three hours of labour I would be presented with my half-crown and would cycle wearily home to begin my weekend proper.

Ken, aware of my Saturday job and of the little financial gain it offered, asked me if I could help out with his own part-time job for a widowed lady up Cowpasture Road on the other side of town. One evening a week should do it. I was not keen, but felt obliged to accept, simply to avoid letting him down.

I don't think the widowed lady took too kindly to a young lad filling in when the Parks Foreman himself could not attend. She was decidedly sniffy, and her housekeeper even more so. But here at least I got to work among the rosebeds, rather than in the shrubbery, and I was even allowed to bed out in early summer. But she never seemed satisfied with what I had done. 'I'm not sure that Kenneth would have done it like that.' She never called him Ken; always Kenneth.

I smiled my most indulgent smile, and went on wielding the rusty trowel she had given me to work with (the better one was reserved for Kenneth), committing the petunias to the bare earth that bordered the roses, and trying not to mutter profanities under my breath.

I battled on for a year and did my best to prune the roses properly, keep the lawn edges tidy and deadhead anything that looked faded. In the end the old lady took to her bed, and it was not long before Ken told me that my services would no longer be required. I can't say that I was sorry, and from that day to this I have steadfastly avoided digging anybody else's soil. Except for *Ground Force*, of course. But that was different.

IT'S CALLED *Simple Gardening*, it's by R. P. Faulkner and it was published by W. H. and L. Collingridge the year after I was born, 1950. It is not an impressive book to look at, and I remember thinking it a bit dull when I took it down from the little bookshelf at home and opened the first of its one hundred pages. It's a small, slim volume with four intricately penned line drawings on the pale green dust jacket—taking a chrysanthemum cutting, building a dry-stone wall, using a besom to sweep loam into the cracks between freshly laid turf, and planting and staking a tree. There are no photographs inside, just more line drawings, and the author's credentials are given on the front flap: 'Mr Faulkner became head gardener at the School of Agriculture, Nottingham, and here became well qualified to write on the practice of the art of gardening. In this book he explains clearly to the beginner' . . . that was me, so my ears pricked up . . . 'how to choose tools and dig ground and then how to plan and maintain his garden. Lawns, hedges and paths, which are the backbone of any garden design, are discussed in detail. A selection of plants for the shrub garden, perennial border and rose garden is given and the suitability of plants to provide flowers for cutting is considered. Fruit and vegetable culture are fully described. Throughout the book the text is amplified by clear line drawings, plans and diagrams.'

And all in a hundred and sixty pages. I read and absorbed it, noting, in my youthful keenness to do everything by the book, that rosebushes 'should be planted twenty-one inches apart', that quality tools 'are stocked by all good-class ironmongers', and that most pests could be 'controlled by spraying with DDT'. I bought a puffer pack.

Reading it now sends a shiver down my spine—not the recommendation of DDT, long since banned as being as much of a health hazard to humans as aphids, but because it can spirit me back and remind me of the excitement I felt when I first read it fifty years ago. *Simple Gardening* was the start of a lifelong addiction to books—not just gardening books—that has continued unabated.

In their eagerness to promote the speed and comprehensiveness of information that can be provided by the Internet, its advocates forget one thing—the physical pleasure of books. The tactile thrill—and it really is a thrill—of actually holding one, new or old, fine leather binding or glossy dust wrapper, light or weighty. Books also have their own smell; the acrid, acidic tang of a Victorian volume; the synthetic aroma of fine colour plates.

*Simple Gardening* was not my very first gardening book. That distinction goes to Beatrix Potter's *The Tale of Peter Rabbit*, which I have always thought of as a gardening book. All those descriptions of vegetables, and the drawing of Mr McGregor's boot kicking over the geranium. The images have stayed with me. So, too, has the delight at feeling the glossy paper as we turned the pages—me and Mum, or me and Dad—when I was six or seven, in the twilight of the back bedroom at Nelson Road.

From Mr Faulkner I graduated to Mr Thrower, having watched him on the BBC's *Gardening Club* every Friday night, when he hung his jacket on a hook on the back of the greenhouse door—the greenhouse with no glass in it. But then it was in a studio. I knew it must be, because the sun was always shining and there was never a cloud in the sky. And the soil in his flowerbed always had the texture of John Innes potting compost.

*Percy Thrower's Encyclopaedia of Gardening*, with its glossy orange spine, shone down from my bookshelves. I used this A–Z reference book all the time. Then there were the slightly strange 'Expert' books that I could buy from Woolworth's for one shilling and sixpence (seven and a half pence). *Be Your Own Lawn Expert* by Dr D. G. Hessayon fell apart in the end. The 'Expert' books were not as thick then as they are now—they were more like booklets than books, but they were great value—and packed with information laid out in a unique 1950s, almost comic-book style that was soaked up by a young lad eager to learn.

Day release at the Institute meant the acquisition of more serious volumes—*Lowson's Textbook of Botany* and *Farm Machinery*, by Harris, Muckle and Shaw, the names so fitting they almost seem made up. They were worthy and earnest—reference books, rather than the sort you read for pleasure.

It was much later that I discovered the works of my now favourite gardening writer, Christopher Lloyd. That other great gardener, Beth Chatto, did not start writing until the 1970s and although Vita Sackville-West was penning weekly pieces for the *Observer* as early as the 1950s, we took the *Daily Express*. The likelihood of me discovering the works of the chatelaine of Sissinghurst was about as great as me discovering Proust.

What I did discover were the monographs—books on a single type of plant. To have a book that deals in depth with magnolias, pelargoniums or lavenders is akin to possessing that knowledge, or at least having it at your fingertips. So it was that I came to be the proud possessor of *A Handbook of Crocus and Colchicum for Gardeners* by E. A. Bowles, *The Old Shrub Roses* by Graham Stuart Thomas and *Snowdrops and Snowflakes* by Sir Frederick Stern. These later volumes were acquired when I had a little more money and experience, and felt that I had 'grown out of' general gardening books. It did not cross my mind that I would one day write them myself.

The collection of wild flowers that I made at junior school, sandwiched in a scrapbook between the sheets of tissue paper that had been used to wrap our daily bread, and which won me the only prize in my entire scholastic career, was founded on *The Observer's Book of Wild Flowers*. For my twenty-first birthday Uncle Bert and Auntie Edie bought me the Rev. W. Keble Martin's *The Concise British Flora in Colour*. Written by a Devon clergyman, it represented sixty years of painstaking watercolour painting of almost one and a half thousand wild flowers of the British Isles, not singly on separate sheets, but woven together family by family. The pages displayed not just the colour and beauty of the flowers, their descriptions and locations, but also the relationships between them.

In addition to learning the Latin names of the plants, I was now learning how they fitted into the greater scheme of things—what was considered to be related to what, and those mouthfuls that were family names, which usually ended in *aceae*—*Ranunculaceae*, the buttercup family, *Iridaceae*, the iris family and *Papilionaceae*, the pea family. Of course, even here there were exceptions to the rule (one of the frustrations of botany)—*Umbelliferae* or cow parsley, *Labiatae* or dead nettles, and *Compositae*, daisies—along with the plates at the back of the book that were monochrome rather than colour, perhaps because of their assumed dullness to the common man—plates of *Gramineae*, the grasses.

But these family names, along with genus and species, variety and cultivar, wormed their way into my affections and my conversations with the ease and regularity that a social climber might litter their conversation with the names of dukes and duchesses. Botanical name-dropping. Comforting and reassuring. They gave me, I suppose, the kind of satisfaction that the early learning of dictionary words had given me. Not that there was anyone in particular to impress with them, except myself. To others in gardening they were common currency—no one was much impressed if you knew that snapdragons belonged to the family *Scrophulariaceae*, though occasionally I could discover a more unusual plant family that the other students would not know existed and which contained perhaps only a single genus. Few know, for instance, that *Thesium humifusum*, the bastard toadflax, belongs to the family *Santalaceae*, or that the horned pondweed, *Zannichellia palustris*, is in its own family, *Zannichelliaceae*. Mind you, even fewer care.

There is, however, comeuppance for those who rest on their laurels. Botanists are forever changing plant names as research reveals hitherto undiscovered relationships or species that have been previously described as something else. For all I know, *Zannichelliaceae* has by now been lumped in with *Potamogetonaceae*. If you really want to know, go and look it up in a book. You won't, though, will you? You'll go straight to the Internet.

Me? I'll stick with the Rev. W. Keble Martin. I know where I am with him.

THE THING ABOUT aspirations is that they start small and grow out of all proportion. When I was fifteen I wanted nothing more than to garden day in, day out. So why then, after three years of working on the nursery, did I feel the need to follow Ken Wilson's advice and embark on that mapped-out career path—college, Kew, Wisley or Royal Botanic Garden Edinburgh and that strange place called The Grotto? The answer is the same whatever the career—because it offered a challenge.

Oh, there were moments of great fear; more than one occasion when I could have stayed where I was, doing what I was doing. Why rock the boat when you are happy with the present voyage? Well, because you don't know if you will enjoy what is round the corner even more than where you are. Because you need to be stretched. And although we all make mistakes, the errors we generally regret are the errors of omission rather than commission. At least if you do something and it goes wrong there is no more 'what if?' That was my reasoning. I think.

The horticultural college most local to me was Askham Bryan, near York. Like all horticultural colleges it majored in agriculture, and so the student clientele would be a colourful mixture of farmers and gardeners or, as I was now learning to say by way of giving myself respectability, horticulturists.

I applied, as instructed, at the age of eighteen (so biddable I was, back then), with a view to starting a one-year full-time residential course that autumn, which would lead to the National Certificate in Horticulture.

I was called for an interview and turned up at the college—an imposing, if not daunting, brick-built pile that stands at the top of a ridge on the main road to York—one blustery spring day in 1967. My recollection of the day is hazy, but I do remember sitting in front of Lance Gilling, the tall, bespectacled principal who had the friendly but distinguished air of an agricultural patrician, and talking about bell-ringing. He asked me nothing, as far as I can remember, about gardening, sorry, horticulture, just about ringing bells, which I had obviously put on my application form under 'hobbies'.

I thought our chat went rather well. But I didn't get in.

The letter informed me that impressive as my interview had been (I had obviously acquitted myself well on the campanology front), it was felt that older applicants should be given the opportunity to attend this year. The college would be prepared to take me the following autumn, when I had reached the age of nineteen.

I was a bit disappointed. And in order to make absolutely sure of a place in the last year of my teens, in 1968, I applied to another college, Oaklands in Hertfordshire, which also ran courses in both agriculture and horticulture and which specialised in glasshouse work. I have absolutely no recollection of the interview, except that the subject of bell-ringing was not touched upon.

It can't have gone too badly. A few weeks later I received a letter explaining that I had been accepted by Oaklands and, if I chose, I could begin the course that autumn. I did choose. I accepted the place, and left home on the last day of September 1968 to begin my new life at college.

There was no leaving 'do' at the nursery. Just mumbled good wishes and nods. Old Harry said, 'Aye, well, good luck to you,' as he cycled slowly up the drive of the nursery and out of sight. Young Harry managed, 'Well done, lad. You'll come back and see us, won't you? No point in saying "goodbye" properly.'

# LOOK AND LEARN

I was worried, more than anything, about being homesick. For goodness' sake! I was nineteen! But the longest I had been away from home until then had been a weekend camping trip to Pateley Bridge with the Scouts when I was eleven, and that had not been significantly successful.

At least I would have a bit of space to myself. Every student—a hundred-odd of us, with only half a dozen of them women—had a room of their own. Two-thirds of the intake were agricultural students, most of them farmers' sons, a fair proportion with red hair. The rest of us were there to study horticulture—mainly commercial, although a few of us were enrolled on the attractively titled 'Amenity Horticulture' course. We were the arty lot who liked growing plants because we thought they looked pretty, rather than because selling them could make us money.

Before the 1969 riots in Paris, which changed student life for ever, so we are told, those of us in colleges this side of the Channel were ruled with a rod of iron. Not for us the freedom of university students. We were treated, to all intents and purposes, like pupils at a private boarding school. The college had responsibility for us and therefore made sure we were under control at all times.

The college grounds were basically a large farm—acres of cereals, cattle, pigs and the like, which were the province of the agricultural students—and then the glasshouses, orchards and ornamental grounds, which belonged to the 'hortics'. Here, in enormous 'aeroplane' glasshouses—the sort with span after span of glass ridges—were grown tomatoes and cucumbers, all-year-round chrysanthemums and carnations, pot plants and other 'protected' commercial crops. There was a smaller nursery area where a wide range of ornamental plants was grown and propagated. Apples and pears graced the sweeping grassy rides of the orchards, and the areas closest to the college were laid out with beds and borders replete with everything from subtropical bedding to alpines, from trees and shrubs to flowering bulbs.

We were up at 6.30 a.m. to be ready for 'practical work' from 7 until 8. Here we undertook operations that varied in their monotony from washing leeks in cold, muddy water and packing them for market, to cutting and defoliating cauliflowers, packing tomatoes into trays, grading apples and pears or digging over vacant ground. There was nothing too taxing at this early hour, lest the half-asleep students should make a mess of it and cock up the reputation of the college in Covent Garden market where our crops were sold.

At 8.15 a.m. we breakfasted in the cavernous dining hall. By 9 a.m. we were on the move to the lecture rooms. Here we would be given the information that would arm us for a life in horticulture. We learned the Ministry of Agriculture's blueprint for growing tomatoes (doled out in deeply serious tones as though we were being schooled in breaking the Enigma code), and some weeks later, when that was completed, cucumbers.

There were lectures on botany from a lady who looked and carried herself rather like the Queen. Her hair was always immaculately coiffed in the style of the monarch, and her vowels were rather strangulated, so that there was a strange yet sensual quality to her pronunciation of xylem and phloem, mitosis and meiosis. To listen to her explaining the behaviour of chromosomes was a bit like hearing the Queen talking about sex.

The mycology lecturer was at the other end of the spectrum—a bouncing academic, fresh from university, he could make the driest facts about fungi seem as vital as the six o'clock news. Not that he always had a satisfactory answer to our questions. 'Why do some fungi have gills and others don't?' I asked. 'Why do you have five toes on each foot and not six?' came the rejoinder.

In 'crop protection' lectures we were apprised of the complex life cycles of the bugs, beasts and bacteria that would be likely to attack our charges, and of the full range of poisons with which we could assault them. Some of these had to be applied via spray lances with the operator wearing a space suit powered by a roaring machine that pumped air into it. There would be no stamping out of the flames on little piles of nicotine shreds here. Rachel Carson's *Silent Spring* was handed round by subversive students who had the courage of their convictions.

Along with lectures on top fruit, soft fruit, climate and soils, records and accounts (oh, how I yawned during those, the only bright spot being the red ink we used on the debit side of the page), glasshouse flower crops, ornamental horticulture, nursery practice and glasshouse construction, we were schooled in the use of machinery. The lecturer here was Mr Telford, a balding, middle-aged technocrat who loved nothing more than explaining the intricate workings of a Satchwell Duo-tronic Control for glasshouse temperature modulation. It is to his undying credit that I can remember what it was called. I fail him, alas, in forgetting quite how it worked.

Mr Telford was a softly spoken gent who always wore a white coat, even in his oily workshop. Deciding that we had quite enough pressure on us when it came to examinations, at the end of each of the three terms he would show us how to reverse a tractor with a trailer, or how to draw a diagram of a Vicon fertiliser spreader, and examine us on our efforts there and then while the operation was fresh in our minds. I have never used a Vicon fertiliser spreader since, but I can reverse my car with a trailer and I can also wire a three-pin plug, for which I owe Mr Telford a greater debt of thanks than I owe the lecturer who fed me the Ministry of Agriculture's blueprint for growing tomatoes, which, forty years on, is now hopelessly out of date.

After a hearty lunch, we would have an afternoon of practical work in one of the various departments—the nursery, ornamental areas or fruit and market garden, where we were taught the practical skills of growing plants. True enough, I had learned a lot during my four years on the nursery, but there were always fresh techniques to acquire, from sharpening a knife properly, to whip and tongue grafting, budding roses and stratifying seeds. These terms, previously just words in a book, now took on real meaning.

I surprised myself by actually taking on board information at an astonishing rate. I had begun to do so at Shipley Tech, but now the learning was full-time it seemed easier to get the momentum going. The fog began to clear, and the mind I had thought incapable of proper reasoning or even of remembering facts seemed, like a muscle almost, to benefit from the exercise and increase its capacity.

I relished the chance to learn the life cycle of pests and diseases, and to bottle leatherjackets and wireworms in formaldehyde, the better to identify them. I won a prize for the best dried flower collection (my junior school training having given me a head start and the collecting bug coming to the fore) and spent night after night of private study (6 till 8 p.m.) in my tiny cell writing down botanical names and committing them, and the plants they described, to memory.

One afternoon a week was set aside for sport. Bearing in mind my scholastic sporting record, and my slightness of build, I was not a natural choice for games. I did try rugby once, but within half an hour I had my head crushed between the scrum half and the goalpost. The concussion sealed my fate—I settled instead for cross-country running. I enjoyed the solitude, if not the scenery, which I found flat and dull compared with the moorland runs of Yorkshire. But it got me out into the fresh air and cleared my head.

After high tea between 5.30 and 6 p.m.—when the rush for extra chips seemed to be the nightly athletic activity—and private study until 8, we were allowed out until 10.30 p.m. This usually meant a walk of a mile or so to the nearest pub, the Bunch of Cherries. There began my introduction to the social life of the student; to beer and skittles, girls and the way to handle them.

IF I THOUGHT that college life would offer rich female pickings I was about to embark on a steep learning curve. There were 101 students in the 1968 intake at the Hertfordshire College of Agriculture and Horticulture. Just seven of them were female. But then one should always look close to home to start with, even if the competition is fierce. Not that the seven were exactly magnificent, though one of them did possess a brooding presence strangely reminiscent of Yul Brynner and James Coburn. She was one of the four farming girls (by far the most glamorous of the seven) but, alas, already attached to the hunkiest of the agrics.

The girl in question had shoulder-length fair hair and an hourglass figure, together with a liking for wearing a black bra beneath a white blouse. Whether they had been together before they embarked on a college education I am not sure, but they were confident enough in each other's company for him not to mind when she pounced on a weedy agric in the dining hall and gave him a love bite on his neck by way of a joke.

One down, six to go. But that makes the situation sound more hopeful than it really was. For a start, one of the six was at least thirty-five, and when you are nineteen, thirty-five seems as old as God. Then there was the extrovert. Well spoken and exuberant, with the proportions of a cottage loaf and the bounciness of a beach ball, she seemed to have stepped straight from an Angela Brazil schoolgirl saga—'Winnie, the terror of the fourth'. Pillow fights and midnight feasts that majored on iced buns were probably her speciality. A big girl. You could do a lot with her. One of our number did. He looked exhausted every morning.

The tiniest student of them all kept herself to herself. A short, stocky girl with short, stocky hair, I hardly remember her speaking and she certainly evinced no interest in men.

There were two girls on the sandwich course, which involved one year in college, one year working outside in the industry and one year back at college. They were embarking on their final year now. One had been to Amsterdam and seemed incapable of beginning a sentence without the phrase 'When I was in Holland . . .'. I'm not sure where the other had been. They were both pleasant enough, but the confidence they had accrued by travelling the world (all right then, Holland) made them a touch intimidating. Fortunately one of them was hitched up to a fellow student and the other had met . . . a Dutchman.

One left. Quite a looker she was, fine featured with expressive hands. But emotionally fragile. You could be talking to her one minute, her face a picture of joy, and the next her features would crumple and she would burst into tears and dash from the room. No one quite worked out why. Within a month the poor girl had disappeared due to some kind of mental breakdown. We were all very sympathetic. But lonely. There was nothing for it but to look further afield.

The nearest field was the Bunch of Cherries. The landlord had two daughters whose thighs . . . well . . . whose thighs were memorable, maybe on account of being encased in white patent-leather boots. Of the ninety-odd male students at Oaklands, not one claimed to have been successful with the landlord's daughters, but that may have been because the landlord was a tall, strapping man with sensitive hearing.

Anyway, there wasn't anything very exciting you could do of a weekday evening within sight of the landlord when you had to be back in college at 10.30 p.m. But on Saturday nights we could be back as late as 11 p.m.—midnight if we had had the foresight to sign an exeat form (Roedean must have been easier to get in and out of than our college.) That meant we could make an expedition in the direction of Watford and two all-female colleges by the names of Wall Hall and Balls Park whose inmates would hopefully be grateful for the influx of a load of farmers and gardeners to brighten their Saturday night.

From 9 till 11 on a Saturday morning we had practical work to do in the orchard or the market garden, the glasshouses or the grounds. Then there was a plant identification test—twenty plants to describe with the names of their family, genus, species and variety—before lunch, after which we would set off into town. A new shirt maybe, or a pair of shoes, in preparation for the evening's entertainment—a film, or a night at the pub or, best of all, a bit of a bash at Wall Hall or Balls Park.

Within a few weeks of our arrival we had formed small groups of friends, the hortics and agrics generally sticking together, since our worlds collided only at mealtimes, and the proximity provided by eight or nine hours of practical work and lectures meant that we got to know each other better and more speedily than could be managed over breakfast, lunch and dinner when the conversation was minimal and the appropriation of chips was of paramount importance.

And so, with Dick from Somerset, I would set out on a Saturday evening with high hopes and a drip-dry nylon shirt, hoping to meet the love of my life and live happily ever after. The back of Dick's van was equipped with a generous supply of cushions, a sort of den of iniquity on wheels. He wished. But then he did seem to have more success than I did, probably on account of his laid-back technique.

Having selected his quarry, he would chat her up in a refreshingly laconic style which involved rolling his 'r's more than usual and winking rather a lot. When it was clear that the two of them were going places he would lean forward into the snog, putting one arm round her, holding his fag and his pint in the other hand, and shifting his weight onto one leg as he raised the other off the ground. I once asked him why. 'Turns 'em on,' was all he said in reply. I couldn't work out how that could be possible, since the girl usually had her eyes closed. How could she have noticed that he was standing on one leg when she was leaning backwards? It only served to reinforce my belief that I knew nothing about women.

Until the night of the hospital dance. Freshly washed, shaved and reeking of Aramis, Dick and I set off an hour in advance of the scheduled time in order to partake of a stiffener before arriving at the appointed venue. It was winter, but it did not take long before our thick jackets came off in the heat of the dimly lit hall, where the sounds of The Hollies and The Dave Clark Five pulsated through the overamplified sound system. Pints in hand, we scanned the sides of the hall for putative conquests. Dick's eye fell on an especially unprepossessing girl with a low-cut dress.

'Why her?' I asked.

'Because her face might not be up to much but she'll be good for a grope.' And off he loped, with that rolling gait of his, in the direction of the unsuspecting nurse. I watched as he grinned at her and winked, and she melted into his arms in readiness.

I, on the other hand, had spotted the girl from the movies. Or so it seemed. One of my parents' favourite films was *South Pacific*. Liat, Bloody Mary's daughter, is a slender, dark-haired Oriental girl with devastating good looks. She falls in love with the dashing Lieutenant Cable and he with her. In the face of the Chinese nurse with the long, shiny black hair and the limpid eyes, I saw the look of Liat. Summoning all my courage I walked across the floor and asked her to dance. She smiled, Liat's smile, and took my hand as I led her to the floor. We danced to the sound of the Moody Blues, and then to Procul Harum, 'A Whiter Shade of Pale'. She put her head on my shoulder and I wrapped my arms round her waist. Later we kissed. I kept both feet on the floor. We said goodbye at the gates and I took the telephone number of the nurses' hostel.

I agonised for days. But I never did call her.

THE POINT HAD COME where I did wonder if I would ever meet anybody. It was possible, of course, and seemed increasingly likely, that I would go through life on my own. Or that I would have to adopt Dick's standards and settle for a good grope. But then he had a van filled with cushions and I didn't.

Then, one night, fate smiled and I noticed a tiny girl with a perfect figure and long blonde hair standing at the side of the dance floor with her dark-haired mate. Dick saw the direction in which I was looking. 'You go for her and I'll take the friend,' he offered.

It is the longest walk known to man—the walk of the adolescent male across the dance floor in the direction of his quarry. For this reason, a little geography homework is worth doing on arrival at any dance hall. First, locate both the bar and the gentlemen's lavatory. That way, should your advance be rejected, you can adjust your subsequent movement so as to avoid retracing your steps. You can, instead, go straight to the bar or the lavatory.

Mentally I was walking towards the gents before I had even asked her, so it came as a bit of a surprise when she said that, yes, she would dance with me. Boy, was she a cracker. I could see the envious looks of the other students as I put my hands round her waist when we got to the slow, smoochy number, and she raised her arms and put them round my neck. She had on the shortest of minidresses and had the perfect pair of legs.

I got her phone number. Dick was silent in the van on the way home.

'You all right?' I asked.

'Waste of time that was. Right stuck up. Not interested.' I smiled to myself. A self-satisfied smile. A new sensation.

At lunch in the dining hall the following day the conversation turned, inevitably, to women. One of the ginger-headed farmers nodded in my direction. 'I like his,' he said. It was a novel sensation. Not that one evening out proved that she was 'mine'. But I did have her phone number and I did ring it.

We went out several times. Happily, I thought. And she was devastatingly good-looking, with her long blonde hair held in place with a black velvet Alice band, the short skirts and the perfect legs.

Eventually she asked me to meet her at her home before we went out for the evening. I arrived at the Hertfordshire farmhouse—rather smarter than I had imagined—to find her deep in conversation with her parents. She seemed a bit petulant. Going on to her dad about her horse.

I sat at one end of the chintz-covered sofa while the sun shone in through the French windows. Helen sat on the arm next to me. Her minidress allowed me a good view of her slender legs, but I tried to avoid looking at them in case her father noticed.

'I really didn't want to have him cut,' she protested.

'Well, it's too late now,' he said, leaning on the mantelpiece with a glass of Scotch in his hand. 'He's been done and that's an end to it.' He drained his glass and left the room.

I felt slightly uncomfortable. Not least because I hadn't a clue what they were on about. Maybe she preferred her horse's mane long and her dad had cut it off. I was, for many years, unaware of the finer points of equine castration.

The conversation having ended, Helen got up from the sofa and said, 'Come on.'

I did as I was told, and we went out for a rather gloomy evening at the pictures. She didn't seem too keen on being kissed that night and I felt a bit short-changed. She agreed, somewhat reluctantly, to meet again the following Saturday. We would go to the county show and she would show me the horses.

I met her at the appointed time, in the appointed place—at the end of the cowshed where bulls and heifers were pawing the ground. At first I did not recognise her. The minidress had gone, to be replaced with jeans and an army combat jacket. The Alice band had gone too, and with it the long blonde hair. It was the first inkling I had that it was not her own. She looked, if anything, a little dowdy, and her manner was that of a sulky child. Nothing I could say or do seemed to lift her mood, and we walked, in desultory fashion, past horses, cut and uncut (did I but know it), pens of sheep and suckling sows. By lunchtime she had clearly had enough and I asked her if she wanted to go home. 'Yes,' she said. And made it clear that she would be travelling alone.

And that was it. My one real conquest evaporated into the agricultural light of day and I caught the bus back to college.

# TO THE PALM HOUSE

I didn't expect to get in. I don't think I really expected to get an interview. There were apparently several hundred applications for the twenty places that became vacant each year at the Royal Botanic Gardens, Kew. But the letter calling me for interview arrived in the spring of 1969 and I turned up at the appointed time to be faced with three serious-looking men in suits sitting behind a large mahogany table. The chair that sat in front of them seemed like a lonely island in the middle of a darkly patterned carpet.

I looked at the men as earnestly as I could and made eye contact with all three, as well as with the stern faces who looked down at me from the gilded frames on the wall behind them—the likes of Sir Joseph Hooker, William Aiton and Sir William Thiselton-Dyer, past directors of Kew who had made their mark on the gardens that were founded in 1752 by Princess Augusta, the widow of Frederick, Prince of Wales.

'When would you prune *Caryopteris* x *clandonensis*?'

It was, I had to admit, not the first question I had expected. But it was the first question I got. I riffled through my mental card index. *Caryopteris* x *clandonensis* . . . a summer-flowering shrub. Fluffy blue flowers carried on new wood. You'd have to prune it late. After it had flowered, but probably not in winter lest its wood be damaged by frost. If it were pruned in spring it would then send out the new wood that would carry its late-summer flowers.

'April.'

'I'd prefer March.'

'Oh.'

So far, so hopeless. But I persevered, and tried to appear personable. I suppose the fact that I had served four years of a five-year apprenticeship on the nursery, and then been to college and managed to get my National Certificate in Horticulture, plus my College Certificate with Credit, must have counted for something. Had I remembered to tell them that I had won first prize for my dried and pressed flower collection? Too late now.

More questions followed. About rock gardens. About Wisley. What did I think of the rock garden there? I tried to be diplomatic. 'Very nice. Very . . . well landscaped.'

Kew's curator, Dick Shaw, an Edinburgh-trained Scot, smiled indulgently. 'Don't you think it has a touch too much rock?'

'It does have a lot of rock, yes.'

He grinned and signalled to one of the two others that it was their turn. And so the gentle grilling continued until the moment I knew I could do no more.

'Thank you for coming. We'll let you know.' They rose from their chairs. I rose from mine, shook all three hands, smiled, I hoped winsomely, and left the room.

Several weeks later the letter arrived saying I had been awarded a place on the September 1969 intake. My parents were over the moon. They bought me a transistor radio, and that autumn I took it with me on my journey down south to work and study in a botanical garden that had started up the rubber industry in Malaya, had been responsible for the breadfruit expedition that led to the mutiny on the *Bounty*, had benefited from the voyages of Captain Cook and whose first director had been Sir Joseph Banks. I was about to take my place in history—albeit a very small and insignificant one—as a student at the most famous botanical garden in the world.

Unlike the day-release system at Shipley, or Hertfordshire where we had lectures in the morning and practical work in the afternoon, the student's life at Kew was divided up into separate concentrated periods of theoretical and practical work. The lectures were grouped together in a three-month block, October to December for first-year students, January to March for second years and April to June for the third years. For the other nine months the students would work their way through all the gardens' departments—tropical, temperate, herbaceous and alpine and arboretum, gaining, if they paid attention, experience from and knowledge of the greatest collection of plants in any garden on the globe. There were no lengthy summer holidays as at university, only three weeks' paid leave a year plus the odd bank holiday. At the end of the course, if you were successful in both exams and practical work, you would be awarded the Kew Diploma at Pass, Credit or Honours level.

The first problem was finding somewhere to live, a task not made any easier by the fact that the list of suggested accommodation was at least a year out of date. From late September, when I started, until late November, I lodged in a tiny room in a seedy house on the Mortlake Road, accompanied by the roar of traffic and an assortment of insect life with which I shared the bedding. The 8ft by 6ft room—one single bed, one chest of drawers, one wooden chair and one hook behind the door—was lit only by a twenty-five-watt light bulb hanging from the ceiling and an orange street lamp on the pavement outside my window.

Breakfast was usually a banana, lunch would be in the local café or the works canteen, and the evening meal, provided by my less than fastidious landlady, would be of massive boiled potatoes accompanied by watery fish or leathery and unidentifiable meat. I wondered if I was cut out for life in London if all it could offer was bedbugs, boiled potatoes and bare light bulbs.

Then I had the great good fortune to take over a room in the end cottage of a little terrace that ran down to the river. It had been vacated by one of my fellow students who had decided to get married, and for the next five years, as it turned out, I lived in this stylishly decorated little house—mahogany furniture, scrubbed pine floors and assorted works of modern art—with Mr and Mrs Randall Bell.

Randall was a rotund surveyor who played golf once or twice a week, for which he would wear voluminous plus fours. His wife, Eileen, was a painter, potter, admirer of the Bloomsbury Group and author of children's books. They took me under their wing, assumed responsibility for my cultural education—concerts at the Albert Hall and Festival Hall, visits to art galleries and museums—and generally brought me out of myself. He was known as Badger, and she as Cat. And that's what I called them for as long as I knew them. They died quite recently, both in their nineties, and both bemused and chuffed in equal measure at what had happened in the years that followed to 'Titch', the wiry Yorkshire youth who came to live with them.

THE ROYAL BOTANIC GARDENS, Kew, are divided into three sections—the herbarium, home to several dozen botanists who busy themselves naming and classifying around seven million pressed and dried wild flowers, added to at the rate of 30,000 a year (I can't think they would have been impressed with my modest little prize-winning collection), the Jodrell Laboratory where the plant scientists work on research, and the gardens themselves, now referred to as the Living Collections Division (just in case you were in any doubt).

The students work in the Living Collections Division, in between their lecture blocks, and hope that it is still alive when they have finished. In 1969 we first-year students were thrown in at the deep end of academic work as soon as we arrived—day after day of lectures in the raked theatre of the Jodrell Laboratory, weekly plant identification tests (twenty plants at a time), and examination after examination at the end of each three-monthly session.

The plant identification tests are regarded as an important part of the course, since Kew aims to turn out *plantsmen* as distinct from mere *gardeners*. For this reason they were undertaken every week of the year, not just during the three-month lecture block, and with several hundred thousand plants to choose from, the ante was upped a bit from my college days when only a few hundred plants grew on the student campus. Plants were chosen, generally, because they were in flower or looking good at that particular time of year, so if you kept your eyes open as you walked round the gardens, you could probably narrow the field. But tests devoted to ferns or conifers could be real stinkers. Only those students who could identify pine trees by the number of needles in each cluster and their relative length—the nerds of the botanical world—would light up at the sight of twenty of these seemingly identical lumps of tree. With pines, I still struggle.

Over our three years of lectures we were instructed in the finer points of structural botany, plant anatomy, mycology, entomology, genetics, plant taxonomy and plant physiology. The botanical aspect was nothing if not thorough. In the third year we would graduate to landscape design and construction, and—least favourite of mine—management.

We were still woefully short of women—there was only one in each year—and by the end of the first term's examinations, three or four students would have fallen by the wayside and been unable to cope, either with the new life away from home or the intensity of the lecture block. That whittled us down to a hard core of fifteen or so who then usually stayed the course for the full three years.

IN ALL WALKS OF LIFE there are choices to be made. One of the most important at Kew was whether to wear clogs or Wellingtons. We were offered a pair of either during our first week there. It was simply a matter of going down to the stores in the Melon Yard—a range of long, low greenhouses or 'pits' where the exotic fruits used to be grown and where all manner of tender plants were now propagated—and asking Arthur, the grey-haired man with the moustache and the brown coat, for a pair of our chosen footwear in the appropriate size. Arthur was the dead spit of Ronnie Barker in *Open All Hours*, though without the stammer.

'Clogs or wellingtons?'

'Er . . . clogs, please.'

'Size? And don't say sevens because I haven't any left.'

'Eights then.' Pause. 'Have you got any thick socks?'

'Don't do socks.'

Students of a romantic nature would plump for clogs as their daily footwear when working in the gardens. They had stiff black leather uppers, leather laces and wooden soles equipped with irons on sole and heel that resembled horseshoes. It was impossible to get around in them quietly. My romantic inclinations should have led me to request them, but on this occasion practicality outweighed any fanciful thoughts and I stuck with the wellies, being of the same disposition as Greta Garbo—unable to function properly unless my feet are both dry and comfortable. (She wore carpet slippers underneath that crinoline for *Queen Christina*. I just drop it in in case you're interested.)

Those who did opt for the clogs would generally capitulate to their discomfort after a couple of weeks and go grovelling to Arthur for a pair of wellies. He'd shrug and disappear into the dimly lit bowels of his storeroom—'I haven't got any sevens, so don't ask'—before returning with a dusty pair of boots and handing them over with a resigned 'Sign here', pointing to the equally dusty morocco-bound ledger on his wooden counter.

The lecture block over and exams behind us, we would now be distributed throughout the gardens, to benefit the plants and more lowly members of staff with our new-found knowledge. The man in charge of the 'Living Collections Division' was the Scot who had asked me about Wisley's rock garden at my interview, Dick Shaw.

The herbaceous and alpine department was presided over by George Preston, known, rather rudely, as 'Piggy'. He was a bulky man in a tweed suit whose face, while not exactly Gloucester Old

Spot, did have something of a meaty appearance. Like all the Assistant Curators he got round the 300 acres of gardens on a bike, his particular machine being identifiable by its wicker basket on the front. I never saw anything in it. Not a sausage.

The decorative department was responsible for the displays of bedding throughout the gardens—those large flowerbeds down either side of the Broad Walk, for instance, and the conservatory known as 'Number 4', which my landlady Mrs Bell always referred to as 'Bournemouth' on account of the fact that it reminded her of the winter gardens in that seaside resort, or what she *thought* they might look like. The decorative department came under Brian Halliwell, a plantsman of great knowledge who hailed from Halifax. Mercurial of temperament, he could go from laughter to anger quicker than anyone I have ever known. If he looked like having one of his black moods, the quickest way to divert him was to talk about theatre, which he was as passionate about as he was plants. I spent some time in his department working in the office, and learned as much about Noël Coward and Laurence Olivier as I did about nicotianas and lupins.

The temperate department came under the gum-chewing and inscrutable Ian Beyer. He was a sallow-skinned man who talked to you as though he knew quite a lot but did not want to let you in on the entire story. His eyes would dart this way and that, as if looking for the nearest exit, or for a tribe of Indians who were about to come over the hill with bows and arrows. His territory consisted of the Temperate House, the Palm House and the Australian House, perhaps the most pleasant climate in which to work—light and airy and not too hot, with no sign of any Indians.

The arboretum—Kew's magnificent collection of trees, many of them several hundred years old—was managed by George Brown, a Devonian with a rolling West Country burr and the most laid-back attitude of any of the Assistant Curators. What George Brown did not know about trees you could have written on a pinhead. However much of a rush he might have been in, he always had enough time to talk to you—about trees, about the weather, or about what was in the news, though one always had the feeling that certain things about life baffled him: 'Oh, I don't know, Alan. Do you?'

The joy of all these departments was to come, but the first one to which I was posted was the tropical department. This consisted of a range of nursery glasshouses—the Tropical Pits (sunk into the ground by the Victorians to help preserve heat, hence the name), the ferneries where Kew's tender ferns were grown, and the 'T-range', named after its shape, like a capital 'T'. This was a conglomeration of glasshouses that has since been replaced by the grand Princess of Wales conservatory. It sheltered, among other things, cacti and succulents in a couple of ordinary greenhouses, and one lean-to whose back wall was painted with a desert scene.

Other greenhouses were devoted to orchids and to the giant water lily, which grew in its own pool of warm water that was filled with a shoal of grey guppies. The atmosphere here was truly tropical—steamy and humid, with the pinging of four-inch-diameter iron heating pipes all day long.

Stan Rawlings was in charge of the entire tropical department, though I seldom saw him without an overcoat. I suppose he felt the cold when he went out. A Londoner with the voice of a market trader, he brooked no nonsense from his students. In spite of the fact that I am pathologically punctual, I managed to sleep in twice during my first week in his department. On the first occasion I was greeted with a raised eyebrow. I was only a quarter of an hour late.

On the second occasion—twenty minutes—it was suggested to me that on the next Saturday morning I go into Richmond and purchase a new alarm clock.

I got the message. I got the alarm clock. I was not late again.

Under each of the Assistant Curators were Gardens Supervisors, a rank equivalent to that of foreman, from which title it had been changed only a few months previously. Responsible for Kew's orchids, and my immediate boss, was George Nicholson, a shambling southeast Londoner whose off-white shirt with rolled up sleeves seemed always to be escaping his trousers, and whose gap-toothed smile revealed a certain shyness. He spoke in a hesitating manner, rather like a schoolboy who had just been reprimanded by a headmaster and who needed to explain that he hadn't really meant to do that but it had just sort of . . . happened. The orchid family is the largest in the plant kingdom, with 880 genera and around 22,000 accepted species—twice as many species as in the bird kingdom and four times more than the number of mammal species. While he might not have encountered all of them, George knew his subject inside out.

AT LEAST DURING THE WINTER we were warm in the T-range. Temperatures seldom fell below 70ºF in the warmer houses, though one or two of the cooler ones, where the cymbidiums lived, were allowed to drop to 60ºF. In summer life here was akin to the Caribbean and most of us wore shorts and T-shirts, though never George, whose grey flannels, off-white shirt and tie seemed never to change. Cockroaches loved the place. Turn on the light in the potting shed attached to the greenhouses after dark and you would see them scuttling away under our lockers and behind the potting bench. I never did grow to like them. When we rearranged boulders around the lily pool they would run out and we would squash them underfoot. They cracked, then squelched. Eugh!

When it came to characters the little enclave of the T-range would have made a mini-soap opera in its own right. As well as George Nicholson it was peopled by Gregory, a camp Barbadian who wore Bermuda shorts, flip-flops and colourful shirts, but who changed out of his work clothes every evening to go home on the bus. He would put on a crisp white shirt and tie, a neatly pressed pair of trousers and a shortie raincoat, slip on his highly polished black shoes, splash on some fragrant floral aftershave, and catch the number 27.

Cathy had been an art student in her youth and was a fine illustrator, but had taken to gardening, and orchids in particular, as a second career. She was a bit nervy, and good company for J.C., a tall, rather fey character who resembled Frederik of the pop duo Nina and Frederik, with a ginger beard. J.C. was never happier than when wandering among his charges wielding a hosepipe and eventually transferred to the laboratories, where he put on a white coat and grew orchids from seed under aseptic conditions.

Joy was the girl who could turn the head of all the male students at Kew. Slender as a pencil, she wore bell-bottomed jeans and a T-shirt and had her long, silky blonde hair held up behind her head with one of those leather-and-wooden-peg things from which it would perpetually try to escape. She wore hardly any make-up. She didn't need to. Naturally beautiful, with a ringing laugh, she was, alas, married to a third-year student and so beyond reach. The words of the hymn 'And with Joy we'll persevere' were a cruel reminder that there was little point.

Into this maelstrom of humanity came, each year, a fresh batch of students for them to get to grips with. It's a wonder anything grew at all.

We learned the difference between terrestrial orchids (those that grew in the ground) and epiphytes (those that clung to trees for support, as opposed to parasites, which extract nutrients from their host). I loathed the fat and blowzy cattleyas that always reminded me of the mink-coated ladies who would pin them in a corsage to their bosoms, and felt only slightly better disposed towards the cymbidiums whose long flower spikes, in the cooler of our orchid houses, could last for weeks on end.

Cultivation seemed to be a mixture of repotting, maintaining humidity by damping down the floor with a hosepipe three times daily, and raising and lowering the slatted wooden blinds, which were, at least, less labour-intensive than painting the green whitewash of 'Summer Cloud'.

The giant water lily had a house to itself. It was named *Victoria regia* by Sir Joseph Paxton in honour of Queen Victoria. Paxton was the first to flower the plant at Chatsworth in 1849, beating the Royal Botanic Gardens by several months, to Kew's lasting chagrin. I suppose Kew's revenge was to insist on the name change to *Victoria amazonica*, that being, the botanists claimed, the first correctly published description, so consigning Paxton's supreme grovel to botanical history.

We grew it in its own tank of warm water in a large glasshouse at the centre of the T-range. It was raised afresh from a seed the size of a dried pea every January, and grown on in a little water tank until it was ready to plant out in the centre of its final home. Over the course of the summer it would grow into a massive plant, with at any one time half a dozen leaves fully six feet across, heavily ribbed and spined on the undersides, the better to make them float and to protect them from hungry predators. The leaves were said to be able to support the weight of a baby, and to prove the point we displayed an old photo of the feat by the side of the pool (no current member of staff being prepared to risk the life of their own infant).

So hot was it in the Victoria house that the pool, with its three-foot-high high stone sides, needed topping up once or twice a day to replace water lost by evaporation. It was all too easy to forget that the tap had been left on and to go about other duties, only to remember an hour later and run back to find guppies flapping their way across the path in the last gasp of life to the horror of passing members of the public. It was for this reason that we tried to do our topping up in the morning; the greenhouses opened at one o'clock in order to let us get our watering and general tidying done free of enquiring members of the public who might trip over a hosepipe if they were allowed to wander around willy-nilly.

After six months of orchid and fish management it was time for another move . . . now that I knew all there was to know about orchids. Well, you could only learn a fraction in that time, really, but I knew more about them than I had when I arrived.

OF ALL THE STRUCTURES at Kew—and there are many, from the Pagoda, that eighteenth-century exemplar of the fashion for chinoiserie, which was designed by Sir William Chambers for Princess Augusta, to King William's Temple by Sir Jeffry

Wyatville, which was completed in 1837—it is the Palm House, I think, that is the most iconic. Its very shape says to most people 'Kew Gardens'. The engineer of the structure, which was completed in 1848, was the Irishman Richard Turner, but the architect Decimus Burton is generally credited with the final design, having simplified Turner's elaborate Gothic excesses.

While most students were moved round the gardens every six months, from temperate to arboretum, decorative to tropical, I managed, for some reason, to spend a year of my time working in the Palm House. It remains a period of my life that is dear to my heart.

If you look at the Palm House from the pond that lies in front of it you will see a high central domed area, flanked by two lower 'wings'. The left-hand wing houses Kew's collection of cycads—primitive plants that have survived 'since dinosaurs roamed the earth'. At least that's what I seem to remember reading in the guidebook. Cycads look like palm trees, except that their fronds are much tougher, harder and spinier. They are also much slower growing.

The Gardens Supervisor in charge of the Palm House was Ruth Storr, a pretty, elfin-faced woman whose slight physique belied her capacity for heavy manual work. She took a while to get to know, but once she felt she could trust you she opened up a little, sharing her knowledge of her charges and her sense of humour in equal measure.

On a summer's morning in 1971, I pushed open the tall, heavy iron door in the central dome of the Palm House and walked in. I was nervous. Not of Ruth, but at the prospect of looking after plants in this horticultural equivalent of Westminster Abbey. Massive palms towered above me, their frothing heads almost out of sight up among the curving white-painted rafters and glazing bars. Two spiral staircases twisted through them, seemingly into infinity, and everywhere was the steady drip-drip-drip of water falling through ornate iron grilles that covered the floor into the dank depth below.

My feet echoed eerily in the silence as I made my way to the small wooden shed that sat, enveloped in foliage, at the centre of the house. Always dimly lit, this 'mess room' had a single forty-watt bulb illuminating its simple interior, with half a dozen chairs pushed against the walls, a sink, an electric kettle and a telephone—a link with the world outside this pocket-sized jungle. There was little else to see, apart from half a dozen tall, slender, grey-painted steel lockers for staff clothing, and a few old magazines stacked in a corner. And Ruth's copy of H. F. Macmillan's *Tropical Planting and Gardening with special reference to Ceylon*—a green cloth-covered book dating from 1946 that was still the bible of cultivation for all those of us working in either the tropical or temperate departments. It lay on a chair in this modest nerve centre from which the Palm House was run, and to which staff would return for their morning coffee and for lunch.

There was no answer to my tentative 'hello', so I dumped my bag—holding my apron and a spare pair of shoes—on one of the chairs and went exploring. It really was like being on another continent. The interior of the glasshouse was so tall, so wide and so densely planted that only the formally arranged paths gave away the influence of civilisation. Those and the plant labels, of course. Every single plant at Kew has a rectangular black plastic label engraved in white showing its family, genus, species and date of introduction to the gardens, along with its coded 'accession number' that allows its history to be checked in central records.

I walked underneath the coconut and date palms, through tightly packed cocoa, tea and coffee bushes, past cotton plants laden with foaming balls of white wool. The light grew brighter now under the airy canopy of a grove of papaws, the whorls of leaves held aloft like parasols, each one fingered like a man's hand, but ten times the size, with fat green fruits clustered round the central stem like gigantic beads. Banana plants pushed up their thicket of succulent sheaths, unfurling their scrolls of paddle-shaped leaves in dappled sunlight that turned each one of them into a stained-glass window. Their long, trailing flower stems were packed with hands of embryonic bananas and terminated in a purple podlike flower that dangled beneath them like an elephant's willy. Such was the imagination of a student gardener.

I found Ruth eventually, hosepipe in hand, watering pot plants on the staging to one side of the house, and I heard then, too, the distant voices of other workers about their chores, their voices and whistling echoing around in the palm-filled heavens.

'Come with me,' she said, and led me to the section reserved for cycads. 'This is your end.'

Ruth thumped the side of a large wooden tub. It was taller than she was, and from it erupted a great knobbly stem, like the deformed leg of an elephant, topped by a massive fountain of spiny green leaves. 'They're a bit sensitive to overwatering, so be careful. And some of them are quite rare.'

'I see.'

'Stick your hand inside and feel the compost—if it's dry give them a really good soak.'

'And if it's damp?' I asked, knowing, in my heart, what the answer was.

'Leave them alone and try again the following day. Whatever you do, don't give them too much.'

'Right.'

She must have seen my expression.

'Don't worry, you'll soon get the hang of it.'

It didn't help that one of the plants had a label attached to it saying 'The rarest plant in the world' and that another bore the legend 'The oldest pot plant in the world'. Disbudding carnations wrongly was one thing, killing a plant that had been in Kew's possession since the time of Sir Joseph Banks and Captain Cook was quite another. But fate was kind, the plants both survived twelve months of my ministrations, and they are still there to this day, frightening the life out of students who are convinced that they will be responsible for their demise.

The cycads are not the only remarkable plants protected by the Palm House. The giant bamboo, which rejoices under the name of

*Gigantochloa verticillata*, is one of the most astonishing. It can grow, in summer, at the rate of a foot every day. It is the plant everyone thinks of as having built the bridge over the River Kwai—though teak also played a part—and is frequently used for all manner of construction work in its native Burma thanks to its strength and durability. Even in the Palm House, a long way from its native home, its stems quickly reach the roof and have to be cut off before they punch a hole in the glass. But beware! The papery sheaths, glossy and parchment-like, that protect the growing point, and which eventually fall away as the plant grows, are covered in fine, silky hairs that look soft and delicate. They are not. They are capable of perforating human skin with the efficiency of a needle, but invisibly, leaving no trace of their entry. Make the mistake of picking up one of these attractive scrolls without wearing gloves, and the irritation persists for several days, and the hairs are so fine that they are impossible to extract.

We used to erect a scaffolding platform around the palm trees to remove faded leaves, but taking the top out of the giant bamboo required an even greater head for heights, a certain amount of agility, and nerves of steel. The way to get to them is via a curving ladder, affixed to the inside of the dome and about two feet away from it. To climb this you must face inwards. This is all very well on the lower part of the glasshouse, which is vertical, but once the structure starts to curve, you will find yourself climbing out across space, looking downwards. It is not a job for the faint-hearted. Added to which, you must make the journey carrying a long-handled saw with which to remove the offending stems.

Picture me then, on a hot July day, with the sun beating down through the glass, endeavouring to remove the top of a bamboo stem, lying on my stomach looking downwards sixty-three feet up in the air above the canopy of luxuriant palm fronds. It was a novel but effective way of staying slim. I mean, there cannot be many men five foot nine inches tall who weigh only eight stone. Forget your fancy diets—try a year in the Palm House at Kew. It worked for me.

# ON THE BOARDS

London in the early 1970s was, pretty much like today, exactly what you wanted it to be. There were drugs around in abundance if you mixed in 'that sort of company'. I think my parents worried about it. But then I didn't really mix in that sort of company. Drugs frightened the pants off me. Or rather the prospect of the effect they could have. I was quite happy drinking too much wine of an evening in terms of having a good time. At least the effect of alcohol was predictable: I would become happy; I would become more talkative (if that were possible); I would become good-naturedly argumentative, and then I would fall asleep and wake up with an almighty headache. Every single time.

I was invited to only one party where I knew drugs would be a part of the scene. The invitation came from a swarthy Peruvian-born youth working in the tropical department. He called everybody 'man', regardless of gender, and had a hoarse voice that women apparently found irresistible. I did resist and found an excuse not to go, without, I hope, losing too much face—the main reason, I think, why so many kids succumb to drugs today. I was lucky and, as far as I'm aware, so were the rest of my student friends.

I was less fortunate where girls were concerned. 'Late starter' seemed to apply to most aspects of my life—not through choice, but through circumstances. Heather was my first Kew love. A suitably horticultural girl by name at least. She worked in the alpine department—a far cry from her native Australia, which is not renowned for its snow-clad mountains. Maybe she enjoyed the change of scene. Heather was deliciously voluptuous with long blonde hair. Things seemed to be going rather well. I asked her out and she said 'yes', which was at least a hundred per cent improvement on my previous track record in this postal area.

We went out once or twice a week for a couple of months. I even plucked up the courage to whisper 'I love you' in her ear, sitting on the window seat in the Roebuck at the top of Richmond Hill. I'd never whispered it to anybody before. She didn't whisper it back and I wondered if she had heard me properly. I thought it best not to check. The following Saturday we went to a party in one of the student's houses. I looked around after half an hour or so and couldn't see her. I went upstairs to the loo and happened to glance into one of the bedrooms. She was sitting on a bed kissing a Canadian. Perhaps she was just improving Commonwealth relations. It was the end of ours.

A few months later she returned to Australia, and some time after that a middle-aged couple came up to me while I was working in the gardens. They introduced themselves as Heather's parents. They were on holiday. I did my best to be nice to them and I enquired after her. She was very well, they said, and had asked them to find me, wherever I was, and pass on her best wishes. They did not ask if I knew where the Canadian was working. Maybe they'd found him already.

Next came Nita, who worked in the arboretum. She was small and petite, with long, *dark* hair (time to try a change of colour), tight jeans and wellies (always wellies) and dark brown eyes. We smiled at each other across wheelbarrows full of autumn leaves and finally managed to find ourselves in a corner at a student dance. She wore a long navy-blue velvet dress that hugged her neat figure. I was totally smitten. Again. We kissed, but I sensed—rightly—that I was the one making the running. Later in the week she slipped me a note saying, as nicely as she possibly could, that she was going back to her boyfriend. I had caught her on the rebound.

Pam was another brunette. She asked me back to her place for coffee and a snog on the bed. The trouble was, she couldn't stop talking. She did have a rather fetching pair of red velvet hot pants, but when you're trying to get to grips with the physical side of a relationship on a single bed, to find that your inamorata is intent on spouting obscure botanical facts is a bit of a turnoff. I gave up on her.

It was time to look further afield than the gardens. I joined the local operatic society.

I CAN TRACE the beginnings of my interest in 'play acting' to 1956, when, aged seven, I was given the painted cardboard head of a mallard drake and told to leap out of the way of Peter Crowther who, by virtue of his Christian name, was given the title role in the little dance we did at infants' school to Prokofiev's music for *Peter and the Wolf*. My final leap (before I was eaten) was particularly admired, so athletic did it seem for a small boy. As sporting prowess goes, it remains the zenith of my achievements. It is the only thing in life at which I have peaked early.

There followed a series of plays at secondary school—everything from *Tom Sawyer* (schoolmaster) to an abridged version of *The Merchant of Venice* (I gave them my Shylock) to an adaptation of John Steinbeck's *The Pearl* (a snake) and the complete *A Midsummer Night's Dream*. Alas, I was permitted to give neither my 'Puck' nor my 'Bottom'.

I played a monkey in André Roussin's *The Little Hut* for Ilkley Players (non-speaking, with a brief appearance only at the end of the play), but by the time I left school I thought my dramatic aspirations would probably have to be sacrificed now that I was going into gardening.

And so, for the first two years of my working life I did not have much of a social life. The solution presented itself courtesy of Joyce, our neighbour and mother of twins. She could be heard warbling gems from *The Count of Luxembourg* and *The Merry Widow* as she dashed away with her smoothing iron. Quite how she persuaded the seventeen-year-old boy next door to go with her one evening to the King's Hall where Ilkley Amateur Operatic Society were auditioning for *Oklahoma!* I will never know. But I'm glad I went. In a funny sort of way it changed my life.

Not that I had a large part, and it was hard convincing my father that there was a good reason why I should, at one point, prance across the stage like a horse to the music of 'Surrey with the Fringe on Top'. It was not quite what he had in mind when he suggested that I broaden my horizons.

Rodgers and Hammerstein's *Oklahoma!* was followed by Lionel Monckton's *The Quaker Girl*, so in my first year 'on the boards' I had a taste of both American and Edwardian English musical comedy. And I loved them. I loved their air of romance and escapism. I loved the tunes, the magic of the footlights and the 'otherworldliness' of theatre. It took me out of myself to a place where I seemed to have confidence and a degree of ability.

It also allowed me to meet girls. Not that anything lasting came out of Ilkley Operatic or, as my mother liked to call them, 'your amateurs'. I did borrow Dad's old Borgward one night and take out a girl from Guiseley who was in the chorus, but she went a bit faster than the car and scared me off. Pathetic really.

I managed only two seasons with Ilkley Operatic before I went to college, and then I was into five years of concentrated study with little time for anything other than a pint in the pub of a Saturday night and the odd visit to the theatre or the Albert Hall. Regular rehearsals would be out of the question.

But when my student course had ended and I was poised to stay on and work at the gardens, I reckoned it was time I had another crack at it. And at broadening my horizons socially. Clearly I was not destined to get it together with another gardener. Or even a laboratory technician, which was about as far as lateral thinking would get me at Kew.

Quite how I ended up at Ye White Hart in Barnes—a Thames-side pub on the last bend of the Oxford and Cambridge boat race course—I am not sure. I had sat in the audience of Kingston Operatic Society's productions at Richmond Theatre, and of Barnes and Richmond Operatic Society, who also performed there. I could have joined either. But the Barnes lot looked younger and livelier. More my own age and, I hoped, disposition.

None of my Kew mates was interested in dramatics, so I was well and truly on my own. It might not have been a long journey by train from Kew Bridge to Barnes Bridge in terms of miles, but it was in terms of confidence. I almost didn't bother. But I steeled myself, plucked up the courage and pushed open the door of the upstairs function room of a London pub where fifty folk were belting out 'Flash Bang Wallop'. I never looked back. That December I played the role of 'Buggins—a pessimist' in *Half a Sixpence*. Casting, I hope, against type.

I felt the same sort of camaraderie and friendliness of spirit during the rehearsals for that show as I had felt when I had gone along to the King's Hall for rehearsals of *Oklahoma!*. It seems rather facile now I come to set it down, but meeting a group of folk who laugh at the same things you laugh at, enjoy the same sort of music you do and share your own love of theatre is a potent and magical mixture. It is not about egos so much as companionship. There were folk there with whom I had little in common other than a vocal score. But there were others who became, and remain, my best friends.

Amateur theatre can, in some circumstances, be a hotbed of intrigue and a place of naked rivalry. It would be futile to deny it. But the half-dozen true friends I made during the years I was a part of BROS were and are as interested in enjoying each other's company as they are in getting parts and showing off.

Mind you, I quite liked that bit, too. In my operatic career (1972–81) I performed at Frank Matcham's masterpiece, Richmond

Theatre, in such virtuoso roles as Ko-Ko in *The Mikado* and Sir Joseph Porter in *HMS Pinafore*, Simplicitas (sounds like sanitaryware) in *The Arcadians* and Fyedka in *Fiddler on the Roof*—standing on a table to reach the top notes. I had a passable tenor, but sometimes it needed a helping hand. I also played in *Cowardy Custard* and *Oh What A Lovely War!*, and even essayed the classics, playing Second Gravedigger in *Hamlet* for Richmond Shakespeare Society.

Aside from the music the operatic society meant meeting new mates of the same age but different backgrounds. A solicitor (Steve, with whom I would later go on holiday to the West Country), a baker, a bank manager, an accountant and a milkman.

But the best thing that came out of my brief but memorable dramatic career was meeting the woman who would become my missus. She was a dancer in *Half a Sixpence*. We went on our first date on New Year's Eve 1973 and her dad had to come out and get us in his Ford Cortina at one o'clock in the morning because there were no taxis to be had. It was foggy. He wore an overcoat over his pyjamas. He didn't look best pleased. But he looked happier when I married her a couple of years later.

BY THE BEGINNING of 1972 I had realised that I was going to have to make a decision about my future. I quite liked it where I was. Could I stay on? I made enquiries.

It seemed that the post of Gardens Supervisor with responsibility for the Queen's Garden—the seventeenth-century garden immediately behind Kew Palace—was coming up. Would I be interested in that? I said that I would. I passed my diploma, with credit, but fate intervened before I could take up the post.

The new curator, John Simmons, one day summoned me to his office. I was nervous. Maybe he'd decided I wasn't up to the job on offer and they'd have to let me go. I wiped my feet on the mat, cleared my throat (nervous habit) and knocked on the large mahogany door of his imposing office.

'Come in.'

At least the words were delivered brightly and with passion, but then John Simmons's words almost always were. Short and stocky with short, dark wiry hair and a goatee beard and moustache, he was the only member of the gardens staff to have a bike like my old one back in Ilkley—the one with the small wheels.

'I gather you've been offered the Queen's Garden.' He tugged at his beard—another habit—and sat on the edge of his desk. 'Only I've had an idea and I wondered if you might like to be involved.'

It was a statement as much as a question, and one that seemed vague in outline. I could do little more than look interested and wait for him to continue.

'Staff training. We don't do enough of it. And what we do is not very well put together. A bit ad hoc. I think we need some proper courses for members of staff—teaching them the basic gardening skills and some theory, too—how plants grow, that sort of thing. Pests and diseases, bit of botany, but mainly practical stuff. Give them a certificate at the end to show they've done it. I think that's important. What do you think?'

'Well, yes. I think it's very . . . interesting.' Interest seemed to be the key here.

'I'd like you to be Gardens Supervisor with responsibility for staff training—setting up the courses, running them and training the staff. What do you think?'

'What about the Queen's Garden?'

'Well, you couldn't do both. The staff training job will take up all your time.'

I was a bit overwhelmed; it was not the kind of thing that I could have seen coming. 'Could I think about it?'

''Course. Let me know by the end of the week.' He tugged his beard again, then chuckled and slid off the desk to shake my hand warmly. 'I think you'd enjoy it.'

I mumbled my thanks—I hoped effusively enough—and went back to work.

What to do? I had just got my head round taking over the

Queen's Garden, and now this bolt from the blue. But I had always toyed with the idea of teaching. I had even sent off for a prospectus for one of the teacher training colleges when I was at Oaklands, with the aim of teaching rural studies in secondary schools. Maybe this was my way in to the world of teaching. Training the staff in the basic horticultural skills. By the end of the week I had made up my mind; the Queen's Garden—much as I loved it—would have to find another guardian and I would take up the challenge and set about organising a series of courses on practical gardening. It couldn't be that difficult, could it?

## STAYING ON

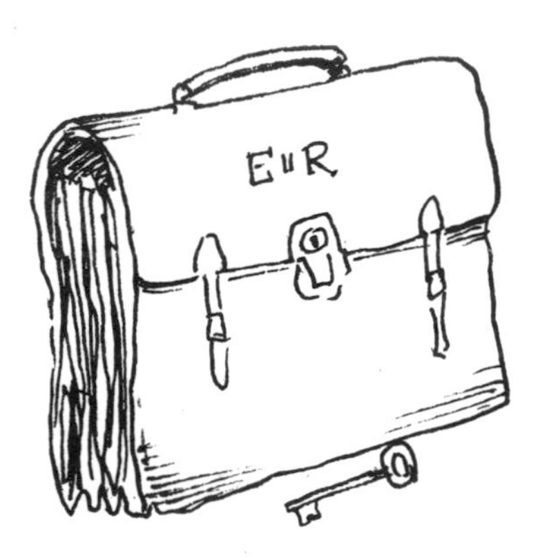


THEY HAD TO FIND me an office, of course. I ended up in the attic room of Descanso House, a dusky red-brick building in a corner of the gardens close to Kew Green. It had been built in 1760 as the residence for William Aiton, who worked for the founder of the gardens, Princess Augusta, and then as head gardener to King George III. It was Decimus Burton, designer of the Palm House, who recommended that the house eventually be turned into offices, so it is to him I owe my thanks for having to walk with a sideways lean, my room being in the very apex of the pantiled roof. The name Descanso is an odd one and was given to the house by George Willison, its tenant from 1888 to 1892. Willison had been a merchant in Brazil, and the word comes from the Portuguese name for 'a resting place'. I was to find it anything but.

I was sent to the stores to see Arthur. He smiled. I had gone up in the world now: no longer a student but a Gardens Supervisor—a rank that held certain entitlements. Arthur stroked his moustache and opened his ledger. I came away from his stores on that day in September, not with a pair of size eight wellingtons, or ill-fitting clogs, but with a bicycle, a black briefcase stamped with the gilded cipher EIIR and a large key on which was engraved the words 'Royal Gardens Kew'. The key to paradise. I was ridiculously proud. I even took it with me up to Yorkshire to show Mum and Dad.

The initial euphoria did eventually wear off, but I never tired of riding round the gardens on my bike (they even let students do it nowadays—standards have slipped), or of letting myself in through the side door with my key.

I set to with a vengeance. The courses were to begin in October and would be set at two levels—one for beginners and one for those who had more experience. I needed charts and felt-tip pens, graph paper and a large diary, all helpfully supplied by the stationery department and delivered by uniformed messenger. This was pre-computer age and anything I needed printing had to be duplicated on a simple Roneo machine, reeking of methylated spirits and printed out in an attractive shade of purple.

The classes I had to organise would be in the form of day release. Some of them would be lectures and others practical demonstrations, so at least I could still get my hands dirty, and I would still be among the plants.

Wellied and jacketed, I showed gardeners how to dig, how to hoe and the proper way to use a rake, with the words of my Shipley fruit-and-vegetable lecturer Lennie Best ringing in my ears: 'The rake is not for *breaking down* soil, it is a levelling tool'. With confidence I passed on his sage advice that a fork was the tool of choice to reduce clods to a fine tilth and that the rake be used simply to level the surface; over-rake—making the particles too fine—and the soil surface would turn into a crust in the first shower of rain. This handy hint has stayed with me. It might even have stuck with some of the gardeners I taught.

I organised plant identification tests, but steered clear of pines and ferns on humanitarian grounds.

At the end of each term there were tests to administer. I organised an intricate timetable of who should be where and when—potting up at 10 a.m., pricking out at 10.30 a.m., seed sowing at 11 a.m., and so on—and arranged for the compost, the benches, the pots and suchlike to be in the right place at the right time. They all managed to muddle through somehow, and when they looked confused or panicked I did my best to relax them.

Within a couple of weeks they'd all been up to my attic room individually to collect their certificates—stamped with the seal of the Royal Botanic Gardens and signed by yours truly—as an indication that they had undertaken their basic training. Soon it was all systems go for the next intake and a repeat of what had gone before, with lessons learned and, hopefully, improvements made.

I managed to stick it out for two years. I loved being a part of the place we fondly referred to as RBG Kew. I enjoyed the fact that I could cycle around the place, and that I worked with one of the greatest collections of plants in the world. And yet the repetition of the courses was something that I found difficult.

I found myself, one day, standing up in my attic room with my hands in my pockets, gently banging my head on the sloping ceiling. It shook me when I realised what I was doing, and why I was doing it. I was bored. Simple as that. No longer challenged, no longer stimulated.

There were several options: I could ask for another job in the gardens, but that seemed akin to admitting defeat. I could go into parks, but the thought of working in a local government office did not appeal one bit.

I decided that I would ask Leo Pemberton, the Supervisor of

Studies, what he thought, when I had worked out how to broach the subject. Curiously, before I could pluck up the courage, fate took a hand once more.

Leo strode into my office one morning, waving in his hand a copy of the *Gardener's Chronicle*. 'Who do we know with a literary bent?' he asked.

I grinned up at him. 'Me.'

Leo dropped the magazine onto my desk and stabbed his finger at one of the adverts. 'You'd better apply for this.'

The job was that of Assistant Editor, Gardening Books, with the Hamlyn Publishing Group. Not a particularly exciting address: Astronaut House, Feltham, Middlesex. Very 1960s. It couldn't really compare with Royal Botanic Gardens Kew, Richmond, Surrey. But then I had done the prestigious bit.

I went for an interview with Hamlyn's Gardening Editor, Robert Pearson, a tall, white-haired, quietly spoken man in a dark suit, whose name I knew only through his column: he was gardening correspondent of the *Sunday Telegraph*. Bob was one of those men who seem permanently preoccupied, his thoughts elsewhere, as if composing his next column, but he was incredibly polite and seemed interested in my career so far, so much so that he almost gave me the job there and then, but said, in the interests of decorum, I suppose, that he would let me know.

A week later the letter informing me I had got the job arrived, and a few weeks after that I handed in my bike and my briefcase and my key to Kew Gardens. Funnily enough, handing over the key was the saddest part. It seemed like a talisman. I did even think of hanging on to it—not to use, just to keep—saying that I'd lost it. But my conscience got the better of me and so I slid it across the wooden counter where it disappeared into Arthur's vicelike grip. It had not been a new key. It did not have engraved on it 'Royal Botanic Gardens' as the later ones did, but simply 'Royal Gardens Kew'. It was probably a century or two old—it certainly looked and felt it—and I wondered who might have used it before me.

Too late now. I had decided to make the move and so I went by train, not bike, to Feltham, known for its young offenders' institution rather than its botanic garden, wondering if I had made the biggest mistake of my life.

IT DID NOT TAKE me long to work out why Bob Pearson had been keen to employ a man. Until my arrival he was the only male in the gardening department. The atmosphere was certainly different. The office itself was quiet for a start. I rather liked that. I've never been able to work with music blaring or endless chatter. When I'm not working—writing, that is—I'm as noisy as the next man, but writing (or editing, come to that) is, for me, a silent occupation. I can concentrate better that way.

Susanne Mitchell was Bob's deputy. Able and kindly, she went on, some years later, to become the Royal Horticultural Society's editor. Alongside her worked Moyna Kitchin, the archetypal lady editor with a matchless grasp of English grammar and punctuation. Wiry and birdlike with a grey dome of hair and a passion for cats and orange lipstick (though never together), she was ever ready to give me an exposition on the correct use of the semicolon or to stand up for the apostrophe. From her and from Susanne I would learn all I needed to know about caret marks and transpositions, metrication of measurements, the use of parentheses and italics, and the meaning of the marginal markings wf and np (wrong font and new paragraph).

In 1974 computerisation had yet to arrive, so book proofs were still in the form of 'galleys'—sheets of paper around three feet long and nine inches wide, on which a column of text was printed. But the book would arrive from the author in manuscript form—typed out, double-spaced with any luck, on sheets of A4. It was the editor's job to go through the copy and correct spelling, punctuation, grammar and general sense before the manuscript was sent off to the typesetter. When it came back, the galley proofs had to be checked for 'literals'—spelling mistakes—and any other errors, since spellcheck was a facility not possessed by 1970s typewriters.

Mistakes would, with any luck, be spotted, but the author, too, was sent a set of galley proofs to check, two pairs of eyes being better than one. The odd howler would occasionally creep through. I cherish the memory of the day when, proofreading a gardening book authored by a particularly prim lady, I spotted a 'literal' under the entry for lungwort—pulmonaria. In the manuscript it was described as having 'leaves spotted with white', but the galley proof read 'leaves spotted with shite'.

Once the copy was sorted out, there were the illustrations to find, which involved letters to assorted garden photographers who would obligingly send in colour transparencies by the hundred. Finding good (and previously unused) illustrations was sometimes difficult, but necessary to prevent all gardening books from looking the same.

Illustrations and galley proofs would then be sent upstairs to the art department where they were crafted into pages by the book's designer, the galleys sliced up with a scalpel and stuck down on spreadsheets with aromatic cow gum before being sent off to the typesetter once more. A few weeks later they would come back as page proofs. Oh, and there were captions to write for all the illustrations—in those days the province of the editor, rather than the author. (I bet nobody's listening.)

The book's jacket design (then as now a source of great angst and rivalry between the editorial and the marketing departments) would eventually be agreed upon and the whole kit and caboodle sent off to the printers, in those days frequently in Czechoslovakia or Italy for both economic and technical reasons.

A few more weeks would pass, and then we would have finished hardback books—shiny glossy jackets, crisp pages, illustrations that were, hopefully, the right colour, and a price tag on the front flap of something around a fiver.

One of my authors was the man who, in childhood and early youth, had been my hero. They called him Britain's head gardener and he broadcast every Friday night on BBC TV, even before it became BBC1 and BBC2. *Gardening Club* it was called at first, and then it became *Gardeners' World*. His name was Percy Thrower.

What I envied most about Percy was his delivery. It would now, I suppose, seem a bit old-fashioned, a bit measured—slow even—but in all the years I knew him it never changed. He had the ability to say almost anything and make it sound like the voice of God. He had been brought up in Buckinghamshire, then worked at Windsor Castle (where he married the head gardener's daughter) and Derby before becoming Shrewsbury's Parks Superintendent in 1946 at the age of thirty-two. His accent, overlaying those deep, rich vocal tones, was suitably rural and yet readily understandable. And he smoked a pipe.

Originally he had broadcast in a three-piece suit, hanging up his jacket on the back of the greenhouse door in the TV studio, which had no glass. The later broadcasts would come from his garden, or from Clack's Farm, the home of Arthur Billitt, who became his co-presenter in the 1970s, and then he would wear an open-necked shirt. So great was his fame that he was immortalised in Madame Tussauds and appeared on the *Morecambe and Wise Show*.

I worked with Percy on his book *How to Grow Vegetables and Fruit*, travelling up to his house The Magnolias at Bomere Heath outside Shrewsbury (he was retired now as Shrewsbury's Parks Superintendent) and recording tape after tape with him, describing his cultivation techniques for everything from apples to strawberries, which I would then transcribe. Always he was affable, always there was a roast lunch—the joint cooked by his wife Connie and carved by Percy—and always the merest hint of friendly rivalry: the older, established gardener aware of the youngster snapping at his heels. I now know how he felt.

During my time at Hamlyn I edited several of his books, including his autobiography *My Lifetime of Gardening*. I learned a lot from Percy. I learned the importance of not being precious. I learned how to handle members of the public and leave them feeling happy and not short-changed. I learned a lot about broadcasting simply from watching him, and I began to understand even more the importance of words—their rhythm and music, how they could evoke mood and emotion, and how they were tools every bit as important as your spade and your fork, whether they were spoken or written down.

He was, in short, inspirational. And I had always said that I wanted to be Percy Thrower when I grew up. I was not a Parks Superintendent, but I had my gardening knowledge and experience, and while at Kew I had taken my O level in English Language just to prove to myself that I could do it. I passed, and that, coupled with a little help from Moyna and Susanne, equipped me for the editing job. It even emboldened me to think that I might be able to write.

## WAITING FOR THE MUSE

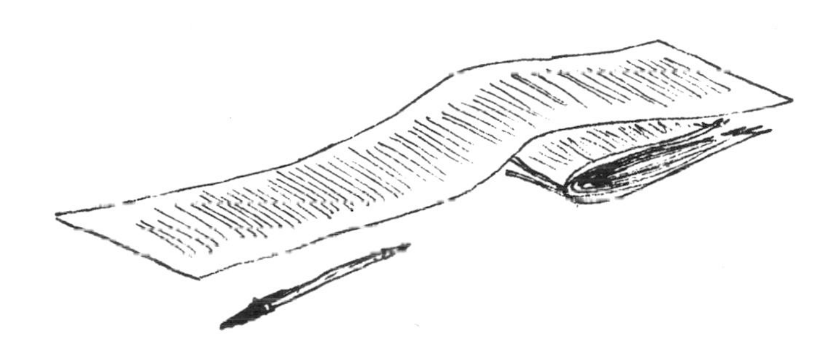

I have, to be honest, always been paid for my words. I suppose they were other people's words first of all, so then I was paid for punctuating them, correcting spelling and putting them in the right order. That is, in effect, what editing is all about. But it does embolden you to think 'I could do this', and so I waited for the opportunity.

It came in the form of a paperback book on house plants, written as a giveaway with a magazine called *Wedding Day and First Home*. Well, a chap has to start somewhere. I only landed the job because whoever it was that Bob Pearson had lined up to write it had let him down. I think he was wary of entrusting me with it, and when I turned in a reasonable job his relief was palpable. So was mine—it meant I earned a little more, and funds were not exactly in ample supply. Oh, and I was about to get married myself.

With the prospect of a mortgage on the horizon I needed all the help I could get, and so I sent a sample article to *Amateur Gardening* magazine. It was a piece I called 'Fur and Feather'—all about plants with furry and feathery foliage. (I did avoid over-alliteration in the article itself.) They took it, changed the title to 'Fur and Feathers' (oblivious to my witty allusion to a shooting periodical that features in the tales of Beatrix Potter) and sent me a few quid. Could I write for them every couple of weeks? they asked.

I was on my way, and Bob, having been happy enough with my booklet for newly married house plant investors, asked if I could write a proper book. About greenhouse gardening. I bit his hand off, and in 1976 *Gardening Under Cover* (a hardback illustrated with line drawings, price £2.99) hit the bookshops. I was now an author. Wot larks!

Alison and I were married in 1975 and moved into a tiny end-of-terrace house—three up, three down—in Sunningdale, Berkshire. At first I wrote in the spare bedroom—pine table, pale blue Laura Ashley sprigged wallpaper—but eventually (when Polly came along) I built a shed in the garden. It was a tiny garden, and so it was a tiny shed, more like a corridor, four feet wide and eight feet long. It had a shelf down one side on which to put my typewriter, and bookshelves floor to ceiling on the other. To reach it I had to cross a wooden plank bridge over a tiny pond that divided the garden in two. We used a baby alarm as a walkie-talkie to summon me into the house for a phone call or a meal.

The garden itself was barely fifteen feet by forty feet but I didn't waste an inch of space. I planted old-fashioned roses—'Cardinal de Richelieu' and 'Belle de Crécy', 'Rosa Mundi' and 'Maiden's Blush', and those two disease-free rugosas, 'Fru Dagmar Hastrup' and 'Roseraie de l'Haÿ'—filling in around them with border perennials. A 'Doyenné du Comice' pear tree was already established, dropping its hefty fruits into the pond each autumn like depth charges.

An old, gnarled wisteria wrapped itself round the front of the house, dripping with purple flower trails each April and scenting the entire house through the open bedroom window. The soil was Bagshot sand, fine as dust but easily cultivated, even after a thunderstorm. It simply swallowed up compost and manure.

At the bottom of the garden I planted a golden-leafed *Robinia* 'Frisia' and built an eight-foot-by-six-foot cedarwood greenhouse with my dad—the second time we'd done that together. It was rather poignant. You can see it on the back of *Gardening Under Cover*. Alison took the photograph. I don't think she ever got paid.

I stayed with Hamlyn for two years, and then a job came up at *Amateur Gardening* magazine. It was a weekly publication on which life would, I reasoned, move a little faster, offer me a different sort of publishing experience. In 1976, a year after we were married, I took a job in London proper—on the umpteenth floor of King's Reach Tower in Stamford Street, as Assistant Editor of the magazine we all called *A.G.*

It was almost a year before I was rash enough to confess to another member of the magazine's staff that I hankered after a bit of broadcasting. You might have thought that by now any thoughts of being the next Percy Thrower would have evaporated in the cold light of day. Apparently they had not.

'That's funny,' said Graham Clarke, the magazine's subeditor. 'We had a letter last year asking us if we knew anyone who could talk on Radio 4.'

'Well?'

'We said we didn't.'

'Oh.' My timing was obviously out.

'Hang on; I've got it here somewhere.' He fished around in his desk drawer among the rubber bands and paperclips, the old files and document wallets. 'Here you are.'

I smoothed out the creases and read the letter. In my lunch hour I set about drafting a letter of my own that I hoped might, somehow, get them to try me out on the radio. I thought it was long gone, but a few days ago, in a drawer of my own I found the carbon copy that I had kept. This is what I wrote to a producer by the name of Denis Lower:

30th August, 1977

Dear Mr Lower,

I believe that some time ago *You and Yours* were looking for someone to act as a kind of 'gardening correspondent' on the programme. If this is still the case might I express my interest? A keen gardener since childhood, I have thirteen years' experience in horticulture ranging from work in a small parks department, to full-time training and subsequent employment at Kew Gardens, and three years in journalism.

I am still only twenty-eight, still enjoy gardening, write frequently in *Amateur Gardening* and am keen to broadcast.

If there is an opportunity on your programme I would be very willing to discuss any contribution I might be able to make.

Yours sincerely,
Alan Titchmarsh
*Assistant Editor*

I love the 'still only twenty-eight'. I don't quite know what the significance of that was, but the letter did the trick.

A MONTH LATER, while I was in the middle of writing a column on the construction of the perfect compost heap, I got a phone call at work. From a lady at the BBC called Marlene Pease (nice name for gardening, I thought). She asked me a few questions. Well, more than a few actually. I wittered on, trying to sound interesting; concise without being monosyllabic. At least, that's what I hope I did. She listened to see if I could string a few words together without sending her to sleep. Then, after what I suppose would have been ten minutes or so—though it seemed like half an hour—she said, 'Can you do us a bit on laying turf?'

'When?' I asked.

'Tomorrow.'

I did my homework. I had chapter and verse on the relative

merits and costs of a lawn made from seed and from turf. But how to put it over? I thought of all my broadcasting heroes, from Percy Thrower to Peter Scott, and wondered how they would perform. Over the next few years I tried to be everyone from Phil Drabble to David Attenborough but decided, in the end, that I had really better be myself. And I suppose that's what came through in that first broadcast.

Like most people, I don't really like the sound of my own voice. I have become used to it. Learned to tolerate it. But it would not be one I would pick off the shelf. I'd rather it were deeper and richer in tone, like the man who interviewed me on that very first broadcast for *You and Yours* back in 1977—Derek Cooper.

Derek looked like a retired colonel—he had a thick military moustache and peered at me, albeit with a kindly expression on his face, over the top of horn-rimmed half-moon glasses. He asked, in a voice that could have been minted by a gravy manufacturer, about the merits of both seed and turf, and the costs, and how one would go about making a new lawn. I tried to sound as personable as I could—chatty without being overfamiliar.

The piece was recorded for the Sunday edition of *You and Yours*, now long gone, though the programme continues to air every weekday lunchtime on Radio 4. As a result, I had not heard Derek's introduction when I was with him in the studio—we just went straight into the interview. On that fateful Sunday Alison and I sat at home and listened, having turned the radio on at least an hour before transmission so we did not miss it.

And then the moment came. Derek set up the item and introduced me. As Alan Titchfield. I looked at Alison. She looked at me, sympathetically. 'Never mind,' she said. 'You sound fine.'

And then it was all over and Derek went into what is known as the 'back announcement': 'I must apologise to Alan Titchmarsh for calling him Alan Titchfield. Dynamic he may be, but no thunderbolt. I'm sure we'll be hearing more of him.'

It was a nice touch. Flattering even. And he was as good as his word. *You and Yours* called me in every week or so to 'do a piece'.

I'd do seasonal and sometimes news-related items. I'd sit with the presenters and chat about the finer points of hybrid teas and floribundas, spider plants and weeping figs, gradually learning my craft, avoiding 'ums' and 'ers' and passing on information in what I hoped was an entertaining way. I've always felt quite strongly that entertainment—or, more accurately, engagement—was just as important as knowing your stuff.

THE MAIN CURRENT affairs programme on Radio 4 back then—as now—was the one that 'set the agenda' for the day: the *Today* programme. In the summer of 1979 Britain was invaded by a foreign army. It was an army of greenfly and it had come across the English Channel on a southeasterly current of air. This was no thinly scattered regiment, but a dense airborne squadron of aliens intent on making their mark on British soil. And they did. They plastered the rosebushes of southeast England in their millions. They stuck to emulsion and to gloss and ruined the handiwork of decorators from Margate to Dover.

What could the nation do in the face of such an unexpected invasion? We'd had no way of knowing it was going to happen. There had been no intelligence. We should have been told about it. What was the government doing? The powers that be at the *Today* programme, ever willing to ask the questions the nation needs answered, got on the phone immediately to someone who would know. They rang me.

Could I come in the following morning and tell Britain's gardeners what to do in the face of an unprecedented invasion of aphids? Was it the end of gardens as we knew them? Would this epidemic ever end? Mercifully the terms 'global warming' and 'climate change' were unknown back then, and it was all put down to that comforting state of affairs: 'an act of God'.

At 5.30 a.m. the following day a sleek black saloon pulled up outside our little cottage in Sunningdale and I was whisked off. Live radio this time. Not recorded. I sat down in the *Today* studio in Broadcasting House at the appointed hour, with the grizzly, bearded Brian Redhead and the florid-cheeked John Timpson quizzing me like a pair of secret-service interrogators. I gave my opinion on the current state of the nation vis-à-vis greenfly.

I left the studio some time after the programme had ended, having declined all offers from its presenters of Scotch whisky, toast and marmalade. This was, after all, the end of their day, even if it was the beginning of mine. By the time I arrived at the offices of *Amateur Gardening*, the phone was already ringing. I took the call. It was from the early-evening television current affairs programme *Nationwide*. 'We heard you on *Today*,' said the voice at the other end of the line. 'Would you like to come in and advise our viewers on how to cope with the greenfly invasion?'

And so, at the other end of my working day, another black saloon car came to take me to the BBC's Lime Grove studios where *Nationwide* was beamed around the country. In my smart blue-and-white-striped shirt and my navy-blue tie with the white spots, I wove as best I could between rosebushes and sprayers, specific aphicides and syringes (organic gardening being but a twinkle in my eye back then) and told an anxious nation what I thought they could do to rid themselves of these turbulent insects.

'Wonderful,' they said at the end. 'You must come back and do some more.' I was over the moon. Live television was a great buzz. It sort of concentrated your energies, knowing that you only had one chance to get it right. A bit like theatre, I suppose.

I went home on a high. 'What was it like?' Alison asked. 'Well,' I said, 'it was a bit like tasting blood.'

I THINK MY MUM had been pretty devastated when I left home. It also coincided with the onset of rheumatoid arthritis, which was to deform the most beautiful hands I have ever seen. She didn't complain, of course, being the 'get up and get on' woman that she was, or had been. In a way that made it even worse. She just gritted her teeth and battled on, though she did become more crotchety, more difficult to live with. You can't really blame her.

Dad remained his old self. 'Yes, dear' was his most oft-used line.

But to assume that he was a henpecked husband in the mode of those Bamforth Comic seaside postcards would be to do him a disservice. He put his foot down when he needed to.

There was three months' difference in age—Mum was born in January 1924, Dad in March of that year—and they lived just a couple of streets away from one another in Ilkley. They went to the same school and then, when the war came, Dad was called up and sent to India—Bangalore, I think—as a craftsman sorting out tyres for lorries. A curious job for a plumber. But the war ended shortly afterwards—Dad told us that they had heard he was coming. Mum went to Lister's Mill in Addingham, wore clogs and worked on the looms. They met at a dance in the King's Hall in November 1946 (Mum had ditched the clogs that night). 'Was it love at first sight?' I once asked her. 'It must have been something,' was her reply. They courted for six months, were engaged for six months and got married on 3rd December, 1947.

The trouble was, they had little or no money saved, what with the war and their low wages, so they moved in with Dad's mum, Florrie, or Grandma Titch as my sister and I would later call her. Anyway, in the autumn of 1949 they found their own place—number 34 Nelson Road—which they bought, on a mortgage, for £400. I would have been six months old. My sister, Kathryn Victoria, arrived in 1954.

The great thing about having a plumber for a dad was that we were the first house in the street to get central heating—second-hand, mind; taken out of somebody else's house when they went for an upgrade. But as well as being a plumber, Dad was a great handyman—he made everything from wardrobes to toy forts, kitchen cabinets to vivariums.

Mum was handy too. Only our underwear was shop-bought. And our socks and shoes, of course. The rest was hand-knitted and hand-sewn—jumpers, shorts, trousers, coats and the regulation winter balaclava. We lived in Nelson Road until 1965, when we moved to a pebbledashed semi up the posher end of town in Victoria Close, the year after I had started work—£3,250, that cost.

Mum did not work while we were growing up. Well, not for money. She washed and ironed, cooked and baked and cleaned, shopped and looked after the garden, as well as two children, which seemed to fill the week to overflowing.

We had no car until my dad was given a firm's pick-up van in the early 1960s, in which we would journey up the dales for 'a run out' on Sunday afternoons. That was after we'd been to church, mind. Both Dad and I sang in the choir, and all three of us, Mum, Dad and I, rang the bells. Mum became 'enrolling member' of the Mothers' Union and, later, Brown Owl of the church Brownie pack, all before the arthritis began to curb her activities.

Dad worked all day as a plumber, and his part-time job as a fireman saw him cleaning the shiny 'appliance' and checking hydrants on Tuesday nights. Then he'd go to the pub for a drink. Mum would go out one evening a week to her 'hens'—four friends who had known each other since their youth and childhood, and who would meet in each other's houses on rotation to chat and sew and knit and have a light supper together.

They'd go out to the pub together on a Friday night, with a couple of friends, and sometimes on Saturdays, too, often up the dale to Addingham where the pubs stayed open an extra half-hour until 11 p.m. Looking back I find it hard to imagine how on earth they managed on Dad's lowly wage. But, apart from the mortgage, they never owed anything.

We would have a one-week family holiday each year—usually to Bispham, which Mum considered the select end of Blackpool—and it was not until I was twenty and at Kew that we had our first foreign holiday, to Majorca. Mum loved the warmth, which eased the pain of her arthritis, but Dad never seemed comfortable with foreign food, which almost always disagreed with him.

WHEN MY SISTER and I had both left home, their lives changed. Well, Mum's did. She went to work in her brother's grocer's shop on Skipton Road. When Alison and I married, we would be sent home from our visits to Yorkshire with a wonderful food parcel of free-range eggs and slices of ham, freshly ground coffee and assorted pickles—a real help in the early days of our marriage when our funds were short.

Mum was the outwardly dominant of the two, but she depended entirely on my father for her stability. He was as solid as a rock—a small man, a little stooped and very slight—but he was straightforward, honest as the day is long, quiet about anything to do with emotion and with one or two surprising gifts. He had a fine tenor voice and he also had the neatest handwriting I have ever known. When he filled in a crossword it looked almost printed. Oh, and he could make a newspaper last almost all day. He was the only man I ever knew who read all the small ads. Maybe he just enjoyed the peace and quiet to be found behind the *Yorkshire Post*.

Mum was more gregarious than Dad by nature. A born flirt, she enjoyed the company of men more than women, whom she seemed to consider as rivals, though she was always steadfastly faithful to my father. As a couple they were totally devoted. Apart from Mum's hens and the fire service they did nothing without each other, so when my father died suddenly of a heart attack in 1986, the bottom fell out of her world. She was devastated.

I had been working in Stoke-on-Trent at the garden festival. There were no mobile phones in those days. I drove back home to Hampshire, oblivious to what had happened, and only when I got there could Alison tell me the news. I walked up to the top of the garden and stood for a bit. Leaning on a tree. Then I came back to the house, packed a bag, got in the car and drove up to Yorkshire.

Mum never did get over it. The first year was the worst, as it always is, with all those anniversaries to be got out of the way. It did not help that I lived 200 miles away and that Kath took the brunt of Mum's grief. But we built her a granny flat above the garage and Kath and her family then moved into the house. Mum had a stairlift, and when she turned it on and it hummed into life, it was like hearing the approach of the ticking crocodile in *Peter Pan*.

It is a common predicament, and one that is universally acknowledged, that absent sons are often thought of more highly than the ever-present daughters who do all the work. I owe my sister more than I can say for hanging on in there while I juggled radio, television, writing, a family and, to a lesser extent, the well-being of my mother.

The nicest thing is that my mum, and my dad to a lesser degree, saw me 'getting on'. I say this, not from an egotistical point of view, but simply to prove to them that their early confidence, thought by some to be foolhardy, was not misplaced.

It was impossible to realise, until they were gone, just how much of my life revolved around them. Whether or not it is healthy or normal I cannot say, but since their passing I have realised just how much I did to impress them. I know in my heart that it is the natural order of things for children to oulive their parents—and the reverse option is intolerable—but when they go they leave a massive hole in your life.

Mum soldiered on without her man for sixteen years, but then in December 2002 she had a stroke and was taken into hospital. Another one followed and it was clear that she was unlikely to pull through.

The last time my sister and I were with her she made some silly joke about my not hearing what she said. 'He needs a blow through,' she said, and made a blowing motion with pursed lips. Silly the things that stick in your mind.

I went back one last time on my own before I had to return to Hampshire, where we were moving house. It seems so dreadful now that I did not stay with her, but I could not leave the family to up sticks without me, and it was unclear how long Mum could carry on. I'd be able to return as soon as we were settled in. I sat with her and held her hand. She drifted in and out of consciousness and smiled at me from time to time.

After an hour or so I got up to go and she opened her eyes. 'You going?'

'Yes. Will you be all right?'

She nodded.

We had never, as a family, been especially outspoken in our sentiments. We kissed and hugged every time we met, but we never *said* anything. You just didn't do that in Yorkshire. Not back in the fifties and sixties. But now it didn't seem to matter any more. I squeezed her hand and told her that I loved her very much.

She squeezed it back, with as much strength as she had. 'Not as much as I love you,' she said.

I kissed her forehead and got up to go. At the end of the hospital ward I turned round and looked back at her. She slowly waved her fingers above the sheets, and winked at me.

It was the last time I saw her. Two days later she died peacefully in her sleep.

With money she left me I bought a little hexagonal summerhouse. Pale blue it is. Sitting in the sunshine across from where I write. Mum wasn't mad about my writing—not about the novels, anyway. She had heard they were a bit saucy, and found any excuse not to read them—in the normal hardbacks the print was too small for her; in the large-print version the book became too heavy. It was a neat way out.

But what she did always love was the gardening—the books and the television programmes. That and the fresh air. She would never be in the house without a window, and preferably the back door as well, wide open. She did not like, as she put it, 'being fast', meaning stuck or unable to get out.

I had a plaque made for the back wall of the summerhouse, which is open on three sides, just as she would have wanted. I didn't want to put anything too maudlin on it, but I did want it to be a reminder of her. It's not flashy, just a simple oval of slate:

In happy memory of<br>Bessie Titchmarsh<br>1924–2002<br>who loved being outside.

I think she would have liked that.

# GOING IT ALONE

I had now reached the heady heights of Deputy Editor on IPC's *Amateur Gardening* magazine. Not bad at the age of thirty. Secure. Pensionable. Not unhappy with my lot, seeing that I was able to write columns for the magazine during the day and books in my spare time. Except that meant I did not *have* any spare time.

But then a timely spanner was thrown in the works. The magazine, it was decided, would move to Poole in Dorset, one of IPC's country outposts where, not unreasonably, it was thought that a gardening magazine might be suitably stabled. Except that neither Alison nor I wanted, at that time, to move to Dorset. Well, not to be tied to a job that I did not intend to keep for life. And what about our friends? They all lived in and around London.

We had already had the family discussion about my workload. It had become a bit weighty. I would journey up to London by train early in the morning, work all day in Stamford Street (not my idea of Shangri-la), come home for about 7 p.m., watch television, chat and eat until 8p.m.—a whole hour to ourselves—and then go up into the spare bedroom to write until bedtime at 11 p.m. This was the Monday to Friday routine, which would explain why the young married couple became rather tetchy with one another in the launderette on a Saturday morning. We did eventually get our own machine, but that only partially solved the problem.

Mrs T, with her usual capacity for common sense, suggested that something had to go, and that she would rather it was not her.

There was a lot of soul-searching. Lots of sums. I worked out that with the amount of freelance work I now had we would be able to survive—just. But it would mean a drop in salary. Still, *Amateur Gardening* had said they would keep commissioning columns every week and now I would be paid for them. And there was the radio work, and the occasional TV. It was, we decided, worth the risk, and I did hate commuting. What could be better than writing about gardening in a shed halfway down the garden?

The answer to this rhetorical question came six months later with the arrival of Polly. I thought I liked being a gardener, but being a dad, at the risk of becoming far too sentimental, was and is just the best thing of all. Bar none. I worry, of course. Dads do. About all kinds of things. Not least the amount of space children take up, which was why, in 1981, we moved down to Hampshire so there would be more room. Camilla arrived in August 1982. Since then I have shared my life with three women. Even our three dogs have been bitches. There are the cats, of course. They were boys, yes, but cut out for a bachelor life. It is, I maintain, good to be the undisputed master of one's own household. And if you believe that . . .

After trying me out a little, and discovering no discernible reduction in viewing figures, *Nationwide* created a Friday slot for me. 'Down to Earth' it was called, with refreshing candour. I had a potting shed and a lawn, situated up on the roof of Lime Grove during the summer months, and in the studio during autumn and winter. At least that way the sun always shone. Having been interviewed for my first few appearances, I was now allowed to go solo and do 'pieces to camera', since they clearly had no difficulty in getting me to talk.

But what to wear? I discounted Percy's three-piece suit. And country tweeds. I plumped instead for rugby shirts. Suitably casual and appropriately rugged, I reasoned. Quite why I was persuaded a year or two later to go into hand-knitted picture-fronted sweaters I cannot imagine. It was my first fashion faux pas and one of which I am regularly reminded when some well-meaning soul brings an old copy of *Woman's Own* or *Amateur Gardening* for me to sign. There I am, with my gap-toothed grin, proudly sporting a pullover decorated with a prize marrow, complete with 1st Prize rosette, or a desert island with palm trees, or a country scene with sheep. Why, oh, why, oh, why . . .?

By now, *Nationwide* had transformed into something called *60 Minutes*, and so the programme which had once brought us the skateboarding duck, but which, more importantly, gave Britain a sense of identity, with correspondents in all the regions chipping into the network every evening, began its rather inglorious descent into broadcasting oblivion.

*Breakfast Time* was the first successful early-morning TV programme, surprisingly trouncing the much-heralded *TV-AM* with its bevy of stars: Angela Rippon, Michael Parkinson, Anna Ford, David Frost and Robert Kee. It was anchored by Frank Bough (with whom I had worked on *Nationwide*) and Selina Scott. They had launched the programme in 1982 with a West Country gardening expert by the name of Don Hoyle, who had died suddenly and unexpectedly before the first twelve months were up. Considerately they had not replaced him, but on the programme's first anniversary they had decided to fill the hole Don had left, and they asked if I would like to take the job.

Instead of one live spot a week on the regulation Friday night (gardening being something that people only do at weekends), I was offered two—a Tuesday phone-in and a 'straight piece' on the Friday. I leapt at the chance, and for the next four years I rose at 4.30 a.m. two days a week in time to get to the studio for 5.30 a.m. and be on air an hour later.

For the first time in my life I felt completely at ease with what I was doing—writing and broadcasting about something I am passionate about, and being allowed to do so from home.

'How do you discipline yourself?' People ask it all the time. My reply is always the same. There is no need to discipline yourself to do something you love. I don't feel as if I *work*, really. I just *do* things.

And then there is the other question. If you had to give up writing, or broadcasting, or gardening, which would it be? That's like asking someone which is their favourite child. Luckily, I don't have to give up any of them. Well, not until they give *me* up. Which they probably will. Eventually. Telly will be the first to disappear. When bits of me start to fall off. Or I lose my marbles. Until then I'll keep on trying to get away with it.

*Breakfast Time* gave me an opportunity to enthuse about my passion to a wider public. Several million of them, rather than the few hundred thousand that the gardening magazines could offer. Practical gardening has always been my forte—just growing plants, and putting them together in a pleasing way.

As well as demonstrating the craft of taking cuttings on live early-morning television (try not to perforate the skin with a sharp knife—the resultant gore might put people off their bacon and eggs), I also undertook country walks, proving, I hope, that gardening and a love of nature are inextricably entwined.

TO HAVE ONE PLANT named after you may be regarded as good fortune. To have six looks like boastfulness. That's what Lady Bracknell would have said. It is, truth to tell, a bit embarrassing. I suppose I should have a flowerbed in which they all grow, but I can't bring myself to do it, lest some garden visitor should enquire what one of them is called, and then another and another. They would think the needle had got stuck in the groove.

The sweet pea was the first, back in 1985 when I was gardening on *Breakfast Time*. I had a letter from Robert Bolton, a famed grower of the flower. Could he, he asked, name a variety after me? I did have the presence of mind to ask if I could see it first. He sent me a bunch. In a box. I unwrapped them and discovered they had no scent. I rang him up. How to put it tactfully? I talked round the subject until he eventually said, 'Of course, you won't smell, having been in the post for a day or two.'

'I do have a decent perfume then?'

'Good heavens yes! Wonderfully delicate but quite marked.'

So I thanked him and graciously accepted, and 'Alan Titchmarsh' the sweet pea has survived now for twenty-four years. He can be a bit tricky. Sometimes he gets bud drop. But in a good year he is cream, flushed pink with frilly edges and a delicate scent. And he has won medals, probably thanks to a good, stiff stalk.

After twenty years or so, when Robert Bolton had died, it looked as if 'A. T. sweet pea' was on his way out, to be superseded by other newer varieties (it is in nature as it is on screen), but he was rescued by an old Kew student, Dave Matthewman, and is now firmly planted on his seed list. I'd like to think Dave resurrected me because I'm worth growing, rather than just for old times' sake. I keep meaning to have me growing on one side of the front door and 'Percy Thrower' (he's lavender blue) the other. I'd rather like that.

The garden pink came next, a good fifteen years ago now, raised by Steven Bailey. I do have stamina. I'm white with a green eye that is slightly bloodshot. (A stickler for accuracy is Steven Bailey.) Try me next to 'Doris' if you like, though to be honest I'm more comfortable with 'Mrs Sinkins', in spite of her split calyx.

The lupin was launched a few years ago now, tall and yellow and bred by the Woodfield brothers of Stratford-upon-Avon. I've never grown 'me' the lupin. Well, I'm on chalk, and they don't much like it. Their leaves become yellow and chlorotic. But I'm flattered that a plant as tall, stately and elegant as a lupin bears my name. It's all very well being squat (the pink) and a good climber (the sweet pea) but both tendencies are open to criticism.

The 'Alan Titchmarsh' fuchsia, raised by Carol Gubler, is what they call a 'good doer', and the 'Alan Titchmarsh' hosta from Park Green Nurseries has wonderfully bright leaves—soft green with a butter-yellow streak right down the centre. (I don't think they were being funny.)

But it was in 2005 that my dream came true and I finally

became a rose, thanks to David Austin. David is famous for his 'English Roses'—shrub roses that are repeat flowering, unlike a lot of the older varieties that have but a single flush of bloom in late June and early July.

The English rose 'Alan Titchmarsh' is . . . well, modesty forbids that I should describe myself. I will simply repeat the poetic description of me from David Austin's book *The English Roses*:

> This variety bears quite large, deeply cupped, full-petalled, slightly incurved flowers that are well filled with petals. The outer petals are pale pink, the centre petals of a much stronger, glowing warm pink. 'Alan Titchmarsh' forms a quite large shrub of elegant, arching growth. This rose has very good disease resistance.

So there you are. I have a border of me just outside the house. Do I have any faults? Well, my neck is perhaps a little weak—the flowers nod gracefully—but I am, as David says, very disease resistant and after a year or two I make a splendid and statuesque plant. In short, I like to think that, in spite of some minor faults, I am worth persisting with. It is in the garden as it is in life . . .

MY FIRST TASTE of Chelsea Flower Show came when I was at college in May 1969. I'd like to claim that it blew me away. It would make a better story. The truth is that I have little recollection of it except the flapping canvas of the Great Marquee, show gardens that were staid and restrained by today's standards—rectangles of lawn and formal pools—and in the Great Marquee the floral seasons strangely mixed together—daffodils with roses, strawberries with chrysanthemums, delphiniums with tulips. Odd.

I went there every year after that and got to know it rather better, but it was not until 1983 that it became a part of my life and since then it has been a permanent fixture in my diary.

By 1983 I was writing a gardening column for *Woman's Own*. They decided, at one of those meetings they have every hour on the hour in magazine offices, that it would be a great idea to have a garden at Chelsea Flower Show and raise the horticultural profile of the magazine. At least, I imagine that's what they thought. They asked me what I could come up with. What I came up with was a family garden. It was not at all elaborate, or large—about twenty feet by forty feet with a stretch of lawn, a swing, a sandpit, a bright pink parasol and a millstone water feature, which was then quite a novelty.

Three weeks we had to build it, me and Mike Chewter and his mate Ray. Mike was a Chelsea veteran who had been recommended to me and in whom I found a trustworthy and hardworking project manager. We were rather pleased with the result. We won a Silver Gilt Medal, and I won a place on the BBC television presentation team.

By this time, Peter Seabrook had been presenting the Chelsea Flower Show coverage since 1976, with a different 'floating' presenter every year—either a broadcaster (usually a woman) or someone who was involved with the show in a professional capacity—a garden designer or an exhibitor in the Floral Marquee.

I had been on the box for about three years by this time so thought I knew the ropes, but putting together an hour's worth of television at an outside broadcast is a world away from four minutes in a studio, as I was to discover.

Not that I was simply invited to participate. I was asked to come in for a chat with Neil Eccles, the executive producer, in his office in Shepherd's Bush. Peter Seabrook was there, too, and took part in the light grilling that followed. At the end of this flexing of presentational muscles—the old hand making sure that the new boy was up to the job—I was asked if I'd like to be a part of the team. I said that I would, and went home with barely suppressed glee and the usual helping of apprehensiveness.

Back then the Chelsea coverage amounted to two hour-long programmes, one that Peter did on his own—*Growing For Gold*—about the build-up, which transmitted on the Sunday night before the show opened, and one evening programme on the Tuesday of show week. The latter would be where I was involved. We filmed from the Sunday right through until Tuesday afternoon, working twelve-hour days and often laying down the voice-over as late as ten minutes before transmission.

This is hard enough work on its own, but when you are also building a show garden it is totally exhausting. I'll be grateful to the old man until my dying day for his generosity with facts and information, which he shared unstintingly with the young presenter wished upon him. He was an absolute brick.

This sort of presentation is a steep learning curve. With cameras in position, an assistant producer will come and ask you to talk for two or three minutes on anything from cauliflowers to flower arranging, cacti to orchids. You'll be taken to the stand, introduced to the exhibitor (if you're lucky) and have a couple of minutes to pump them for information before you have to stand in front of the camera and speak as though you are an expert on everything that meets your eye. Well, you are, to some extent, but it's the nitty-gritty bits that often catch you out. What year was this plant raised? Who bred it? What sort of growing conditions does it like?

Anyway, I can't have done too badly, since they asked me back the following year. The year after that, 1985, I made another garden for *Woman's Own* and this time landed the Holy Grail—a Gold Medal. It was a country kitchen garden with fruit and vegetables, flower borders and daisy-studded grass, a brick and flint wall with a little gate in it, two Chinese Chippendale benches from Chatsworth Carpenters, a little rill—oh, it did look lovely.

What's more, the Queen came to look at it. Along with other members of the royal family, she pays a private visit on the Monday afternoon before the show opens to members of the RHS on Tuesday. She seemed impressed. She said, 'I like your onions. They're nice and small.' Then, seeing that I looked a little crestfallen, she added, 'When they're big they taste of nothing at all.'

The garden was, by today's standards, modest in aspiration. I charged *Woman's Own* £11,000 for making it, which included all my time as well as the plants and the building costs. The garden that was awarded Best in Show in 2009, by comparison, cost £350,000.

In the intervening years the show coverage has changed dramatically. The contract was awarded to Channel 4 for a couple of years at the turn of the millennium, and then came back to the BBC and so, with just a couple of years off, I have been presenting the coverage for twenty-seven years. Best be quiet about that or they'll start to think it's time for a change.

For the last twenty years I've been the main anchor of the television coverage, which now stretches over seven days, with a half-hour at lunchtime and at least an hour most evenings. Where once we offered an hour's coverage, we now supply around twelve hours over the week.

My own Chelsea week begins on the Saturday night before the show, when I move into a local hotel with a week's worth of clothes. 'Don't you have a London flat?' I get asked. My answer is that it's rather nice to have someone else cook supper when you get back in the evening, so I prefer a hotel. It is, I reckon, a necessary perk. I'll rise at 5.30 a.m. and be in the grounds of the Royal Hospital at around 6.30 a.m. on Sunday, filming right through until 6 or 7 p.m. That sort of regime will continue for the rest of the week, ending on Saturday at around 6 p.m., when those who have been stalwart enough to stay for the sell-off will stagger home with hanging baskets dripping with fuchsias, towering delphiniums, monstrous tree ferns and whatever else they can lay their hands on.

I get ribbed about the clothes. Sunday will be relatively informal—a jacket and an open-necked shirt—but Chelsea is still a part of that uniquely British phenomenon called 'The Season' so I like to do it the honour of smartening up. On Monday—Press Day and the day of the royal visit—I'll wear a suit and tie, and keep the tie and a jacket for the two members' days that follow. Then, when the show opens to the public for Thursday, Friday and Saturday, it's back to a jacket and open-necked shirt. Does it really matter? Does anyone really care? Well, I like to think we don't get enough 'special' in our lives, so I try to keep Chelsea special. I reckon it's worth more than a T-shirt and jeans. Must be my age . . .

Then there's the badge. It gets a lot of comments, mainly because it glints in the sun. I wear it on my left lapel. It's the Victoria Medal of Honour—the Royal Horticultural Society's highest award, limited to no more than sixty-three horticulturists at any one time, the same number of years as Queen Victoria's reign. They gave me it in 2004 and it came as a bit of a shock. In 2009 they made me a Vice-President, at the same time as Lord Heseltine. I'm hoping for a seat in government very shortly.

As for the style of the show itself, it changes each year. Some things remain constant, of course—the height of the delphiniums, the succulence of the National Farmers' Union vegetables, the outrageousness of the National Association of Flower Arrangement Societies' stand—but the prominence of a particular group of plants, sometimes cottage garden flowers, sometimes orchids, is often a reflection of plant fads and fashions and the way our gardens are going.

Chelsea, more than ever, offers a wake-up call each spring to anyone who thinks that gardening is unimportant or stagnating. I don't mind if it sometimes irritates, provided that the irritation results in a positive outcome and makes people think about their surroundings. It can also put them off, of course, since it is a counsel of perfection and in its way quite unreal. How can anybody hope to achieve a garden that looks like a Chelsea garden? They can't, of course. Chelsea gardens are designed to look perfect for one week in May. They would look pretty dreary in September or February. But what I hope the show does do, more than anything else, is inspire people to at least have a go.

I'VE ALWAYS FELT SAD that we can't, as a nation, decide on who should occupy the fourth plinth in Trafalgar Square. It seems to me a sign of mean-spiritedness rather than egalitarianism that we can't agree on one mortal who deserves this country's approbation. Anyway, in my case there is no disagreement whatsoever on who my own heroes are. The people who chivvied and encouraged and who could spot latent talent. Well, what they *thought* was talent. Or something.

It started with Granddad Hardisty, of course, on his allotment.

But outside the family, Harry Rhodes must count as my first real hero. He taught me for only a year when I was nine, but his influence was profound and long-lasting. His enthusiasm was boundless and in evidence both in the classroom and at Sunday school. I don't remember him ever being rabidly evangelical—that was not his style, and anyway Ilkley All Saints was Low Church, understated rather than happy-clappy. He taught us Religious Knowledge in the same way that he taught us English and sums, matter-of-factly but always brightly.

But the reason that he is a hero is twofold. First, because he was always pleasant and encouraging, realising that such an approach was more effective than the reverse, a concept strangely incomprehensible to many teachers back then. Second, because he was a keen gardener. Each autumn, at the church bazaar in the King's Hall, he sold cacti and succulents that he had grown in his greenhouse at home. I bought them for sixpence apiece and grew them first on the lavatory windowsill and then—when that overflowed—in my little polythene greenhouse. Mr Rhodes taught me my first botanical Latin. *Bryophyllum pinnatum*, a succulent that produced tiny plantlets along the serrations of its leaves and gave a young gardener the easiest possible introduction to plant propagation.

I've probably said enough about Percy Thrower, who was my second hero. If meeting him for the first time was a thrill, then getting to know him a little better over the space of thirteen years was just as rewarding. I still aspire to his level of professionalism, the smoothness of his delivery and his relaxed style of broadcasting. He, more than anyone, influenced my television career, and I can only hope for a fraction of his charisma and watchability.

Not all my heroes have hopped the twig. Beth Chatto is very much alive, and she is a heroine to countless gardeners. I have known Beth for almost as long as I have known my wife—around thirty years—and we swap regular letters and the occasional phone call. Why is she a heroine? Well, not just because of her astonishing gardening expertise and skill with plants, but because she is such good company and still curious, still learning. Beth will ask you for your opinion on almost anything—from plants to music to painting—and listen, and evaluate, and reason and then come back with her take on it. She is stimulating, in the same way that Christopher Lloyd—another hero—was stimulating.

Christo's garden at Great Dixter in East Sussex was, and is, a mecca for keen gardeners, but he was a tricky old stick to deal with. The secret was to stand up to him and give as good as you got, politely but firmly, and never to bluster or pretend you knew something you did not. Oh, he would have a go at you—'Fancy you not knowing that, Alan; well, you do surprise me!'—but always with a twinkle in his eye.

His plant knowledge was prodigious and practical; he knew what grew well with what, but took great delight in shocking people, planting clashing colours to make visitors raise their eyebrows. And he was no respecter of tradition, ripping out the rosebeds at Dixter to make a tropical garden. Sometimes his schemes worked and sometimes they didn't, but it was trying them out that gave him such pleasure.

I'd put any one of these four on the remaining plinth in Trafalgar Square. How fitting it would be to have among the warriors and kings someone who had made their mark through the peaceful occupation of growing things.

There is, of course, an alternative hero who fits the bill on two counts. First, he is royal, and second, he is as good a champion as the natural world has ever had. The Prince of Wales takes more flak than most, for doing a job he did not choose to do and doing it with every ounce of energy he possesses. I have never known a harder worker. He takes on architects and he takes on governments. There are those who think he should pipe down, but I reckon he's the best royal voice the people have ever had. You might quarrel with some of his opinions, but public opinion seems to be coming round to more and more of them. And when he rattles those in high places who think they are beyond criticism I feel a sense of satisfaction at their discomfort. He is a keen and knowledgeable gardener, a passionate environmentalist and a born countryman who deserves to be judged on things other than an unfortunate marriage. The achievements of the Prince's Trust alone—unmatched by any government initiative—qualify him for heroic status. Yes; he'll fit the fourth plinth very nicely.

## MAKING GARDENS

In 1986 I had an offer I almost refused and which was to change the direction of my life altogether.

Between breakfast time and lunchtime the BBC showed either schools' programmes or the test card. By the mid-eighties it became clear that an opportunity existed to fill more of the airwaves, and daytime television was born. I was asked by a man called Roger Laughton, who was given charge of the hours between 9 a.m. and 6 p.m., if I had ever considered doing any television other than gardening. I told him I had not.

'Do you fancy auditioning for a new programme we're planning to run late morning? A viewers' feedback programme. Like *Points of View* but longer and with more teeth. It will be called *Open Air*.'

I hummed and hawed. But it did sound like a challenge, so I went up to Manchester and auditioned along with a pleasant, fresh-faced chap called Peter Bazalgette. It was a baptism by fire—sitting in a studio fielding phone calls and conducting interviews for an hour and a half, when previously, apart from the Chelsea Flower Show, I had presented nothing longer than four minutes. Anyway, I got the job. Peter didn't. Instead he went on to found Bazal Productions, which became part of Endemol, which came up with the ideas for *Changing Rooms* and *Ground Force*. He's now a powerful media mogul. Funny how life works out, isn't it? And it says a lot about Peter that he never bore me a grudge.

I was offered the anchorman's job, five days a week. I turned it down, explaining that I was a gardener first and foremost, with writing commitments on top and that I would be prepared to do just one day a week—Fridays.

Looking back I am astonished that a) I had the nerve to be so picky and that b) they agreed to take me on under those terms. So who did they get to do the other four days? An Irish lad called Eamonn Holmes.

Along with Eamonn and Pattie Coldwell I presented *Open Air* for a year, and was then offered the chance of having a crack at a lunchtime show to be transmitted from BBC Pebble Mill. By now I had the bit between my teeth. I simply loved live television—I still do—and the chance to front a magazine programme for an hour every lunchtime, rather than simply talk about last night's TV, was too good an invitation to turn down. I took the job and along with Pamela Armstrong (for the first year), Sue Cook, Judi Spiers and Floella Benjamin, presented *Daytime Live*, which eventually morphed into a chat show called, simply, *Pebble Mill*.

The programme ran for ten years between 1987 and 1996, and during that time I had a chance to talk to a wide range of heroes, from Alan Bennett (who had a fresh pear and cold tongue for lunch in the canteen) to Dirk Bogarde, who chatted amiably about his life as we sat in the stalls at the National Theatre. I leaned on Sir Georg Solti's piano in his home in St John's Wood while he played Mozart, and sat next to Placido Domingo as he took Evelyn Glennie's hand in his and sang 'Your Tiny Hand is Frozen'. I can still see the rapt expression of incredulity on her face.

There are those who are sniffy about daytime television. To me it doesn't matter what time a programme is transmitted; what matters is that production standards remain high regardless of the hour. They don't always, of course, but I like to think I've done my bit to help. There is, I reckon, a world of difference between popularising and dumbing down. Sadly not all critics see it that way.

It was while I was billeted at Pebble Mill that I was asked to present *Songs of Praise*. It was the shortest job interview I've ever had. I bumped into the series producer Roger Hutchings in the corridor. 'You go to church, don't you?' he asked. 'Sometimes,' I said. 'Fancy presenting *Songs of Praise*?'

I was very wary at first, not wanting to be seen as holier-than-thou or a 'God botherer'. My faith is at the heart of my life but I do shudder when someone comes up to me and says, 'You're a Christian, aren't you?' as if to imply that I am somehow different from the common herd. My beliefs are private; my business and nobody else's. If folk think I've 'got religion' they might steer clear of me. That's what 'Low Church C of E' does for you. It is a suitable faith for a Yorkshireman—deep maybe, but understated and tacitly accepted, rather than something to make a song and dance about. But I reasoned that there are moments in everyone's life when they need to stand up for their beliefs, however tentatively, and I do think it is important that *Songs of Praise* remains on television on a Sunday evening, shunted from pillar to post though it might be, to accommodate more 'mainstream' programmes. (I wonder what God makes of the fact that He is not considered 'mainstream'?)

So I overcame my reservations, telling myself that in the interviews that are a part of the programme I would be taking the standpoint of 'everyman' rather than an evangelist. In the five years that I presented *Songs of Praise*, alternating for the most part with the delightfully cheerful Pam Rhodes, I saw more of the world and the UK than with any other programme I've been involved with before or since, and it gave me a heartening view of humanity—I met people who had overcome the most fearsome obstacles and tragedies in life with stoicism and good humour, backed up by a faith that might sometimes be shaky but which had, in the end, seen them through.

Of all the things I saw, the images that stay with me the most strongly are those of refugees queuing in Bosnia—doctors and businessmen carrying their lives in a plastic bag, lining up with the long-term poor—and the abandoned babies in serried ranks of cots in a Romanian orphanage. I stop and think, every now and then, what might have become of the dark-eyed infant called Cosmina I held in my arms, and who wrapped her fingers round mine. Where is she now? Is she being looked after?

PEBBLE MILL came to an end in 1996. 'It has run its natural course,' they said. I was about to find myself without a job, on television at least, though the writing seemed set to continue unabated. And then they asked if I would like to take over *Gardeners' World* when Geoff Hamilton stepped down. Like most other things in my life, it came out of the blue.

The funny thing about fate is that while you can help it along, you can't force its hand. I had auditioned for *Gardeners' World* back in the early eighties—when Geoff had ended up landing the job. They said that Geoff's garden was more relevant to the majority of their viewers because Barnsdale was in the Midlands, rather than mine which was in the south. They were probably just being kind. Geoff was a more experienced broadcaster than I was back then. But by 1996 he was ready to leave, having presented the programme for seventeen years.

He and I had known each other for a long time; I had even written for him in the 1970s when he was editor of *Practical Gardening* magazine. We chatted about when he wanted to step down from *GW* and when I would take over, and agreed that Easter 1997 would be a good time. But fate stepped in again, this time in the saddest of ways. Geoff died of a heart attack in the summer of 1996 and I was thrown in at the deep end to complete the series.

It was probably the toughest job I had tackled up until then. The sadness of his premature death infused the first few episodes, and it was only when the programme returned in the spring of 1997 that I felt I could really start to make it my own. I was not

Geoff, I told myself, I was me. I could only be myself, and those who tuned in would have to take it or leave it. So from then on I did my own thing. I cherish the remark made by one correspondent whose letter began unpromisingly:

> *When you took over* Gardeners' World *from Geoff Hamilton my heart sank.*
>
> *I have been watching you closely over the past few months. You'll do.*

It was, for me, a turning point, and I shall for ever be grateful to the viewer who took the trouble to write and let me know.

It was in that first 'proper' year of *Gardeners' World*, 1997, that *Ground Force* came along, and that the names of Charlie Dimmock and Tommy Walsh became part of the nation's vocabulary, along with 'water feature' and 'decking'.

Nobody expected much at all of *Ground Force*. I certainly didn't. I very nearly turned it down. I mean, gardens evolve, you can't make them in two days. But John Thornicroft, the producer/director who Peter Bazalgette had charged with persuading me to have a crack at it, was like a dog with a bone. He knew that the way to get me to agree was to suggest that I could *not* make a difference to a patch of ground in two days. 'Of course I could,' I replied.

With Tommy to take charge of the hard landscaping, along with builder's mate Willy, and Charlie to help me with the gardening, we tackled our first challenge in West Wickham, near Croydon. The rest is history.

The programme was so successful that we were moved from BBC2 to BBC1, and the repeat of that very first programme pulled in twelve million viewers—second only to *EastEnders*. You've got to smile. Twelve million folk watching a gardening programme. Wonderful! Of course, some said that it wasn't a gardening programme at all, it was entertainment. The very idea! That gardening should be entertaining. Whatever next?

I do have one or two regrets. I know that I will for ever be associated with decking, which is perhaps not as classic as York stone paving but it is cheaper and easier to lay. I know that I had a predilection for blue-painted fences. Cuprinol even brought out a timber preservative called 'Barleywood Blue'. But then we used to wear bell-bottomed trousers and kipper ties. Fashions change. At least the programme got people talking about gardening and, hopefully, doing it as well.

I stayed with the programme for six years and designed a total of sixty-seven gardens, by which time I realised I was in danger of running out of steam and ought to quit while I was—marginally—ahead.

The highlight has to be the garden we made for Nelson Mandela in the Transkei. He really is an extraordinary man, with the quietest and most powerful charisma of anyone I have ever met, and that human quality I prize above all others—generosity of spirit. When we met, I asked him why he was not bitter. His reply: 'There is no time for bitterness. There is too much to be done.'

To sit down and talk with Nelson Mandela is a rare privilege. Like many great people, he has that knack of making you feel that you are the only person in the room—or the garden, in my case. I have a copy of *Long Walk to Freedom* that he signed for me. It is inscribed: 'To Alan, Best wishes to a competent and caring journalist. N. Mandela.'

And so, when others accuse me of incompetence, I can say that Nelson Mandela thinks otherwise. I'm grateful for that.

'DESIGN', AS SUCH, really only entered my consciousness at college. Up until then I knew the things that I wanted in a garden, and it was simply a matter of arranging them like the pieces of a jigsaw so that they fitted together properly—greenhouse in the best-lit spot, vegetables down the far end so that when they looked horrible in winter you wouldn't see them, and a nice big lawn in the middle. Neat. Tidy. I like orderliness. I am a naturally tidy person. At Kew the process of designing was taken much further in Landscape Construction and Landscape Design lectures, but it was with Mrs Bell, my landlady at Willow Cottages in Kew, that I first felt the exhilaration that comes from a well-designed garden. In a way that's perverse, because her garden was anything but 'designed'; it just seemed to happen. And it was tiny. But she used a range of plants that I had hitherto been unaware of—shrub roses in particular—to create an arty-yet-artless mix that was full of atmosphere and the most wonderful place to relax at the end of a long day.

My first garden—if you don't count the ones I commandeered from my parents—was the fifteen-foot-by-forty-foot patch in Sunningdale where I built the greenhouse, the shed and the pond that cut the garden in two. But my scope there was limited. It was not until we moved to Barleywood in Hampshire that I really had a chance to flex my muscles.

The garden was on a northwest-facing slope, eighty foot wide and an eighth of a mile long. It had a gradient of 1 in 4 on the steepest part, and the soil was chalk, clay and flint. Why make a garden there? Well, because we loved the spot, we could afford it—it was far enough away from London to be reasonably priced—and the house sort of felt right.

The house was at the bottom of the hill and the garden rose up from it. Friends asked if I was going to terrace it and were surprised when I said 'No'. But if you terrace a garden when the house is at the bottom of the slope, all you see is a series of risers—it's like standing at the foot of the stairs. When the house is at the top of a slope terracing makes great sense, for then the garden is presented to the house. But in my situation, the garden was already presented to the house, all I had to do was sculpt it.

Making a garden is a combination of things—art, obviously, by which I mean sculpting as well as painting the picture, but also craft—a skill that needs to be learned and then adjusted depending on the site in question.

The garden should complement the house, or at least resonate with it in some way, rather than seeming to be tacked on. There is no reason why it should not contrast with the house, provided that the contrast is either pleasing or exhilarating, or preferably both.

Barleywood was in a Hampshire village. It was nothing flashy. It had originally been one of a series of corrugated-iron shacks, each built on an acre of land to accommodate men returning from the Boer War. It had been built round and added to in the 1970s (and we added to it even further in the 1980s) but it was basically a chalet bungalow—a house with bedrooms in the roof, illuminated by dormer windows.

My taste in gardens has altered over the years. These days I am as formal as I have ever been (though not necessarily in my mode of dress), but Barleywood was a country garden that needed to be treated as such. Nevertheless I have always liked good lines, and so I made a zigzag path up the garden, which was part lawn and part gravel or cobbles set in cement, and filled in between it with billowing banks of flowers. Good, strong lines softened by planting have always appealed to me.

I had a veg patch, too. I've always had a veg patch. We had an allotment in Sunningdale when I could not squeeze any fruit and veg into the garden itself, but I have always been a fan of *small* kitchen gardens. Manageable ones. Stagger your sowings, too, to avoid gluts and that all-too-familiar sight of long rows of lettuces running to seed. Only grow what you like eating (obvious, perhaps, but often overlooked) and site as near to the kitchen as possible to avoid long, soggy journeys in wet weather. If the kitchen garden is too far from the kitchen you'll find any excuse not to go there. End of lecture.

Barleywood came with an acre and a third of land. The third of an acre was the steep slope immediately behind the house, and above this was an acre of paddock where the ground flattened slightly. It was not until I started presenting *Gardeners' World* that I took the paddock into cultivation and created a sweeping series of borders that could be home to different styles of planting. The challenge was to make the garden work as a cohesive whole, as well as accommodating a series of features that would provide inspiration for viewers with less space. It also gave me room to have a large greenhouse divided into three sections and surrounded by a formal Mediterranean garden.

It was fun making the garden at Barleywood, though it took me twenty years to do so. We'd been there for fifteen years before I started presenting *Gardeners' World*, so the lower portion was well established by then. The extra acre gave me the opportunity to try things I had not tried before—a tropical garden and a woodland garden—and to grow plants that I loved but had no space for lower down, tree ferns particularly.

We were lucky enough, over the years, to be able to buy additional land at the top, where we planted trees by cajoling friends to turn up one Sunday and 'Plant a wood in a day'. We managed to get in over 1,000 trees—oak, ash, beech, birch, wild cherry and the like—between dawn and dusk. They were little six-inch-high whips that were protected from deer and rabbits by tree shelters. I gave demonstrations on how to do it and Alison provided soup and bacon sandwiches. It was a real achievement and is now, eighteen years on, a fully grown wood that we used to visit every now and then on *Gardeners' World* to show tree planting or, in the patch of older woodland we bought, the glory of bluebells.

In the last few years, other presenters came and joined in—Chris Beardshaw and Rachel de Thame, Pippa Greenwood and Joe Swift, who designed the border at the back of the greenhouse. Much as I enjoy their company—and they all four rank as friends—it is tricky having other people digging your soil. They tease me about the fact that I used to hand them a fork after they had done a piece to camera standing in one of my beds or borders, but they all got used to having to fork out their footprints. I told you I was tidy-minded.

Why is it hard to let others loose in your garden? Well, because we all do things differently. The gardens I like best are those that reflect the heart and the soul and the personality of their owner—something you never find in a garden that has been designed by committee or run by an institution. Kew and Wisley are superb gardens, but they are impersonal in a way that Great Dixter (Christopher Lloyd) or White Barn House (Beth Chatto) are not.

Hidcote (Lawrence Johnston) and Sissinghurst (Vita Sackville-West) were designed and planted by individuals and then taken over by an institution (the National Trust). They have become hybrid gardens where the personality and spirit of the founders can still be felt. If planting and restoration are handled sensitively, this will continue to be true. But there is an ever-present danger that the gardens' original character and atmosphere will be lost. It is inevitable, since no two gardeners are alike in their approach—good gardeners, anyway.

After twenty-one years we moved from Barleywood to an old Georgian farmhouse a couple of miles down the road. It was a wrench after twenty-odd years—and we did hang on to Barleywood's woodland—but I felt that I had one more garden in me, and I had always wanted to make one round a Georgian house. It's not grand, more like a small doll's house, really, with a door in the middle and two windows on either side on two floors. The new extension, the kitchen, was built in 1777—the date is scratched on a brick. It is a friendly sort of house and has about an acre of garden, plus three acres of wild-flower meadow and a pond behind the long, low barn that sits alongside it. The barn is where I write.

The garden is flatter than that at Barleywood, and the soil not nearly so flinty, having been enriched by farmyard manure for hundreds of years. Thanks to the assiduous work of a local historian we now know the name of every owner and lessee of the house dating back to 1066.

In the early 1800s it was owned by Sir Thomas Miller, although it was not grand enough for him to live in. Jane Austen, who lived a mile away, wrote to her sister Cassandra recording his demise: 'I treat you with a dead baronet in almost every letter.' So that's nice—not his death, but the fact that Jane Austen knew the owner of our house.

Because the house sits squarely in the centre of the acre, and is (hurrah!) surrounded by a brick and flint wall, I designed the garden on more formal lines than Barleywood. There's a York stone terrace running right round the house, formal beds and borders close to, and an informal winding path beyond them that snakes through tree ferns (I'll never give them up!) and woodland plantings. I tried curves nearer the house when we first moved in, but they simply did not work. In the end I went for the obvious, which is often a guide as to what is most natural, and used straight lines that complemented those of the house.

I like intersecting vistas and axes with focal points at the end (not original, I know, but pleasing), and plotting these and getting them to interlink is a great challenge. I also have a circular, raised, formal pool with, at its centre, a cheap copy of Verrocchio's *Boy with a Dolphin*. I never did get the Queen's Garden at Kew, but at least I have the statue to remind me of it.

There is lots of topiary—clipped cones and balls of yew and box. I worry, sometimes, that the place looks like Trumpton, but evergreens offer form and solidity in winter when deciduous trees are bare, and when they are formally clipped they look much less like the planting in a cemetery.

Behind the barn the land is not so much a garden as a conservation area. We made a large wildlife pond and planted a mixture of British native broad-leaved trees as well as three cedars and a lot of country hedging.

Two years ago we acquired another couple of acres, to take us up to four, and I sowed these with a wild-flower mixture. Now the meadow is a delight. First came marguerites, then vetches, then wild carrot and knapweed and scabious. Crested dog's tail mingles with cocksfoot and sterile brome, and I scattered some yellow rattle to help weaken the grass on what was previously rich farmland—it is a parasitic plant that saps the strength of competing grasses that might otherwise overpower weaker wild flowers.

The birds and the butterflies love this haven—painted ladies and commas, ringlets and meadow browns, and the occasional blue, flit among the flowers and lay their eggs on the grasses and in the hedgerow.

Last summer I went round with the Reverend Keble Martin's

book under my arm. I totted up seventy-five different species of wild flower, and those were the ones that I knew and that I could see, which probably means there are around a hundred different species growing there.

Of all the things I have ever done, I think sowing a wild-flower meadow and planting a wood are the most satisfying.

I'm lucky to have been able to do it, I know, but on the other hand it means I will be leaving behind a piece of ground that is in better heart than it was when I took it on. In that way I feel I've paid my rent.

## WORDS AND MUSIC

WHEN I WAS A BOY there was one night above all others when my family would watch television together. *The Last Night of the Proms* was a must, and Mum and Dad would sit in their armchairs happily singing along to 'Land of Hope and Glory' with the rest of the audience more than 200 miles away in the Royal Albert Hall.

Cookie next door would be brought in to join in the fun; beef and onion sandwiches and a glass or two of Double Diamond would help the evening go with a swing, and then we would all go to bed, having reminded ourselves that we were British and proud of it, and that we really did have some wonderful tunes.

It never seemed insular, prejudiced or—a word we never heard back then—jingoistic. It was just a part of our lives, and pride—not the sort that goes before a fall—was very much a part of it.

Nearly fifty years later I was to be given the best seat in the house at the BBC Proms—the box at the centre of the Grand Tier. Except that I had to sit with my back to the audience and keep talking when they had fallen quiet.

I had presented the occasional Promenade Concert on television, having been involved with music programmes on BBC Radio 2 since the 1980s. Now I present a programme on Radio 2 every Sunday evening and get a chance to play an hour and a half of my kind of music, everything from music hall to opera, musicals to classical fare. It really is a great treat. But of all my musical presenting, the four years I spent as anchorman of the Last Night of the Proms from 2004–2007 are the highlight.

It is an evening of tremendous atmosphere, with 'promenaders' queuing up overnight to make sure of seats for the grand finale of the season. The hall is never less than packed to the rafters, and tickets are at a premium. The orchestra rehearses in the morning, and the presenter for the television coverage arrives at about midday to begin the technical run-through, sitting in the Grand Tier box and being kept in touch with what is going on via an earpiece through which the producer and director in the massive scanner parked behind the Albert Hall offer advice and timings.

The evening is introduced with the presenter on-screen, and the artists and the conductor are introduced off-screen as they make their way onto the stage. In the presenter's hand is a four-inch-thick pile of cards containing not only the script (in case the autoscript on the camera fails) but also details of everyone performing. These are handy if gaps need to be filled and information passed on to the viewer.

There are in-vision interviews to conduct in the intervals between the music, and with any luck you will get a musician who can string a sentence or two together, and a musicologist who has the ability to speak in a style understandable by the common herd as well as the cognoscenti.

Once the second half is under way and the broadcast has switched from BBC2 to BBC1 (the first half of the concert is generally considered too highbrow for the more popular channel) the presenter kicks off part two and is then out of vision for the last section of the programme. But by now the adrenaline is flowing, and before you know where you are, 'Land of Hope and Glory' is ringing out through the Hall and you can glance at your family sitting in the box next door (a perk of the job) and join in with them, singing at the top of your voice, waving your Union Jack and hoping that both the camera and the microphone are switched off.

The Prom concert I will never forget is the one that was performed for the Queen's eightieth birthday. I cannot remember now what music was played. I was simply aware that when the audience fell quiet after the applause for each musical item, I had to carry on talking in a normal voice as usual. The Queen was in the next box but one to mine and, out of the corner of my eye, I could see her leaning forwards and looking in my direction to see why I was still wittering on.

Added to this, I was sitting on two stacked chairs, rather than one, with the object of raising my head above the brass rail in front of the box, which would otherwise appear to run through my head. It is rather a perilous position, but provided I sit still it is unlikely that I will topple over the edge.

After the concert all the performers—and me—were instructed to make their way to the room at the top of the Hall to be presented to Her Majesty. I found myself standing next to Bryn Terfel when the Queen approached. She chatted to Bryn, who is a delightful and unassuming man whose basso profundo can rattle windows. Then she turned to me. I apologised for continuing to talk during the quiet bits and said that I hoped the Queen did not mind. 'No,' she said. 'Not at all. It was just your chair. We were worried that you might fall off.'

I WOULD NOT WANT YOU to think that all I have ever done is to wait for opportunities to present themselves, and gone where others suggested I might go. Well, I have a bit, but then I've also taken a few risks. And done things which, really, it would have been wiser to have avoided. Like writing novels.

I mean, there I am, plodding along nicely with *Gardeners' World* and *Ground Force* and writing gardening books. Why rock the boat by having a bash at fiction? Never mind putting your head above the parapet, writing a novel is like jumping stark naked from the battlements. And yet . . .

At school, I loved writing stories. I loved writing them rather more than Miss Weatherall liked reading them, but that's by the by. And then I grew up. A bit. And I realised, when I grew up, that unless you are an artist, or a composer, or a novelist, you never get to use the one thing that gives so much pleasure as a child—your imagination.

They always say, 'Write about what you know', so I wrote (or started to write) the story of a young TV gardener, Rob MacGregor, and his love life. I had in mind a sort of romantic adventure story, believing myself to be both romantic and adventurous. I received one rejection slip, one request to see more and one invitation to lunch. Having always taken rejection badly, and never wanting to do more than I have to, and because I can never resist a hearty meal, I went to lunch with a man by the name of Luigi Bonomi. It is not made up. He really does exist and, as far as I am aware, in spite of the sound of his name, he is not a fully paid-up member of the Mafia. Rather he's a good egg. A very good egg.

Luigi found a publisher. The book came out. It sold well. I have now written seven novels, all of which have made it into *The Sunday Times* top ten. But the great joy is that I have found a method of self-expression that I had hitherto only dreamed of. It's also another string to my bow and one that I hope I can carry on employing for a few years yet.

Writing fiction is agony and ecstasy in equal measure, depending on how the day is going. I do not write ground-breaking literature.

Neither am I of the deeply cerebral or highly esoteric school. I write what I hope are well-crafted stories that will take you out of yourself. They tell stories of ordinary people in often extraordinary circumstances. They do, in their simple way, reflect human nature. There are smiles. A few tears. But above all I hope they just take the reader off into another world in the company of characters who they may like or loathe, but at the very least about whom they care.

Having written about forty gardening books up to this point, I began *Mr MacGregor* in the winter of 1997/98, in the shed at the top of the garden at Barleywood. I have always written best in the morning—I'm a lark, not an owl—and so I would sit down at around 8.30 a.m. and write solidly until 1 p.m. or 2 p.m., then collapse, exhausted. My usual rate is around 3,000 words at a sitting. Sometimes more, sometimes less. One really good day is usually followed by a poor one, so the numbers even out.

After a light lunch I'll potter around in the garden and think about where I am going. But even then, things don't always work out as one imagines. I learned that within days of starting on *Mr MacGregor*. I had planned for our hero and his girlfriend to go up the Dales for supper that evening. He suggests the idea to her. I tapped away at the laptop and discovered that his girlfriend had other ideas. She was going out that evening with her boss.

I actually sat back from the keyboard and wondered what had happened. I had it in my mind that they were going out that night, and yet she had contradicted me and said they were not. Maybe this was what it was like when you were writing fiction. Maybe the characters *did* take over. I had a choice: either I could *make* them go up the Dales that evening, or I could hand over the plot and let them decide. I plumped for the latter, and that's what I've done ever since.

I feel a touch pretentious setting all this down; as if what I write has some kind of literary merit, when I really just tell stories. But folk are often curious as to where such stories come from. How they get a life of their own. The truth of the matter is that I wish I knew, but I do enjoy helping them to unfold. Acting as a 'medium' in a funny kind of way, for the characters who exist only in my imagination and, hopefully, come to life on the page.

THEY ALWAYS SAY, 'Be careful what you wish for', the implication being that when it happens it might not turn out quite as you imagined. As a child I had always wanted to be Percy Thrower; that dream came true, in a manner of speaking, and it lived up to expectations. But before the gardening bug bit, it was 'nature study' that captivated me. I wouldn't say that I wanted to be Peter Scott or David Attenborough but I did admire them. They were the sort of people who spoke my kind of language (albeit with longer words) and liked the kind of things I liked—animals and birds and, to a lesser extent, plants and flowers.

I had been presenting *Gardeners' World* for six years (and I was wondering just how long I wanted to carry on) when an approach came from the BBC's Natural History Unit.

It put me in a bit of a quandary. The problem with being a gardener, and being married to a garden as well as a wife, is that you cannot simply push off and leave it for months on end. I said that what I would really love to do was a series about the wildlife and natural history of the British Isles. It seemed to me that we had enough about meerkats and lemurs, lions and tigers and camels, and all too little about dormice and starlings, red squirrels and Glanville fritillaries—the wildlife on our doorstep and the countryside we need to cherish.

The NHU listened patiently as I explained my feelings, and promised to come up with a strategy that would enable us to work together. That was in 2001. The result was *British Isles: A Natural History*, a series exploring the foundation of our islands, their geology, geography, climate and natural history, over the last few million years. It took two years to make this eight-part series, and I managed to be away from home for only a week at a time, so that my garden would not become totally overgrown.

What this commitment did mean was that I could not possibly

continue presenting *Gardeners' World*. And so, at the end of 2002, I relinquished my tenure as 'the nation's head gardener' and moved on. The autumn of 2002 became a turning point in so many ways: in October I stopped presenting *Gardeners' World* and *Ground Force*. On 16th December we moved house and on 17th December we went to Yorkshire for my mother's funeral.

But there were happier things, too. During that same year I worked on a series I had longed to present, one that would go right back to basics and make gardening easy to understand. *How to be a Gardener* was made in several small gardens local to me in Hampshire, since I knew that we would be moving and could not base it at Barleywood. I showed folk how to sow seeds and take cuttings, but also explained the 'Why?' as well as the 'How?'

Of all the gardening series I have ever made, it is *How to be a Gardener* of which I am most proud. It was produced by Kath Moore, whose way of bringing out the best in a presenter has yet to be equalled. 'Give me a bit more heart,' she'd say, tapping her chest with her fist. 'Just a bit more heart.' I gave *How to be a Gardener* all of my heart, and it ran for two series.

So did my natural history programmes. *The Nature of Britain* followed *British Isles: A Natural History* in taking a closer look at wildlife habitats—from mountain and moorland to streams and rivers, fields and hedgerows—explaining the interdependency of plants, animals and humans in an ever more pressurised world. But I have always believed in being positive about natural history, not being the prophet of doom. Drone on at folk for too long about how this is threatened and that is on the verge of extinction and they will switch off, believing that there is little they can do to redress the balance. A celebratory, though not head-in-the-sand, approach is, I reckon, far more effective. Get them engaged, without browbeating them, and they will do their bit for conservation and stewardship of the countryside.

Of course people need to know how fragile is the land on which they live, and how its future lies in our hands, but show them how they can make a difference, and explain the adaptability and opportunism of the wildlife that inhabits it, and they will see that it is not a hopeless cause but rather something they might feel able to participate in.

LOOKING BACK, the one thing I know for certain is that I have been extraordinarily blessed. It doesn't do to say so, of course. It makes you sound soppy and sentimental. But I consider myself so very fortunate in the things I have been allowed to do and in the people I've encountered on the way who were confident enough in my abilities to encourage me in my endeavours.

I have made my way in life, as Sir David Frost put it, 'by trowel and error'. In 2008–09 I had the honour of being the High Sheriff of the Isle of Wight. It is an ancient office, and one which allows you to commission a personal coat of arms from the College of Arms in London. Those arms contain a motto. Mine is short and sweet: *et stilo et rutro*. Translated from the Latin: 'by pen and spade'. Two implements that haven't done badly for me, all things considered.

# Dawn French

## *Dear Fatty*

Dear Dad,

So you're still dead. It's been thirty-one years and every day I have to remind myself of that fact, and every day I am shocked.

I'm not nineteen any more and so many things have happened that you haven't known, so I have decided to write this book for you. I want to remember our time together and I want to tell you about lots of stuff since.

So far, it's been better than expected . . .

Dawn French in 'Dear Fatty'

# DEAR YOU,

Hello. I have decided to think of this book as a memoir rather than an autobiography. As I understand it, the latter means that I have to be precise about chronology and touch on all aspects of my quite-dull-in-parts life. I think that would be quite dull because in quite a lot of parts my life has indeed been quite dull. You wouldn't want to read about those bits, believe me. They would be mainly about puddings I've enjoyed and when I've set the washing machine on the wrong cycle and my quest for comfortable shoes. You don't want to know about that ol' faffle. So, I've decided instead to concentrate on those memories that are especially important or vivid to me. The parts of my life I can still remember the taste and feel and smell of.

Here's what I've learned writing this book. Memory doesn't begin with or end in 'what happened'. In fact, I don't think it ends at all; it goes on changing, playing a kind of hide-and-seek with our minds. Some of my memories are nearly fifty years old now and sometimes the startling clarity of them makes me doubt their reality. Do all of the people I write to in these pages remember what I remember? My dad, mum, brother, daughter, friends, lovers and so on? I am lucky that I've kept diaries for large parts of my life on which I can anchor many of these memories. Even so, most of my diary-keeping doesn't tend to remind me of my true emotions at any particular juncture. For that I must rely on my rapidly deteriorating grey matter, and a lot of investigative chatter with my nearest and dearest. I shouldn't really be so surprised by the alarmingly speedy erosion of my memory; after all, my waistline has disappeared entirely. Like wearing a nappy or the Lost City of Atlantis, my waist is now only a vague memory, or may even just be an ancient myth for all I know.

So, it's in this spirit of reminiscence that I offer you this memoir of my life so far. I have decided to tell my story through letters, because this way I can address my life to the people I've actually lived it with. It's not that I don't want to tell it directly to *you*, it's more that I know these people well, and hopefully, by the end, you might know me well too. I do hope you enjoy it. If you do, feel free to tell all your friends. If not, please replace the book neatly where you found it, and if you're in a residential area, be thoughtful, and leave quietly. Thank you.

## DEAR DAD,

So, you're still dead. It's been thirty-one years, and every day I have to remind myself of that fact, and every day I am shocked.

You and I had only nineteen years together, and so when I think of you, I am still nineteen and you are . . . What age were you? To me, you were just the right age for a dad. Old enough to be clever and young enough to be handsome. Probably about the age I am now. Blimey, that's weird. I will soon be older than you ever got to be. That's not right somehow. A parent is supposed to be older at all times. The natural form is, *I* get older and you get . . . just old. *Then*, and only then, should you be permitted to die. Even that should happen in front of the telly after a bowl of stew and a cuddle up with your missus. Not the way you died. Not like that.

I'm not nineteen any more, Dad, and so many things have happened that you haven't known, so I have decided to write this book for you.

I want to remember our time together and I want to tell you about lots of stuff since. So far, it's been better than expected . . .

## DEAR DAD,

I'm having trouble remembering my very first memory. Each time I try I think I'm stealing other people's first memories that I've either read or been told of. I *can't* remember looking out of my pram at an adoring mother, I *can't* remember being shocked at the first sight of my own pudgy baby fingers.

There is something I *can* remember vividly, and when I experience it now, the effect is visceral. It takes me thundering right back to a very early, blurry memory. The smell of Mum. A heady aroma that embodies birth and life and strength and sex and safety and fags. Whatever perfume she adds (currently she's favouring JLo's new honk, I noticed, when I was last in her bathroom), this smell is always there as the baseline, and for me it's magnificent and it announces that I'm home. I guess the scent is the code, the method of imprinting between a mother and child. Sometimes even now I snuggle up to Mum just to get another headful to nourish me till the next visit.

I don't have such a strong early memory of you, Dad, although I do have one of something that happened when I think I was about two or three. I remember creeping into your bedroom while you two slept and crawling under your bed. I'm not quite sure why I did this. A sort of delicious invisibility. Anyroadup, you might remember, a frightening thing happened. The bed was the kind that had low metal bars and bare springs beneath. I must have had my hand inside one of the springs when one of you moved, resulting in a crushing pain as my little fingers were trapped. I shrieked and woke you. You leapt out of bed, full of confusion and dadly alert. You reached under the bed and, with a bit of gentle coaxing, pulled me out to safety and I ran into Mum's arms for comfort. All of this was fairly unremarkable except for one thing. You were completely naked and, although I was in agony, I couldn't take my eyes off that weird dark, dangly wrinkled thing. What *was* it? I'd never seen you without your pants on and the first conclusion I jumped to was that you were being attacked by some kind of nocturnal bed-intruding vicious hairy saggy mole-snake creature.

Naturally the correct course of action, considering you had just rescued me from certain finger-death, was to reciprocate, so I lunged at your assailant, thwacking it as hard as I could, trying to dislodge its tenacious teeth from your groin. However hard I hit, it would *not* let go or fall off. Inexplicably, both of you seemed helpless with laughter, and you even seemed to be resisting my help as you pulled on your pants and let the biting thing stay INSIDE them. I never saw it again so I guessed you'd had it put down at the vet's or perhaps left it at the zoo.

## DEAR GARY,

Dad was at RAF Valley and we were living in Holyhead, Anglesey, so I must have been three years old and you must have been six when Hunni the dog turned up. I remember she was named after a little girl called Honey Hindley-Maggs who you were at school with and who you lost your heart to. Did she know you named a dog after her? Did she feel special as a result of that, I wonder? I think the dog, a cairn terrier, was officially supposed to be *your* dog, but I just want to let you know that she definitely preferred me and I loved her back with a fervent passion.

After a certain amount of initial resistance she gave in to my efforts to make her lie down next to me for hours on end. I wanted to feel her tiny body breathing calmly, sleepily, next to mine and I wanted her to be like a Disney or Lassie dog, who could understand me and all my three-year-old problems, so I endlessly blethered on into her ear.

She was also very handy as a baby or dressing-up doll. Quite a lot of my doll clothes fitted her and even suited her. She looked better in pastels—it contrasted well with her sandy fur—and I was stunned by how becoming she was in a mobcap, although I had to bite holes in it for her ears to poke through. Too much wriggling prevented any true representation of an entire outfit.

One thing Hunni was *always* up for, probably due to the delicious taste, was liberal use of Mum's lipstick, a stunning burnt sunset-type orangey red. Wetness of nose, hirsuteness of lips and constant licking made application tricky but, with effort and tenacity, not impossible. The overall effect was stunning and in no small part reminiscent of early Dusty Springfield. Excellent.

I'm pretty sure she favoured this sort of girly activity over the silly exploits *you* got up to with her—like walking, throwing and catching, running after rabbits or wrestling. Honestly, what were you thinking? She was a *dog*!

## DEAR MUM,

I've been thinking about what life must have been like for you around the time I was born, when Dad was stationed in Anglesey. When I look at pictures of you pushing me in a pram, with a toddler Gary by your side, you look so glamorous and so happy. Then I look at other pictures from that time. We must have been in RAF quarters but there I am having a bath in a bucket in the back yard. Maybe this was just for a laugh—we must have had a bathroom, surely? I know that the camp was miles from the local village and the shops in Caergeiliog and that you had to walk for hours to get a pint of milk. I also know that Anglesey is hellishly windy and flat and remote. It must have been exhausting to drag both of us such a long way in that raging raw weather, and I know that often when you arrived at the shop, it was very hurtful when people chose to speak Welsh only, to refuse to help you in English. I know you often felt lonely and rejected, but I prick up my ears when I hear Welsh. I like how dangerous and dark and a bit caustic and secretive Welsh people seem. I was born there, but I wasn't bred there and I'm not *from* there, yet Wales and the Welsh prompt an acute sense of tribal belonging in me. Perhaps what I'm feeling is a distant sense of your alienation, Mum. Because you were made to feel the trespasser, I want to belong, on your behalf. Maybe it's a bigger issue. Dad's being in the RAF meant that you (and we) followed him wherever his work took us, so we didn't get to belong anywhere. Sometimes we were in our home for less than a year. You might have only just got a job, we might have only just settled at school, and we had to move on again. Sort of legit Gypsies really. Moving to a new camp, new town, new county, but strangely and rather comfortingly, always the same house—same layout, same G-Plan furniture. We seemed to have very little of our own. Just ornaments and books and odd items with which to try and personalise yet another RAF standard red-brick house.

It's no wonder both Gary and I did so much sleepwalking and sleeptalking when we were growing up. We probably harboured our fair share of new-school stress, constantly having to try carefully to negotiate our way into new groups of friends. The RAF kids were easy to befriend—they had the same itinerant experience and were sympathetic. It was the gangs of local kids that were harder to crack. They were fed up with forces kids turning up, and then buggering off before true friendships could be forged. I vividly remember the first few days of arriving anywhere new, when it was imperative to make a good show of yourself, make sure all your wares were on display attractively—humour, hipness, kindness (but with a hint of steel), intelligence, comprehensive knowledge of hit parade, courtesy, eloquence and skipping and twoball prowess. If that failed (which it usually did due to pathetic lack of élan in any of above skills), employ bribery and giftage techniques swiftly, sometimes even deploying own toys as bait. On rare occasions, this modus operandi backfired and we were judged to be spineless tossers for buying affections. Then, *and only then,* would I employ my master plan, a strategy that never failed, but demanded tireless acting. I would concoct a terminal illness that meant I was not long for this world, and would elicit sympathy and pledges of eternal friendship. RAF kid 1–local kid 0. Result. I'm sorry, Mum, if it meant you regularly had to answer strange questions from concerned parents about your sickly daughter's tragic condition, but somehow I eluded retribution and moved on to the next camp with renewed vigour. This nomad life, which incidentally also rewarded us richly with experiences all over the country and later in Cyprus, was no doubt part of the nagging core feeling I had: that we didn't belong anywhere.

If it's any consolation, Mum, believe me when I say that everywhere we went was our home because you made it so. You were and are the absolute centre of all of us, and you kept us anchored when we could so easily have felt lost and confused. There might have been endless new doors but behind each one were you and Dad, making a safe and happy place for me to be. Any confidence I have had since stems from that one unassailable fact. I am loved.

Thank you.

## DEAR DAD,

I think I was about four years old or so when you were posted to RAF Leconfield and we all moved to Yorkshire. It was a long way from Grandma and Granddad French in Plymouth, and on the journey Gary and I would physically fight the entire time, mean pinches and punches and stabs and Chinese burns. You tried word games and songs to distract us, but we were compelled to battle. That was our kid purpose. If any of our squabbling became too dangerous, or if Gary was winning, I would be sure to whinge loudly to you and appeal for justice. Gary accused me of being 'a girl'. A girl?! How very low.

Another reason I recall these journeys on family visits is the smoke. I don't know how many fags you and Mum were smoking a day but it *must* have been a hundred each. One cigarette lit the next and we travelled along in this stinking, acrid foggy tin box for hours. Gary and me and the dog in the back seat, sucking up thousands of fags' worth of used smoke and gasping for air in a desperate attempt to stay alive. For years I thought I was a sufferer of carsickness until I travelled in a smoke-free car and realised that smoke was the reason for my queasiness.

Anyroadup, I remember one particular journey back up North because there was only one topic of conversation the whole way. The Queen Mother. You told us that you had been selected as a typical serviceman, a chief technician with an average family—one boy, one girl, one nursery-school-teacher wife, dog (comes with or without clothes). A perfect family, safe and presentable enough to display to a visiting royal on a very special day for our air-force base. She was coming to visit and inspect in two weeks' time! All I could think was, 'Why is she called the Queen Mother and not the Queen's Mother? Was my mum therefore the Dawn Mother?'

Do you remember the Dawn Mother flew into a flurry of excitement and didn't sit down or sleep once in those two weeks? *Everything* was dusted, mopped, antisepticked, hoovered, pinned up on the line and beaten, including us kids. Gary and I had haircuts, new outfits—mine was a tartan kilt and new red patent-leather Start-rites which I had been longing for, so yay and respect to the Queen Mother for those; Gary's was a grey suit. The Dawn Mother had a twinset and a perm and you of course wore your bluey-grey uniform, which I always loved because you looked so spruced and tiptop and important. You shone in it, and it shone on you, with all buttons and belts and medals and significant regalia-type badge things duly buffed till they glinted.

We practised bowing and curtsying for hours until our backs and knees buckled and bled. We tried to rehearse being humble and quiet. The little pamphlet on royal etiquette gave us some tips: we were to speak only if spoken to (royal rules, not family rules). Could we try on her crown? Or feed sugar lumps to the unicorns that would pull her pink carriage? After the initial 'Your Majesty' we were to address her as M'am, rhymes with Spam, *not* M'arm rhymes with farm, and never M'erm. This threw me into a panic because I felt sure I would mistakenly call her Spam from start to end.

The day came and, boy, were we prepared and perfect. Beds made with crisp hospital corners, books neatly on shelves with spines facing *out*wards, teddies and dolls scrubbed and lined up on the pillow. The house smelt of furniture wax and Mr Sheen. A newly baked cake was on the table and the best—in fact, the *new*—china was arranged beside it. The Dawn Mum was virtually still licking us clean like a mumcat when *SHE* arrived (do I remember it correctly, Dad?) in a *helicopter*! All the neighbours were out in the road to watch. She first went for a quick visit to a suitably presentable officer and his family at the other, pedigree, end of the camp. We were always segregated like this from the commissioned officers—they had posh detached houses with huge gardens front and back whereas us oiks lived in rows round a central play park.

And so we waited and waited for her to come. Finally, she walked up our garden path. I had a quick glance at the stunning outfit with the matching huge hat (hang on, where's the crown?!), before taking a very low stoop into my curtsy, holding my tartan skirt out at the sides for maximum effect. Gary did his gentlemanly bow simultaneously, and both of us remained like this for an uncomfortably long time—possibly two days. As I stood up, and the blood rushed away from my head, I blinked in the light and looked directly into the face of the mother of the Queen. She was about my height (I was four years old and three foot), which surprised me. I smiled my special show-every-tooth-in-your-head smile, carefully avoiding saying hello first and definitely *not* calling her Spam (*don't* say hello Spam, *don't* say hello Spam). She then reciprocated with a huge ear-to-ear beaming smile and—horror of horrors—she had a mouthful of BLACK TEETH! What? Eh? No carriage, no crown and now she turns out to be a fully certified evil witch! And she's coming into *my* house! I was dumbstruck and with my heart beating fear in my ears, I hid behind your knees and grabbed on to your legs. I remember you trying to shake me off, but I wasn't going anywhere. She was in our house, chatting and drinking tea for all the world as if she *wasn't* evil incarnate! She looked at Gary's train set, she asked polite questions and complimented us on our lovely neat house. Had no one else noticed? I knew what to do. Hold on to your leg and refuse to either speak to her or look her in the eye. So that's what I did. I said one word when she asked me about my school. I said, 'Nice.' That was it. She left our house and went off to spread her evil seed elsewhere, after twenty minutes or so. The scariest twenty minutes of my life. Does she get back in the helicopter or simply hop on her broomstick to get home? I'm only four, there's nothing more I can do. No one believes me. I'm helpless, hopeless, inconsolable.

I was left with this deep, hidden fear for years, and then I happened to meet the QM at a reception for the arts many moons later and found her still to be alarmingly short, but much less evil, with lovely teeth.

Thanks, Dad, for the use of your leg that day. It saved my life.

## DEAR HANNAH,

From the moment you were born, on Boxing Day 1993, and when I first looked into your eyes, I knew we were linked in a profound way. I have watched you grow into your teenagehood, negotiating the assault course of your childhood using exactly the same techniques as I did. I see your thinking, I see your actions, I see your doubt and I see your method, and I know them as my own. Is it the family connection? Whatever the reason, I am so glad you're here, that you're my niece, and I cherish our mysterious sameness.

I can't apologise enough for the lifetime of comparison to me you have already had to, and will in the future, endure. The endless comments about how you and I are so similar must be agonising. I understand how alarming this comparison must seem. For a start, how could anyone be alive and *so* very fat?! Well, all I can say is that I am just as surprised as you. I honestly cannot fathom the dimensions of this curious body I've been given. I was aware, from *very* early on, that it wasn't quite like anyone else's. None of the laws of physics, nature, chemistry, biology, art *or* universal order seem to apply. I know I am a human life form, but not as we know it, Captain. Why, for instance, am I *so* short? I know the Frenchies are not tall in the genes department, hailing as we do from labouring stock, heavy, beefy men who built the first tar roads in Cornwall and from fishermen who, again, need to be robust and sturdy to haul in their living. Surely, though, their proportions were not quite as startlingly dwarfish as my own? What is my physical category, actually? Plump? Rotund? Squat? Corpulent? Buxom, possibly? No, I defy these definitions. I am more hobbitish, with a big dollop of Weeble. You know, the ones that wobble but don't fall down? You would think that in return for the shocking lack of leg/arm/torso length, God might have been prepared to bless me with elegant long fingers suitable for pianos and rings, or even exquisite toes for sandal and nail-polish use. No no no. Not to be—got the dumpy Wall's sausage fingers and the cocktail-sausage toes. Thanks, God. What about an arched neck? No no no. Got the full, direct-from-chin-to-chest fortification, with impressive turkey-gobble flaps attached. Above all, what in the name of all that is holy is the purpose of these massive ocean-going buoy chests? I know bosoms are womanly but these surely belong to *many* women. I would happily share, given half a chance. I'd love to see my chipolata toes again—it's been so long. I'd love to run and still see ahead on every other stride. I'd love to lie down on my back without gathering underarm beach balls. I'd love to pick up a bra catalogue and find my size in *all* ranges rather than turn each page ever more forlornly till I come across the trusted industrial 'Doreen' in white polyester—the only bap-scaffolding that comes in my staggering 42H. I have tried to customise the 'Doreen' so many times—I've added lace, I've hacked away at it with pinking shears to create a sexular-looking shelf-like effect, I've covered it in intriguing fabrics in an attempt to make it more comely. On one occasion, fortified by drink, I wore it back to front.

Anyroad, I know you will look at me from time to time and dread the onset of this odd body shape. Fortunately, I think your mum's genes might save you. Evidence thus far points towards early intervention of good strong height genes. You even seem to have an actual neck, which goes in under the jaw and then down, providing you with a place where necklaces apparently go. How lucky you are. But should this fleshy strangeness befall you, I want to allay your fears a tiny bit and tell you that it's not all bad. I have discovered that big breasts can precede you into a room and announce the arrival of someone to be reckoned with. This can be very useful if you are feeling nervous or shy, because the knockers do the attitude for you; meanwhile, you have enough breathing time to let your courage catch up with them. I've also experienced big bosoms as a sort of theme park for boys. They just can't seem to resist them. They just can't. You will have to train boys to treat the pleasure domes with all due respect and to cherish them like the magnificent cherishable things they are.

I once went to the theatre with a chum and noticed a woman in her fifties having a pre-show drink in the bar, with the most splendid front I have ever seen (the woman, that is, not the bar). She was very grand and she held herself so proudly. I was in awe. I couldn't stop looking at her, at them, at it, at the whole fabulous, majestic thing. Imagine my delight when, quite by coincidence, she sat down next to me. I was breathless with admiration. She was glancing at the programme. I tried to resist, truly I did, but I couldn't—I leaned over and said, 'Excuse me, I hope you don't mind but I am compelled to tell you that you have the most magnificent bosom I've ever seen.' She looked beatifically at me over her bifocals and said, 'Yes. I know,' and smiled. And the lights went down and we watched the play side by side. Me and the lady with the remarkable chest. We didn't speak again. And it was delicious.

Don't forget that although you have a deal of 'French' blood in you, to a certain extent the shape of your body can be YOUR CHOICE. I've heard that exercise and a lean, healthy diet can make a big difference. I've always known this but I can't help it—personally, I would rather read a book or watch *Big Brother* than go to a gym and jump about with a flushed face. However, I have to admit that those who put themselves through it often look bonny in the end, so the fact is—you do have a choice. I am a sedentary person, I've got the kind of well-spread bum that is perfect for sitting and watching, and that's what I do best. I'm sorry to boast but I really am good at it.

Some things *are* worth moving for, and for those beloved and special activities I have been known to move with alarming speed and tiptop energy. The 'worth moving fast for' list is as follows: (1) doing sex, (2) swimming, (3) tennis, (4) walking by sea with dog, (5) going into town to get a pasty, (6) doing sex, (7) dancing, (8) running away from evil people, (9) running towards delightful people, (10) doing sex.

Talking of dancing, sweet pea, you are *so* good at it. When I watch you perform, I nearly burst with joy. You are supple and expressive and dazzling. I hope your enviable connection to your body and the confidence it gives you will last the rest of your life. That's the key, you know, confidence. I know for a fact that if you can genuinely like your body, so can others. It doesn't really matter if it's short, tall, fat or thin, it just matters that you can find some things to like about it. Even if that means having a good laugh at the bits of it that wobble independently, occasionally, that's all right. It might take you a while to believe me on this one, lots of people don't because they seem to suffer from a self-hatred that precludes them from imagining that a big woman could ever love herself because *they* don't. But I *do*. I know what I've got is a bit strange and difficult to love but those are the very aspects I love the most! I've never been particularly attracted to the uniform of conventional beauty. I like the adventure of difference.

Ever since I can remember, people have told me I have a 'pretty' face. When I was little, I used to feel so chuffed and grateful, and I know it was meant to make me feel good. The older I got, I sometimes had the distinct feeling that it was a not very clever way of saying 'Oh my God, look at your huge unpleasant body, at least you've got a nice symmetrical face for us to look at'. Now, even older, I have found myself really thinking about this whole 'pretty' thing. What is it? Correct amount of features in a pleasing formation? Lack of deformity? What?! My biggest problem is how can I accept the compliment when I haven't accomplished *anything*? I haven't even tried! I was given this face by my parents just like you were given yours by yours. That's all. Nothing accomplished—just luck.

Mind you, with us, Hannah, you and me, it's not just about the looks we share. Something else, something much more fundamental, is going on. We can share our fears and our joys. I sort of *get* you, so rest assured I've got your back, babe, and I'll fight for your right to be whoever you best think you are, making lots of necessary and glorious mistakes along the way. Oh, the places you'll go . . .

## DEAR BF,

Being balanced, both psychologically and emotionally, is supposed to be an attribute, isn't it? I'm not entirely convinced that it *is*, and I am further unconvinced that it is an attribute that can be attributed to me! I have often, even sometimes by you, my beloved Best Friend, been told that I am a 'balanced' person. Is the apparent ability to empathise with both sides of a situation an enviable quality or is it a sort of curse which renders one incapable of having a definite opinion or position? I don't know—aaargh there, see? Jennifer, for instance, is often exasperated by my interminable seesawing.

People have suggested to me that I am unfeasibly fair because I am a Libran. This smacks of über-hogwash to me. No, I think if I *do* have this tendency, it's because of two concurrent and utterly opposite family relationships, with my grandmothers. My dad's mum, Grandma French (Marjorie), and my mum's mum, Grandma O'Brien (Lil). Two mighty women who both did much to shape me. I surely walk in their shoes, although one is a teeny-tiny, sparkly, perfect pointy ballroom-dancing satin shoe which I can barely squish the chipolatas into. The other is a colourful, loud, high and clacky anklestrappy, saucy strumpet of a shoe, too roomy for me, therefore inherently perilous!

Let me tell you about my experience of these two polar opposite matriarchs. First, Marjorie French née Berry, much beloved mum of my dad. Typical Berry, she is diminutive and compact with a kind, smiley face and the sparkliest, naughtiest, most expressive eyes in the firmament.

You've met her several times. You know that she's remarkable. A ninety-nine-year-old woman who insists on living independently, who will get down on the floor to play with any visiting toddler, who will race out to the kitchen to make a cup of tea (powdered tea, that is—an acquired taste) and offer a saffron bun to allcomers. She is the anchor for a massive group of people, she is our family's history and our rock. She is the keeper of all the secrets and she is the purveyor of all the comfort and advice any of us need. She has never, *ever* made a judgment about me or anyone else in my earshot that isn't positive or encouraging. She might often have a good laugh at some twit's shortcomings or do funny impressions of people who amuse her for one reason or another, but she has no malice in her. None.

Recently I took from her house a handwritten manuscript (in faultless copperplate, I hasten to add) she has been writing for some time about her life. She writes of when she went into service for a family in Plymouth, and she is discreet but frank about falling out with the father of the family. Her love for her siblings is palpable, and her admiration for her parents through feast and famine is so moving. Her knowledge of Dartmoor is astonishing: she learned so much about its landscape and wildlife, her Arcadian life dictated by the seasons and the mysterious supernature that permeates the area. Whenever I've taken her there for a jaunt in the car, she insists that we pull over here and there, so that she can tell me relevant stories, or strange moorland legends that live on. She remembers meeting my grandfather Leslie, who was tall and handsome and rode a motorbike and whom she kept waiting and waiting for his first kiss. And waiting. He drove through regular snowdrifts on high parts of the south moor to see her on their rare days off. He lost his bike once in a huge mound of snow and had to return to dig it out. The snowy weather even threatened to ruin their wedding day. Only a few guests made it and those who did had to dig a path to the church through a snow barricade!

My Grandma French is a minx, always quick with a gag and a wink and, to be honest, quite saucy. On one of our moorland outings, I was directed to the impossibly tiny house her whole family lived in while her father was in service as a chauffeur to a posh family near Two Bridges. The big house where the posh family lived is next to the tiny house and is now a hotel. I suggested we went in for a cream tea and she said she couldn't possibly go in, that she wasn't 'allowed', which of course was a throwback to her childhood. Eventually I persuaded her and we sat and had a slap-up tea and a good gossip in a room she had previously been forbidden to enter, a trespass that somehow made our scones even more delicious!

As we were driving away, up the long driveway, she pointed at a big, bushy tree on the right-hand side and said, 'See that tree? That's where me and your granddad first—' and she winked. First what?! First let him kiss her after waiting so long? First let him go 'upstairsies outsidies'? First held hands? Surely not first . . .?! I asked her, carefully, and she just tapped her nose. So I guess I'll never know, but she obviously remembers it *very* clearly. Lucky her!

My granddad Les was a real catch, albeit a bit of a rogue. I remember he had an amazing thick shock of hair and huge hands. He was very manly and always busy. He had been a milkman, but later, when I was very young, he was a newsagent with his own little shop on a housing estate called Ernesettle in Plymouth. He got up early every day to do the papers and to run a mobile newsagent from the back of his van at the Bush factory nearby, providing all the workers at the start of their day with supplies of fags and sweets and papers. He managed his team of paperboys like an army squadron. I clearly remember the bottom room of the shop where the papers were sorted into the bags and numbered with stubby pencils so's the boys knew where to deliver them. It was a loud, vulgar, cheerful atmosphere. The place and the boys smelt of ink. There was shouting and rude jokes and cussing and *BOYS*.

There was always a shop dog, an Alsatian, for protection. Carlo was the first one that I remember. A huge, handsome dog who was *so* patient and tolerant, sitting on the front step of the shop while endless children came up and hugged him and poked his eyes and tickled his ears and kissed his nose and fed him sweets. Then one day I witnessed a change in the behaviour of this dog that made me respect him and his like for ever after. Granddad had locked the shop at the end of the day and he was doing some finishing up in the bottom room, the sorting room. I was with him, and someone tried to break in at the door. The dog switched into a total killing and maiming machine and barked and snarled and slavered. This was a supreme working dog with utter control over the right response at the right time. There were no break-ins at the shop when that dog was presiding. There were also no incidents of biting or grumpiness around the kids either. He was a bit of a hero for me. Carlo the Great.

Grandma and Granddad lived at the top of the hill near the shop, in St Budeaux, in a cosy little bungalow where Grandma still lives today. Down the side of the hill towards Ernesettle was all woodland with a huge creek at the bottom, and Granddad would walk Carlo in this woodland every day. He had a sort of allotment in there where he kept geese (his passion) and lots of chickens. I loved going on these steep walks with him and the dog, our breath visible in front of us and our feet crunching through fallen twigs and leaves.

I have many lovely memories of my granddad, a very powerful one being his eccentric obsession with bargains. For years, he had two pairs of enormous department-store front doors leaned up against his shed. He had no use for them as far as I knew, he'd just got them for a good price. Likewise, he used to go to jumble sales and pick up stacks of ties. Eventually they had to move the thousands of ties into a caravan parked in their drive. Pretty soon it was impossible to get into the caravan at all, so if anyone had thought to hitch the caravan to a car, the ties *could* have actually gone on holiday to the seaside.

Another love of Les's was his aviary. He had various versions that I can remember, but the main one was in a shed in the garden. He chiefly bred budgies but he also had parakeets and lovebirds and canaries. I never tired of seeing his huge hands delicately holding those tiny, colourful birds, like jewels. He was not always so sensitive with us mini-humans. He was quick to chide or discipline us if we put a foot wrong, but he was also fair and ultimately wanted to have a laugh, so all was forgiven. We all loved him.

Where was I? Oh yes, I was telling you about how inspirational Marjorie is to me. So long as her beloveds are well, she asks for nothing more. She has always been generous with what matters most: her time and her care. Due to the geographical distance, she and I have always written to each other about once a month. In this way, she includes me in the vital family loop, making sure I know exactly what's happening with my cousins and my aunties and uncles. She makes sure I am not a 'celebrity', that I am a granddaughter, as equally cherished as the others. She earths me so that any sudden lightning that strikes, be it some glitzy prize or scary trauma, can be grounded through me without toppling me. I am safe in the certain knowledge that she will always love me, flaws and all. She is my ultimate proof that love is *always* the answer.

It is my heaven to be around her. I recall sneaking into her room, and snuggling up in bed with her along with various cousins, on cold mornings after Granddad had gone to work. Condensation on the windows, and stories, sometimes read and sometimes made up.

I remember fitting into her shoes when I was about six or so because her feet are so very tiny—I think she takes a size 2. She was a gifted dancer and in her rather unlikely (heightwise) but strangely hypnotic and graceful partnership with Granddad, the two of them not only taught but won lots of trophies. Somehow, when we granddaughters tried these shoes on, we borrowed a tiny bit of her innate glamour and elegance.

There was one other phenomenal world that Grandma let us into. The parallel universe of wondrous joys that was the loft. A small metal ladder would be winched down and, if we were lucky, she would invite us up the ladder and through the small attic opening in the ceiling of the hall. This was a portal to her personal domain, which was a twinkling constellation where all the tiny little stars could shine, and each star was a doll.

It was a staggering, magical collection that enchanted every kid who saw it. Like Santa's grotto at Christmas, it sparkled and gleamed and delighted us. I went up those little steps into the loft recently to find a small empty space with no trace of the former magic. I thought I might have dreamt it. I asked her if I had remembered it correctly and, again, she just winked and hugged me.

So that's Marjorie, my lovely dinky fairy grandmother who smells like cake and only comes up to my shoulder and has sent me a tenner in every birthday card for fifty years. A dainty little lady with a towering powerhouse of strength inside her who has guided us Berrys and Frenchies through two warfuls of hell and all kinds of sun and storms for ten decades. She is my yin and I call her Good Granny.

Then, of course, there is Evil Granny. The yang. Grandma O'Brien. Lillian. Fag Ash Lil. Did you meet her? I can't remember. She wasn't evil really—just very, very bad. She died a few years ago at the age of ninety-three, I think. Actually, some of the most fun I had in my teenage years was with her, but I was nearly always aware that whatever we were doing was probably illegal and certainly unhealthy. All around Lillian were lies. Lots of lies. She would encourage me to lie so as not to get into trouble if we were up to something illicit, she told me lies about her childhood and her marriages, she told her own kids lies about many things and she lied to get her own way. On top of that, we all lied around her—elaborate lies about how we were going to be abroad at Christmas so that we didn't have to witness more drink-fuelled rantings and bad moods. Lies about how much pocket money I had in my purse so that she didn't scrounge it all.

Lil was a tricky woman with a colourful history, a sharp tongue and a short fuse. She had a first marriage that nobody seems to know much about, to a boxer, and she lived in Polperro where my mum's eldest sister, Wendy, was brought up until Lil married my mum's dad, John McArthy Alfonso O'Brien, and came to live in Plymouth. McArthy was in the Royal Navy, then left and ran various pubs with Lil, who couldn't have been better placed to indulge in her favourite hobby of tasting lots and lots of alcohol. It was when the two of them were running a pub called the Antelope in the Octagon on Union Street in Plymouth, that my mum gave birth to my brother in the upstairs room. A real Plymouth 'bey' (boy)!

From what I can gather, Lil didn't seem to have a single maternal bone in her body. This did not prevent her from having more children: my mum Roma, Terry, Owen and Michael. She seems to have regarded her kids as either troublesome pests or domestics, except her first-born, Wendy, who was prized, protected and praised. Their upbringing was pretty tempestuous, with Lil dishing out physical and verbal abuse in equal measure. By the time the grandchildren came along Lil had mellowed a bit. She could hold forth when in her cups and she could often be a complete selfish pain in the arse, but I loved how uncontrolled and tough she was. She was sly, and never short of a con or two, always on the lookout for a way to make a few bob, at whatever cost. At some point she had worked on a stall in the Pannier Market, a beautiful, light, airy, covered market in Plymouth. She knew how and where to get a good deal in secondhand jewellery. On one occasion, I had need of her skills in this murky area.

I was about fifteen and a friend of mine from school, Patsy Ritchie, had invited me to come home with her to Gibraltar for the holidays. I desperately wanted to go, but my parents didn't have enough cash to spare. So my dad struck a deal with me: if I did a paper round for him for a month, he would pay my wages and then double it to make up the required amount. But however hard I worked, I fell short by £40 even with Dad's help. Mum noticed how sad I was and came up with a brilliant solution. She went and furtled about in the attic for a while and returned with a flat velvet box. She explained that inside was a set of jewellery which she had never liked—they were pearls, and she had always superstitiously believed that they bring bad luck. My mission, should I choose to accept it, was to take the jewellery to the market and get the best possible price for it. She said I would certainly be able to get £40 but that I should barter, vigorously. OK. Off I went.

As I entered the vast hall, who should pop up from nowhere but Lil. We went for coffee and I explained my predicament. She took the box with the pearls from me and told me to leave it up to her. I sat tight until she returned, smirking, ten minutes later.

'Who's your favourite gran?' she said as she sat down and triumphantly counted out the tenners on the table. One, two, three, four—great, that's my target. Then, oh God, here comes more—five, *six*. £60! I couldn't believe it. What a result! Big victory hugs all round, more coffees and some celebratory dough cakes too, which I happily paid for, oh and some bread and cakes for her to take home for later. Of course, my pleasure.

I went straight to Mum to show her my winnings. When I told her about the £60 she didn't look as pleased as I'd hoped. I explained about meeting Lil and letting her do the dirty deed. She grabbed my hand, muttering things like 'I'll kill her' and 'canny old cow' and other, ruder, grumblings under her breath. Within minutes, we were at my gran's flat in Rendle Street and Mum

Outside Madame Tussauds, where a man placed a monkey in my arms and another in Gary's and we had our photo taken. It marks the day my monkey-love began.

Jaw set, on bed in Akrotiri, Cyprus, quite determined to conquer the world of ballet despite shortness and roundness of stature.

My whole family drowning a lilo in Cyprus, when Dad was in the RAF and we lived on air-force bases at Nicosia and Akrotiri. Gary was an accomplished lilo surfer.

Me, on holiday, trying to attract males the beach at St Mawes in Cornwall. My schoolfriend Angie—'the Cornish rebel'—came too.

Filmin 'Slags' in 1984—one of several short films written for television by Fatty and featuring performers from the 'Comic Strip' comedy club in London.

Len loves comedy. He is the most effusive audience member I've ever known. If something tickles him he surrenders to fits of joyous laughter. It's wonderful.

Performing 'French and Saunders' with Fatty, live on stage at the Shaftesbury Theatre in London's West End.

Fatty—a chum to bounce ideas around with, to have a career with and laugh your tits off with ...

marched me in, demanding that Lil give me the rest of the dosh. Lil looked a bit sheepish and eventually relented and reached into her handbag. Then laid three more tenners on the table. I was aghast. Mum said, 'And the rest!' Eventually there was £100 on the table. I was speechless. She had done a deal for £160, but she had decided to pocket £100 of it as a sort of commission. My mum had known all along the pearls were worth a lot; she wanted me to have the experience of finding that out and doing a good deal for myself; she hadn't anticipated Evil Granny interfering. I always kept my eye on Lil after that. She was very quick. And slippery.

Lil loved to have a good time. A drink, a song, some darts and a fight would be the perfect evening for her. Any chance to put on a rabbit-skin fur coat, *lots* of lairy bling, a big gash of red lipstick and some click-clacky shoes was all right with her. She took me to arcades and pubs and bookies. I got drunk, I caught nits, I occasionally walked home on my own when she was too pissed to remember I was with her. It was never dull.

When her marriage broke down, she moved in to the council flat in Rendle Street where my two great-uncles lived, her brothers, Bill and Jim. Both had been badly injured in the war serving with the Royal Devonshires. Uncle Bill was still in terrible shock from the unspeakable sights he had seen in Belsen. Uncle Jim had to have a full-body skin graft and lost several fingers, when he was the last off the roof of a bombed building in Greenland. He was the sergeant and, thus, final man to go down a precarious rope which burnt and snapped, plunging him, on fire, to the ground where his legs and ankles broke. When he was at the field hospital, they had set his legs wrong and covered his burns in sticking plaster which took months to soak off when he returned to England, where his legs had to be broken again and reset. In later life, he was the projectionist at the Plaza cinema in the Barbican while Uncle Bill built submarines in the dockyard and slowly contracted the asbestosis which eventually killed him, although no one would admit it. Neither of these lovely old guys had married, and I always found it touching that they slept, Morecambe and Wise-like, in the same big bed just like they had as young lads, trusting only in their loyalty to each other. This meant, however, that there was a spare room and Lil wasted no time foisting herself upon them and somehow convincing them that they needed her to look after them. She also demanded payment for it! An extortionate pecuniary arrangement was set up, and those poor brothers were stuck with their monstrous sister, charging *them* for living in *their* home. Another brilliant coup for Lil.

It was during Lil's time at this flat that another elderly relative, Aunt Fan, came to live out her final days with them. She spent most of the time in bed in Lil's room. She was a gentle, sweet lady who we all loved, and even Lil softened to care for her in those last weeks.

When my career kicked off a bit in the eighties and occasionally a picture of me turned up in a magazine, Lil would cut it out, mount it on card or frame it, and display it in a corner of her flat I liked to refer to as the 'temple'. Once, after coming to see me perform in Plymouth, she demanded I sign a 4 x 6 publicity photo to her as follows: 'To my darling grandma, I love you *so* much, thank you for everything, from your devoted granddaughter, Dawn French xx.' This too was then placed at the temple altar. I tried several times to dismantle the temple since it caused me untold embarrassment and was beginning to send trouble ripples through the family, who were rightly furious. But she wasn't having it. Woe betide any visitor who might come in and *not* know I was related to her.

Y'know, even after all the weird and bad stuff she did, I was really sad when she died. I felt like a mould had been broken. In her curious way, she loved me very much and I loved her, but it was the kind of love that you only show when you've got your full armour on, just in case of an unpredictable attack.

So, you see, these two women have had a massive influence on me. Two extremes, two entirely different legacies. And I am grateful to both because without either of these opposing powerful forces, I don't think I would stop to balance things up as often as I do. It may frustrate me, but it's just the way I am.

# DEAR JACK,

When I was about six and your dad was about eight—only a couple of years younger than you are now—we went with our mum and dad to live on a hot island in the Mediterranean called Cyprus. Our dad, your granddad, who sadly you never met (you would have loved him, and boy would he have loved you), worked for the Royal Air Force and his bosses sent him to live over there for a few years. At the time we arrived, a frightening war was taking place on the island to do with the people who live there, called Cypriots, wanting their country to be separate from Great Britain. There was also some fighting between the two different types of people who lived there, the Turks and the Greeks, who had a long history of disliking each other, so all in all it was pretty scary.

The first house we lived in was in a place called Nicosia, which is in the north of the island. The house was big and painted white and pink with iron railings round the balconies. There was an older house next door where a Greek family lived and we all became friends. The mother of the family was called Androniki and she was very loud and bossy but very kind to us. She never stopped kissing me and your dad—you can imagine how much he liked that! *NOT!* This lovely lady always used to call me Haravghi Moo instead of Dawn. She explained that the Haravghi bit is the Greek for dawn, as in the sunrise at the start of the day, and the little 'Moo' bit on the end of the name was in fact 'Mou' and is the way Greek people call you darling or sweetheart. So, all the time I lived in Cyprus, our family called me 'Haravghi Mou', which slowly changed to just the plain old 'Moo' that you will have often heard your dad call me. At least, I *hope* that's why he's calling me that.

While we were living in the big white and pink house, quite a lot of fighting was going on nearby and we would often hear gunshots and loud bangs, which were terrifying. We had to be safely locked up in our house by a certain time in the evening, as did everybody else. This is called a curfew, and it lasted for some time. Our dad was busy at work and occasionally couldn't get home in the evenings so we were confined to our house and reliant on the radio to get instructions from the people who were in charge of the British on the island. Our mum, your granny, had to be very strong and she helped lots of other families in the same situation.

I remember one day that was particularly alarming. Granny kept telling Gary and me not to look out of the window and down into the street. There were gunshots very close by and it was really dangerous to be near the windows. Of course, as you know, I am a champion nosy parker and I couldn't resist a peek. I have never forgotten what I saw. A man was lying on the road right next to our house. I knew straight away he was dead. He had lots of blood on him and was lying in a strange crumpled way. He was a Turk and had been shot by his enemy, a Greek. Granny was aware that gunmen, snipers, were aiming at the roof of our building and anyone who was on it. Honestly, Jack, you won't believe what she did. She marched up to the roof *still* wearing her apron, and she shouted at the gunmen to go away and leave us alone, that she had a family with young children inside to protect and that they should know better. She told them they were welcome to go and kill each other elsewhere, but not near her family and friends, thank you very much. As you know, Granny can be pretty fearsome when she wants to be, so they apologised and moved elsewhere to continue their deadly fight.

The body of the Turk stayed there on the road for a few days though, and I tried not to look but I kept wondering when the poor dead man would be returned to his family, who must have been feeling so sad not knowing where he was. Then, one day, he was not there. He was younger than my own dad, but he was dead, and that was hard to understand.

During this difficult time, Cyprus was divided into two parts with a big border across the middle of the island from left to right, west to east. North of this line belonged to the Turks and south of this line belonged to the Greeks. We were moved to an air-force base in the south, called Akrotiri, near Limassol, and although the island was still at war, we were much safer and we were all together with other RAF families, and life returned to relatively normal.

Well, Jack, let me tell you what 'normal' was like. Us kids would go to school between 7 a.m. and 12 noon and then we would go to the beach *all afternoon, EVERY DAY!!* Fantastic! Sometimes a grown-up who wasn't working would come with us but often we would be dropped there, a group of about a dozen RAF kids ranging in age from six to sixteen, given a picnic for lunch and then be picked up again just before dark. Those long sizzling afternoons have remained in my memory as some of the happiest times I've ever had. Swimming and splashing with your dad and our mates, building huts and dens and sand sculptures. Exploring among huge ancient rocks. Hearing stories of Greek gods like Aphrodite, the goddess of love. Daring each other to dive-bomb into the sea from higher and higher rocks. Eating olives and smelling eucalyptus. Pretending to be mermaids and pirates. Inventing our own underwater towns and having jobs in submerged shops and factories. Befriending strange dogs on the beach and worrying about their welfare. Playing with local kids and not noticing for one second that we didn't speak the same language. Learning from them where the best caves and treasures were. Keeping secrets for each other, cutting our fingers on purpose and fusing our blood to become a forever conjoined family. Snorkelling in brightly coloured masks and darting through shards of underwater light chasing fish and octopuses. The unsurpassable, exhilarating sense of freedom.

Most of the time we lived on the RAF base, your dad seemed to be dressed as a Roman centurion, wielding a huge toy sword, and roaring. Does this sound a bit like you, I wonder? Gary was very close to a little dog who lived with us called Whiskey, who I think we inherited from another family that were leaving. This was common practice among forces families. Pets were constantly passed round since they couldn't be shipped home. He was a great dog, springy and keen, and could see no other purpose in life other than to play. He often came in quite handy as a centurion's mascot or a hunting dog in Gary's games. He was also an accomplished lilo surfer.

Away from the beach, my playtime was taken up with four main activities: (1) Roller-skating. Up and down the road for hours on end. I was sort of addicted to roller-skating and would occasionally do it well after bedtime and on into the night, I loved it so much. I didn't really learn any nifty tricks or turns, I just loved the rhythmic swaying and feeling of speed. (2) Horse riding. Not a real one—a horse's face painted on the end of our fence with strings attached for reins which I jiggled about on for hours (!) pretending to be in endless imaginary gymkhanas and western movies. Oh, the joy. (3) Hairdos. Your granny had a friend who was training to be a hairdresser and she needed hair models so Granny volunteered me. This lady was mainly perfecting the art of bridal hairstyling, so twice a week I would be the proud owner of an elaborate 'do'—usually 'up', and festooned with masses of curls and plastic daisies; that's what we liked in the sixties. Sometimes the hairdo would be so fancy and flamboyant and flowery that my neck could not support it and I would simply fall over. (4) Ballet. I was a divine dancer, so light, so graceful and renowned the world over as a champion junior prima ballerina who could leap higher than anyone else in the land. The trouble was, all of this was only true IN MY HEAD! I loved my ballet classes but your dad spied on one of my classes and said we looked and sounded like a herd of hippos. I soon gave up ballet for good. I blame him for my lack of success in that area. I'm pretty sure I could have been internationally acclaimed.

Hard as it is to believe it now, Granny and Granddad were really 'groovy' young parents back then. They really loved each other and were always smooching and dancing. They loved pop music like the Beatles, and Granddad especially loved Nat King Cole and Ella Fitzgerald and the Ink Spots and the Platters, and Johnny Cash and Matt Monro.

A really special thing happened to me one Christmas, Jack. Houses in hot countries don't have chimneys so I was obviously very worried about how Santa was going to get in with all our stuff. Granny told me not to worry, that he would find a way. Well, you can understand, I found it hard to sleep due to the worry and fear of disappointment. At about midnight, I heard the faint, very faint sound of bells, which grew louder and louder until there was a definite thud on our rooftop that shook the house. I ran to the window and opened the shutters and right there, outside *MY* window, was Santa himself with his sack. He asked if he could come through my bedroom since there was no chimney, so of course I let him in and he went through to the front room where the tree was. He rustled about a bit and then came back through with the empty sack and told me to go back to bed. I did. Straight away. But then I heard the bells again, so I shot over to the window and saw Santa in his sleigh, being pulled by all the reindeer rising higher and higher into the sky. I saw it with my own eyes! When I told them all about it the next morning, my dad said I must have been dreaming because Santa never lets you actually see him, but I'll tell you something, Jack. I did see him. I did.

## DEAR SARAH WALTON,

I had to write to you because you were one of the very few 'civvy' friends I made as a kid. As you know, us air-force brats generally stuck together, but when we came to live at RAF Turn Hill near your house in Market Drayton in Shropshire, we hit it off straight away, didn't we? You were so welcoming to me at quite a tricky time. It was only tricky really because I was eleven years old and my body was a hive of hormonal confusion and my brain was a soggy pink sponge of girly emotion ready to drip with inexplicable tears at any moment.

I always valued the security of the RAF base where I knew all the faces, but there was something magical about your house. I remember it as big and rambling and friendly with a toasty country kitchen. Am I right, did it have a mezzanine with banisters where you could see the entire first floor as you went up the stairs? There was a new litter of curly-haired chocolate-coloured puppies that was a source of great delight. We lay on your lawn for hours playing with them and naming them and hugging them and dressing them and not minding being bitten by their tiny sharp teeth. How lovely it was to be in your orbit and how loving your family were towards me.

I remember when we decided to do a little double-act turn for a talent contest at our school. We performed Esther and Abi Ofarim's extraordinary hit 'Cinderella Rockefella'. I wore a leather jacket and took on the male role and you were the pretty one in the dress. We mimed, I freely admit that, but we went down a storm and, best of all, people LAUGHED! So, two big lessons were learned by me on that day: (1) ham it up and give the audience permission to find you hilarious, and (2) it doesn't matter if your impressions are pants so long as they're funny. Oh, and (3) try to get the other one to wear the leather jacket and be the Boy as often as poss to avoid cumbersome costume and stubble rash. Thanks for being the first of several successful partnerships I've had on and off stage!

When you and I weren't at school or petting animals, we did a lot of dreaming, didn't we? Mainly about being bridesmaids. I loved those conversations about how our dresses would be, how our tresses would be, how very like princesses we would be . . . If only somebody, ANYBODY, would ask us! I thought it would be quite good to offer ourselves as a brace of bridesmaids. We were friends, which surely helps to sidestep ugly bridesmaid rivalrous wars that inevitably end in tears and a certain amount of hair damage. We were prepared to practise bridesmaid tandem walking for *hours* so's we could be perfectly harmoniously in step. Elegant, light and breezy with a perky symmetry, if a bit chunky. Would there be gloves? Would we be permitted make-up? Just a smattering of mascara perhaps or the lightest brushing of a mum's shimmery coral lipstick? Oh, we could only dream.

Then, one blessed day, it happened. My mum told me that my beloved Uncle Owen and his lovely fiancée, the irrepressible Joan, were coming to visit and that the bride-to-be wanted to have a chat with me. At last, I was on the brink of bridesmaidhood for sure. I wasn't going to forget you, though, you were definitely part of the deal, although of course you weren't actually part of the family and had never actually met Joan, but somehow, through sheer righteous force of the plan's perfectness, I would surely persuade her that you were to be included.

The day of their visit came and Joan asked if we could go for a walk together. Oh my holy God. This was it. We had never 'gone for a walk' before. I suppressed my excitement and cocked my head and tried desperately to appear to be listening. 'Hurry, hurry, I might faint if you don't get to it. You know you need me. Just ask! Oh, and by the way, my friend Sarah and I are sort of joined at the hip, could she be one too?' I thought. Hang on, now she was telling me about her family and all the little girls in it who would make suitable bridesmaids. Tune in, Dawn, what is she actually saying? Something about too many nieces, odd numbers, how I will apparently have lots of other opportunities and for me not to be too upset, and am I OK? What is she telling me? My tear ducts seem to get wind of the devastating rejection before I do, and start to do impulse crying. Auntie Joan has her arm round me and is apologising. I haven't passed. I'm not in. Me no bridesmaid. It was quicksilver. It was there. Then it wasn't. I was a bridesmaid. Then I wasn't.

I managed to reassure her that despite my silly tears, I really didn't mind. Yeah, sure I didn't mind. The rabid injustice of it all sputtered inside me until it grew into a full howling tornado of hurt and anger which made me want to spear all bridesmaids everywhere immediately with my red-hot sharpened rods of spite.

As it was, we returned home and through gritted teeth I explained to my mum that there was indeed to be a full complement of fluffy bridesmaids but that I was not to be one of them. Never mind, eh? Mum saw through my pretence instantly and took displacement action. A week later we drove to Manchester and we spent too much money on an outfit for me. I ended up at that wedding in an eye-catching, extraordinary and (like all revenge buys) ill-advised get-up. It took the form of a bright pink trouser suit. The trousers were flared, the top was a cape with gold braided buttons at the Nehru neck. The hat was jockey-inspired, also pink. The blouse was frilly-fronted, also pink. The shoes were black patent leather with a T-bar. The socks were school (mistake). Certainly I was noticeable. If only for all the wrong reasons. Thank heavens that, a short while later, my very cool, jazzy, clever Uncle Mike and his equally groovy fiancée Trish finally granted my wish and asked me to be bridesmaid at their wedding. It was a real sixties wedding and Trish's lovely sister Heather had to play your part, Sarah, because we had moved by then, and also mainly because she was Trish's sister. Anyway, I got to do it and it was utterly dreamy and included gloves *and* a fancy hairdo *and* a small heel. Praise be.

I never found out if you managed to be a bridesmaid. Hope you did. Otherwise you might still be as dangerously murderous as I was. Any time you would like to do synchronised slow walking, with fabulous hairdos and matching accessories, let me know!

## DEAR DAD,

I am trying to book a holiday. We haven't got enough time to go abroad, and besides, I don't really want to do that—I'm feeling a bit carbon-footprint guilty, plus I hate flying. Since we only have a week, two flights don't add up to funsville for me. No, I want to find a British-based holiday. Quite difficult considering the different needs, likes and dislikes of all three of us. I like sea, art, food, naps, telly and dog. Len likes books, heat, pictures, tunes, wine, comics and walks. Billie likes bed, phone, PlayStation, Facebook, iPod, boys and dark rooms. Usually we try to do a bit of all of the above, but that often results in no one being satisfied.

We *have* had some splendid holidays, the like of which we could never have imagined as kids. We often stay in private rented houses so as to keep away from eager Brits with camera phones. I don't normally mind if people want a quick photo, but I have an entirely different mindset when I'm on holiday, and I feel strangely shocked that my work-life 'stuff' like photos and autographs has intruded on my private family time. It just feels inappropriate and I get quite embarrassed. I find it hard that people don't read the obvious signals, when you're meandering about hand in hand with your old man and your kid, nosying in art galleries or quietly reading a book in the back of a café. It is so clear that I am off duty, so to speak. Some people can be unbelievably rude. We've had photos taken from the balcony of our hotel *into* the bedroom, and on one excruciating occasion, Len and I were on honeymoon in Kenya and the dining room full of Brits joined in a loud chant of 'We know what you've been doing' as we entered. Exit swiftly stage left. Room service, thank you, goodnight.

The worst ever occasion of such thoughtlessness wasn't on holiday, it was at a sports event with Billie. She is a bit of a dab hand at the ol' shot-put, and she's not bad at discus either, and running. She takes part in various athletic competitions as a member of her local club. Imagine that, Dad, I am the mother of an athletic kid! Who'd've thought it, eh? I have been suddenly launched into a world of track suits, running shoes, personal bests, pep talks, endless packed lunches, safety pins for numbers to be attached to shirts, energy drinks, pulled muscles, Deep Heat, orders of events, statistics, long circuitous journeys to old stadiums at the arse end of brown towns, and loud, utterly biased hollering from the stands. The fab thing about a local athletics club is that it unites everyone, whatever colour, background, school, religion or anything else. I have been astounded to see the dedication of the coaches, who are all volunteers, to these kids, and equally the parents who sacrifice so much of their spare time to join in and support. The folk at Bracknell Athletics Club were immediately welcoming to Billie and to us, with a palpable sense of 'nothing special'—thankfully—just a new kid joining and some new parents supporting. We were in the team, and therefore we had to pull our weight and join in.

The day came for our club to be represented in the Southern

Counties Women's League at Kingston. There were about eight to ten clubs competing and the stadium was heaving. Our Bracknell lot decided to camp out on the grass, close to the discus net and the shot-put sector. It was a warm but blustery day and the events went well for us. Then, something terrible happened. Billie had thrown well in her shot-put event and we thought she might even bag first place but couldn't be sure till the official announcement was made. There was a hubbub of group excitement building, and then the familiar, loud, tinny voice from the speaker announced: 'In the under fifteens shot-put . . . third was Katie blah blah . . . with blah metres . . . second was Tanisha blah blah with blah metres and first was Billie Henry with blah blah huge amount of winning metres!' We started to cheer and I grabbed Billie for a victor's hug. But Mr Tinny Official hadn't finished his announcement. He went on . . . 'Billie Henry, whose mother, the celebrity DAWN FRENCH, is here with us today, ladies and gentlemen, sitting over there on the grass. Nice to see you out today with all the normal mums and dads!' I'm sure on reflection he meant no harm, but his careless and misguided attention started the rumblings of a volcano of foaming fury inside me. I found myself in a reflex action, charging purposefully towards the official's booth on the other side of the track. Billie was tugging at me, pleading, 'No, Mum, it's OK. I don't mind! Just leave it!' but I was hell-bent on a meet and right retribution. I was going to give it to him in an eloquent but savage verbal attack he wouldn't forget. How dare he highlight me over my daughter's hard-won achievements? How dare he make this day about anything other than the kids? How dare he sully this lovely, pure, clean, happy moment with the filth of 'celebrity'?! As I approached the booth, I caught my first sight of the enemy, three elderly, silvered ex-athletes in their authoritarian whites beaming at me with expectation and joy. I opened the door and the main culprit, Official Tin Voice, a lofty and superior old fox, greeted me with: 'More tea, vicar?!' What fresh hell was this? I was so staggered by his blindness and insensitivity that my hitherto torrent of emotional lava somehow instantly diluted.

Instead my body made an alternative choice—to blubber like a baby. Oh dear God, no. Not now. Come on! I need some steel! I endeavoured to use words, but I couldn't. This, maddeningly, prompted a big hug from all three of the enemy. I did manage to blurt out a version of the 'How dare you?!' speech, but it manifested itself mainly as 'My daughter! Blub blub my daughter!' which they understandably misread as over-effusive pride. Billie was crumbling with embarrassment behind me, and led me away to the car. By now I was only liquid, so I poured myself into the driver's seat and tried to compose myself while she packed the car. Various members of our club came over to sympathise and to share their annoyance and offer support. The journey home was glum and sniffly for me. I felt that this was another opportunity to have a full and frank chat about the drawbacks of being in the public eye. We have often talked about it, and Billie is in no doubt about my utter disrespect for the culture of celebrity. I didn't get the chance to know how you would have felt, Dad, about this strange phenomenon of celebrity befalling your own daughter. I suspect you would have mistrusted it as much as I do. In my opinion, fame, money and politics are among the most corrupting influences we live with. Mostly, recognition is debilitating. It disables your ability to judge or behave normally because you are constantly reacting to people's preconceived perceptions of what or who you are, or what you need and want. Plus, you are constantly on guard to resist the bluster of gushing praise which is blown up your bum. I find the status and value system in our country confusing—how have we come to this place where footballers and singers and jesters are prized above teachers and doctors and carers? Don't get me wrong—I don't underestimate the importance of entertainment, not at all, *BUT* why are we paying so much attention to the wrong people? I have benefited hugely from this perverse social structuring, I don't deny that. I don't feel guilty, I feel baffled. While life's hierarchies are so topsy-turvy, it is even *more* crucial not to confuse lustre with importance.

Anyway there I was, apologising to Bill for the idiocy of adults who are impressed with the wrong thing. I was explaining how helpless I felt when her achievement was eclipsed by a stupid error of judgment. I told her it would be so great to be able to turn off the fame knob when it suited and that is practically always when I am around her. Billie told me to chill out, that she sees it coming a mile off every time, and finds it *hilarious* to watch the behaviour around the shiny quicksilver that is celebrity. She found the whole episode funny and embarrassing, not least my phenomenally entertaining overreaction! She patted my hand and said, 'There, there, dearie, you'll get over it. You'll worry when no one notices you.'

Anyway, I started this letter talking about holidays because, given only a week to find a good one, I wondered whether we should hire a canal boat. I remember all those lovely holidays we had on that tiny Fibreglass motorboat you bought. Gary and I would sleep at the back, under the cover at night, while you and Mum were in the cabin. It was so exciting. Chugging round the canals and rivers during the day, negotiating the locks and the islands, and mooring up at night wherever we fancied. Reading *The Hobbit* and Spike Milligan aloud by the light of the Tilley lamp and holding on whenever the wake of a passing vessel rocked us too hard. I loved that you assumed the role of captain too seriously, that we had to use nautical terminology for everything and be mindful of safety issues at sea. Not that we ever were actually 'at sea'. We were on canals in Shropshire and Lincolnshire and Yorkshire and the Midlands.

We must have looked an odd sight on the canal. You in an ostentatious captain's hat, barking *Navy Lark* orders at your junior matelots. Mum holding Poppet, our Westie, over the side so she could do her business, and a sparrow in a cage on deck. Oscar the sparrow, a little no-hoper fledgling who fell out of his nest when he was only a few minutes old, was miraculously nursed to full adult birdhood and only wanted to hang around with humans because he was convinced he was one. The door of the cage was often left open for him, and he would occasionally hop about and stretch his wings, but his preference was to stay near us, his human buddies, who were just like him, human. OK?! Now back off and make with the seed.

I can't remember ever going abroad on holiday as a kid. We went to Scotland once, and drove around looking at castles and mountains, didn't we? Gary and I were teenagers then and holidays with you guys were totally uncool. I think my own kid has reached that same point. She agreed to come on a sailing holiday last year where we bobbed about exploring various Greek islands, but she was mainly preoccupied with sending texts home to friends saying things like 'Am being forced to be interested in Greece. Send help' and 'Dull parents laughing all day—why?' and 'Saw fit guy who seemed interested but no, yawn, we had to "eat in a taverna" instead'. Yes. I know I shouldn't be reading them. On her phone. After she's gone to bed. Checking if she's doing any international drug deals. If it's any consolation, it takes ages to decipher them since the above messages read something like 'dl pts. Laffg al dy —?' and 'Sw ft gy—intd—bt no, we "et @ tvn"'. So, if she didn't really enjoy the Greek boat experience, is it likely she is going to enjoy the British canal experience, where she will have to live up close and personal with her 'dull parents' for a whole week? I think not. Mmmm, better rethink holiday idea. Maybe stay at home? All do stuff we want to in separate rooms? Sounds sublime.

## DEAR BILLIE,

When I was about thirteen, I was invited to a party by my friend Karen. I was *so* excited about this party because I knew that there was going to be a boy there called Mark who I really liked. Although we had some mutual friends and we had been in the same room on various occasions, he had paid me no attention whatsoever. I found this heartbreaking and I was determined to get him to notice me. I planned to summon up my courage and somehow do this at the party that Saturday night. In order to impress him, I decided to wear my new purple suede hot pants. Hot pants were what we called shorts back then and they were the singular most fashionable item you could own. I saved up my pocket money for AGES, I did odd jobs for extra cash, and eventually I had enough to go to a big shop called Trago Mills and buy them. They didn't really fit me, they were far too tight, but I wanted them SO much I didn't mind how uncomfortable they were. Everyone wanted hot pants, but as is so often the cruel injustice of fashion, they suited very few people. I *wasn't* one of those chosen few. It was definitely an advantage to be tall, thin and have long, shapely legs. I had none of these attributes but I convinced myself I could carry the hot pants off nevertheless. My whole outfit was new. Starting from the bottom up (the bottom of my legs, that is, not my actual bottom): brown suede wedge heels with espadrille straps round my Miss Piggy ankles. American tan tights. The bright purple suede hot pants with shiny buttons on the pockets. Above the waist was a considerable overflow of puppy fat, which was forced upwards and outwards by the too-tight waistband of the hot pants. On top of this was a cream cheesecloth smock top with stringy lacing down the front, slightly see-through, with flared sleeves. Many Indian bangles about the wrists. Large dangly earrings. Long straight hair parted in the centre with no fringe, a bit like Ali MacGraw, but only a very tiny bit. Green suede shoulder bag with tasselly fringing. Big round sunglasses worn permanently on head. I glanced in the mirror and decided I looked pretty damned fine. Actually I didn't feel this at all but I knew I would have to fake feeling good in order to leave the house. So it was with this pretend confidence that I went to look for my dad to arrange my lift home. He asked me to come in to the front room for a quick chat. He closed the door behind us, and asked me to sit down. My heart sank. I thought I was in for a good talking-to. I was right about that, but it wasn't the usual precautionary drill, it was something else. Something I've always remembered, especially if I'm feeling a bit insecure—which we all do sometimes, don't we?

It was a long time ago but, to the best of my memory, it went something like this:

DAD: Sit down, puddin'. Actually, before you sit down, give us a twirl. Wow, you look really lovely, a right bobby-dazzler. Are those shorts? Or lederhosen?
ME: They're hot pants, Dad.
DAD: Where did you get those? Millets?
ME: No, Dad, Trago Mills.
DAD: Well, you look very . . . pretty. They are quite short.
ME: Yes, because they're shorts.
DAD: I see, well you look really super in them. Very dandy.
ME: Can I come home late?
DAD: Hold your horses there, missus. Before we talk about arrangements, there's something I want to say. What's that black stuff in your eyes by the way?
ME: Kohl. It's Indian. I've worn it before.
DAD: Have you? I've seen black stuff on *top* of your eyes before, but that looks like it's right inside . . .
ME: That's where it's supposed to go. Millions of Indian ladies haven't died of it yet.
DAD: Anyway. This party tonight . . .
ME: It's fine, Dad. There won't be any alcohol.
DAD: I should hope not. Alcohol? You can't drink alcohol!
ME: I know. That's why there won't be any. Karen said there wouldn't be any. Her parents'll be there, they're going next door during the party.
DAD: Here's the thing I want to say . . .
ME: Can we hurry?
DAD: How much do you think Mum and I love you?
ME: Um . . . a lot?
DAD: More than a lot, Dawn. Much more. When you were born, you had scarlet fever, and for a couple of days there, it was a bit touch and go . . .
ME: I nearly died?
DAD: Yes, and when we thought we might lose you we realised just how much we loved you already; even your brother was worried . . .
ME: Yeah, worried I might survive!

DAD: Don't be facetious, which by the way is one of the few words in the English language with all the vowels in the correct order. No, we were all very anxious. We had so much to look forward to, so much to learn. So much to do, so much fun to have. Mum and I fought hard to be together and to make this family. I know it's been a challenge sometimes. We haven't had much money, no surplus certainly, but we have saved and shared everything together, haven't we? In this family, no one is lonely because we're always there for each other, the four corners that keep our square whole, all connected to and looking out for each other, equally. You are a vital part of that. You and your brother are our life, our reason and our happiness. We adore you both and we feel blessed to have you, and to witness you grow into the remarkable young people you are becoming. Never forget what a treasure you are, and if your faith in that ever wobbles, have a look in the mirror and have confidence in what you see. You are a rare thing, an uncommon beauty, a dazzling, exquisite, splendid young woman. Look! You must know it's true, you're a corker. How lucky any boy would be to have you on his arm. They should fight tournaments to win your affection, they should kill for your favour. Don't you dare be grateful for their attentions, you utterly deserve it and, more than that, you deserve the very best. Don't think for one second you should settle for other people's rejects. *You* are the princess, you are the prize, so be choosy and take your time. You decide how, when and where, *not* them. They will wait. Of course they will. Who wouldn't wait for someone so priceless? There is no one better. Know this: if anything ever happened to you, Moo, our lives would fall apart, we would be devastated and this family would never be happy again. So, you must take care of yourself, you must guard against danger. When you are out of this house it is up to you to protect yourself, your reputation and your dignity. We love you and we need you. OK. That's all. You can go now. And yes, you can come home late, 1 a.m. at the outside, understand?
ME: Yeah . . . Thanks, Dad.

Off I went to the party, feeling ten foot tall and fabulous in my hot pants. Mark did come to talk to me that night, but I wasn't that interested. He wasn't really good enough, to be honest . . .

My dad gave me armour that night and I have worn it ever since. I could never quite buy the bit about being the best, but I *do* believe I am worth something. My self-esteem, still surprisingly intact after quite a few attacks, is still my strong centre, my metal, and I owe that to him.

The comforting thing is, Bill, I may not have my dad around any more but I do carry his values and his belief in me. When I think of what he said to me—every word applies to you. I'm so sorry you didn't get to meet him because he would have loved you so much and you would have loved him back. The only gift I can give you from him is this letter and the hope that you will read it, imagining his sentiments are addressed to you, through me and Dad. Hopefully, with time, you will come to know a greater and truer self-worth and know how valuable you are to us and to the family.

That's all. You can go now. Be home by 1 a.m. at the outside, understand?

## DEAR DAD,

I loved Lincoln, I thought it was the poshest city we had ever lived near. There was something grand about it. There's that big ancient bow arch you can walk under, and an elegant river that runs right through the middle, reminding you what an important place you're in. Plus of course a cathedral you can't miss. I haven't visited Lincoln since we left when I was fourteen years old but I clearly remember being in awe.

RAF Faldingworth was also impressive to me, but in a different way. The quarters and the NAAFI were quite compact and cheery but the actual base where you worked seemed sprawling and, as I recall, a large part of it was empty and virtually derelict. It was like being in a spooky episode of *The Avengers* or *The Prisoner* where someone nearly always ends up doing plenty of fast running and hiding and dodging. The perfect location for a teenager to get up to eight kinds of no good. And sorry to say, Dad, we did. We had secret parties where I was introduced to the mixed blessing that is sweet cider. We had romantic liaisons behind the doors of storage cupboards. We had terrifying seances where we tried to summon up the spirits of dead relatives. I once attempted to connect with Granddad McCarthy and was utterly petrified when the glass on our homemade Ouija board hurtled round accurately spelling out various clues about our family which no other soul there could have known. I was shaken to the core by this experience. This explains why I have never tried to communicate with you through any of these odd channels which I find too eerie and strange to understand.

Do you remember taking me to look round Caistor Grammar, my first experience of senior school? I only spent a year there but I had a good time except for the hideous weekly cross-country torture. Otherwise Caistor was just fine. It *was*, however, the venue for my first criminal activity. There was a sweet shop just outside the school gates and, yes, it was expected of you as a measly first-former to steal sweets for the older girls. You were a cretin and a smell if you didn't and you would also be forced to suffer the humiliation of being actually killed, which I didn't relish.

There was an officer's daughter called Heather (not her real name—her real name is Hannah Black). She was big and bold and brave. She *loved* stealing. It was her passion and she was extremely talented at it. She was cool, she was a bobby-dazzler, she was a hepcat. She was *it*. I was swept along with this frothy tide of admirers, and somewhere along the way I convinced myself that stealing was actually OK, that it was only our parents' archaic morals that had fooled us into eschewing such exciting, rewarding delights. I wanted to be like Heather. I wanted to be a proper thief, yay. We would go into town at lunchtimes and I would watch and learn from the Grand Mistress. She had no fear, she was cunning and stealthy and extremely smooth. My first attempt was in Smith's. She advised me to start small, with something inexpensive so I could feign ignorance if caught. OK, here I go—a packet of six pencils. The 'grab' was awkward and the packet edges grazed my flesh as I shoved it up my sleeve. I went a bit sweaty and telltale red in the face, but I did it—I nicked the pencils. My tutor was delighted with her protégée and promised a bigger, brighter, lucrative future if I stuck with her.

I went home that night and looked at my swag. Six lovely red pencils, sharp and perfect. My booty. Mine, all mine, and I hadn't parted with a sou of my precious pocket money. How great was this? Yes, it was. It was great. Wasn't it? So why wasn't I feeling great? I felt awful. Full-of-guilt-and-self-loathing awful. In the end, I tossed 'n' turned in bed, feeling steadily worse as the night wore on. I was plagued with guilt. It was a massive dragon breathing hot fire down my neck until eventually I could bear it no longer and I came to speak to Mum and confessed all. She was very understanding but said that you, Dad, needed to be brought into the loop to make the big decisions about how we should proceed now that she was fully informed of how hopelessly miscreant I was. So, you sat on my bed and what followed was the most serious and sobering conversation I had ever had. Thanks for holding my hand, by the way, but it didn't comfort me much during your frank assessment of the dire situation. You explained that in light of my villainous underhand dealings there were only two options open to us: A, to call the police and inform them how bent I was, or B, to try to replace the contraband without anyone knowing. I had never known you be so solemn. You then commended me for my honesty and said it might take time to come to terms with the shame and the potential dishonour brought upon the House of French. Then you promised to make a decision the next morning and we went to bed.

Well, we were outside the door of Smith's at opening time. Putting those pencils back was SO difficult! People around me were noticing my shifty behaviour and looking at me with accusatory and disgusted glares, but, somehow, I replaced them. I left that shop and my former crooked life behind that day. I was no longer a low cur; I had cleaned up and was back on the straight and narrow, all thanks to your wise counsel. You surely saved me from a life of pure, base wickedness. So that's good then.

Heather was disgusted and said she'd let me know when she'd found a spine donor for me. She went on to some truly awesome thieving, including large hi-fi equipment and TV sets. Eventually her dad found it all in a cupboard and she got a hiding from hell. Wonder what she's up to now? Probably something in government, I s'pect.

It was at RAF Faldingworth that you set up the big youth club, wasn't it? I think you must have noticed how vulnerable bored teenagers are. Maybe you could see that shagging and stealing weren't going to lead us anywhere good, that we needed distractions. All of my mates loved you for it—you reclaimed a building from dereliction and we all decorated it till it was a perfect teen meeting place with a coffee bar, tuck shop, ping-pong, games and a dance floor with disco lights. I loved those dances except for one thing—you were *always there* keeping a watchful eye on the proceedings, so it was double difficult for Gary or me to get a snog or a puff. The kids there knew you well, and thought you were dead groovy and told us how lucky we were to have parents like you.

This was only a small part of what you did for young people everywhere we went, and only now do I see what a phenomenally selfless thing it was to do. It took up a lot of your energy and often tested your patience, but Dad, you did a wonderful thing—you gave your time up to improve the lives of so many young men and women. I hope you knew how proud we were when you received the BEM in the honours list for this work, because we really were.

## DEAR DAVID ECCLES,

Oh heck, even writing your name there has given me a little flutter of flushed embarrassment. It is only momentary though, because if I scrunch my brain up hard enough to remember . . . yes, there it is—I can still smell your sweet breath and taste your divine lips. Your lovely, lovely mouth. How bloody fabulous it was to kiss you.

You came along when my Dad was posted to RAF Faldingworth in Market Rasen. As I recall, you were Gary's best friend on that camp, just before he went away to start boarding school in Plymouth, and even after, when he came home on holiday. I can't quite remember how we started with the kissing, I don't think we actually dated as such, did we? I loved how tall and funny you were (are?!) and I was doubly impressed with your Swiss army knife expertise, and the whole camouflage flak jacket and bobble hat thing you had going on. You looked like you might go all Rambo at any moment and disappear into the forest to live on grubs and bark, start your own campfires from brushwood kindling and stab any evil-doers who crossed you. I liked that.

Both my parents were out at work all day and my bro and I were latchkey kids. After school there were a good couple of hours of parent-free home time in which to pretend it was actually our own house and we could behave any bloody way we wanted. We could be true renegades and put chocolate powder in our milk or even chuck our knives and forks carelessly in the sink thereby making quite a clatter. We could play Deep Purple records at volume six and everything. So we did. Other kids would come round and sit about untidily, putting their feet up on the sofas *with* their shoes on and taking dangerous single sips of Amontillado sherry from a six-year-old bottle. It tasted like vinegar, because by then it actually was, but it didn't matter, it was alcohol of sorts, and in a virtually teetotal household, that was precious. It was during these crazy, wild escapades that you and I eventually made contact. I was praying that you would fall under my bewitching spell when I caught your eye and gave you my well-practised come-hither head toss, the like of which I had seen working for Marilyn Monroe in films. I'm not sure how you held back for so long, but eventually you stopped kissing every single *other* girl available and gave in to my utterly resistible siren techniques.

Do you remember the joy of sitting on that couch and doing industrial-strength kissing? Sometimes for an hour and twenty minutes without a break? The sudden revelation for me was that you can move your face about while in the throes of a delicious snog . . . and *breathe* . . . and make little snuffly, grunty noises of pleasure. The thousand ways of using your lips with someone else's lips—the nips and the sucks and the different pressures—were a sensual wonderland, but the mother of all epiphanies was the power of the tongue. I was giddy with delight, and instantly became obsessed with you, with the potency of kissing you. I am for ever indebted to you for showing me the ropes kiss-wise. You were a generous, accomplished instructor and it has been a struggle to find a match of your élan ever since. Perhaps we never can recapture the unique thrill of first love with its heady, exciting blood rush. Perhaps we're not supposed to. Perhaps other, later relationships have to be built on stronger foundations, more durable than pure kissing genius alone. A good kisser is hard to beat though, and hard to find; and believe me, I've tried!

It seems to have fallen to me to continue the quest for ever. Or at least as long as I can get away with it. I have never passed up the opportunity to lock on to the face of a willing party in pursuit of that rare beast, the talented kisser. In this hunt, I am bold and unshakeoffable.

In my desire to test drive as many lips as possible before I am too ancient and repulse my accomplices (I'm aware that, sadly, I may well have passed this point of no return), I have been unfeasibly lucky. For an early Comic Relief charity show, I decided to wangle a kiss from Hugh Grant by involving him in an elaborate ruse where

I pretended to be a swollen version of his then beloved, Liz Hurley, wearing a giant version of 'that dress' she wore so effectively, with the safety pins down the side. I wore it with considerably less panache but with quadruple the comedy, I felt. Jen and I wrote the sketch with the sole intention of landing his lips on mine, and may I say, 'HOWZAT!' We raised a million quid. Very quickly I realised that if the reason was funny enough, I could elicit these smackers at a prodigious rate. Thus I have proceeded to claim quite a few impressive trophies along the way, and none of the participants have seemed in the slightest bit offended. Lucky me.

Just thought I might make a little list of some of the more memorable liptastic moments I've had in case you're interested. Try not to be too jealous.

1. A boy called Michael Le Pellier when I was about four—functional and edifying.
2. A dog called Hunni—hairy.
3. You—heavenly.
4. Assorted guinea pigs (long AND short-haired)—split lips and large teeth—alarming.
5. A girl called Lisa—soft and fragrant and confusing, involved lipstick.
6. Assorted friends of brother—unremarkable, worse than guinea pigs.
7. A horse called Shula—huge velvety lips with spiky hairs, but bliss.
8. A farmer's son called Mark—new stubble, passionate.
9. Nick Brentford—meaningful and lingering.
10. A clever boy called Charlie who played Falstaff when I played Mistress Quickly—onstage, covered in talcum powder he had put in his hair to age him. I longed for him to kiss me off-stage but he wasn't interested.
11. A French sailor on Plymouth Hoe—cold, with nose dribble involved, but was given the little red pompom from his cap in return for the kiss, so v. romantic.

12. Plymouth College boys on Saturday nights at the OPM club—all tasted of cider or lager.
13. Various girls in dorm—but doesn't really count as was only practice.
14. Neil, a marine—light, almost not there.
15. Graham Inman—oh, how I wished.
16. Biker boys in the car park opposite Burgh Island—not a word spoken, furious and slavering and brief.
17. Jerry, the art teacher's son—sensitive but distant.
18. A chef at the Salcombe Hotel—utterly revolting. Bad teeth.
19. David Smyth, a navy sublieutenant—many, many soft Irish kisses with lots of laughs in between.
20. Students of the acting course at Central—too self-interested, were only imagining kissing themselves.
21. Colin—wouldn't, shame.
22. A saxophone player—too much suck and blow.
23. Steve—first experience of a moustache. Furry.
24. A rugby player—gay. Lived with mother. Cried.
25. Scottie—gay. Fag-hag kisses. Good technique.
26. A Welsh actor—poetic, heart-stopping.
27. Keith Allen—bossy, smug, scary and disappointing.
28. A musician on the Red Wedge tour—exciting.
29. Robin Ellis-Bextor—very tall, stepladder needed.
30. Lenworth G. Henry—the brightest, the best. Loves kissing anywhere, anytime. The King of Kiss.
31. Every boy at the Comic Strip—joy in the workplace.
32. Jennifer Saunders—in a play—passed messages in note form or gum. Lovely.
33. Frances Barber—in *Murder Most Horrid*—temptress with fabulous lips.
34. Hugh Grant—professional with odd chuckle, very game.
35. Jonathan Ross—for a joke. Never again.
36. Boyzone—enjoyable, varied.
37. A cat's arse—less enjoyable, but better than Jonathan Ross.
38. Brad Pitt—angel in male form. A woman's mouth, bliss.

39. Johnny Depp—sweet, respectful, as if I was favourite aunt. Not long enough or full enough or penetrative enough. Resistant.
40. Jamie Theakston—second-best kisser in the world.
41. Stephen Tompkinson—skilled, heartfelt.
42. Clive Mantle—strong, savouring, powerful, with occasional slurping.
43. George Clooney—bold, unashamed, clasped my face in both hands.
44. Richard Armitage aka Guy of Gisborne, or 'Man of Pleather'—shy, giggling, loving.
45. Richard Curtis—kisses like a butterfly has landed on your lips.
46. Len Henry again—sorry, but truly, he's really good.
47. Oh yes, and Alison Moyet—Alla—in a video. She knows how, that girl.

So, you see, it's been quite a journey, liply speaking, and believe me, my work is not yet done. I have you to thank though, David Eccles, for starting me up, and keeping me revved. I intend to tick over until I stall, and I hope my final breath is on someone else's lips, doing this kissing thing you are so darn good at. Mwah mwah.

## DEAR GARY,

Perhaps I should finally, belatedly, apologise to you for writing rude notes for you to find in every drawer in your bedroom when you came home for the holidays from boarding school. 'Nobody here likes you—true' or 'Go back to Nam!' I didn't really know what 'Nam' was. I just knew it was bad and so it'd suit me for you to go there. Yes, I *should* apologise for that but then I also remember quite a lot of torture coming my way too—the barrage of pinches and punches and Chinese burns.

Eventually, after a year at Caistor Grammar, I began the big boarding-school experience myself. Like you, I went to board in Plymouth so's we could be a stone's throw from the wider family and, like you, the RAF paid the bill, which meant both of us were in schools with people who were well out of our social and economic class. I think boys are crueller about all that stuff and I suspect you had a harder time than me, although both of us seemed to keep friends from schooldays for years afterwards, so we must have forged *some* loving and lasting links along the way.

Thanks, by the way, for bringing home a variety of different chums in the holidays from Plymouth College. I appreciated these offerings. Most of them were of great interest to me! I remember one incident where a boy from your school took me to a party in his car on a Saturday night and, forgetting that you were present, started boasting to his friends back in school on Monday morning about the many wild exploits we had been up to in the back of his small, dull car. All lies, of course, and according to your friends who related this to me later, you 'sorted him out'. Ta for that. I remember when you did something similar in Cyprus when some boys were trying to pull my gym pants down for a look when I was about six. Ta for that too. You have always been protective towards me and I do appreciate that, especially in later years when we have sometimes needed to look out for each other as the road to Adultville has become ever more twisty and turny. Underneath your good-humoured, easy-going exterior, Gary, I know you are made of strong stuff and I have been glad of it on lots of occasions.

I imagined St Dunstan's would be one long round of midnight feasts and jolly hockey sticks with plenty of clandestine liaisons down the dingle thrown in. It wasn't, of course. It was a small, traditional girls' public school set in the grounds of a beautiful Gothic abbey, where staff and pupils rubbed along trying to do the education stuff the best way they could. Do you remember Hazel Abley, my headmistress? She was everything a good school head was supposed to be—fair but austere, and very, very clever.

In the evenings after supper some of us used to volunteer to help out in the kitchen. It wasn't quite as altruistic as it may sound, since this favour elicited two important returns: (1) big hugs from Lavinia the cook, who was huge and generous and loving and was a kind of temporary mum substitute in occasional moments of homesickness (I'm sure you remember those), and (2) Lavinia sometimes doled out goodies like biscuits and hot sweetened milk.

Funny how we were all drawn to the kitchen, to some vestige of home life, of normality, at the back end of the day, to calm us all before sleeping. Are we all always looking for home? Don't get me wrong, I wasn't the achingly sad and lonely type of boarder—I met plenty of those and their sorrow consumed them. I didn't feel like that, partly, I think, because it was made so clear to us, wasn't it, how difficult and strange it was for Mum and Dad to send us there in the first place. We don't come from a posh long line of generations of public-school sprogs, of whom it is expected that they will be shushed away like troublesome flies. No, our mum and dad did *not* get this kind of education and they were determined that you and I would benefit from everything they were convinced they'd missed out on. The RAF would provide most of the fees, but they still had to find the funds for uniform, books, trips, trunks, name tags and all the other endless minutiae of a boarder's requirements. In order to find this cash they gave up fags and holidays and treats.

I think, for both of us, the boarding-school experience was a challenge and a test of our sense of identity. We were kids from a working-class West Country background whose father's job meant we travelled so we didn't grow up where we belonged. Add to that a father who refused the chance of a commission out of the ranks because—why?—presumably he feared the judgment of those above him who he clearly knew to be from a different, higher class than his. He preferred to stay down, to be at the top of his game, in his 'rightful' place. On top of that, Mum hailed from an even lower class than Dad, and boy didn't she feel it when she first got together with him. She experienced plenty of snidery and even actual resistance to their marriage. I think it's true that Grandma and Granddad French didn't speak to her for a year or so when she married Dad and only relented when you, their first grandchild, came along and they couldn't resist the chance to know you. So, we had parents who felt the weight of class and limitation on their shoulders and were determined to push up, push through that prejudice. For them, education was the answer. Boarding gave us stability; we wouldn't have to keep moving from school to school every time Dad was posted elsewhere. They wanted us to become confident, brave people who would not be daunted by class or intellect or authority.

It wasn't easy being the first from our family ever to go through the public-school system. We were mixing with kids who were very different to us economically and socially. I stayed some weekends with girls who had *ponies* in *meadows* and *sinks* in the corner of their bedrooms. Whose houses had driveways and beige carpets where you had to take your shoes off, where the heating was on all the time in the whole house! Girls who were presented with a new car on their seventeenth birthday. Girls who went skiing. All unfamiliar, all exciting, all *so* middle class, all so new. I regarded the whole confusing experience as fascinating drama—look how these people live, look how they think, look what they say, look what they wear, look what they love.

There were some girls like Nicky Varley whose dads were in the forces, some who were on scholarships, some like Nikki Rowe whose dads were butchers, or salty Salcombe girls who were just wild and adventurous and naughty like Kirsty Lamont. I loved being with those girls, and I never detected an iota of grandeur about any of them, but they were in the minority. For me, this school was the height of everything our parents wanted for us, so I found the lofty disapproval of snobs insufferable. This was *our* school, our team, our tribe, our world, and my parents had made seismic sacrifices for me to be there and I loved it. I wore my Downton House badge with unquestionable pride and used my hockey stick as a cudgel to defend the honour of my team against any snivelling enemy wing attack. We rarely won a match but we forged everlasting tribal bonds, and bore the scars of our many defeats with pride. I still have them. Inside and out.

I remember coming to watch you doing the same thing playing rugby. Donating your knees and ears and teeth for brief moments of glory, and a profound sense of belonging. Funny, isn't it, how now that we are so much older, after both having lived in many different places, countries even, we have returned here, to the West Country, where we feel the strongest call. I don't think it's just the sea and the light and the green and the cream. I think there are echoes for both of us of those cold sports fields and those cold dormitories, of Mum's tears and Dad's brave face on the first day of term. Of what it cost us as a family. Of discovering our sibling glue and liking it, liking the security of having a brother inextricably linked to me. Of our filial relationship with that area. Echoes of grandparents digging the ground for your roots to be secure. Knowing you'll return. And we have, haven't we?

## DEAR FATTY,

You and I have often talked about our respective school lives, the friends, the teachers, the whole caboodle. In fact, over the years, we have plundered that rich seam for material for our show. You went to the local grammar school and I went to public school, but when we have discussed our experiences, the difference is minimal, I think. So minimal that we even shared the same friend, but at different times. Her name was Camilla Leng. I think her dad was something impressive in the army and she lived for a short while in Plymouth and was in my class at school. She was a fantastic, larger-than-life character, a force of true naughtiness. It was Camilla who dared to attach notes declaring 'I'm so sexy' and 'Kiss me now' to the backs of the muted lavender cardigans of the most elderly teachers. It was Camilla who persuaded me to go into a long, dark, dripping cave by the river near Rock in Cornwall, where we were searching for dabs in the sand. She made scary noises—screeches and wails—using her natural ventriloquist skills, each time claiming she was not to blame. I loved being around her, basking in the heat of her boldness and her humour. Then, years later, I think it was during an interview, you and I discovered that we had *both* known her, and that before she came to Plymouth, she had lived near you and been your chum also.

Both you and I also took care to judge the safest and most enjoyable route through the canyon of danger and death that is an all girls' school. Keep your enemies close and beware bandits and fair-weather friends. Dodge the quicksand and use the oldest, tallest, widest trees for shelter and camouflage. Occasionally it is important to prove your colours as a leader and instigator in order to earn respect, but, equally, it's vital to entertain and amuse your fellow troopers. Hence the clowning and the mimicry. Let's all have a good laugh because it's nigh impossible to laugh and hate simultaneously.

St Dunstan's Abbey school in Plymouth was no longer a convent when I arrived in 1970, but it had all the trappings of one. It was grey and Gothic and ghostly. The floors creaked and the wind whistled through the covered cloisters to whip our calves. In stark contrast to the cheerless ash grey of the building, some ancient sadist had decided that dark blue, light blue and yellow stripes would be a good idea for a school uniform. We wore ties and blazers in this awful gaudy pattern and looked like escapees from a glee club for dwarfs. The hats were blue bowlers with a ribbon in the school stripe round the brim in winter, and boaters with the same ribbon in the summer. We might as well have been branded with 'twatty little toff' on our foreheads. There were some strange folk in town who regarded us as a kind of human coconut shy: they hurled verbal insults at us and, on some occasions, actual missiles.

Yep, the uniform identified us all right. It marked us out as young and vulnerable. Never more so than on one particularly distasteful occasion.

Boarders at St Dunstan's were not, repeat NOT, allowed out without permission or parents between Monday morning and Friday evening. OK?! This rule was made crystal clear. The consequences were dire and could include capital punishment. Mind you, I would happily have chosen eternal Stygian darkness over the worst punishment of all, which was meted out for 'being seen outside school in uniform—but hatless'. If caught committing this heinous crime, we were subjected to the arse-wrenching humiliation of having to wear the hat ALL DAY at school. However, one evening, a friend and I agreed we would risk extermination in order to go into town for half an hour. But we weren't total nihilists, we would, *of course*, wear our uniform.

We slipped out the side door and giggled all the way into town. We had a singular, important purpose. We needed to go into the Co-op and spend all of our pocket money on the photo-booth machine. We had planned a series of hilarious face contortions we knew would stick together to make a funny cartoon-style story about . . . well . . . about two girls in school hats in a photo booth in the Co-op, pulling faces. Excellent! With this task in mind, we dived into the back of the multistorey Co-op, which led us through the food hall where the photo booth was. We were just about to put our money in the machine when a burly man in a suit called out, 'Hey, you two—stop that!' We froze as he approached. 'What do you think you're doing?!' he asked, sternly. I ventured, 'We were just going to use the—' but before I finished he interrupted, and my heart sank as he said, 'As you well know, one of you has stolen a packet of tights. I am the store detective and I clearly saw you sneak the tights under your jumper. You have two choices: (a) we can call the police, and since you're Abbey girls that means informing your head; or (b) you can choose to be searched and we can settle this matter here in the shop.' I flashed a look at my friend. I was furious—how could she ruin our trip into town for a pilfered pair of tights? We both knew we would be in all kinds of trouble if anyone alerted the school, so we took the search option.

The man instructed us to follow him and we went up one floor and I saw that there wasn't a soul around—there were scaffolding and ladders and paintpots blocking the way. The Co-op was undergoing a makeover but the worksite was completely still; the men had obviously finished for the day. Big dust sheets covered the floor and stairs and hung from the ladders. He indicated that we should push past the dust sheets, so we did, and he told us he would conduct the search right here himself. Although it did occur to me that this was a strange place to do it, I was quite relieved that we didn't have to endure further humiliation with any other witnesses. He asked me to lift my jumper up, which I willingly did. After all, I was utterly innocent and he would find no contraband on me. No sir-ee. On finding nothing, he asked if I had hidden the tights inside my blouse. Absolutely not, I said, have a look. He did, and he put his hands right round my back to check. All of this was done in a most professional way, you understand. Fast and emotionless. Had I hidden the packet *inside* my bra? He then deftly checked very thoroughly. Indeed. No sign, of course. Had I hidden the packet up my skirt? Inside my tights? Inside my pants? No I hadn't thank you very much, and please to check. Which he did. Very thoroughly. You see? Nothing. NOW he searched my friend in exactly the same way. Very thoroughly indeed. She looked worried, which I took to be an unmistakable sign of guilt. As he proceeded further and further I was gobsmacked to see how well she had hidden this elusive packet of tights. Where *was* it? I was amazed when his search proved fruitless. It was a mystery. He told us that we had been *very* clever with the hiding and to run along and not do it again.

We raced away from there so fast. Halfway back up the hill towards school we finally stopped running and sat on a wall to catch our breath. 'Where did you hide them?!' I puffed. 'I didn't nick any tights, I thought you had . . .!' It was only then we realised what had happened. A sleazy git had just groped us. He had expertly taken advantage of our fear and lured us into a vulnerable situation where we were willing to let him fiddle with us, to let him put his filthy mitts all over us. It was so easy for him. How many times did he do it to others? Did he ever do anything worse? I hadn't properly remembered the incident until I came to write this letter to you, so I don't think I could ever claim that it scarred me in any deep way. Sadly, it has melted into my memory as just another one of those difficult and unpleasant moments that young women experience all the time with dirty old men. Luckily, I was shaken but unhurt and I learned a big lesson about how crafty and manipulative predatory men can be. What strikes me as one of the worst aspects of the whole sorry episode was the fact that my friend and I kept this story to ourselves. We felt stupid and embarrassed and, most of all, we were so afraid because we were breaking a school rule!

Have you and I taught our beloved daughters enough to keep them safe? While we pray they never have to face anything too scary, surely we also know they can learn to navigate their way through life by occasionally butting up against something a bit frightening and realising they can indeed cope with it. Perhaps they will more readily tell those uncouth codgers to cock right off. I wish I had.

## DEAR NIGEL,

May I just say what a delight it has been to be your number-one fag hag all these years. May I also say that you deserve major regalia-type bling for the remarkably long and loyal service you have put in as BBF (Best Boy Friend). You ought to have a medal. But perhaps you would prefer an ankle bracelet? Needless to say, it will involve Diamonique in ample measure.

How I loved the teen-slouching round your kitchen table in Plympton with you and your twin bro Gareth, eating your mum's Welsh cakes, and raging about the injustices of the school youth drama club and life in general. We didn't take any action, of course, that wasn't the point at all, we just wanted to moan and grumble long into the night. We had lots of dates, you and I. We went to the theatre and films and exhibitions and concerts. We performed onstage together, learned lines together and wrote sketches together. Probably the first bit of comedy writing I ever did was with you. I think it was a piss-take of a Harold Pinter play with jokes galore about pauses and dot dot dots. But the most wonderful, inventive and thrilling part of it all was the letters. At least once or twice a week, you wrote to me as many different characters, inviting responses from me in the character you had addressed your letter to. So, it was my mission to reply in kind, becoming one of these many people, inventing a whole life around them and a situation in which the two might be corresponding. Sometimes they were engaged in a torrid affair, or in the midst of a petty row, or they might be gossiping about the news of their time. It might be present day, or Edwardian, or Elizabethan, or anything. The joy of these letters filled many a long evening of boarding-school life, and often entirely replaced prep. I only ever wanted to make you laugh and I hungrily sought your approval. So, in a way, you were my first script editor.

Obviously, admitting this does not commit me to any form of pecuniary reimbursement. You will have the ankle bracelet, and that's that. We're quits.

May my suffocatingly enormous love for you smother you to certain death.

Your devoted hag.

## DEAR BF,

I have always enjoyed partnerships. It's how I think and work best. A chum to bounce ideas around with, to have a career with and laugh your tits off with, like Jennifer. A chum to trust and to go into business with, someone who inspires and motivates you, like Helen Teague. A chum to dress up in bridesmaid gear with and share dreams of hairdos and bouquets, like Sarah. A chum to guide and listen, to share home truths and teenage wrangling tips with, to be continually delighted with their direct-from-heaven-via-nowhere-else talent, like Alla. A chum to gossip and chirrup with like Di

Cracknell. I have needed every one of these important partnerships and I have greedily gorged on all of them, and felt grateful to know and care for these wonderful women. And to be cared for *by* them.

You. You have so generously encouraged me to give myself to these remarkable relationships because you know the utter joy they have given me back. The bigness of your love is astounding. You are selfless. I don't know how you are able to be the phenomenon you are. I don't know anyone else like you and I never will, it's too tall an order for any other human to emulate the beauty you have.

Meeting you at college was my saving grace. I arrived late for the start of term, and I didn't really fit in. The groups had forged themselves and I was a sort of lost puppy bounding hopefully between them, looking for a way in. My dad had committed suicide a matter of weeks before and I was dripping with sadness. But of course grief is invisible and suicide is tricky to introduce as an ice-breaker, so I kept it to myself until I knew and trusted people more. You have an extrasensory superpower, and it wasn't long before you sniffed me out as the walking wounded, which was remarkable considering you weren't even in my year. Central School of Screech and Trauma was run under a regime of separation. The actors didn't speak to the lowly teachers, the speech therapists were distinctly aloof, so only those on the stage-management course were friendly with everyone else, and that's because they were too knackered to put up any resistance. Anyway, it was unusual to mix with folk from other years and you were someone who refused to be limited by that. I remember very early on, you required of me a proper, formal commitment to this new friendship. I think you must have been subconsciously searching for a 'bestie' for ever, and when we set our sights on each other there was, frankly, no other avenue open except total devotion. I knew instantly that I would know and cherish you till my dying breath, or yours. I would truly lay my life down for you, give you my kidneys, my eyes, my teeth, my tits, whatever you ask for. That's the key though, isn't it? You never do ask, for anything really, which is why I belong to you. Our friendship is a labour of love, a pledge to keep watch over each other and to stay constant. It is a quiet arrangement. Deep calling to deep. I will never leave my post, I will remain vigilant, I will not falter, I will always forgive. These are our unspoken vows and I respect them. You know any secrets I have, you know my fears, my demons and my delights, and I yours. I feel honoured to have obligations to you. You make a mirror for me in which I used to seek out my shortcomings, but with your ceaseless support I have learned to recognise my strengths. What a very grown-up thing to do.

Being grown up isn't exactly a mainstay of our partnership though, is it?

Do you remember when Billie was about to come to us? Len and I only had a week or so's notice and I had to somehow get every bit of baby kit together in one day, without rousing any suspicion. We wanted her to come home without any fuss and to nest in with her away from any noisy publicity. It was the most important thing we had ever done and we were very serious and protective. Fatty swung into action, helping me to walk out on a *French and Saunders* series that was in production by taking over the crew, the studios, the whole obligation and plonking her new sitcom idea *Absolutely Fabulous* right down on it instead. It fitted well. She has since said that she needed that kick up the bum to force her to develop the idea we had written in a sketch on our show a year or so before.

On the day in question, Len and your chap Barrie remained at home putting up shelves and trying to navigate their way round the construction of a cot. Potentially disastrous. We drove the 40-odd miles into London and parked behind Mothercare in Hammersmith. Your mission was to pose as the heavily pregnant first-time mother, and I was there as your mate, helping you to select all your baby kit. You shoved our sofa cushion up your front to look convincing. We went into the store and you were immediately offered seating and a glass of water, which you graciously accepted. You stumbled about a bit when a young assistant asked 'how far on' you were and when the 'little one' was due. You had to do some quick mental maths—never your strong point. With my hasty calculations you were confidently informing her the baby was going to be eleven months in gestation . . .

Our elaborate system of coded winks and blinks and coughs meant that in reality I was making every choice. The downside was that I had to load up the car while you looked on smugly from your chair in the shop, nursing your 'swollen' ankles. With the car now full of baby stuff, we went home, where you gave birth to your cushion in a hilarious display of torturous labour.

We go back a long way, you and I. Thirty years or so, I reckon.

We have witnessed the big stuff of each other's lives haven't we? The loves, successful and disastrous, the weddings, the IVF, the miscarriages, the births, the adoption, the kids, the families, the deaths, the birthdays, the meals, New Years, the houses, the schools, the pets, the shoes, the choices, the phases and the fads. We keep each other safe and steady, and because of that, we can take the chances we do.

Big respec' to the BF.

## DEAR NICK,

I haven't seen you or heard anything about you for a lot of years now. Whenever I was visiting Plymouth or Cornwall, I used to get little snippets of information about you. Such was the residual strength of our adolescent relationship in the minds of others, they felt the need to update me about you. I haven't heard anything for some time now, though, so I hope you're all right. I suddenly feel concerned for you, and that concern is very familiar. I was always worried for and about you. Your life seemed so stormy and often very difficult.

I was sixteen. You were the first boy I felt the right to call 'my boyfriend' in public. Plenty of boys disliked this kind of proprietorial display, but you were cool about it. I liked that. We were included in each other. I was part of you, and you were part of me.

Rather than boisterous evenings in big gangs, I preferred the quieter times, because in you I found probably the first boy I could talk to properly, about virtually anything. I was consumed with thinking about you all week at school. Images of you, constantly pulsing through me, and I couldn't wait till Friday afternoons when we could be together again. I loved how funny you were, and how utterly irreverent. You were without doubt the cheekiest chap in Cheekyville.

My friend Jane was dating your friend John, and a considerable amount of time was spent sneaking off to a flat somewhere in Mutley. Do you remember? We took cheap Spanish wine-inspired liquid, and laughed A LOT. The booze helped with any shyness or awkwardness. It was fabulous to be in a proper flat, pretending we all lived there, slobbing about, drinking and listening to Thin Lizzy, T. Rex and The Sweet. Eventually the laughing and flirting would dwindle, and in our separate partnerships and on opposite sofas, we got down to the serious business of petting. Hours and hours of mutual, delightful exploration. I can still remember the excitement of going practically all the way but stopping just inches this side of trouble, pulling in to the temptation lay-by for refreshments and a cool-down. All blood returning from groin to brain, momentarily. Lovely. Safe . . . And then we'd be at it again, just to test if we dared go further each time. I'm not sure you can ever reclaim the bliss that was those endless hours of innocent twiddling.

I remember you lived in Modbury, an impossibly pretty town built on a huge hill. When I first knew you, your mum ran the café called The Teapot, I think, which stood at a forty-five-degree angle to the steep gradient of the high street. I liked your mum Mary very much, she seemed liberal and exciting to me. You and your brothers and your cool, handsome dad could so easily have run any mum ragged but she seemed to revel in the testosterone-charged energy in that house. It was a loud, muscular, masculine environment, but she was the feisty feminine buoy you all tethered your roaring adolescent engines to. Lots of men and then Mary, running her tea shop with great panache, and with *great* scones.

It seemed pretty much perfect, our tender, young relationship. Somewhere in the midst of the perfectness, you arranged a party. The excitement of it all was massive. I remember lots of frantic phone calls. Who should come? What music should there be? What to drink? Eat? Wear? We were determined that we should all get a bit drunk, but the skill was to be drunk enough to party but not so bladdered that anyone was sick all over your nice house thereby compromising any future parties.

The day of the party came and I remember we spent quite a lot of time and effort making the house ready. Your mum and dad had agreed they would stay out of the way and watch telly upstairs. Contrary to your typical party-thrower's last-minute paranoia, our mates actually turned up and the party started. It was just right. People got drunk quite quickly and unexpected couplings started to happen, which is the stuff of a great party. You were in your element as the host, chiefly finding interesting new mixes of alcohol. I'm not sure vodka and lager were ever going to be happy bedfellows but I was glad to be part of their inaugural outing. The atmosphere was loud with the tapes blaring out and the clamouring of teenagers trying to be heard above the music. There was laughing and sobbing and singing in equal measure. The room oozed hot hormones and alcohol, and we couldn't have been happier.

The next thing I remember was your mum shrieking for you. The kind of shrieking that pierced the din like a pin through a balloon. The party lumbered on but through the swaying bodies I saw you stumbling towards your mum and I saw fear in her eyes. You disappeared upstairs with her and my memories of the following hour or so are a jagged, blurry collage of strangeness and horror. I waited a while, then I started to climb the stairs to find you. One of your brothers stopped me and said something was wrong. Your dad. He had passed out. Get everyone out. Stop the party. Your mum crying. Turn off the music. You shouting and telling everyone to go home. Tears in your eyes. People staggering about, drunk and confused. You darting out to the front door to check for the ambulance.

Teenagers on the dark street. A creeping dread. Still your mum crying. Your brothers shaking. You pacing like an angry animal, ashen and anxious. A taut and strange stillness. The ambulance arriving. The rush of fresh air coming in with the paramedics. Some quiet mumbling from the upstairs room. Heavy footfalls on the stairs. Your dad on a stretcher. A glimpse of his pallid face. I knew. I knew. Random puzzled party kids colliding with the stretcher by mistake. Apologies. Sirens. You were gone. All your family were suddenly gone. Only the chaotic debris of a broken party was left.

I can't remember what happened next. How did I get home? Who locked up? Did we clear up? I don't know.

My next memory is the following day at home, sobbing into my dad's chest and feeling the hard buttons of his shirt making marks on my face. He held me so tight and stroked my head. It was the first time I ever dared to imagine a death in the family or what it might be like to lose my own father. How were you, Nick, going to cope with it? I knew I would be devastated if it was him, *my* precious father. It was unthinkable. Then my dad spoke to me about you properly for the first time. How one of the things he liked about you was your irrepressible cheek. He said your pluck and wit combined to make you a person of substance. He told me that you would feel bereft but that you were a survivor, whose close-knit family would sustain you through your grief and prop up your courage.

My dad spoke very softly to me about how your life would have to change now. How, as the eldest son, you would probably have to grow up very quickly, prematurely, in order to support your darling mum and brothers. He also told me that I had a role in this, to support you if that's what you wanted. He said you might attempt to live your life right, as a tribute to your dad. I could see a purpose in that.

I went back to school the next morning, feeling exhausted and aimless. I didn't want to call you because I was aware you were in the tight centre of your family, but I longed to speak to you, to know how you were. I was also a bit scared to call your home lest your mum should answer. I was sixteen. What does a sixteen-year-old say to a woman who's just lost her husband? Nothing felt right so I kept quiet and I kept my distance.

I was surprised when later that week *your* mum phoned *my* mum to say that you were refusing to leave your bedroom at home and she thought it might help if I came to see you. We drove to your place and the minute I saw your mum I started to blub and stammer some kind of rubbish condolence. Mary immediately released me from that hell by saying she was so glad I had come, that I really COULD be of some use if I would go and see if I could persuade you to come out of your room.

So it was that I climbed up those same stairs I'd seen your dad being carted down a few days before. As I approached I heard the sound of you thumping eight kinds of hell out of the drum kit you kept in there. This wasn't practice, this was fury. I knocked. Silence. I said it was me. A more silent silence. Then you opened the door and there you were, wide-eyed, shirtless and crazy with the madness of it all. The room was humming. It smelt of stale sweat and tears and agony. You let me in and I shut the door behind us.

I didn't leave that room for three days, other than trips to the loo on the landing outside. Your mum pushed trays of food in sporadically. I think we both grew up quite a lot in those three days, don't you? It's not for me to say what happened in there. It would be disrespectful to you. I just want you to know that I'm glad I was there, I felt privileged that you would let me weather that storm with you. I learned a lot about profound sadness and extreme hurt. It was raw and loud and honest. Then it was tender and careful. In the end I think we were flushed out by the sheer rankness of ourselves. We were pretty feral and strangely euphoric. You can never know, Nick, just how useful that time was for me later. It gave me permission to flex every muscle of my own grief when it came. By then I knew that anything goes when you are deranged with sorrow.

Our relationship fizzled out naturally some months later and I remember feeling a sense of shuddering injustice for you when I heard that your mum died also. That's not fair. That's really not fair.

Do you remember when we met briefly on the sea tractor going over to Burgh Island? Blimey, it must have been fifteen years ago or something. Len was with me and it was a bit surreal. Impossible really, to encapsulate so much, so many important memories in the briefest of moments. I truly learned a lot from you, Nick.

## DEAR BIG NIKKI, LITTLE NICKY, ANGIE, JANE AND PATSY,

The six years I spent at St Dunstan's were very important, and remain tinging clear in my memory, and I couldn't move on from thinking about that time without writing to you, my beloved school friends, who I still know and still love. It's impossible to chart those years in detail in one letter, so I want to try and concoct a sort of mnemonic scrapbook to celebrate our time there together. I'm going to pluck moments as they occur to me. Here goes:

I arrived at school a bit after everyone else, in the second rather than the first year. I had to navigate my way carefully through the treacherous waters of the established friendship groups. I had to put on quite a display of personality fireworks in a desperate attempt to attract your attention and be accepted. Look how funny I can be! I can fall over! I can pull faces! I can dance! I can clown! I can mimic! Roll up, roll up! In actual fact, all of you were incredibly welcoming to me straight away, and for that—cheers!

I remember dormitories, with huge, high arched windows, iron beds and one little locker in between. There were about ten or twelve beds in each big dorm and as we grew older, we shared smaller rooms in twos and threes and then finally in the sixth form we had our own hallowed room. Mine was between the chemistry and physics lab and smelt of Bunsen burner gas.

A regular entertainment in our dorm was to leave a mysterious object, a note or a piece of jewellery perhaps, on someone's bed, then hide under your own bed till that person came in and discovered it. The utter joy of eavesdropping on their confusion and being invisible was bliss. It wasn't unusual for me to be stranded under the bed, motionless and soundless, for three hours! Meanwhile, I enjoyed the general comings and goings of a dorm full of people who didn't know I was there—hidden, secret and naughty.

I remember loathing the new matron who had come to fill in temporarily for our beloved kind matron, Mrs Coombes. This new beast very quickly alienated all of us with her strict rules and loud handbells in the morning. She was ash grey and made entirely of granite, not dissimilar to the school, and seemed impervious to our efforts to oust her. In the end, we were forced to take serious action. Little Nicky and I decided to sneak into her room and sprinkle her bed with mice droppings or, even better, rat droppings if we could find them. But try as we might, we couldn't find ANYTHING revolting at school, so I was determined to bring some form of odious poo from home at the weekend. After a fruitless search round our cottage, I had to resort to the guinea-pig cage. I smuggled in half a shoeboxful of guinea-pig-poo missiles, which Nicky and I spread over and in Matron's bed on the Thursday night. Suffice to say, she didn't return on the Monday.

I remember turning our radios on early in the morning and Noel Edmonds would wake us up with lots of gags and silly voices and tunes from Mungo Jerry and Slade and Diana Ross and Benny Hill. It was perfect, because that first moment when we opened our eyes was the very instant we missed our mums the most, and he helped us get past that bit.

I remember working out that French was taught precisely the same to each year, day for day. Therefore, Patsy's prep on a certain day would be EXACTLY the same for me, the year below her, on the same day the following year. So I could copy her prep from her previous year's book, word for word. I got away with it for about a month, getting better marks than I ever had before! Then two bad things happened: (1) Mrs Whitfeld (who I loved and respected) totally knew and didn't even punish me, just whispered in my ear that it was most disappointing, and (2) I didn't learn any French. A huge regret. Bugger. On both counts.

Do you remember the night we clambered up to the high windows in the dorm in our nighties and flirted with some boys down in the street? All of a sudden they started climbing up the walls! In a trice they were into our dorm. BOYS! IN OUR DORM! AT NIGHT!! This was both thrilling and threatening. A heady mixture. We tried to shush them but they were loud and boisterous. Oh God, I wish they could have stayed longer. We were starving for them. In no time at all, Mrs Coombes heard them and they bolted. The police were called and the boys were rounded up and paraded in front of us. We had to identify them so's they could be charged with breaking and entering. As one, we refused to do this and, even under threat of parents getting involved and expulsions, we kept our quiet. A tiny moral victory. Miss Abley was fuming. We didn't do it again.

I recall the anxious moments in the morning, when the post was handed out, and how vital it was to get some, any. Valentine's Day was especially horrendous, but every day mattered. Thank God for my regular correspondence with Nigel. All letters, however, from parents, brother, boyfriends, girlfriend were—are—*so* welcome. I have never ceased to feel the same joy every time a proper letter arrives. My nearly 100-year-old grandma has written to me every few weeks for the best part of forty years. Our connection is strong and continually nurtured through those hundreds of wonderful letters.

I remember the staunch, tough façade you presented, Nikki R. You were my first experience of a person my age with a strong moral centre. An unshakable sense of justice and left-ness. Being a day girl, you brought in a fresh breath every morning, the astringency of your big, loving, boisterous family. Others (idiots) mistook you for grumpy and severe, but I knew and know you to be a fierce protector and an insanely loyal advocate. And you were so physically fit and determined. It was you who introduced me to soul music, to blues, to Motown and all those fab girl groups. You had your mojo workin', maid, and still do.

And you, Nicky V, 'little' Nicky Twobells. Always dodging and diving, nervous but keen, sporty and sensitive. A girl so desperately in need of approval from parents who, inexplicably, seemed to withhold it. So you sought it elsewhere, making sure you were appreciated by many. Your cheek and your beauty enabled you to pilfer our boyfriends from right under our noses but somehow I never minded because you deserved them, and they adored you. I remember how kind you were to some of the very young boarders, discovering how lovely it was to be needed. I remember our chambermaiding exploits together down in Salcombe, to make money in the summer holidays. The endless disgusting sheets, the sticky rooms, the trolley laden with individually wrapped biscuits too delish to resist, taking photos of each other's bums on residents' cameras for them to discover in Boots when they returned from their holidays. Fighting off randy chefs and barmen, far too old for us. Sharing a bedroom in the attic of the hotel, for protection.

I remember the endless rows about the school uniform, among all of us. In the sixth form we were finally allowed to ditch the dreaded stripy blazer with blue serge kilt and heavy jumper. Each new sixth form were allowed to choose their own uniform, a chance to be unique and expressive. How, then, in the name of cock, did we end up with brown and mustard as our palette? What were we *thinking*?!

I remember Miss Abbott, our drama teacher, with her beautiful clear diction and her twinkly eyes. I begged my mum to let me have extra lessons after school with her, where we sat in a tiny, musty room and discussed plays and writers, new and classic. We worked on voice and we prepared pieces for exams. I wanted to *be* Miss Abbott, and if I couldn't be her, I wanted to be *like* her. She had trained at the Central School of Speech and Drama in London, and she told me all about that. Very early on I decided it must be a fine school, if Miss Abbott went there. So I would go there. And I did. I would be a drama teacher. And I was . . . briefly.

All because of my crush on the fabulous Miss Abbott.

I remember you, Angie. The Cornish rebel, by far the most defiant of us all. You were the first with the boys, unafraid to experiment and full of confidence, which was *so* appealing. I used to worry that you might slip up, or be disappointed somewhere inside the anarchy, but you were too astute for that. With all this firebrandery bubbling inside you, I was amazed that you were able to conceal it with the flip side of your nature, the no less real nurturing, motherly and astonishingly upright character you also are. A woman of fascinating and fabulous contradictions, you are one of the most enthusiastic and energetic people I know. So much of this came to bear when later in our twenties we shared a room together in a flat in London. I had no hesitation jumping in to that adventure with you because where you are, there is thrill.

Jane. Janey. Or 'Sausage' for some reason I've forgotten! The stylish, clever one among us. You always played your cards close to your chest and I had an abiding feeling that you were finding most of our school life highly amusing in a very internal and sophisticated way. You were quick-witted and observant, and I loved sharing jokes with you. I have pictures of you and I outside our house, writing songs and strumming guitars. The songs were *very important* tortured songs about love and loss, neither of which we had experienced at that stage, but about which we were experts. We used to go to a folk club called Friars and believed that we were genuinely much better than everyone who performed there. Except Ralph McTell of course, who we idolised because he sang of *exactly* our pains and joys, right? Yeah. The other man who was singing just to us was Jim Morrison. You and I fancied we were very like Ali MacGraw in *Love Story* except we weren't American or dying of cancer. We favoured the long, dark, parted-in-the-middle-and-worn-in-bunches-or-plaits-like-a-squaw-type hairstyle that Ali did and we thought it looked pretty good. I'm looking at the photos. It didn't. Since your dad was the housemaster of Mannamead House at Plymouth College Boys' School (where my brother went),

I spent some time staying with you there. Which meant staying inside a boarding house. Full of boys. Your room was literally one wall away from about SIXTY boys. I could smell them! No, seriously, I really could smell them . . .

I remember Goodbodies coffee shop just off Mutley Plain, where we would go on a Friday after school. The preparations for it would begin around lunchtime, when we would sneak into the loos and start the makeover. It was of the utmost importance that the teachers should *not* notice any added make-up or change of clothes etc., so all was executed with great subtlety, e.g. the yanking up of bra straps to force teen bosoms into a more upright position, the rolling over of the waistband of the school kilt to raise the hemline of the skirt, loosening of a button or two on the blouse. A *tiny* amount of orangey Avon spot-cover and foundation and perhaps the merest hint of pale lipstick. Silently we counted down the seconds to the end-of-the-day bell. Then, and only then, could we race to the loo, hastily slap on the full orange grouting and many, many, many layers of thick, gloopy mascara, eye shadow, blusher, roll-on deodorant, breath freshener, brush teeth, brush hair and let hang loose, roll up skirt even further, put on jewellery, spray Aquamanda perfume, whisk off tie—hey presto!—pop in some gum and off. Being a weekly boarder I was always dragging my suitcase, but I didn't mind. A thirty-minute brisk lug up North Road, past the train station, over the top of Pennycomequick, on to the bottom of Mutley Plain and into the café. There they were, the pantheon of prized Plymouth College sixth-formers all sitting at one table huddled round hot chocolates. Bliss. The key was to make it seem coincidence that we were all there together. We purchased one Nescafé or one Coca-Cola and we sat at the furthest table. Oh boy, did we ignore them. It was delicious to turn our backs on those boys. Our plan seemed to work. They also ignored us. We took this to mean they were gagging for it. We were often in there for three hours, not communicating at all. Eventually the time came when one group had to leave, and would slope off without so much as a grunt to the other. Result! Once outside we would burst into skittish fever pitch, twittering about how amazing it all was. We were overintoxicated with arousal. Fit to burst. Excellent. What a trip. Phew. Let's do it again next Friday.

I remember quoting *Monty Python* sketches word for word, and retelling Dave Allen gags and copying endless Pan's People dances with solemn and supreme accuracy.

I remember us all going to Nikki R's family beach house at Gwithian after our A levels in '76 and running into the sea as a triumphant cleansing rite of passage, a marker of the end of study FOR EVER! It wasn't, but it felt like it then. There was a drought and the country was baking, but we were eating Fab ice creams and listening to our Marc Bolan records so we didn't care. We lolled about in bikinis getting nutty brown and fanning each other, loving and hating the sizzling heat.

So, that was school as I remember it. I wonder if you remember it the same way?

One last thing—I know that segregating children into 'houses' at school is divisive and potentially dangerous because it can create hierarchy and unnecessary competition. Yes, I know that, but all of you need to face one irrefutable fact. Downton House *is* best. Sorry, but it's true, and you know it, you losers!

## BELOVED BILLIE,

It is Mother's Day. I am on a *French and Saunders* tour and I am in Manchester, so I am not with you. You are not with your mother and I am not with mine. That's three generations of wrong. I woke up this morning and thought it might potentially be a truly grim day but then I remembered that when your dad visited briefly to watch our first night in Blackpool on Friday, he stuffed a big brown envelope in my case and said, 'Open that on Sunday.' So I did. A card from you. A handmade card. Honestly my uttermost favouritest gift ever. I am astounded you remembered at all, considering everything that's going on for you at the moment, during the maelstrom that is this strange age of sixteen. The words in your card are simple, 'I couldn't ask for a better mum. I love you so much . . .' You cannot begin to know how gladly I read those words because I know what it costs you to write that.

I have had to stop writing here to have a little self-indulgent weep, as I allow the significance of your easy forgiveness for my absence, and the sheer warmth of your appreciation, to flood through me. I should be with you today. I don't feel guilt about it, I just feel the pain of separation, which confirms for me how connected we are. That in itself is a kind of miracle considering what you and I regularly go through together, especially at the moment. Apparently it is quite usual for mums and daughters to war when the daughters are rampaging through their teens with all guns blazing. I suppose I knew that, but actually, I don't remember much in the way of big shouting at my mum. Plenty of sulking and violent inner thoughts, but not outright raging. That's what you do. You roar. You blast us with your bellowing. You insist that you are heard, and y'know what, Bill? Good for you. Be heard. Be loud. Get it out, whatever it is.

You have a lot to feel furious about. Anybody who is adopted as a baby has the right to a fierce hurt. You will probably wonder how on earth your mother could have looked at you, at the perfect, beautiful, tiny new you, and still make the decision to give you up. Do you think perhaps you just *weren't* perfect enough or beautiful enough for her to instantly adore you? Or maybe she was a dreadful, selfish or mad person who would never know how to show you love? Perhaps, worst of all, you are not lovable? How unthinkable.

The truth is, Billie, none of the above suppositions are real. Quite the opposite. The details of your adoption are private to you, and you know all about it as far as we know anything. There is nothing hidden from you, but there is part of it that will be hard for you to imagine at this point. This much I know: your birth mother *did* love you. Undeniably, enormously, as much as any mother has ever loved any baby. Her heart is connected to your heart for ever and no one can cut that properly sacred thread. The pictures we have of you as a newborn are palpable proof of how hard that decision must have been for her, because you were the most wondrous baby. Fact.

The pictures show a bright-eyed beaming little face, with wide, open features and flawless caramel skin. Your mouth was a perfect, kissable little O with full, plumptious lips. Your dear little face was round and irresistibly cute with a ready grin and a winning twinkle from the off. You were marvellous, a perfect, tiny, wriggling example of one of God's own masterpieces. A rare thing, an exquisite baby with unparalleled beauty. Your mother *must* have been instantly besotted. So, Bill, try to imagine how hard it was for her to look at you, at this splendid little shining thing, and to know she had to make what was probably the hardest choice of her life. The choice to give you a better life than she might have been able to, to put *your* interests before her own powerful maternal urges. Personally, I think that she did a mighty thing that day. She prized you above herself, above her own desires. That is a feat of love, Billie. Big, powerful, priceless love.

I will always be thankful to her for having the enormous courage to make that decision, because otherwise we would never have had you, that splendid little spudling, in our lives. And although I often think about her grieving, I thank God daily for her choice. She is our link to you and we don't forget that. Our little triangle has an invisible fourth side, which is constantly in my thoughts. I'm sure she must be in yours too. Especially on Mother's Day. We are related to each other, all of us. In the spirit of that bond, I accept this card to a mother on her behalf too, because as a testament of her love for you, she gave you to me, to my keeping, and thus I am truly blessed. There *is* no greater love than that. You say, 'I couldn't ask for a better mum.' And in the truest sense, you're right. You couldn't.

Thanks, Bill.

# DEAR MUM,

It was 1973 and I was sixteen. As you know, I was obsessed with horror films and the most scary horror film ever, *The Exorcist*, was released that year. What a stir it caused! There were protests outside the cinema, representatives from many different religions objecting to it, local councillors, mothers' groups, all manner of moral defenders. It was crazy and of course served to make me all the more determined to see the film. You gave in quite early on when I begged you to take me. I think you knew I would go anyway come hell or high water, but Mum, I also know how little you would have wanted to see that film yourself. You worked such long hours and always had a long drive home down into Cornwall, so I appreciate the effort you made. Anyway, we went together and because I was with an adult, in we swanned, past the barracking and jeering. You were, apparently, sacrificing your daughter to Satan's power. Wow. Great. Lucifer, here I come, your willing handmaiden!

I don't think you and I had been to the pictures together since I was a little kid when we went to see Jerry Lewis or Elvis Presley or Disney films. I experienced the strange juxtaposition of feeling very grown up because I was about to witness an X-rated film, but also feeling decidedly junior because I was with you, my mum. My discomfort was exacerbated by the fact that the couple directly in front of us decided to eat each other's faces off, and you started to mutter your disapproval of that. By the time the lights went down, I was a strong beetroot hue, and wanted to be almost anywhere else. It didn't help that the folk behind started to crinkle their sweet wrappers for which further admonishment from you was apparently necessary. Just when I thought the torture of mum-next-to-you-in-a-cinema-ness was over, there was fresh hell. Before the main film, there was a short B movie. You *must* remember this?!

Which buffoon was it that sat down and thought, 'OK, the main film is a sinister and distressing voyage to the dark side, what shall we give them as a warm-up? Oh, I know, nude hippie dancing.' So here we are presented with three naked hairy rejects from *The Joy of Sex* via Woodstock, who jumped about, wobbling their genitals. By now the extent of your distaste was clear to the entire auditorium. Mercifully, the naked jangling was relatively short and at last the haranguing stopped, and we could relax into an hour and a half of soothing evil as we witnessed the noxious possession of an innocent child. Which was lovely.

As we left the cinema you picked up where you'd left off with plenty of 'Well, honestly, what a load of old rubbish that was. Really. I can't begin to understand why you like this sort of nonsense. It was just silly. Utterly unbelievable. Pointless' – all the way back up to school where you dropped me off with a kiss and 'See you on Friday, Moo, night'.

You would think the running commentary and the damning review would help to dilute any fear that film might have instilled in me, but no, frankly. I had nightmares about it for months afterwards. Nightmares to remind me of the nightmare that evening was.

I love you, Mum, but I'm not going to the pictures with you again. So there.

## DEAR DAVID,

Thank goodness we didn't get married. I thought we were a perfect match, a couple who complemented each other, like yin and yang, or Little and Large, or Jack Sprat and his missus, but on reflection, that was wishful thinking. Really, we were, and are, like chalk and cheese, and if we're honest, they don't go together, do they? I've never had a successful chalk-and-cheese sandwich, for instance.

This difference was all too evident when we met that afternoon a couple of years ago, for the first time in, ooh, nearly thirty years. We went for tea at what is, in my opinion, simply the best place to take tea in London, the conservatory in the Lanesborough Hotel at Hyde Park Corner, or, as I prefer to call it, my London office. I chose that place to meet because, firstly, they pride themselves on their amazing choice of fine teas and since you are a tea man by trade, I hoped you would feel comfortable with that. Secondly, the cakes are sublime. Boy, did we need the mediatory benefits of cake that day. The purpose of our meeting was an apology, from you to me, for making the fundamental error of speaking to a hack about me. No friend or lover or family member had ever done that before, and I was truly shocked that you were so easily tricked by her artifice. For some reason I still don't entirely understand, you decided to talk to her at length, giving her details of some particularly private moments between us. How very ungentlemanly of you. Were you caught off guard? Or were you flattered? Or what?! I was keen to hear why you had made this rather uncharacteristic choice. Within ten minutes of sitting down with you, I was reminded of a key aspect of your personality. You were *annoyed* that your accounts of our time together were so ill reported. You weren't *sorry* at all. You were one part blameless to two parts patronising. As I say, thank goodness we didn't get married.

The telling aspect about your account of our relationship is how very favourably you depict yourself. I guess we *all* do this to some extent, remember our past selves with a rosy glow. Woe betide we should reflect on any decisions or actions and recognise moments of true cowardice or dismal failure or even regret. I include myself in this department of flattering self-delusion. Writing this here book is, in itself, an exercise in trying to remember the *truth* of a moment rather than the edited highlights where I figure as the heroine. It's so tempting and easy to cast oneself as a tad splendid, but ultimately that would be daft. Since it is so clearly not accurate.

I *think* we met at a party in Liskeard. I must have been about seventeen or eighteen and you were about twenty-one, twenty-two.

I was instantly attracted to you. Oh yes, that's for picking-cotton sure. You are a handsome man, David. Flawless skin, twinkly pale eyes, a strong masculine jaw and the most heavenly mouth. The hands were a crucial factor—could they cup a 38DD? Yes, with ease. Then there was also your easy manner and soft Irish brogue. Back then, you were a navy sublieutenant. You were recently out of Dartmouth and on HMS *Hermes*, if my memory serves me well.

You and I fell for each other pretty heavily and pretty quickly. You introduced me to your brother Ian and took me on my first visit to Ireland, to your home town, Belturbet in County Cavan, to meet your ma and pa. A tiny clue to our mismatch became evident even way back then. You insisted on buying me an outfit to meet your folks in. I suppressed my hurt and attempted to find the right thing. It's hard to shop for clothes when you don't know who you're supposed to be. I have had similar experiences since, when trying to choose costumes for a character I'm playing. The clothes provide vital clues to the person and it's important to get it right. The mission back then was to find clothes that would earn me the parents' approval. What *are* those clothes? Well, I look at the photos now, and apparently the perfect parent-meeting clothes are a white blouse with a Princess Di lacy collar, an A-line flowery skirt, matching bolero with trim and bows in the same floral fabric, tan tights and a good low court shoe. Or two. It seemed to work. Your parents were delightful and I *think* they sort of approved of me. Well, not really, because they weren't actually meeting *me*, they were meeting some strange clothes with a person inside trying desperately to be like the person who was wearing those strange clothes.

Clothes were important on various occasions with you. Being a navy officer meant lots of formal 'dos' where everyone dressed up to try and look as grown up as their job suggested. Little boys and girls in grown-up uniforms and long dresses being allowed to play like the adults. I have to admit, the uniforms were pretty spunky. I liked yours most of all when it was hung on a chair at the bottom of the bed.

You were always a natty dresser, with classic, conservative taste. You always appeared to be a man of reckoning, definitely in charge, with ambition and a plan. I don't think I did it on purpose, but I do remember constantly trying to puncture the air of slightly smug confidence you exuded. To reach in and find the exciting, impetuous you I felt sure you were hiding. In fact, I think, on reflection, I was plainly attempting to just change you into a more suitable boyfriend. At one stage I even persuaded you to wear dungarees and sandals and, bless you, however much you must have loathed it, you did! If I were you, I wouldn't forgive me for that, ever.

Costumes notwithstanding, we managed to have a lovely time together. I have such happy memories of driving trips in England and Ireland, staying at funny little B&Bs and enjoying calling ourselves Mr and Mrs Smyth. Because that's who you properly are. Mr Smyth. I remember lots of romantic suppers and robust political debates (another clue!) while we both worked out who we were and what we thought. I remember skinny-dipping at night, on Slapton Sands, in Devon. Oh, and thinking about beaches and the sea, of course I remember the most important moment of all . . .

I was eighteen when you and I were planning to go camping in Cornwall, by the sea. I told my mother you were supplying the tent. She was silent for a moment, then she said, 'Don't you mean tentS?' And I said, 'No, tenT.' And that was it, I was telling my mum what was about to happen, giving her a warning shot across the bows. She didn't like it. A young man who had waited patiently, with great restraint and respect, and an anxious, excited young woman finally ready to be cherry-picked!

We drove down to the beach in your car, with the venue for the main event, the tent, packed in the boot. I had waited for this day, I had imagined it and dreamt it. Now it was here and we were en route to it. To 'it'. 'It' was going to happen. Tonight. In that tent. The excitement of it all was too much for me, and instead of erotically enjoying the anticipation, I decided to counteract it, to dissipate the tension, as I always have done and always do, by talking.

Happy talk. Non-stop. Jokes, stories, anecdotes, more jokes, other people's anecdotes, items in the news, family gossip, football scores, list of favourite names, pop-chart info . . . ANYTHING. I didn't stop talking for the two-hour journey. I didn't stop talking while we put the tent up, in fact I talked more, faster, when I saw it, the *actual* arena, the scene of the imminent crime, the pleasure pavilion, the sinning site. We decided to go to the pub. By now I was in a total spin, chattering away, a hundred to the dozen. I was utterly hysterical with apprehension. I effervesced myself into a manic, frothy, verbal vortex until, finally, the effects of the several gin and tonics started to take control. It didn't stop me babbling, but at least I was also breathing now. We walked back to the tent. I was still jabbering. We undressed. Still blethering.

You took my face in your hands and said, 'Just . . . *please*, Dawn . . . It's time to shush now.' 'Yes but, ha ha—' 'No, *shush*.' And then you shut me up with a kiss, and you opened me up with a touch so exquisite and gentle and careful, I felt myself actually swell and bloom.

The next morning we woke and clambered out of the fuggy tent and silently walked hand in hand over the dunes and into the sea. Oh, the beautiful beauty of it. I was finally quietened by it, by the bigness of it all. We laughed and shared muted intimate mutterings. We played in the sea. I was new and definitely different. I felt sort of glossy. Loved. I hope you remember it this same way—it's so clear in my head. The noise and then the quiet. Splendid.

Soon after this, in September 1976, and while I was still utterly besotted with you, I went to America for a year and you went off to sea on your bloody huge big boat. I won a scholarship with the English-Speaking Union, through all the debating and public-speaking competitions Miss Abbott had encouraged me to take part in at school. In the final round of the competition, our local politician, Michael Foot, seconded my attempt and voted for me to win. As you know, I did, and winning meant an exchange year. Twelve American students were going to come from the US to study in British schools and I was to be one of the twelve British students going to America. You and I were to be separated, for quite some time, and I dreaded that part. The American scholarship part, however, was AMAZING. My placement, when it came through, was New York. Manhattan. At that point in my life I had not yet lived in a city and had absolutely no desire to. I couldn't think of anything worse than Manhattan, a place where you would DEFINITELY get murdered. On a regular basis. It was going to be all concrete and crowds and cabs and I didn't like any of that. I was furious that I had been sent to the most exciting city in the world.

My year in New York was, of course, unbelievably fab. I missed you very much and wrote to you every other day and I still have your letters back to me. They chart our relationship during that thrilling year. Your attitude to navy life was changing. You speak of getting out, of getting a job, of us being together more. I sense perhaps you were a little anxious that we might grow apart, that I was having too good a time? Well, yes, I was having too good a time.

I was nervous about how I was going to cope in this big, bustling city, and so I employed a technique which still serves me well today. I imagined myself as someone who relished new, exciting opportunities, who was utterly unafraid and perpetually optimistic. My theory was that if I *behaved* like a confident, cheerful person, eventually I would buy it myself, and become that. I always had traces of strength somewhere inside me; it wasn't fake, it was just a way of summoning my courage to the fore. This method worked then, and it works now. I tell myself that I am the sort of person who can open a one-woman play in the West End, so I do. I am the sort of person who has several companies, so I do. I am the sort of person who WRITES A BOOK! So I do. It's a process of having faith in the self you don't quite know you are yet, if you see what I mean.

When I first arrived in New York that September, the first family who had agreed to put me up were the O'Neils, who had a spare room in their apartment and were kind enough to let me stay. I attended the Spence School, a highly academic private girls' school on the East Side, and, in effect, repeated my last year of school again, but in the American system. It was *so* different to my recent experience of A levels. Instead of taking three quite focused and advanced subjects, I was taking five different subjects each term, including American literature and anthropology and art history and photography. It was bloody amazing! The facilities at the school were breathtaking and the staff were funny and friendly. The canteen was phenomenal—a buffet where you could *choose*! Wow! That canteen gave me the first of many satisfying encounters with the wonder that is tuna mayonnaise. And bagels. And pizza in single slices. And pastrami. And potato salad. And . . . well, basically, food. I got fat very quickly in New York. There was something new and remarkable to taste everyday!

Anyway, apart from food, the best thing about that year was the people who looked out for me and let me live in their homes. The Butler family and the Slussers, and the Wallers whose daughters were at school with me and who made it their priority to give me a great time. They took me *everywhere*. We went on boat trips and sightseeing tours, to art galleries, shops, museums, the theatre, movies, skiing trips in Vermont, and holidays by lakes to see the fall in New England. I went to Yale with Winnie, a girl in my class, on a three-day college visit. For the first time ever, I was the only white person in a hall full of hundreds of black students going through the process of positive discrimination and minority admissions. I was brought up to speed very quickly about the situation for black students in Ivy League colleges, which was both shocking and hopeful. I had a week in Washington, DC, living with a clever writer who made it her mission to familiarise me with US politics and culture.

Some of the best fun was had when my Uncle Mike, who was a professor of American history at the University of Michigan in Ann Arbor, came to visit me in NY. He took me down to the Village to hear Stan Getz in a smoky jazz club, and to see the Andrew Wyeth exhibition and out to Ellis Island to see the Statue of Liberty and to understand how New York had evolved, with all the tired immigrants arriving by boat with one suitcase each.

Of course, my entire year in the States was spent longing for your visits and you did come to see me as often as you could. On your first visit, you came to spend Christmas with me, do you remember? You arrived on December 19 and my diary reports that I woke up with 'butterflies in my heart'. On December 20 you took me out for supper to a restaurant on West 48th Street called 'A La Fourchette', which I think is French for 'don't make any hasty decisions', and you asked me to marry you. I was overjoyed. I wanted so much to be Mrs Smyth. Mrs Dawn Smyth, wife of David Smyth. Lovely.

We spent Christmas in snowy Ann Arbor with Uncle Mike and Auntie Pat. It was so cold, our tears froze on our faces and we could pick them off. I loved the little solitaire diamond on my left hand. I looked and looked at it. I looked at it in the mirror, I looked at it flopping off the side of the sofa in repose, I looked at it when my fingers were linked with yours. We spoke to our families on the phone on Christmas Day, and told them we were engaged. They were a bit surprised but they seemed pleased for us. We spent the holiday making snow angels and kissing a lot. It was very romantic. Except for one evening when Auntie Pat read our tarot cards and told us we wouldn't end up together. Party-pooper . . .

When you went back to work, I went back to school and showed off my ring to my American chums, who were utterly baffled and couldn't work out why anyone would want to be married at nineteen years old. By this time I was included in the goings-on of an off-off-Broadway theatre company whose home was at the Church of the Heavenly Rest, close to the school. The school secretary, Molly Grose, was part of it and asked me to come along and help out. So, for the best part of a year, I was tea girl, lighting assistant, runner and general factotum for this company. I had a proper apprenticeship, watching and learning how a play comes together, and being part of a backstage team.

I ran out of money in New York. I didn't want to ask you for any, or my parents who really didn't have any, so I decided to utilise the misguided American impression of a young Englishwoman travelling abroad. Friends of the families I stayed with often used to say that well-spoken young Englishwomen reminded them of Mary Poppins. So, I put an ad up on the staff-room notice board and sent word about that I would be willing to do some childcare at the weekends or baby-sitting in the evenings. The response was amazing, and some weeks I would babysit *every* night. I looked after kids called Chandler Bigelow III, and Zorro, and Clymer, and Nancy. They were very different to English kids, more relaxed and proper little city dwellers. I earned tons of lolly and that meant I could complete my American trip by spending the last few months in LA, where I stayed with a crazy nurse on the ocean in Santa Monica. Just before I went there, though, was graduation day in New York, which was a big deal at Spence. All the girls had to attend, looking like virgins, in big white dresses. We sat for our photo, pretty maids all in a row.

At the end of that summer I returned home. I had missed my mum and dad very much and couldn't wait to see them. They came to collect me at the airport and I was shocked by my dad's appearance. He looked haggard and drawn. I knew he had been through the mill a bit since he'd had a nervous breakdown the year before. They were living in Saltash and I knew his business wasn't going very well. He was also sporting a huge beard and moustache, which totally wrongfooted me. I had never seen him look so different. I'm so glad you met him, David. It was very important to me later, that you knew him and he knew you. I think my family were a bit concerned about our future together, especially my brother, who knew me as a bit wild, and he could see that you were much more strait-laced. My dad, however, never expressed any doubts to me but did advise me to take things slowly, which, of course, I didn't. He liked you well enough. I think he knew I was safe with you, which was true. I *was* safe. You would never be cruel to me or intentionally hurt me in any way. Safe isn't *it*, though, for the long run, is it? Not for you, or me.

I remember after Dad died, when I went to college in London and lived in a cramped room in a flat in Kensal Green, you left the navy. We wanted to be together more. I was bereft after my dad's death and you were incredibly comforting. Then you landed that job with Lipton's as a new young tea-taster with great future potential for rising up through the company. Then they sent you to Calcutta. Of course they did. Duh. Tea comes from India.

So I went to college and started to work out who I was, a sort of lefty hippie, and you went to work and discovered that you were a company man with right-wing tendencies. I was red and you were blue. It was doomed really. A hopeless mixture. In love and doomed.

## DEAR MUM,

When I was about eight, I bought you a present from an antique shop. It was a brass wall plaque. It had a picture of an ancient granny in a rocking chair doing her knitting, and below that was a verse I still remember:

> *Who is the one who ne'er finds fault,*
> *Who never seeks to blame?*
> *To whom you go when troubles come,*
> *Whose love remains the same?*
> — *Your mother.*

How ridiculously sentimental. How archaic and cheesy. How revolting. How true.

Something I've always admired about you, Mum, is your ferocious independence. Only recently have you allowed any of us to properly do things for you. Perhaps retirement has given you permission to be more vulnerable? I don't know, but I certainly do remember all the remarkable things you have managed to pull off on your own. I remember once returning home to Stoke in Plymouth to find a giant wardrobe in a different room. How had you moved it alone? Impossible. I think you've always regarded difficult and seemingly insurmountable problems as challenges, daring you to solve them. And you usually do, somehow.

My favourite faux pas of yours (sorry, Mum, but you *are* hilarious sometimes, and long may you continue to be!!) was when I managed to get great tickets to see Elton John perform on the Argyle ground at Home Park in Plymouth. Argyle hadn't hosted a rock event before and the city was abuzz. I'd bought tickets for eight or so of us in the family and you were due to babysit for Jack, who was too young to go. Only as the hours crept by did I realise you were a bit put out about it. I saw the ol' lemon lips setting in and asked you what was wrong, remember? You told me that you were sad not to be going, that you adored Elton John, that he was one of your favourite singers ever, that you would have loved to go. Cousin Keiren stepped up and heroically sacrificed his ticket for you in favour of an evening of fun with Jack instead. What a guy! I apologised for my oversight. 'I didn't know how much you loved Elton's music,' I ventured. 'Yes,' you replied, 'he's wonderful. My absolute favourite song of his is "Ben". I love that one.'

After we'd all changed our pants from laugh damage, we explained that that song was in fact Michael Jackson's, and giggled all the way to the stadium. Just before the show we popped in to say hi to Elton, who is always the most genial of geniuses. I felt a daft amount of pride that he'd come to our stadium, and I wanted to show our support as a family. Sorry if I embarrassed you, Mum, but I just *had* to tell him what you'd said. It was worth the bruise on my ankle when you kicked me for doing it! When he was halfway through his blisteringly great set, Elton said loudly into his mike, 'This one is for Dawn's mum, Roma. Sorry it isn't your favourite but maybe this will do instead. It's "BEN . . . NIE AND THE JETS"!' The song boomed out over our hallowed stadium, we winked at each other and sat back to lap it up. Thanks for all the laughs, Mum. I know they weren't intentional but they were delightsome all the same.

*Whose love remains the same? Your mother.*

Yay, yay and thrice yay to that.

# DEAR DAD,

I KNEW you were ill. I didn't know *how* ill. You and Mum were very clever at concealing any trouble from Gary and me. We have tried to work out if we'd ever noticed anything amiss while we were growing up. Here's what I know: I know you suffered dreadfully with migraines and often had to lie in a quiet, dark room. I know that leaving the RAF and rejoining civvy street was extremely stressful for you. You'd been in the air force since you were a teenager, and civilian life was full of uncertainties and responsibilities you weren't used to. I think, as well, that you missed the camaraderie of the air force.

As the eldest son, you were expected to take over from Granddad at the newsagent in Ernesettle. I know the constant barracking from customers about late papers (not your fault—there were endless train strikes back then) was difficult for you. On top of this, you had the shadow of Granddad at your shoulder with whom this business had been so clearly identified for so long. You were the new blood. Gentler and quieter. Traits that are often mistaken for weakness in business. I think it was difficult for you to pick up the baton and very difficult for him to relinquish it.

The grinding erosion of your energy, working those slavishly long hours, was evident. You aged a lot in a relatively short time. There were issues with debt too. When you left the RAF you assumed the entire costs of the school fees and mortgage, which I know were beyond our means. I also know that, despite the money problems inside our own family, you were supporting other people, specifically your brother-in-law who needed help with his own newsagent's in Devonport. I know that after a lot of agonising you eventually sold the Ernesettle shop, which must have been difficult for lots of reasons, and I know you started a business breeding rabbits! I knew very little of the difficulties for two reasons:

you were skilled at hiding them, and I was far too wrapped up in my own exciting world, utterly ignorant of any signs of your depression, which, I'm sure, is just as you would have wished.

Mum knew the financial situation was bad and had taken steps to avert a crisis. Mum is a problem solver, and made of strong stuff. You know that, you married her. Ever resourceful, she took herself off on a course to train to become a 'canine beautician'. She loved and understood dogs, she was a hard worker, she was prepared to learn and she knew there was a gap in the market. While Mum was on her course to learn this bizarre trade, I remember you, Dad, locating and procuring a shop on Market Street in Plymouth and turning it into 'Felicity's Pet Parlour'.

She set about making the shop a success. Downstairs was a pet shop, selling all kinds of pet supplies, from the necessary, like food, to the novelty, like jewel-studded collars and leads for the more barking of the pooches and their owners. There was cat-wormer and budgie seed and flea powder and pigs' ears and, of course, there was the livestock. We had parrots, some fish, occasional kittens, but mostly small rodents like gerbils and hamsters.

Upstairs, Mum had her parlour. There was a row of kennels, some big sinks and a central table where the drying and snipping took place. It was hot and smelly, and dangerous. Dogs generally don't enjoy this process, so they try to kill you lest you dare to apply shampoo.

Mum had so many dodgy moments in that place. On the whole, she loved the dogs and would give them all a chance not to bite her, but if they persisted in objecting she would have to muzzle them to get the job done. She dealt with droolers and farters and nibblers and panic wee-ers. And that was just the staff! Once, a big black poodle got his head stuck in between the bars of the kennel and the fire brigade had to come and saw him out while the owner waited, unaware, downstairs. I remember some old dogs simply found the whole experience too overwhelming and would faint. Or, even worse, die!

Mum took allcomers, from cheeky Heinz 57-variety mongrels

to aloof pedigrees, and endeavoured to send them out perky and clean. Our own dogs, a couple of dirty-grey West Highlands, looked on with great amusement.

I remember how tired Mum was after a day of such labour-intensive work. I remember how hot and dirty she used to get, how the dog hairs would stick into her pores (she said they felt like a thousand tiny jabbing needles) and how they would sometimes get infected, just like the endless bites she sustained. She was constantly boosting her tetanus levels, in order to give the dogs another chance. And in order to give us another chance. This second income was crucial at this time, so she had to make her business pay.

I expect it didn't help your self-respect to realise that, conversely, things were sinking your end. Nobody in our family would have echoed that feeling but you were an old-fashioned man, believing the head of the household, the man, ought to be the one bringing home the bacon.

I have written fondly in my diary about a time, before I went away to the States, when I was off school for a couple of weeks so I could be at home with you. Mum had to keep working, Gary was away at uni, and it was obviously deemed necessary for someone to be with you, watching you, watching over you. Did people fear then that you might take drastic action? I write that you'd had a nervous breakdown and were feeling 'poorly'.

You were in bed for a few days but then I write that you are up and about, laying a floor in our bathroom and we are laughing a lot together, drinking coffee in the garden. I like to think that I was unknowingly part of your recovery on that occasion, maybe serving to remind you how much your family loved you.

Then I went away for the year in America, where we all kept in touch by letters and phone calls. I came back to find you bearded and gaunt. There's no doubt that you had a haunted look about you. You told me things were a bit rough with work but that it would all be OK and not to worry. On the long drive back to the West Country from Heathrow, we babbled on, hardly stopping to draw breath, catching up on all the stories, all the gossip. You hadn't laid eyes on me since I had become a 'fiancée'. I fancied that I looked entirely different, more mature and desired and mysteriously unattainable. No, you assured me, I just looked more American.

Back in Saltash, I made contact with all my pals and family, rushing about recounting details of my exchange-year experience, boring them all with tons of photos. David was due back from a long trip on his ship and I was beside myself with excitement to see him. You liked him, I think, yes?

I can't remember much about this period except that I was so happy to be home. I knew that you had a horrible bout of piles, which had been a regular ailment, and that, to avoid waking Mum in the night, you were sleeping on the sofa or in the spare room. It was difficult for you to move about easily, and you were tired from lack of sleep. I didn't know that this discomfort was just the tip of the iceberg, that underneath, inside, you were in hell.

On September 10, 1977, I waltzed off with a casual farewell to you and Mum. I was going to stay with David at the home of a friend of his and the friend's wife who lived in navy quarters in Devonport. It was one of those nights where I was playing at being a grown up. Well, I grew up fast the next day.

How did it start? Was there a phone call? I can't remember, but suddenly, early in the morning, David and I were dressing hurriedly and racing back to Saltash in his car. When I arrived home, Mum was sitting, ashen-faced. Gary looked like it was raining inside him, grim and beaten. Oh God. What? Where's Dad? What's happened? Who told me? Mum, I think. Yes. It was Mum, because she said you had been suffering badly all day, and that last thing you went upstairs together, with quite a struggle due to your discomfort. You kissed her good night. You told her you loved her. You shuffled out to the other room. So as not to disturb her sleep.

When she woke the next morning, she said she had a strong sense of disconnection immediately. Something felt wrong. She called out to you and there was no answer. Then there was a panicky frantic bit where she and Gary searched for you, shouted for you in the garden. The car was missing. Gary drove, on his motorbike I think, up to the field where you kept some of the rabbits, near Pillaton. He found you. God. That must have been dire, sickening. You had planned it. A hose on the exhaust, fitted carefully, fed through the window of the car. A bottle of sherry, so that a teetotal man might drink himself into the oblivion necessary to start the engine and lie back. And sleep. For ever. No more hell. Did it feel lovely? Like anaesthetic? Did you feel giddy? Or were you howling in agony, raging in your depression? Did you go out still fighting? Or did you surrender to the stillness, willing it to take you? Did you weep? Did we cross your mind? Did flashes of our life together show inside your head like a splendid movie? Or did you have to extinguish any thought of us so that you could do it? Did you say goodbye? To the night sky, or the inside of the car, or the life lived? Did you sputter and drown? Did you choke? Struggle? Did you just float away? Did you see a light? Did you hear a voice? Did dead beloveds hold their arms out and welcome you to their dead place? Is that where you are? I've lost you. Where are you? Can you see me? I'm in f—ing agony, you selfish bastard, don't you care? How could you do this to us? How dare you steal our happiness? Was it our fault for not noticing? Did you want us to stop you? Did you pray that someone would knock on the car window at the very last moment and drag you out? Did you consider that we couldn't—can't—live properly without you? So, you lied when you told me you would always be there for me? Did you think we would be better off without you? Did you think you had failed us? Did you suppress your sadness so much that it started to eat you from inside? Did you decide not to drag any of us into your black pit with you? Did you think this was the most selfless thing you could do? Did you think it was the *only* thing you could do? Did you just need to go? Away from the clanging racket of your mistakes? Were you racked with wretchedness and unable to see light, anywhere?

Was it dark and terrifying in your head? Did you want to be in a light place, to be hushed and tranquil? What did you hope it would be like? Like a lazy hot sunny day on the moors, or like a walk on the beach in Rock, or like bobbing about on the ocean? Like going home, maybe? Or did you just want it to be *anywhere* but here? The unbearable place where you felt savaged. The misery was too much. Maybe our happiness was too strong a contrast to bear? You wanted us to be happy but it tore you apart to not be able to include yourself in it any more. Your torment was a monster, and to kill it, you felt you had to kill you. That was the only way it would die. You were slaying the monster so that life could continue for those who deserved to live it. You were being the dad. Protecting your family. From you. I understand. At least, I understand that I don't fully understand. But if I love you, I have to try to understand. And I do love you. So much. And I miss you. Profoundly miss you. And I do forgive you. Because what do I have to stay angry about? That you have found your peace? That you did what you needed to do, however heartbreaking that is? I feel no regrets for you, no shame. Just awfully, awfully sad. For myself. For a nineteen-year-old with your skin, your eyes, who felt strangely responsible until I worked out your illness wasn't my fault. And even *that* I worked out by tapping into a synergy I always had with you. By thinking, 'What would you wish for me now, in this pitiful grief?' and, of course, you would wish me to live my life to the full, and not waste a single second or a single chance at happiness. You would want me to relish those chances, and I do, Dad. I live my life fully, as a tribute to you and in the full knowledge that you couldn't so I will, for both of us. I carry you with me, not as a heavy weight or some kind of sorrowful burden, but as my energy and my engine. You are around me and part of me, my father, my dad. My darling dad. Denys Vernon French.

We were utterly broken, Gary, Mum and I. All of us just kept on breathing, but we weren't really living. We were numb with grief. Mum tried to be strong and distracted herself with getting on and organising stuff. I offered to stay at home for a year, to defer my place at college, and stay with her. There was no altruism in this—I was in pain and wanted the comfort of home. Mum was stunning—she refused outright to let me stay. She said that we had to work through it and be busy, that she couldn't endure any pity heaped on top of the harrowing heartache.

The house was full of family, my clearest memory being of Mum's three brothers, Terry, Owen and Mike, the triumvirate gathering round her. She had cared for and looked out for all three in their lives and now it was time for them to look after her. They helped with everything, the funeral, the money, the planning. Gary became the man of the house the day he found you, Dad, and it was hard for him, but he took his role seriously and has been there to watch out for Mum and me ever since.

I couldn't go to see your body. I hadn't seen you since that night when I casually breezed out of the door, chucking goodbyes over my shoulder in my haste. I can't even remember what you said, what your last words were. It could so easily have been 'I love you', you said it so often. Was it that? Did you know that what you were saying to the back of my head as I rushed out was the last thing you would ever say to me? No matter really. It just crosses my mind sometimes. I only pray it wasn't 'Don't go'. I didn't want to see you because I was afraid I would have that final lifeless image of you etched on my brain instead of all the vital happy memories that were and are so clear. Mum said you looked like you were having a nap. So that's good.

Mum became very quiet and soft in the days leading up to the funeral. I think she was girding herself for it and trying not to die of the misery which was threatening to swallow her whole. She told me that David could sleep in my room. I was gobsmacked! Under her roof it was her rules, and this was a definite no-no ordinarily. But this wasn't ordinary and she wanted us to have all the comfort we could. So, for the first time, David and I slept wrapped up in each other in my tiny single bed in my teenage bedroom surrounded by my dolls and my posters of Steve McQueen and

Steve Harley. I cried a lot and woke up startled in the night many times, reliving again and again the shock of what had happened. David was there and he held me close through each night.

The funeral was excruciating. It was in the church where you and Mum were married in St Budeaux, behind the old Blue Monkey pub which has gone now. We always called it the Blue Monkey church. Following the hearse was harrowing, Gary and I on either side of Mum, all clinging on to each other for dear life. Yes, dear life. I was so touched when we pulled up outside the church, and I saw so many of my friends there, who had all loved you, Dad, who wanted to say goodbye, or 'chio' as we say in Plymouth. I can't remember the service except being fixated on that box where you were—but I do remember getting back in the awful big black cars and, again, following the coffin, with you inside it, up to Weston Mill Crematorium. Up, up the hill, and into that little chapel where there was more pointless blether. More platitudes and clichés and metaphors. Blah blah. Shut up! You didn't know him. Then, it happened. That woeful moment when the vicar is saying something about committing you to God and suddenly a buzzing starts and the curtains begin to close round your coffin like a macabre matinée finale. This was suddenly a palpable, final, finite moment. I wasn't ready for it, it was too much and I started to sob uncontrollably with Mum and Gary. I have never before or since felt such aching despair.

We couldn't face a 'do' after the whole dreadful thing was over. The family were probably perplexed by this, but we preferred instead to go home, get the dogs and go for a long walk on the beach at Rock. We were closer to you there, where we had often walked, where we had laughed and loved each other as a family. Looking out at the sea that day, the significance was overwhelming. I realised that your suicide was the wave crashing on the shore. The wave was sinking back into the ocean, and I was left standing on the shoreline without you, utterly lost.

The next week, bruised and broken, I left home and went to college in London.

# DEAR DAD,

Mum was right, as always. It made sense to go to college straight away, and not to delay. I was distracted from my big you-grief by the thousands of new things that were suddenly happening.

A friend of a friend's daughter had a room to let in a flat she shared in Leighton Gardens, Kensal Rise. I didn't know London at all really, except for the few times I'd been there with you and Mum when I was little, to do tourist stuff like visit Madame Tussauds—outside which a man placed a monkey in my arms and another in Gary's and we had our photo taken. One of the more surreal memories I have of childhood and marking the day my monkey-love began. After that, I nagged you to get me a pet monkey about twice a week, till I was sixteen.

So, anyway, the flat in Kensal Rise. Yes. Well, I didn't really have a bedroom—it was one of those awkward half-rooms where you might store an exercise bike or perhaps a Hoover. Just large enough to fit a single bed if the last six inches were sawn off. Large enough for that, but nothing else other than that. Just the mini-sized single bed touching the walls on three sides, that's all that fitted in there. Well, no, maybe I should take my foot off the exaggerator, there was also room for a cup of tea on the floor, so long as you were inside and the door was shut. I did, very briefly, consider kipping on a chair instead, which would free up a couple of square feet for a chest of drawers, but decided against it in the end in favour of sleep.

I didn't know my flatmates very well, and when I discovered that one of them, a guy, was taking copious amounts of drugs, I retreated further and further into my little cubbyhole. I should have been living in the new, exciting, huge, buzzing city, but in reality I was living in a cupboard. I couldn't afford to venture out much, I was gobsmacked at how much everything in London cost, especially travel—the flat was a long way from the college in Swiss Cottage and practically all of my grant was spent on travel. The grant itself was another problem. The amount was calculated by the local authority at home, who took into account the income of you and Mum. The figure they gave me for the year was supposed to include support from both of you. Of course, you weren't around any more, Dad, on top of which Mum was dealing with a bankful of enormous debt. She was already having to sell the house and buy a flat in Plymouth on Mutley Plain, she was broke, I couldn't ask her to stump up more. I went to the bank and organised a small loan, but no spotty student was allowed much, and luckily one of the hero trio of uncles stepped up to help out a bit. Uncle Terry lent me enough to get through the first year, on the strict understanding that the loan would be paid back by such-and-such a time with such-and-such interest. I know he was teaching me a lesson about borrowing, he was trying to be a substitute for you, Dad, helping me to manage a budget. Once all the books and equipment for the course were bought and my rent and travel was paid, I was left with less than two pounds a week to buy toothpaste and other essentials. Like food. Of course, I should have bought vegetables and pasta and made big hearty soups that would sustain me and last all week, but I chose a different, edgier route. This was the first time I had ever lived on my own, so I did what I ruddy well liked thank you and went cocking crazy and spent all of the two pounds on chocolate, milk and crisps. Every day. For a year. Wild.

My journey to college each day found me at Finchley Road station with a long walk to Central School of Speech and Drama, which was great for exercise but added hours on to my day, and was a bit scary when, as was often the case, we finished late at night. I had just come from New York, widely regarded as one of the most dangerous cities in the world, and yet I was more afraid walking home in the dark in Kensal Rise.

My first day at Central was a shock. I was a couple of days late because of the funeral, so I was nervous that I hadn't been part of those crucial first few moments where everyone is in the same boat. By the time I arrived they were already on their boat, it had left harbour and I was rowing furiously behind in my little dinghy to catch up. The first class of the day was Movement. I had no idea why something was called 'movement'. I knew how to do movement. I did it all day, didn't I? That's how I got about generally, by moving. I had the same confusion about classes on the timetable labelled 'Breathing' or 'Voice'. For a misguided instant, I imagined that perhaps only West Country people knew how to move, breathe and speak. Perhaps these natural skills weren't as widely practised as I had taken for granted. Wow. I was an advanced mover, breather and speaker already, without even trying because, frankly, I'd been doing all three my whole life! These other suckers better catch up.

Oh, how very wrong I was. I clambered into the regulation black leotard and tights with added ugly jazz shoes and slunk into the movement studio. A terrifying space with huge mirrors and barres. Terrifying because we could see the full horror of what we looked like in the black all-in-ones. Leotards don't look good on anyone. Even Madonna. And she looks better than everyone else who's ever worn one.

So there we were, the teachers' course class of 1977–80, known as 'T80'. A sorrier bunch of stooped, bewildered, crushingly embarrassed subhumans you have never seen. This was the environment in which I first laid eyes on Jennifer, my beloved Fatty. Her disdain for the whole leotard experience was obvious. She barely made an effort with the shake-out and warm-up, and the leg-swinging was an affront. Somehow, in this torture chamber of lycra lunacy, she maintained an air of cool. She was as lumpy as the rest of us but she refused (publicly at least) to acknowledge the humiliation of the leotard, so her controlled demeanour remained intact. No nylon nightmare was going to ruffle her. I noticed this seeming self-assurance immediately and chalked her up as unattainable, out of my league, too sophisticated. She didn't make much eye contact with me, but then again, outside the class I *did* wear beige corduroy A-line skirts and a back-to-front baseball cap and I did call biscuits 'cookies' and think everything was 'neat'. That's what happens when you have no taste and you live in America for a year when you're nineteen years old. I mistook Jen's lack of connection with me as low-level loathing. I now know how shy she can be, which is an explanation for her sometime coolness, alongside the equally likely probability that she was mostly distracted by thinking about what she might have for her tea. Fatty is a consummate daydreamer. Unlike most of us amateur daydreamers though, she doesn't visit woolly, blurry places where your mind can have a little dance and a rest, or if she does, it's only for a short time. No, her mind whisks her off to vivid, fresh places where she can live at the pace her brain is constantly working at, which is quite a lot quicker than most mortals. She is constantly running a cynical, internal parallel tape of her real life—what she sees, hears, reads, eats, loves and hates—and it never ceases to amuse her. It's this sharp skill of observation that gives her the comedy spurs she uses to jolt her mind on from a trot to a canter when she is improvising or writing. On the surface, though, all is calm. Calm to the point of catatonia, of procrastination until the urgency kicks in. It's usually a deadline that provides the fear and that is the cue for her to switch to shark mode. It's as if she has smelt the blood in the water, her eyes focus and she swims very fast, very skilfully towards the target, using all the muscle of a new idea that's been slow-cooking during her reveries, as the power to thrust her forward. It's an awesome talent to witness. Back then, though, I thought she was a snobby git.

After a year of Kensal Rise and only seeing David on the odd weekend, he was sent to India to work for Lipton's. It was ironic really: one of the reasons he had left the navy for the tea trade was that we didn't want to have so much time apart and now here he was, off to abroad. I didn't want to stay in the pot-reeking flat any more and I was overjoyed when one of my favourite college mates, Gilly, mentioned that her boyfriend Malcolm, who owned some properties, had a new conversion available for eight flatmates to share in Steele's Road, Chalk Farm. This meant only a ten-minute walk to college and a spanking new flat. The rent was more expensive than I had been paying so I knew I would have to share my room. I knew my old schoolfriend Angie was looking for accommodation, so that was that. Gilly was putting together a group of us to share the flat, some people from college, an American student called Cici, one single guy called Tom, and she said that Jennifer Saunders from our course was also interested. I was definitely underjoyed by the prospect of that. It wasn't that we actively disliked each other, not at all, just that we had been on the same course for a whole year by this point and not really found each other, not really bothered, both assuming that the other wasn't our type. I thought she might be the only one in the flat I wouldn't be able to relate to.

Then we moved in and, of course, within days we were walking to college together and getting to know the virtual strangers we were to each other. She made me laugh so much, she was bright, and leagues and layers deep. She was, and is, incredibly attractive in lots of ways. She is a bit mysterious and it takes an effort to know her well, but once in her orbit it's a very cockle-warming place to be. We could subvert any seriousness about our college course by finding it all a bit ludicrous, and taking the piss. We equally sought out chances to puncture any pomposity or pretension we saw around us. This meant that the only point of each day was to make each other laugh. On one memorable occasion we decided to see what it would be like to laugh heartily out loud, non-stop, from the second we stepped out of our flat till we reached the steps of college. Of course, loud laughter is pretty funny and contagious so by the time we reached college we were uncontrollably lost in genuine laughter, exhausted, and suitably damp of crotch.

It was so good to find a buddy to laugh with like that. I needed to laugh—there hadn't been much to laugh about for a year or so. In fact, probably the last time was with you, Dad. Laughing with you remains a powerful memory for me. I remember how much

John Cleese made us laugh in *Fawlty Towers*, helpless, falling-off-the-sofa laughing till we were begging him to show mercy and stop being so funny. Cracks and gags and affectionate teasing were a mainstay of our life together. To share a sense of humour is such a privilege, such an intimacy and such a love. I wasn't at all surprised to find, then, that this was the same for Fatty and her dad. I went to her home in Cheshire that November because her parents were having a bonfire party. Their house was big and rambling and friendly. I suppose she must have told her parents about my situation having just lost you, and from the moment I met her dad, he took great care to ladle me with lots of love. I will never forget his kindness at a time I was starved of dadness.

College was a bit disorganised. There were several people at Central for whom getting there had been an ordeal. They had worked to save for it, and they were furious that the course was such a shambles, so they formed quite a militant force and made complaints. The complaints were justified, but most of us in T80 were very young and having a ball just being in London. We weren't that bothered about learning, we wanted to have fun, and magically have a degree by the end of it. I remember one particular exam—was it theatre history? We all filed in, sat down and turned over the question paper. I didn't know ANY of the answers and immediately assumed it was because I was thick or had revised entirely the wrong subject (not unusual). Pretty soon it became obvious that no one could answer anything because we simply hadn't been taught it. The grown-ups of T80 took a stand—literally—and we all followed, marching out of the exam room in revolt. It was quite handy having eloquent and assertive people to represent us, to lead the mutiny when necessary and to shake up the college, which was a bit sleepy. Further education is often the time when we formulate our political leanings and it was fantastic to be in such a lefty environment, listening and learning. And for the last year and a half of our course, we had Margaret Hilda Thatcher the milk snatcher as our foe, so boy didn't *that* unite us under a common enemy. Nothing like a spitting, spouting monster to bring even the loiteringest sluggards out from the back of the cave to stand their ground. Even me.

We were required to do some twatty things during our time there. There was one exercise where we had to wrap each other in newspaper with Sellotape to form human eggs. The lights were dimmed in the studio and we were instructed to stay inside our 'eggs' for as long as we needed until it was time to slowly break out, reborn into an entirely different world where we had to invent a new language and find a new, utopian way to live together. You can imagine how seriously I took this. I figured outright giggling wouldn't go down well so I opted instead for a little snooze inside my hot paper egg. When I woke up, I had no idea how long I'd been asleep, so I thought I'd better break out pretty sharpish in case they were all waiting for me, imagining I was being introspective and interesting. I pierced the paper with my finger and made a hole big enough to peer through. In the gloaming, I could just make out that everyone else was still inside their eggs. I must have only nodded off for a few seconds. Drat. The teacher saw me peering out and gestured encouragement to give birth to myself and come out into the brave new world. So, very slowly, I ripped my shell open and crawled out, muttering my 'new' language, which I had decided would be a slowed-down, slurred version of Elvis's 'Can't Help Falling in Love'. So, I was shuffling across the floor, spreading like a lumpy puddle, gurgling, 'Wahse—meen—saay—ooonleee—foolz—ruuuhsh—eeen . . .'. This went on for an eternity. I was alone in the nightmare until some other sucker finally joined me. The minute I saw Fatty pop out of hers, that was it. I couldn't control the laughter any longer, and was eventually asked to gather myself outside. Honestly, hard-working folks were paying taxes for us to arse about like this!

Of course, there was the flipside where we did serious classes which, had I bothered to concentrate, would have come in very handy later on. Voice, for instance. By the time I left I didn't know the difference between a uvula, a vulva and a Volvo but, astonishingly, I somehow had the qualification to teach it! Phonetics would have been another good one to have had under my belt, the language of language. Phonetics would have helped me to write down accents and nuances in shorthand and replicate them later. I have needed this skill a thousand times and, stupidly, I haven't been equipped, because back then I was too busy doing laughing to focus on anything important. How I achieved the degree at all I have no idea.

Meanwhile, life in the flat was peachy. Angie and I loved sharing, except for the not infrequent occasions she had a gentleman caller, whereby the form was that I would vacate our shared room for the night and kip on the sofa.

We had a cleaning rota and each took our turn, or not, to clean certain areas of the flat, which inevitably led to hilarious arguments. We made marks on the side of milk bottles to ensure no one was illegally slugging our precious pints, we ate huge six-day-old stale pasta soups with grated cheese on top, and quiche, and mash, and bread with butter and sugar sprinkled on top. We had big, loud, themed parties, tarts and vicars, togas, rival drama colleges, all sorts. We took weekend jobs chambermaiding or in the local pub or cooking for firemen to make a few bob, which we then spent on punky clothes at Camden Market. We were pathetic punks, not properly committed, just dressing up at weekends. We went to see *The Rocky Horror Show* again and again, we went to watch bands like the B52s and the Eurythmics. We had the most excellent tea parties with our classmates. I had a crashing crush on Rowan Atkinson, who lived nearby, and I felt sure he would love me if only we could meet. I agonised over whether to drop a note through his door. Luckily, I lost my bottle, and didn't put him through it, but we *did* go to see his live show and considered him a genius only hindered by a geeky sidekick I later found out to be a man called Richard Curtis.

I loved the company of my new friends. Of Gilly, who had set the flat up for us, who drove her Mini like a madwoman while cradling hot coffee in her lap, and who had a comprehensive collection of Lladro figurines which I considered to be supremely elegant and sophisticated. She was dating Malcolm, our landlord, who was the most dashing and handsome man in Chalk Farm. That was good, it was unlikely we would be evicted while that lasted. (It has now lasted about thirty years, and provided me with the dream-boat that is Sophie, my first godchild.)

Then there was Jobo, or Yoyo Knickers as I called her. What a woman. Tall and gangly and *über*-clever. She had just returned from Kenya, from some relationship with an exciting chap, and she was like no one I had ever met. Fatty was drawn to her and they were very close by the time I started to know her. She was an exuberant, daring minx with a love for elaborate pranks. She would do anything for a laugh or a dare. It was too irresistible not to challenge her. She would perform her tasks with enormous panache, like, for instance, shouting out her love for strangers on the street, or pretending to be blind at the wheel of her car and asking passers-by for directions while wearing two eyepatches. Getting entirely naked driving through central London and staying so for the whole journey. Wandering about in the street below our flat with our laundry basket on her head and no trousers, and on and on with the gags. She is fearless and wild and beautiful. She was unafraid to fake fits when difficult exams were due, to tell elaborate porkies to staff in order to explain the lack of essays she submitted. She lived in a fabulous crumbling old house in swanky Chelsea and no one believed her when, late once again for lectures, she explained that the ceiling had collapsed at her house, when of course it had. She had fabulous long legs and occasionally did a bit of advertising work for Pretty Polly tights—or did she? Who knows! She *said* she did—anyway, she had a bit of cash and was always free with it. I will never forget when she noticed how hard up I was, and how embarrassing it was for me to completely run out of dosh by the end of the week. Somehow she obtained my bank details and anonymously put money into my empty account which saw me through a whole month. I didn't know who had done it for ages, but found out later that it was she who had been so fabulously generous.

In our last year at Central, there was a student union-organised cabaret evening. We didn't ordinarily bother with these shows at college because it seemed to us they were yet another opportunity to have to witness the actors showing off and loving themselves to bits. The courses were so divided. They didn't want us there, and we didn't want to support their ego-fest. But this time, Fatty and I were encouraged by our friends to do a sketch.

By now we had been amusing ourselves for a year or so, inventing characters at home in the flat. We used to put our hated leotards on backwards, we sewed tassels onto our ladybumps and thus we launched the 'Menopatzi Sisters'. Ta-da! We decided they were the last in a long line of an Italian circus family. They were useless acrobats who performed pathetic feats of weakness and ineptitude. It was such a simple pleasure to jump about like daft dafties for the entertainment of our chums. We improvised other characters too—Americans obsessed with spiritual wellness, and punk duo the 'Menopause Sisters', and lots more. Never for one second did we think these little amusements would become more than private.

When our friends encouraged us to perform at the cabaret evening, we were a bit hesitant initially, but eventually we decided to go along in order to prevent it being yet another exclusive night where the teachers were unrepresented. We had very little nerves—what did we have to lose? The evening went well, we performed our American sketch and the Menopatzis. People seemed to laugh in all the right places. I'm extra pleased that Gary happened to be there that night because on reflection I realise that it was a seminal moment, a turning point. We hadn't shamed ourselves and we'd had a good laugh—and frankly that's pretty much been our yardstick ever since. I try to make her laugh, she tries to make me laugh, and if anyone else enjoys it too, then that's a bonus.

I wish you could have seen us, Dad; I think you would have liked it. You certainly would have liked her. She's dead funny, my friend Fatty.

## DEAR FATTY,

I thought you might be interested to hear that a strange thing has happened in a pub near me. A couple of weeks ago, a chap walked in there, casual as you like, and asked for a pint. I don't know of what. Maybe Scruttocks Old Dirigible with twigs and bits of beak in it, as Alexei used to say. He used to do that a lot, say things that weren't quite true for comedy effect. Anyway, anyway, anyway, this chap ordered his beer and the barman went off to the cellar to change the barrel since it had run out. To my mind, he should really have changed it before that, then he wouldn't have had to keep the customer waiting and feeling neglected. He obviously wasn't keeping his eye on the levels as closely as a good landlord oughta. Do barrels have levels? Like petrol gauges, or a dipstick? I wonder. I wouldn't have been so tolerant if I had been the customer and thirsty for my Scruttocks. I personally wouldn't actually be thirsty for that of course, because I detest beer. It is the urine of the devil with all its froth and rancid flavour.

Anyway, anyway, anyway. While the barman or landlord (he could of course be both) was away from the bar, the man took the opportunity to look around and saw that there was absolutely no one else in the pub. I'm not sure why. Maybe someone, a regular perhaps, had died and everyone else was at the funeral except the barman who was furious he still had to open up because the brewery are strict about things like that? Or maybe there had been tell of a ghostly headless horseman charging through the pub which had frightened everyone off? With headless horsemen, by the way, is it the horse that's headless usually, or the man? Or perhaps it was just a Tuesday before lunch and everyone was at work? We'll never know.

Anyway, anyway, anyway, while he sat there at the bar on his own, the man inadvertently started to pick at a bowl of nuts on the counter. I wouldn't do that myself because of the statistic about every bowl of nuts containing at least twenty specimens of different wee from dirty folk who don't wash their hands after the loo. He obviously didn't know this fact, or he didn't care, or he might even have been some kind of wee connoisseur or appreciator. In which case, what a freak! Anyway, anyway, anyway, he was aimlessly popping the bar snacks into his mouth when he heard a little voice in his ear say, 'Goodness, you're handsome!' I mean, honestly, how very forward was that? He looked all around, very confused, and of course, nobody was there. And he hadn't even had his pint yet, so we can't blame the alcohol at this point. Before you could say, 'Time, gentlemen, please! What is the time, gentlemen please?!' he heard another little voice, this time saying, 'Wow, those slacks really suit you.' Again, he was utterly confused because he couldn't work out where these little voices were coming from. Just as he heard the barman's footsteps coming back up from the cellar, there came a third and final comment: 'Mmm, you smell lovely, like limes on a summer evening in the Algarve.' Well, you can imagine what state he was in by then, really quite flummoxed, and he was glad to see the barman emerge. Apparently he then told the barman about his bizarre experience, to which the barman responded casually, 'Oh, don't worry about that. It's the peanuts. They're complimentary.' Can you believe that?

## DEAR DAD,

My last year at Central was a bit crazy. I was aware that David and I were growing apart but I wasn't ready to face it full on because I still loved him very much. Isn't it mad the way we postpone the most important stuff? I was living a liberated life in London, free of the immediate restraints of a big relationship because my chap was thousands of miles away. I missed him a lot, and I was always utterly faithful to him, but I was also having a great time discovering who I really was, which turned out to be *not* somebody who should marry David, or who David should marry. As you know, David was quite a forceful personality and liked to be in charge. Surprise, surprise, that's who I was becoming too, someone quite assertive who knows their own mind. At the time I still slightly reverted back into a somewhat meeker role when I was with him because that's how it had always been. Old dynamics die hard. Plus, to be honest, there's a big part of me, like a lot of people, that loves to be looked after, protected and sheltered inside a partner's love. I didn't realise then, as I so clearly do now, that it was all possible on a much more equal footing. On reflection, all the signs were there, but I was blind. And reluctant to let go. In fact, I took the polar opposite action and charged ahead with arrangements for the wedding. Fatty was to be a bridesmaid, the Blue Monkey church was booked and we were investigating various venues for the reception. Oh what a circus, oh what a show.

It was the Easter holiday 1980 and the last time I would visit David before we were to be married. It was an important trip because I was going to stay in the house where we would live together afterwards, the marital home. By now he had moved from Calcutta and was living in Colombo, Sri Lanka. I loved India—the colours, the sounds, the smells, the incredible, mystical difference of it all—but I didn't really warm to expat life. The exclusive clubs and the drinking and the non-working wives and the separateness from local life. Most of all, I found it difficult to stay at his flat surrounded by servants. SERVANTS! I was addressed as Memsahib and bowed to. It was too strange.

Outside, it was even stranger. Parts of Calcutta were beautiful, with a faded grandeur, but the poverty was horrific, and I was constantly confronted with situations and sights direct from a Bruegel nightmare. Half-bodied people scooting along next to me on little carts, women with dead babies in their arms, pleading for money, other beggars with alarming facial disfiguring, lepers with gnarly stumps and famished, emaciated children, all tugging at me, wanting a few paise. Here I was, a fat young white woman, shopping for fruit and beads in the market while all around me was despair. The clash was revolting. I started by giving money to everyone, but of course that caused further begging, more insistent and louder, until I was forced to retreat inside in utter shock.

Meanwhile, David and I would be invited to posh dinners inside lavish homes with dozens of servants providing for our every need. Or there would be balls—Caledonian balls with only white people there, and again I never quite looked or felt or *was* the part. The part of a company wife, quietly supporting her upwardly mobile company man of a husband. Who was I? Who was he? Where was the spirited young Irish lad I had known? He was certainly highly prized by the company and I was often told by his colleagues that he was tipped for great things. I was proud of him, *for* him, but, Dad, I didn't belong. So, this visit to Sri Lanka mattered. We would arrange the teaching job I was going to take, we would hire staff together, we would hang out with all the people who would be our friends for the next couple of years.

When the plane landed, as soon as I'd gone through passport control I saw him, on the other side of the glass, waving at me, while I waited for my luggage. There he was, my handsome fiancé whom I missed so much—there—at last—he was. So why was I feeling nothing? Why was my heart not pounding out of my chest as it usually did? Come on, heart, wake up! There he is, smiling and waving, we've waited for this—come on! I did the waving-back thing but something was wrong, Dad, terribly wrong.

We reached the house; it was beautiful and colourful and hot. We drank tea, amazing, well-chosen, well-mixed, top-quality tea, we chattered, and we went to bed. I felt totally numb. Nothing was right, it was all very, very wrong. Something was missing. Everything was missing. What had happened? We slept, uneasily. We went to his club the next day. He introduced me to his new buddies.

Other tea men, businessmen, nurses, wives, my future friends. I felt as if I was drowning.

That evening, with two more weeks of the holiday to go, we finally talked the way we should have talked for the past year. We spoke about so much, about how different our lives now were, how we had grown apart and changed into people neither of us really recognised, how we were political polar opposites, how much he loved the ex-pat life and how little I did, how much I disliked our his 'n' hers scuba-diving kit, how it made me feel 'owned'. All this was reasonable and understandable. Then, and only then, after all that, he told me he was sleeping with one of the nurses he'd introduced me to at the club. So, you're shagging someone else and she's allowed to inspect me? I asked if anyone else knew about it. Yes, he finally admitted. It seemed everyone knew. So he had taken me to meet a group of people who all knew my fate? It was just me, miles from home, miles from my friends, who *didn't* know? Why didn't he tell me before, stop me from coming? Was *that* what I was feeling at the airport? Did I sense then that it was over? And if so, was I just sensing that it was over for me, or for us? Or was the love just . . . gone? On both sides? I had no answers to any of this but I had to get away.

I was back at the airport the very next day, and after a tearful farewell and a weepy flight home, I ran into the arms of a love I could depend upon, my brother, who took me back to his flat in London and listened to me blub on about the injustice of it all for days until he gently reminded me, mid-rant, that I had already known it wasn't going to work out. It was better for everyone that it ended now, *before* the wedding. He was right of course. I called Fatty and she came. She was the only other one I talked to at that point, until I could work my way through it and steel myself to call the various parents to explain what had happened.

David and I met again briefly a few months later, when I returned the ring, and a few bits 'n' bobs of his old kit. I was afraid that when I opened the door to greet him I might be revisited by a rush of the familiar old love and realise we had made a huge mistake, but no. There was, instead, a rush of nostalgia, a tender remembrance of the younger, happier times, but we both knew it was right to have ended it.

So. That was over. I had been at college for three years, turning away from every possible opportunity of big sex fun with a bucketful of delish fellow students. Now I had a single term to catch up. Wahey!

## DEAR DAD,

Other than my friend Scottie, no one on the acting course at Central spoke to me, or to any of us student teachers. They refused to make eye contact, let alone converse. I think they believed they might catch something off us. And indeed they might have. Manners, for instance.

Annoyingly, their iciness made them all the more enigmatic, and there was a definite elite of blessed, golden, chosen ones. They were, on the whole, good-looking, usually blond and quite fit. We used to refer to them as the shampoo brigade, because their hair was always so perfect. There was one in particular who I thought was divine—I used to see him skulking about being moody and interesting. The foyer of the college was the actors' main posing arena—it was directly outside the cafeteria, thus commanding a captive audience—they would throw interesting shapes against the wall while perusing their timetables and various notices. My particular darling, whom I shall refer to as the 'Golden One', was quite brooding and James Dean-ish. He was a good actor, I saw him in various plays at the Embassy, the theatre at the centre of the college. For some preposterous reason, we, the teachers, were not allowed into the theatre at any time except to watch the actors performing their plays. All of our productions took place in the studio spaces, which were fab but just not as exciting as the proper proscenium-arch grandness of the forbidden Embassy. The most memorable play that I saw the Golden One in was Bill Morrison's *Flying Blind*, where he spent a deal of time naked. Yep, I saw that play several times, each night occupying a seat in the auditorium closer and closer to the front. I wanted to get a really good look at the ... play.

One day, I was having coffee where I could see the goings-on in the foyer. The Golden One was there doing expert leaning against the notice boards. He was alone. This was unusual, he was unguarded and vulnerable, so I decided to seize the moment. We had been attending the same college for nearly three years and if I didn't take action now, college would be over and all hope gone. I wasn't entirely stupid; I knew I couldn't compete with the beauty of the girls of the shampoo brigade, but I had something else to offer. My sparkling wit, surely? In that instant, I decided to embark on Operation Flirt by winning him over with a flurry of hilarity—the romance would surely follow later. I stood up and crossed the foyer. He was caught unawares. I advanced upon him in all my beige corduroy splendour, deciding that my opening gambit would be, 'Hi. Hello there. Yes it's me, I'm talking to you at last after three years. I bet you can't believe your luck, eh? You must be so frustrated that you know nothing about me. Well, that agony stops right here, right now, and you, mister, are gonna know everything you've ever wanted to know and more about me, Dawn Roma French ... Right, I'm going to start at the very beginning, stop me when you're in love.' He looked genuinely afraid and was backing up towards the wall, which meant I had to continue with the gag until he *got it*. He will get it eventually ... won't he? So I valiantly soldiered on. 'So, um, right, I was born in Holyhead in 1957, and luckily for my mother, I was a baby.' Nope, nothing. Carry on. 'I was a chunky child, bold in nature, a real rusk-taker ...'. He's right up against the wall now. Don't give up, keep going. 'You will probably be keen to know exactly what inoculations I've had, well ...'. And on. And on. Still no response except clearly utter revulsion, and the squeaking of leather belt on wall as he tried to slide away. I *had* to persevere—you know me,

Dad, I'm nothing if not tenacious! I think after about six minutes of solid talking, and a tiny bit of physical restraint, I had reached as far as infants school, and was about to launch in to the junior-school years and regale him with many hilarious anecdotes about that, when suddenly the bell rang indicating the start of the next class. I was momentarily startled and the Golden One grabbed the opportunity to run, run like a hunted fox, for his life, off up the corridor to his Tumbling class and out of my life for ever.

Or so I thought. Cut to about three years later. I was in a queue at the bank in Swiss Cottage. I was still banking there although I had long since left the area. I was inching my way slowly towards the front of the queue when out of the blue I heard my name. 'Dawn! God, darling, how great to see you!' I turned round and it was him, the Golden One, advancing upon me with his arms wide open, gathering me up like a precious thing and giving me a huge, effusive, loving bear hug. I found myself in a situation I would have given good money to be in just a few years earlier. Now I'm not saying that things changed so completely and so utterly because I was by then working with the Comic Strip making eight films a year and we were always casting. No, I'm not saying that. But. It was odd.

And here's *another* odd thing. The same man, who had spurned me, was, shockingly, struck by lightning. Actual, real lightning. On his head. Now, Dad, I'm not saying that it's *very* unwise for any man to ever actively resist my charms. But it *is* weird, isn't it?!

## DEAR BF,

How the knob did we get away with calling ourselves teachers? I still see people now, grown women with children, especially in the Camden Town area, who shout after me, 'Miss French!' A clanking reminder of an extraordinary year you and I spent teaching at Parliament Hill School for Girls. 1980–81, wasn't it?

Dear Lord, we were both just out of 'school' ourselves.

Parliament Hill. A big girls' comprehensive between Camden and Highgate, set in beautiful grounds backing on to fields, with William Ellis boys' school right next door. Huge and well equipped (Parliament Hill that is, not the boys), it was a massive education machine stuffed with boisterous, confident kids and dedicated staff. I was a bit intimidated, but it helped that I'd had my final teaching practice there, so it was more of a natural progression than getting a new job in an entirely unfamiliar school. My teaching practice before that had been up the road at a big co-ed comp called Acland Burghley, which had one of the most inspirational dance/drama departments in the country, so I had hoped Parly would be the same.

Well, it wasn't quite, was it? There *was* a small basement studio but the staff room for our department was in the old toilets next door. Our cupboards were toilet stalls, with toilets still there. We balanced files on washbasins and we made a little seating area under the mirrors at the end. It was a cold, damp, smelly, depressing place, wasn't it? I think the atmosphere had slowly eroded the head of the drama department's enthusiasm and she wasn't coping so well. She had some ill health and I was quite often thrust into her position. Me, the rookie newby twit, in charge of all the O-level, CSE and A-level drama courses, about which I knew *nada*. Thank God you came in part-time. You really helped me out Babe, and into the bargain we had an opportunity to spend more time together, cementing our friendship even further, united in fear and confusion. Quite often, I would spend the evening learning the theory I was teaching the next day from the course textbooks. I was about two pages ahead of my students at any one time. And what students! The older A-level kids were bright and inquisitive and quite a challenge—after all, I was only four or five years older than them. For most of the time I was really wishing we could abandon the studying and gossip about telly and boyfriends. The O-level and CSE groups were the main ones we taught together. What a hoot! Once we could get them *into* the studio we could have great sessions. But getting them there wasn't so easy. Parly had a culture of repeated truancy among certain groups of students. It wasn't unusual for me to go scouting about in the fields or the shops or even to their homes to herd them in. I had to throw in the towel eventually when it turned out I was spending more time on the prowl than in the studio teaching. Of course, what I later realised was that if the classes could be fun, or interesting enough, word would spread and the attendance figures would rise anyway. I learned this from the completely fab PE department where I found two mad but inspirational teachers, Rosie and Gill, employing this technique: Connect with the kids properly and they will slowly come to respect you and turn up regularly. For drama classes, like PE, teamwork is crucial—there's no production if there's no cast. Many would fail if a few let them down, so it was my dearest wish to get the full complement of kids as often as possible, and enable them to feel a sense of achievement when their group pieces were well received.

The actual work, when they turned up, was mindblowing. These kids had real-life dilemmas to draw upon, the likes of which I couldn't begin to imagine. Issues to do with race, religion, weapons, drugs, bullying and abuse were way out of my experience, and yours. We stood agog while a kaleidoscope of their real lives was revealed to us. They put my lesson plans to shame. Some of the kids suggested their own dilemmas, like, 'How do you stop your mother shooting up in front of your younger brother and sister?' or, 'My dad beat me up till I passed out, but I don't want him to be taken away otherwise me and my sister will go into care.' The classes often turned into a kind of group therapy where the kids gave each other advice, and they were the ones who really knew *what* advice, much better than us. So it was proper drama, real-life drama, being talked about and acted upon right there in front of us. Slowly the drama space became a place where kids would come to hang out at lunchtime and after school; I realised they were using it as a sanctuary.

The younger classes, the eleven- and twelve-year-olds, were my absolute favourites. They had only recently arrived at 'big' school and hadn't learned yet to be 'cool' and suppress their excitement for the subject. Their imaginations were bursting, and since there were no awful exams to stunt their enjoyment, they would trip down the stairs like a herd of happy gazelles with their new shoes clacking like hooves on the stone steps. They found it hard to keep still or listen, but when they did we had fantastic adventures, didn't we?

I do remember getting it wrong a couple of times, though. Once, we were doing a big improvisation about Captain Cook discovering Australia, a voyage of adventure on the high seas, on a big old ship built from chairs and tables in the studio. We had lookouts, and someone at the helm (a plastic hula hoop) and tots of non-rum and sailors cooking (chopped lettuce) in the galley and sails (sheets) being hoisted and pirates and all sorts. One particular kid was selected to be keel-hauled as punishment by her bosun for not coiling the ropes properly. We had talked before about what this involved, dropping her over the side and dragging her under the hull (canteen tables) at the widest part of the ship, where she could scrape off the barnacles on the way. So, we tied a rope round her middle and put her over the side, which, in effect, meant jumping off a chair and then scrabbling under the tables. I was distracted at that point by someone in the crow's nest shouting out she'd seen land ahoy! We all busied ourselves getting our galleon into port where I noticed our keel-haul victim sitting, arms and legs crossed, very cross indeed, under the table. I realised we had abandoned her at a crucial moment and tried to encourage my deckhands to 'Quick, pull her up, pull her up, me hearties!' But she sat still. 'No point,' she said glumly. 'I've drowned. And you'll have to tell my mum.'

Another enjoyable idea that backfired on me was when I implemented the 'rule' that all students should bow to me at the start of class and repeat the following: 'We beg you, Your Majesty, to teach us, and teach us *now*!' The kids loved it, and we always had a laugh doing it, it helped to focus them at the beginning of the lesson and it was a kind of unsubtle comedy message that I was in charge. The kids got it, but some of the parents didn't. I was hauled in front of the head for that when one of the parents complained that her daughter was being forced to be my 'subject'. As I say, people develop at different times and some parents' comedy development was severely stunted. Luckily the head had a twinkle in her eye when she reprimanded me.

The head was wonderful, wasn't she? You and I always had a laugh with her. Mrs McKeown. Is that the right spelling? She was a relatively new head but very popular, as I remember. She was very helpful to me when I had to make a crucial decision, and actually, on reflection, her shrewd judgment was the deciding factor in my choosing to pursue a career in comedy.

About halfway through that first teaching year, Jennifer called me up and said she had seen an advert in the *Stage* looking for women to perform at a new comedy/cabaret venue called the Comic Strip inside a strip club at the Boulevard Theatre in Soho. The audition was hilarious, mainly because we only had a couple of seconds of material, from the silly sketches we'd done at college. It wasn't as if we'd honed it into a perfect showpiece, because neither of us had intended to take it any further. I was teaching daily with you; Fatty was living on the dole and spending most of her day drinking and doing crosswords and having a lovely lazy bohemian time in Chelsea with Jobo. Her attitude to the advert was, 'Hey, why not?' So we shuffled along to the tiny red theatre in Soho, to find the auditions in progress, with a man on the stage juggling lobster pots in a comedy way. We did our American sketch, not very well, and lo and behold we were in! Only later did we realise that *any* women who had walked in the door on that day would have got the job. They were desperate for women in the line-up of an all-male comedy group, which consisted of Alexei Sayle, Ade Edmondson, Rik Mayall, Nigel Planer, Peter Richardson, Arnold Brown and occasional others like Keith Allen and Chris Langham. So our qualification for the job on that auspicious audition day was, basically, breasts. We had those in plentiful supply between the two of us, so—result. This meant I was teaching during the day, covering for the head of department who was ill, then moonlighting onstage in Soho, *every* night of the week, meeting a whole new gang of people and, by sheer luck, becoming part of a group at the forefront of what was mistakenly, to my mind, labelled 'alternative' comedy. The Comic Strip show gathered momentum and popularity, and became the place to be if you liked comedy. Robin Williams performed with us, and people like Jack Nicholson and Bianca Jagger were in the audience. It was sort of bonkers and I kept praying that no member of staff or parent of a kid at Parly came to see the show. I don't know now how I found the energy but then I loved being so busy with two very different jobs.

My first priority, though, was the school and getting the kids through their exams. It was while I was focused on this that two opportunities arose simultaneously and sent me into a maelstrom of indecision. Mrs McKeown offered me the chance to take up the post of head of department officially because the present one was leaving. It would mean skipping eight years of hard upward slog, and nearly doubling my salary to about £8,000 a year! Plus, I would be in control of my own little universe doing the job I'd always wanted, and had trained for. At the same time, the Comic Strip, as a group, was offered the chance to go on tour round the UK and to the Adelaide Festival in Australia. If I didn't go, Fatty probably couldn't go—we were a double act after all. Teaching or tour? Career or bit of a lark? That's how I saw it then. I discussed it with you and with my family and with Keith Allen, who I was doing a bit of jig and poke with round that time. His solemn advice was to stay with teaching a hundred per cent.

I was nervous, but I felt compelled to come clean with Mrs McKeown and so I told her about the Comic Strip and my moonlighting escapades. She could have been furious, she was my employer after all, but instead she considered for a moment and reasoned that, although she needed me at the school and it was a tricky transitional time for my students, they would survive it, and she could always find another head of department. She had the foresight and generosity to say that I would probably always regret it if I didn't take the opportunity to go to Australia. She was so right about that, but y'know, if at that moment she had chosen to remind me of my obligation to those kids, emotionally blackmailing me to remain, I would have, because I was so torn and felt so guilty. It's all thanks to her savvy and her mental poise that I went off with my comedy chums Down Under, for some of the best times I'd ever know.

## DEAR DAD,

The Comic Strip was a phenomenon. Peter Richardson was the force that drove it on, and he was—still is—a very talented, determined chap. By the time Jennifer and I joined, it was already thriving. I had never seen a show like it. A repertory of eight or so regular performers with guests each night. Most people on the 'circuit' at that time had done the endless rounds of pub gigs, and back then the burgeoning Comedy Store was the hub of it all. Also based in a Soho strip club, the Comedy Store was ruled by a gong and the idea was to perform five to ten minutes without being gonged off. Considering that a large portion of the audience was drunk and thought they were there to see a strip show, the gong provided a perfect opportunity for them to be cruel. Some acts were gonged off as they walked onstage, even before they opened their mouths. You would have hated it there, Dad; no gentle humour or meandering understatement could survive in that boozy, gladiatorial, competitive arena. It was loud, uncouth, extremely masculine and—consequently—strangely thrilling. Fatty and I were already safely ensconced at the Comic Strip, which was much calmer—no gong, a regular income—but we knew we had to have a go at the Comedy Store for the sake of our credibility. Very few women were performing back then, unsurprisingly. The ones that did were fairly tough with confrontational political material, or very dirty (good dirty, I mean!) or poets. We didn't fit into any of these categories. Our 'material', such as it was, was character-based and chatty. Two people talking about something, that was us. From the minute Fatty and I went onstage at the Comedy Store the very first time, oafish drunkards started shouting, 'Show us your tits!' I just couldn't abide the rudeness, Dad. I switched into teacher mode, stepped completely out of the sketch we were attempting, and ordered them to sit down and be quiet. Oddly enough, it worked and we finished our sketch with no further interruptions. However, we *did* perform it at eight times the usual speed! Maybe it was genuinely better that way.

Life at the Comic Strip was altogether more genial, though, and we were under the watchful eye of Alexei Sayle as our MC. There we could write and experiment with new material. Fatty and I used to try to perform a new sketch each night. She would come to Parly where I was teaching and we'd take advantage of the studio space to work up new material. It took us a while to realise it was the audience that changed each night, so the material didn't have to—in fact we could have a good few weeks to work on it and edit it. Doh!

Jen and I didn't have a proper name for our act at first. We spent ages trying to come up with something vaguely amusing, for instance we seriously considered calling ourselves 'Kitch 'n' Tiles' . . . Oh Lord. Luckily Lexei soon tired of our indecision and eventually one night, exasperated, he introduced us with: 'Ladies and gentlemen, please welcome French and Saunders.' I thought it sounded a bit like a new brand of mustard, but it seems to have stuck.

Although we had joined the group late on, we very quickly felt part of it. It was like having six older brothers who made you laugh a lot, teased you mercilessly and played a bit rough. They all operated out of one big smelly dressing room and we had the little one next door, which we shared with occasional visiting girls. The Boulevard Theatre is in Walker's Court in Soho, right at the heart of the red-light district. Every other building was an 'adult' shop or a strip joint. The Boulevard contained two theatres and a bar.

One of the theatres was ours and the other was a strip club, which we passed through nightly to get to our dressing rooms. I loved the strange mixture of comedy and erotica in that building. On some more surreal occasions, the audiences for both shows would be thrust together in the tiny bar during the intervals. Our lot would be young people in acres of new-romantic ruffles and leather, ladles of make-up, big hair and shoulder pads, and their lot were mainly Japanese besuited men who came over all bashful when they encountered our audience. Two entirely different groups united by their common determination to be entertained. Wherever they are, comedy clubs and strip clubs have virtually the same decor and the same ambience, or so it seems to me. They are usually dark red with a small stage area and an abiding atmosphere of intensity and alcohol. They are fuggy, edgy dens where anything can and might happen. One of the most powerful sensory memories I have of the Comic Strip was the smell. Our dressing room wasn't so bad, or if it was, it was masked by a heady top note of hairspray, perfume and deodorant. The boys' room was a rank, acrid, humming place. They used to sweat a lot with nerves, then sweat more onstage, then take off their stage outfits, hang them up on the floor and never wash them. I think they thought it was unlucky to do so, or something.

Jennifer and I recently returned to the Boulevard to do a gig to help launch some try-out nights for the BBC Comedy Department. I was delighted to see that very funny Miranda Hart was the MC for the night, but other than her, the line-up was still staunchly all-male. And the smell in the dressing room was exactly the same: eau de nervous comedian. Mmmm.

The Comic Strip tour in Australia in 1981 was fantastic. The day we travelled was just like being on a buzzy school trip. We all rejigged our seats on the plane so's we could sit together and drink and laugh for most of the very long flight. The minute we arrived at the Oberoi Hotel in Adelaide, we checked in and agreed to meet five minutes later at the swimming pool. We were in a hotel! In Australia! It had a swimming pool! So much for the supposed cool disdain of young, alternative comedians. We raced down there in our swimmers and, on a count of three, jumped right in with a ferocious splash, and had a shouty freestyle race just like a gang of six-year-olds. I remember that the Pina Bausch dance troupe were also staying there, and were relaxing on their loungers, watching us scream about. There they were, all lithe and brown and elegant and slinkily nonchalant. There we were, all overexcited and goofy and fat and white. And so, *so* British.

I have rarely felt so clearly defined by my nationality as on that visit to Oz. Of course, being a Brit you're a constant joke target for the Aussies, and we had plenty of that. Australians are so full-on. It takes a bit of getting used to, but I found it really refreshing. They do, at least, like to *commit* to everything and rush at all aspects of life with a cranked-up, full thrust of brio. The energy at the festival was swirling and we enjoyed the attention our show was getting. Conversely I witnessed a couple of incidents that shocked me rigid. One such was when I took a cab. I was chatting to the driver, who seemed perfectly friendly. We pulled up at some lights, and found ourselves next to a slumped Aboriginal guy. He was obviously the worse for wear and I was worried that he might roll onto the road into the oncoming traffic. I asked the driver if we could get out and at least help him to the other side of the road. The driver yelled a definite no. He then proceeded to wind down his window, and shouted to the unfortunate man that he was a 'dirty lazy rock ape', and spat on him. The lights changed and we sped off. I was speechless. I couldn't believe what I'd seen. Then the driver tried to re-engage me in breezy chat, as if nothing had happened. I asked him to pull over and I got out and walked back to the hotel in a dazed state of shock. I had never before witnessed one human being relating to another in this despicable way, I didn't know how to process my reaction other than feeling sick. I tried to talk about it to work out what had happened to make relations so bad. I was surprised by the general dislike for the indigenous population from folk I had previously regarded as pretty liberal and broad-minded. People I expected to be humanitarian and left-thinking. People in the arts! I quickly realised that this subject was a minefield, that I was ill-equipped to wander through it until I was better educated about it. I knew the history of relations between Aboriginal Australians and white Australians was tricky but I didn't know just what a total mess it had become. This was evidently a big ol' can o' racist worms and I wasn't about to enter into it until I knew more. Nearly three decades later, I'm still baffled. That was my first revolting taste of racism, which has since reared up many times in my life.

We were very much a team on that tour and my favourite memories are of the social time we spent together, after the shows, the picnic we had at Hanging Rock, the BBQs with giant prawns, burying each other in the sand on Bondi Beach and boozy trips to vineyards.

Alexei used to sing his weird hit 'Pop-Up Toaster' as the finale to the show, and it was the only time all of us were together onstage. Previously the boys had been the only ones to get together for this song but now we were invited and the finale became a girl-friendly zone. That small gesture marked a big difference in the dynamics of the group and gave us a strong springboard from which to launch into, first, the British tour and, second, the following twenty years' worth of Comic Strip films together.

Those films are quite a body of work when I think about it now. I recently did some publicity for the big DVD box set of all things Comic Strip and I realised just what a huge and influential part of my life it had all been. Oh Dad, I wish you could have been around for that. Remember all the Enid Blyton books I read as a little kid and how much I loved them? Here I was years later taking the right royal piss out of them and being part of ground-breaking film-making at the launch of Channel 4. Our first film went out on the opening night. There were plenty of rows about what we were making and complaints galore, but we were basically left to conceive, write and produce a series of films of our own choosing. Pete Richardson and his writing partner Pete Richens wrote most of them, but we all had a go somewhere along the line. We still had the old rep company attitude to making the films. We were paid equally and we were cast equally, which avoided any squabbling. You always knew that if you only had four lines in this film, you might have the lead in the next. We spent a lot of time away together making the Comic Strip films and came to know each other very well. I knew Fatty already of course, but it was great to get closer to Ade, who is quite a dark horse, a complex and profound person, as serious as he is funny. He is a shockingly bright chap, passionate about music and his family. Of all the Comic Strip boys he is the one I feel the most sisterly towards. I'm drawn to his shadows, to the hidden. He knows I love him and he loves me back in the most affectionate, unlimited way. Ade is the most sincere supporter you could wish to have. He has come to see me in virtually every play I've ever done and has always been honest with me, for which I respect him very much. When he and Jen *eventually* got together (after no small amount of nudging, I hasten to add), I felt that they had found, in each other, a proper mate.

Rik I knew and know less. He was probably the person who made me laugh the most. I took any chance to watch him work onstage because he is a consummately funny man. There are rich comedy strata only Rik has access to and he is king of them to this day. He was not only hilarious, but also quite beautiful with the clearest, hugest eyes and the most expressive face. I also have Rik to thank for pointing out, at one particularly auspicious Comic Strip meeting, that Fatty and I were being paid half as much as the boys! We knew nothing of this and so were at once horrified and delighted to be awarded the pay rise. Rik is honourable in that way.

Pete Richardson, or 'Mad Pete', was our Clint Eastwood. Brooding, lip-chewingly anxious and utterly committed to making films. Pete is an unusual man, whose otherness is the foundation on which everything good he does is built. He didn't really seem to have watched telly, so he didn't have the same references as the rest of us.

He liked to mix up ideas, like when we did a film called *Strike!* It was about a writer, played by Lexei, being asked to write a movie for Hollywood about the miners' strike. So, there were lots of levels—as much a comment on LA gloss as it was a chance to do impressions (Jen as Meryl Streep as Mrs Scargill, me as Cher playing Joan Ruddock, Pete as Al Pacino as Arthur Scargill etc.), as it was a satirical, topical romp.

Pete was always prepared to push us as far as he could to get 'the shot'. Both the crews and ourselves worked ridiculously long hours, sometimes sleeping on the set, sometimes for only six hours before we were back on again. I can't imagine doing that now, or even asking a crew to do that, but we all loved it and loved him, so no one really minded. We were young, no one had kids or hatchback cars yet, and anyway, why would we want to go home or have days off when all our best mates were on the set?

A lean and handsome fellow, Pete was wound up as taut as a coiled spring and would lose his temper as quickly as he would become helpless with childish laughter. I was on the receiving end of his irritability once when I took against a last line he'd written to a film I was in, called *Susie*. My character, the eponymous teacher, was, not unusually, a bit of a nymphomaniac and had bonked virtually every guy in the story. In the last scene, after romping with Ade in a wheat field, I was in an ambulance. The scene required Susie to flirt with the paramedic to prove how irrepressible she was, even in the face of death. It was very funny but the last line was awful and lame, and at the read-through weeks earlier we had all agreed (including Pete) that it needed a rewrite. The moment came to shoot it, the light was fading and it was the last shot of the day. I asked Pete for the rewrite. He ignored my request for the new line by looking at me when I asked for it but pretending not to hear me, just looking straight through me. It was a very weird, defiantly stubborn thing to do. The atmosphere in the tiny ambulance with all of us crushed inside was electric. Everyone knew this was a stand-off. We were all in such close proximity, the tension was hard to ignore. On Pete's command, the ambulance started to move, and he called for 'Action!' I did the scene exactly as written, until the very last line, whereupon I paused, looked at camera and smiled. All in character. But I did *not* say the awful line, whatever it was. Pete shouted, 'Cut!' and then said, 'You seem to have left off the last line, Dawn,' in a strict geography-teacher sort of manner. I repeated that I was not going to say the line, that it was bad, and would let the whole film down, as we had *all* agreed. He called for the shot to commence again. 'Action!' Again, I stuck to the script till that last moment, then I said, 'La la la la la la la.' Pete shouted, 'Cut!' The ambulance stopped again and Pete asked me to step outside to 'discuss' it. The crew were silent. I climbed out of the ambulance onto the country road where Pete was waiting, red with rage. The veins on his neck were visibly pulsating his fury, and his eyes were blazing. The 'discussion' very quickly escalated from some pretty muscular accusations to full-on loud streams of obscenities (from both of us) until suddenly Pete started to poke me hard in the shoulder, screaming the repeated chant: 'You will say it! You will say it!' I replied, just as loudly: 'No I won't! No I won't!' The poking became pushing, pushing became shoving, shoving became tussling which took us off the side of the road into a field of corn where we had a proper wrestle (hilariously echoing the scene we had just shot in the wheat field). A genuine fight, an actual ruck! Eventually we both stood up, brushed ourselves off and he hissed one final seething 'You will say it!' I so much wanted to stand firm and respond with an equally decisive 'No I won't', but the spat had unnerved me, and woken up the latent girly girl inside me who decided it was a good time to cry. Bugger and bollocks! Just when I wanted to be tough. So the tears streamed down my face, while Pete had a quick drag on a roll-up and then went back to the ambulance. I composed myself as best I could, readjusted my wig and climbed back in. I sat in my place. There was no air, just tension, and I said, 'I will say the appalling line, Pete, but then I will go back to the hotel and leave immediately.' We still had four more days of shooting so I knew that would scupper the film. He looked me straight in the eye and said, 'Action!' I started the scene, but the lovely cameraman, my friend Peter Middleton, stopped the filming and told us that the light had gone, and on top of that, my face was too blotchy from the crying. Pete gave up with a groan, and we drove back to the unit base in a silent huffy huff. Once out of costume, I headed back to the hotel, hell-bent on packing and leaving. Of course, Pete came into my room to placate me and eventually we sat on the bed apologising to each other profusely. We went to the bar for a drink and, naturally, continued the filming the next day. Incidentally, the last moment in *Susie* is the first take, the look to camera, the smile . . .

The episode served to confirm to me Pete's complete passion for our films. He is one of those people who is nine parts genius to one part knob, and he is one of my closest friends. I almost love the knobby part of him the most. Not his actual knob, you understand, just the part that is a bit of a knob.

Nigel Planer was always a really good actor. He is now also a poet and a writer, but back then I only knew him as an actor, and as a colleague, of course. He was the most fastidious of us all, employing proper techniques to find his characters—like getting the shoes right and caring a lot about the costume, and learning the bloody lines! He is attentive to his health and well-being and he didn't get drunk as often as many of us. Nige is kind and sensitive and willing to take a risk. He can play small and subtle and real as easily as he can choose bigger broader strokes, as he did in *The Young Ones*, which meant that he could play literally *any* part. And he did.

Alexei is a force of nature. I smile immediately when I think of him. Back then, he enjoyed his reputation as a larger-than-life, prickly firebrand. An angry political comedian. A spitting, shouting, foul-mouthed commie ranting on about evil social workers and the loathsome middle class. Oo-er, he was a bit scary. True, his stage persona, which was a heightened representation of his real self, *was* aggressive, but hey, this was the era of punk and retro-ska and two-tone and skinheads. Lexei was all of that and more. His physicality is the first thing you notice. Sort of angry panda. He is Russian in physique. Muscular and hairy and yet strangely light on his feet. He's a good dancer, agile and very musical. He is highly intelligent, widely read, good at art, good at writing, good at jokes, good at driving. He is an intriguing mass of lovely contradictions; he seems to be a big sulky bear but actually he has great patience. He looks like a fighter but is in fact a peacekeeper. He appears to be angry when in fact he is often perfectly content. He is thought to be motivated mainly by politics, but actually he is just as comfortable with the silly and the surreal stuff of life. He looks like he wouldn't give a toss when in truth he is a thoughtful and attentive friend. He is a tart for a laugh, and when he does laugh, it's big and round and full. Consequently he's the sort of person you *want* to make laugh. You want his approval, his generous warmth wrapped round you. He is quite shy at times and so it can take some trial and error to creep into his affections, but when you're there, it's grand.

Ben Elton was unbelievably supportive to us, always encouraging us to try new material and to be brave. He was prolific, coming up with acres of his own new gear every night, and absolutely no one matched his writerly ability. Passionate, determined and hard-working, he forged his own unique path with breathtaking force and commitment. He didn't consider himself an actor, I don't think, but he is certainly one of the most powerful stand-ups I've ever witnessed. As for his writing, his huge successes both in print and on stage speak volumes about how popular his particular brand of incisive comedy is.

Robbie Coltrane joined us for the films and very quickly became a regular because we couldn't face filming without him. He made us laugh like no one else on set. His big chippy Scottish style was so different to everyone else. He played around a lot on set and yet on camera he is clearly in utter control. He was the one who had big feature-film-sized presence.

Keith Allen was a reluctant member of our team. He was torn between enjoying the work and the company, and his ever-demanding need to appear cool. Being part of our group was so *not* cool. He was a solitary, renegade, lone wolf of a figure and the thought of an association with us was so obviously abhorrent.

However, he was, I think, very fond of Pete, and when he deigned to take a part, he was always very good because he is such a talented actor. Keith's desire for a reputation as a bad boy was a key factor in his demeanour. He decided, somewhere along the line, to be a threat, so that's how he presented himself. He relished the disruptive power of turning up unannounced at the Comic Strip and setting up his band without so much as a by-your-leave while somebody was mid-act. It must have been exhausting to be so Keith Allen.

Arnold Brown was one of my favourite people of that time in the eighties. He's a Scottish comedian in a tidy brown suit and tie. He had been an accountant for most of his adult life and was giving comedy a go at a much later age than the rest of us. He stood out. In a good way. His comedy was gentle and self-deprecating. He spoke quietly. He was then—and still is—a fabulous oddity and a truly funny man. He didn't join us on the films because he didn't really do the acting thing—his strength is live stand-up.

So, Dad, that was the line-up of people I spent the best part of twenty years working with. People who are, for the most part, still my good friends today. People who helped shape who I am, and who directed me towards a greater understanding of just how bloomin' lucky I was to have such a great living. All that stuff you and Mum used to gently tell me off for, like being loud and showing off and being attention-seeking—guess what, Dad? That's my job!

## DEAR DAD,

When the live Comic Strip show was at its height, people I admired came to see it, people you knew of and appreciated, like Peter Cook and Michael Palin. I was stunned every time I was introduced to folk such as these, my comedy heroes. I remember sharing with Michael Palin the fact that we had received a bad review in the London listings mag *Time Out*, which I found very hurtful. He told me about the initial, appalling reception he'd had from the press for virtually every job he'd ever embarked upon, especially for *Monty Python*, and said to take heart, which I most certainly did. I have since endeavoured to avoid all reviews of any live work, until the very last night when I enjoy a little ritual of reading 'notices' with a glass of rum when I get home, after the party, when the whole shebang is put to bed. By this time the reviews can't hurt me or influence me or even puff me up, and if there is anything useful there for me to take forward to the next job, I can take it in. Reviews for TV work are different. The job is done, the show is made, and usually my involvement is over by months. I will have watched it, maybe edited it, and so I have already formed my opinion of what I like or dislike about it. A review is handy for the audience perhaps, but even then you know very quickly if an audience enjoy something, because they continue to watch, or not, and that's reflected in the viewing figures. The response is that tangible, that quantifiable. I learned a big lesson when the first series of *The Vicar of Dibley* received one memorably vile review which was especially personal about me. When the same series was repeated later in the year, the exact same fool wrote a glowing review claiming that Richard Curtis and I must have taken heed of his previous comments because this second (so he thought) series was much better, blah blah . . .

Anyway, sorry, meandered off-piste and up my own bum there. I was telling you about the various remarkable folk who came to watch us at the Comic Strip. One night, I heard very loud, distinctive, deep, rolling laughter in the audience. It was constant, throughout the show. This was the kind of big infectious laughter you crave when you're a comedian. You hunger for it. Someone generous-spirited was *really* enjoying the performance. We all felt it, and it was lovely. That person turned out to be Lenny Henry. He and Chris Tarrant were in to see the show, and especially to see Fatty and me because they were doing a new late-night, adult version of *Tiswas* called *O.T.T.*, and were looking to cast some women. Don't get me wrong, I loved *Tiswas* but I found Len a bit loud, too broad, for my taste. They came backstage. I don't really remember much about it except thinking what a huge, impressive-looking man he was. To this day, he remembers every word of that first meeting and can repeat them back to me, as a kind of torture, doing a far-too-accurate impression of the much younger, misguided me who was at pains to explain that, 'We take ages to write our stuff, yeah? And I'm not sure we could be involved with a show where we aren't, like, totally in control of it, we're just not going to do that, OK? And we don't want to be token women, right, that's not what we are, we're not just token, we actually *are* women and that's not really the point anyway, cos we're performers, not women, and anyway, if there's gonna be women in bikinis we wouldn't honestly be involved anyway. Cos it's demeaning. Sorry.' Yes, that is how much of a pretentious arse I was back then.

I didn't come across Len again till maybe a year or so later when Alexei was in a TV show called *Whoops Apocalypse* which was filmed in front of a live audience at London Weekend Television. I went along with my friend Angie to support Lex and, while we were waiting in the queue, I felt a tap on my shoulder and it was Len with his friend Davey who had also come to see Lex. Of course, by then they were good friends because Lexei had gone on to do *O.T.T.*, the show I had been so very sniffy about. So, we started chatting in the queue and ended up sitting next to each other in the studio. Throughout the show, I witnessed the close-up phenomenon of that big laughter I had heard before at the Comic Strip. Len loves comedy. He is the most effusive audience member I've ever known. If something tickles him he surrenders to fits of joyous laughter, longer and louder than anyone. It's a wonderful thing.

Something else, parallel, was going on that evening. My friend Angie was getting on *very well indeed* with Len's mate, Davey. They were flirting a-go-go. After the show, it was obvious the two of them wanted to go on somewhere else, to have a drink, so really, Len and I tagged along like lemons. Or is it gooseberries? Well, like some kind of tart fruit anyway.

We went to a bar and had a few drinks then Angie suggested we all went back to the flat I shared with my friend Gaynor in Paddington. She was the leaseholder and I was the tenant. It was small but smart, with a balcony that looked out over leafy Cleveland Square. Gaynor was a precise, neat person, which is why the flat was so lovely and clean. Gaynor was a teacher, but she was much more diligent than I'd ever been, and went to bed early each evening with ear-plugs in to get a good night's sleep. I was always tiptoeing around in a concerted effort not to disturb her. I enjoyed living in that flat, but I never entirely relaxed in it. Sometimes Gaynor went home to her family at weekends and I knew she wasn't there on this particular night, so it would be OK for the four of us to go back.

By the time we tumbled into the flat, it was pretty obvious Angie and Davey were hot to trot, and before long they had commandeered my bedroom. Len and I were left to chat on the sofa with the giggles and shrieks of their fun time as the soundtrack to our evening. We were both a bit awkward at first, but then, slowly, we chatted and relaxed. It was so revealing, Dad. I was witnessing a whole other side to him, the quiet, bright, interested person he really is. Quite serious and, even more unbelievably, shy. We talked and talked and talked. It must have been four in the morning or so when we realised the bedroom had been silent for some time. They must have fallen asleep in there. We were also pretty weary, so I pulled out the sofa bed in the living room, and we camped down on that. It was all so innocent. Two gooseberries taking comfort in each other's company, that's all.

By morning, I was in giant love with him. In proper, big, marvellous, astonishing love. It completely shocked me, Dad, how in tune we suddenly seemed to be. I hadn't experienced anything like it before. Most wonderful of all, he seemed to feel the same and didn't want to leave.

The other two had to be up and out but Len lingered on and I made a huge fry-up with the full works. He has never forgotten this breakfast, he remembers exactly what was on the plate and where!

He didn't leave the flat for the best part of a week. The morning of the breakfast, I was due to write with Fatty, but my head was in a spin and I totally forgot about the arrangement we'd made.

She knocked on my front door and, seeing that it was her through the peek-hole, I opened the door half an inch and hissed, 'Go away!' She said, 'Don't be silly, let me in, what's going on?' I replied, 'Can't explain, can't work today, fallen in love, go away, sorry,' and shut the door! Never before or since have I been so rude to her. But Len and I were genuinely in a love-fug, and I didn't want anyone to interrupt it, especially *not* Jennifer who I always have regarded as an utter beauty and far preferable to me for any guy. Somewhere in my insecure mind, I thought that if he met her, he would surely love her instantly, and I wanted to hang on to him even if it were only for a few more deluded days. Luckily we are close enough, Fatty and me, for her to overlook this strange behaviour, and frankly, in the Book of Jennifer, a day where work is cancelled is a good day!

In that week, Gaynor got used to seeing Len around the flat. It wasn't easy because the flat was small and Len himself isn't exactly petite. In fact, let me describe him for you, Dad. He's about six foot two inches, very powerfully built, with a big chest and strong arms. His arms are amazing. They're long and wrap round me easily and that's no mean feat. He's got big hands and the best legs I've ever seen on any man, long and sturdy, with much might in them. He is a sort of reinforced-looking person physically; he is solid and strapping, which I love. When you're a big woman like me, you need a man who won't break. Len won't break. And his face, Dad, his lovely face. It's broad and open with appley cheeks and the most excellently expressive eyes, and a beautiful soft mouth. If he wants to, he can do things with his face that would persuade you to believe it's made entirely of rubber. He can move it about like a human shouldn't be able to, which led me to believe that perhaps he *wasn't* entirely human. Usually, though, his face is in repose, and he maintains a lovely calm, quite serious demeanour. So much so that people often shout at him,

'Cheer up, Len!' The one thing he can't do with his face, though, is lie to me. If I need to know something, anything, and I ask him, his face speaks volumes he can't control. Of course, that doesn't mean he hasn't got or can't keep secrets, but if asked outright, he is an open book. It's like he's brimful of honesty and it overflows onto his face all the time.

That's Len physically, but Dad, what a tiptop chap he is. It sounds so trite to say I wish you could have known him, but I do so wish that. I don't waste my time dwelling on it but there is no doubt that, apart from Gary, you and Len have been the most important men in my life, and I would have had so much pleasure witnessing you discovering each other. I think both of you would have laughed a lot and I also think you would have been quick to spot the softer, perhaps more troubled places in Len, and you would surely have been a good listener for him. But, hey-ho, that ain't how it turned out. The really wonderful thing, Dad, is that I often hear your advice in my subconscious, so maybe vicariously you are still influencing our lives in some significant way. Who knows? You certainly set the bar for me, as so many dads unknowingly do for their daughters. I knew I wanted a man who was as kind and supportive as you, and I certainly have that. Len is a gentle soul. He hates conflict and will do anything to avoid it. He is extremely romantic and continually surprises me with new ways to express his affection. He writes the most fantastic, moving poetry. He is a voracious reader and consequently has a really broad palette of knowledge and taste. The same applies to music, which is in every molecule, every atom of his body. He especially loves hip hop but he will listen to Radio 3 and get passionate about a symphony and listen to only that for a week. He loves blues, soul, jazz, rap, reggae, swing, grime, dance, jazz-funk, pop, rock, not country so much but Dolly Parton is allowed, not indie really, definitely not Dean Friedman (he 'lost' all my DF albums in one house move. I still haven't forgiven that). He can listen to acres of Brian Eno mood music and other strange soundscapes, or chanting or liturgical music, or world music, while he reads. He plays the piano really well. He has an amazing voice. He has a band. He has great taste in suits. He always carries a bag on his shoulder that is heavier than his own body weight. He loses stuff all the time. He's clumsy and he breaks things. He doesn't like pets but he has loved all of our dogs more than he cares to admit. He has enormous feet and has to have his shoes made. He smells great. He gets very dry skin and rubs coconut or almond oil all over.

He can do a very funny dance featuring his privates. He loves movies. All kinds. He hates *Big Brother*. He is open to learning new stuff. He actively pursued the education of which he'd been deprived, starting when he was in his twenties, taking O levels while doing a summer season in Blackpool. He followed that with an Open University degree and now he's doing an MA. He writes all the time. He is a great dad. He strives to be a better person, always. He investigates his inner, spiritual life. He loved and still loves his beloved mum. He values his family. He loves wine. He loves food. He cooks. He loves Sundays. He loves kissing . . . and stuff. He loves his daughter till he's in pain. He doubts himself. He is not afraid to fail, and learn from it. He drives too fast. He gets lost a lot. He leaves the cooker on. He leaves the back door open (burglars, ignore please). He gets lonely easily. He lives and breathes stand-up comedy. On occasion, he's quite grumpy. He will help anyone. He's a Commander of the British Empire. Sometimes we refer to him as 'Commander'. He can ride a horse. He can play tennis. He will NOT swim until he's ready. He's curious. He loves *The Sopranos*. He fancies Judi Dench and Sinéad Cusack and Jessica Lange. He does the school run with no complaint, ever. He reads Harry Potter books aloud, doing all the voices. He knows lots of good jokes. He is a great, great man. A big, great, dignified, bright, beautiful man.

The first time I saw him perform, in about '82, I'd gone with him to a gig at an army base and we were held up in traffic en route so he was late. The crowd of squaddies were baying for his blood and were chanting racist stuff. It was a horrible, aggressive atmosphere. He came on to the tiny stage and within five minutes he was utterly, masterfully in control of a potentially explosive situation. Anyone who continued to pipe up was very quickly dispatched with a clever put-down. It was totally his room and he made them laugh solidly for an hour, until they were calling for encores. Of course, I'd seen plenty of comedians work, but all the lads I knew worked in comedy clubs where the audience were usually receptive. Len's apprenticeship was in working-men's clubs and nightclubs where he was eighth on the bill so he had to learn to win people over and be heard above the din.

Eventually, after a few messy moments, when we both had to extricate ourselves from relationships we were in, we 'came out' as a couple to our friends and family and did lots of introducing. By then, I was living in a house in Goldsmith Avenue in Acton, with Fatty. Len was much better known than me, and that's when I got my first taste of unwanted press attention when a couple of photographers loitered around in front of the house for a week or so, taking pictures of us coming and going. I found it excruciatingly embarrassing. I still do. He's always handled it better than me. He is obliging and courteous but brief. The only time I've seen him lose it was when press people were shoving our daughter and he couldn't abide that. What good dad would?

A key moment in those early days was when Len took me home to meet his mum, the remarkable Winnie, or 'Momma'. What a woman! As tall as Len, she towered over me—the whole family did. It was like walking into some kind of Jamaican episode of *Land of the Giants*. Len is one of seven siblings. The eldest is Hylton, who is an impressive six foot six, a benevolent, soulful fellow. Then comes Seymour, a true Jamaican with a passion for his homeland, always with a new plan hatching, cooking up some ism or schism. Then there's Bev, the spiritual, bountiful mother figure, the respected, wise older sister, the focal point in the family. Then Kay, the generous, ambitious, determined, tenacious, career-minded, spunky sister. She was the one who made Len pretend to be Paul McCartney, her hero, so's she could get hitched to him in a play wedding when they were eleven or something. Then comes

Lenworth George, the first to be born in England. Then Paul, the younger brother, who lives in a small town outside Dublin, who is funny and observant, a brilliant chef and a writer. Then the baby, Sharon, or the 'Queen of the Mad Bitches' as she likes to be known. She is a supremely bright young woman with a sharp tongue, coruscating wit and a degree in minxiness. And that's the Henry Posse, who were headed up by Momma, an extremely powerful force of a matriarch.

She told me that in the fifties she had travelled alone on a boat to England, following the lure of the promises made to so many Jamaican people, of amazing jobs and fortunes to be made in the UK. She lived in grey old Shepherd's Bush, and shared a room where she slept in the bed at night and someone else who did night shifts slept in it during the day. Imagine, coming from the bright warmth of Jamaica where fruit grows on trees by your back door, to rainy Shepherd's Bush where it doesn't, and where she had various menial jobs. She put in long hours of backbreaking work and suffered a great deal of abuse on the streets. In the end, she headed up to Dudley to settle near family members who had already secured jobs in factories there. She went without, saved her wages and gradually, one by one, she brought all of her Jamaican-born kids over to join her. She gathered her brood and her husband to her and went on to have three more children on British soil. She had always worked hard, and I loved the evidence of that in her huge hands. She made me feel welcome. Momma ordinarily spoke with a strong Jamaican accent but she sometimes used to temper it with careful, posh pronunciation to help me understand her. When I first knew her, she used to get the best china out for me. That nonsense stopped pretty quickly when I, thankfully, passed the Momma test. She was an amazing cook and she sat me down at her table where I was presented with 'mi dinna', which was a plate piled about a foot high with rice and peas, curried goat, salad, plantain, okra, fried chicken and cucumber, with slices of buttered sourdough bread on the side and a 'nice-coppatee'. I did not hesitate. My task was clear. Eat it all or leave now and never return. The grub was delicious, and I set about it. A clean plate—save a few bones. I passed. I was in.

Momma and I always got along. So long as Len and I were happy, she was happy. She visited us many times, and I have the most touching films of her wandering round our garden on Len's arm. This film is precious because she was diabetic and when complications with ulcers later set in, both of her legs were eventually amputated and she was confined to a wheelchair. She was an enthusiastic born-again Christian, and when I think of her, I remember her in her smart dresses, her Sunday best, wearing her special hats like crowns, beatific in the bliss of her beliefs. Her faith was awesome, solid and unflinching, and sustained her through a prolonged and painful illness. We would visit her in hospital where Len and Billie, who was then about seven years old, would read aloud from the Bible while I moisturised those strong unforgettable hands. The same hands that held Billie when she was a newborn and were bigger than the baby's whole body. We held her hands often while she spoke, without fear, about her holy delivery into Christ's hands.

I sometimes wonder how it works after death—does this notion of a welcoming committee exist? If so, were you on Momma's welcoming committee? Was there a heavenly reception for her with a soaring celestial gospel choir, where she was offered her favourite drink, Guinness punch, made with Guinness and condensed milk and nutmeg, where she could sip on Saturday Soup and eat hot peppers from the jar and where she would have her beloved Jesus?

The day I missed you more than any other day, Dad, was our wedding day. It was bloody fantastic! By then we were living in Sinclair Road, Shepherd's Bush, in our first ever joint home, a little basement flat that backed onto the nuclear train track. We had a brass bed and a cat called Aretha who was the Greta Garbo of cats. Gorgeous but unavailable. Len bought her for my birthday, which was a selfless thing to do since he openly loathes pets, especially cats. I very much enjoyed teasing him about 'the correct way' to introduce a cat to its home. I told him that a tried and tested way to stop her running off was to smear butter on her bum and lick it off. His face crinkled into a rugose mask of horror as he digested this information. I explained that it was just replicating what the mother cats did, that it would be over quickly, that everyone who had a cat did it and to hurry up. He considered it for a good minute and was about to do it, but I couldn't keep a straight face long enough to see it through. I also knew I wouldn't want to kiss him if he did that.

Anyway, the day of the wedding drew close and the excitement mounted. I had, stupidly, decided to embark on a ridiculous diet. For some reason, I didn't think it was OK to be a fat bride. I had started a rigorous regime which involved paying a fortune to a Harley Street charlatan, getting injections of what I later realised was probably speed, taking orange and green pills (probably more speed—I didn't ask) twice a day and only eating meat and citrus fruit. By the day of the wedding, October 20, 1984, my body had really eaten itself. I was down from a bonny size 20 to a starving size 12, and my breath stank from all the rotting meat inside me. Yeuch. Len had asked me to stop and questioned who I was doing it for. He reassured me that he loved me the way I was and was concerned for my health. Still, I continued till the actual day, and my friend Sue who made my dress (an inspired combination of shepherdess and whore, realised in champagne satin, net and ribbon—well, it *was* the eighties) had to take it in twice.

On the day, I got ready at our flat. The mums, so different, tall and short, chalk and cheese, went off in a big car, the BF and the bridesmaids—Len's nieces Babette and Donna—went off in another, and I was left for the last few single-girl minutes with my lovely brother, who was being you, Dad. He poured us both a gin and tonic and urged me to have a few calm moments to gather my thoughts. He wisely reminded me to clear my head and focus on what it was really all about. It was about me and Len, and he told me to look at Len and to be in the moment and remember what I was saying and why and how very important it all was. It was such good advice, which I always try to pass on, because otherwise my memories of that day would have been full of unimportant nonsense. Instead, I remember Len. And his face. And how happy I felt, how in love.

We raised a toast to you, Dad, and off we went, with him at my side walking me up the aisle in St Paul's Church, Covent Garden, towards my old school chaplain, Reverend Gordon Cryer, with the soaring, joyful strains of the London Community Gospel Choir ringing round the beautiful Christopher Wren building. I was aware of all that was happening, but all I saw was Len.

Yes of course a pigeon flew in and shat on people. Yes of course the price was still on the bottom of Len's shoes for all to see when he knelt down, yes of course we were interrupted by the din of the street performers and fire-eaters in the piazza outside, and yes of course Len stood on the train and ripped the dress. That's us, we always get it a bit wrong. We don't do perfect, but I tell you, Dad, that day was as near perfect as I ever want a day to be.

I stored my bouquet, with its traditional sprig of myrtle from the Bishops Garden at St Dunstan's, in the freezer at home while Len and I went off on honeymoon to Kenya. On our return I brought it down to the Blue Monkey church in St Budeaux in Plymouth, and I quietly laid it on the tiny little plot where your ashes are, for you.

## DEAR ALLA,

Thirty minutes ago I was on my feet clapping like a greedy seal at SeaWorld, celebrating your encore at the Hammersmith Apollo. Who would have thought that twenty-five years on 4,000 people would roar for the triumphant return of Yazoo? It was so touching to see you hand in hand with Vince, lappin' up the love, and what a bloody lovely night it was. I was expecting a comforting retro meander down electro-pop lane among a bunch of my-agers, only occasionally straining our middle-aged knees and rising to our feet to bop along to favourites. Not a bit of it. I'd forgotten how sharp the art is when you two are together. Of course, being a techno freak, Vince is on it with state-of-the-art music technology. Something about his cool mastery brings out the supreme soul mistress in you, to cut across his electric soundscape with your vocal super-nature. The walls were thumping and my ears were full of swirling noise. Everybody was dancing and sweating and remembering. It was fabulous.

We all tried to sing back at you the songs you gave us, singing so loudly you would be in no doubt how much we know and love them. Some particular songs we wanted you to sing only as the backing track for our tribal rendition, like 'Only You'.

I watched you in the environment where you are most at home. So easy in front of a mike, being a sexy mofo and exploring the extraordinary shining excellence you are blessed with—your phenomenal, phenomenal voice. Are you ever as amazed with the sound it makes as I am? Does it surprise you when you reach so far inside and find those notes that no one else can make? You are a vocal archaeologist, finding treasures in hidden places and digging them up for our pleasure. Is it right that notes are made up of three other notes? Someone told me that once, and tonight it struck me that what I hear with you is all three parts of each note. The top, the middle and the bottom are all there in one glorious whole, a consummate resonance.

Quite besides the utter pleasure of the gig, I watched you with awe. I feel massive pride when it comes to you, and I am properly honoured to be your pal—maybe because I admired you before I knew you.

We met, I think, at a party at the Wag Club in Soho in the eighties. I don't know why I was there, though I have a vague memory of the party being something to do with Elvis Costello, who we both knew a bit. Anyway, I remember spying you across the room and getting very overexcited at the nearness of you. After much unsubtle staring, you eventually returned my glance and then we sort of flirted with each other by having a kind of competitive funny-dance-off from a distance. How divine it was to enjoy those surreptitious moments with a kindred spirit. No one else was aware of what was going on, just us, in our own little bubble, displaying our comedy feathers to each other like peacocks. It wasn't long before we spoke and we haven't stopped speaking since really, have we? Two forceful birds with plenty to say, that's us. Our time together is so limited that sometimes we speak simultaneously so's we can cover more ground. I speak, you speak; I also listen, you also listen—just all at once! We don't always agree, and we aren't afraid to flesh out a difference of opinion at considerable volume. You are moved by much that happens around you. Maybe that's why your lyrics are so insightful—you notice everything. I am less precise, more of a bletherer, keen to experience everything quickly, soon, now—usually without thinking enough about it first. I am a doer, you are a thinker.

We have been good counsel for each other through many phases, I think. There have been so many times when you have been the one who says the key, opinion-changing, intelligent thing which provides the pivotal moment. The change of the mindset. When Len and I went through a rough patch, I talked endlessly with my mum, my BF, Fatty, my brother, all of whom were supportive and helpful, in so many ways. But *you* were the one who spoke to me about what forgiveness really means. How it isn't something you withhold for power purposes if you truly love someone, about what a weight it is, how much lighter you feel the more of it you give away. Give it freely, you said, Not recklessly. Make sure to learn from what's happened, but don't amass a backlog of fury because it will kill you. Be generous and understanding and kind. That's what you told me. Don't judge, just help each other to heal. It was the only thing that made sense to me. You also reminded me of what a remarkable man he is, just at the moment I could have tipped myself, for an inviting wallow, into a vat of Len faults. You nipped that in the bud, which was a tad frustrating at the time. We all enjoy a good self-pitying moan, don't we? But you knew it wouldn't help and would only serve to extend the unforgiving time. The dangerous time in any conflict where one person takes a higher ground from which to do their superior judging. You reminded me how much Len loves me and you cited literally hundreds of instances when you had witnessed that love. You drew a picture for me of a man I adore, a family I belong in, a world I've invested my life in. Then it was obvious that I should fight to keep it and make it stronger. To concentrate on the important stuff and to ignore the crap. And that's what I did.

We continually share a lot about our kids, you and I, and help each other by reminding ourselves that we are benevolent, well-meaning women just trying to do some good parenting in the face of the frightening tsunami that is teenagehood. On many occasions, we have come to agree that teenagers are selfish little buggers who are, for all their faults, the fundamental point of our lives, the basic underpinning of our reason for being here. *They* are what has made us different and better. *They* are the leaven that has raised us up from being the selfish big buggers we were before they came along! If we still over-loved them like it was easy to do when they were teeny, the inevitable separation would be so traumatic we would surely collapse and die from utter grief. This way, their behaviour forces us to create a distance, to slacken the ties and allow the disconnection. They will still be moored to us, just by a long, long, long, long rope.

We often spoke of how much we would love to work together. We had already had a few little jaunts, like the time Fatty and I appeared in your video for 'Love Letters' and when I shook my tail feather on your 'Whispering Your Name' video. One of my greatest thrills was coming onstage with you at the Albert Hall and shoogling around you like a demented eejit. But as well as all these daft times, we wanted to find a proper opportunity to work together, didn't we? We embarked upon an extraordinary adventure which resulted in us both appearing in a West End play called *Smaller*.

Do you remember the brief? We wanted to commission a piece from a tiptop writer, something that gave us both a chance to flex our muscles (if only we had muscles—I haven't had sight of a muscle on this Mr Bumble-ly spherical body I live in for years!), and operate slightly outside the ol' comfort zones. We knew that without being pretentious the play had to speak to people our age about the complex nature of the relationships women have inside a family. This was an area we had foraged about in before, fully aware that it was hazardous, stony ground.

To begin with, we imagined it would be a two-hander. Simple and stark. Very early on I called Kathy Burke, my great friend and the most knowledgeable person I know about new writers. She always has her ear to the ground for formidable new talent. Her first instinct was the person we eventually approached, Carmel Morgan, who was part of the award-winning writing team propelling *Coronation Street* towards top plaudits at the time. So, I met up with Carmel, who, by the way, wins the prize for best swearer I've ever met. What a potty mouth. Top. She told me straight away that she had an idea for a play that had been brewing for years, involving a mother and a daughter. The mother, whose life was becoming slowly 'smaller', was in the grip of a powerful degenerative disease, and the daughter was the carer. Carmel suggested that she could well add a sister into the mix, your part, and that would bring another dimension she hadn't considered before. Plus you would write songs specifically for the piece. Alla, the songs you brought to that first rehearsal were unbefeckinlievable. The best I had heard you sing or write for ages. Both of us were delighted when Kath agreed to oversee the writing process and direct the play.

Kathy is a careful and thorough director, who encouraged us to sit and talk about the play for a whole week or more before we got to our feet. By that time we had June Watson on board to play the mother, we had classes on lifting a disabled person, we learned about the wasting disease our mother character had, and we talked endlessly about the confines and the freedoms of this explosive triangular relationship. Sometimes she was strict with us, insistent that we face our worst fears and deal with them in what was a truly emotional roller coaster of a play.

I remember the day we realised that there was need of an extra song. A really important song that you would sing in the funeral scene when finally the two warring sisters are united in grief for their dead mother. It was the very thing you had asked us not to do. To put you under pressure to write a song quickly. You left on the Friday with an air of grump to propel you into the weekend. On the Monday you played us the Catholic funeral hymn you had written in two days, with your buddy Pete Glenister. Alla, that was one of the most splendid moments of my life. What talent. The hymn, a quiet then soaring paean of exquisite love and beauty, a gift from a daughter to a mother, and most importantly a holy and sacred song, reduced me to tears every night I stood next to you and heard it.

I had one other blissful moment like that with you. Do you remember when we went to Jamaica on holiday? You and Malcolm and me and Len. What a laugh. I remember when we went on a lazy raft trip. Len and me in front. You and Malcolm on the raft behind. We floated aimlessly down a river in the gorgeous sizzling heat. All was calm and silence till you were taken with an irresistible urge to sing. You sang out, clear and strong, filling the air with magic. I couldn't see you but I could hear you, your beautiful voice providing the soundtrack to a heavenly, perfect moment.

I knew then that, as you often tell me, I would always 'love the bones of you'.

## DEAR LEN,

Really, this book should be called *Dear Len* and simply be one big long love letter to you. It's hard to know how to sum up everything I want to say to you in one letter. We have been married for twenty-four years now, and we were together a couple of years before that, so half of my whole life is you. You. You. Obviously there are things I can't and won't write about in these pages because we both, but especially you, are quite rightly very private about our life together, but when I think about who you are to me, and what I want to say to you, it is, essentially, thank you.

THANK YOU for filling out the all-purpose, multiple-choice questionnaire I devised for you when we first met. This helped me to ascertain whether you really wanted to eschew all opportunities of bendy dancer girlfriends and go out with a Weeble such as me. It also told me whether you could take a joke or not. You could.

THANK YOU for getting down on your hands and knees and helping me to trim the carpet at Gaynor's very clean flat with nail scissors (all I had) when you had stepped in the cat-litter tray and walked the poo round the whole flat, and she was due home in twenty minutes.

THANK YOU for doing eighty-six astonishingly accurate impressions of different famous people saying Happy New Year to me on New Year's Eve, and for knowing that, for some reason, New Year makes me gloomy and I needed cheering up.

THANK YOU for being the kind of person who fell for the lady in the shop's patter and therefore bought the most expensive ring with which to propose. Thank you for not having a suitable face to go with the moment, so twitching like a demented Disney rabbit in anticipation. Thank you for not minding in the least that the ring has spent twenty-four years in a safe because it is beyond hideous.

THANK YOU for not chucking me when I took you to a romantic place I told you was 'magical', which turned out to be an old railway carriage set into the dunes on a beach in Cornwall where we were both very cold because it was winter.

THANK YOU for taking me to Jamaica to meet your wider family. For not minding when I laughed a lot after you were trying out your best Jamaican accent and the man you were asking directions from just looked and said, 'You is an Englishman.'

THANK YOU for doing a five-month summer season, two shows a day, seven days a week, at the end of the North Pier in Blackpool, to pay for the wedding.

THANK YOU for insisting that all birthdays are celebrated, even when I can't be arsed. I remember when you insisted I go to Le Gavroche posh restaurant on my birthday despite my many protestations that I was too knackered to go out because I was filming. I begged you to let me stay at home and celebrate with a candle in a Big Mac. You persuaded me to go because when my supper arrived under its silver dome it was revealed to indeed be a hamburger with a candle in it, Gavroche-style. It was delicious and the kitchen staff were buzzing with excitement—they'd never ever served a hamburger before.

THANK YOU for buying me a white Pagoda soft-top 1964 Mercedes.

THANK YOU for putting up with the many pets, all of which you hated to begin with, and only three of which you came to love. Aretha the Cat, Delilah the Dog and Dolly the Smaller Dog are winners, but Hale and Pace (goldfish), Rodent (hamster), Oscar (guinea piglet who was eaten by Delilah the Dog on Christmas Day, the day he arrived), Holly (replacement guinea pig bought on Boxing Day), Hoppy (rabbit), Dracula (vampire rabbit) and Stickys 1–23 (stick insects) were *not* beloved by you.

THANK YOU for opening up a world of music to me. Music I would never have listened to if I didn't know you. Thanks for all the tapes and CDs you've made, especially those which were for special reasons, like when I did *Smaller* with Alla and every song had something to do with small or little, or songs to celebrate anniversaries, or songs with stories, or songs with gags, or songs that start with talking, or songs that start with the letter D.

THANK YOU for not minding too much when, embarrassed and horrified by the price, which we could ill afford, I returned the very early model of a computer you'd bought me as a birthday gift in 1983, to the shop. Sorry I've never learned to use one yet and thanks for printing things out for me or even occasionally typing things for me. I will catch up eventually. Probably. Will I? No.

THANK YOU for being such a loving son-in-law to my mum, and

starting jokes 'My mother-in-law is *so* nice', '. . . *so* genial', '. . . *so* supportive', and so on. I guess I felt the same way about your mum. The only time it was dangerous to be around them was the regular Christmas Turkey Tussle. We used to cook it very slowly overnight, remember? My mum likes it to be moist but fairly plain with perhaps an onion up its bum for flavour. Your mum would sneak down, yank out the onion, slam in some peppers and a pineapple and cover it in rum; two hours later my mum would creep down and remove all that and replace with an Oxo cube; your mum would later discard that and add chillies and sweet potatoes, and on and on all night. The wars of the mums. Whoever raped the turkey last was the victor, leaving the other one to pout and sulk, lemon-lipped, over the Christmas dinner table. Yuletide joy!

THANK YOU for offering, without hesitation, to let me put our house up as collateral to get the loan to start my big-girls clothes business, 1647 Ltd, with my African partner, Helen Teague, in 1991. Still chugging along all these years later, we haven't made a penny, but we have provided lots of big girls with some decent clobber that fits their booty-licious bums!

THANK YOU for never complaining when endless streams of friends and family come to stay, often bringing further, even more unwanted pets into your life.

THANK YOU for understanding the nature of my very close relationship with my cousins Keiren and Ellie and knowing that I never want to be without them, and so allowing our door to be open to them at all times of night and day. Sometimes people are placed in our lives for a purpose and these two have a hundred per cent been given to me so that I may learn about the profundity of family love. Thing is, you see, I looked out for them a bit when they were younger and now they return the favour and look out for our kid. There is a natural symmetry in it all.

THANK YOU for your patience and understanding and total commitment to the endless rounds of heartbreaking IVF failures we endured together, while quite often simultaneously celebrating yet more arrivals of new babies in the lives of our chums. The sneaking in and out of clinics, often at night, to avoid press interest. The discoveries of various problems, on both sides. The support we gave each other. The awful, painful injections you had to administer to me at home and your sweet crinkled face, so reluctant to hurt me with them, but so determined to try and make it work. The isolation of not being able to speak about it to others, for fear of alerting the media. The miscarriages and the grieving. Two of us quietly forging ahead together in our great yearning for a baby. The giving up. The reawakening. And then, the uphill adoption process. The hours of interviews, the reports, the questions, the counselling and the minute scrutiny of our marriage by strangers. The intrusion. The breath-holding and, eventually, the utter joy. Thank you so much for being such a mensch through it all. We sailed together in one small boat on this most private and personal sea of troubles, safeguarding each other throughout. We brought a baby back to a united and happy home.

THANK YOU for being such a genuinely great dad. For breaking a mould and being the kind of dad you had no example of, for making it up as you went along. For holding fast through terrible twosomeness tantrums which lasted ten years and immediately turned into tricky teenage tantrums, most of which appeared to involve the exact same dialogue.

THANK YOU for saying, 'Every day, clean slate.'

THANK YOU for doing so much devoted parent stuff during all those nights I couldn't be there when I was onstage. I've counted up the evenings of my absence from bedtimes since Billie turned up. It's over two years' worth. You had all those evenings on your own with her and you never once complained. Thanks for giving her that unquestionable security, the surety of her dad's love. I, for one, know just how important that is as a foundation for every other relationship she will have. She doesn't know it yet, but she will.

THANK YOU for telling me the truth when, like most marriages, ours was buffeted by a tornado. There's a reason we vow to love each other for better and for worse. It's because there will always be a *worse*. Otherwise how do you know what the better is? Or the even better? We work apart a lot, we meet interesting, attractive people and they are interested in and attracted to us. Some stuff's gonna happen and mostly, so long as no one is hurt or embarrassed, it's unimportant and ignorable. I genuinely believe that. We are, none of us, robots or perfectly perfect people. We are flawed and weak and tempted. Often. What compounded the situation in this particular instance was that certain facets of the press decided to whip up an infidelity maelstrom. You had made some grave errors of judgment, yes. It was frightening and humiliating to be doorstepped in the night by two journos in macs who I was convinced were police. You were driving home from a gig that night, so when I saw them I thought that they were here to tell me you had died in some awful crash. Instead, they were at my door to gleefully dump their buckets of sleaze and Schadenfreude on me. Oddly, I was relieved! I thought you were dead. You weren't dead; you were just careless and a bit daft. No one wants to hear bad news like this, and no one wants the entire country to hear it, and worse, no one wants the entire country to hear a bizarre, and in so many instances, fabricated version of it. BUT we are in the public eye, and when you trip up, unfortunately everyone's going to know about it. In an effort to lure us out of the silence we chose to keep, several newspapers ran supposed 'Exclusive Interviews' where we were both apparently quoted verbatim. Since neither of us has ever spoken to anyone about it, those brazen lies really shocked me. Meanwhile, we were forced into a strange utter-cards-on-the-table kind of congress at home, both of us. We needed to know every single incident, harmless or otherwise, from sixteen-odd years of marriage, so's we could be armed against the bomb attack. The most remarkable thing was that, once again, our natural instinct was to pull tighter, towards each other, unite, hold hands and walk through the storm together. There was no single moment when separation was a possibility. We needed to remind each other what was worth fighting for, and my darling Bobba, you are worth fighting for. The most terrible thing about the whole palaver was that it had all come at a time when you were already feeling a bit midlife-sad, your mum had died and you were in the grip of that slippery old snake, grief. You had thrown yourself into too much work, both TV and touring, and you were knackered. All of this humiliating shit publicity on top of already feeling shit made life shit to the max. That's when you had a total wobble and I knew you needed to talk to someone, to work out what was really wrong. That's when you went into the Priory, which was the last place on earth I would have wished for you to be, believing like so many others that it was a guilt hide-out and spa for frazzled pop stars. Of course, the reason so many people go there, mostly unfamous, is because it's frickin' good, simple as that. The main doctor who was recommended to work with you couldn't treat you unless you went there, and we particularly needed his help. The Priory is not a spa, it's a hospital, with many people on the edge of their lives for one reason or another. You didn't have an addiction, but you certainly had a life-toppling, debilitating crisis of utter, all-consuming sadness and it was awful to see. You firstly needed sleep, proper big long sleep, and you needed to be safe in the hands of someone who could help you unpick the mental mess you were in. You are emotionally bright, you could put yourself back together so long as you could understand why you fell apart. Which you did. Quite quickly. It was amazing to witness you logically fitting your personal jigsaw back together. You love reason, you get it. It was a fabulous example of proper help for emotional and psychological trauma. I so wish this was the avenue my own father had been able to take. He struggled on alone with his private torments till it was all too much and he sought his own, tragic way out. You didn't. You took quantum leaps of courage and examined your flawed self, you drew conclusions and made decisions about how to live your life to avoid that sadness as much as possible. That, for me, has been the most remarkable, courageous and bloody brilliant achievement you have had, in what is a life chock-full of achievements, frankly! I bloody loved your fortitude and your humility and your openness at this frightening time. I saw your phenomenal backbone righting itself and I saw you walk upright again, in the face of much scorn and derision. I also thank you for, at that time, going to the homes of everyone on both sides of our immediate family and sitting them down to tell them what happened by starting with 'Look, I've been an arse . . . I wonder if you can forgive me?' By dint of that humility, you is a proper man.

THANK YOU for all the poetry, the letters and the cards. You haven't let a month of our marriage go by without reminding me of something meaningful. You *always* point me towards the bigger picture when, oftentimes, I'm busy doing frantic colouring in with felt-tips in the corner.

THANK YOU for not giving me surprise parties. I would *hate* them.

THANK YOU for always working so hard to keep our family (including the many and various dependants who you also never complain about) ticking over. You are so selflessly generous, it sometimes takes my breath away.

THANK YOU for showing such strength in the face of the inordinate amount of racism you experience. Knowing you has shown me a whole raft of mainly insidious, quiet racism that I had no knowledge of before. Those tiny, constant snidey jokes at industry gatherings, like 'I know the invite said black tie, Lenny, but that's taking it too far, sonny' from a much respected older comedian. Strange how the reference to you as 'sonny' is the more painful dart in that jibe. I remember you being interviewed on radio by a presenter who consistently referred to you as 'this little black boy from Dudley' throughout. Stealth racism. The references to me in the papers as 'his blonde girlfriend'. I've only ever been blonde once, for three weeks. It meant 'his *white* girlfriend'. Of course, we have had the big showy stuff too, the excrement smeared on the front door, the scratching of racist names on every panel of the car, the lit petrol-soaked rag through the letterbox, starting a fire on our doormat at 3 a.m. Luckily, I smelt it in time. The many letters with lurid racist obscenities sent to both of us. The most memorable of which came to you at a gig, threatening to kill you after the show because 'you are a filthy cone'. Racists can't spell so well, it seems. Remember when a Jiffy bag dropped through our door and it contained a broken tile with the image of a knight on one side and on the reverse it said, 'You have been visited by the Ku Klux Klan'? No we hadn't. We hadn't been visited. Visitors make themselves known. And stop for tea and cake. People who drop something hateful through your letterbox and scurry off into the night aren't called visitors. They're called cowards.

THANK YOU for knowing that, although I am usually resolute, sometimes my strength fails me. Thank you for sensing when.

THANK YOU for coming to Cornwall with me. It's not your home, it is mine. You will inevitably be the 'only black in the village' and you are a long way from the beloved bustle of the city. We will, of course, have dollops of that, when we need or have to, but mostly we will be together quietly, in what I genuinely believe is the most beautiful place on earth, and where I truly belong. It didn't help, did it, when we were first thinking of settling down there and I took you to Padstow to seduce you with delicatessens and great pubs and great music and art and stuff. My heart sank when locals regaled us with stories of their famed annual celebration of 'Darkie Day' . . . where they black up and dance in the streets! I knew it would be difficult to reverse out of this arcane cul-de-sac with any iota of reasonable explanation. I tried a pathetic attempt at: 'It's ancient, it's to do with fertility, it's not racist, it's tradition.' 'Yes,' you replied, 'traditionally racist'. We had some silence. Then I ventured: 'It's a bit like the Black and White Minstrels—you know, sort of odious and outdated but with nil malicious intent.' I had you at that. The Black and White Minstrels? Hadn't you been the first genuine black man to perform with them? I know you hate being reminded of it. I know it's a hideous blip in your past, I know we don't have it on telly any more for VERY GOOD REASON, and Cornwall might be some way behind when it comes to catching up with PC ancient rituals.

But . . . you said, 'OK, so what do I do on annual Darkie Day? Do I have to stay indoors? Or will I be burnt for the amusement and general warmth of the gathered townsfolk?' We have yet to see, but anyway thanks for risking life and limb.

THANK YOU for loving me so very well, and for being an allround tiptopmost chap.

## DEAR SARAH,

I've never had a sister, but I always wanted one. Badly. Then my brother married you and suddenly I had one!

You are quite simply the best person he could possibly have chosen. He is such a spontaneously emotional man, and when he was younger, I sometimes feared he would let his impetuosity get the better of him and he would choose someone wildly wrong. But he didn't. He chose you. And you are so perfectly right. Your tolerance, your patience and your optimism are the gifts I'm so grateful to you for, because inside your love, my brother has come to know and trust how loved he truly is. He carried a heavy load at too young an age from the moment our dad died, and with you he can share that and be lighter. You have been there, side by side with him, through lots of potentially scary decisions. I know your support gives him courage. Can I thank you, too, for making my favourite niece and nephew and letting them come out to play with me so often? How sublime it is to know that we will all be there for each other whatever happens. (Unless of course you murder someone, in which case I won't be there for you at all. I will show no mercy or forgiveness and I will reject you and all your family in a heartbeat. Otherwise, I'll be there for sure.)

I thank God for you, and I love you.

Your sister-in-law.

# DEAR RICHARD,

Been watching the news? Big hoo-ha about the possibility of female bishops for the Anglicans. Obviously there are those for whom the notion is abhorrent, a monstrous offence against God. They're probably the same protestors as last time, who then couldn't deal with the idea of female vicars. Remember them? They were the ones who were furious about our series, quite often sending me tracts about the sin of women being allowed to speak in church *at all*, citing verse thirty-five and the like. I could never have anticipated receiving hate mail from Christians.

Of course, they were a tiny minority and I guess their fear was that you might write something funny enough or popular enough to normalise this new situation in the way that television so easily can. In that respect, their fears were well founded, because I think that's exactly what you did. You and Paul Mayhew-Archer together posited the idea of female priests as a natural and sensible state of affairs. Mainly, Geraldine just got on with the job of ministering, didn't she? Along with plenty of snogging and chocolate scoffing of course, which ought surely to form a large part of any decent vicar's life. Thanks, by the way, for all the choc. I know it didn't often figure in the original plot but was crowbarred in as an added component for my delectation. Some actresses might have objected to the large quantities that were required to be eaten on camera, but in that respect, I am extremely fortunate because I have such an active metabolism that I can scoff tons of chocolate and it doesn't seem to show on me at all . . .

I think it was some time around 1992 that you first mooted the idea to me of *The Vicar of Dibley*. I think you'd been to a wedding where a female lay preacher had officiated in some capacity and I knew you thought it made total sense, seeing as it's nearly always our mums we run to for support and guidance in times of emotional or personal need. Anyway, I remember you giving me an outline of an idea which I think I read on a plane. I remember thinking that this was a very Richard Curtis kind of a project. The idea of a parish council full of odd bods, most of whom were no doubt based on people you knew or knew of when you were living, as you were then, in a tiny little cottage with wild roses round the door in a village in Oxfordshire. I couldn't understand why quite so many men of your age working in telly lived in Oxfordshire until it eventually dawned on me, like the dolt I am, that, of course, you'd all been to Oxford and sort of stayed there. A bit like modern day lost boys.

At the time, I didn't really have much to do with you Oxbridge lot. We at the Comic Strip regarded you as the privileged, old-school-tie brigade who would, naturally, be propelled into top jobs at the BBC because all your mates and forefathers and everyone you ever knew were already there. Although founded in a certain amount of truth, this theory was laced with bitterness and chippiness, which didn't make for great relations between you, the toffs, and us, the proles. You, of course, ignored the general wrath, in true Curtis style, and crossed the divide when various of our tribe like Rik and Robbie Coltrane appeared in *Blackadder* and when almost all of us did various bits 'n' bobs on the very first Comic Relief stage show and subsequent video, and every Comic Relief event ever since.

I've always admired you, Dick, for being such a persuasive and soothing negotiator. It is virtually impossible to deny you anything. I'm sure anyone who's ever worked with you and for Comic Relief will agree with me. It must be exhausting for you to be so constantly pleading, scrounging favours and explaining, on behalf of others, but only you can do it with such panache. You launched Comic Relief (with Len alongside you), and it certainly would have crumbled without you continually driving it forward.

I first encountered your irresistible, devilishly clever powers of persuasion after I had read that first brief document about how you envisaged the series. I could see it would be rural and green and British and pretty. I could see why all the characters were extremely funny. Except mine, who appeared to be a sweet, kind, wise, nurturing sort, around whom everyone's stories and troubles would swirl. She was to be the fulcrum, the heart of the village. All good—'cept where's the cockin' jokes? I wondered. I couldn't conceive how the lead in a sitcom could be so bloody nice and still be funny. My personal favourite sitcom characters were big ol' monsters, full of pomposity like Captain Mainwaring or misguided snobby twots like Basil Fawlty, or louche fashion victims like Edina and Patsy, not nice, kind vicars like Geraldine. Do you remember meeting a few times in your rosy cottage to talk it through? That was the first of many times I saw a glimpse of that stubborn chap who lives inside you. You ran out of patience with me and my procrastination quite quickly and sent me a list of other, more talented and available actresses including Miriam Margolyes, Alison Steadman and Julie Walters. That certainly jolted me into affirmative action. Thank God I said yes, because honestly, making that series for the next thirteen years with you was some of the most fun I've ever had.

For me, coming to work with you every day was the ultimate lure. I suspected it would be fascinating to watch you sculpt the scripts with Paul, at close hand. I suspected I would learn a lot about teamwork and tolerance and keeping an open mind. I suspected I would laugh all day. I suspected we would forge lasting friendships and feel part of a loving, generous family. For all of that, and much more, my suspicions were confirmed. What I *hadn't* anticipated was how much I would come to love you as a true, loyal, decent, understanding, lifelong bosom pal.

Let me remind you of some of the lasting memories from what were, for me, golden days:

- Meeting the legend that is the wondrous Reverend Joy Carroll, one of the first young women to be ordained and your inspiration for the character, and bombarding her with intimate questions. Watching her officiate with great tenderness at a funeral. Going to her wedding. And having her on set to advise us and be our ally. Having her blessing. Realising that knowing her is a blessing.

- The day Paul Mayhew-Archer brought his teenage son to work on 'go to work with your dad' day. How much Paul wanted to impress his son, so he leaned back on his chair with his arms behind his head at the read-through table in an effort to appear cool and thoughtful and writerly. Of course, he leaned too far and toppled right over backwards. His son was consumed with embarrassment (as was Paul) and informed his father on the journey home that he was a total 'f—wit'. Henceforward Paul carried that nickname. He is, needless to say, nothing of the sort.
- You, Dick, running in after every take, sometimes with a cushion strapped to your aching injured back, nervously twanging an elastic band between your fingers and grinding your teeth, with some inspired new thought or suggestion to try.
- Giggling helplessly with James Fleet.
- Seeing Trevor Peacock's willy, when he did his Full Monty routine.
- Listening to Roger Lloyd-Pack trying valiantly, but failing, to master the tuning of 'Oh Happy Day'.
- Delicious gossiping with Emma Chambers.
- Listening to John Bluthal's old stories about Spike Milligan.
- Sly conspiratorial glances with Gary Waldhorn.
- Liz Smith's utter inability to pronounce the word 'taramasalata' in front of the audience.
- Getting plastered in thick gooey chocolate custard from the chocolate fountain episode, which had to be the last shot of the day. Getting in the shower to clean up and realising when I got out that everyone had gone home and I was locked in at Pinewood.
- Being stuck in a strange Dibley amber, age-wise. I celebrated my fortieth birthday as Geraldine when I was in fact forty-seven, and you even suggested, for a brief, deluded moment, that I should have a baby with my new 'husband' when in the grown-up real world I was forty-nine. Ta for the compliment but I'm a broad

who welcomes age and all its creaky, dry and hairy wonders.

- Having the following shouted at me more often than I can cope with:

  'More tea, Vicar?!'
  'Hey, Vicar, where's Alice?!'
  'Let's see your knickers, Vicar!'
  'Hey, Vicar of Dimbleby!'
  'Hey, Vicar of Doubleday!'
  'Hey, Vicar of Dribbley!'
  'Hey, Vicar of Drimbly!'
  'Hey, Vicar of Dumbledore!'
  'Hey, Vicar of Dublin!'

- Filming in beautiful Turville, under the shadow of the windmill on the hill. Finding out the windmill was the one in *Chitty Chitty Bang Bang*. Doing a dance of excitement.
- Finding out a *Sun* photographer lived in a cottage on the green and constantly took photos of punch-line moments and gave them away.
- Noticing all our kids growing up as they regularly visited the set over the years.
- Hearing my then four-year-old daughter explain to one of the extras that her 'mummy is a vicar' and her 'daddy is a chef'.
- Me getting an actual crush on Peter Capaldi. Then me getting an actual crush on Clive Mantle. Then me getting an actual crush on Richard Armitage. Then me getting an actual crush on Johnny Depp. Me realising I am an actual dirty harlot.
- Having fab directors like Ed Bye and Gareth Carrivick and Dewi Humphreys who returned again and again.
- The undeniable holiness we all felt when we shot the Christmas episode where the Christmas story was told in a farmyard, ending up with Alice giving birth in a stable. There had been lots of jokes all day, all evening, then suddenly, at midnight, when the little newborn was handed to Emma for that final shot, we were silenced by how sacred it all was.
- You, Dick, being unable to speak in the presence of the

divine Miss Kylie Minogue when she came to do a guest appearance.

- Receiving written requests to perform christenings, weddings and exorcisms for actual people in their actual lives!
- Witnessing the regular 4 p.m. doughnut and cake tray turn up on the set, and by 4.02 p.m. every crumb would be inside a Turville resident rather than the intended crew or cast member.
- Not being able to continue filming for some time when Trevor Peacock as Jim Trott spoke his astonishing lines about wanting to have sex with a poodle. Neither the cast nor the audience could continue until we had a little break to compose ourselves.
- Great parties. So much dancing. So much vodka. So much errant misbehaviour. I remember doing some extremely over-enthusiastic dancing to Shakira's 'Hips Don't Lie' during which I actually dislocated my hip and had to walk with a stick for four weeks. So thanks, Shakira—the bald fact is your hips *do* lie, madam.
- I very much remember at the wrap party, after the final episodes, saying a tearful thank-you and last goodbye to everyone. Then, as I was leaving, the producer came up to me and said, 'Just so you know, Richard's asked us to store the set . . .' So, Dick . . . what was I saying about those female bishops . . .?

Bless you.

## DEAR ALFRED,

I think I would have missed out on my foray into the world of opera if it hadn't been for you. When the call came through in the autumn of 2006, from the Royal Opera, I thought it was some kind of elaborate joke. Please would I consider being in the Donizetti opera *La Fille du Régiment*? Me? Just for one tiny deluded, pathetic second, I found myself feeling flattered that perhaps, just maybe, someone had overheard me singing and realised that my voice was an undiscovered jewel, a hidden treasure, raw, naive and beautiful. Who could have guessed that I possessed such a latent, undeveloped well of brilliant virtuoso talent? Nobody could have guessed. Nobody did guess. Because, of course, in reality my voice is remarkably average. Below average really. Average to poor. Pants, in fact. My voice is pants.

Did I ever tell you about the day this was proven to me in the most humiliating and painful way? The producer and the director of *Mamma Mia!* asked if I would consider being the funny fat one in the film version. I hadn't even seen the stage show at this point so I hurried along to take a look. Never before have I felt like such a pooper at a party. The audience were *lovin'* it and, apart from the great Abba music—that's a given—I couldn't connect with it at all. I didn't get why the broad humour was so appealing, and I didn't feel remotely emotional about the story. Yet the entire rest of the audience most certainly did. There's no doubt it has a magic, the show. Anyway, they told me that Meryl Streep was on board to play the main role. Wow—Meryl Streep! Big heroine of mine. She's got great taste, maybe I was wrong about the show, maybe it's utterly brilliant and I'm the only person in the world who doesn't get it? So, drunk with the idea of working with her, and also just a little bit actually drunk, I agreed to take the next step, which was a voice test.

I was quick to explain that I am NOT a singer, that all the singing Fatty and I do in our shows is written by us and arranged by our trusted musical-director chum Simon Brint (ex Raw Sex band leader and all-round genius) and that he goes to great pains to fix everything so's it's in the right key for us and so on. In other words, he makes the music fit our very limited ability. *It* comes to us, so to speak. With the Abba music, I would have to go to *it*. Everyone knows and loves this music. It would be awful to sing it badly. I voiced all of these concerns and they reassured me that with Björn in charge of the music, even if I bellowed like a cow in labour, they would be able to cope. But they encouraged me to have a safe little plinky-plonky no-strings friendly singalong with their musical director just to check. I agreed to this, with the proviso that we do it somewhere ultra private. I pootled along to HMV and bought an *Abba's Greatest Hits* and punished the air in my car with some pretty confident renditions for a week or so. I hate it when you're caught singing your head off by other drivers on the motorway, as I often am on the M4, and you have to pretend your gaping jaw action is all down to dreadful toothache and start looking at your mouth in the vanity mirror, don't you? Oh, don't you? It's just me then.

Anyway, the day came to meet the music guy. The audition was arranged in a 'quiet' room at the very top of the Palace Theatre in Cambridge Circus. The lift was broken so we walked up the 8,462 floors to the top. A small, pert man, he bounced up the stairs ahead of me. A big, fat, lumbering woman, I hauled myself up behind him, puffing all the way. By the time I reached the top I knew I would need to sit down and recover with a Kit Kat and a cuppa for about three weeks, without moving, never mind singing. He introduced me to a bevy of bright-eyed chaps working in the office next door to the room we were to be 'private' in. A couple of the dandies made comments like 'Ooh, we're so excited', 'Can't wait to hear you warble'. I asked Mr Music if we really would be 'private' as requested. Yes, of course, he assured me. We went into the small room, which had a sofa and a keyboard. I sat on the sofa and started wall-to-wall nervous fast gossiping so as to delay the awful moment. I noticed that I could hear the guys next door quite clearly and deduced that the reverse must also be true. I thought we might start with some gentle scales, a little warm-up perhaps, but no, he sat at the keyboard, invited me to share the piano stool, and off he went pounding away at the keys, and before I had time to draw breath, we were away, one song after another, 'Dancing Queen', 'Take a Chance on Me', 'Chiccyteeta' or 'Chicken Tikka' or whatever that one's called. It was fast and loud and furious. Each one was worse than the last, and the first was appalling. For some reason I don't understand, not only did I sing dreadfully, but I sang worse than I ever have before. Worse than dire. An entirely tuneless, croaky, wailing, drony caterwaul of a noise. Horrible, horrible, horrible. All credit to Mr Music, he was tenacious, he was trying to remain optimistic, but very quickly I sensed he was beaten. After half an hour or so of this excruciating slaughter, the punishment was over and Mr Music bade me farewell with tears of pain in his eyes reflecting the damage to his ears. I rushed out, offering a hasty 'Bye!' to the poor witnesses next door, most of whose hair was standing on end and all of whom couldn't look me in the eye for shame. My shame.

As I beat a speedy retreat, I turned my phone back on to see if there had been any calls, and it was ringing with my agent's name flashing on the tiny screen. 'Love, it's not going to work out.' 'But, Maureen, I've only just left—' 'It's just not going to work out, love—' 'Maureen—?' 'It's not going to work out, love . . .'. So that was that. I can't sing. At all. Fatty was very supportive when I told her about the horror of it all, and in defiance, we decided to sing 'Thank You for the Music' at the end of our show on tour every night. We sang it loud and proud and I was gradually clawing my way back out of the pit of zero confidence voice-wise and was really enjoying performing it with gusto until someone told me there was a reference to the song in a review which said we were 'hilariously out of tune'. I surrender to the gods of music, to Pan, to Apollo, to Björn, Benny, Agnetha and Frieda. I am not your servant or your handmaiden or your daughter. I am your jester. That much is clear.

Anyway, sorry, Alfred, back to the opera. Of course they didn't want me to sing. No, they wanted me to take a speaking part, a comic cameo. Well, I had no reference for such a proposal so I called you toot sweet. You are, after all, my encyclopedia of all things opera. I love our ritual. You call up, you have tickets, it's *vital* to see this particular production because of this singer, that director, this conductor, that composer etc. etc. I come to your flat in Fulham, we eat scrambled eggs and smoked salmon, we listen to a recording of said opera, you educate me about the story, the background and, my most favourite part, the gossip. Which diva is shagging which divo. Who was booed off at La Scala and had a hissy fit, all that stuff. You are not only the font of all high information, you are the deliciously dirty dealer of the low. That's what makes it all the more intriguing for me. I can then watch the opera appreciating not only the soprano's excellent coloratura, but also her bravura bosoms, knowing which divo has had his mitts on 'em!

So, do you remember when I called you and told you about the production? 'Who is in it?' you asked. I told you. Juan Diego Flórez is the tenor, Natalie Dessay is the soprano, Laurent Pelly is the director, and so on. 'There is only one word to use regarding this decision, Dawn,' you said, 'and that word is "must". You MUST do this. If you do not do this I will kill you. No, seriously. Kill you. A slow, lingering, merciless death. Understand?' Message received. You went on to explain that these people are the *corps d'élite*, prodigious talents at the top of their game, and the time was right, this particular opera hadn't been performed at 'The Garden' since Pavarotti and Joan Sutherland did it in the sixties. It's rarely staged because the tenor has to hit nine extremely difficult high 'C's in one demanding aria and there are very few singers alive who can do it well. Juan Diego is one such singer. And what's more, you explained, he's Peruvian and drop-dead gorgeous. Sold.

What a bloomin' roller coaster! Opera is such a different world to the kind of theatre I am used to. My part was in French so I had to attempt to conquer that, which I never fully did, so we decided Franglais was a good, funny, alternative route. To be directed in French was quite an experience. I had to make myself understood with gesture and posture, which is suitable for big opera in a big opera house. I was also aware that my part was tiny and that a great big muscly machine of a production can't wait about for one fat ol' comedienne to arse about. It needed to be grand and slick, and funny. The day comes eventually, when, after endless costume, shoe, wig, jewellery, make-up tests and fittings, you actually get on the stage for a dress rehearsal. Finally, the many different elements who've been rehearsing in many different rooms come together at last. That's when the chorus are there to join in and when the singers sing out for the first time. That's when my head was nearly whipped off with the full force of the sheer blast of power of their huge, impressive voices. It was fantastic!

Luckily, the show was well received, and no one seemed to mind me, the impostor, too much. When opera audiences love a show, they *really* love it. We would bow our way through ten curtain calls with the entire opera house on their feet. It was utterly thrilling and I'm so glad I took your advice, Alf, to do it. I made some good friends, and I had an onstage seat every night to hear and see such phenomenal talents at their peak.

During the run, I kept complaining that I would finish my time at the opera house having never sung a note. Surely, I ought to be entitled to *one* note?! Then I'd be able to claim for ever that I had sung onstage at the Royal Opera House Covent Garden. My final exit each night from the stage was a big huffy flounce off, accompanied by a loud, angry roar because my character had been thwarted. It comes about three minutes from the end. So, on the very last night, instead of roaring I decided to sing that last moment of fury. I waited, I waited. The moment came, and I sang out loudly, one note, one word, '*Merde!* '—and exited. Yes, ladies and gentlemen and my beloved Alfred, I have indeed sung onstage at the Royal Opera House Covent Garden. I thank you.

## DEAR DAD,

We've never been a family where any one person's achievements matter more than anyone else's, so I really want to make sure you know about all the amazing stuff Mum and Gary have done.

Gary, it probably comes as no surprise, has been adventurous. He's travelled a lot, especially in his twenties and thirties. He would work hard for a couple of years to fund each next journey, where he would have phenomenal experiences—for instance, actually building the main part of a hospital in a leper colony in India, or living with and helping Tibetan refugees. Then, when he'd exhausted his funds, he'd return and put his nose to the grindstone again. He's worked mostly in housing, in London and in Devon and Cornwall. At one time, he was finding housing for people on probation, and he was later the instigator of an amazing 'Foyer' scheme in Plymouth. He'd seen a version of this scheme working on the Continent, where young homeless people are given a place to stay and access to an IT centre and careers advice which they can use to springboard them into jobs and consequently further housing. They are given counselling and lifestyle advice to help them bridge the gap between home and work. It sounds like the sort of thing you would have been involved with, Dad. Perhaps he is more of a chip off the old block than we know. He has married a fantastic woman, Sarah, with whom he has had two gorgeous kids, Hannah (the Heavenly) and Jack (the Lad). He is a great dad, for whom family comes before everything. They live happily in Cornwall, where Gary and Sarah both worked hard in housing—until recently, when Gary made a huge decision of which you would be so proud. He decided to change his life completely. He runs the café that overlooks Burgh Island at Bigbury on Sea in Devon. He is his own boss, he cooks the grub and makes the decisions. I've rarely seen him so happy. Who knows what he'll do next. He is willing and open and creative. Gary knows himself and has listened to his heart. He's still fiery-tempered, always fighting for the rights of the underdog or the unheard. He is remarkably unmaterialistic and generous of spirit, and he is a great listener. Certainly for me and for Mum. He loves his dog, his family and his friends, he loves to sail, he loves to read, he loves music, and chickens and pigs and food and Cornwall. Tangible happiness is his motivation and I really think he's done that rare thing and found it.

Mum rose from the ashes like a phoenix. She turned her grief and her loneliness and her fear into a snowball of energy that gained and gained momentum. One Christmas, maybe 1982 or so, I noticed she had an unusual amount of cards on her fireplace. As I read them, each one was more effusive than the last: *Dear Roma, you are the light in my darkness, To Roma, thank you for saving my life*, and on they went. When I asked who these people were, it turned out she was opening her home to allcomers, glue-sniffers and heroin addicts and alcoholics alike, to have a place to come and talk. I was a bit concerned for her safety, and I felt that she would be more use to people if she had the proper training.

Well, Dad, she was amazing. Mum, who had left school at sixteen, took herself off for, firstly, a foundation counselling course, then further qualifications to enable her to help the people she most wanted to. She was gripped with a desire to change what she saw was useless practice and bad law when it came to young mothers with drug problems. The typical process was that, once the mothers were discovered to be addicts, the social services would immediately take the children into foster care until the women had been through rehab and proven they were clean. It all had to go through the courts, so very often this process could take years, during which the mother and children were separated. Mum's theory was: keep them all together in a safe place. They must recover and heal together because the kids need to witness their mum's recovery in order to trust her again. Meanwhile, alongside the rehab, the mum also gets cooking and parenting classes, the kids go to local schools and they all work together to slowly, carefully feed the family back into society when they're ready.

In order to achieve this, Mum had to find the funding to buy properties that could be transformed into safe flats for the families, with a rehab centre attached. She somehow raised the cash, through a mixture of charity, fundraising and the local council, to set up, with a colleague, the Trevi House Project in Plymouth. The ongoing success rate was so good that the government consulted with them to use their method as a blueprint for other projects around the country. As if that wasn't astounding enough, she went on to acquire the magnificent ex-admiralty Hamoaze House at Mount Wise and with a dedicated team she created a drop-in centre there for drug and alcohol abusers and their families in Devonport, Plymouth, which has been a huge success. She has worked tirelessly for other people's benefit for thirty-odd years now, and when she retired a couple of years ago, the city gave her a posh lunch to thank her for all she'd done. And, like Gary, she's done it all quietly. No hoo-ha. I took your lovely mum, Grandma French, along to the official opening of Hamoaze. I saw that there were four generations of our family there. If ever a family have been committed to the improvement of a city, the Frenchies have been to Plymouth. Your city, Dad.

Mum lives happily alone, by the sea in Cornwall, on a cliff overlooking a fishing village. She says the view and the air are healing. She's very high up. I think she feels closer to you there.

## DEAR SCOTTIE,

I want to own up at last to what happened with your ashes. Much as you predicted, your death was quite a drama, and I'm glad that you decided to put me in charge of it because then, at least, I had something to do to distract me from the misery. I love a bit of organising, you knew that.

I clearly remember when we met, as we so often did, for supper at Julie's restaurant, it must've been about 1989 or so, and you told me you had HIV. I felt the ground beneath my seat shudder. I tried to remain calm, but one of my best friends was going to die quite soon, and I didn't feel calm at all. I felt scared and panicked. Typically, you had everything in hand and you told me your plans. You'd always been in control like that. I remember loving that about you when I first knew you at Central. That and the fact that you were virtually the only actor who spoke to me for the whole three years at college. I hate not knowing what's happening. It unnerves me. You explained that you were going to the States where they were more familiar with HIV and where there were more advanced medicines available. You knew where you would stay, where you would go for treatment, everything. My job was to visit you occasionally in New York and be ready for your return, which you told me would indicate that you were in the final phase. And who knows, you explained, they might find a cure in the short time you thought you had left, but probably not. So, hey, that's enough of that, you said, let's talk about important stuff like which one of us is the more likely to get a shag with George Michael. If he was blindfolded. On a desert island. With only us two to choose from. Yet again, I was the loser, just like in the same game previously, featuring k.d. lang.

So, you went to America. When you weren't ill, you had a great time. You fell in love. He had HIV too. Then you came back in 1992 to the serious business of dying.

The Middlesex Hospital was the venue, and the Broderip Ward, an Aids ward—the campest place in London—was your deathbed of choice. There were nurses in drag, and a cocktail trolley at 6 p.m. I remember your key nurse, Mark, very well. He knew and loved you and was determined the finale would go as well as it could. With boas and glitter wherever possible.

You were pretty bad by the time they moved you into a private room. We all took it in turns to sit with you, and while you were conscious we managed a lot of laughs.

Although I arranged the funeral, you had, of course, stage-managed and designed it to perfection way ahead of time. The music, the coffin, the flowers, all chosen for perfect dramatic effect. You chose the quiet room at the Lighthouse, the Terrence Higgins Trust hospice, for the ceremony and decided exactly how the room should be set out. As we sat there, crying to Louis Armstrong singing 'What a Wonderful World', I looked at the coffin and I couldn't erase the thought of your tired and ravaged body inside it. Then my eye wandered to the artwork on the wall beyond, which was a huge photographic triptych of a mass candlelight vigil in Trafalgar Square with thousands of young gay men singing. Then I saw you. Right in the middle, young, healthy, with your hopeful, happy face bathed in candlelight and your lover's arm round your shoulder. The old Scottie. It was a fabulous final masterstroke, you absolute drama queen.

So, to the ashes. I know you asked for them to be flung off the top of the Empire State Building while we incanted favourite lines from various show tunes, BUT it wasn't that easy, Scottie. Len and me and the BF and her fella Barrie went to New York for New Year specifically for that purpose. We had booked a table for supper at the Windows on the World at the top of the World Trade Center for 10 p.m. to see the New Year in and to raise a glass to you. So, earlier on in the evening, your old friend Michael Way joined us as we traipsed up to the viewing platform at the top of the Empire State Building with the urn containing your ashes. On arrival we discovered that there are fine mesh nets all around to prevent people jumping off, or falling debris killing innocents on the street way below. We didn't want you to be caught up in that mesh, so we climbed in a yellow cab and drove to the river on the West Side to scatter you there. But, of course, there are huge fences and barricades, so we climbed back in the taxi and asked the now impatient and confused driver to take us back to our hotel via Times Square. That way, at least you'd be scattered on Broadway.

By now it was raining and the cabbie really couldn't understand why we needed to divert through the busiest square on the busiest night of the year. We eventually persuaded him and Len distracted him while we attempted to get the ashes ready in the back as we approached Times Square. Then, to our horror, we realised that the cab window only opened two inches, so we had to sort of flick you out in the fervent hope that most of you would end up on Broadway. Job done, and recovering from the fit of hysterical giggles the process had reduced us to, we headed back to the hotel to get ready for the evening. We paid the driver and gave him a fat tip for the favour he didn't know he'd done.

Later we stood against the windows at the top of the world at midnight, looking down on all the firework displays. We improvised a quick show-tune medley, and raised a glass to you. To Scottie. The gayest and fairest of them all.

## DEAR FATTY,

So, here I am, nearly at the end of my book, and here we are nearly at the end of *French and Saunders*. I'm glad we decided to do one last tour, aren't you? It feels right to finish it as we started, with a live show. Don't you think it's amazing how we have jointly and happily come to this decision to stop now? It feels completely timely and undeniably the correct choice to say goodbye to that part of our work lives while we still love it, and while we still have the audience for it. I know you felt like I did, privileged and grateful, to be taking the show round the country and personally bidding farewell to our audience from the stage each night. It has been so rewarding to experience the appreciation, and to notice that there were often three generations of the same family who came to see us. Blimey, how old are we? I'm only fifty as far as I know, and aren't you the same? Yet we have the support of three generations. How bloody gorgeous is that?!

Doesn't it get your goat when interviewers *always* ask how often we fall out? To my knowledge, I don't think we *ever* have, have we? Sure, we have a few grumpy moments and an occasional bit of skilled sulking goes on and some extremely enjoyable ranting about whoever or whatever has annoyed us, but as for outright fury *at* each other, I can't remember any. I think we have a well-tuned mutual gauge of each other's mood, attitude and taste. We know what could be potentially awkward so we don't travel there. I'd rather spend time seeking out and enjoying what we both love about each other. There are those who would call this avoidance. These are the people, in general, to avoid. Avoidance is good. It's what compromise and maturity are made of. In order to avoid, you have to identify that which you are avoiding, and know that to avoid it is a choice. Avoidance is a loud and clear inner language, which we all speak and hear with various levels of clarity. You and I know each other. *Really* know each other. And so I think we make these intricate and sophisticated decisions *all the time*. We try to work out what matters to the other one, what would make us happy or sad, and we make constant, attentive fine adjustments so that nothing needs to come to such a head that it unbalances us, knocks us off-kilter. I think that's why our partnership has endured. We relish our similarities and respect our differences, of which there are many of course.

Can you remember the people we were when we first met? We've shed a few skins since then, I think, but essentially we are the same two bods who have grown through so much, learning all the time. I have such vivid memories of our friendship. Mostly, it feels like we came out to play as often as possible, both with work and home life.

I remember you going off on Sundays to cook for the local firemen to earn a few extra quid when we were students. One day you were running the customary thirty minutes late and so you borrowed my foldaway bike to make up time. I watched from the top-floor window of our flat, as you sped away on the bike, then I watched the bike folding away underneath you as you frantically pedalled, gradually bringing the handlebar closer and closer to your hilariously bewildered face. You must have forgotten to put the necessary pin in or something. This image tickled me so much, I laughed about it for weeks.

I remember, later, writing *Girls On Top* in Ruby Wax's flat in Holland Park. You fell asleep a lot, so your character ended up as a sort of dormouse who didn't speak much. Thank God for Ruby, whose energy was the generator for both of us. No wonder she was often exhausted, she was constantly pushing the two of us lazy lardbuckets up the comedy hill to work. Do you remember Ruby pretending to be blind so's she could utilise the disabled taxi pass she'd mistakenly been sent in the post? The chutzpah of the broad. A clever, funny, self-deprecating and daring woman who motivated us, and who made us laugh all day long.

How lucky we were that the BBC took a long-term view of our career there. And how lucky we were to have the remarkable Jon Plowman as our faithful producer, who always defended and fought for our jokes. Our first series was well meant and showed glimpses of promise but was pretty shabby, wasn't it? In the present climate at the Beeb, we wouldn't be permitted to go any further for sure. Back then, the head of 'light entertainment', Jimmy Moir, decided to take a gamble on us (or, in his words: 'I've got my dick on the table for you ladies'), to give us time to develop and learn, to nurture us, and to take the long view. Thirty years later, we still wonder occasionally if they want us . . . I think it's quite good to doubt. It puts us on our mettle. Forces us to keep inventing and experimenting with new ideas. This desire for fresh challenges is why it's so important to bid farewell to our sketch show. We need time and room to work on new, different ideas. Stuff we've been cooking up together and individually for years, but which there's been no time to concentrate on. Besides which, I think we both agree that sketches are a youngster's game, they're so demanding. Personally, I look forward to cheering on the next batch of female funnies.

Talking of change, how did you manage to change so skilfully from being the mistress of effortless understatement in the early days of *Girls On Top* and *Comic Strip* and *French and Saunders*, to the queen of pratfalls and big, broad, loud monsters, like Edina and Viv Vyle? I guess the switches were imperceptible over time, but on reflection you have run the gamut and back when it comes to versatility. How very annoying to discover that everyone has noticed your huge talent. I selfishly imagined it was for the benefit of my own private pleasure.

Do you remember once, when we went to see our friend

Gareth Snook playing Prince Charming in panto in about 1986 or something? Buttons came on to play games with the audience. I love panto and was already a bit overexcited when he held up a giant troll and explained it was the prize for the winner who had the lucky number on the back of their programme. I glanced at the back of mine—number thirteen—huh, not much chance. I wasn't surprised to see such an unlucky number, I'd never won anything in my life, never. My concentration was wandering slightly when Buttons shouted, 'Number thirteen, come on down!' I simply could not befeckinlieve it. I'd won! I'd won the giant troll! I'd always wanted one of those . . . I remember screaming at you, 'I've won! It's me!' as I stood up to rush and collect it. I felt you clawing at my clothes and urging me to sit down. But no. I wanted that troll, I deserved to claim my rightful prize. I pushed past everyone in our row and ran down to the front, with such euphoric glee, waving my programme with my prize-winning lucky number aloft as proof of my great good fortune. It was only as I reached the stage, and I started to tune in to the resounding laughter, that it dawned on me that this was a joke—EVERYONE in the theatre had number thirteen on their programme. It was only me that didn't click until it was too late. The elderly had got it, the children had got it, the three rows of mentally challenged people at the front had got it, the whole audience had got it. It was just me, twatty thick ol' me, that hadn't. The walk back to my seat took five years. Thanks for trying to comfort me in my utter humiliation, by the way, and for not disowning me at that awful, cringing moment.

Another memory that stays with me is the time, many years later, when we performed with Darcey Bussell onstage at the Opera House in a benefit for the Benesh Institute. We achieved a major ambition of mine that night, by simply having, on the door of our dressing room, a gold star and a list of its occupants as follows: Miss Darcey Bussell, Miss Sylvie Guillem, Miss Viviana Durante, Miss Jennifer Saunders, Miss Dawn French. We were prima ballerinas for the night! What a laugh it was. We did our silly sketch where I pranced about, echoing Darcey's steps in a giant mirror (a routine we later repeated on *Vicar*), and you played a bossy dance teacher (good toes, naughty toes). We had been asked to bring alternative costumes to wear for the finale, so I had a friend make me a preposterous outfit where I looked like an old-fashioned ballerina in a tutu over a huge swan with tiny dangling knitted ballerina legs hanging over the swan's back. The swan's neck was held by a handle and its legs were, of course, my legs in black tights with huge ungainly flippers for feet. The effect was just plain silly and hopefully very funny. Well, *we* laughed anyway. I know I looked ridiculous, that was the point. Ordinarily when you do a big jokey sketch with a big jokey costume, you endeavour to get out of it pretty quickly. When the gag's over, it's over. Unfortunately, as you may remember, that night we all had to remain onstage to receive the Royal Blessing of the institute's patron, Princess Margaret. She obviously knew a lot about ballet and seemed familiar with many of the dancers onstage, who were the crème de la crème from round the world. She moved along the line, chatting and congratulating everyone till she got to me. She leaned round the swan head to shake my hand, and looked me full in the face with full-on pity in her eyes, quietly said, 'How brave,' and moved on. I think she thought I was special needs or something, being given a chance to jump about with the real dancers. On second thoughts . . . she was right, really, wasn't she? Tee hee!

I love it that we still have so much fun together when we come out to play in our civvie life. Like when we started a book club to encourage us to read more, and to have a chance to meet our favourite mutual female chums for literary criticism and alcohol in equal measure. Or going to see Dolly Parton over the years, witnessing both her waistline shrinking and her genius ever expanding. I love that we have been part of each other's family. I'm *so* glad you had three girls, all older than my daughter, all very different, who I could watch and learn from. I have gained so much from seeing you and Ade bring them up so beautifully.

I will never forget the cloak of protection you flung round me when the press were on my tail trying to exacerbate an already sensitive and tricky situation with Len and me. We'd just started a new sitcom, *Let Them Eat Cake*, at the BBC, and I was trying to be light-hearted and funny, when I was actually feeling hounded, and anxious for Len. You were like a gladiator, fiercely guarding me, and calling for coffee breaks whenever you sensed I was a bit wobbly. You deserve a proper gladiator name for that. How about 'Defender'?! Yeah, sounds good.

I watched you the other week, at your fiftieth birthday party, looking more radiant and confident than ever, basking in the love of those who care so much for you, and I was reminded in one blinding instant how lucky I am to have you.

So, as I say, here we are, at the end of an era. Saying goodbye to *French and Saunders* with a last shout in London at the Theatre Royal, Drury Lane. I've said some important work goodbyes recently—*Vicar*, *F&S*, and so on. You'd think I would feel sad. I don't. I feel more alive and more creative than I have for years, and I can't wait to say hello to LOTS of new projects. I think both of us are now busier than we've ever been, in every way. But we mustn't forget to stop for a breath occasionally and enjoy the moment. Because it's a glorious moment. We're fifty. And it's bloody fantastic! There are only two things to look out for as we get older. One is loss of memory and . . . I can't remember the other one. I bow to you, and bring on the next fifty!

As we move our gear into yet another dressing room for the last time, I remember all the other dressing rooms. How they are all so different and yet the same. The sharing of hair dryers and make-up and rollers. The chocolates and the nuts and the Berocca! The speeded-up running of lines in a bid to reassure ourselves that we know the show. The no-nonsense notes to each other, no punches pulled, no time for politeness. Speak up. Wait till I've finished before you move. Don't do that thing to the audience at that moment. Energy. Pace. Clarity. Don't blether. God, I hate this. Are your flies done up? God, I love this. This is going to be a good one. Remember they've paid. I need the loo. A quick handshake for luck. You arsehole. You twat. The *F&S* theme tune. The lights. We're on!

There's just no buzz like it.

I think we might miss it, you know.

## DEAR DAD,

It's time to stop writing now, but I feel frustrated by all the stuff I *haven't* managed to tell you about. There's so much. Nearly a lifetime's worth. I've forgotten more than I can remember. It's clear to me that when I reflect on everything that's happened so far, it's not the work or the career I remember so much as the people. Somehow I've been on the receiving end of such plenty when it comes to the folk I know. It's an embarrassment of riches. They are the ones who, with my family and the BF and Fatty and so many others, shore me up and love me so well.

In the end, y'know, I'm wholly convinced that 'the love you take is equal to the love you make'. I'm further convinced that you can only know *how* to give love if you've been given it yourself. And I have, Dad, in bucketloads. Starting of course with you and Mum. My steady stream of unwavering love from you was stemmed far too soon, but Dad, for me to feel the lashings of self-worth I do, is a clue to how deep and wide that flow must have been. I only know how to love others because of your huge, unquestionable love for me. That's a gift that keeps on giving.

Don't misunderstand. I can be ornery. I am extremely stubborn about probably far too much. I am unforgiving of those I don't trust or who have betrayed me, or who are needlessly unkind, or who threaten my beloveds. But whenever I catch sight or sound of myself in the full grumpy flow of despicable thoughts or words or deeds, I repulse me sufficiently to try and stop, thank goodness.

It's far preferable to seek out the good than dwell on the bad. A bit like Mum with the dogs in the parlour, I endeavour to give everyone at least a chance, y'know, before I condemn them to the eternal fires of hell!

It feels difficult to finish these letters. Even the simple act of writing 'Dear Dad' at the start of a letter has been comforting and has given me a closeness to you I have missed so much. Dad. It's such a short, dapper word. Just like you. The palindromic perfectness of it is beautiful. Dad. A little word that contains a whole world of meaning. Like 'Mum'. I use that word often, I use it on the phone to her, I call it out when I'm with her, I use it to check if she wants a coffee, or to see how her day is. I use it to write in my diary about her, or to include her in a list of things to do, or an invite, or on a note that goes with flowers, or a card at Christmas or on her birthday. Or for a thousand reasons. I've written that word 'Mum' so often. But I haven't written 'Dad', I don't think, for about thirty years when it's directly to you. I write it now—'Dad'. There, with such tenderness. It's a treat to write it, an excellence. I don't want it to stop . . .

But it must. It must stop because it's time to properly say goodbye, isn't it? After your funeral, when I was nineteen, I stood on the shoreline at Rock, feeling entirely bereft without you, feeling that you were gone with the waves sinking back into the ocean. Writing these letters to you has helped me to wade out a little way, and dive in. That's all I needed, to swim about and play for a while. To connect with you and feel your nearness again. I'm surprised how easy it is to do. I didn't know how near you are. You are close by, aren't you?

About five years ago I went to Skibo Castle and one evening a medium from the Black Isle came to tell us our fortunes and read our tarot cards. It was all for fun, a light-hearted distraction. I went in, a little worse (or maybe better) for whisky and sat down. She was quiet, and then she looked at me and said, 'Oh, I see your dad is with you!' This shocked me. 'Yes, there he is, standing right behind you with his hand on your shoulder. I hope you're not offended by this but he's calling you "Dumpling" and "Moo".' I had to leave. I wasn't offended, I was heart-thuddingly touched. How did she know? Was this trickery? I went for a walk outside and sat on a bench in the clear moonlight. I don't know if you, or some form of you, was there, I don't really hold with 'all that' ordinarily. Actually, it doesn't really matter what she said or saw, her words to me transcended the rational. What mattered that night, as it has mattered to me through this whole book, is that we are always connected, you and I. Always. It's the memory of you and the love you gave me that remain. Death is merely the horizon, the love is eternal.

There's an astronomical term, 'syzygy'. It means the alignment of celestial bodies in the same gravitational system along a straight line. Apparently it's rare when it happens. That's how I think of you and me in this book. For a brief, excellent moment, we have aligned in the same gravitational pull, and we've been together. But now it's time to go about the rest of my life. I don't know what you'll do. I like to imagine you in a sort of five-star dead men's dorm with Eric Morecambe and Elvis and Kenneth Williams and Tommy Cooper for company.

As for me, I pootle on, with you in my heart for warmth and fortitude, and I do all I can to have a good life. And it is a good life ... with knobs on. And then some more knobs!

Chio then, Dad.

*Editors' Note*: In 2010, Dawn French and Lenny Henry issued this statement: 'Dawn French and Lenny Henry are sad to announce they have decided to separate after twenty-five years of marriage. They made the decision last October and since then have been living together in constant, open and honest discussion. The separation is entirely amicable and they fully intend to maintain their close relationship. Their priority is to commit to the future joint parenting of their daughter.'

Patrick Swayze
& Lisa Niemi

*The Time of My Life*

*We were performing an exhibition of classical dance at a school auditorium in 1972. Lisa and I had learned and rehearsed the 'pas de deux' from the ballet 'Raymonda'.*

*Just before we stepped out on stage, I kissed her on the cheek for good luck, but that wasn't the magic moment. The magic happened when she took my hand to start dancing.*

*I looked into Lisa's eyes, and we moved together as one. It was a fleeting moment . . . but I never forgot it.*

*Patrick Swayze in 'The Time of My Life'*

# *Prologue*

In late December 2007, life was looking pretty good. I had just wrapped shooting on the pilot of a new TV series, *The Beast*. My wife Lisa and I were enjoying a second honeymoon after a long, difficult period in which we had grown painfully apart. I was feeling excited about new work, new directions, and the promise of the future.

Lisa and I were planning to spend New Year's Eve at our ranch in New Mexico, as we'd done for the past few years. But first, we stopped off in Aspen to visit a couple of friends. It was there that I got the first hint that something was wrong.

I had been having some digestive trouble for a few weeks but I've had a sensitive stomach my whole life, so I hadn't thought much about it. In Aspen, though, when we all raised glasses of champagne for a toast, I took a sip and nearly choked—the champagne burned like acid going down. I'd never felt anything like it, but not wanting to ruin the festivities, I said nothing to Lisa. I just didn't drink any more champagne that night, and didn't think anything more about it.

Three weeks later, in January 2008, I learned that the burning in my stomach wasn't some minor irritation. It was the result of a blockage in my bile ducts, which was caused by pancreatic cancer—

just about the most deadly, untreatable cancer you can get—so when my doctor at Cedars-Sinai in Los Angeles told me that my chances of surviving for more than a few months weren't high, I had no reason to doubt him.

A LOT OF THINGS go through your head when you get a death sentence handed to you. Once the shock wears off, it's hard not to sink into bitterness, to feel that you've been singled out in a way that's not fair. For me, that initial shock quickly turned to self-criticism and blame. Did I do this to myself? Is it my fault?

In those first few weeks after my diagnosis, amid the whirlwind of figuring out treatments and medication, I struggled, with Lisa's help, to make sense of what was happening to me, to counteract all the negative emotions that kept welling up. I needed to find a way to accept what was going on, but I just couldn't. I wasn't ready to go, and I was damned if this disease was going to take me before I was. So I told my doctor I wanted to understand exactly what I was up against so that I could go after this cancer rather than waiting for it to beat me. And in the year and a half since my diagnosis, that's exactly what I've done, with every ounce of energy I have.

Fighting cancer has been a challenging and eye-opening experience and it has sent me on an emotional journey deeper than anything I've felt before. Facing your own mortality is the quickest possible way to find out what you're made of. It strips away all the bullshit and exposes your strengths and weaknesses, your sense of self. It exposes your soul.

It also leads you to confront life's hardest questions: Is there a heaven? Will I make it? Have I lived a good life? Has this life counted for something other than just my own narcissism? Am I a good person? It's easy to dismiss these questions when you have your whole life ahead of you. But for me they suddenly took on a whole new meaning.

There's a scene at the end of *Saving Private Ryan* that really resonates with me. As an old man, Private Ryan muses aloud about his life. 'I tried to live my life the best I could,' he says. 'I hope that was enough.' It's hard to judge the mark you've made in this world. Writing this book has been, in part, a quest to do that for myself.

Spending time with Lisa looking back at our lives has been really illuminating. I have never felt that I had all the answers, and I certainly don't claim to now. Yet the one thing I realised as Lisa and I retraced the arc of our life together is that no matter what happened, we never, ever gave up—on each other, or on our dreams. I'm far from perfect, and I've made a lot of mistakes. But that's one thing we both got right, and it's the one thing that's keeping me going today.

As I write this, sitting in our beautiful ranch home in New Mexico with the sun beaming down on the mountains, I realise yet again how much more I want to do in this life. Together with Lisa, I'll keep on pushing, keep on believing in the future. Because that, in the end, is the greatest gift we have.

*Patrick Swayze*
*June 2009*

As Patrick and I have been writing this book, I couldn't help but be amazed by all the stories of things we've done and been through. It was surprising to me how hard we've both worked, how focused and single-minded we've been. Always striving to be more, do better. And that drive has served us well, particularly with all that we're going through now.

Looking back, I wish I had done more to 'stop and smell the roses'. So many gorgeous things have happened in my life and I was too busy moving forward truly to recognise and enjoy them. I'm different now. Today I'm much more willing to take luxurious pleasure in a beautiful day, in the wonderful smell of my favourite mare's hair, in the overflowing love I feel for my husband. You'd think that when someone close to you receives a death sentence it would inspire amazing insights and lessons about life. I know that's what I thought. But after Patrick's cancer diagnosis, and after I started to recover from feeling I was trapped in a perpetual nightmare, I looked around and couldn't see a damn lesson in sight. Yet, slowly, as I've been dealing with the initial grief and fear, living each day that comes, getting to do this book, the lessons have started to ease out into the open. I couldn't force them out any sooner. They come in their own time when they, and you, are good and ready.

There's a lot of wisdom in the idea of living one day at a time. And when you might not have someone for long, that's what starts to happen.

I used to be afraid of time—that I'd run out of it, that I wouldn't have enough to do all the things I wanted. Now I'm seeing each minute that passes as a victory, something I'm proud of. It's as if I can gather all these minutes into my arms like an enormous mass of jewels. Look what I have—another moment! A kiss, a stroke of the skin on my husband's arm, the light coming through the window just so . . . Each of these jewels gives me the confidence to stand up and look Death in the face and say, 'No one's going anywhere today.'

I can help Patrick—I can love him, track his medications and calories, be there to kick him in the pants or just hold his hand if he needs it. I can't save him, of course, and I try to remember that, but I've got the best possible weapon on my side: Patrick himself. He's such a fighter. He's so amazingly strong and beautiful.

You know, we were in New Mexico a couple of years after Patrick had broken both his legs in a life-threatening horse accident. We walked out into the fresh mountain air, and he had taken off his shirt to enjoy the sun as we strolled in to our beautiful pasture to visit our five spirited Arabian horses. Patrick was rubbing one of them on her neck and I had walked away for some reason. I turned round in time to see him grab a handful of mane and swing himself up on the mare's back. No saddle, no bridle, nothing.

She and the other horses started to trot off together and then, in a tight group, they launched into a full gallop, Patrick riding bareback in the middle of them through the open field. I couldn't believe it. I couldn't help but see how fantastic and free he looked. And I couldn't help but be pissed off. I mean, he'd just broken his legs a year or so earlier and he was going to risk doing it again?

The horses had their joy ride and slowed to an easy trot. Patrick hopped off blithely and walked over to me a little sheepishly, waiting to see if I was going to admonish him. But I couldn't. I could only shake my head and smile.

This is the man who's taken on cancer. As always, he's on the ride of his life. And I know that he's going to ride this horse as far as it'll go.

*Lisa Niemi*

# Chapter 1

Halloween night, 1970. It was a balmy Saturday evening in Houston when I ran onto the field with my Waltrip High School football teammates, ready for a big game with our crosstown rivals, the Yates Lions. We were pumped up to play, since we'd heard there would be college scouts in the stands checking us out. Little did I know then, but this night would change my life for ever.

It was my senior year at Waltrip, and this was my chance to show the scouts what I could do. Yates was a good team, physical and aggressive, and the stands were packed with screaming fans, so the stage was set. At five foot eleven and 180 pounds, I wasn't your typical big, bruiser football player, but I was fast, running the hundred-metre dash in just ten seconds. With those scouts in the stands, I was hoping to have a big game—we didn't have enough money for me to go to college, but a football scholarship would take care of that.

High-school football isn't just a game in Texas; it's more a religion. There's something magical about the smell of freshly cut grass, the coaches yelling, the fans stamping their feet, and the twenty-two men on the field going at one another hand-to-hand. I loved the competition and the rough physicality. Whenever I took my position on the field, I wanted to run faster and hit harder than anyone else.

But that night, I was the one who got hit hardest. On a midgame kickoff, I caught the ball and started to run. With blockers in front of me, I ran up one sideline, then cut back against the grain and tried to outrun the shifting defenders. But a couple of their big guys launched themselves at me, helmets first. One came in high, the other one low on my blind side. And they hit me at the exact moment my left leg planted on the ground.

My knee snapped, bending grotesquely, and I went down like a shot. In that moment, most of the ligaments in my knee ripped in half, completely destroying the joint. But all I knew at the time was that even though my knee felt like it had exploded, I wanted to get up and walk it off—to show they hadn't hurt me, even though they had.

I tried to get up, but collapsed, as my left leg couldn't bear any weight at all. I got up again, but again I fell to the grass. Finally, the coaches ambled over to check on me. One of them looked down at me and sneered, 'Too much dancing, huh, Swayze?' This was Texas, and even a star football player was the target of mockery if he happened to be a dancer, too. I glared through a haze of pain and said nothing as they finally lifted me up, put me on a stretcher and carried me back to the locker room.

As I lay on a table in the room, the pain in my knee began to dull, replaced by shock. And that was enough to make me want to keep playing.

'Let me get back out there!' I told the trainer. 'Let me just finish out the game!'

'Nope,' the trainer said. 'You're done.'

But I wouldn't take no for an answer. I slid off the table, but as soon as my left foot touched the floor it felt as if someone had jammed a dagger deep into my knee. It buckled, and I fell to the floor, passing out. The next thing I remember was hearing sirens and seeing the flashing lights of an ambulance.

My knee joint had been pretty much destroyed and I ended up having major surgery. The doctors repaired as much damage as they could, after which I spent three months in a hip-to-toe cast.

This left my knee joint hopelessly stiff, and while being in a cast was difficult and painful, it was nothing compared to the agonising rehab process of physically breaking and loosening the scar tissue that had formed in the joint.

I remember lying in my bed at home, hearing my mother crying in the next room. It scared me.

Obviously my days of playing football were over, but what would happen now to my dreams of competing in gymnastics, or dancing professionally? In all my eighteen years, I'd never questioned my ability to do anything I set my mind to do. But now, for the first time, thanks to that one fleeting moment on a high-school football field, I was facing a true test.

MY FAMILY'S ROOTS go way back in Texas, and my parents' relationship was the classic Texas story of the cowboy who falls in love with the city girl. Jesse Wayne Swayze, known to all as 'Buddy', was a one-time rodeo champion. He was unpretentious and bright, and worked for years as a butcher, then put himself through home study to get a degree in drafting. He got a job with an oil company and continued his studies, earning another degree and becoming a mechanical engineer. He put all the money he had into his family, especially into the dance company and school my mother ran.

My mom, Patsy Swayze, was a choreographer and teacher, and one of the founders of Houston's dance scene. Mom was an amazing teacher but a demanding one, and we kids worked hard to win her approval.

I was the second of five kids, and the oldest boy. My older sister Vicky and I both studied dance with our mother from the time we could walk. Mom's studio, the Swayze Dance Studio, was like a second home for us, a place where we spent endless hours hanging out and studying dance. My mother never asked Vicky and me if we wanted to study dance—it was just expected of us.

And not only that, but we were expected to be the absolute best at it. In fact, my mother chose the name Patrick for me because she thought 'Patrick Swayze' would look good on billboards. But like my dad, I went by the name 'Buddy'—or, when he was around, 'Little Buddy'.

Our younger siblings, Donny, Sean and Bambi, also felt the constant pressure to perform in whatever activities they undertook. We called it 'growing up Swayze'—an almost manic drive to lead the pack in whatever we attempted. Both our parents were very accomplished: Dad had been a Golden Gloves boxer and Mom was one of the leading lights of Houston dance. But that's where the similarities between them ended.

My mother was a perfectionist and she expected the same in her children, no matter what we did. This was a double-edged sword, as her pressure implanted in me a burning desire to be the best at everything, but it also led to a near-constant, deeply rooted feeling of inadequacy. My dad was more laid-back, the gentle cowboy. He was the rock our family was built on, a steady and stable presence in our lives. In some ways, we were nurtured more by my father than by my mother, and growing up with a father who was both strong and sensitive made a huge impression on me. It made me realise that having a gentle side didn't make you less of a man. In fact, it made you a better one.

We didn't have a lot of money, especially while my dad was working in the butcher's shop, but my mother always carried herself with dignity. I can remember feeling embarrassed while walking into Mass at church one morning, since the sole of one of my shoes had partially torn off and made a flapping noise all the way down to my pew. I can also remember that our neighbours in North Houston kept their distance, since we were 'those arts people', not a label anyone really aspired to in 1960s Texas—a fact I learned all too well as a young male dancer.

By junior high school, everybody knew I was a dancer, as I was always performing in theatre productions. I got picked on, called 'fag', and beaten up more times than I can count, but it wasn't until one particularly bad beating, when I was about twelve, that my dad—who'd been a serious boxer— finally stepped in.

Five boys had jumped me at once, and although I fought back

with everything I had, those are bad odds for anyone. When I got home, my face all bruised and cut, my dad decided it was time for me to learn how to fight his way. So, in addition to dancing, I spent the next couple of months studying how to box.

When my dad thought I was ready, he drove me back up to the school. He walked me into the football coach's office and said, 'I want you to pull those five boys out of their classes so we can settle this thing.' When Dad went on to say he wanted me to fight these kids again, Coach Callahan just stared at him. 'But this time it isn't going to be five boys on one,' my dad said. 'It's gonna be one on one, fair and square. They think they're tough? We'll see how tough they are.'

Times were different then, and Coach Callahan quickly deemed it acceptable educational policy to pull boys out of classes, put us in the weight shack by the football field, and let us fight it out. Dad and I walked down to the shack and the coach soon met us there with the five boys.

I won't deny that I was scared. My father obviously believed I was strong enough, and a good enough fighter, to beat all five of these boys. As I prepared to square off against the first one, I could feel my adrenaline pumping—not because I was afraid of getting hurt, but because I didn't want to let my dad down. But I felt my senses sharpening and my heart beating faster, and I had a realisation. I suddenly understood that you can conquer fear by making it work for you. And so I did. I beat all five of those boys that day, one by one.

That didn't solve my problems at school—in fact, once word got round that I was the new 'tough guy', everybody wanted to fight me. And since I was playing violin at the time, the 'tough guy' was an even more inviting target, with his ballet shoes stuck in his back pocket and a violin case in his hand. I got into plenty more scrapes with boys at school, but I never forgot the lesson of how to turn fear to my advantage—a lesson that has served me well my whole life.

And although my dad had taught me to fight, he also taught me two unbreakable rules about when and how to do it.

'Buddy,' he always said, 'if I ever see you start a fight, I'll kick your ass. And if I ever see you not *finish* a fight, I'll kick your ass.' I learned from my father that you might not always win, but you never, ever give up. And since that day in the weight shack, I never have.

When I was about ten years old, I had climbed onto the roof of a two-storey house being built down the street. 'Hey!' I yelled down to the construction workers below. 'How much will you give me if I jump?'

The men looked up and saw a wiry kid, hands on his hips, perched at the edge of the roof. One of them shook his head. 'You want us to give you money to jump off that roof and break your goddamn neck?' he yelled up at me.

'How much?' I asked. 'Come on!'

'I'll give you twenty-five cents,' the man replied, while the others chuckled.

'Give me fifty cents and I'll do it!' I yelled back.

He nodded and waved his hand. 'Well, go on, then.' And this was the moment I'd waited for. Everyone's eyes were on me, my blood started rushing, and I jumped off that roof—right into the sand pile they'd been using to mix the cement. I hit the pile and rolled, my momentum carrying me right back up to my feet after a couple of turns. The man reluctantly fished a couple of quarters out of his pocket and handed them to me.

I might have looked crazy to the men, but with all my gymnastics and dance lessons, I'd spent my whole childhood running and jumping and flying through the air. I knew how to fall and how to roll. I knew my body inside out, and knew exactly what it was capable of.

As soon as my younger brother Donny was old enough to run with me, he and I charged through the woods near our house like a couple of daredevils. I always loved heroes like Doc Savage and Tarzan—not superheroes with special powers, but ordinary guys who pushed themselves to do extraordinary things. I'd play Tarzan and we'd swing around on a network of vines hanging from the trees behind our house, wearing our specially made Tarzan suits: old Speedo swimsuits, cut to look like loincloths, with a belt round the waist.

Doc Savage was a particular hero of mine because he was not only physically daring, he was also a Renaissance man. He could do anything—he was an explorer, a scientist, an inventor, a martial-arts expert and a master of disguise. I wanted to be like Doc Savage, to be able to do absolutely everything. When I wasn't flying around, jumping off buildings and racing through the woods, I was up in our tree house with my chemistry set, trying to invent the perfect rocket.

The space race with the Russians was in full swing, and model rocketry was our latest and greatest hobby. I'd built and launched a few model rockets, but then decided to take it a step further and make my own fuel, too. I got my hands on some zinc dust and sulphur and began mixing it up. Unfortunately I knocked my Bunsen burner right onto my mound of zinc and sulphur, which took only a few seconds to ignite—just enough time for me to fly out of the tree-house door and tuck and roll to safety.

The explosion was deafening, and as the tree house went up in flames I looked back at the smoke billowing out and thought, Well, I'll just have to build another one. I had no concept of the danger I'd put myself in, that I could have been hurt or even killed. Like most teenage boys, I felt invincible—a feeling that would continue well beyond my teenage years.

At the same time as I was being the wild man in the woods, I was continuing to study dance, gymnastics and violin, and performing in musicals. I spent hours at Mom's studio, sweating and pushing to become the best male dancer Houston had ever seen. I loved the grace and strength of dance, and the sheer physical demands of it.

My mother saw that I had talent, and although she let me mess around in the woods she did set some other rules to try to keep me safe. The one I hated most was that she wouldn't let me have a motorcycle. She'd had two uncles in the police force who both died in motorcycle accidents.

'If I ever see you on a motorcycle,' she'd tell me, 'I'll chop it up with an axe.' My mother was strong and had a quick Irish temper, so I knew she was capable of doing it.

But I wanted a motorcycle more than anything, so I decided if she wouldn't let me have one, I'd make one myself. First, I took an old bicycle frame, welded a plate on the bottom, and put some fat tyres on it. Next, I stole the engine from my dad's lawn edger and mounted it on the bike frame. Once I got the engine hooked up to the sprocket, I had myself a homemade motorbike. It didn't go all that fast, which is maybe just as well since the only brakes it had were my two boots pushing on the front tyre.

I'd tear around on that motorbike while Mom and Dad were away, riding all over the neighbourhood. But one afternoon my mother came home early and I got caught. Just as she'd said, she went after that motorbike with an axe, destroying not only the bike frame but Dad's edger engine as well—putting me up shit creek with both my parents, though I suspected Dad secretly admired the ingenuity I'd shown. But that was the last motorcycle I had for a while.

ALL THROUGH JUNIOR HIGH and high school, I continued to pursue all the things I loved doing: sports, music, dance, gymnastics, martial arts, sailing, skating and diving. I was a Boy Scout too, rising to the rank of Eagle Scout. I ran track, swam and roller-skated competitively, and took up diving, which I did well in, thanks to my gymnastics training. In my determination to become Doc Savage, I wanted to try out—and master—every skill I possibly could. And of course the place where I could really earn the jocks' respect was on Waltrip's football team. I didn't particularly like the locker-room culture of football, but I did love showing people what I could do on the field.

Also, being the son of a cowboy, I had grown up with horses. I'd loved horses all my life. Our family didn't have much money, but horses were cheap in Texas, so we kept a few at some run-down stables near our house. We'd barter with the stable owners, exchanging chores for boarding, so from the time I was small, I learned how to muck out stalls and care for horses. And because those corrals were so dilapidated, the horses needed a lot of attention, for things like splinters and hoof injuries.

But with all that said, the number-one priority in our family was always the stage. Dancing, choreography and teaching performance were my mother's life's work—and I was her golden boy. Throughout my childhood, junior-high and high-school years, I performed in summer stock musicals—*The Sound of Music*, *Gypsy*, *The Music Man*—always honing my ability to sing, dance and act on stage. I pushed hard to be that perfect golden boy.

All the hard work paid off in my early teens, when I received scholarship offers to study with the Joffrey Ballet and the American Ballet Theater in New York City. But I turned them down, deciding instead to continue to study with my mother and dance with the Houston Jazz Ballet Company, which she founded, and making myself available for the sports training that fell during the summer. At that point, I wasn't sure I wanted a life as a professional dancer. In fact, I was having real trouble figuring out what I wanted to do, with so many options to choose from. Gymnastics? Dancing? Sports? How could I possibly decide among them?

But then came that fateful high-school football night and the injury that threatened to derail all those dreams. Lying in bed with a hip-to-toe cast after knee surgery, all I could think was, Can I come back from this? Will I be able to do everything I could before?

It wasn't long before I decided on the answer: Yes, I could, and I would. Failure was simply not an option, so from that point on, it didn't matter how hard I'd have to push, or how much pain I'd have to endure, I would will myself through it.

As soon as the cast came off, I began working out my leg again—lifting weights, stretching, running, anything I could do to get it back into shape. By now I was in my last semester of high school, and my next step depended on being back in fighting form. I had decided to accept the offer of a gymnastics scholarship to San Jacinto Junior College, about an hour's drive from Houston.

I rehabbed my knee all spring and summer and by September I

was working out daily with the San Jacinto gymnastics team. It still hurt, but soon I was back to doing everything I'd done before the injury. My goal now was to compete in the Olympics, and my coach, Pat Yeager, told me I had a shot at it. He had coached the US Women's Gymnastics Team and he was also a member of the Men's Olympic Gymnastics Committee, so he knew something about world-class gymnastics.

I couldn't have known it then, but the best thing about having got my knee back into shape wasn't going to be the Olympics—it was the fact that I could continue rehearsing and performing at my mom's studio, which had merged with the Houston Music Theater. So I was there when a particular fifteen-year-old girl with long blonde hair started showing up.

## Chapter 2

I noticed Lisa right away, with her lithe dancer's build, her long blonde hair, and the look of indifference she had whenever she passed me by. Unlike the other girls, she usually acted like I wasn't even in the room, so one day, when she walked by close enough, I decided it was time to get her attention. I reached down, pinched her rear end, and said, 'Hey there, cutie!' She turned and glared at me as if I'd just farted in church.

Now, in my defence, I'd grown up at the studio and I'd been pinching and flirting with girls there ever since I was about three foot tall. But Lisa wasn't like the other girls. Also she'd been told that I was something of a Casanova and that when I walked into a room, you had to raise the roof to let my head in, it was so big.

The truth was, though, I'd had a couple of girlfriends and liked to go out, but never anything serious.

The second time I met Lisa, I was auditioning for a musical we were doing at the Houston Music Theater, and when I noticed that Lisa was watching with a few other girls, I decided to ramp it up a notch. I sang the song with all the gusto I could, then ended with a spontaneous back flip. Lisa and the other girls just rolled their eyes.

Lisa was the opposite of me—quiet, introverted and mysterious—and I'd never met anyone like her. In Houston in the seventies you were either a surfer, a doper or a cowboy. Lisa had a reputation for being a doper, and although she did occasionally smoke pot, her reputation stemmed mainly from the fact that people didn't know what to make of her. Most girls in Houston weren't quiet and self-contained, they had big hair and personalities to match. Lisa came from a Finnish family, the Haapaniemis, a cool, blonde, self-confident bunch that included five brothers, none of whom would be thrilled if the 'Casanova' Buddy Swayze tried to move in on their little sister.

IN THE FALL of 1971 I started at San Jacinto Junior College on my gymnastics scholarship, but was still living at home, driving to campus each day. When I wasn't in classes or practising with the gymnastics team, I was either at my mom's studio or working at the ice rink in the Houston shopping mall. I liked working at the ice rink: I'd sometimes catch sight of Lisa hanging out at the mall.

I'd see her coming and going with her friends, and although she was as blonde and pretty as a cheerleader, she had the air of a 'bad girl' about her, mostly because she seemed so hard to get to know.

But when Lisa started her freshman year at the High School for Performing and Visual Arts, she discovered dancing. At first, she wasn't as interested in dancing as she was in theatre, but to her surprise, she fell in love with it, and by the spring of her freshman year, she'd made up her mind to become a professional dancer. She took a part-time job at the Parfumery, located at the opposite end of the mall, to raise money to move to New York—so now I'd see her going to and from work, a new sense of purpose on her face. And occasionally I'd 'casually' wander down to talk to her and just check out what was going on.

I still had my dream, too—of making the Olympic gymnastics team—and I trained long hours at San Jacinto to make it happen. But that dream came to a crashing halt during my freshman year.

It happened at a gymnastics competition, as I was warming up on the rings. This was my strongest event, all the more so because I didn't have to worry about my knee on anything but the dismount—success on the rings depended almost entirely on the strength of my arms and torso.

On this occasion, though, at the end of my warm-up I forgot for a split second that I was on the lower rings, not the higher ones. So when I began my dismount I thought there was more room than there actually was between me and the floor. I executed what would have been a perfect dismount for the high rings, spinning into a somersault—but then I crashed hard to the mat, jamming both legs into the ground.

Blinding pain shot through my body and I knew I'd injured the same knee again. It was agony to lie on the mat, knowing I'd hurt myself—and knowing it was because of a stupid mistake.

For the second time in two years, I was faced with surgery, a cast and rehab. So, as I'd done the first time, I just made up my mind again that no matter what and no matter how hard it would be, I would get myself back into shape.

I continued at San Jacinto, and the more time I spent away from home, the more I began to realise that there was a whole big world out there waiting to be explored. Even if I couldn't be an Olympic gymnast, there were still a million other things out there that interested me. Yes, gymnastics had been my dream, and it stung like hell to know I'd missed my chance to achieve it, but I somehow knew instinctively that when one dream dies, you have to move on to a new one. The unhappiest people in this world are those who can't recover from losing a dream, whose lives cease to have meaning. I wasn't going to let that happen to me.

Once again, I faced the question: What did I want to be? Who was Patrick Swayze and what did he have to offer the world? I still wanted so much—to dance, to sing, to act. I also wanted to become a pilot, and I learned that if I finished two years at San Jacinto, getting my associate arts degree in aviation, I could go into the military and hope to get into flight school. For a while, that's what I decided I would do, even though the Vietnam War was raging on the other side of the world and sucking young men like me into its jungles.

But before long, I realised the performing bug was just too strong for me to consider doing anything else. I rehabbed my knee again and kept working out at Mom's studio, which of course, meant I would see Lisa, who was studying dance there now.

I was still intrigued by this mysterious, beautiful girl, but she was acting as cool as ever to me. But then for the first time we danced together on stage. And suddenly, everything changed.

We were performing an exhibition of classical dance at a school auditorium in 1972. Lisa and I had learned and rehearsed the *pas de deux* from the ballet *Raymonda.* Just before we stepped out on stage, I kissed her on the cheek for good luck, but that wasn't the magic moment. The magic happened when she took my hand to start dancing, and our eyes locked.

It felt as if an electric charge suddenly coursed through my body. I looked into Lisa's eyes, and we moved together as one. It was a fleeting moment and, after the dance was done, I didn't mention it to her, afraid that the feelings had been mine alone. But I never forgot it.

Not long after that, we were paired up in yet another dance—one that threatened to make it embarrassingly clear how I felt about her. We were at my mom's studio, rehearsing a more avant-garde dance with some pretty provocative moves. Well, you can imagine the effect this had on me, a healthy twenty-year-old guy wearing tights. At one point, I was afraid that someone might note my 'primal stirrings', and quickly turned away to stretch and adjust my leg warmers. Needless to say, I couldn't wait for the next rehearsal, so I went ahead and asked her out on a date. Fortunately, she did agree to go out on a few dates with me, but they were hardly the stuff of great romance. When you start to like someone who used to be a friend, you get shy—and that's how I felt. I suddenly didn't know what to do with myself when I was around her.

First, I'd show up at her house, and one of her five tall Nordic brothers would answer the door. He'd give me the third degree—Where was I taking Lisa? What time would I bring her home? Then, we'd go to dinner and have awkward conversations, which basically consisted of me telling her about how great I was and her seeming utterly unimpressed. I wanted her to like me. I just didn't have any idea how to make that happen.

As my time at San Jacinto drew to a close, and I was mulling over what my next step might be, I got an invitation to play Prince Charming in the *Disney on Parade* travelling shows that toured all over the United States, Canada and Latin America. I loved dancing and the idea of playing Prince Charming, so I signed up. Time to see the world.

*Disney on Parade* was a huge travelling show, with dozens of dancers and a giant stage set. We would perform in arenas and coliseums, with billowing blue lamé curtains, a full-scale castle with towers, and a huge egg-shaped screen projecting the stories of *Snow White*, *Fantasia* and other Disney classics. I was excited to have my first performing job outside Houston—and excited to be travelling to places I'd only read about in books.

The dancers made $125 a week, which felt like a lot of money, especially since we all doubled, tripled and quadrupled up in our living arrangements on the road. Most of the dancers were women, and of the few who were men, even fewer were straight men. So the opportunities for me in terms of finding women to date were just about endless.

Unfortunately, I still didn't know how to communicate with women, or anybody else. I just sounded like an egotistical ass, because I couldn't stop going on and on about myself. For one thing, my knee was giving me no end of trouble. It got so bad that I had to go to the hospital in every city to get the fluid drained from the joint. And the more knee trouble I had, the more I had to talk about it.

But after a while people started realising that I wasn't really egotistical, just insecure, and I ended up making a ton of friends. Like a puppy learning not to chew on things, I learned not to talk about myself all the time.

I began dating one woman who was in the show, a good-looking blonde who had a party-queen reputation. She was a wild one, the kind of girl who liked trouble, and at first I was drawn to her dangerous air. Part of me just wanted to see if I could win her, but once I did, I realised she wasn't at all the kind of woman I was looking for. It sounds corny, but I really did believe in Snow White and Prince Charming—I wanted to find a woman with whom I could ride off into the sunset and share my life. I'm not sure I was aware of it at the time, but subconsciously I was comparing all the women I met to Lisa.

Meanwhile, Lisa was back in Houston having problems of her own. She'd been experiencing a lot of trouble sleeping, and her insomnia eventually got so bad she had to drop out of high school. She'd always had trouble fitting in, and now, with the onset of a creeping depression, she felt even more alienated. This was the beginning of what she later called her 'blue period'

Things at home were tough, too—her parents had a very contentious relationship and it affected the entire family. This was a scary time for a teenage girl who had come to feel that no place was safe. Finally, she decided she had to get out of her parents' house, at least until things cooled down a bit. So one day at the studio, she asked my mom if she could come stay at our house for a while.

My mother, who could be so hard on her own kids, had come to adore Lisa. For one thing, Lisa had started dancing very late—no serious female dancer starts in her teens, as Lisa had. But Lisa was determined, and highly gifted, and she'd experienced a life-changing moment at the age of fifteen when she made the conscious decision to pursue dancing seriously. She began working out at my mom's studio seven days a week—she even got the key from my mom so she could work out when nobody was there.

Lisa's dedication thrilled my mother, who in return was a

mentor to her, providing validation and emotional support. So when Lisa asked if she could move into the Swayze house for a couple of weeks, my mom didn't hesitate at all before saying yes.

As it happened, I was home for much of that time. Early on, before she really knew Lisa, my mom had told me, 'Buddy, I don't want you dating Lisa. She's bad news.' But then my mother had watched Lisa transform herself into a serious dancer, and now she had a slightly different message. 'Buddy,' she said. 'I don't want you dating Lisa. I don't want you messing her up.'

My mom didn't know it, but the attraction between Lisa and me had been growing for some time. Lisa had seemed indifferent to me all those months, but it turned out she was interested in me too—she was just shy, and acting like she didn't care was her way of covering it up. But during those two weeks when Lisa stayed with us, she and I took every opportunity to steal time together. When Mom was in the kitchen, we'd be behind the swinging door in the dining room, and after everyone in the house had gone to sleep, we'd sneak out to the living room and fool around on the couch. We still weren't technically 'dating', but man, we couldn't get enough of each other.

WHEN *DISNEY ON PARADE* ended, it was time to figure out my next step. After all the rigours of the show, my knee was pretty wrecked, and I looked forward to it having some time to heal. But then I received a scholarship to study with the Harkness Ballet in New York City.

Touring with *Disney on Parade* had made me realise how deeply dance was rooted in my soul. Of all the things I loved to do, nothing came close to the feeling dancing gave me—a feeling of complete emotional and physical freedom, as if your spirit was soaring in all directions at once. It's hard to capture in words the sheer joy and fulfilment that the act of dancing can bring. All I knew was, I wanted to do it for ever. And Harkness was my chance to do it professionally, at the highest level.

My mother, who had pushed me and pushed me as a young

dancer, didn't want me to accept the scholarship. She knew that ballet dancing is just about the hardest thing you can put a knee joint through, and a company like Harkness was guaranteed to push me to my absolute limit.

Of course, if there's one sure way to get Patrick Swayze to do something, it's to tell me I can't do it. You don't think I can dance with one of the greatest professional ballet companies in the world? Watch me.

So I packed up a couple of suitcases and got ready for the move to New York. This was it—Buddy Swayze was heading for the bright lights and the big city! I was excited at the chance to test my stuff against the best dancers in the business. And I knew exactly who I wanted to spend my last evening in Houston with: Lisa.

I invited her to dinner at St Michel's, a fancy French restaurant in town. We talked for hours. Lisa and I had got more and more comfortable with each other, and we talked easily about dancing, life, and the future that stretched enticingly ahead of us. At the end of dinner, she gave me a fifty-cent piece. 'This is for luck,' she said, pressing it into my hand. In return, I gave her a broken Mickey Mouse watch I'd got during *Disney on Parade*.

I didn't realise yet that I was falling in love with Lisa, but I did know she was the kind of person I always wanted to have in my life.

I gave her a card that which that she's kept all these years. It gives a pretty good idea of how I was feeling about her:

> *Lisa, I really can't tell you how much you've come to mean to me in such a short time, as a friend, and as someone I could really care for. Remember the happiness we shared, and I hope in your mind you know that I don't want what we shared to end! I'll miss you very much and will think of you often. Work hard at your dancing and I'll do the same, and maybe, someday . . . my heart will be united with yours,*
>
> *Buddy*

It was a magical night—or at least, it was until I dropped Lisa off at her house and was driving home. As I was making my way through the suburb of Bellaire, I looked in my rearview mirror to see police lights flashing. My stomach fell. Earlier that day, I'd realised the licence plates on my car were out of date, so I'd foolishly taken the plates off my dad's truck and put them on my car. The police were pulling me over because they'd run a check and discovered the plates were on the wrong vehicle.

The police in Bellaire had a reputation for being nasty and aggressive, and they certainly lived up to it that night. After they pulled me over, I tried to explain why I'd switched the plates, but the officers weren't having any of it. They pinned me hard up against a chain-link fence, frisked me, and put me in the back of their car to take me down to the precinct. I was under arrest.

I spent half the night in jail, until my dad was able to come down to bail me out. He didn't have enough cash on him to do it, though, and there were no ATMs then. So I fished around in my pockets and gave the police the rest of my cash, too—including the lucky coin from Lisa.

Getting arrested and thrown into a jail cell certainly wasn't the big send-off I'd hoped for. But at least the next day I was on my way, with fingers crossed that my luck in New York would be better than my luck on my last night in Houston.

# Chapter 3

My first apartment in New York City was at 45 West 70th Street. Unlike the clean, upscale neighbourhood of today, New York's Seventies then were still rough round the edges. My street was at least decent and affordable, and it had the bonus of being close to Central Park. But the apartment itself turned out to be less pleasant than the surroundings.

I was moving into a basement apartment with a fellow Harkness dancer, and as I descended below sidewalk level, I realised it wasn't going to be pretty down there. The lack of natural light was depressing enough, but it wasn't nearly as bad as the musty smell and the water stains on the walls. My family didn't exactly live in a mansion in Houston, but I could hardly believe this was the place I'd now be calling home—it was a hovel. At a Harkness trainee stipend of just forty-five dollars a week, though, it was all I could afford, even working extra jobs in my spare time.

I was scared to death about how my knee would hold up at Harkness. Part of me knew it was crazy even to have accepted the scholarship, but I wasn't going to let that stop me. I'd made a huge amount of headway in my life trading on the invincibility of youth: this would be no different—I would just dance and grit my teeth whenever it hurt. And it would be worth all the pain when I made the leap from trainee to company member.

For all the fear I felt about my knee, I should have been equally afraid of the infamous Harkness regime. In addition to the physical stress of dancing in up to six classes a day and pushing your endurance to the limit, Harkness also put some of its dancers on a special diet aimed at virtually eliminating body fat. The Harkness diet allowed dancers to consume just five hundred calories a day—basically, lettuce and a few bites of turkey, plus vitamin shots.

And that wasn't all. The Harkness doctors also came up with a shot that was said to encourage your body to live on its own fat tissue, so that even those who had almost no body fat to begin with still dropped pounds, as the small deposits of fat between muscles melted away. I had always been lean, through constant training, but my arms and shoulders were big—I looked like Godzilla compared to the other male dancers. But under the Harkness regimen, I transformed my body. I dropped fifteen pounds and developed the streamlined physique of a dancer.

The women in Harkness had it even rougher. At this point, nobody had written an exposé like Gelsey Kirkland's 1996 book *Dancing on My Grave*, which detailed the dark side of the professional ballet world. Gelsey was dancing with the New York City Ballet and American Ballet Theatre at the same time I was at

Harkness, and I often partnered her at *pas de deux* class. The tales she told in her book of the eating disorders, drug use and emotional trauma that dancers could face, matched what I saw during those years.

Female bodies aren't really supposed to look like the bodies of ballet dancers, so no matter how thin a dancer was, she was always encouraged to lose more by the Harkness tribunal, which kept tabs on dancers' progress. 'Lose five more pounds' was the mantra, even if the women had already shed pounds on intensive, crazy diets. The pressure was so bad that two women died during my time at the ballet. They just pushed themselves farther than their emaciated bodies could handle.

Everything my mother had said was true—the amount of suffering you had to undergo to become a professional ballet dancer was overwhelming. I stuck to it, dancing and dieting to prove that I was ready to take my spot in the company. But the one thing I couldn't control, of course, was my knee. And with the daily abuse of dancing, it got worse than ever.

As had happened during my days touring with *Disney on Parade*, my knee began swelling up after I danced. I would put ice round it to bring the swelling down, but at times there was just too much fluid in the joint and I'd have to get it drained. This was an unpleasant procedure: one of the company orthopaedists who worked with Harkness would insert a long needle into my knee to let the fluid out. There were times when the joint was so inflamed I'd watch it swell right back up just after having it drained. Then I had no choice but to go home, put more ice on it, and just hope it would be ready for class the next day. Yet even if it wasn't, I'd have to dance anyway.

At one point, I felt a strange burning sensation I'd never had before. The joint swelled up worse than ever, and when I went to the doctor to get it checked out, he told me I needed to stay overnight in the hospital for treatment. I told him that was impossible—I had too much to do. I couldn't miss any classes, and I didn't want anyone to think my knee wasn't strong enough.

The doctor looked at me with a grave expression. 'Patrick,' he said, 'this is a serious staphylococcus infection. If we don't nip it in the bud, you could lose your leg.'

I stared at him, stunned into silence. I had been pushing myself so hard, it had never occurred to me that I could actually be putting my health in danger. Ever since I'd hurt my knee in that football game, I had forced myself to operate as if it was fine, as there was no other way to do all the things I wanted to. The doctor's words scared me, but I knew that after I got it treated, I'd have to push on as before. I'd have to find a way.

If it hadn't been for my knee trouble, I would already have made the Harkness company. Even though I had lost some weight and muscle mass, I was still a rarity in the world of ballet, a male dancer who actually looked like a man on stage. Most male dancers were slender and graceful, amazing dancers—but they didn't look like what the ballet companies wanted. On the most fundamental level, the purpose of the male dancer was to make the woman look beautiful, and my performances were geared towards exactly that strong and masculine look.

I was a good partner, and a good soloist, which of course made me all the more reluctant to give up.

AMID ALL THIS DANCING, dieting and worrying, I had to find ways to bring in more money. The stipend wasn't enough for anyone to live on, so despite the fact that we were often exhausted from workouts and rehearsals, many of the dancers did extra jobs to pay the rent.

I worked for a time at a Hallmark card store, and also lifeguarded at a subterranean men's health club near my apartment. I sang and played guitar in the clubs down in Greenwich Village, which was a hotbed of creative energy. New York in the 1970s was rough, a little wild, with an anything-goes feel to it. Energy seemed to pulsate through the streets, and being young there made you feel as if you could do anything. And that anything could happen.

The next job I got was a perfect example of that. In early September 1973, I got word that the Harkness Ballet's benefactor, the oil heiress Rebekah Harkness, had specifically requested me for a rather unusual assignment.

Mrs Harkness had commissioned Spanish artist Enrique Senis-Oliver to paint a gigantic mural for the brand-new Harkness Theatre then being built at Lincoln Center. Called *Homage to Terpsichore*, the painting was to stretch from the stage to the top of the proscenium and down both sides, and would consist mostly of what *Time* magazine later called 'an agonised, thrusting morass of naked dancers'.

Well, those naked dancers were me. Over a period of several weeks, I posed and flexed so Enrique could paint my nude form over and over in the mural. Enrique and I spent many exhausting hours perched on scaffolding thirty feet off the ground in the freezing theatre while he painted the ceiling. As a thank-you he painted my face on the mural's centrepiece—a towering twenty-foot-high portrait of me leaping naked towards the sun, with a cape of peacock feathers trailing behind me.

As a letter I wrote to Lisa shows, the fall of 1973 was a very good time for me in New York. I'd just returned after seeing her in Houston, and I was filled with the excitement of being in the city, and having my life ahead of me:

*Well, Lisa,*
*I'm back! I was really dreading coming back while I was on the plane, but now that I'm back, it's great! Everything is fine, my rent is paid, and everything is well at Harkness.*

*I went walking tonight, and the street was bustling, and the fountain at Lincoln Center was so neat, and everything seems to be going my way, that I just started running and singing! People thought I was crazy but I didn't care!*

*Well, I've got tons of work ahead of me but I'm looking forward to it. There is hardly anyone in class because of the summer students being gone, and it's really fine! You know, I didn't leave sad, Wednesday, I really felt good; that is about you. I know if we are meant to be, that we'll get it together one day. Over such a short time, you've grown to mean a lot to me, I want to always be great friends. Work hard and maybe you'll be up here before you know it!*

*I miss you much and hope it's the same. Tell everyone 'Hello' and I miss 'em, okay? Stay happy, and write!*

*Missingly yours, Buddy*

My feelings for Lisa were growing, but I was still scared to admit it outright—either to her or to myself. I was hoping against hope that she'd get a ballet scholarship too, and I was dropping her name at Harkness, trying to help her secure one. I even offered to have her stay at my apartment whenever she did make it up to New York. 'It will save quite a bit of money,' I told her, presumably with a straight face. I knew Lisa's parents wouldn't approve of her living with me in New York, but I wanted to plant that seed anyway.

Despite the intensity of the feelings Lisa and I obviously had for each other, we both were trying very hard to protect ourselves. We both came to the relationship feeling like, 'I don't want this person to get to me'—we were afraid of being too vulnerable, afraid of getting hurt. So we made a big show of just wanting to be friends, at least until the other person made the first move.

We kept writing back and forth and talking on the phone, though, so our relationship continued to grow even if we didn't quite know where it was going. And it probably would have continued that way, except that in 1974 Lisa finally got her scholarship to Harkness. She was coming to New York City, and despite her mother's hope that she'd move into the Barbizon Hotel for Women, she'd decided to take me up on my offer to live with me at the new place I'd found for myself on West 74th Street.

LISA MOVED to New York in the summer of 1974 and, as I soon discovered, she had very distinct ideas about what we'd be doing together—and not doing. Despite the fact that we'd had plenty of intimate times in Houston over the years, she made it clear we'd be living together as room-mates, not as lovers. Lisa, who was now eighteen, had been dancing seriously for three years and she was absolutely driven to make it as a dancer. Now that she'd made it to

New York, she didn't want any distractions getting in her way.

I wanted to make the Harkness company, too, of course, and I was focused on that goal. But my feelings for Lisa grew stronger and stronger the more time we spent together. After just a few weeks, I had no doubt that Lisa was the woman I wanted to be with. She was deep, talented, driven—and beautiful. As I played one of my favourite records of that summer—*The Best of Bread*—Lisa would catch sight of me gazing at her whenever the song 'Baby I'm-a Want You' came on. She knew what I was feeling, and it frightened her.

But the attraction between us was so strong, and the intensity of our emotions so high, that something eventually had to give. And boy, did it. When Lisa and I finally got together in the winter of 1974–5, a few months after she'd moved in, it was like the dam had broken and the flood came rushing in. Up to then we'd never had sex together, but once we did—well, suffice it to say I'd never felt such passion in my life, and I couldn't get enough of it. We were intoxicated by each other, and when we weren't dancing or working, we were at our apartment spending every hour we could together.

We'd stay up all night, talking, laughing and just enjoying each other. The intensity of it was thrilling—I never thought I could feel so strongly about another person. We were discovering so much about each other, and learning about ourselves, too, all in the excitement of first love.

Lisa felt it, too, but she was also scared. She worried about giving in to her feelings for me when she wanted to be totally focused on dancing. Years later, she dug up her diary pages from that time, and they show how deeply torn she was over what was happening between us:

*I really don't know what to do (concerning Buddy). I'm so frightened. I want to sit down and talk it over with him, but I'm afraid I might startle him too much or make him think I'm jumping to conclusions . . .*

*Sometimes I wonder whether I'm being shallow and just getting carried off like so many girls I know always do. God, I'm so afraid. I've never done anything like this before and I feel danger in getting close to a person and caring more than I should . . .*

*I wonder if I should move out. I might have to. But I'd see him every day anyway [at Harkness] so there's not much good for my head in that. What I should do is find a way to get out and away as often as possible. I can't get my life too tied to his.*

I had no idea Lisa was considering moving out, which was a good thing, as it would have scared me to death. I'd have felt that she was rejecting me, which would have rocked my fragile self-esteem to the core. My feelings for her were now so strong, and I was so sure of them, that I'd have felt paralysed at the idea that I might lose her.

I wanted to lock in our relationship and our love. Lisa and I had talked a little bit about where our relationship was headed and I had never got the sense that she was anxious to commit to anything long-term. But I was. I wanted to marry Lisa. And one night in the spring of 1975, as we were playing around on the couch, I decided it was time to raise the subject.

We were wrestling and tickling each other, just messing around, and all of a sudden I said, 'Lisa, why don't we get married? Why don't we just go ahead and do it?'

Of all the responses a man hopes to hear to this question, dead silence isn't one of them. But Lisa was quiet for a moment before responding slowly. 'Yeah, sure,' she said. 'That could happen.'

I sat up, every nerve ending on alert.

'When do you want to do it?' I asked her.

'Well,' she said, pondering, 'how about fall of next year?' Meaning, the fall of 1976—nearly a year and a half away.

I could feel panic rising from my chest to my throat. For some reason, I just knew that unless we got married right away, it was never going to happen and I would lose Lisa for ever. 'No,' I said. 'If we're going to do it, let's do it right away—like, next month.'

Now it was clearly Lisa's turn to panic. She tried to buy herself some time—but I wasn't having it.

'Lisa, we need to get married right away,' I told her. And that was that—I wouldn't take no for an answer. I told her that I loved her and needed her and couldn't live without her. I even told her that if she wouldn't marry me now, I'd run my motorcycle into a stop sign. I'm not proud of that particular moment, but it's evidence of just how afraid I was to lose her. No matter how confidently I projected myself on stage and in everyday life, inside I was still a scared boy—afraid of rejection and willing to do whatever was necessary to stave it off. At the same time, I really believed that even if Lisa didn't love me now, she would love me later. I would win her.

This wasn't the best of circumstances for starting a marriage. To my relief, though, Lisa said yes. But the sting of her first cautious response stayed with me for years. For the first decade of our marriage, whenever we had a fight, I'd accuse her of not loving me enough. 'Well, you didn't want to marry me anyway!' I'd say. 'You only agreed because I pushed you into it!' This was a tremendous insecurity of mine, and it took a long time before enough trust built up for me to feel confident in her love for me.

LISA AND I got married in Houston on June 12, 1975. We didn't have much money, so we cut corners wherever we could. The ceremony was in her family's back yard, the reception was at my mom's studio, and Lisa made both her wedding gown and the three-piece suit I wore.

In photos taken during the ceremony, both Lisa and I have deer-in-the-headlights expressions. I think neither one of us could quite believe what was happening, and we both felt some fear about taking this step. Lisa cried through the whole wedding, except for one moment—when she tried to put my ring on and couldn't quite manage it, she smiled a sweet little smile. As she stood there with tears in her eyes, all I could think was, 'She's crying because she doesn't want to marry me.' But she was actually just overwhelmed with emotion.

In fact, she later told me she had a realisation during the ceremony. Looking at me, she had seen my vulnerability, and she suddenly had the thought that marrying someone is just about the nicest thing anyone can do for you. It's making a decision to hold nothing back. I was making a public vow to commit myself to her for ever and she was touched by how profound that was. Unfortunately, I mistook the look on her face for horror.

Thirty-four years later I can say that marrying Lisa was the best decision I ever made. But looking back, I'm struck by how very young we were, and how little we really knew about each other. Or anything, for that matter. There was a real passion between us, but that's not what made it last. It's the commitment we made—and kept—to work on the relationship as much as was needed in order to keep it going. Everybody goes through rough times, and we certainly ended up having our share, but we've always found a way to come back together, which is easier said than done.

For our honeymoon, Lisa and I borrowed a motorcycle and rode to Lake Travis, about 180 miles outside Houston. We were pretty much broke, of course, so we just camped and brought along a little cookstove for meals. We stayed for a week, and although it was about as low-cost as you could get for a honeymoon, we both had the time of our lives. For all the anxiety we'd felt at the wedding, we were happy and excited to begin our marriage together out in the natural world, just the two of us.

This was the beginning of our life's journey together. But as we discovered when we returned to New York, it wouldn't all be sunshine and roses.

## Chapter 4

BACK IN NEW YORK, the Harkness Ballet was sputtering to an end. Despite the support of Mrs Harkness and the sparkling new theatre at Lincoln Center, the company folded—and with it, my dreams of becoming a Harkness company dancer ended too. Lisa had already left Harkness to train at the Joffrey Ballet, so she was set. But I needed to find a new place to continue pursuing my dream.

I managed to win a spot in the Eliot Feld Ballet, one of the most respected companies in New York. Every dancer in Eliot Feld was a soloist, so the quality of the dancing was extremely high. I was excited to join the company and immediately began striving to move up within it. I wanted to become a principal dancer, to get the best roles I could. The level of artistry in my dance was rising, and I wanted to make it to the top of the ballet world.

But as a letter from Lisa home to her mother describes, my knee problems were continuing to threaten my dance career:

> *Yesterday Buddy went to a doctor because his knee was giving him a lot of trouble again. A Dr Hamilton, really good, specialises with dancers and has written books on their injuries.*
>
> *Nothing really new about the knee except the arthritis has set in faster than was expected. The bones are grinding flatter and flatter. He was given lots of exercises and we bought a brace to prevent it from moving too much*
>
> *Dr Hamilton said that Buddy has the knee of a 45-year-old man, and that in five years it will be that of a 100-year-old man. This is cause for serious thinking. He might not be dancing much longer—a year is the limit . . .*

This news had been especially painful to hear, because it came just as I was making real headway with Eliot Feld. Lisa's letter goes on:

> *. . . Kinda awful because right now he's at a crossroads and it's just now that things are rushing out to greet him. Eliot is crazy over him, the things he has said to him are more than anyone could hope to hear. Cora [Cahan, Eliot Feld's company manager] says he's not just good on stage, he's fantastic. And he is, and it's just now beginning to be noticed . . .*

But she also noticed something else, something deeper. One thing I've always loved about Lisa is her ability to see beyond the obvious things. She's very intuitive and uncovers things most other people can't see. And at this point, she was realising things about me that I didn't even see myself.

> *... One thing about Buddy is that he can be equally fantastic if he does something else. His charisma shines as great. I think it will turn out well, he doesn't have to stop dancing altogether, just not be in a situation that demands too much. And there are so many things he wants to do, but never has the time: writing, his songwriting, is an important part of him.*
>
> *Everything's kind of a blur right now, but something just hits me that Buddy will bloom when he has the freedom to give himself to all the things he wants to do. His reasons for dancing confuse him so much. He can enjoy it, but something drains him and downs him. As he said, this would show if it was dancing or not. I personally at this point think that dancing is a big part of him, but not his whole life.*

Lisa was right—dancing was, and had always been, a source of conflicting feelings for me. It stemmed from trying to please my mother, from trying to make myself not just a good dancer but the perfect dancer, and from pushing myself beyond my limits. Everything Lisa said in this letter was true, and although I didn't realise it yet myself, it was what would eventually save me when I had to stop dancing full time—a time that was closer than I thought.

Meanwhile, our life in New York was a complete whirlwind. Between rehearsals, teaching, singing and side jobs, we were constantly in motion.

I've always been this way, trying to pack in as much as I can in a day, but looking back I don't know where we ever found the hours to sleep.

In addition to the dancing, training and part-time jobs, we also spent the first couple of years auditioning for musical theatre roles during the ballet's off-season. I performed in *Music Man* at the Paper Mill Playhouse in New Jersey, and did the role of Riff in *West Side Story* at the Northstage Dinner Theater in Long Island. But although these roles were fun to play and brought some money in, they were considered a step down for serious dancers. For a ballet dancer, the only real dancing is ballet—everything else just pales. Even dancing in Broadway shows.

Still, in 1975 I was happy to be cast as one of four featured dancers in *Goodtime Charley*. The show starred Joel Grey and Ann Reinking, and it ran for 104 performances. It was my first time dancing on Broadway—and also my first time meeting the cute, curly-haired young woman who would later play a big role in my life: Jennifer Grey. Jennifer is Joel's daughter, and she was fifteen that summer, a bubbly, outgoing, sweet girl. Neither of us could have known that twelve years later, we'd star together in a movie that would change both of our lives.

In the midst of our whirlwind of activities, Lisa and I still had just one overriding goal: to become principal dancers in a ballet company and achieve the highest possible level of artistry. I hoped that the Eliot Feld Ballet would be the place. And, in early 1976, I was offered my big break.

THE COMPANY WAS PLANNING to tour South America in May, but during rehearsals, Eliot's principal male dancer, George Montalbano, had to pull out because of injuries. That hole had to be filled in all the ballets he was dancing—and Eliot chose me to fill it. Suddenly I was going to be performing principal roles in the South America tour, but that wasn't all. Eliot had big plans for New York performances upon our return. He started choreography on a new work that would have three company dancers—including me—dancing with none other than the great Mikhail Baryshnikov, who was coming in to perform as a guest star. This was a huge opportunity for a young dancer, the big chance I'd been waiting for.

Eliot Feld was one of the premier American choreographers of the last fifty years. He had choreographed more than 140 ballets and won numerous awards. He could be a hard-nosed bastard, quick to berate his dancers and stingy with praise, but when he expressed pleasure at something you had done, it was the greatest feeling in the world.

Now Eliot started rehearsing me hard to get me ready, and I pushed myself even more. My knee was giving me as much trouble as ever, so a couple of months before the tour was to launch, I had one more knee surgery in an attempt to stabilise the joint. Even so, I still had no choice but to keep draining the knee, as it was swelling up after eight to ten hours of rehearsing a day.

But as the tour dates drew near, I found myself having second thoughts about what I was putting myself through. For one thing, I wasn't thrilled to be leaving Lisa for two months. I'd even be missing our first wedding anniversary, which upset both of us. Also I was afraid of getting my knee drained in South America, worried that conditions there would be less hygienic than those in New York. I'd already had my leg threatened by one staph infection and I feared the same thing might happen again.

But could I really bow out of this amazing opportunity? After all the work and sweat of the last three years, I was going to tour South America with one of the most respected ballet companies in the world, not to mention performing back in New York with Baryshnikov. How could I possibly step away now? Wasn't this exactly what I'd been working for my whole life?

But then, one afternoon, a freak incident changed everything.

I was riding my motorcycle on the West Side of Manhattan, heading downtown for a rehearsal on a bright, sunny day. The lanes narrowed as I approached the West Side Highway overpass and suddenly a car cut right in front of me. I braked, but he'd cut too close—I had to manoeuvre to the left, trying to squeeze between his car and the guardrail. It was a dangerous moment, but it looked as if I'd managed to avoid a collision—until I suddenly saw a boy on a bicycle directly in my path. He was riding the wrong way down the street and now there was nowhere for either of us to go.

I knew in a flash we couldn't avoid colliding, so I hit the rear brake and let my motorcycle shoot out from under me, sliding sideways along the road. That way, the motorcycle would hit the kid's bicycle, rather than the kid himself. If we hit head-on, he'd probably be killed.

The manoeuvre worked perfectly: my motorcycle slammed into the boy's bike and he flew off, ending up with scratches but no serious injuries. I was okay, too. I had some cuts and bruises, but was still able to rehearse that day. Emotionally, though, this accident really shook me up.

All the rest of that day, I was haunted by the thought that if the accident had happened slightly differently, my dance career would have been over. It was as if I realised for the first time that a dancer's whole professional life hung by a thread, and that I'd been fooling myself thinking I could have a ballet career, even without the knee problems I had.

The next day I still couldn't shake these feelings, and all of a sudden I realised it was over. During a break in rehearsals, I talked to our dance coach, Cora Cahan. I broke down in tears, saying, 'Cora, I don't think I can do this any more.' She didn't want to hear it. She tried to talk me out of leaving, but I knew I was done. I just couldn't go on—not even for the chance to dance an important New York season with Baryshnikov. That week, I told Eliot I wouldn't be going on the South America tour. Just like that, my career as a professional ballet dancer was over.

It's hard to describe how devastating this decision was. I had worked so hard, and come so far, and now I was walking away. I still get emotional thinking about it even with all the amazing experiences I've since had as an actor; nothing really compares to the sense of joy and exhilaration dancing gives you. Leaving the ballet world created a void in me that I spent years trying to fill.

Lisa tried to console me, pointing out that I'd gone incredibly far considering the injury and pain I was constantly dealing with. But it all sounded hollow. For so long I had been Patrick Swayze, aspiring ballet dancer. What would I do now?

Back when I was at San Jacinto Junior College, I'd had to deal with watching my dream of competing in the Olympics go down the tubes. That had been a huge disappointment, but it was not even close to the devastation I felt now. But fortunately I had learned an important lesson from that first loss: when one dream dies, you have to move on to a new one. I could have fallen into serious depression when I left Eliot Feld, and very nearly did. But the lesson in self-preservation that I learned from that first disappointment saved me in the second one.

Two other things helped to keep me going. One was that I knew I had Lisa standing by my side, no matter what. The other was my growing interest in different spiritual teachings, including Buddhist philosophy, which I had begun studying after I moved to New York.

Ever since I was a boy I'd been interested in the whole range of beliefs out there in the world. I'd gone to Catholic Masses and even considered becoming a priest at one point, but eventually I became disillusioned with Catholicism. The Catholic schools I'd attended were populated by the kind of mean nuns and knuckle-rapping priests you read about in books, which didn't do much to lead me further into the faith, and I even got into trouble once as an altar boy for sneaking sips of wine in the vestibule.

I was always curious about spirituality, though, so I started exploring other options. In high school I devoured Kahlil Gibran's writings, Antoine de Saint-Exupéry's *The Little Prince* and Eugen Herrigel's *Zen in the Art of Archery.* These books spoke to me in a way church sermons didn't. And because I had studied martial arts, I was also familiar with the notion of *chi*—connecting with your true self.

Once I left Texas, I continued on this spiritual journey. New York in the 1970s was a hothouse of spiritual exploration—everyone was looking for meaning in their lives and the one philosophy in particular that really spoke to me was Buddhism. I had begun doing meditation and chanting and found that not only did it help me stay focused, it calmed the voices that were forever trying to undercut me. What struck me about Buddhism was that it didn't exclude other religions. You could be Catholic, Jewish or Hare Krishna and still be Buddhist. And, unlike some religions that required you to look outside yourself for God, Buddhism was all about finding God from within—you had everything you needed within yourself. This philosophy had very deep appeal for me.

But the spiritual journey we were on wasn't ultimately about finding answers. It was about understanding the questions. Once you think you have the answers, you stop growing. Yet if you keep exploring, seeking and opening your mind, you'll find that the learning never stops. This thought has helped me immeasurably in the difficult days of my life, from dealing with injury, to career disappointments, to the most trying days of all, as I fight now to keep on living through cancer.

WITH MY BALLET CAREER over, it was time to figure out the next dream. Performing was in my blood and I wanted to continue doing it, so I began studying with Warren Robertson, one of the best acting coaches in New York. Lisa was still dancing, but she was broadening her horizons and had started doing TV commercials and auditioning for theatre. She started studying with Warren, too, in anticipation of career opportunities to come.

Warren was an amazing teacher, perfect for young people because he knew how to break down your 'act'. Each of us has a way we present ourselves to the world—the 'act' we show to other people as opposed to the true self, which we try to protect. Warren taught us that the degree to which you believe your own act is the degree to which you're limited in drawing from the deep well of characters inside you. This was especially liberating for me, because although I'd been acting since boyhood, it was almost always in musical theatre—the 'presentational' school of acting. Warren showed us a totally different approach, a more organic way of approaching acting.

Even as we studied with Warren, we kept one foot in the dance world by taking teaching jobs. Living on a shoestring in New York, Lisa and I would take whatever work we could get—we taught jazz, acrobatics and gymnastics classes in places as far-flung as Pennsylvania and New Jersey. We'd ride out on our motorcycle, through snow, rain, sleet or whatever. The days were long but the teaching brought in extra cash and kept us dancing.

Another way we made money was by doing carpentry. Growing

up, I had always enjoyed building things—the homemade motorbike was just one example—and while I was still at Harkness, I'd decided it would be a great idea to do a little woodwork on the side. I didn't know much about it, but that didn't stop me. How hard could it be, after all?

I had put word out that I was available for carpentry jobs and it wasn't long before Bill Ritman, the set designer for Harkness, approached me. Could I finish converting three floors of an Upper West Side brownstone into an apartment for him? I had to stop my mouth from falling open. This was a far bigger project than I'd anticipated—and it was for the Harkness set designer, who knew a little about quality work. Any sensible person would have owned up to not having the experience, and perhaps not being up for it.

'Sure!' I told Bill. 'Ready when you are!'

I showed up at the brownstone with a backpack full of tools, but unbeknown to Bill, the most important tool of all was my *Reader's Digest* do-it-yourself carpentry guide. Let's just say I spent a lot of time in the bathroom on that first job, flipping through that book and trying to quickly teach myself how to do all the things Bill was asking of me. Fortunately, it was a good guide, and I was a quick learner. The brownstone work went off without a hitch and I was on my way to making money as a woodworker.

Lisa joined me in the woodworking business when I got a job building a hi-fi and TV entertainment centre. I started working on it in our bedroom, and at some point I said to her, 'Lisa, can you hold this board for me, please?' From that moment on, we were partners. We built that entertainment centre together, and in the months to come we worked on tons of projects, doing the work in our bedroom (and ending up with sawdust in all our clothes) and stacking the finished items in the living room. Our apartment ended up looking like a furniture showroom.

When we finished a project, we'd deliver it the same way we got everywhere else—on the motorcycle. We'd carry it down the five flights of stairs and I'd get on the back of the motorcycle and try to balance whatever we'd made while Lisa drove. Fortunately, we had a big cycle—a Honda four-cylinder model, practically a car on a frame—so at least we weren't teetering along on a little bike.

Lisa and I got a decent number of these jobs thanks to recommendations from friends and the dance companies. But we still weren't making very much money, so every week we'd budget how much was coming in and how much we could spend. If we had at least twenty dollars for food, that was a good week. The only way we had been able to get the motorcycle, in fact, was by managing to get a credit card and then immediately maxing out our limit to buy it. We spent the next five years paying off that debt.

We got very good at saving money, doing our shopping at a market downtown, and making dishes that would keep. Lisa became an expert at making turkey last for days—she'd make turkey casserole, turkey sandwiches, turkey soup. When we got sick of turkey, she'd make whatever she could with the meagre cash we had.

Every once in a while, we'd land a job that paid pretty well, especially compared to the pennies we'd made as ballet dancers. We got hired to sing and dance in industrial shows—trade shows for companies like Ford Motors and Milliken Carpets, where we'd get flown to other cities, put up in hotels, and paid what felt like a fortune. Sometimes the companies even gave us samples of their products. Milliken, for example, gave us high-end rugs, so although our apartment was sparsely decorated, a little dingy, and often covered with sawdust, we at least had beautiful floors.

Around this time I got in touch with a talent manager named Bob LeMond. Bob was originally from Houston and my mother had helped get him into the managing business. I'd known Bob my whole life, and had always thought of him as just a quirky little guy from Texas, a would-be dancer who didn't dance nearly as well as he talked. But by 1977 he had become a big-time manager—he represented John Travolta, among many others.

Bob's office was in Los Angeles, so I didn't call him the first couple of years I was in New York. But after rising in the dance world, and getting respectable musical theatre credits under my belt, I decided it was time. I made an appointment through his secretary, and when we met in New York he had one question for me.

'Buddy, why didn't you call me before this?' he asked. 'Where have you been?'

'Well, Bob,' I said, 'I wanted to wait until I felt I'd earned it. You know, I've always been Patsy Swayze's son, especially to you. I wanted to make a name for myself before coming in.'

'That's your first mistake,' Bob said. 'You've got to use anybody you can in this business to get you where you want to go.' I just looked at him, but he wasn't done yet. 'Don't you ever do anything like that again in your career,' he said.

Bob didn't take me on as a client just then but he told me he'd help me out. I knew I was in good hands. He was acquainted with absolutely everybody in the business, and his charming manner brought people's guard down. As one director I know joked years later, 'You know, Bob and I would just talk, and he's got that southern thing and is so friendly, and we have such a good time—and then he leaves and I realise I just got screwed.'

During the seventies, there was one long-running show in particular that Bob used as a breeding ground for his clients: the Broadway production of *Grease*. The musical had opened at the Broadhurst Theatre in 1972, and when I hooked up with Bob it was still playing. I hoped I might become the latest protégé to win a role in the show—and sure enough, before long Bob had arranged an audition.

As Lisa revealed in a letter to her parents:

> *Buddy is up for (I don't know whether to say it or not) a role in Broadway's 'Grease'.*
>
> *Physically Buddy is the best choice, his voice and appearance couldn't be closer to what the role requires. They just have to see if he's an actor now. I guess we all do. I've never seen him do anything before. He has done acting but it was quite a while ago.*
>
> *It's a very big part, the lead, as a matter of fact. He's perfect for the part, I know he could do it 'cause he's always playing around here exactly as Danny Zuko does on stage. He just has to do it for them. It's so exciting, I keep trying to stay objective*

*and not start thinking of what it would do for him if he gets the part. I feel like I'm auditioning. Cross your fingers and we'll let everyone know.*

In that same letter, Lisa described the show she was in—a revival of *Hellzapoppin'*, which had been the longest-running Broadway musical back in the thirties and early forties. The revival starred Jerry Lewis and Lynn Redgrave, and Lisa was a featured dancer—but the New York critics savaged Lewis, who was politically unpopular at the time, and the show unfortunately never made it to Broadway.

Seeing her name printed in the programmes, Lisa began to wonder if 'Haapaniemi' wasn't too much of a mouthful as a stage name. Before long 'Lisa Niemi' would begin appearing on playbills and cast and crew lists, as she embraced her new name and budding career.

I WON an eight-month stint in the role of Danny Zuko in late 1977, and started on January 3, 1978. The movie version starring John Travolta and Olivia Newton-John hadn't come out yet, but legions of theatre patrons knew the story of Danny and Sandy from the show's nearly five-and-a-half-year run on Broadway.

My performance got good reviews. I was doing eight shows a week—slicking my hair back with a combination of Groom 'n' Clean and hair spray, and singing, dancing and acting my heart out. Although the schedule was exhausting, I loved being on Broadway—the excitement of the crowds, the adrenaline of performing live on stage. And for the first time, crowds started gathering outside the stage door, waiting for me to sign autographs.

And there was another reason I was happy to be on Broadway: the pay cheque. Lisa and I had been saving for so long, it was nice finally to have the cushion of a little more money. As soon as we found out I'd got the role, we moved to an apartment up on 115th Street, across from Columbia University. We still didn't have any furniture to speak of, but we did buy an actual bed—the first one we ever owned together. No more sleeping on a mattress on the floor!

Lisa and I loved our new place, and we loved New York. But *Grease* began opening new doors for me, and soon Bob LeMond planted the seed of an idea. He told us we should come to Los Angeles, where he was based, to explore movies and television. At first, neither of us was interested. As I told an interviewer at the time, 'I may love doing TV and movies, but I don't want to leave New York—that's where the training and creativity are.' However, as my time in *Grease* began winding down, we found ourselves thinking more seriously about a move to Hollywood.

Lisa's theatre career was just starting to take off, so this would be an especially hard move for her. But she knew as well as I did that we had to grab the momentum I'd got from *Grease*. There were far more jobs for actors in Los Angeles than in New York, so if we wanted to have a chance to seize that life, now was the time. We discussed it and made the decision together that, all things considered, this was the best move.

Over the course of a few months, we saved up about $2,000 for the move. We called Bob to let him know we'd be flying out to Los Angeles in a week or two. 'Great!' he said. 'Call me when you get here!' We booked our tickets, packed up our two cats and a couple of suitcases, and said goodbye to New York. Because we weren't sure things in California would work out, we sublet our apartment in case we needed to come back.

## Chapter 5

After Lisa and I landed in LA, the first thing we did was call Bob LeMond's office to tell him we'd arrived. An Englishwoman picked up the phone. She asked who was calling, and I told her 'Patrick Swayze', expecting she'd recognise my name.

'I'm sorry,' she said. 'Who did you say you were?'

'Patrick Swayze,' I said. 'Bob just took me on as a client. My wife, Lisa, and I just flew in from New York.'

'I see,' she said. There was a pause. 'Mr LeMond is out of town and won't be back until next week.'

This wasn't good news—we'd thought Bob would be able to help us find a place to stay and get settled in, but now he wasn't even going to be around. And in those pre-cellphone days, it wasn't that easy to get hold of people. We had no clue where to go—neither Lisa nor I had ever been to Los Angeles before.

'Well,' I said, 'would you happen to have any suggestions for a place we might stay? We don't really know the city.'

'I believe most of our clients who come into town stay at the Beverly Hills Hotel,' she said. 'I will let Mr LeMond know you called.' And with that she hung up. Welcome to LA!

We made our way to the rental-car counter, packed the cat carriers and suitcases in the car, and headed towards Beverly Hills. But as we drove along Sunset Boulevard and saw the Beverly Hills Hotel, we didn't even bother pulling in—it was a gorgeous hotel, obviously way beyond our means. We had a total of $2,000, which had to last until we got work. Staying in that hotel, our money would have been gone within a week.

Lisa and I looked at each other, and though we didn't say it, we were both thinking the same thing. Had we made a mistake? We'd sublet our beautiful apartment in New York and left a wonderful life there, thinking Bob would take care of us. But he wasn't here, and his office didn't even know who I was. Had I misunderstood what he'd said?

We'd have to figure that out later, as right now we needed to find a place to stay. 'Well, where should we go?' I asked Lisa.

'How about Hollywood?' she said. 'That's why we're here, right?' So I took a quick look at the little map provided by the rental-car company, and we made a U-turn to roll back down Sunset towards Hollywood.

Most people think of Hollywood as a glamorous place, but there are parts of it that are as seedy and run-down as any poor urban area. We pulled up to the first hotel we saw, and I went in to check on rates while Lisa waited with the cats. I walked back to the car shaking my head.

'What's wrong?' Lisa asked.

'Well,' I said, 'they don't rent by the day.'

She looked confused. 'What does that mean?'

'Lisa, they only rent rooms by the hour,' I said. She understood what I meant. I got back into the car and we took off.

Unfortunately, we ran into the same situation at the next two hotels we stopped at. By now, we were getting desperate. Darkness was starting to fall and the streets of Hollywood seemed to be populated with hookers and junkies. Our cats were meowing in the back seat and we were tired from our cross-country flight. We felt like hamsters on a treadmill, with no clue how to get off.

Eventually, driving farther along Sunset Boulevard, we saw the Saharan Motor Hotel on the south side of the street and pulled in. I asked the man behind the front desk if he had any vacancies, and told him how desperate we were. 'We just need a place for a few nights,' I said. 'Please, anything you've got.'

'Well,' he said, 'I do have one lady who comes to town sometimes on business and, when she's not here, her room is available. But I'll have to call and ask if she's allergic to cats. Come back in an hour or so and I'll have an answer for you.' Reluctantly, we got back into the car and drove around some more. But when we came back, the man said the room was ours. We had found our first 'home' in LA.

At that time, the Saharan was the kind of place where you didn't want to walk barefoot on the carpet. It also was never quiet: even at night you could hear the Laundromat next door, the occasional scream from the alleyway outside, and sirens going by. But although the Saharan was pretty dire, the guy at the front desk was always smiling and kind. When we finally checked out a week or so later, after we'd found a place to rent, he said, 'Come back and see us after you make it in Hollywood! You're welcome any time.'

We managed to find a really nice, cheap apartment in the Hollywood Hills, in the lower half of a house owned by two friendly women. It had a kind of bohemian glamour, and because it was built on a hillside we had a fabulous view of Hollywood. The women upstairs were real characters and one of them seemed always to have a tumbler of Scotch in her hand. We loved the apartment—now we just had to find work to pay the $500 a month rent.

Our $2,000 were going fast. Between staying those nights at the Saharan, paying rent at our new place, and eating, we were just about broke. At night, I'd drive up to a spot on Mulholland Drive that had a beautiful panoramic view of Los Angeles. I'd sit there, looking out over the lights of Hollywood, and say, 'I am going to conquer you.' It was like a ritual, a way to gear myself up for the fight ahead. If I was going to make it in Hollywood, I really had to believe I could do it.

WHEN BOB FINALLY got back into town, he apologised for the mix-up and assured us he was taking me on as a client. He knew absolutely everybody in Hollywood and right away started arranging interviews. I'd go to six in a day, one right after the other, then come home and hope the phone would ring. Having performed in a lead role on Broadway certainly helped open doors, but it didn't guarantee that I'd get anything. Then, just at the moment our $2,000 had been whittled down to almost nothing, I got offered a role in a movie called *Skatetown, USA*.

In the late 1970s, especially in Southern California, roller disco was king. You'd see skaters everywhere, half of them toting giant boom boxes playing the latest Earth Wind & Fire or Jackson 5 songs. Walking in Venice Beach, you'd be swarmed by skaters in bright socks and short-shorts, twirling their way down the boardwalk. So when I read the script for *Skatetown, USA,* I knew that even if it wasn't great art, it was at least part of a genuine cultural phenomenon.

It also had a cast that included some of the hottest TV stars of the seventies. I was cast as Ace Johnson, a bad-boy skater in tight leather trousers who battles the hero, Stan, played by Greg Bradford.

I had roller-skated competitively in my teens, but hadn't done much since then. I was hell-bent on doing some amazing things on skates for this movie, so I had my dad send me my top-of-the-line figure skates from Houston and began practising moves on any open paved area I could find. By the time we started filming, I was pumped—I wanted to bust Hollywood wide open with my first role.

Unfortunately, I almost busted my ass on my very first stunt. I was supposed to jump over a Fiat parked at the end of the Santa Monica pier, using a small ramp. I raced down the pier, going faster and faster, and when I hit that ramp I shot up into the air—a lot higher than I expected to. In the footage, you can see me yell 'Charge!' as I take off, then the look on my face changes from determination to wide-eyed surprise. The camera cuts away before showing me landing, flat on my back, on the cement. I had the breath knocked out of me, but we did get it in one take.

My scenes at the roller rink with world-champion roller skater April Allen, where I could show off my dance training as well as skating, went more smoothly. I'd skated with April years earlier in Houston. We were friends from way back.

April was an amazing skater, and she and I heated up the set with a skate-dance scene that was powerful, sensual and sexy. I also had a solo skate that led to the review that launched my career, when the *Los Angeles Times* wrote, 'Not since John Travolta took the disco floor in *Saturday Night Fever*—no, not since Valentino did his tango in *The Four Horsemen of the Apocalypse*—has there been such a confident display of male sexuality as when a lithe newcomer to films named Patrick Swayze hits the rink . . . Swayze ought to be on [his] way in films.'

This was flattering, of course, but on another level it was the last thing I wanted. I wanted to be a serious actor, not a dancer-turned-actor or hunk-of-the-week. Not long after *Skatetown* came out, Columbia offered me a multipicture deal to star in teen idol-type movies, but after talking about it with Lisa, I turned it down. We both knew that if I accepted, even though the money would be fantastic and it would be guaranteed work, no one would ever take me seriously as an actor.

As I had just arrived in Hollywood, it was hard to turn down a multipicture deal. But Bob LeMond gave me a piece of advice that made it easier. 'The only power you have in this business,' he told me, 'is the power to say "no". More careers have been screwed up by "yes" than anything else.' I took Bob's advice to heart and we turned our attention to finding better roles.

But, to my frustration, the one role I really wanted that year was one I couldn't have: Bud Davis in *Urban Cowboy,* which was filming down in Houston.

I'd have been playing a Texas cowboy who loved to dance—a role that had my name all over it. But John Travolta was flying high after his successes in *Saturday Night Fever* and *Grease*, and the part was his for the taking. It tore me up to think of how that character would have launched my career. It was also frustrating because my mother was the choreographer for *Urban Cowboy*, and she had hired Lisa to work with her. So Lisa was working down in Houston on the movie I'd wanted, while I was alone in LA, finishing up *Skatetown, USA.*

As soon as we wrapped, I flew down to Houston to join Lisa. One night we ended up hanging out with John Travolta and teaching him a few steps, which frustrated me even more. I hated giving someone else tips on how to play a role I was born for, but what I really hated was that he was so good at it. John was an absolute natural. He's also a generous and kind-hearted person and Lisa and I liked him right away. We became quite close on that movie and have been friends ever since.

After I turned down the Columbia deal, I kept auditioning for other, better roles. I got my first TV role in the made-for-TV movie *The Comeback Kid.* It aired in the spring of 1980, and though I was proud of my work, I still wanted bigger, better roles. I got my wish when I won a part on *M*A*S*H.*

*M*A*S*H* was a long-running, incredibly popular show—but that wasn't what got me so excited about working on it. It was the fact that the stars of *M*A*S*H* were very well respected in the industry—talented actors like Alan Alda, Loretta Swit, Harry Morgan and Mike Farrell. Winning a part on *M*A*S*H* meant that the producers believed you could hold your own among them. Playing Private Gary Sturgis was my first great role in Hollywood and, oddly enough, it had a plot twist involving cancer.

Most of my scenes took place with Alan Alda, who played Dr 'Hawkeye' Pierce. My character, Private Sturgis, has hurt his arm in combat. He gets sent to the *M*A*S*H* unit at the same time as his buddy, who's more severely injured and needs a blood transfusion. Sturgis desperately wants to give blood to his buddy, knowing they share the same blood type. But Hawkeye tests Sturgis's blood and discovers he has leukaemia. When Hawkeye tells him, Sturgis breaks down—he had no idea he was ill.

Playing Sturgis was an amazing experience for me. It was a dream to act opposite Alan Alda. I just followed his lead, and the emotion poured out of me. Using the process I'd learned in my acting classes, I was able to tap deep wells of anger and bitterness at how unfair the diagnosis was for this young kid.

But through those first two years in LA, parts like that were few and far between. I kept holding out for good roles, but as a result I wasn't working much. In the meantime, Lisa and I acted together in a play, *The Brick and the Rose*, at the Attic Theatre on Santa Monica Boulevard.

We both got good reviews, but theatre work didn't pay the bills, so Lisa and I started up our woodworking business again on the side. We built stage sets and also did some work for Jaclyn Smith, whom I knew well from Houston. Jackie had been a student at my mom's studio in the seventies, but now she was a Hollywood star thanks to her leading role on *Charlie's Angels*. Yet she never acted like a big star—she was always welcoming and warm to Lisa and me, and supported us however she could, even making an appearance at the premiere of *Skatetown, USA*.

Meanwhile, my parents had left Houston too. After working on *Urban Cowboy*, my mom decided she wanted to choreograph more Hollywood movies, so she and my dad pulled up their Texas roots and moved to Simi Valley, just north of Los Angeles. I was happy to have them nearby, even though our busy schedules kept us from seeing each other all that often.

But even having my parents just up the road didn't help when, during our second year in LA, Lisa and I found ourselves dead broke, without even enough money for food.

WE HAD BEEN WORKING pretty steadily on carpentry jobs, but the pay was minimal. The rest of our time was taken up with auditions, acting classes and other totally unpaid activities. Somehow, we must have lost track of our income and expenses, because one day around Christmas Lisa checked our account and discovered we had about three dollars left. We were expecting a little bit of money for a job we'd just finished, but that was already earmarked for rent and bills.

All of a sudden, we realised there was no money to go home to Texas to visit Lisa's family for Christmas, no money for presents, no money even for food to eat.

'How the hell did this happen?' Lisa asked. She did a quick update of our bank statements and chequebook—something we should have done months before. Our monthly expenses stood at about $1,200, which was a huge sum compared to what we'd been spending in New York.

After a year or so of living in the Hollywood Hills, we had moved into an apartment in West Hollywood, on La Jolla Avenue. The saving grace of our new apartment was the orange tree in the back yard, which ended up feeding us for the difficult weeks we spent trying to pull our financial life together. We managed to scrape together enough coins to buy a jar of peanut butter and some bread, and that, with the oranges, was what we ate.

Although my parents were in Simi Valley, I was too proud to ask them for money or food—I didn't want them to know we were in such dire straits. Lisa did tell her mom what was going on, but her family was strapped at the time too, and couldn't send anything to tide us over. The couple of times when friends invited us over for dinner, we didn't let on how hungry we were, but we were completely demoralised, and once again found ourselves wondering, had we made a big mistake leaving New York? We had never been this desperate there.

There's a difference between simply being broke, and being broke while not knowing where your next pay cheque will come from. But now, after working for two years in Hollywood, we didn't have any new work on the horizon. We started looking round at what we could sell, and I thought of those nights I'd sat out on Mulholland Drive, vowing to conquer Hollywood.

We had done some carpentry work for a man named Green, so in a last-ditch effort to make some quick money, we called him and threw ourselves on his mercy. 'Do you have anything that needs doing?' I asked him. 'Anything at all?' And Mr Green, sensing the desperation in my voice, came up with a laundry list of small tasks for us. The biggest was building a doghouse for his two German shepherds, a task Lisa and I jumped on as soon as I hung up the phone.

But just as in a Hollywood movie, real life in Hollywood can change in an instant. In the midst of our despair, as we worked on the doghouse for the few dollars that would tide us over, I got a call about a new TV show I'd auditioned for a few weeks earlier. It was called *The Renegades*—and I was being offered a leading role!

Just like that, I soared from the depths of despair to the heights of euphoria. Getting a role on a TV series was a huge leap for a struggling young actor, bringing with it the promise of job stability and a really good pay cheque. I couldn't believe my luck. And I couldn't wait to tell Lisa.

But first, I made a stop at a place I'd wanted to go for the past two years—an auto dealership selling DeLoreans. These were the cars with gull-wing doors designed by John DeLorean, who made only 9,000 of them before shutting down production in 1982. In the early 1980s, the DeLorean was the emblem of style and slick automotive design, and I'd wanted one ever since the prototype came out. Now, with my new job, and if I could manage to talk them down in price, the car would be within my means. So

I went straight to the dealership, and then called Lisa.

'Hey, Lisa,' I said. 'I've got some news for you. I'm buying a DeLorean.'

'You're *what*?!' she said, surprise and excitement in her voice. She knew there had to be more—either that, or I'd completely lost my mind.

'I got a leading part on *The Renegades*!' I said, and whooped. It was such a great moment—and it was all the more amazing because it came just when we'd been on the edge of despair. Lisa was thrilled, of course, though she did have one concern.

'Shit,' she said. 'Now I'm going to have to build that doghouse all by myself!'

After I bought the car, Lisa and I drove up to Simi Valley to show it off to my parents. I'll never forget my dad's response when he came out to see us pulling up in the sparkling new DeLorean, with its stainless-steel panels and flat, square hood.

'Well, what are you doing driving around in a kitchen sink?' he asked, a big smile on his face.

It was obvious how proud he was of me, and that was worth more than any role or any car would ever be. It was one of the best moments of my life.

## Chapter 6

*The Renegades* was an updated version of *The Mod Squad,* a ground-breaking cop series that ran between 1968 and 1973. I played Bandit, the tough-talking leader of a gang of street thugs, although in my chic leather trousers and sleeveless vests, I looked as much model as tough guy. It was fun, and I was happy to have steady TV work.

Things were looking up. I was making good money, and Lisa and I were taking acting classes with the respected teacher Milton

Katselas. We loved our apartment on La Jolla Avenue and our circle of friends was growing steadily. Almost three years after moving to LA, we at last felt like we were settling in. We even made plans finally to move the rest of our stuff from New York.

Then, one day when I came home from shooting, everything came crashing down.

I pulled into our driveway and walked into the two-car garage we'd turned into our woodworking shop. I'd just started messing round with a project we were working on when I felt Lisa walk up behind me. To this day I couldn't tell you how I knew it, but I knew right away something was very wrong. Lisa put her hand on my shoulder and said, 'Buddy, could you come into the house? I need to tell you something.'

I wheeled round. 'What is it?' I said.

I could see she'd been crying.

'Tell me now.'

'Your mom called,' she said quietly. 'Your dad had a heart attack. He's dead.'

My knees buckled and I sank to the floor. I felt sick, like I'd been sucker-punched in the stomach.

'He was walking with the dogs out behind their house,' Lisa said, rubbing my back. 'He died instantly. There was no pain.' This would be a small consolation later, but I wasn't ready to be grateful for anything yet. I just couldn't believe my dad was gone.

My dad, the gentle cowboy, was my source of unconditional love while I was growing up, the steady hand on the rudder. My mother loved us with a fierce, proud, demanding love, while my father loved us without qualification. Big Buddy had taught me what it meant to be a man. Seeing his example while I was growing up had been a huge influence on me.

Born and raised in Wichita Falls, my dad had grown up on a small working ranch in the Texas Panhandle. There, he learned how to do all the things a cowboy does—doctor and brand cattle, repair fences, ride and groom horses. He was a cowboy in his blood, not just for show. And although his life wasn't easy and they never had much money, he always had a smile and a good word for everyone. In turn, everyone loved Buddy Swayze.

Dad and I had always loved being outdoors, and it was comforting in some ways that he died outside, with his dogs, in the beauty of nature. We used to go out into the wilderness together, with just a few supplies and his knowledge of living off the land to sustain us. I treasured those days with him, exploring the landscape and learning the most basic human ability: how to exist in the natural environment. I've always been grateful for the skills I learned with him, and I still think of him whenever I'm outside, living off the land, or even just appreciating the sights and smells of nature.

As stabilising a force as my father had been in life, his death had the opposite effect on me. Everything was suddenly out of kilter. I'd never been much of a drinker, but one of the first things I did after my dad died was buy a case of his favourite beer, Budweiser. I hated the taste, but I popped open can after can, trying to get myself drunk. No matter how much I drank, I couldn't feel anything.

My dad's death was devastating for many reasons. For one thing, it devastated my mother, who had loved and depended on him for all those years. She was crushed, and she felt angry and alone. My mother is a strong woman, but her emotions run strong too. And losing him nearly put her over the edge with grief.

My brothers and sisters were devastated. Losing a parent is hard. But for me, my father's death meant my very identity had changed. My whole life, he'd been Big Buddy and I was Little Buddy. But now that he was gone, I was the oldest male in the family and now I had to step up and be the Big Buddy. This marked a new level of responsibility and it started right away. Lisa and I had to plan my father's funeral and take care of all the details leading up to it. This was difficult enough, but there would soon be one truly horrible moment that showed me just how strong I needed to be.

It happened just before the viewing at the funeral home. I went down before the rest of the family arrived to make sure the undertakers had prepared his body and everything was set. But when I looked in the casket, I was shocked. The man lying there looked nothing like my father—they had put too much blush make-up on his face, and he looked like a clown. Rage rose in my chest, and I knew it would break my mother's heart to see him this way.

'Take him back there,' I said to the undertaker, my voice tight. 'I'll do his make-up myself.'

In the back room of that funeral home, I gently wiped my dad's face while the tears streamed down my own. I desperately wanted to make him look like my dad again, but I just couldn't get it—until finally, after a few fits and starts, I got the make-up right and managed to fix his hair the way he always wore it. When I was finished, I wiped the tears from my eyes and took him back out for the viewing. It was the hardest thing I'd ever done.

We buried my father in a simple wooden casket. I don't remember much about the funeral, but I remember wanting to carve his initials into the casket before we lowered it into the ground. I didn't end up doing that and I regret it. He'd always carried an Old Timer knife and I did, too—it was part of our identities as Swayze men. But when the last moment came, I just watched as the casket was lowered, and then we threw dirt over it, and he was gone.

IN THE MONTHS after my dad died, I began drinking as I'd never done before. I was trying to get drunk, but I never could feel it. In some strange way, I felt that I was honouring him, doing something he loved to do—drinking beer.

One thing about being a Swayze is, you never do anything halfway. Lisa was concerned about how much I was drinking, but I didn't choose to stop. Then, late at night, I'd take my DeLorean up to Mulholland Drive—the twisting, steep part through the Hollywood Hills where car aficionados would come to race. I'd put a case of beer on the seat beside me and go, taking on any and allcomers to do suicide runs. I never got into an accident, but it wasn't safe or smart and Lisa was understandably worried about me.

In all my life, I never drank for the sake of drinking; it was always a response to some kind of emotional difficulty. Drinking for me was a symptom of a problem, but it certainly caused problems between Lisa and me. She would plead with me to cut back, but every time a memory of my dad came into my brain, it turned into a fresh, open wound again. His death had thrown me completely off-balance and I didn't know how to cope with it.

I was still trying to find an identity for myself. Who was I? Was I just some teen idol, a piece of beefcake? In that case what had all my training been for? When my father was alive, I had his unconditional love to anchor me. Now that was gone and I felt angry, as if he'd abandoned me.

Lisa loved me unconditionally, too, but I wouldn't let myself believe that. I still felt stung by her initial response when I'd asked her to marry me. Our relationship has always been passionate, in both positive and negative ways—our love for each other was incredibly intense, but so were our fights. This was the first really tough period in our marriage and it scared us both.

I knew all too well what had happened to so many young creative artists—James Dean, Janis Joplin, Jim Morrison, Jimi Hendrix—who got swallowed by their ambitions and destroyed by the choices they made. I had studied their examples to make sure I didn't end up going down that road myself. But, as I soon discovered I was in a cycle, I didn't know how to stop.

So I did the only thing I knew to do: I buried myself in my work. At my dad's funeral, I'd made a vow to live in a way that would have made him proud. The moment when he'd beamed at me in my new DeLorean was forever burned into my memory and I wanted to live as if he was still watching me.

After I became an actor, I realised my life had had a certain pattern to it. I had always needed a goal, something to push towards. And I had always feared what would happen to me if I reached the top of a given profession and then had nowhere else to go.

But acting was different. For the first time, I was throwing myself into something that could never be mastered. Acting wasn't like sports—you didn't win the world championship and then settle into retirement. No matter how great an actor you are, you can *always* be better. Every role is different and the learning curve is endless. I was excited to find something that would never stop challenging me, and I was humbled by the chance to make a living at it.

And then, by an amazing stroke of good fortune, soon after my father died, I was given a chance to stretch my acting ability even further by working with one of the greatest film directors in history, Francis Ford Coppola.

THE AUDITIONS for *The Outsiders* were unlike any auditions I'd ever been to before. Based on the best-selling book by S. E. Hinton, *The Outsiders* focused on a group of 'Greasers'—a gang of high-school toughs trying to find their way in the world. Throughout the movie, the Greasers clash with the 'Socs'—pronounced 'soshes,' short for the social upper-class kids. It's a classic coming-of-age story, fuelled by testosterone and violence, and Francis Ford Coppola wanted to find young male actors who could disappear into those characters.

The movie's climactic scene is a giant fight or 'rumble' between the two factions. So, for the auditions, Francis invited dozens of young actors to stage improvised fights on a sound stage. Usually when you audition, you're alone in a room with the casting director, director, and maybe a few other people. Auditioning with a huge group of talented young actors brought out the competitive fire in everyone. And because Francis was a legend, having already made *The Godfather* and *The Godfather II* as well as *Apocalypse Now,* everybody was fired up to impress him.

There was method to his madness, because he ended up with an amazing cast of up-and-coming male actors. Matt Dillon was already a budding star, having played lead roles in *Little Darlings*, *My Bodyguard* and *Tex*, but the rest of us were just starting out. And we were anxious to make our mark.

We lived these roles. We became like a gang ourselves, hanging out together, smoking, drinking and just generally running wild.

Those were crazy days, with drugs and alcohol fuelling everything—and the Greasers' drug of choice was beer. And Francis ratcheted things up a notch with his style of directing, which was aimed at bringing out the most realistic emotions possible.

Francis was all about instinct and the pursuit of perfection. He was one of the most demanding directors I've ever worked with and he stopped at nothing to get the performance he wanted. He'd talk to you and draw you out, finding your deepest, darkest secrets. Then, on set, he'd announce them over a loudspeaker for everyone to hear. This had the effect he wanted—my blood would pound when I'd hear his voice over that speaker—but it's a brutal way to bring out an emotional performance.

Francis and I also clashed after I asked him about camera angles for a couple of scenes. I was curious about the art of film-making, and here I was working with the master—I figured it was as good a time as any to ask questions and learn how it was done. But when I asked him about why he chose to shoot in certain ways, he misunderstood.

'Ah, everyone knows that all dancers are really interested in is looking at themselves in the mirror,' he said.

This was a real insult, and it was all the worse coming from him. I didn't care about how my face looked on screen—I wanted to be the best actor I could. And if he didn't believe that was so, why had he cast me? His comment really pissed me off, but there wasn't much I could do about it, except show him how hard I would work in my performance. Which is probably what he was angling for in the first place.

With all that said, I loved Francis and would have worked with him on anything. He brought out performances we never thought possible. Anything went on that set—it was as if he'd given us all permission to create these amazing characters and live in their skin. In the climax of it all, the final 'rumble' between the Greasers and Socs, we didn't just act out a massive gang fight; we really *had* a gang fight, with fists flying and blood running and guys pounding each other.

Francis brought in a bunch of local kids, and on a day when the rain came pouring down, he put us all together in a giant muddy lot to battle it out. He whipped us up, telling us to make it as realistic and violent as possible, and when he set us loose, everyone went crazy. Guys were beating on each other, punching and kicking and wrestling in the mud. In the middle of it, one guy came charging at me with a wild look in his eyes. He was coming to lay me out and the only way I could keep from getting hurt myself was to hurt him. I punched him hard in the face and knocked him unconscious.

There was actually some choreography planned for the rumble, with each of us fighting specific people, but by the end everybody was just whaling on everybody else. And the really interesting thing was that all of us Greasers stuck together, watching one another's backs as if this was a real gang fight. Our survival instincts kicked in, and we fought with a kind of primal animal fury. It was a brilliant, reckless piece of film-making.

Tom Cruise had the smallest role of any of us, but even then, at age twenty and with very few credits to his name, he was as driven as anyone I'd ever seen. For the scene in the movie where the Greasers are heading out to the rumble, Tom's character does a back flip off a car in excitement. I taught Tom that move, and in fact Lisa and I taught most of the other Greasers gymnastics moves to use in the rumble. I was the big brother in the movie, and I felt like one on the set, too.

I had a blast working with all the guys, and in spite of all the beer my own personal drinking problem kind of cured itself. I particularly bonded with Tommy Howell. We'd met on the set of *Urban Cowboy*, where his dad was a stunt man, and we had a shared love of the cowboy life. Tommy was a true cowboy—he loved horses and had even been a junior rodeo champion, and he and I remained close after *The Outsiders.* In fact, over the next year and a half, we would act in two more films together: *Grandview, USA* and *Red Dawn.*

When *The Outsiders* came out, the posters and promotional

materials showed all the Greasers posing in denim and leather, looking tough with our hair slicked back. We all got a lot of attention from the film, including the inevitable magazine photo spreads for girls. Tom Cruise didn't want to do those photo shoots, since he was self-conscious about his teeth and thought he wasn't good-looking enough. But he got roped into it just like the rest of us, and before long he became the biggest movie star of all.

ONE THING I've always loved about being an actor is getting the chance to travel all over the world for work. In the course of our careers, Lisa and I have been fortunate enough to travel to places as far-flung as India, Namibia, Hong Kong, Russia and South Africa. It was just after *The Outsiders* that we got to travel to our first exotic location—Thailand—for the 1983 film *Uncommon Valor*. I traded in the first-class plane ticket the studio bought me for two economy seats, so Lisa could join me in Bangkok.

Starring Gene Hackman and Robert Stack, *Uncommon Valor* was about a group of Vietnam veterans who return to Southeast Asia to rescue a buddy who'd been taken prisoner in the war. I was excited to be working with Gene Hackman, who was already a huge star. Getting this role was another step in the right direction, continuing the momentum that was starting to build in my career.

It was a big break to be cast with Gene, and he took me under his wing on the set. He was unfailingly professional and very generous with his time and insight. He also taught me a very big lesson about acting, telling me, 'You're not here for yourself. You're only here to serve.' This fed right into everything I'd studied in Buddhism—that it's only through learning to serve that you can become a master. Gene devoted himself to his movies: even if it took twenty takes for the other actor to get it right, Gene would be right there, delivering his lines with the same energy and dedication. Every single time. It was mesmerising to watch him work.

Meanwhile, my role called for as much fighting as acting. I played a cocky young Special Forces soldier who's brought in to train the Vietnam vets. On the set, I was taught by ex-Special

Forces guys, learning hand-to-hand combat techniques from the best in the world. In addition to travelling, that's another of the things I love best about my job—getting the chance to learn new skills from the top experts in each field. I've been lucky enough to study martial arts, kickboxing, surfing, skydiving and many other skills on movie sets.

For one scene in *Uncommon Valor*, I fought a character played by Randall 'Tex' Cobb—a former boxer turned actor who'd gone fifteen rounds with heavyweight champion Larry Holmes just a year earlier. Tex's character in the movie, Sailor, was crazy—but no crazier than Tex himself. He was a classic bar-room-brawler type, a huge man with a fleshy nose that lay flat against his face, reportedly because he'd had the cartilage removed so he could take more punches. The beating Tex had taken in his fight with Holmes had been so severe, commentator Howard Cosell retired from calling boxing matches in protest that the fight hadn't been stopped sooner.

When Tex and I went at it in the river for our big fight scene, he was really hitting me—pounding and pounding my upper body in an exhausting series of takes. The man was a professional boxer, and the blows he landed were solid. I didn't want to look like a wimp, but I finally had to speak up.

'Tex,' I said, 'I know you're supposed to kick my ass in this scene, but you've got to back off a little bit here.'

'What's the matter, Little Buddy?' he spat back. 'You can't take it? Is it too much for you?' I liked Tex, but the sneer on his face as he taunted me was too much. And when he started pounding on me again, finally knocking me down hard in the river, I lost it.

Tex had punched me hard enough to spin me round and put me on my hands and knees in the river. I got up slowly, and without looking at him I took a hitch step backwards, went one running step, and hit him square in the face—harder than I'd ever hit anyone in my life. The blow rocked his head back, and when it came forward again he had a big old smile on his face. And then he laughed.

'Is that all you've got, Little Buddy?' he said. I just stared at him. I'd hit him with all my strength and he hadn't even felt it.

But as crazy as Tex was, he and I ended up becoming good buddies. Nobody else would share a dressing room with him because he was too much of a wild man, so I did. Then his partying ways got to be too much for me too, and I pitched a tent for myself nearby. Tex loved Bangkok's red-light district, Patpong, and spent plenty of nights there—as did many of the other guys in the cast and crew. But only one guy decided to stay behind after we wrapped filming: Tex. He cashed in his plane ticket home and the last we saw him, he was heading back to Patpong. We did eventually see him a couple more times over the years, but whenever I'd ask how he finally made it out of Thailand, he'd just say, 'Little Buddy, you don't want to know.'

*Uncommon Valor* was a good movie, for what it was. But I still wanted to find roles that would stretch me more as an actor. And I was tired of playing characters younger than myself—I easily looked five or ten years younger than I was, so that's how I was always cast.

But after *Uncommon Valor*, I was cast in *Grandview, USA* as a more mature man, Ernie 'Slam' Webster, a Demolition Derby driver in a love triangle. Slam Webster had something of the wild child in him too, but he was more mature than my other characters. Tommy Howell was cast as Tim Pearson, my rival for the hand of Michelle 'Mike' Cody, played by Jamie Lee Curtis.

Lisa worked on the film too, choreographing a dream dance sequence—the first time she and I worked together on a movie. I was especially happy she was there because the town where we were shooting—Pontiac, Illinois—had only about 10,000 people, so there wasn't a hell of a lot of local socialising. In fact, Pontiac's main claim to fame was its prison, which employed or incarcerated most of the people in town. Just about the only half-interesting place to go was the Courtyard Hotel, where the Teamsters and other movie crew members stayed. We called it the Gorilla Villa.

My next movie was *Red Dawn*, and everything on *Red Dawn* was epic in scale: the hard-core training, the controversial plot, the insanely rigorous shoot, and the antagonism between myself and a certain young actress—one who would later dance with me in the movie that shot us both to stardom.

# Chapter 7

'You can call me the General,' *Red Dawn* director John Milius announced. 'Swayze, you are my Lieutenant of the Art, and I'll direct these little fuckers through you.' With those words, Milius put me in charge of the cast of *Red Dawn*—Tommy Howell, Jennifer Grey, Charlie Sheen, Lea Thompson and others—for the gruelling shoot in the mountains of New Mexico.

*Red Dawn* was a controversial movie right from the start. Five minutes into the film, Soviet and Cuban paratroopers float down to a small Colorado town and open fire with machine guns, launching World War III with an invasion on American soil. In the early 1980s, when we made this movie, the Cold War was raging and fears of a Soviet attack ran high across America. But nobody would touch it as a movie plot—except Milius, who was just the man for the job.

Milius was a wild man and a military freak. He had a collection of firearms and an encyclopedic knowledge of arms and armaments, and he even kept a loaded gun on his desk at the 20th Century Fox offices. Milius wrote *Apocalypse Now* and co-wrote *Dirty Harry*, and he loved war games. He consulted military experts while co-writing *Red Dawn*, even reportedly asking former secretary of state Alexander Haig for help. Milius wanted his film to be as realistic as possible, so he started with training his cast as if we were really a band of scared teenage soldiers rather than actors on a movie set.

I played Jed Eckert, the leader of a group of high-school students who manage to escape to nearby wooded mountains after the Soviet invasion. The movie follows our group—dubbed the Wolverines, after the local high-school mascot—as we survive a freezing winter, foraging for food and skirmishing with Russian soldiers who track us down. To prepare us for our roles, Milius arranged for real mercenaries to train us in military tactics, after which we would take part in real war games with a National Guard unit before filming.

The mercenaries taught us all about military manoeuvres and survival techniques. We fired weapons, learned how to camouflage ourselves and undertook stealth manoeuvres through the woods. It was dirty, tiring and physically demanding—and I loved every minute of it. When our training culminated in a giant game of Capture the Flag, with the ragtag Wolverines going up against the newly arrived National Guard troops, I wanted more than just to show off what we'd learned. I wanted to capture that flag and win.

Our objective was to start from the cover of a forested mountainside, cross an open valley, and take the flag planted on the other side of the valley. We had three days to do it, with hundreds of trained National Guardsmen trying to stop us.

From the moment we set up camp on that mountainside, I became Jed Eckert. Right away, this game became a matter of life and death—I almost felt like my life really did depend on capturing that flag. And I treated the other Wolverines that way, too, yelling and pushing them to their absolute limits in the game. Charlie Sheen and Tommy Howell loved it—they were as gung ho as I was. But Lea Thompson and Jennifer Grey seemed taken aback at my intensity. In fact, it's probably safe to say Jennifer couldn't stand me once I started barking orders at everyone.

Getting across the open valley was going to be tricky, and I doubt the seasoned National Guard troops expected much from us. But we had a plan. With the help of some crew members, we dug a network of shallow trenches and camouflaged them as best we could. Once they were covered with plywood and dirt and sod, you could even walk on them in some spots without realising anyone was underneath. In fact, during our eventual assault across the valley, which took place at night, one National Guardsman almost stepped right on my face—and he never even knew I was there.

When we captured the flag after our all-night valley crossing, the National Guard troops were stunned—and pissed off. Milius, on the other hand, was elated and couldn't wait to start shooting. He had his real Wolverines. We had bonded out there in the trenches, and we had transformed ourselves into a pack of high-school mujahideen, just like he wanted.

THE HARD PART was that once I became Jed Eckert, I didn't ever want to step out of character. I really became this mercenary warrior, this almost savage kid turned military leader. When Lisa came out to the set, she couldn't reach me—I was afraid to just be Patrick again, fearing that if I dropped the character, I wouldn't be able to get him back. It was frustrating for Lisa, and yet I couldn't stop. This was a huge role for me—my first real leading role in a big Hollywood film—and I had to nail it.

The film's setting added to the realism. We shot in the area round Las Vegas, New Mexico, which—smaller than its more famous namesake—had its own rough-and-tumble reputation. A hundred years ago, Las Vegas had been the last point on the Santa Fe Trail to get supplies, get drunk and get laid before heading into the Rockies with your wagon train. It had been a tough-guy kind of town, and it still wasn't the most welcoming place.

This was especially true of the town's bars, which were the kind of dives where the men carried knives, and half of them got pulled out on any given night.

One night, Charlie, Tommy, Brad Savage and I went to one of these bars to play some pool—Charlie was a great player, and he was giving us some tips. I never knew what started it, but suddenly all hell broke loose. Blood and beer were flying everywhere, and I looked at my guys and thought, 'I gotta get them out of here!' Tommy and Brad were just kids, about eighteen years old, and I was their leader, responsible for getting them safely away.

I grabbed a pool cue and broke it in half, then started swinging it wildly at whoever was in the way, trying to make an opening for us. Charlie, Tommy and Brad pushed in behind me, shoving and punching all the way, and we finally got to the front door, where I threw down the bloody pool cue and we took off. The Wolverines had escaped the enemy again!

The funny thing was, Lisa and I ended up buying a ranch in that same area years later. And when we brought up the subject of that bar fight with a few locals, they remembered it. Apparently it was one of the biggest brawls in the history of Las Vegas, New Mexico. And it'll probably never be topped now, because the town's seediest bars have all gradually disappeared in the years since *Red Dawn*. It's now a quaint, friendly town with a colourful past.

Despite *Red Dawn*'s dead-serious theme—or maybe because of it—the pranks we played on the set were epic. It was a violent war movie, with hundreds of explosions from bombs, machine guns, missiles and grenades, so the crew had every kind of explosive available. And, unlike some directors, Milius was as wild as the rest of us, so I aimed pranks at him as much as at anyone.

One time, I rigged the toilet in his trailer with charges—M60s, which are like little one-eighth-size sticks of dynamite. I packed them into a steel tube, so they wouldn't blow shrapnel everywhere, and taped them under his toilet. When Milius went in to do his business, I detonated them—and the explosion sent him running out of the door in a panic. He'd barely got the words 'Swayze, you son of a—' out of his mouth when I set off a second round of explosives, blowing two garbage cans sky-high and scaring the shit out of him.

Another time, I hid a bottle-rocket launcher in his room, so that the next morning, dozens of tiny rockets flew at him. Day to day, he never knew what might be coming at him—and he loved it.

Milius had gone to amazing lengths to make sure everything on *Red Dawn* was authentic. I still get chills when I think about the scene where the paratroopers float out of the sky, landing on the field next to the high school and then opening fire with machine guns. All the helicopters, tanks, planes and missile launchers were absolutely true to the era. Watching it today, you can still feel the fear that was so rampant throughout the Cold War.

The realism was also aided by the fact that we really did camp out during what was the coldest winter in years, with temperatures plunging at times to thirty below. My fingers became frostbitten from all the hours spent in the elements, and to this day they throb painfully whenever it's cold. We really became those characters—scanning the skies for helicopters, rationing our food, riding horses across the mountains. And we even had to perform our own heroics when a freak accident nearly led to disaster one afternoon.

The actors playing the Wolverines were riding in a van that was towing a horse trailer behind it. The mountain road was steep, icy and treacherous, with a sheer drop to one side. As we towed the horse trailer up the road, it began sliding on the ice, right towards the edge of the cliff. The trailer slid to a wobbly stop just on the edge of this massive drop. If it went a yard or two further, it would go down—and pull the van and us right over with it.

Tommy Howell and I jumped into action. 'Get the door open!' I yelled. 'Don't get out of the van in case that sends the trailer over. But get in the doorway so you can jump if it starts to go anyway!'

While the others crowded into the van's doorway, Tommy and I jumped out to deal with the horses. There was a gap between the road and the horse trailer's door, so we'd have to get the horses to jump across to safety. The problem was, the horses were going crazy with fear. We gingerly made our way back to the trailer, unlatched its door and guided the horses one by one to the road, urging them across the gap. Somehow, we managed to get them all to safety—and once the horses were out of the trailer, it was light enough for the van to pull it back up to the road. Tommy and I were as elated as if we'd single-handedly repelled a Soviet air attack.

I loved playing Jed Eckert, and I enjoyed every minute of being the leader of our ragtag band, even if my performance was a little intense for some of the others. As I've mentioned, Jennifer Grey was probably the least impressed of all—she really chafed when I ordered her around, and rolled her eyes when I stayed in character between takes. But there was a moment near the end of the film when she seemed to warm to me. It was when we shot her character's death scene.

Jennifer's character, Toni, has been mortally wounded following a Soviet aerial attack, but Jed doesn't want to leave her to die. In that scene, I scoop Toni up onto the back of my horse and flee the attack, but it's too late for her. Toni and I end up taking refuge under a tree, where she asks me to finish her off with a pistol. But I can't.

It's a very tender scene and, as I stroked Jennifer's hair, it was a genuinely emotional moment. This was the first meaningful scene she and I had had together, and I think it endeared me to her after all the friction we'd had. Most of the scene ended up being cut, but even in the shorter version that made it into the film, it was clear to anyone watching that Jennifer and I had chemistry together.

IN THE SUMMER of 1984, *Red Dawn* came out, just as Lisa and I were starring together in a very different kind of performance. In fact, the stage show *Without a Word* was just about as far as you could get from the freezing Cold War drama of *Red Dawn*. It was an intimate, deeply emotional reflection on dancing, dreams, and what happens when those dreams die.

It had all started months earlier, when Lisa and I danced in a special performance for our acting class. We were studying with Milton Katselas, a legendary acting coach in LA. We had waited years to get into his class, but it was well worth it. Milton pushed us further and made us dig deeper than ever before.

We weren't the only dancers in Milton's class—in fact, it wasn't unusual for former professional ballet dancers to turn to acting. And one thing we noticed was that all these people felt like we did, that nothing really filled the void left by dancing. Lisa and I became close to one in particular, an amazingly talented dancer named Nicholas Gunn. We'd hang out together after class, sitting at diners and talking about the passion and pain of dancing, and how we'd drop everything in a heartbeat for the chance to do it all again.

These were little more than idle conversations until we were invited to dance for a special scene in acting class. There was a cellist in the class who was also studying acting, and he wanted to explore different forms of expression through music. He asked Nicholas, Lisa and me, and another dancer and actress named Shanna Reed, to perform dance pieces on stage at the Beverly Hills Playhouse, while he played, with the class watching.

Lisa and I prepared a pas de deux. And the feeling I got while being on stage, dancing ballet once again, with the gentle moan of the cello guiding us, was far more intense than I had expected. It had been so long since I had danced in front of others, and so long since I'd felt that amazing soaring in my spirit. It was beautiful, and painful, and in the end, devastating. No matter how much success I had begun to have in the acting world, nothing compared to the sheer exhilaration of dancing.

When the performance ended, Lisa and I went backstage and I just broke down. I was overwhelmed with feelings—all the feelings I'd buried when I had to leave Eliot Feld. I had forced myself to cope after leaving because I had to. What I now realised was that I had a lot of emotional unfinished business related to leaving the ballet.

Lisa and Nicholas felt the same way I did, so we resolved to do something about it. It was time to explore all those feelings, to give them an outlet. And Milton Katselas offered a vehicle for us to do it. He had started a programme called Camelot Productions, which offered free space for people who wanted to develop new plays. We could write about all these pent-up emotions, create a combination drama and dance work, and produce it at Camelot.

Lisa, Nicholas and I got right to work, coming up with ideas and scenes through improvisations. Lisa would write all our ideas down and shape them, and we worked to make seamless transitions between talking and dancing. We wanted the dancing to say as much as the speech, which eventually led to our title: *Without a Word.*

The centrepiece was three monologues, one each by Lisa, Nicholas and me. We wanted to express our innermost thoughts and feelings about dance, making the work extremely personal. The day we decided to create these monologues, Lisa went straight home and started writing. She was so driven and focused, she wrote the entire thing in one night. And the next day, when she read it to Nicholas and me, we just looked at each other. Nicholas said, 'Well, she's certainly set the bar high.'

Doing *Without a Word* was both frightening and exhilarating for me. One of the most important themes in my life had been learning how to seek out another dream when one died. Too many people get swallowed by disappointment when their dreams don't work out, and I had always made sure I wasn't one of those people. But now I was digging back into that disappointment, exploring it. The result was a tremendous outpouring of emotion. A catharsis.

We put on three preview performances of *Without a Word* in the summer of 1984, then reworked it for a month-long run at the Beverly Hills Playhouse that fall. Every single show sold out, and audiences left the theatre in tears. A *Who's Who* of Hollywood stars came to see it, including Liza Minnelli, Drew Barrymore and Melissa Gilbert. Gene Kelly came to a performance, too, and he particularly loved Lisa. He and Liza Minnelli pressed Lisa and me to take *Without a Word* to New York or make a movie of it, and separately Gene encouraged me to pursue more musical projects.

When all was said and done, we received six LA Drama Critics Awards, including Best Play, Best Direction, Best Actress for Lisa and Best Actor for me. As an artistic endeavour, it was an amazingly satisfying experience. But that wasn't the best thing about it.

The best thing about the play was the response we got, and continued to get even years later, from people who'd seen it. For years, people would come up to Lisa or me and tell us about the dreams they'd had, and how they'd fallen by the wayside—until seeing our play. People were actually finding the courage to go back and follow their bliss, encouraged by what they'd seen on stage.

*Without a Word* touched a deep emotional chord in so many people, and of all the endeavours we've undertaken, Lisa and I both remember this as one of our proudest artistic moments.

By the time *Without a Word* premiered, Lisa and I had been together ten years. We'd been through a lot in that time: the untimely end of our ballet careers, moving across the country, going broke, my dad's death, my foray into too much drinking. But through it all, I still felt a magic with her, which our emotional work together on *Without a Word* confirmed.

Lisa wasn't afraid of anything, and jumped right in to whatever we did, from woodworking to acting to playwriting. She was game for everything, and she never lost her sense of humour. The longer we were together, the luckier I felt that we'd found each other. And I even began to let myself believe she wanted to be with me, too.

One reason we fitted so well together was that we shared so many interests. We both loved dancing, acting, travelling, being out in the wild. We also both loved horses, and shared a dream of owning a few some day. But when we finally took the first step towards that dream, it was more like a funny misstep.

While we were on the set of *Red Dawn,* both Lisa and I had fallen in love with a horse in the movie named Fancy. As shooting was winding down, I asked the movie's horse wrangler if he'd sell Fancy to us. We still lived in an apartment, so we couldn't keep him at home, but we figured he could live at the equestrian-centre stables in LA. Fancy was a gorgeous, high-stepping Morgan parade horse, with his head always jacked up so high that sitting on him was like sitting on the back of a sea horse.

I offered the wrangler $150, hoping it would be enough. To my relief, he agreed. He led Fancy out of a trailer and held out the lead rope. 'He's all yours!' he said.

I'd just bought a horse! What was I going to do with him now? I took the rope and began to lead Fancy away, and at that very moment one of the old ranch hands was walking by.

'This is my new horse!' I said, a big smile on my face.

'That horse is lame,' the old-timer replied. He pointed at Fancy's legs, and I was forced to admit what I'd noticed earlier but tried to ignore. Fancy had a slight limp in his right rear leg. We'd bought a lame horse, with bowed tendons, but I loved him anyway—he and I had been through that freezing winter together. And, despite his limp, Fancy still turned out to be a great first horse for us.

I'd loved horses all my life, and we even had an Arabian mare when I was growing up. She wasn't well bred, but she was an Arabian, and we bred her to have a foal, whom we named Princess Zubidiya of Damascus. We called her Zubi. I rode her every chance I got. And I learned horsemanship from a master—my dad.

My dad was beautiful in the saddle. He was like John Wayne. He'd been riding since he could walk and he came from a long line of cowboys. His father—my grandfather—had been a foreman at the King Ranch in Texas, which was the size of Rhode Island, and one of the biggest ranches in the world. My grandfather was shot to death by cattle rustlers before my dad was born and, according to family lore, the killers had sat there smoking his cigarettes while they waited for him to die.

My grandmother remarried after that, and my stepgrandfather was a cowboy, too, up in the Texas Panhandle. When I was growing up, I used to go there in the summers and work with him on the ranch. His name was Cap, but we kids called him Pe-Paw, which he hated. Later, when we'd go into bars together, he'd say, 'Little Buddy, you call me Cap in this bar; don't be calling me that piece of shit Pe-Paw!' I loved him to death, but of course I'd call him Pe-Paw just to drive him crazy.

These were the men who passed on to my dad—and me—the cowboy way. Even though I moved to New York and LA, becoming a dancer and an actor, I never lost that cowboy blood. My dad and I used to talk about owning a ranch together some day, with a stable of horses and big outdoor spaces. He died before I could make it happen for us, but I kept that dream alive and swore to myself that Lisa and I would buy a beautiful ranch in his honour when we had the money.

In late 1984, five years after moving to Los Angeles, I finally got the TV role that would enable me to do just that. And, ironically enough, I'd be playing a man who spent much of his own life on horseback.

## Chapter 8

Orry Main, the swashbuckling Confederate Army soldier in *North and South*, was the role that sent my career soaring. *North and South* was a twelve-hour mini-series, and it was a TV event that rivalled the epic *Roots* mini-series of the late 1970s.

The story revolved round the Confederate Orry Main and his Union soldier friend George Hazard, played by Jim Read. Orry and George meet at West Point, and the mini-series follows their friendship through the tumult of the Civil War and beyond. *North and South* was a huge undertaking, with more than 130 cast members, thousands of extras, nearly 9,000 wardrobe pieces, and 15,000 props and set decorations. It was a certifiable Big TV Event.

I was very excited to win the role of Orry, and not just because he was the kind of Renaissance-man, courageous southern gentleman I'd always aspired to be. Playing Orry meant that I would be starring alongside the most amazing cast ever assembled for a television series. Elizabeth Taylor, James Stewart, Olivia de Havilland, Johnny Cash, David Carradine, Lesley-Anne Down, Gene Kelly, Robert Mitchum and Jean Simmons all had parts in *North and South*—and that's just a partial list.

Of course, being me, I was determined that, even though I'd be playing opposite some of the greatest actors of all time, I'd try to be cool about it. After all, Jim Read and I were the leads of the series, and I wanted to project confidence. But when, early in the shoot, I heard James Stewart's distinctive voice as I walked towards the set for our scene, and saw him sitting behind an ornate desk, in character as Miles Colbert, I simply couldn't believe I'd been lucky enough to be cast opposite Hollywood legends like him, and my knees turned to jelly. For a young actor, it was the opportunity of a lifetime.

In addition to feeling lucky to be on that set, I also loved everything about my role. *North and South* was set in a time of courtliness and southern gentility which really appealed to my old-fashioned side. I loved walking down the streets on the set, seeing the men in their military uniforms and the women in their corsets and gowns, fanning themselves in the heat.

The set even came equipped with 'leaning boards', as women couldn't sit down in their giant ball gowns without crushing them. Instead, they'd prop themselves gently against the leaning board, resting without sitting. Walking by a row of corseted beauties, dressed in my sharp Confederate Army uniform, I felt I'd gone back in time.

We filmed all over the South, in Mississippi, Arkansas, Louisiana, South Carolina, Texas. And because we were making not only the twelve-hour *North and South*, but also *North and South: Book II*, we ended up shooting for a year and a half. It was amazing to have that much guaranteed work, and at a really good salary. Even on *The Outsiders,* which was not only a Francis Ford Coppola movie but also did very well at the box office, I'd received only the basic scale pay. It was worth it, of course, to work with Coppola. But both Lisa and I were really happy to have some real money coming in now.

The shooting schedule and conditions were intense. We shot six days a week, for no fewer than twelve hours a day. And some of the longest days were right in the middle of the South Carolina summer, when we'd sometimes spend up to eighteen hours shooting, wearing heavy woollen uniforms. I even fainted once on the set, slamming my face into a cement column. But when Jim Read and I asked permission to take our coats off for one scene on a train, the director, Richard T. Heffron, first had to confirm with a Civil War expert that it would be historically accurate before he said yes.

The producers did everything they could to ensure historical authenticity. Some of the costumes were made with nineteenth-century silk, and others were borrowed from historical collections. The best source of costumes, however, was the hundreds of Civil War re-enactors who played in the battle scenes.

This was my first time meeting hard-core re-enactors, and I was amazed at how particular they were. Some of them were descendants of soldiers who had fought in the battles we re-created, and they not only wore clothes that were true to the period, even down to their underwear, but they also didn't eat any food or use any tools or weapons that weren't available during the Civil War.

The cast also had coaches, to help ensure we stayed in character. Our dialect coach, Robert Easton, made sure everyone spoke with the proper drawl or brogue, and dance historian Desmond Strobel taught us how to dance an authentic 'Sicilian Circle' and 'Lancers' Quadrille'. The result of all this attention to detail was a background that looked, sounded and felt like a real Civil War setting.

DEPENDING ON the cast and the general mood, film and TV sets can be pretty wild places. On *Red Dawn,* we'd got into some crazy pranks, partly to defuse the tension of the shoot, which was both physically gruelling and emotionally draining. But on *North and South,* the cast wasn't into pranks so much as having a good time. It was a fun group, and Lisa and I loved hanging out with everyone in the evenings after shooting.

We did a lot of filming in Charleston, South Carolina, which is packed with fantastic restaurants in its tree-lined, beautifully preserved old section. One restaurant in particular, Philippe Million's, became a cast hangout. We'd head there nearly every weekend, drawn by the kitchen's excellent nouvelle cuisine. Some actors could be found there several times a week, in particular Lesley-Anne Down, who we'd heard had her own reasons for wanting to spend as much time as possible in expensive restaurants.

Lesley, who played my love interest in the series, had already starred in countless TV shows and films, including *The Pink Panther Strikes Again* and the BBC's popular *Upstairs, Downstairs.* At the time we were shooting *North and South*, she and her husband, the director Billy Friedkin, were heading towards a bitter divorce, and it seemed that she was aiming to spend as much of Billy's money as she could before it was final.

So on the nights she was at Philippe Million's, the champagne flowed and the food kept coming—courtesy, unbeknown to him, of Billy. She must have spent tens of thousands of dollars at that restaurant. We'd all eat and drink to our hearts' content, then head out to a nearby place to dance. It was a pretty lively group, and there were a lot of late nights.

Lesley also treated herself to an upgrade over the cast housing in Charleston, which was already nothing to sneeze at. She chose a penthouse suite with a fantastic view of Charleston. And she was generous with that, too, inviting us all up a couple of times for drinks.

On one of those evenings the last thing I remembered was talking with David Carradine, and the next thing I knew, I was waking up the next morning in my hotel room, slightly hung over.

The following afternoon Lesley said to me, 'Patrick, I was so worried about you last night!'

'Why?' I asked.

'Well,' she said in her clipped British accent, 'you and David were out on that tiny ledge, outside the window, doing karate. I was scared to death!'

I just stared at her. I had no recollection of going out on the ledge—why would I do a crazy thing like that? After all, her suite was up on the twelfth floor. But apparently, it was true. David was a serious martial-arts guy—he'd played the lead in the seventies TV series *Kung Fu*—and he and I had apparently gone out to the ledge to demonstrate our balance skills in kata, a form of slow-motion shadowboxing. Thank goodness that, even with alcohol in our bloodstreams, our balance had been good enough to keep us from tumbling to the beautiful cobblestones of Charleston, twelve floors below.

Needless to say, Lisa wasn't in Charleston with us that particular weekend. Otherwise I wouldn't have been up there in the first place. I definitely tended towards more drinking and late nights when she wasn't with me—I never have been able to stand the inside of a hotel room alone. When I was missing Lisa, I just wanted the nights to go by faster and staying out was my admittedly imperfect way of trying to make that happen.

But as much as I loved partying with my fellow cast members on *North and South*, I probably loved the horses even more. There were some gorgeous horses on that set, including John Wayne's last horse, Parsons. Parsons and I developed an amazing connection—it was almost telepathic. All I had to do was think about what I wanted him to do next and he'd do it.

There were plenty of good horse scenes in both parts of *North and South*, but the best one came in *Book II.* Orry, who by now is a general, is riding away from camp with two of his aides when suddenly the camp comes under attack. The three of them have to turn round and come to the rescue, with guns blazing.

Just before we shot the scene, I had an idea. I was always trying to figure out ways to make the action scenes more exciting, and I knew I'd hit on something great with this: we should hold the horses' reins in our teeth so we could fire our rifles with both hands as we raced through the battle.

The two guys who played my aides were hard-core re-enactors. They had the long hair and grizzled look of real Civil War soldiers, and this was how they spent their leisure time—travelling round the country, putting on re-enactments and handing down knowledge of the Civil War era to future generations. These were men with full beards, powerful builds and leathery skin. I just knew they'd be ready to up the ante on this scene.

We were all three astride our horses, and just as the director was about to yell, 'Action!' I said to the two guys, 'Hey, dudes—we've got these double-barrelled short shotguns; let's ride with the reins in our teeth so we can fire with both hands!'

The guys just shook their heads. 'No way,' said one of them, sitting back in his saddle.

'Well, why not?' I asked, exasperated.

'Teeth,' the guy said. And he reached up and popped his front teeth right out of his mouth. It was a denture.

'Oh shit,' I said. 'How'd that happen?'

'Riding with the reins in my teeth,' the guy replied, and calmly placed the bridge back in his mouth. 'If that horse trips, it'll pull your teeth right out of your head.'

Just then the director yelled, 'Action!'

We all took off and, despite the warning, I held the reins in my teeth for the whole shot. I kept my back as rubbery as possible, trying to absorb every little jolt with anything but my teeth. But I didn't need to worry: Parsons was such a good, sure-footed horse that he raced silkily round every obstacle. The shot turned out well, and fortunately all my teeth stayed in my head.

THE FIRST INSTALMENT of *North and South* aired in November 1985, and suddenly Jim Read and I found our faces plastered all over newspapers, magazines, billboards and TV shows.

ABC had ratcheted up its publicity machine, and that, combined with the Americans' enduring interest in the Civil War, established the mini-series as a huge TV event. The television landscape wasn't so fragmented in the 1980s as it is now, with hundreds of channels competing for attention, so millions of people tuned in to see the instalments as they aired.

The floodgates were officially open. Patrick Swayze fan clubs appeared and interview requests were pouring in. Now, whenever we went out, Lisa and I would find ourselves surrounded. Before *North and South*, people might sometimes recognise me on the street and ask for an autograph. But after the mini-series aired, fans were suddenly everywhere, approaching us no matter where we were. I have to admit, it was kind of cool.

But as the level of fame went up, the level of courtesy sometimes went down. People would interrupt our conversations, even jump in front of our car to ask for an autograph. And when we went to events, the organisers would often take my arm and try to lead me away, completely ignoring Lisa. In those cases, I'd interject loudly, 'Have you met my wife, Lisa?' and they'd get the picture.

Yet we've always tried to accommodate fans' requests. After all, we both know we wouldn't be where we are if it weren't for the fans, and we're appreciative of the support they've given us over the years. For the most part, people are very nice so it's easy to be nice back. And, of course, I'm a guy who always wants people to like me, so I have extra motivation for being nice to those who approach us.

Lisa, too, has always taken the attention in her stride, even when women fans get a little more aggressive. She's not the jealous type. And besides, she knows as well as anyone that all the attention has been good for my career.

But even though we were happy about my career taking off, we had to deal with some difficult situations after *North and South*. For one thing, my manager, Bob LeMond, who'd brought us out to LA and helped us get started, died of complications from AIDS. Bob had been a real mentor and friend, and we'd known him since our days in Houston. Losing him at this point in my career, just three years after my father died, was devastating.

Lisa and I also realised that we'd now have to take steps to protect our privacy. There were paparazzi all over Hollywood, not to mention overzealous fans who weren't above staking us out at home. Luckily, though, the role of Orry Main allowed us to buy a five-acre ranch, where we could keep dear old Fancy and enjoy nature without being disturbed.

But although Lisa and I saw the potential on our new property for the home we'd always dreamed of, when others saw it they were shocked. They thought we'd just bought ourselves a nightmare.

Nestled in the foothills of the San Gabriel Mountains about twenty miles north of Hollywood, the piece of land Lisa and I fell in love with was just a weed-choked lot.

Used-car parts sat rusting, and dead tree limbs and river rocks lay scattered across it. The house was just a couple of run-down cabins connected by a breezeway. The floors needed finishing, the kitchen needed renovating, the walls were made of plywood, and everything was generally a mess. But right from the start, it looked like heaven to us.

Ever since our first days of doing carpentry back in New York, Lisa and I had felt ready to take on any project, no matter how large or small. This would be a very big one, but when we looked at those cabins and that land, we didn't see work and toil. We saw the potential. Lisa and I both had plenty of ideas and we couldn't wait to get to work making them a reality.

We knew we'd need help, so the first thing we did was make it fun for friends to come out and join in the labour with us. We built the pool first, before fixing up the house, so everybody who came out and sweated with us could have a nice cool dip afterwards.

We invited friends to 'rock parties' that had nothing to do with music: we'd fan people out across the property to collect up all the rocks, then have a big barbecue for everyone afterwards. And we turned weed-cutting from a boring chore into a sword-fighting lesson. I outfitted everyone with sabres and we thrust and parried into the weeds, theatrically attacking the common foe. It was during one of these clean-up sessions that one of our friends gave our new home its name: Rancho Bizarro.

It was wonderfully liberating to be out in nature again after all our years of city living. Our ranch adjoined the Angeles National Forest, which made it feel as if our little five-acre lot was really a million-acre spread—we could ride horses deep into the wilderness from right outside our back door. The air was fresh and the smell of sage and oak permeated everything.

We worked on the ranch itself every chance we got, creating a beautiful kitchen with terracotta floors and refinishing the wood floors ourselves—which Lisa says she'll never do again. We got to add our own special touches: over time, we built trellised patios, a master-bedroom wing, a music studio, a dance studio, a guesthouse and an office.

We also built a sixteen-stall pinewood barn, because living on the ranch wasn't just about fresh air and privacy. It was also about reclaiming the cowboy life. The smell of dirt and horse sweat and the raw masculine power of working on horseback was energising for me and I wanted to get back into it.

Lisa and I were lucky enough to know someone who could now help us get some really good horses. Gene McLaughlin was a world-champion trick roper and his son Cliff had been a stunt double in *North and South.* To make ends meet between rodeos and trick-roping shows, Gene would buy horses down south and truck them to Los Angeles in a trailer, where he could sell them for three to five times what he'd paid. We bought our second horse from him—a fantastic, talented gelding named Cloud.

Cloud was small but rode big. He and I would explore the mountains in the Angeles National Forest behind our ranch, sometimes going out for days at a time. I'd pack some food and water and a sleeping-bag, and we'd just hit the trails. Some of my happiest memories are of Cloud and me exploring the deepest reaches of the woods together, miles from people and civilisation. It reminded me of being with my dad, to the point where our journeys together felt almost spiritual.

Cloud was also an excellent calf-roping horse. Calf roping is the hardest rodeo sport, in my opinion, as it requires lightning reflexes and excellent timing. You have to rope the running calf off your speeding horse, then use the horse's stopping to propel yourself forward and land on your feet running. You then hit the calf and grab the feet, lacing them with string in a nice bouquet.

The whole thing takes about two seconds, but one wrong move can result in injury to you, the horse, the calf, or all three. Gene trained me and I was off to the races—I loved getting down in the dirt and honing my skills.

With the pinewood barn finished and plenty of room for more horses, Lisa and I started thinking about buying the most beautiful, regal animals of all: Arabians. But even with the money I'd made on *North and South*, we still weren't sure we could afford them.

Arabians are the steeds of the gods and expensive to buy. Originally bred in the Middle East, they have a proud bearing and gorgeous bone structure, with arched necks and high tails. An Arabian is the kind of horse that can make you gasp as it prances by. And not only are they stunning to look at, they're also smart, with boundless energy. Arabians aren't the easiest horses to train but the result can be a real partnership between horse and rider.

I'd always wanted to own an Arabian and, as well as Gene McLaughlin, Lisa and I were fortunate enough to know two of the best breeders in the country, Tom and Rhita McNair. So we decided to stop by and see the McNairs one week when we were in Houston visiting Lisa's family. We'd just told them we weren't sure we were ready to buy, when a horse named Ferouk came trotting out of his gate. Ferouk was a stunner, an impressive, powerful, well-trained horse.

'This one's a winner,' Tom told us. 'You could win Western Pleasure competitions with Ferouk.' Looking at that horse, with his gliding stride and dark, intelligent eyes, we knew it was true.

Lisa and I wanted to own Arabians to learn more and improve our horsemanship, but we also wanted to show them competitively. Tom knew this and Ferouk seemed to understand it, too. He looked at us with those big brown eyes as if to say, 'You and me! Let's go!' So we asked Tom how much it would cost to buy Ferouk—and his answer was a lot less than what we'd expected.

Lisa and I looked at each other and we both knew we were about to buy our first Arabian.

And that was how we began showing horses. We didn't know much about it, but being dancers we picked up the physical nuances quickly. Your bearing and carriage have to be impressive, as the horse takes its cues from you. After taking her first lesson in how to show, Lisa entered a competition the very next day—and was placed third. She was hooked.

Ferouk was a smart, savvy horse, and he and Lisa bonded right away. Soon they were an amazing team. Lisa was a natural, and less than a year later she took him all the way to the US Nationals competition. She competed there with people who had been showing horses their whole lives, but her skills were phenomenal, and she was placed in the top ten—an incredible achievement. And I went top five in Region Nine, the most difficult region in the country.

We competed seriously for a while, travelling all across the United States for horse shows. People were surprised that we did everything ourselves, from mucking out stalls to scrubbing down the horses to staying in the same motels as our trainers. I suppose they expected a couple of prima donnas, but to us the whole point was to be one with the horse and not to stand out.

Unfortunately, the more famous I got, the more difficult it was to compete in horse shows. Working with horses, like working with ballerinas, teaches you that it's not about yourself. It's about bringing out the beauty and precision and perfection of your partner—in this case, your horse. But as fans began to realise that I was showing horses, they'd come out to the arenas and hang over the rail, shouting, waving photos for autographs, or even taking flash photos right in my horse's face.

I tried switching from riding horses to showing at halter, where you have the horse at the end of a lead rope. You teach the horse to stand in a certain way, pulling up the head and neck, and then you run, leading the horse through paces meant to show off its conformation and movement. This worked out a little better, though eventually, after my next movie, I'd have to stop showing altogether. It just wasn't fair to the horse or to the other competitors.

As Lisa and I worked to get Rancho Bizarro in order, we accumulated more and more animals. Soon we had dogs, cats, horses, peacocks and a chicken house. I loved being around animals and felt a connection with them that I felt with only a few people. If an animal was upset, I could talk it down and soothe it—and they could do the same for me. Surrounded by acres of gorgeous land and our growing menagerie of animals, we felt that the ranch was a true haven.

And we'd soon need that haven more than ever, as 1987 would mark the release of my biggest movie yet—and the start of the craziest period of our lives.

## Chapter 9

I read the script for *Dirty Dancing* one evening in our new house. Right away it filled me with emotion—but not the kind it was supposed to. I didn't like it. It seemed fluffy—nothing more than a summer-camp movie. Lisa read it, too, and she felt the same way.

But at the same time, we both could see the kernel of a great story in there. The ideas behind *Dirty Dancing* were fascinating. There were elements of class conflict, relationships, sexual awakening, family issues—it had a little bit of everything. And though the screenplay was weak, with some work on it to create a strong story filled with compelling characters, it could explore all those elements.

Potential is a wonderful thing, but would the writer and director be open to rewrites? The next morning Lisa and I talked about how the script could be better. And despite our initial reservations, we began to get a little excited. I was scheduled to go in and read for a role in it that seemed perfect for me, but I also wanted to find out if we could really turn it into a great movie.

One thing that attracted me to *Dirty Dancing* was the fact that Emile Ardolino would be directing. Emile didn't have a mile-long Hollywood résumé, but he came from the dance world and had done award-winning work, including a televised presentation of *Baryshnikov at the White House* and a documentary about Jacques d'Amboise that had won an Academy Award. *Dirty Dancing* would be his first feature film, but he was a class act and really knew dance. If anyone could pull this off, it was Emile.

But I still had reservations. Even if the script could be vastly improved, I wasn't sure this movie was the right step to take in my career.

The response to *Skatetown, USA* had made it clear that I could have my pick of similar roles—and make a lot of money doing them. But it was also clear that if I did choose that route, I might never be able to escape it. I'd always be seen as a dancer-turned-actor. So in the eight years that had passed since *Skatetown, USA,* I had avoided roles that involved dancing or had any kind of teen-idol flavour. I'd turned down that four-picture deal with Columbia that would have shot me to fame. I'd taken acting classes, and I'd been constantly on the lookout for stronger, more demanding roles.

Now, with *Dirty Dancing,* I had a choice. Should I stick to my guns and refuse to take a dancing movie? Or was this a different kind of movie, that would allow me to dance but would also stretch me as an actor? I was scared that if I said yes I'd be undoing what I'd worked for the last eight years to build. But at the same time, both Lisa and I believed that *Dirty Dancing* had the potential to be a wonderful movie.

So, after many conversations with Lisa, I made my decision: I would go for it. Part of me was excited about doing a dance movie, of course, and then again, we now had house payments to make, too. So that afternoon I said to Lisa, 'Okay, here we go.'

THE ROLE OF JOHNNY CASTLE wasn't mine for the taking. Once I'd established that Emile was looking at how the script could be improved, I had to go in for a couple of auditions, first where I read, and then where Jennifer Grey and I danced together.

Whenever I read for auditions, I prefer to improvise rather than doing all the lines straight up. So for that first reading, I talked about growing up without much money in Houston, and how dance was a magical form of escape. The truth is, I really identified with Johnny. He was a blue-collar fighter whose soul was stirred by the beauty of dance. He was the kind of man who combined a tough exterior with a gentle soul—the kind of man my dad had been and the kind I was trying to be. In that first audition, I didn't act out Johnny. I *was* Johnny.

For the second audition, Jennifer Grey and I went in to dance for writer Eleanor Bergstein, choreographer Kenny Ortega, and Emile Ardolino. Eleanor was very close to the material—she'd based her story partly on her own experiences in the early 1960s, when she was a teenage girl called 'Baby' dancing in the Catskills, and the movie was really an important labour of love for her. So she was the one who came forward to show Jennifer and me what we needed to do.

Eleanor put on some music and half-talked, half-danced us through what she wanted. I wasn't exactly sure what she was looking for, so I decided to wing it. Jennifer and I had never danced together before and she probably still thought of me as that half-crazed forest warrior from *Red Dawn*. But as I led her through a couple of steps, we soon found ourselves in a comfortable rhythm together.

I moved her round slowly at first, pulling her towards me and spinning her back out. I wanted her to feel confident in her dancing, enough to lose herself in it and not feel self-conscious. She was a little bit giggly at first, but she soon got more comfortable. We started doing more complex moves, and as we danced I decided she was lithe enough and balanced enough to try a lift.

Lisa was in the room, too, so we showed Jennifer how the lift would work. Lisa and I had done it so many times, we made it look effortless. I knew that if I was to lift Jennifer successfully, she'd have to feel completely safe with me—and after sitting and watching me lift Lisa a couple of times, she seemed ready.

It's not easy for a female dancer to execute her first lift. She's got to trust her male partner completely and give in to the momentum he sets for her. Otherwise, one or both partners can get hurt. Jennifer got up and took Lisa's place, and as we continued talking with Eleanor and Kenny, I just took her and gently raised her over my head. I showed her I could control her completely—she would never tumble if she made no sudden moves.

Jennifer did break position a couple of times, which was a natural reaction for someone who's never done lifts before. 'Don't worry,' I told her. 'No matter what position you're in, I can put you down safely.' The next time I lifted her, she posed beautifully, and I lowered her slowly to the ground, with our eyes locked on each other. It was a lovely moment.

Jennifer smiled when I put her down, and from that moment on, I knew we had it. We did a couple more dance moves and when the audition was over Eleanor had made up her mind. As she told us later, at that point she felt that if they didn't get me for the role of Johnny, they didn't have a movie.

Once I'd been cast as Johnny, Lisa and I started looking at the script. Eleanor, Emile and others were doing the same thing, so it was definitely a group effort, but I was as grateful as ever for Lisa's insights. Whether rewriting scripts or honing my performance, she and I have worked together on every movie I've ever done—she has an amazing ear for dialogue, a great sense of story, and knows how to zero in on performance. More important, she's absolutely truthful, even if it's something I don't want to hear. I always know I can trust her completely—which has become more and more important as time goes by and my stature in Hollywood has grown.

A lot of actors surround themselves with 'yes-men'. They like to be told that everything they're doing is great—it helps boost their confidence. But I'm the opposite. I want to know what's weak, so I can work on improving it. Whenever we work on a script or scene for a movie, we always try to think through what the writer intends here. What does the director see? Could the story have higher stakes? Is this how my character would react? Do these people talk like real flesh-and-bone human beings? Once you've done this, when you get back down to the words on the page you know right away what works and what doesn't.

That's how Lisa and I work together: we find the intention and emotional flow of a scene and the words follow naturally. As the great director Elia Kazan once said, people are often revealed by how we conceal our emotions, not how we show them. So, good writing has a lot do with how much your character conceals, rather than reveals. For example, it touches the audience's heart far more to see somebody go to the ends of the earth not to cry—than to watch someone over-emoting, crying in their pretzels.

The draft of the script we'd read only hinted at deeper sociological and emotional currents, but we all knew that if we could just push the characters a little further, and explore them a little more deeply, we'd really have something. So everyone jumped right in, working day and night to tear apart things that weren't working and deepen the parts that were. Eleanor's script had strong bones, but now we were adding the flesh to them—and we'd continue doing so all the way through filming. And by the time we were done, we had a beautiful script.

Some of what Lisa and I suggested made it into the film, and some didn't. We'd be working on new dialogue right up to shooting—and then continue fixing it between takes. Lisa and I stayed up the entire night before filming the final scene, where Johnny grabs the microphone in front of everyone at the resort, so we could rewrite his big speech. We never stopped trying to make it better.

One line that I absolutely hated ended up staying in, though. I could hardly even bring myself to say 'Nobody puts Baby in a corner' in front of the cameras, it just sounded so corny. But later, seeing the finished film, I had to admit it worked. And it became one of the most-quoted lines in the entire movie. I even quote a version of it myself these days, saying 'Nobody puts Patrick's pancreas in a corner' when people ask how I'm doing.

But it wasn't just the rewrites that required us to put in serious overtime. We also spent hours perfecting the dance moves that would really make the movie pop. Lisa spent many late nights working with me, rehearsing and honing these sequences.

Following the lead of choreographer Kenny Ortega, everyone

in the cast spun and twirled and danced until we were ready to drop—Cynthia Rhodes later said she lost ten pounds during the shoot, despite drinking milkshakes every day. But Kenny had an infectious energy. He was like Gene Kelly, whom he'd studied with. He was always dancing with a huge smile on his face, and having so much fun you couldn't help but have fun too.

Kenny was a real hoofer, a talented dancer who could cross genre barriers. I loved the fact that he worked in so many kinds of dance—jazz, swing, salsa. Jazz in particular had been a very big part of my early dance education, since my mother had pretty much created the jazz scene in Houston.

We all worked incredibly hard, but we had a hell of a lot of fun too. Shooting many of the scenes really was like a party—just rock and roll and everybody sweating on the dance floor. The actors and dancers in the movie were so game and so talented, they just tore it up.

I drove the van between locations, with Kenny and Jennifer and Cynthia and whoever else wanted to come along. We all spent hours together in that van, singing songs and talking. We were like a posse—a gang of young, energetic artists who'd been thrown together in a beautiful old colonial-style hotel, with nothing to do but create. It was one of the most exhausting shoots I can remember—but also one of the most fun-filled.

WITH ALL THE DANCING and jumping and running around, it's no surprise that my knee began swelling again. I'd ice it after shooting the dance scenes, but as filming went on, I had to start getting it drained again—just as I'd done back in New York. But it wasn't dancing that caused me the most knee pain of all. It was a scene where I'm balancing on a log with Jennifer, above some rocks.

It looks like fun in the movie, but shooting that scene was dangerous and physically taxing. When you're balancing like that, your joints are working overtime, making constant tiny adjustments. After spending a couple of hours filming that log scene, I had to go straight to the hospital to get my knee drained. It was definitely more painful and difficult than anything I did on the dance floor.

In fact, I often pestered Kenny and Emile to give me more serious dance moves. All Johnny's dirty dancing was fine, but I had to subordinate my ego for the role, and this of course was absolutely right as I was actually a far more highly trained dancer than blue-collar Johnny. In the end, the closest we got to letting Johnny do anything difficult was in the final scene of the movie, when I leapt off the stage and did a double pirouette and double turn.

Shooting scenes indoors could also be unbearably hot, especially early on, when temperatures outside hit the nineties, and inside, with the cameras and lights, they soared to above one hundred. Several dancers and actors passed out from all their exertions, but everyone hung in there, fighting through the heat to do multiple takes and get everything perfect.

Jennifer Grey worked as hard as anyone, and did an amazing job considering that she had never been a professional dancer. In my life I've encountered very few people who have the natural talent she has. She learned quickly, was game for anything, and as time went on, everything became easier for us both, because she never hit a plateau in terms of her ability or willingness to try new things. She had courage—emotional and physical courage—and the movie wouldn't have been half as good with anyone else in her role. I believe that Jennifer's performance was really underappreciated. In many ways, she made the movie.

As the summer turned to fall, we wrapped up filming. The shoot took only forty-four days, but even so we ended up shooting later in the year than planned. The leaves had begun to turn, so the crew rushed to spray-paint them back from orange and red into summer green for the last few scenes. Everyone—Emile, Kenny, Eleanor, and all the actors and dancers—seemed proud of what we'd done. And I felt really invested in this film, with all the dancing, acting and rewriting. Not to mention the addition to the soundtrack of a song I wrote with Stacy Widelitz, 'She's Like the Wind'.

I've always written music, and I'd been singing on stage since my music theatre days. I studied violin and guitar growing up and, ever since, there's nothing that relaxes me more than noodling around on a guitar. Music has always been a huge part of my life, so it was natural to try to integrate it into my movies, too.

Stacy and I didn't write 'She's Like the Wind' for *Dirty Dancing*; in fact, I started writing it for *Grandview, USA*, and Stacy later helped me finish it. I was disappointed when the song didn't make it into that film, but I didn't give up on it and when I played the demo for Emile he liked it enough to pass it on to the music supervisor, Jimmy Ienner. Jimmy loved it and he ended up picking it for an extended sequence in the film.

In the mid 1980s, movie soundtracks weren't a big business yet, so I wasn't thinking in terms of record sales—I was just happy that the song would finally get heard. Movie soundtracks had never been great sellers so the music companies didn't charge much for the use of old songs. In fact, the entire *Dirty Dancing* soundtrack cost just $200,000. But it ended up changing the music business for ever—just as this modest little $5.2 million movie would change all our lives for ever. We just didn't know it yet.

AFTER EMILE and his team completed their final cut of *Dirty Dancing*, the producers set up a private screening so we could go and see it before it was released. We'd heard that the first cut hadn't been very well received—in fact, one producer was rumoured to have said, 'Burn the negative and collect the insurance.' But Emile had gone back into the editing room determined to make the movie as great as we all believed it could be.

So, Lisa and I walked into that private screening knowing that everyone involved had done good work, but not having any idea what to expect beyond that. With all the thousands of little decisions that go into making a film—in writing, shooting, sound, lighting, cutting, editing—it's impossible to know how the final product will turn out.

We settled into our seats and the lights dimmed. Almost two hours later, when the credits rolled, Lisa and I turned to each other and smiled. The story had turned out better than we'd hoped for, all those months before in our kitchen. It wasn't just a shallow movie about two people sucking face—it was a moment in time when two very different souls really do connect. And Jennifer and I had achieved that together on screen.

Even so, we still figured it would be a modestly successful movie, and not much more than that. Lisa thought it was the kind of story people would be drawn to, where the good guy falls in love with the funky girl. We had no idea what was coming—that after the movie opened we would be swallowed by a tidal wave of fame and attention.

In the meantime, Lisa and I headed for a place about as far away from Hollywood as you can get—geographically, spiritually and otherwise. We flew to Africa to make our first feature together: *Steel Dawn.*

# Chapter 10

Lisa and I peered out of the window as the small plane we were in descended towards Swakopmund, on the western coast of Namibia. We were exhausted, having travelled for more than twenty-four hours, including a ten-hour layover in Frankfurt with nothing but chairs to sleep in. As we looked out at the desert terrain below, I said to Lisa, 'Damn, it looks just like Arizona. Why'd we come all this way?'

Bone-tired from the *Dirty Dancing* shoot, I was only half joking. But we soon found out that the Namib Desert, where we would be shooting *Steel Dawn*, was a magical place. Our time spent there would restore us in many ways, and lead to a lifelong love of Africa.

On our first morning there, we piled into a Volkswagen camper van and headed out to explore. The Namib Desert borders the Kalahari, the largest desert in Africa after the Sahara. And although the word 'desert' conjures dead images of sand and more sand, this desert was alive, especially in the morning.

In addition to wind-sculpted dunes, in some parts of the desert there are whole stretches of crusted black rock, like a moonscape. If you spend the night in that moonscape, and wake up just before dawn, you can watch the whole desert suddenly blossom into green. When Lisa and I first saw it happen, we thought we were dreaming. But the lichen on the rocks was opening up briefly, like a flower, to collect moisture. Then, as the sun rose in the sky, it suddenly closed back up, leaving nothing but scorched-looking rocks and the memory of what seemed like a mirage.

Ever since the days of camping with my dad in the backwoods of Texas, I've always loved learning about how people in different places live off the land. Here in southern Africa, I wanted to connect with local people who could teach me how to live in the desert. Where do you find water, food and shelter in such a desolate environment?

Seeing the desert blossom into green was amazing, and it showed us that sustenance can come from the most unlikely places. Some African members of the crew had grown up in the desert and they told us more—about the roaming herds of ostrich and other animals, and details about how to survive in the desert. Lisa and I connected in a very deep way with the nature all around us and we loved driving out to explore different parts of the Kalahari during the shoot.

But although we loved being in Africa, I was exhausted from *Dirty Dancing*. I'd put everything I had into that shoot, and then I'd moved straight into *Steel Dawn* with no break. My *Steel Dawn* character, Nomad, was a warrior in a postapocalyptic world who travels across the desert fighting mutant sand people and outlaws. We shot a lot of very physical scenes, with sword fighting, martial arts, spear throwing and hand-to-hand combat. All that activity, plus being immersed in this amazing place, was enough to make my head spin.

As always, Lisa was my rock. This was the first time we were acting in a movie together and it was rewarding to share scenes with her on screen, rather than just working behind the scenes with her. She played Kasha, a widow who lives in the desert with her young son and falls in love with Nomad. Lisa is a wonderful actress and I was happy she was finally getting an opportunity to show her stuff. And I found that I was falling in love with her all over again.

I'd always said that the perfect woman for me is someone who's interested in all the things I like to do—not someone who says, 'No, I don't want to get my hair wet!' When we were shooting *Steel Dawn*, I saw once again how open Lisa was to new experiences. She loved going out into the desert and loved learning everything about Africa. Spiritually and emotionally, we were just amazingly compatible.

After we wrapped *Steel Dawn*, Lisa and I went on a safari, staying at the place—Mala Mala—where Elizabeth Taylor and Richard Burton were married. It was marvellously romantic, a beautiful bungalow situated in the lush African landscape. By the end of our time in Africa we felt refreshed and renewed. It was a good thing, too, because when we got back to the United States and *Dirty Dancing* exploded into theatres, our relationship would be tested like never before.

THE DEAUVILLE American Film Festival takes place every year in a beautiful resort town on France's Normandy coast. It's a prestigious festival, attended by the biggest movie stars, directors and producers in the world. And in 1987, to our excitement, the organisers chose *Dirty Dancing* to open the festival.

Emile and Eleanor both flew to Deauville for the screening, and Lisa and I joined them there. We weren't sure what kind of reception the movie would get, since the French are very picky moviegoers, and this was just a modest little film about 1960s

America. We settled into our balcony seats and waited nervously as the lights dimmed. And as we watched *Dirty Dancing* all the way through for just the second time, I was struck again by how well it had turned out. But we still weren't sure what the audience was thinking.

When the movie ended and the lights came on, we stood up to leave. But all of a sudden, everyone in the theatre turned round, looked up at us in the balcony, and broke into a thundering standing ovation that must have gone on for five minutes. Emile, Eleanor, Lisa and I just stood there, dumbstruck, as the audience whooped and applauded. It was an incredibly gratifying moment and gave us our first hint about how this 'little movie' would ultimately be received.

A party had been planned for after the screening and it seemed as if half of Deauville showed up. After a sit-down dinner, everyone danced into the wee hours of the morning, trying out their dirty-dancing moves and bringing a little bit of sixties America to the French coast. It was the perfect kickoff to a crazy time.

*Dirty Dancing* opened in the United States on August 21, 1987. It shot to the number-two spot, and within ten days it had sold more than $10 million in tickets—a huge amount back then. People went to see it multiple times, starting a trend that would ultimately lift the grosses to more than $60 million in that year alone. Made for just over $5 million, it was on its way to becoming a bona fide phenomenon.

*Dirty Dancing* was everywhere you looked—on TV, in magazines and newspapers, and playing on multiple screens at the cineplexes. People dissected Johnny and Baby's relationship, debated about Penny's abortion, and talked about their own relationships with their fathers. We had never dreamed the movie would become anywhere near this big. Suddenly we were engulfed in a total whirlwind.

Lisa and I had got used to people stopping us on the street and asking for autographs, but now everything was turned up a few more notches. Rather than having people approach us politely, we were getting mobbed. People were knocking on the windows of our car, surrounding us as we walked into restaurants. Paparazzi began trailing us and even hanging around outside Rancho Bizarro, waiting for us to come out. Obviously we were thrilled at the success of *Dirty Dancing* but, on the other hand, it was becoming harder and harder to live anything like a normal life outside the haven of our ranch.

It's hard to describe exactly what it feels like to be thrust into this kind of fame, but 'whirlwind' comes pretty close. Everything around you is spinning. You try to touch it, to get a grasp on it, but it just spins faster and faster. If I had found myself in the middle of something like this when I was younger, when I first came to Hollywood, it probably would have destroyed me. In many ways, dealing with fame is the purest form of dealing with your demons.

The easiest way to destroy people is to give them exactly what they want. You might not realise it at the time, but the struggle to achieve something is, in many ways, much more satisfying than actually getting it. The very act of striving is what keeps you alive, and it keeps you grounded. But then, when the thing you've been fighting for is suddenly in your grasp, it's all too easy to look around and say—is this all there is?

Also, despite how proud I was of finally making it big, I was also torn about how I'd finally got to this place. All the fears I had about giving in to 'dancer-turned-actor' typecasting were crystallised one evening when Lisa and I happened to catch a segment about *Dirty Dancing* on *Entertainment Tonight.*

We were getting ready to go out of town, and had the TV on in the background as we were packing. I heard the announcer say something like, 'After the break, Patrick Swayze bumps and grinds his way into movie history!' My heart sank. I turned and looked at Lisa, who just shook her head. This was it—my worst nightmare come to life. I'd worked so hard to be taken seriously, and now this would be my legacy. I was definitely proud of the movie, but 'bumping and grinding' was not what I wanted to be remembered for.

Yet it wasn't only my role as Johnny Castle that was stirring up the whirlwind. The *Dirty Dancing* soundtrack shot to number one on the Billboard charts—and it stayed there for eighteen weeks. 'She's Like the Wind', the single I wrote with Stacy Widelitz and performed with Wendy Fraser, went to number three on the Billboard Hot 100 chart and number one on Adult Contemporary. Along with 'I've Had the Time of My Life', it became one of the signature songs of *Dirty Dancing*.

Lisa and I flew to New York City for a record signing at the height of the *Dirty Dancing* craze. I was scheduled to sign copies from nine or ten o'clock in the morning, but when the reps picked us up in a limo and brought us to the store, we could see that people were already lined up all the way round the block. 'They've been lining up since about 6 a.m.,' one guy told us, 'just sitting out there on the sidewalk.'

The limo pulled up outside the store and about fifteen security guys materialised to shepherd us through the crowds. Everyone started screaming when Lisa and I got out of the car—it was a madhouse. We had to go only twenty feet or so, from the kerb to the door, but hundreds of women were pressing in, trying to get a glimpse of us. The noise was deafening.

When we made it into the store, we could see all the fans outside, lined up and pressing against the plate-glass windows. My head was spinning, taking everything in, when the guy from the store leaned closer and said to me, 'Now you know what it's like to be the Beatles.' And he was right. Looking out of those windows was just like looking at those vintage reels of screaming fans.

But, strangely enough, when you're in a sea of people like that, it's actually a very lonely feeling. I was glad to have Lisa at my side, glad not to be facing this pandemonium alone. She stayed nearby as I smiled until my face hurt and signed so many CDs that my hand began to cramp. I kept going well past the allotted time, because I couldn't imagine turning someone away who'd waited for hours on the sidewalk, and who was looking for only a few seconds of my time. So we stayed and stayed, until the last person had got through the crush.

And it was like that when people wanted autographs. If one person stopped me on the sidewalk to sign something, then someone else would come up and then another. Once, at a baseball game, I must have signed a thousand autographs. These people were paying me a real compliment, and the last thing I wanted was for anyone to walk away thinking I had too big a head to find a moment for them.

It could be hard on Lisa, though. Once I even made her stand in the snow, shivering, in high heels and a little dress. Learning how to balance the needs of the fans with Lisa's needs, and my own, was a process that took some time.

The one thing I couldn't abide was when people got aggressive. I'll spend all day accommodating you if you're polite about it, but if you're rude, that's another story. But even so, when people did get rude, I was still never comfortable just walking away.

Once, I was scheduled to make an appearance in West Germany, and even though there were at least a dozen bodyguards, the crowd managed to break through. Suddenly, people were climbing over people and grabbing at me, and the bodyguards were completely overwhelmed.

Suddenly I had an idea. Rather than resisting the crowd or trying to push back, I just started shaking hands. 'Nice to meet you!' I'd say, shaking a hand, then following with, 'No need to push. How you doing? I'm Patrick. Let's make some room here.' I shouted to the bodyguards to do the same. 'Say hello to people! Shake a hand, keep smiling.' When the bodyguards started doing the same, turning the energy from hostile to friendly, the fans soon stopped shoving.

I learned little techniques like that for crowd control, like patting someone on the back as you shake hands, then gently guiding them to one side. The fact is, once you've talked with people and given them that moment they were looking for, they're on your side. So you can easily turn a group of fans into a second line of defence if others are pushing and shoving. The most important thing to remember is that people really want only one thing: for you to look into their eyes and say, 'Hey, how are you doing? Nice to meet you.' And I was always happy to do that.

The first time Lisa and I really saw what it meant to be famous was back in my *Skatetown, USA* days. Jaclyn Smith, whom we knew from Houston, had become a huge star in *Charlie's Angels.* And she came to the *Skatetown* premiere as a show of support for us. When she walked out of the premiere, flashbulbs began popping like strobe lights. I was feeling blinded by all those flashes, but Jackie had the most beautiful smile on her face and she barely blinked. She had a completely calm expression, as if she was the only one there. I often thought of Jackie's example all those years later, when I became the one in the strobe lights.

Unfortunately, there's a flip side to all the love you get from fans. The vast majority are perfectly decent people who reach out with an open heart. But once you become famous, some others crawl out of the woodwork—the ones who don't hesitate to go after your money and your reputation, hoping to enrich themselves.

People will sue you for any little thing, claiming you bumped into their car with yours, or even that you injured them somehow with an innocuous handshake. And every incident requires a response from a lawyer. We've had a wonderful lawyer for years, Fred Gaines, who takes care of any issue that comes up, but the fact is, having to respond to every claim takes money and time, even if the claim is totally fabricated.

After 'She's Like the Wind' became a hit, at least five people filed lawsuits claiming they'd written it. These claims just came out of nowhere, from people we'd never met, and one suit even went so far that Stacy and I were no longer allowed to receive royalties. It just dragged on and on, but I knew we'd win because we had written the song. So Fred just kept responding, point by point, and the truth did eventually come out.

AFTER SUPPOSEDLY 'bumping and grinding' my way into movie history, I signed on next to do a serious family drama called *Tiger Warsaw*. I played a drug- and alcohol-addicted loner whose sister accuses him of committing incest—a dark, intense movie that pushed me deeper as an actor but ultimately never really came together. Despite having a strong cast, including the Oscar-nominated actress Piper Laurie, *Tiger Warsaw* was directed by an inexperienced director and didn't do well, making little more than a ripple at the box office.

But the film I shot after that, *Road House*, did very big business at the box office. And while *Dirty Dancing* had launched a kind of cult following for me among women, *Road House* created a cult following of its own among men. With its multiple bar-fight scenes and macho, tough-shit antagonists, *Road House* was an old-fashioned Western-style movie, where the good guy comes to a bad town to clean it up. I knew it wasn't Dostoyevsky, but I still wanted to give my character, Dalton, real depth, and not just play him as a camp hero. There's definitely a guilty pleasure to watching myself in *Road House*, but it still ended up entertaining a lot of people. It was a classic guys' film.

The truth is, in some ways I was built to be an action star. All the running, jumping and falling I did as a kid had taught me how to be my own stunt man. Gymnastics had strengthened every part of my body and taught me balance. Studying martial arts, boxing and sword fighting gave me a base of skills I could use in any kind of fight scene. And I could drive anything—cars, motorcycles, horses, whatever was called for.

For the fight scenes in *Road House*, I trained with Benny 'the Jet' Urquidez, a kickboxing pro who never lost a match. Benny was a short, stocky guy who used sharp, sudden moves to keep his opponents off-balance. But when he tried to teach his style to me, I had a lot of trouble—it just wasn't the way I moved. I kept trying to mimic his technique, but we weren't getting anywhere.

Suddenly, Benny said, 'Wait a minute! You're a dancer! I've got an idea.' The next day, he showed up on set with a boom box. He plugged it in and flipped a switch, and Michael Jackson's 'Thriller' came blasting out.

That was all it took. Moving with the beat of Michael Jackson's music, I finally got a rhythm going, and my kickboxing came together. It was a great moment—all the speed and subtlety of the art form suddenly were mine. And I loved it. *Road House* gave me the opportunity to hone an old skill that I never realised I'd missed.

I soon found out that I'd need all the fighting skills I could muster. This was because the actor who played my primary opponent, Marshall Teague, was ready to kick my ass for real if he could get away with it. Marshall had served in Vietnam and was a Navy SEAL, which meant he was a serious, real-life badass. He had no patience for bullshit and would say so to anyone's face. Marshall apparently thought I was a dilettante pretty boy he could knock over with one of his meaty fingers. But when we started training, he learned otherwise.

He and I started rehearsing our fight scenes, and soon enough he saw that I knew what I was doing, and that I could take a punch. 'Let's put some contact into it,' I told him, well aware that he could lay me flat if he chose to. But I knew if we choreographed it well, we could have some contact without killing each other, and it would look totally real on screen.

When you earn the respect of a man like Marshall, you earn it for life. He and I became friends on the set of *Road House*, and we've been friends ever since. Not that many people understood his mentality, but when I looked him in the eye, we really connected. It was a good thing, too, because the fight scene we finally shot was epic and we very nearly killed each other.

We fought in a river, and I was wearing no shirt, no pads, nothing but sweatpants. So when I hit the ground, I was hitting the ground hard. Since both Marshall and I loved the adrenaline high of a fight, it was easy to get carried away and we really started pounding.

After a few minutes of us kicking the shit out of each other, Marshall picked up a log and swung it over his head. He thought it was a prop log—which would have been perfect for the scene—but unfortunately it wasn't. He realised his mistake mid swing, but it was too late: he cracked me right across the spine with a real log, breaking a couple of my ribs and knocking the wind out of me.

I dropped to my hands and knees, gasping for breath, but the scene called for us to keep fighting. I didn't break character and didn't give up—we kept fighting, and eventually got to the part where I'm forced to kill him. When you watch this scene in the movie, the exhaustion you see on my face is real. I barely had the strength to drag myself out of the river after that fight.

MY NEXT ROLE was as another tough guy, a Chicago cop in *Next of Kin*. But this time, the training I got wasn't nearly as enjoyable as with Benny the Jet. This time, some real Chicago cops decided they'd give me some training I would never forget.

They hung out with me on the set, took me on ride-alongs to get a feel for the streets, and told me all about the dangers they faced on the job. We spent a lot of time together and I really bonded with these guys. They were the real deal, putting their lives on the line every day, and I respected their courage. Then they decided to test mine. Or at least, test how strong my stomach was.

They drove me to the Chicago morgue, pulling the squad car up out front. I already knew what I was in for—they were going to show me dead and decomposing bodies, to test my mettle. But before that happened, there was a funny moment out on the sidewalk.

The cops were walking me up to the door when a couple of junkies lying out front, really desperate-looking guys, peered up at me and one of them said, 'Hey! Aren't you that Dirty Dance dude?' I couldn't believe it—these guys couldn't have been to a movie in years, but I guess *Dirty Dancing* was everywhere you looked, on posters all over the place. I just smiled and said, 'Nope, sorry. You've got the wrong guy,' and the cops hustled me through the door.

It was a beautiful building, all pristine and pretty on the outside and nice and clean on the inside. But then the guys led me down to where the bodies were stored on rows of shelves. Some of them had apparently been there a long time and were in a pretty advanced state of decomposition.

The guys chose a particularly gruesome body to show me, hoping to make me puke. It was a kind of tough-guy game—could I stand this, or was my stomach too weak? These guys had seen everything already, so they had a clinical detachment. They just wanted to see whether I could handle it. I couldn't, but I didn't let on. I felt the bile rise in my throat but managed to swallow it back down. I wasn't about to show these cops that I couldn't handle it.

There was another, more serious reason I didn't want to show weakness. Doing this kind of movie is all about showing someone else's world on film. The story is really about them and what they do, and I wanted to be good for these guys. In fact, I wanted to *be* them. So I forced myself to behave and respond as they would. And since I respected them, they in turn respected my efforts to make my portrayal of their world absolutely true.

Lisa was also up for a role in *Next of Kin*, playing my wife, Jessie. She would have been perfect for it—but she was reluctant to appear to be pushing for it on account of her being my real-life wife. Lisa's integrity really came through and Helen Hunt, who'd just started her career, ended up getting the role. Helen was wonderful, but it was frustrating for Lisa, who's a very talented actress.

The truth is, talent takes you only so far in Hollywood. There are any number of other factors that influence who makes it—and a lot of people didn't take Lisa as seriously as they should have, just because she was married to me. If I pushed for her to get a role, that would be seen as nepotism—even if she was the best actress for it. To be taken seriously she had to work twice as hard and be twice as good, which is a very hard obstacle to overcome.

In addition to that, you have to be able to sell yourself in Hollywood. As a Texan, that was something I loved to do—I loved the challenge of winning someone over, making that person want to hire me. Being from a Finnish family, Lisa had inherited a certain reserve. She had been raised to believe that the quality of what you do should speak for itself, that if you try to sell to people, you're insulting their intelligence. If success in Hollywood came from sheer talent, Lisa would be a huge star. But all these factors conspired to keep her down—which was a real source of frustration for her.

Lisa kept working, though, and she got a recurring role in the TV series *Max Headroom*, playing a character named Janie Crane. She went out for auditions whenever we were in Los Angeles, but much of the time she was working with me on my movie sets—rewriting and helping me with my scenes and performance. Every movie I've ever been in, Lisa has had a significant role in fleshing out my character. She also started learning the skills of the director's trade, spending time with the director of photography on each set and asking about the how and the why of a shot, becoming savvy about the inner workings and process of making a movie.

Liam Neeson and Bill Paxton were both in *Next of Kin* and we became great friends. Liam and I enjoyed hitting the town together, going to Chicago's blues clubs and pounding the beers. He was a wild man with a sweet, gentle side and, years later, when his wife, Natasha Richardson, died aged forty-five after a freak skiing accident, I felt for him like a brother.

With *Next of Kin* and *Road House*, I'd now done two macho action flicks in a row. I didn't mind showcasing that side of myself and of course I'd had a blast making those movies. I also had original songs in both of them, so even though I was playing the action star, I still got to show some versatility behind the scenes. But I was feeling the itch again to get a deeper, more fleshed-out role.

The next movie I auditioned for would give me exactly that—but I'd have to get past an extremely reluctant director if I ever hoped to get cast.

# Chapter 11

ONE AFTERNOON in late 1988, Lisa walked up to me in the dining room and dropped a script on the table. 'Buddy,' she said, 'you have to read this. It's incredible.' I looked down at the title page and saw the word 'Ghost'.

After *Dirty Dancing* became a hit, I'd started receiving all kinds of scripts, which were soon piled up on chairs and tables all over the house. I even got offered money to read some of them, but there just weren't enough hours in the day to do everything that needed doing. So, although I trusted Lisa's opinion more than anyone's, I left the script right where she'd put it.

It wasn't until a month later, when Lisa saw it on the table and said, 'Buddy, *please* read this! It's a great story, and you'll love the part!', that I finally sat down and looked at the first page.

And that was all it took—I didn't stop reading until I turned the final page and walked into the kitchen with tears in my eyes. 'I have to do this movie,' I told Lisa. The story was every bit as good as she'd said it was, and she was right—the role of Sam Wheat in it was perfect for me.

Unfortunately, the director, Jerry Zucker, didn't think so. Jerry had just seen the kickboxing, tough-guy Patrick in *Road House*, and he couldn't imagine me in the role of the sensitive boyfriend who gets murdered and comes back as a ghost.

Of course, Jerry himself knew a little bit about going against type. He'd made his name doing a string of off-the-wall comedies, and *Ghost* would be his first real foray into drama. He obviously believed it was possible to move successfully between genres. Now I just had to convince him I could do it as well as he could.

Demi Moore had already been cast as the female lead, Molly Jensen, beating several other actresses who auditioned, including Nicole Kidman, and a *Who's Who* of leading men were under consideration for the part of Sam, but the role was still open. Zucker was convinced I was the wrong guy for it, but he finally agreed to let me audition.

Sam Wheat is a banker, and I wanted to really look the part, so I dressed in a sharp Kenzo suit and tied my hair—still long from *Next of Kin*—back into a ponytail. I walked into the audition, faced Jerry Zucker and casting director Jane Jenkins, and said, 'Do whatever you need to do to check me out. I'm willing to do this entire script from beginning to end if that's what you want.'

And they almost did. They really put me through my paces, asking me to do six scenes, and I put everything I had into them. I wanted this part so badly I could taste it. Jane could feel it too—as she told Lisa later it felt so real, it made her miss being an actress. It was an intense audition and, when it was over, Jerry Zucker was completely persuaded. I'd won the part of Sam.

That left one more role to cast: the store-front medium, Oda Mae Brown. When I first read the script, I immediately thought of Whoopi Goldberg for the part. Whoopi's career had begun to take off in the eighties, starting with a one-woman show on Broadway, and soaring higher with her starring role in *The Color Purple*. She was a gifted comic, but she also had incredible range as an actress. She was perfect, but Jerry thought of her mostly as a comic, and he feared her comedic edge would overshadow the relationship between Molly and Sam, which he saw as the heart of the story.

Finally, I insisted. 'Jerry, at least just put me in a room together with her. We'll see if there's any chemistry.'

At the time, Whoopi was shooting *The Long Walk Home* in Alabama with Sissy Spacek, so Jerry and I flew out to meet her. She and I had met once, briefly, after her Broadway show, but we didn't know each other. However, as soon as we started going through Sam and Oda Mae's scenes, you could feel the electricity popping in the air. Whoopi just took those lines and created a fully fleshed, finger-wagging, hip-shaking character all her own.

Once again, Jerry admitted that his first instincts had been wrong. Whoopi was perfect. He offered her the role and I couldn't wait for us all to get back to LA to start shooting. But first, as with all my movies, it was time to do some rewrites.

IN THE FIRST DRAFT of *Ghost*, the character of Sam couldn't communicate with the living after he died, so he just hovered around in scenes, with no more lines. Maybe that seems logical for a ghost, but we felt the scenes would play out a lot better if Sam continued to be an active character.

That's a pretty major change to suggest, but fortunately the writer, Bruce Joel Rubin, is not your ordinary writer. Lisa and I forged an instant bond with him, and he was always open to whatever changes we suggested. Of all the writers I've worked with over the years, I felt the closest connection with Bruce—he really became like a brother to me. And as I learned later, he was the one who had suggested early on that Jerry consider me for the role of Sam.

I knew that if Sam was relegated to being just a silent apparition, we'd miss out on all kinds of dramatic and humorous possibilities. 'The humour comes from this guy who refuses to accept that he's dead,' I said to Bruce. 'He keeps trying to participate with the people who are alive. So let's make him part of the scenes, give him dialogue.' Fortunately, Bruce agreed.

All three of the main characters needed some rewriting and we worked on them throughout the first weeks of the shoot. But with Whoopi, it didn't really matter what was on the page—what came out of her mouth when the cameras were rolling was whatever the hell came into her head.

This is Whoopi's genius: she goes wherever her instinctual wild-ass world happens to take her. She has so much trust in herself, so much trust in her own instincts, that it freed me up too. The one thing I knew about comedy was, you shouldn't play things for laughs. The best comedy is born out of reality. So, when Whoopi was doing her free-form thing, I played Sam's natural reactions to her—and those funny moments were some of the best in the film.

This also played into an acting technique I'd been using for years. I like to look at every other relationship and every other character before I really look at mine. It keeps me out of my own ego when I approach my character; and also, you learn a lot about people by looking at how they relate to others. Playing Sam straight up, responding to Whoopi's comedy riffs, was the most honest and direct way to bring out his true character.

Demi and I did the same thing—we played off each other and really made up our sex scenes as we went along. All we had to do was go with it, let our imaginations run wild, and then touch each other's arms for the sparks to fly. The best love scenes don't require what I call 'humpage'. You don't really want to see the characters jumping each other. You want to see the intimate, personal moment that conveys desire. That's what I feel is sexy.

Shooting love scenes is really difficult. It's such a private thing, and you're on a set with camera operators, director, lighting technicians—sometimes a dozen or more people milling around. You're trying to make a moment look sexy, in just about the most unsexy environment there is. And I always felt extra pressure, since I was supposed to be Mr Sexy, if you believed all the magazines. Of all the scenes I ever shot, I probably felt least confident in the love scenes.

You can't really choreograph or script these scenes. You just have to have a conversation between the actors and the director, talk about what you want the viewers to feel—and then dive right into it, nerves and all. Luckily for me, Demi was really good in these situations. She was very warm—she showed a vulnerability that was very attractive, and this came through on screen. When Lisa and I saw the finished film months later, I was happy—and relieved—with how it turned out. Demi and I had managed to capture a moment between these two people that made everything that happened later in the story feel that much more wrenching and emotional.

And speaking of wrenching and emotional, there was one scene that nearly tore me apart when we shot it. I didn't have any idea it was going to be so devastating, but I could hardly get through it when the cameras rolled. The scene comes when Sam looks down on his own bloody body in his lover's arms and realises he's dead. A lot of people assume that scene was done with a camera trick—that the body was me, and that we shot the scene twice. But Demi was actually holding a wonderfully realistic life-size dummy of me. In the scene, Sam sprints after the guy who's just killed him, then walks back slowly towards Molly, realising as he draws near that there's someone in her arms. As the cameras were rolling, I walked up to Demi, but when I looked down at the body she was holding a terrible chill shot right through me.

I suddenly flashed back to the moment when I was looking down at my father's body in his casket, eight years earlier—a moment I had completely blocked out. I don't look particularly like my dad, but somehow the dummy in Demi's arms just became him.

My whole body started shaking and my heart pounded. I felt as if I was having a panic attack. I couldn't believe how strongly I felt my dad's presence in that moment. Jerry kept the cameras rolling but he couldn't use this cut—audiences would have had a hard time switching back to the lighter feel of the movie. We shot it again, and the second time I managed to play the scene as written. But I've never forgotten that sickening feeling of horror I felt.

And that wasn't the first time I'd freaked out in connection with that scene. The first time came when we actually made the dummy. I had to get a plaster likeness made and it's not a pleasant experience, believe me.

The special-effects department sent me to a make-up room, where they asked me to take off my shirt and sit on a stool. The dummy needs to be made with the exact pose and expression required for the shot, which in this case meant I'd have to mimic lying dead on the street. We figured out the best facial expression and how I needed to hold my arms, and then a couple of guys got to work.

They started layering me with wet plaster strips from the waist up, creating the dummy's torso. Then, they created a jig system to prop my arms in place, since I'd have to hold them still until the plaster was applied and had dried. They kept laying those plaster strips on me, working their way up my body to my neck, then my chin, then my mouth. At the last moment, they stuck a couple of straws into my nostrils so I could breathe—but already I could feel some of the liquid from the wet plaster seeping into my mouth and inching down my throat.

I felt as if I was about to suffocate. I'd never been claustrophobic in my life but, being completely encased in that plaster cast, I was seriously freaking out. I couldn't see, smell or hear, and I could barely breathe.

As panic rose in my chest, I started clearing my throat loudly, hoping the guys would realise what was going on. Finally, one of them asked, 'Are you okay, Patrick?' I groaned, and he must have realised my distress, because he poked a tongue depressor through the plaster covering my mouth, to let me get a little air in. I calmed down enough to keep quite still while the plaster dried, but once I got that cast off I swore I'd never do anything like that again. Ever since then, I've had little moments of claustrophobia, when I flash right back to that feeling of being trapped.

*GHOST* WAS THE MOST high-tech movie I'd ever done. It wasn't easy, back in 1989, to shoot a convincing ghost scene. But we used a new technique that made the scenes look real, even though some of the effects do seem dated now.

First, the actors would do a run-through of the scene, getting an idea of where each character would be. In one scene, for example when Willy, the bad guy, breaks into Molly's house, Sam still doesn't understand that he can't touch living people, so he takes swings at Willy, but his fist goes right through him. And when Willy tries to go upstairs, Sam hurls himself at him, desperate to find a way to stop him. But Willy never knows he's there.

Once we'd walked through the scene, the crew taped little numbers on the floor, showing us exactly where we had to be at each point in the action. I had a specific spot for every tiny moment, and not only did I have to be right on that spot, but my timing had to be absolutely perfect, because Jerry was going to shoot the whole sequence with each actor separately, and then layer them together to make it look as if we were in the room at the same time.

At least we had a computerised camera that ensured the timing was perfect. But, even so, hitting marks precisely was easier said than done. It's hard enough to throw yourself down a staircase and make it look good, but try throwing yourself down one and then hitting a tiny piece of tape at the bottom. It's tricky.

The other tricky thing was trying to do all this with no one acting opposite me—I was running around, yelling at nobody, swinging at nobody, throwing myself down stairs to grab nobody. It was a very strange experience.

Doing all that in the confines of a closed set was one thing, but doing it outside in front of a crowd of gawkers was another. We used the computerised-camera technique for the scene we shot on location up in Bedford-Stuyvesant, a rough part of New York back in 1989. Not a whole lot of movies got shot there so a crowd of people had gathered round to watch.

This was a big, emotional turning point in the movie. It's the first time that Sam realises his own friend Carl was the one who set up his murder. Sam follows Carl out onto the street, furious and hurt at his friend's betrayal.

I got really geared up for this scene, summoning all the emotion I could to convey Sam's hurt and anger. But, of course, because we were shooting with the computerised camera, I did the scene completely alone. There was no Carl there. So the crowd of people who'd gathered to watch just saw me coming out yelling and swinging like a maniac. And they started laughing.

Looking back, I'll admit that doing that scene alone probably looked pretty funny. But, at the time, I definitely didn't see any humour in it. I stopped and turned to the crowd.

'Shut the fuck up!' I yelled. 'You want to get out here and do this yourself? You think this is easy?' People looked startled, but they shut up. And when we went back to shoot the scene again, you could hear a pin drop. Nobody made a peep until we finished the whole take. When Jerry yelled 'Cut', the whole crowd broke into applause.

After we wrapped on *Ghost*, I did a 180-degree turn for my next role. I went from playing the nice-guy banker Sam to the Zen-surfer-bank-robber Bodhi in *Point Break*.

Bodhi was a once-in-a-blue-moon character, the bad guy who you love because you believe what he believes in—until he believes it too far and kills someone. I loved Bodhi because I identified with his quest for perfection and the ultimate adrenaline high. He's a complex character who can read people instantaneously and knows exactly how to handle them. I could not wait to sink my teeth into that role.

I was also excited about getting paid to be a beach bum. *Point Break* is a surfing movie, so going to work meant hopping into my Range Rover at dawn, heading out to the beach and being on a surfboard as the sun came up. Both Keanu Reeves and I got surfing lessons, but we had world-class stunt doubles for the really big waves. When you get out there in the ocean, you realise quickly that serious surfing takes huge amounts of both skill and courage.

To be a really good surfer, you have to start when you're a flexible little kid and have no fear, because you're trying to ride on a wave that's lifting you higher and higher, sometimes up to the height of a three- or four-storey building. Then, just at the moment you have to be functioning at your highest level, you go over the top and get your brains pounded in. I had surfed in Galveston growing up, so I knew the basics, but this was different. Messing around in these big waves was dangerous, so I just focused on being able to paddle out, pop up onto the board and do a cutback on the wave. I just wanted to be good enough so that when they cut from a shot of me to a shot of my surfer double, I didn't look like someone on the sound stage of a fifties beach movie.

Keanu and I also got to skydive for *Point Break.* I had never done it before, even though my brother Donny had got seriously into skydiving. I knew it was only a matter of time before I decided to throw myself out of a plane too, and *Point Break* finally gave me the opportunity.

The funny thing was, the first time I jumped, I felt no fear at all. I stood at that open plane door looking down, and I should have been terrified, but it's such a sensory overload that I couldn't really take it all in, so I just jumped. It wasn't until the second jump that I suddenly found myself scared—because my brain had had a chance to figure out what was going on. On the videotape of that second jump, you can see the jump master having to rip my hands off the bar to get me out the door.

With all the skydiving, surfing, chase scenes and fight scenes, *Point Break* was one of the most fun movies I've ever worked on.

It was also one of the most painful, as I cracked my left wrist and a couple of ribs, and tore up my shoulder and elbow. But whether I'm dancing, playing sports, acting or anything else, I try never to allow pain to derail me. Pain is a constant companion when you make action movies. It's also just a part of living with a serious knee injury. So I learned how to put the pain elsewhere, how to compartmentalise what was happening in my body.

Pain is nothing more than a sensation, and you can choose to give in to it or choose to control it. It's how I managed to sustain my career for this long, and even how I've managed to fight cancer. Pain, like fear, sharpens your focus, and lets you know you're alive.

But Lisa and I had to deal with another kind of pain during this period, that had nothing to do with physical aches. This one had to do with heartache.

WE HAD BEEN TOGETHER for fifteen years now, and despite some ups and downs over that time, our relationship was strong. We both loved children and definitely wanted to have a family of our own. With my career going so well and both of us in our thirties, this was the perfect time to go for it.

To our excitement, Lisa got pregnant. The idea of having a family together with her made me happier than anything. And I wanted to be the best father I could be—the kind of father my dad had been to me.

About three months into her pregnancy, though, Lisa went in for her latest ultrasound. She'd gone into the exam room before me, and as soon as the nurse showed me into that room, I knew something was very wrong.

Lisa was crying. She didn't have to say anything to me—one look at her face, and I knew the worst possible thing was true. The baby's heart wasn't beating.

I felt completely crushed with grief. I'd been so excited that day, so thrilled at going in to see my baby's heartbeat. And he was dead. I couldn't handle it—when we got to the parking lot, Lisa and I both wept bitterly, holding each other tight. Even now, neither of us can talk about that day without tearing up.

We wanted to try for a baby again, but the loss had been so devastating that we just couldn't do it right away. At that point, we figured we had plenty more years ahead of us. Eventually, we did start trying again, and we kept at it for many years, hoping Lisa would get pregnant again. But she never did.

We always knew we could adopt, and we talked seriously about it. While I was shooting a movie in Russia, Lisa even took a trip to a Russian orphanage to do some research on adopting there. But somehow, as the years went by, we never did it. I'm not sure either Lisa or I could even explain why, but if there's one thing I regret in my life, it's that we didn't have children. It makes me sad for myself, but maybe even more so for Lisa, who would have been a beautiful mother.

# Chapter 12

After *Ghost* came out, the whirlwind started up again, fiercer than ever. The movie shot up to number one at the box office and it stayed at the top for four weeks. The magazine and TV interviews and photo requests kept flooding in—our phone never seemed to stop ringing. It felt great to have such a good movie out, and Lisa was also having a blast, wrapping up her starring role in a TV show called *Super Force*, in which she played a police captain in the year 2020.

The tricky thing about success is, the more of it you have, the more you fear it will disappear. On the surface, we had everything we'd been fighting for all these years. My career was soaring, we had a beautiful ranch, and we had each other.

But what would come next? I was proud of my work in *Ghost*, and I desperately wanted to follow it up with another great role. This felt like my big chance—my best opportunity yet to vault myself into the company of the serious, respected actors who get offered the best parts.

That's when I heard about the role of a lifetime, the chance to work with one of the greatest directors in the business, Roland Joffé. The film was called *City of Joy.*

I had never met Roland Joffé, but I'd seen his films, including *The Killing Fields* and *The Mission*. I knew he was passionate about his work and never compromised on his vision. I knew also that the opportunity to work with him, on a movie that really explored the human condition, had the potential to change not only my career, but my life as well.

*City of Joy* is about an American doctor, Max Lowe, who becomes disillusioned and depressed after a young patient of his dies in surgery. He tries to escape his pain by travelling to India, and there, to his surprise, he has a transformational experience, finding new purpose through helping Calcutta's poor.

I loved the character of Max. In fact, I identified with him. Max never felt he was good enough and, like me he was always battling his inner demons. Max's struggle was one I knew intimately, and I desperately wanted the chance to create his character on screen.

When I walked into the audition I probably looked like a beach bum, my hair and beard still bleached blond from *Point Break*. But Roland and I connected right away, and I opened up with him completely about how much this character and story meant to me. This wasn't like any other audition I'd been on—instead of my reading for the part, Roland and I just talked. We forged a real bond that day, the foundation of a lasting friendship. He pushed me to explore my own feelings and I got very emotional as I tried to explain why I was so drawn to the part.

Roland told me later that one moment in particular had convinced him I was right for the role. It came when I told him, 'If you will have me do this movie, I will give you my heart.' Roland operates on instinct and at that moment he knew I would hold nothing back—and he also knew I would need that kind of passion for what lay ahead.

But when Roland went to the producers and said, 'We have to have Patrick Swayze for Max,' the response was lukewarm. Despite the success of *Dirty Dancing* and *Ghost*, Hollywood still didn't see me as the kind of actor who could carry a serious drama. Some still saw me as just 'that dance guy'. Roland didn't back down, though. He said, 'It's Patrick. That's it. He *is* Max.' Thanks to Roland's perseverance, I finally had the role I'd spent years hoping to get. So it was off to the crazy city of Calcutta.

On the night Lisa and I arrived, the first thing we noticed was the thick, smoky fog that enveloped us as we walked out of the airport. We had never been to India before, but we didn't really expect to find the smog so thick there that you could barely see ten feet in front of you.

We loaded into a car, and the scene as we rode to our hotel was surreal. There were a few streetlights, but because of the soot in the air even their dim light was diffused. So there was a strange, eerie glow outside the car, with apparitions seeming to move in and out of the darkness: women dressed in flowing saris, the men in loose-fitting cotton trousers and shirts and, despite how late it was, there were people absolutely everywhere. Looking out of the car windows, we felt we were in another world.

Roland wanted to throw me right into the type of situation that Max Lowe had found himself in. So the next morning, he took me straight to Mother Teresa's Home for the Dying—the place where the poorest of the poor Indians came to die.

Every country in the world has poor people, but the kind of poverty we saw in India was staggering. Little children with spindly arms and legs, their eyes hollow from hunger. People missing arms and legs, their bodies covered with pus-filled sores. There was a level of suffering among the poor in India that I had never seen before, but there was an amazing spiritual richness, too. And Roland wanted me not just to see it, but to plunge into it—to care for the most destitute with my own hands, just as Max Lowe would do.

At Mother Teresa's, I did whatever the head nurse asked of me. When she saw that I wouldn't shy away from touching the sick, she put me to work with them. I washed the hands of a dying man, sat with a frail woman's head on my lap, helped clean up children who had soiled themselves. Yes, I was doing research for a movie—but this went way beyond that. It was impossible not to be touched by the deep need all around us. It humbled me and made me realise once again how fortunate we are to have such comfortable lives.

The next stop was even more difficult. Roland took us to a street clinic, one of thousands across India that provide medical services for people who have no money. There was a young boy, probably about eight years old, who came in for treatment while I was there. He had been in a couple of months earlier with badly burned arms, and the staff had bandaged them up. He was coming back because those bandages, now filthy, had grafted themselves into his skin. The boy was in a lot of pain and those rotting bandages had to come off.

I took that little arm into my hands and began trying to pick out the putrid bandage threads. All I had to work with was saline water with some kind of milky antiseptic in it, and a Swiss Army knife. His skin was raw and infected, but I just kept picking at that bandage. The boy could tell I was upset, so he reached over himself to try to help, as if he were consoling me. He never shed one tear, which caused me to blink back tears myself. It took a couple of hours, but together we finally got the last remnants of that rotten bandage off.

The third stop of the day was a leprosy clinic. We sat down at a table with the director of the clinic, and before long a young man came in to serve tea. But when I saw a pair of fingerless hands placing my teacup in front of me, that was the moment I had to decide, Am I really in this or not? I didn't know anything about leprosy, and I had no idea if it was contagious or not. But to refuse the tea because of who served it would be beyond insulting. It would be rejecting everything I'd come here to do.

Roland and I drank our tea. It was trial by fire: this was the moment I decided we were in this for better or for worse, the moment I totally committed to what we would be doing here.

During the four months or so we were filming in Calcutta, we faced many obstacles. The shoot took place during the first Gulf War, so anti-American sentiment was running high. Huge crowds would gather outside my hotel, shouting for the American to go home. The producers hired more than a hundred Indian policemen to act as security, but more often than not they'd just slink into the crowd themselves if things got really rough.

A few weeks in, when it became clear how aggressive the mobs were becoming, Roland held a meeting with all of us.

'If you feel your life is in danger,' he said, 'you can go home with my blessing.' There are directors who would have bullied everyone into staying no matter what, but Roland was far too decent and honourable to act that way. No one left. As the cast and crew took to saying, we were on a mission from God.

The Gulf War wasn't the only reason we were unpopular in Calcutta. The subject matter of Dominique La Pierre's best-selling book, *City of Joy*, which the movie was based on, was very controversial in India. Some felt that it showcased the absolute worst side of India and made the Westerner the hero. But Roland believed the story showed universal truths, that it got to the heart of what it means to be human and to be connected as family. He believed strongly in the movie and was determined to make it.

Roland had anticipated trouble in India, so he'd taken the precaution of building a giant set replicating a Calcutta slum. It was huge—five acres in all—and it took eight weeks for hundreds of workers to create its shanties, trash-strewn alleys and running sewers. And it was surrounded by a high wall with concertina wire on top, not only to keep out protestors, but to prevent Calcutta's poor from moving in.

It was filthy on the set, just like in a real slum, and for much of the entire shoot my clothes and skin were covered in dirt. From the dirty water I got conjunctivitis so badly I could hardly see, and I also battled 'Delhi belly', which made me so sick I had to learn how to throw up and have diarrhoea at the same time. (For the record, you sit on the toilet and throw up into the bathtub.) I felt as if I *was* Max Lowe in this movie, feeling the shock of discovering India, and falling in love with it at the same time.

The Oberoi Hotel was a real oasis of luxury, and it was always amazing to come back there after shooting, to clean sheets and room service. But on the night when I settled in to watch the tape-delayed Academy Awards telecast, with all those Hollywood people dressed in their finery, the women draped in millions of dollars of jewellery, it felt totally bizarre.

Then came the special moment. Whoopi Goldberg won the Best Supporting Actress Oscar for her role in *Ghost*—the first time in almost fifty years that an African American had won the award. The audience went crazy as she made her way up to the stage, but then you could have heard a pin drop as she made her speech. It was very short—she thanked her family, Paramount and Jerry Zucker, and then singled me out by name.

'I have to thank Patrick Swayze, who's a stand-up guy, who went to them and said, "I want to do it with her",' she said. Sitting there watching in my Calcutta hotel room, I was incredibly touched by Whoopi's unexpected thanks. It meant more to me than I could ever express.

THE RELEASE DATE for *City of Joy* got pushed up by three months, as Roland's financial backers were anxious to make back their money. Roland had wanted extra time to build the audience, but he didn't feel that he could say no to the people who'd made the film possible. So we ended up with a release date in April 1992.

Unfortunately, this was the month of the Rodney King verdict and the subsequent riots—Los Angeles was gripped by a wave of looting and mayhem, and the mayor declared a curfew over the entire city. So, just as this amazing film was hitting theatres, no one in LA could go and see it. And across the rest of the country, people were watching TV coverage of the riots, instead of going to the movies. *City of Joy* ended up doing weak business in its theatrical release.

I was crushed. I believed that *City of Joy* was an amazing, uplifting movie. Everything I'd hoped for had come true—Roland had brought out incredible performances, the camera work was fantastic and the final cut was beautiful. When I finished work on *City of Joy*, it was the first time I ever really felt I'd done absolutely everything I could on a movie, to the very best of my ability. Seeing it fare so poorly was just heartbreaking.

And, of course, I went straight to a very dark place, thinking that maybe it didn't do well because of me. I had dared to hope it would mark a turning point in my acting career, and the tremendous disappointment I now experienced tapped into every insecurity I still felt as an actor. No matter how obvious it was that external factors had played a big role, I couldn't shake the feeling that I had failed.

I hadn't been drinking very much over the previous year or so, having cut back after doing too much of it for too long. Lisa had been concerned about my alcohol intake for a while, and we sometimes got into fights about it. So I had cut back significantly, and while I was in Calcutta I hardly drank at all.

But the disappointment over *City of Joy* threw me right back into self-destructiveness. I gave in to those demons that were forever trying to undercut me, and I started sliding into serious depression. Adding alcohol was like pouring fuel on the fire. And did I ever pour it on.

THE NEXT MOVIE I worked on after *City of Joy* was *Father Hood*, a drama about a wild man who becomes a small-time hood. There were some interesting things about the character, and the director was fresh and talented. But compared to the kind of roles I'd hoped to get after *City of Joy*, this was a disappointment. Honestly, though, any role less than Max Lowe would have been a disappointment.

I drank more while making *Father Hood* than I ever had before.

One morning after a night of drinking, the crew had trouble waking me up. They were scared that I was slipping into a coma, but they knew that if someone called for an ambulance it would be instantly all over the news. They wanted to protect my reputation, but what if I really needed medical help?

I ended up being fine, but when Lisa came to Las Vegas, the last location where we were shooting, to spend some time with me, she saw my most embarrassing moment of all. We were trying to shoot a scene, but I'd had so much to drink I kept passing out while the cameras were rolling.

For someone who had taken so much pride in professionalism, this was about as low as it could get. I knew I was sacrificing my standards and integrity, but I couldn't stop.

For Lisa, this was agonising to watch. She'd tried everything she could think of, begging, arguing, fighting—but nothing worked. We got into terrible shouting matches. Tempers flared and things got broken. Lisa was almost ready to give up. Her survival instinct was kicking in and she began turning from trying to save me to trying to take care of herself.

Everything came to a head when I returned home to LA after wrapping *Father Hood*. I walked in the door and Lisa could see that I was drunk. She was sitting at the dining-room table with our friend Nicholas, and as she told me later, she turned to him and said, 'I wish he'd just go back. I can't do this any more.'

Lisa didn't say anything to me about it that night. But the next afternoon, when I woke up and came into the kitchen, she said, 'Buddy, what are you planning to do?'

'What do you mean? Why are you asking me this?'

'Because I need to know what I need to do next,' she said. The look in her eyes was as sad and serious as I'd ever seen. And I knew exactly what she was saying.

At that moment, I accepted that I wasn't in control of my life. With drinking, I had always believed I could stop when I wanted to. I'd always felt that alcohol wasn't the problem—the problem was the pain and insecurity. Alcohol was a symptom, not the disease itself. But looking at Lisa's face, I realised I had been in denial about what was happening and how it was affecting her.

'I'm going to go someplace and get my shit together,' I said to her. She thought I meant rehab, though all I knew was that I needed to go to a place where I could get help restoring myself.

Two days later, I checked in to a treatment facility in Tucson. At first, I was put off by the fact that they seemed to want to talk only about alcohol, because there were so many other underlying issues I needed to address. I also didn't like the feeling of being just another actor going to rehab—a victim, or a cliché. But after a month, I began to feel more in control. I began to take responsibility for my own life again and the facility gave me the tools to do it.

One of the hardest things to realise is that taking responsibility is not the same thing as taking on guilt. Saying 'this is my fault' isn't taking responsibility; it's passing judgment on yourself. For me, taking responsibility meant figuring out what was wrong with my life that was causing me to drink. If I'm drinking for emotional reasons, that's when there's a problem. And taking responsibility means being aware of it and taking steps to curb it.

The other thing about rehab, and the reason so many people, including Hollywood celebrities, continue to have trouble afterwards, is that it's not a quick fix—it just starts the process. It's like a muscle you have to exercise every day. Because if you really want to change, you have to want it every day.

After I got back to LA, I tried to keep all these things in mind. But what really helped me get back on track was beginning to pursue a new dream.

I decided to start taking flying lessons. When you fly a plane, you're taking on all kinds of responsibility, so there is no room for wallowing in alcohol or allowing your demons to get the better of you. You have to study hard to get a pilot's licence—it's like getting a college degree in a compressed time period. I threw myself into it, grateful to have a new challenge.

Once I began bouncing back from my drinking and depression,

my relationship with Lisa began to heal. I joined her in New York, where she had been cast as one of the two female leads in *Will Rogers Follies* at the Palace Theatre on Broadway. She opened the show with a solo that showed off her beautiful voice and great stage charisma. Lisa was thrilled to be starring on Broadway, and I was glad to be there for her—offering suggestions for her performance, running errands, and just generally being her cabin boy. We stayed in New York for six months, our first extended stay there since the late seventies, and we loved every minute of it.

In the meantime, I started looking again for good movie roles. Fortunately, the next role I got was a really fun one, playing a character named Pecos Bill in the Disney movie *Tall Tale.* Playing Pecos Bill allowed me to be a cowboy and ride horses all day, which was a balm for my soul. Any time I'm up in a saddle, the world around me just looks brighter. I had a hell of a lot of fun making that movie, and it brought me back into the hero role.

Little did I know it, but for my next big part, I'd be trading in that cowboy gear for a dress.

## Chapter 13

From the first time I heard about *To Wong Foo, Thanks for Everything! Julie Newmar*, I knew I wanted to be in it. It would be a real challenge to transform myself into a convincing woman, and playing a man in drag would really stretch me as an actor.

But, once again it was the same old story. Steven Spielberg was producing, and he wasn't keen on having me audition for the role. A lot of actors were being considered, including Johnny Depp and Tom Cruise, but the part still hadn't been cast. I wasn't about to take no for an answer, so I got in touch with the director, Beeban Kidron, and told her I'd fly out to New York the next day for an audition if she would just see me. She agreed.

Before the audition at a loft downtown, I went to their make-up and wardrobe people. They gave me a dress and heels and a pretty little strawberry-blonde cropped wig, and made up my face to look as feminine as possible. I had been trying out different mannerisms and voices in an effort not to seem like a caricature, and I thought I'd hit on a pretty good tone. Now I was about to find out if anyone else would buy it.

I had read the script for the first time the night before, so when Beeban asked me to perform a two-page monologue, I told her I'd have to improvise.

'No, no, no,' she said. 'It has to be the words. You need to do the scene as it is in the script.'

'I'll do the best I can,' I told her, knowing that I'd have to improvise anyway, and that I needed to absolutely blow her and the producers away with it. 'I may not have everything in the exact sequence, but it'll be close.'

The monologue was a drag queen telling the story of her life, so what I did was take the details I remembered from the script, and then tell it from my own perspective: the story of Buddy Swayze's life if he'd grown up a drag queen in redneck Texas. I talked about getting beaten up by five kids in junior high, and about getting teased by everyone at school. Everything I said was all true, except for the drag-queen part.

'There was nothing special about me,' I said towards the end, my voice soft and low, 'until I became a woman.'

I don't think anyone in that room really expected that the guy from *Road House* and *Red Dawn* could really transform himself into a convincing woman. But by the end of my audition, I knew I had. It was so strange—people didn't talk to me like I was Patrick Swayze. They talked to me like I was Vida Boheme.

After all the auditions were finished, Beeban narrowed the list to the ones she liked best, then took the tapes to Spielberg and the other producers. Everyone agreed that I *was* Vida. I got the part. I was back in the game.

It takes a long time to turn a masculine man into a woman. First, you have to be incredibly well shaved, and not just on your face. All those places where men have hair and women don't—face, neck, even ears—have to be smooth. Then, because men's pores are bigger than women's, the make-up department applies a stucco-like filler, to smooth out your skin.

Then comes the make-up. You'd get a base coat of foundation, followed by powder, lipstick, eyeliner, eye shadow, fake eyelashes—and my make-up guy on *Wong Foo* certainly knew what he was doing. At about six feet five inches tall, he'd once been a towering, gorgeous drag queen himself.

Make-up usually took about three hours, after which my co-stars Wesley Snipes and John Leguizamo and I would go to the wardrobe room. I learned very quickly not to let them dress me in any cute little tight trouser-suits, because that meant I'd have to use an apparatus called the gender bender. This is a special piece of equipment, designed by some sadistic bastard with a sense of humour, which you tuck your manly parts into to push them back and make them 'disappear'. It's a very scary sensation, so very quickly I learned to ask for lovely dresses that allowed things to remain in their rightful place.

I never knew how many categories of drag queen there were until we started doing research for *Wong Foo*. And by 'research', I mean going out to clubs with some of the most beautiful, statuesque, amazing queens I had ever seen.

The level of talent in the drag world is phenomenal. These people could sing, they could dance, they could vamp. Some of the men singing as women had the most beautiful female voices I'd ever heard. We had a blast exploring their world. And Lisa was pleased to get a compliment herself, when a drag queen passed her on the street, looked her up and down, and said, 'Beautiful!'

Spending time with these men was incredibly eye-opening. Not only did they have an amazing sense of humour, they also had amazing courage. They weren't afraid to be exactly who they were, and to expect the rest of the world to catch up. It was inspiring to see.

I loved working with John and Wesley, both of whom looked absolutely fabulous in drag. I really didn't mind wearing women's clothes, but Wesley absolutely hated it. When we wrapped *Wong Foo*, he held a ceremonial funeral for his wig and costume. He burned them and buried the ashes in the Nebraska soil, relieved to be free of them. But I liked my clothes, and even asked Lisa if she wanted any of them after the shoot was over. She laughed and took a one-size-fits-all Armani shawl—the only thing that would fit her.

*Wong Foo* went to number one on its opening weekend, but in the end it didn't do as well as we had hoped. The reviews were mostly good, though, and I received my third nomination for a Golden Globe Award. That was hugely validating, because I'd really pushed myself to become Vida. I loved her, and even missed her a little bit when she was gone.

LISA AND I both enjoyed the *Wong Foo* shoot, and my career was again on an upswing. But, personally, that period marked the beginning of a difficult time, starting with the death of my older sister, Vicky, who committed suicide in December 1994.

Vicky was four years older than me and as kids she and I had been close, even though we'd fought like cat and dog. She was very talented—a beautiful dancer and singer, and an amazing actress. Vicky had the same pressure on her as all the Swayze kids, to be the best and push the hardest, but as an adult she also had another burden to bear. She suffered from depression and was eventually diagnosed as bipolar.

Vicky's struggle with depression was long and intense. Like many families of bipolar people, we suffered through her terrible times and never knew what to expect when we saw her. We weren't sure how to deal with her pain, and although we tried our hardest to support her, both emotionally and financially, it never felt as if we did enough. But the sad truth was, nothing would have been enough.

Vicky's doctors had prescribed a variety of medications, which she hated taking. About two years before she died, we found her a doctor who specialised in getting people off psychiatric drugs. The terrible irony was that although this really seemed to help, it ended with her killing herself.

As her doctor explained to us, it was possible that his different medications allowed Vicky to get just well enough to see how horrible she felt her life really was.

Vicky's suicide really rocked my world. It made me wonder how much of her was also in me. Being a Swayze is a gift and a curse, because we all do possess this kind of wild Irish temperament. That temperament unleashes powerful things in terms of creative work, but it can be an enemy as well. You have to keep it in balance to survive and Vicky hadn't been able to do that. I think all of us Swayze kids felt vulnerable about ourselves after her suicide.

Yet, despite my own self-destructive streak, I've always had an even stronger urge for self-preservation. No matter how much despair I've felt in any given period, I never came close to considering suicide. Deep down, I always believe things will get better somehow. But Vicky's death seriously battered that belief.

I had never allowed myself to feel like a victim before. But it was hard not to feel, sometimes, that no matter what you do, life is going to smack you down. No matter how hard I tried, no matter how good a person I tried to be, bad things kept happening.

When those you love die, the best you can do is to honour their spirit for as long as you live. You make a commitment that you're going to take whatever lesson that person was trying to teach you, and you make it true in your own life. Making that commitment is one way to ease the pain of their absence. But more than that, it's a positive way to keep their spirit alive in the world, by keeping it alive in yourself. I've tried to honour that with my father, my sister, with anyone we've loved who has passed on.

With everything that had happened over the previous couple of years, Lisa and I started seriously to re-evaluate how we were living our lives. For too long, we'd been running in the whirlwind, taking on too many things at once and ignoring the needs of our spirits. Together, we decided to simplify things, to get back to the basics.

At its peak, our horse business—showing and breeding—had included fifty horses, the majority of which we kept in Texas. This was way more than we could be personally involved with, so we sold some and cut back on travelling to horse shows. We also decided to focus more on the things that made us happy, rather than the things that ended up controlling our lives. And the biggest thing we did, by far, was to finally fulfil our lifelong dream of owning a real ranch on a real spread of land.

Ever since we'd spent time in New Mexico during the shooting of *Red Dawn*, Lisa and I had been in love with the rugged beauty of the mountains there. In the late 1990s, we had an opportunity to purchase almost 15,000 acres of gorgeous ranch land, near where we'd filmed *Red Dawn.* It was like buying a piece of heaven, so we jumped at the chance.

For me, I was sorry my dad wasn't here to be a part of it, but I was proud to be returning to my cowboy roots, just as he'd always hoped I would.

Lisa and I were now both pilots, so we could fly ourselves back and forth to New Mexico. And we did, every chance we got. Because being out in the natural world, out at the ranch we loved, always helped restore our spirits.

In May 1998, I was shooting a scene for the film *Letters from a Killer*, when disaster struck.

It was late afternoon, and we were trying to get a few final shots for a big chase scene. My character, Race Darnell, was riding a horse bareback, galloping through the forest with the FBI in hot pursuit. The scene called for me to race my horse right under a diagonally growing oak tree, right by a camera. A small crowd of people had gathered near the tree to watch the action—but they were standing in the path my horse would be racing down. Several hundred yards away, as I waited for my cue to come over the walkie-talkie, I had no idea they were there.

When the director yelled 'Action', I spurred my horse to a gallop. We raced towards the tree, but where I needed the horse to go right he wanted to go left. He'd seen the people blocking his path, and he didn't want any part of it. When he started going left, I quickly had to pull him right again or the shot would be ruined.

Everything happened in an instant. I pulled the horse sharply back to the right and he changed direction so fast that I flew straight off his back. The only thing that saved me from crashing headfirst into that oak tree was instinct: in a split second, I grabbed the mane with both hands and flipped myself over, smashing into the tree legs first.

The impact broke both my legs and tore tendons in my shoulder and I collapsed to the ground. I didn't know right away how badly hurt I was, but I knew something was badly wrong.

My long-time stunt double, Cliff McLaughlin, was at my side in a flash. He heard me say, 'Let me just walk it off. I'll be okay'—the same thing I'd wanted to do on that high-school football field nearly thirty years earlier. But I wasn't going to be walking away from this accident. I tried to sit up, but I could feel myself going into shock, which was dangerous out in the woods, with the nearest hospital miles away.

The set medic wanted to strap my legs together and drive me to it.

'Hell, no,' I told him. 'Do not touch my legs.'

I had a GPS device and a radio that could communicate with air traffic, which would help a rescue helicopter locate us out here in the boonies. We made the emergency call, gave the coordinates, and talked the chopper pilot in to our location, but it still took them over an hour to get to us.

Lisa didn't see the accident, but she got there quickly after it happened. She was worried, of course, but also upset with me for having been riding at all. Cliff had been ready to jump in as my stunt double, but I'd told him to relax, as I really wanted to do the scene myself. I couldn't think of anything more fun than roaring through the woods bareback on a horse—it was the kind of thing I loved to do, and here I was getting paid to do it.

By the time the helicopter got me to the hospital, the pain was agonising. The doctors went right at it, giving me pain medication, CAT scans, the works. I had two broken legs, one a lot worse than the other. My right femur was broken and, luckily for me, the hospital at UC Davis had the world's foremost expert on a new way to treat femur breaks. It used to be that anyone who broke a femur had to have the leg split open and go through months of healing time. This new technique required only a small incision, which meant you didn't have to heal muscles that had been sliced open. Three hours after surgery, the doctors had me get up and walk. And three months later, I was back at work, which would have been unheard of only a few years earlier.

But even though my physical wounds healed quickly, other wounds did not. This was the first accident I'd ever had that really came close to killing me. If I'd gone into that tree head first, I would either have been killed instantly or have broken my neck and been left paralysed, as Christopher Reeve, best known for his role in *Superman*, had been not so long before. I'd done some crazy stunts on horses, but this accident made me realise that no matter how good a rider you are, when you're riding bareback on a horse you're nothing but a human projectile.

It was as if the invisible shield that had always protected me had finally broken. I'd always acted as if I were invincible, because I always felt invincible. Now I realised I wasn't.

I had nightmares where I'd see myself flying off the horse and smashing into that tree. I'd wake up in a sweat, my heart beating like crazy and fear coursing through me. With time, I was able to get back the courage the accident stole from me. I went back to doing everything on horses I'd done before the accident, and loving it. And the nightmares stopped.

But even now, when I remember the feeling of hurtling towards that tree, my heart starts pumping again. Even with all the movie stunts I'd done, that was the first time I'd had a real brush with death.

Less than two years later, though, I was to have another.

# *Chapter 14*

In early May 2000, after a particularly dry spring, the National Park Service set a controlled fire in northern New Mexico, where our new ranch was, to burn off brush and grass. For months, the area had suffered record-setting high temperatures and the landscape was parched. So, when fierce winds suddenly whipped up the flames, the fire quickly got out of control. Within days, huge swathes of New Mexico were ablaze.

Lisa and I were in Los Angeles, but we became more and more worried as we watched the news coverage of the wildfires. Tens of thousands of people were being evacuated and their homes were going up like tinder. News reports showed walls of flames and fleeing residents, and President Clinton declared a state of emergency in several New Mexico counties. All I could think about was that our beautiful ranch—our haven and spiritual home—was in danger.

We sweated things out in LA for a couple of weeks, but as the fire drew closer to our ranch, I knew I had to do something. I couldn't just sit thousands of miles away as the place I loved went up in smoke—and when we heard the authorities were evacuating the canyon where our house was, that was the last straw. I decided to fly out there and get into the canyon somehow, to at least bulldoze a fire break round our house.

Late on the night of May 31, I told Lisa I was flying to New Mexico the next morning. 'You're what?' she said. 'Buddy, they're evacuating the canyon. You won't even be able to get near the ranch.'

She tried to convince me not to go, but I was determined. Because I was at an emotional fever pitch, I hardly slept, and before the sun rose, I threw some clothes into a bag and headed out to the Van Nuys airport. Just before dawn broke I settled into the cockpit of our Cessna 414a to make the three-hour flight to New Mexico.

About a month earlier, Lisa had encountered a dangerous situation while flying the Cessna near the Grand Canyon. She had been climbing to a higher altitude, when all of a sudden she heard a warning alarm noise in the cockpit. The noise startled her, but she quickly realised that it meant the cabin wasn't pressurising properly as she climbed. A valve was probably stuck, allowing the escape of air. We occasionally smoked in the cockpit, and a sticky residue on the outflow valve could be the result of tar from cigarettes.

When a plane's cabin isn't pressurised properly, there's not enough oxygen, which leads to hypoxia and possibly death. Fortunately, Lisa had realised quickly what was happening, so she was able to descend to a safe altitude and finish her flight. And we got the plane serviced right after the incident.

On the morning of June 1, I decided to fly at a relatively low altitude in case the pressurisation problem recurred. I brought the Cessna to 13,000 feet, set the autopilot, and settled in for the rest of the flight. And that's the last thing I remember, until suddenly becoming aware of green and brown around me, and everything spinning. I looked around for blue sky but the plane was at a very low altitude and what I saw was a strip of road with a strange oval at one end. One thought managed to penetrate the fog in my brain: *That must be the airport.*

I hooked a hard left to line up with what I thought was the runway. The next thing I knew, there were electrical power boxes in front of me, and I vaguely remember trying to push the plane over or round them. Then, suddenly, I was on the ground. I sat stunned for a moment in the cockpit, groggy and disorientated.

I had no idea that I'd just had an off-airport landing, or that my plane was damaged.

In fact, I had just landed on the street of what was to become a new housing development in Prescott Valley, Arizona. It was being constructed at the time, so there was hardly anyone around to see my plane descend, clip two light poles and a power box, and still somehow land without crashing.

As I opened the plane's door and stepped down onto the ground, a couple of construction workers came running over. I vaguely remember one of them telling me I'd clipped something on the way down. I walked round the front of the plane to look at the wing and, when I saw that it was damaged, I got upset for the first time—this plane was Lisa's and my baby and I'd hurt it. I still didn't understand what had happened, but, little by little, the truth started penetrating my still confused brain.

The first thing I did was call Lisa—a call I dreaded making, as I knew she'd be upset. 'Lisa, I've had an off-airport landing,' I told her. 'I thought I was landing in New Mexico, but I ended up in a housing development in Prescott, Arizona. I'm okay, but the plane is damaged.'

As Lisa told me later, she just went numb as I recounted what had happened. What made it worse was the fact that I was actually suffering from hypoxia, which slurs your speech, so it sounded as if I'd been drinking. This effect wore off quickly, but because I called Lisa so soon after landing, all she knew was that I'd damaged the plane in an unscheduled landing, and on top of that I sounded as if I was unfit to fly.

The next call I made was to the Federal Aviation Administration, to report the incident. I described what had happened, and the FAA representative told me he'd call the National Transportation Safety Board. So all the official wheels were in motion for dealing with the incident. Then I made a decision that seemed sensible at the time, but that created its own problems later.

I was carrying some beer and wine on board. This was of course legal and I should have just left it where it was, but instead I gave it to the construction workers. There was no doubt that photographers were on the way, and I had a feeling that if word got out of alcohol on board my plane, they'd try to twist the story into 'Patrick Swayze Flies Drunk'. I was trying to minimise possible complications, but when the story came out that I'd got rid of the alcohol—as I should have known it would—people assumed I was trying to cover something up.

One of the construction workers gave me a ride to a hotel, where Lisa and our long-time flight instructor, Frank Kratzer, joined me as soon as they could, and we waited there for the National Transportation Safety Board investigators to arrive at the site, so we could answer any questions they had.

The NTSB investigation later revealed that a hose clamp on the pressurising system had malfunctioned, which alone would have been enough to cause a problem, even at my relatively low altitude. The situation was also exacerbated by the continued presence of tar deposits on that rubber outflow valve, and the fact that I was a heavy smoker. When you have a three-pack-a-day habit, as I had at the time, your lungs don't function as well at altitude as those of non-smokers. The NTSB report noted that the combination of all these circumstances meant I had almost certainly become hypoxic during the flight and had lost consciousness. It found no evidence of alcohol as a factor.

But the really scary thing was this: I had apparently stopped responding to air-traffic control around Needles, California, near the Arizona state line, yet somehow I must have knocked off the autopilot between there and Prescott Valley, which allowed the plane to descend to a breathable altitude. Otherwise, my plane would have just continued at 13,000 feet, flying until it ran out of fuel, and I would have been dead.

Air-traffic control radar showed that between Needles and my landing in Prescott Valley, my Cessna almost hit the ground eleven times. Its route looked like a strand of spaghetti, looping round for about forty-five minutes.

Fortunately, as it approached Prescott Valley, there was enough oxygen in the cockpit to revive me. I woke up at just a couple hundred feet above the ground and somehow managed to land safely. It was nothing short of a miracle.

There was a lot of fallout from the off-airport landing. For one thing, Lisa and I never smoked in the cockpit again. I also offered to make a public-service announcement for the FAA, warning of the dangers of smoking while flying, which weren't widely known at the time.

Even though the problem had been mechanical, I still had to fight to keep my pilot's licence, going through psychological testing and skills tests. That meant it would be two years before I could fly again. But this wasn't nearly as tough as getting through the nightmares I began to have after the incident, dreaming I was heading for a crash or floating aimlessly in the sky, unconscious to the end.

Lisa had a hard time coming to terms with it, too. We had been together twenty-five years by then, through thick and thin, through enough pain and joy to fill a hundred lifetimes. She hadn't wanted me to fly that morning in the first place, but when I did, and then nearly died doing it, she felt betrayed that I'd been willing to risk everything we'd built together. She felt helpless and angry, and it would take some time for those feelings to subside.

THIS AIRPLANE INCIDENT, combined with my feelings of vulnerability after the horse accident, really messed with my head. I had cheated death once again—but what for? What was the point of all this? What was I adding to the world?

Earlier in my life, I had made it through difficult times by always focusing on the next dream. But now I was starting to feel not just tired, but disillusioned. Had all this effort and pain been worth it? Had I created anything of value?

Since my relationship with Lisa had frayed from the stress of constantly trying to prove myself, I wondered if I had been focusing on the wrong things all along.

And even as I kept pushing to find good projects in Hollywood, the whole business of making movies was changing. With the economic downturn of 2000–01, financing for bigger projects dried up and independent films started to become more popular. There seemed to be fewer movies in general, and not as many good roles to choose from. It was tough going, but I did manage to shift gears and get work in a few good independent films—for example, *Green Dragon* with Forest Whitaker, *Donnie Darko* with Jake Gyllenhaal and *Waking Up in Reno* with Billy Bob Thornton.

There was one film, though, that both Lisa and I longed to make. Ever since our play *Without a Word* had been a hit in the LA theatre world back in 1984, we had wanted to turn it into a film. *Without a Word* had only a month-long run in LA, but even all these years later, people still stopped us on the street to say how much they'd loved it. They would tell us how inspired they had been, and they would ask us to please make a movie out of it.

If movies were made through sheer effort alone, we'd have finished this one long ago. Over the past two decades, Lisa and I had done everything possible to try to bring *Without a Word* to the screen. But there are so many factors that have to come together to make a movie—it's like herding cats, and we couldn't get them all together at once.

Early on, Lisa had done a full rewrite, since the play was non-linear and would be hard to adapt for film without a more traditional narrative story line. We had entered into discussions with a variety of possible producers, financiers, directors and writers, but for one reason or another, we were having trouble finding the right blend. We'd start down one road, thinking we were making progress, but then the project would fall apart.

Now, however, we realised it was do-or-die time. We wouldn't be able to do the film's very demanding dance sequences for ever, so we had to make it happen soon—or let it go.

And that's when Lisa really stepped up. She invited Nicholas Gunn, who had co-written the play with us back in 1984, and the producer, Janice Yarbrough, who had run our production company at Fox, to dinner. With all four of us at the table, she said, 'I have to do this script. I know what needs to be done, and I can write it.'

A dead silence fell at the table. Her face showed a kind of determination I'd never seen before. She'd always been the type to defer to others, playing down her own skills. But not this time. She'd worked on nearly all my movie scripts over the years, and had written a theatrical musical, so she was completely prepared for the task. More important, she knew the story in her bones, and I made up my mind at that moment to support her no matter what.

This was the film that finally led Lisa to put herself out there in a way she'd long been reluctant to. It was a huge turning point professionally, and I was thrilled for her—and for our movie.

Although excited about taking on the roles of writer and director, Lisa felt that trying to do both, and act in the film, too, might be too much, so we asked Billy Bob Thornton, who had written, directed and starred in *Sling Blade*, what he thought. 'All the producers have been telling us this isn't possible,' Lisa told him. 'They're saying it's too complicated to direct and star in a movie at the same time.'

Billy Bob's answer was succinct: 'One word: horseshit.'

We took that as a kind of blessing, and with a commitment for financing and some money from our own pockets, we were finally off to the races. Lisa wrote, directed, starred in and coproduced *One Last Dance*, the name we chose for the film. We got an amazing cast of dancers, including the fantastic George de la Peña, a former soloist with the American Ballet Theatre. It's not easy to find people who can both dance and act at the highest level, but George could do both beautifully. He was perfect for the role.

We shot the film in thirty-two days, mostly in Winnipeg but with a few exteriors shot in New York and LA. And when all was said and done and Lisa had pulled the footage together, *One Last Dance* was everything we'd hoped it would be. Everyone in the cast and crew had given their hearts and souls to this movie, and it showed.

*One Last Dance* was released as a DVD and went to number one, and it's still one of the best movies ever made about the world of dance. Lisa showed all the abilities I knew she had and I loved being directed by her. She had a natural instinct for it, and

I was thrilled that she'd finally got the chance to put that talent into action.

I'd never been so proud of Lisa, but I was spent by the end of the process. The shooting had been gruelling, and there's always a natural letdown when you finish a project you've invested in emotionally. *One Last Dance* was such a deeply personal project that I felt that letdown even more acutely. Before I knew it, I became seriously depressed again.

I DON'T THINK I really understood what depression was until this period of my life. I had certainly struggled with deep sadness and feelings of frustration, but my natural optimism had always somehow managed to shine through. In the years following *One Last Dance*, though, that optimism began to desert me entirely. I'd lost the passion and purpose in my life and couldn't seem to get it back.

I started drinking again. Everybody fails in life, but it's when you can't pick yourself up after failure that you're in trouble. I hated sounding like the whiny actor—*Why can't I be more successful? Why can't I get better roles?* But for the first time in my life, I began to fear deep down that I would never bounce back again, that I had no control over my success or failure.

As I sank deeper into this hole, and drank more and more, Lisa got to the point where she didn't even recognise me. I had always been resilient, but this person she was living with was beaten down, defeated. Work had always been my cure for feeling depressed, but now even that wasn't happening any more.

For Lisa, this was too much. Seeing me descend into such despair was scary for her. There was a lot of anger during this period, and a lot of raw emotion that came out in sudden, jarring spurts. In Lisa's eyes, I was going off the deep end. She was afraid one of us would end up dead, and she couldn't take that fear.

So she made a decision. Without telling me, she packed a couple of suitcases and took off one morning before I woke up. She didn't want a fight. She felt she had to leave for her own sanity and safety, and she wasn't about to put the matter up for discussion.

When I woke up and found Lisa gone, I was crushed. And angry. I couldn't believe she'd left me, and I was terrified it would be for ever. We had been together now for more than thirty years, and I couldn't bear the thought of life without her. We had made it through so much—how could we lose each other?

Lisa didn't go far, renting an apartment in the San Fernando Valley, about a twenty-minute drive from Rancho Bizarro. She didn't tell anyone she'd moved out, and somehow, miraculously, we managed to keep it a secret from the tabloids. We talked every day and she often visited the ranch for business. But she was absolutely determined not to come back until things had changed. She kept that apartment for a whole year, which we've never revealed publicly until now.

When Lisa left, I had to completely re-evaluate my life. I was driving away the one person who had always stood by me, who had always loved me no matter what. I still didn't know how to change what I was, but there was one thing I could change. I stopped drinking after Lisa moved out, quitting cold turkey.

The year of our separation was a period of really assessing myself, of learning how to bring myself back from the brink of despair. I was desperately hurt that Lisa had left, but over time I came to understand that she wasn't doing it to punish me. She'd left only when she felt she had no other choice.

My anger and sense of betrayal began to give way to more productive feelings. Instead, I thought about how I could make things better. And how I could win Lisa back.

In the midst of our separation, after I'd been sober a few months, I was cast as Allan Quatermain in *King Solomon's Mines.* This was a godsend—a starring role in one of the great heroic narratives in literary history—and it saved my ass. I was excited to play this courageous, horse-riding hero, and thrilled to be going back to Africa—a place where Lisa and I had found such spiritual sustenance during *Steel Dawn*.

In Africa, I was back doing the things I loved best—acting in a period piece, doing stunt work on horseback, spending time in the beauty of nature. I started exploring the African bush, learning again how to live off the land and regaining that feeling of self-worth it always brings. The weeks we spent shooting felt absolutely restorative, as if a slate were being wiped clean. I began to find again that sense of purpose and passion that I'd lost for so long.

Lisa and I spoke by phone every day, and towards the end of the shoot she agreed to come to Africa for a visit. I couldn't wait to see her, of course—but as the date drew near, I subconsciously began protecting myself from the possibility that she was flying all the way to Africa to tell me she wanted a divorce.

When a week of her visit passed and Lisa didn't ask for a divorce, I was relieved. Maybe she was here just to be with me, after all. So I finally began to let my guard down and enjoy our time together, and when we went for a week-long safari in Botswana, after wrapping up the movie, things continued to get better. I was still scared, but as the days went by and we became more comfortable together, I dared to believe she might still love me.

Yet rifts as deep as the one we'd suffered don't heal overnight. After we returned to California, Lisa moved back home with me, but our troubles weren't over. We still weren't really connecting with each other, and the longer that went on, the worse it seemed to get. It was as if we'd made the commitment to make it work, but didn't have the spirit to follow through. Our relationship was dying a slow death right before our eyes. We wanted to stop it, but we didn't know how.

During that time, the friction between us grew worse and worse. We lurched between anger and despair, our relationship poisoned by mistrust and bitterness. On one occasion in LA, we had a particularly brutal argument, one that made it obvious to both of us that things couldn't continue this way.

'I feel like you're torturing me out of this marriage,' Lisa said to me, her eyes filled with hurt.

'I feel like you're doing the same thing to me,' I replied. We stared at each other for a moment, but there was nothing more to say.

At that point, neither of us knew how to find our way back to the other. Fortunately we were about to get some assistance—from a very unlikely source.

George de la Peña, who had starred in *One Last Dance*, had become a dear friend since we made the movie. In 2007, for my birthday, he decided to give us a consulting session with a woman he'd written a self-help book with. Elizabeth was a well-known psychic and George swore by her abilities.

Lisa and I weren't big aficionados of psychic readings, but there was no harm in getting a new perspective on things. I couldn't tell you to this day if Elizabeth has psychic powers—or if anyone does, really—but the evening she came to Rancho Bizarro, she started picking up on some things very quickly. Maybe George gave her some insight before she came over, or maybe she's just an amazing reader of people and body language. But she cut through the bull-shit right away.

We walked with her through the house, showing her each of the rooms so she could get a feel for our life together, and when we ended up in the office in the barn, she said, 'Let's sit down right here.'

She started talking. She talked about our horses, our furniture, the feng shui of our home. And then, suddenly, she looked straight at Lisa. 'There's something really weird happening,' she said. 'You're sitting right there, but it's like you're not really here.'

Lisa just stared at her. 'Yes. You're here, but you're not really,' she went on. 'It's like you've checked out already.' And Lisa burst into tears.

Elizabeth turned to me. 'She's already gone,' she said. 'You need to really look at what she wants, at how to fix this. Because she is out the door.'

'She's right,' Lisa said. 'In my heart, I'm gone. I'm gone.'

I felt the tears well up, too. What was Lisa saying? Had I really lost her? Was it too late?

'Little Buddy' Swayze aged five. Patrick Wayne Swayze was born on August 18, 1952, in Houston, Texas.

Little Lisa Haapaniemi, already a dancer at the age of three. Aged fifteen, she came to my mother's dance studio and I noticed her right away with her lithe dancer's build.

Our wedding in June 1975. This was the only moment during the ceremony that Lisa smiled—when she had trouble getting the ring on my finger.

Dancing with Lisa in New York.
The training was exhausting and physically demanding—but it was also exhilarating.

On the set of 'Steel Dawn', the first movie that Lisa and I starred in together. We explored the Kalahari Desert and fell in love with Africa.

I shot thirteen episodes of the TV series 'The Beast' in Chicago while undergoing chemotherapy. Lisa directed my favourite one, 'Brother's Keeper'.

I knew that if I was to lift Jennifer successfully, she'd have to feel completely safe with me.
(Still taken from the film 'Dirty Dancing'.)

I would never have dreamed that one person could find so much passion and so much loyalty with another. Spiritually and emotionally we were amazingly compatible.

'What do you want, Lisa?' I asked her. 'What can I do?' She sobbed quietly beside me and my heart just about broke open. I wanted to hold her and never let her go, but all I could do was touch her shoulder gently.

And then a strange and wonderful thing happened. We looked at each other and somehow we each suddenly saw once again the person we'd fallen in love with. I hadn't been able to see that for so long, since we had many layers of pain that had built up over the years. But in that one moment, instead of seeing someone I'd fought with, or felt angry towards, or resented, all of that simply fell away. I felt a surge of love for Lisa that I hadn't felt in years. I took her into my arms and we cried together.

We started talking, really talking. When two people are at odds, sometimes the hardest thing to do is decide who will step through the door first to try to repair things. But now, with the help of Elizabeth, Lisa and I came together again. We both opened our hearts at the same time. And at Elizabeth's suggestion, we each wrote 'I will forget the past' ten times on a piece of paper, then buried it under an avocado tree in our yard. It was time for a fresh start.

People always ask us, How do we do it? How have we kept a marriage of thirty-four years so strong? I don't claim to have any great answers, but I do know one thing. Lisa and I never, ever stopped trying, no matter how bad things got. We never gave up on each other, although in our absolute worst moments, we came very close. If there was a way to save our relationship, we were going to find it. And the very fact that we both always wanted to save it meant that there was a way to do it. Because that desire is the key. As I said to Lisa not long after our experience with Elizabeth, just as an argument was starting to break out, 'We're stopping this right now. I never want to go back to the way it was.'

Our experience with Elizabeth was definitely life-changing. With our relationship back on track, we were ready and eager to face the world again. I'll always be grateful that we were, because the next twist that came was the cruellest of all.

# Chapter 15

With so few good movie roles available, I'd been looking off and on for a TV series, but though I'd read tons of scripts, nothing was ever quite right. I had really enjoyed working on *The Renegades* and *North and South*, and knew if I could find a good character on a solid series it would be worth gunning for. Then, in 2007, I was sent scripts for two new series that both looked very good.

One of the two shows, *The Beast*, was about an enigmatic FBI agent named Charles Barker. Barker was a fascinating, layered character, who constantly surprised me as I read through the script. I loved his world-weary persona, and the fact that he wasn't your stereotypical good guy, but a complex and mature character.

I really liked the writing and the ideas on *The Beast*, but the production team was young and inexperienced, especially compared to the team that would be working on the other series. Going with the young, hungry show would be a risk, but ultimately I just liked the material better. There was something about Charles Barker that really spoke to me, so in the end I turned the other project down.

We shot the pilot episode, and I knew even before seeing the finished product that *The Beast* was going to be really good. If it got picked up, we'd be shooting the full first season in Chicago, and both Lisa and I had high hopes that would be the case. So we went into the Christmas holiday period more optimistic than we had been in a long while—happy to be in love and excited about the future.

Then came the fateful night in Aspen that I began this book with. As we toasted the new year and I felt the champagne burn my stomach, I never could have guessed what lay ahead. I just gritted my teeth and made it through the holidays, assuming I'd start feeling better soon.

Back in LA a couple of weeks later, I noticed something else strange. When I went to the bathroom, I noticed that I had begun losing weight. I'd been having digestive issues, too, so I told Lisa what I'd noticed. She knew I hadn't been feeling all that great and she asked if anything else wasn't quite right.

I walked to a mirror and peered at my face. 'Do my eyes look yellow?' I asked Lisa. She came to look, and I pulled my lower lids down and rolled my eyes around.

'Yes,' she said. 'They do. They look jaundiced.' Lisa's not the worrying kind, but I could tell that she was concerned. 'Let's make an appointment for you to see Dr Davidson tomorrow,' she said.

'I don't think that's really necessary,' I said. 'I'm sure it'll clear up.'

But Lisa was adamant. 'This isn't normal,' she said. So we made the appointment, then got online to see what we could find out about the symptoms I was having. We looked up jaundice and found a long list of things that could cause it, none of which sounded very good—from hepatitis to liver infection to cancer. All the same, we didn't imagine for a second that I could possibly be that sick.

THE NEXT DAY, January 14, Lisa and I went to Cedars-Sinai to see Dr Davidson. We described my symptoms and, after looking at my eyes, he immediately ordered a batch of tests. CAT scans, blood tests, urine test—they put me through the works. The CAT scan revealed a mass on my pancreas. This was very bad news, though it still didn't mean I definitely had cancer. To find out for sure, the doctors would need to do an exploratory endoscopic procedure, to get a piece of tissue for testing.

The endoscopy was scheduled for January 19. An anaesthesiologist put me to sleep, and a gastrointestinal surgeon snaked a tube down my throat. He planned to insert a stent into my bile duct, to open it up and have a better look.

As I lay sleeping off the anaesthesia in the recovery room, two of the doctors gave Lisa the news. 'We need to do a pathology on the tissue to be absolutely certain,' they told her, 'but we're ninety-nine per cent sure that he's got pancreatic cancer.'

Lisa later told me she had needed help to take in this news and help decide what to do next, so she managed to ask them to call her sister-in-law Maria Scoures, who is a respected oncologist in Houston. The doctors got Maria on the phone and she's been a godsend for us both from that moment on.

Lying in the recovery room, I still had no idea what awaited me. When I woke up, Lisa came in to see me, but first she made a decision: she wouldn't tell me about the cancer right away. She wanted me to have one last night of 'normal' life—one last night of innocence before our hardest fight began. She told me she loved me, and spent the night by my side.

The next morning, the surgeon came in and woke us both up to give me the diagnosis. I don't remember much about that conversation, but when he told me I had pancreatic cancer, my first thought was, I'm a dead man.

Fear sliced through me. What the fuck had just happened? I had been so excited about the upswing my life was on. Now it all seemed like a cruel joke. I couldn't be dying—I had too much to live for! I just couldn't face the idea that life as I'd always known it was over.

Neither could Lisa. She had always been so strong, so determined and capable. We had been together through so much, and since then she has helped me through every aspect of this disease with good humour and boundless love, but at that moment, after the surgeon left, she just broke down and cried. She crawled into the hospital bed with me, buried her head in my neck, and we wept together. She knew I couldn't change anything about what was happening, and she was devastated.

There was one last sliver of hope. If the cancer hadn't spread at all, the doctors told us it might be possible to operate. But that hope came crashing down the next day, when another CAT scan showed that it had already spread to my liver. I had what they call Stage IV cancer, the worst possible.

Lisa and I decided to tell only a few people about my diagnosis, at least until we knew for sure what my treatment would be and what my prognosis really was. We especially didn't want to tell my mother, as she was having eye surgery the next day and was supposed to try to keep her eyes dry—no crying—for a few weeks after the surgery.

Unfortunately, those morally bankrupt souls at the *National Enquirer* had other ideas. Someone in the medical field tipped them off, and a *National Enquirer* reporter showed up at my mom's house. She opened the door to have a complete stranger ask, 'How do you feel about Patrick having pancreatic cancer?' And that's how she found out. For the life of me, I cannot understand how anyone can be so cruel, but human decency is apparently an afterthought when there's money to be made selling tabloids.

Lisa and I jumped right into action, learning everything we could about the disease and how to treat it. Maria was a tremendous help, too—she was doing pancreatic cancer research of her own and advised us on how best to fight it. From the beginning, we've done all our own home care—injections, intravenous nutrition and everything else—because we don't want to have an at-home nurse. We want life to go on as normally as it possibly can, because I have no intention of staying alive just for the sake of it—I want to live and enjoy life rather than feel like a full-time patient.

BEFORE THE NEWS of my illness broke publicly, the television network A&E decided to pick up *The Beast* for a full season. This was great news—but of course, they'd ordered those thirteen episodes without knowing their lead actor had just been diagnosed with pancreatic cancer. At first, I wasn't sure I could go through with filming a full season of an action-packed dramatic series—I didn't know whether I'd be healthy enough to do it. But very soon I realised there was nothing I wanted to do more. And I made up my mind that I'd find a way, no matter what.

We got in touch with A&E to let them know about my diagnosis, and I sent along this message: 'Don't count me out. I can do this.' All I could think was, if I'm really going out, I'd rather go out on a high note, doing quality work I believe in. I loved *The Beast*, and felt that I'd done some of the best work of my career in the pilot. I really wanted to have the chance to explore the character of Charles Barker even further.

Once they learned about the cancer, the executives at A&E were under no obligation to keep their offer on the table. It would have been the easiest thing in the world for them to cancel the series. But to their immense credit, they did not. We decided to see how my chemotherapy treatment went, and they'd make a decision after that. If I responded well, and it looked as if I'd be healthy enough to shoot the series, they'd go ahead with it.

Television executives aren't necessarily renowned for their generosity of spirit, but that decision by A&E president Bob DiBitetto was a thoroughly decent, open-hearted act—and he kept his word. After a few months of treatment, when I was feeling pretty good, I invited the writers and producers to Rancho Bizarro. I told them I was excited to do the series and ready to go, and they called A&E right then to ask for the green light. We got it.

Chemotherapy was hell on wheels, and it got worse the longer it went on—but I knew if it was a matter of just pushing through all the pain and discomfort, I could do it. I spent many nights curled up in the foetal position on the bathroom floor, desperate for the pain to pass. But there was at least one side effect of chemo I'd dreaded but didn't suffer: I managed to keep my hair.

As Lisa and I headed up to Chicago to begin shooting in the late summer of 2008, I vowed to myself that no one on the set would ever know if I was feeling bad or in pain. I was going to shoot this whole series, doing my own stunts, right into the Chicago winter—and I wasn't going to utter a peep about anything having to do with cancer or treatment. If I had a 6.30 a.m. call, I'd wake up a couple of hours earlier in order to get my digestive system in order and make sure I was ready to go.

I stayed on that first chemo régime for ten months, which is a long time—most people undergo a round of chemo for just a few months, as the side effects get cumulatively worse. And mine did get worse towards the end of the shooting season, but I undertook an attitude adjustment every single day, reminding myself how fortunate I was to be working on a project I loved, and willing myself to put one foot in front of the other to finish it.

There were definitely tough moments, but some days were good. Once, after a crew member said to me, 'I can't believe you're able to do all this,' I turned to Lisa and said, 'I've worked with hangovers worse than this.'

I continued with chemotherapy all the way through the shoot, but I never took any painkillers, since they dull not only your pain but also your sharpness. If I was going to do great work on this series, I wanted to be a hundred per cent there. Quitting was not an option. In five months of shooting, I missed only a day and a half of work, and that was because of the sniffles.

I didn't take on this challenge in order to become an inspiration to other cancer patients. But when reports came out that I was starting to shoot a new TV series, a full six months after being diagnosed with an illness that kills most people within weeks, we started receiving all kinds of letters and cards from people who found it inspiring. I'm grateful for the huge response from people, but really I just wanted to make a great TV show.

As always, Lisa was an equal partner in creating the character I played. She spent the whole shoot in Chicago, and she also directed one of the thirteen episodes. Working with her again, and watching her craft what became a fantastic episode, was amazingly gratifying. We were in this together, in every possible way—just as we had always been.

It's a fact that Swayze men have never lived to ripe old ages. My father died at fifty-seven, the same age I am now. My paternal grandfather also died young, and most of my uncles never saw the other side of forty.

In some ways, I've always felt as if I was living on borrowed time. I've cheated death more times than I can count. There's something in the Swayze make-up that loves risk, and God knows I've embraced my share over the years. After I passed the age of thirty with my body and mind still intact, I always felt I'd got away with something.

The months I've spent fighting this cancer have been an emotional roller coaster. There are days when I feel determined to live until a cure is found, and truly believe I can do it. And there are days when I'm so tired, I just don't know how I can keep on going. But I have to. I have to keep moving forward as if there's a long future for me. As if this is beatable. I'm not running round like some kind of Pollyanna—it's more of a clenched-jaw determination. I'll just be damned if this son of a bitch is going to beat me.

In all my life, I never gave up in a fight, starting from that day in junior high when five boys were beating me up at once. And I'm not going to give up now.

I have so much to live for. So much I want to accomplish. Since we've had our ranch in New Mexico, Lisa and I have been working on conservation and preservation of the land. We've commissioned a 200-year forest-stewardship plan that will not only maintain forest growth levels, but also improve them. Lisa and I are passionate about being good stewards of this beautiful land, and we want to share the knowledge we've gained with others, to help spread the word about conservation.

When we bought our ranch in New Mexico, it was the fulfilment of a lifelong dream. I swore when my dad died that I would one day own a ranch and return to my cowboy roots. I also swore I'd do everything I could to make him proud for the rest of my life. There's no better way to do both those things than by keeping this land pristine and beautiful for generations to come. I am my father's son, and I'm living the life he dreamed of having. In every way imaginable, it's worth living for.

There's also so much more I want to accomplish as an artist. I've been writing new music in the last few months. I still have the energy to take on new projects, and have no patience for anyone who suggests otherwise. Whenever someone asks me what I think my legacy is, I say the same thing: I'm not finished yet! My work is my legacy.

And of course, there's my relationship with Lisa. I can't even begin to express what she has meant to me over the years. As a naive and insecure twenty-year-old, I would never have dreamed that one person could find so much passion and so much loyalty with another. Lisa and I are a part of each other—I can no more imagine life without her than I can imagine living without my own heart. And feeling that love for her is that much sweeter after the hard times we went through.

In the summer of 2008, just before we went to Chicago to film *The Beast*, Lisa and I decided to renew the vows we'd made to each other thirty-three years before. We put the whole thing together in four days, and invited a handful of close friends and family members to join us. I rode in on a white stallion, and together Lisa and I stood hand in hand and recited the vows we'd each written. As she finished saying the words she'd written for me, tears came to my eyes.

> *While the future is an unknown, the one thing I do know is that I will love you. I'm very lucky to have found you in my life and am grateful that I have had the ability to open my eyes and see just what I have . . .*
>
> *Because what I have—the love, the greatness and enormity of what I feel—informs everything around me, and brings me back to what I cherish most. And in cherishing the most there is for me, I cherish you more.*

And then I spoke the words I'd written for her.

> *How do I tell you how lucky I feel, that you fell into my life? How grateful I am that you chose to love me? I know that because of you, I found my spirit, I saw the man I wanted to be. But most of all, you were my friend.*
>
> *Together, we've created journeys that were beyond anything we could imagine. Journeys that dreams are made of. We have ridden into the sunset on a white stallion, countless*

*times. We've tasted the dust in the birthplaces of religions. Yet you still take my breath away. I'm still not complete until I look in your eyes.*

*You are my woman, my lover, my mate and my lady. I've loved you for ever, I love you now and I will love you for evermore.*

Even with everything we've been through, and everything we still are facing, it was one of the happiest days of my life. And it made me more determined than ever to have as many more beautiful days together with Lisa as I possibly can.

*Editors' Note*: Patrick and Lisa were to enjoy one more year of 'beautiful days' together before Patrick's illness worsened and he was taken from her side in September 2009. His ashes were scattered at the New Mexico ranch where the couple had spent so many happy times.

During his struggle against cancer, Patrick drew great inspiration from the support of his innumerable fans, and his fellow actors were fulsome in their tributes after his death. His *Dirty Dancing* co star Jennifer Grey said of him, 'Patrick was a rare and beautiful combination of raw masculinity and amazing grace. Gorgeous and strong, he was a real cowboy with a tender heart.'

COPYRIGHT AND ACKNOWLEDGMENTS



Spine (from top): Grant Sainsbury/Contour by Getty Images; Liam Duke; Trevor Leighton/Random House; Startraks Photo/Rex Features. Front cover (from left, clockwise): Grant Sainsbury/Contour by Getty Images; Liam Duke; Startraks Photo/Rex Features; Trevor Leighton/Random House. P.6: Grant Sainsbury/Contour by Getty Images; p.30 (top left & right; bottom left): courtesy of the author; (bottom right): Acorn Pictures Ltd/The Picture Desk; p.31 (top left & right): courtesy of the author; (bottom right): Doug Peters/Press Association Images; (bottom left): Alastair Muir/Rex Features. P.160: Liam Duke; illustrations by Alan Titchmarsh; p.190 (top left, bottom right): courtesy of the author; (top right): Alison Titchmarsh; (bottom left): ITV/Rex Features; p.191 (top & bottom left): © BBC; (top right): *Amateur Gardening*, May 1983; (bottom right): Karen Graham. P.294: Trevor Leighton/Random House; p.318: images courtesy of the author; p.319 (top left; bottom left & right): images courtesy of the author; top right: Adrian Sherratt/Rex Features. P.476: Startraks Photo/Rex Features; p.620: images courtesy of the authors; p.621 (top left): courtesy of the authors; (top right): Amy Holliday Sobin; (bottom right): C. Vestron/Everett/Rex Features; (bottom left): Vestron/The Picture Desk.



Printed and bound in Europe by Arvato Iberia

400-499 UP0000-1